TWENTIETH-CENTURY
Chinese Drama

CHINESE LITERATURE IN TRANSLATION

Editors
Irving Yucheng Lo
Joseph S.M. Lau
Leo Ou-fan Lee
Eugene Chen Eoyang

TWENTIETH-CENTURY

Chinese Drama

An Anthology

Edited by Edward M. Gunn

 INDIANA UNIVERSITY PRESS
Bloomington

First Midland Book Edition 1983
Publication of this book was aided by a grant from the
Program for Publications of the National Endowment for the Humanities,
an independent federal agency.

Manufactured in the United States of America

Library of Congress Cataloging in Publication Data
Main entry under title:

Twentieth-century Chinese drama.

(Chinese literature in translation)
  1. Chinese drama—20th century—Translations into English. 2. English drama—
Translations from Chinese. I. Gunn, Edward M. II. Title: 20th century Chinese
drama. III. Series.
PL2658.E5T88   1983   895.1′25′08   82-47923
ISBN 0-253-36109-5
ISBN 0-253-20310-4 (pbk.)
1 2 3 4 5 87 86 85 84 83

Contents

INTRODUCTION

THE TWENTIETH CENTURY has been a period of intense activity and innovation in Chinese drama. Experimenting with operatic tradition and building a new "spoken drama" (hua-chü), dramatists have expanded the esthetic range of Chinese theater and kept the drama at the forefront of social, political, and artistic controversies. Two fundamental considerations should be kept in mind as part of the particular background for this drama. Much of it is derived from Western dramatic literature, which is represented chiefly by plays written by men in their forties and fifties after arduous apprenticeships in well-established European traditions of drama. In China, by contrast, this spoken drama was adopted primarily by younger writers with far less training and fewer theatrical resources at their command. Indeed, for most of the Chinese writers the form of spoken drama itself was an iconoclastic statement, designed to convey broader views for social reform and revolution. Given its inherently public nature and the social views of the writers, spoken drama has been the most assertive form of innovative literature in modern Chinese society. The work of its young writers is offered here not in competition with the pillars of modern Western drama, but rather as studies of what and how this foreign art and its concerns have been translated into the bold experiments of young Chinese writers.

The most immediate form of competition these young writers have confronted has not, then, been the work of their Western inspirations, but rather the highly developed and well-entrenched traditional Chinese theater, the second of our preliminary considerations. The various forms of opera that over the centuries came to form the Chinese theater were still enormously popular at the beginning of this century and have remained so. They order a wide range of emotions into standard patterns of music, and define characters by conventional role categories (clown, warrior, virtuous young woman, young scholar, etc.), each with its characteristic movements, painted face masks, and colorful costuming. They enact stories usually drawn from popular history and legend, illustrating the moral order of traditional society. Numerous formal innovations have repeatedly brought change and variety to the opera, but as of the early decades of this century far less was being witnessed in the way of new psychological or moral vision. Perhaps, too, in drama as a literary form, there had been a decline, with stylistic creativity and the storytelling function too heavily subordinated to the more theatrical arts of spectacle and music. How opera has indirectly influenced the new spoken drama and how modern playwrights have accommodated their work to the traditions of the opera are also topics of concern in this anthology. And, just as it is younger playwrights who have veered most sharply away from tradition, it has largely been older writers with their years of observation and experience in appealing to Chinese audiences who have sought to incorporate the strengths of older forms into the new drama. Their tampering with what both East and West have to offer has been no less controversial.

These broad, fundamental considerations of experience, aims, and influences serve to frame the complex details of theory and practice that the plays in this anthology illustrate.

It was precisely the popular strength of opera in its preoccupation with highly developed, stylized theatricality over its potential to convey new ideas that made it appear to some young Chinese artists and intellectuals as an outward and visible sign of the inward and spiritual weakness that had brought the Chinese nation to its knees as the sick man of East Asia. The intellectuals thought it was time for a drama that educated its audience to new ideas about contemporary issues. The discussions of drama published by the young philosopher Hu Shih in 1919, together with his short play *The Greatest Event in Life*, are generally taken as the watershed in the development of a new theater consciously opposed to the faults of the old.

Hu Shih's work was not without its forerunners. In the late nineteenth and early twentieth centuries other Chinese had been exposed to foreign ideas of drama in a meagre fashion through the simple religious skits of missionary schools or in the glimpses of foreign amateurs entertaining fellow expatriates in Shanghai. More importantly, several Chinese who studied in Japan participated in stylized versions of Western dramas which the Japanese had begun to study, and the Chinese formed their own troupe to produce *Camille* and *Uncle Tom's Cabin* in 1907. *Camille (La Dame aux Camélias)* was a Western equivalent of traditional Chinese tales about courtesans who enjoyed nurturing their young admirers but stood aside, even at sacrifice to themselves, when their lovers were ready for more responsible and respectable roles in society. *Uncle Tom's Cabin* was intended to speak more to the theme of the ethnic Han Chinese determination to overthrow the Manchu minority regime and establish a Chinese republic. Students returning to China from Japan wrote and produced their own plays advocating social reforms and political revolution which became known as "civilized drama" (wen-ming hsi). So identified was civilized drama with sensitive political issues that after a Chinese Republic was declared in 1912 it banned these productions. Once civilized drama was deprived of its leaders and their social platform it went into obscurity to survive as a form of vaudeville. From the beginning civilized drama was characterized by posturing and declamation, less by any well-prepared script, and least by any unified concept of arrangement and production. There were writers more attuned to the craft of Western drama in the early years of the Republic. But they were commercial writers, regarded as hacks by intellectuals; the popular periodicals in which their occasional translations or original works appeared were not taken seriously. Hence, Hu Shih's writings formed the first serious theoretical statements and the first application of them.

Hu Shih saw in the realism of Henrik Ibsen's problem plays a vehicle for the critical examination of social failure. Realism was equated with facing truth and reality, especially the unpleasant truth of unhappy endings, as Chinese opera had largely avoided doing. The realism of Ibsen meant organizing time and action in economical fashion, creating individualism, and embodying the historical evolution of a scientific, objective mind superior to that witnessed in earlier forms of drama.[1] Since Ibsen himself was not a theoretician, Hu Shih was obliged to piece his theoretical statements together from Western discussions of "Ibsenism" (particularly George Bernard Shaw's), from Ibsen's intellectual concerns outside the drama, and from Hu's own observations of Chinese theater. There was never any discussion of Ibsen's own preference for his verse dramas or historical panoramic plays, but this was an obscure fact and it is understandable that it was overlooked.[2] The realism of the problem play was given the value of "truth," and while some of Hu Shih's ideas were ignored or rejected by others in drama, the notion of realism as having a monopoly on truth gained a dominant position.

Part of the pursuit of realism was also the result of the failure of early modernistic experiments to win audiences. The key example of modernism in early Chinese spoken drama is Hung Shen's *Yama Chao*, which concludes with a swirl of expressionistic scenes that baffled audiences. To those concerned with marketing spoken drama as a practical problem, such as the theorist and scholar

Sun Ch'uan-fang, the answer was to turn to the "well-made play," a form of realistic drama emphasizing elaborate plot construction to generate excitement and suspense. This was the sort of work popular in the West, less intellectually demanding than expressionism, and the root of great art, like Ibsen's. Ting Hsi-lin's *Oppression* is a well-known favorite of the 1920s that exemplified the trend toward well-made plays, and the trend also did much to educate the famous Ts'ao Yü (Wan Chia-pao) in dramatic techniques which, when he applied them to complex plots and timely themes in the 1930s, were a tremendous popular success. His early works, *Thunderstorm* (1934) and *Sunrise* (1936), attracted unprecedented audiences to the spoken drama and helped establish the first full-time professional company devoted exclusively to spoken drama.

To politically hard-pressed writers further to the left, including the very active Communist propagandists, this concern with the techniques of realism reduced the concept to "mere" art. By contrast, their theory of realism drew on Zola, with his stress on observation, and Belinsky, with his seminal statement on art as a reflection of life, to argue for "contemporary realism," a sociological slice of life that mirrored economic hardship and social injustice in a fashion which they hailed as "actual life" and not "mere art." Hsia Yen's *Under Shanghai Eaves* is a major example of how such a theory appeared in practice on the eve of war with Japan in 1937.

The association of realism with "life" and "truth" was naturally challenged by some critics.[3] The view that realism perforce meant "contemporary realism" and could only deal with contemporary situations observed by the writer continued to have a life of its own. One finds writers as late as 1957 feeling constrained to defend historical drama as also being capable of realism.[4] With the start of the War of Resistance to Japan (1937-45), Chinese writers had absorbed the various notions of realism and it remained for them to bring the practice of realism to maturity in their work. Their development is evident in a range of plays from Ts'ao Yü's *Peking Man* (which once again explored elements of nonrealism) to the three wartime plays by Ch'en Pai-ch'en, Li Chien-wu, and Yang Chiang that are included in this anthology.

If during the war hundreds of thousands of Chinese came to appreciate and support spoken drama, there were still hundreds of millions for whom realism and spoken drama meant little or nothing. Reaching beyond the largely urban, educated audience already involved in transforming China, to a largely rural, uneducated, and unchanged populace had been the concern of a few dramatists for some time. Ironically, it was the very modernism of Hung Shen's *Yama Chao* which in the early 1920s helped inspire such a populist writer, Ou-yang Yü-ch'ien; for, in the frenzied scenes of the play peopled with the figures and paraphernalia of popular legends, Ou-yang saw a place for traditional theatrical spectacle. Ou-yang joined a People's Dramatic Association in the 1920s which found its guiding light in Romain Rolland's proposals for a "people's theater" in Europe, and seized on the idea of transforming Chinese opera by drawing on instruments and techniques from Western opera as the key to a popular new Chinese drama.[5] The association faded, never to "go among the people," but Ou-yang continued to keep the topic of a modern opera alive. When war came in 1937 and many writers turned to popularizing patriotic propaganda for the widest audience possible, the influence of traditional opera showed ever more prominently in many plays. The notion that the theater was traditionally the means of "educating" (or enculturating) the peasant and was ideal for the purpose certainly antedated the rise of modern spoken drama and Western theories;[6] now that it was time to offer the peasants a new wine, the old bottles still seemed useful, as the saying went. In the Communist base at Yenan this trend reached its extreme, endorsed by Mao Tse-tung in his "Talks at the Yenan Forum on Literature and Art" in 1942, and writers there wove their works together out of local forms of folk entertainment.

The rise of a Maoist theater in the late 1940s brought with it a new set of theoretical considerations. In the broadest terms, Maoists favored a kind of ceremonial drama; that is, a drama characterized by its celebration of communal experience, with generalized or exemplary characters in public roles (as opposed to private conflicts), reflecting positive or good forces opposing negative forces at some turning point in history. Since the events of the play are based on what the community already recognizes as having a unified historical significance, there may be a deemphasis on internal unity within the play, and there may be less importance attached to the verbal aspects of the play, with the conspicuous exception of rhetoric as a strong feature, than to spectacle, music, dance, and even actual ceremony.[7] With the spread of Mao's authority, such a ceremonial drama as the celebration of Communist Party programs began to dominate the stage in the late 1940s. In the early 1950s the drama was increasingly subject to the theory of "socialist realism" developed in the Soviet Union. Socialist realism calls for the portrayal of the "essence" (pen-chih) of an era through ideal types of characters as determined by Party doctrine. The notion of the "typical" (tien-hsing) as essential to realism had long been in currency among a number of writers in the Republican period, but they had identified the typical with the commonplace.[8] By contrast, a Maoist like Yao Wen-yuan in the 1950s and 1960s was committed to the typical as an exemplar of values appropriate to the depiction of the essential nature of socialist development at a given point in time.[9] Yao's insistence on the primacy of the presentation of a consciously and methodically conceived correct model of thought and behavior, which apparently had the support of Mao, dominated prescriptions for writing through the Cultural Revolution up to the late 1970s. After Yao and his associates were arrested in late 1976, critics emerged once again to stress the theory of art as a "reflection" (fan-ying) of reality, whether conscious or unconscious.[10]

With the rise of such theories as socialist realism (later known as "revolution-ary realism and revolutionary romanticism" after the split with the Soviet Union), the term realism lost its formal esthetic denotation, and the discussion of form was subsumed under the Maoist concern for a "national form." Traditionally China had no single "national form" of drama but rather a variety of styles associated with different regions, social groups, and historical periods.[11] When Hu Shih introduced his theoretical discussion of modern spoken drama from the West, he praised it as something decidedly foreign to China and a part of international cultural expression outside the range of Chinese experience. In the first flush of the movement for a new drama there were those who saw Chinese theater as a barbaric, backward form and even urged closing down opera theaters to make way for spoken drama. There was in this the seed of the idea for making spoken drama the national form for drama. A broader understanding of Western drama and the all-important question of audience acceptance tempered this extremism early on, though advocates of spoken drama regarded proposals that opera be considered the national form (kuo-chü) as reactionary.

Spoken drama was not successful among the peasantry, for reasons never thoroughly understood. Over the years the explanations have variously empha-sized form, content, and the irrelevance of some plays to the peasants as factors inhibiting a more widespread appreciation.[12] All of this encouraged the growth of concern with national form under the term min-tsu hsing, a phrase with the same populist coloring as the Russian term narod, referring to both the "people" and their identity as a nation. Mao's "Talks" provided new prescrip-tive guidance, calling for works to have a "national form," neither "ancient" nor "foreign," but acceptable to the Chinese audiences. In this atmosphere various commentators asserted that spoken drama was fundamentally Chinese, not foreign, reminding any who might question this assertion that, however rare and obscure, instances of dramas written without music were known to have existed as far back as the T'ang dynasty and that the late-Ch'ing dynasty "civilized dramas" were not modeled after Western sources.[13] Moreover, state subsidies were provided for some ninety to a hundred professional spoken drama companies in the early 1950s following Liberation, an assurance that spoken drama had a firm place in Chinese theater, next to the some 2,900 opera companies that were also officially supported. In the most practical terms, the role of spoken drama was outlined as the form which "most easily reflects real life and struggle."[14] At the same time, spoken dramas of this period, as exemplified in the works by Yang Lü-fang and T'ien Han, show concern for "national form."

Not content to stand still, theorists offered various proposals for developing spoken drama as a national form. One of the most widely published of these was by the veteran Shanghai director Huang Tso-lin, offering a mild suggestion for innovation based on his appreciation of Brecht and Stanislavski and, in turn, on their admiration for Mei Lan-fang, the most celebrated Peking Opera artist of this century. Huang urged that the narrow nineteenth-century theatrical conceptions of fourth-wall naturalistic realism and their claims to scientific truth, still the heaviest influence on the theater of spoken drama, be abandoned to admit to the spoken drama various techniques employed in traditional opera which had been admired and imitated by such giants as Brecht and Stanislavski. Essentially, Huang was arguing for a Chinese modernism in theater on the authority of Brecht and Stanislavski, but one based on traditional opera and hence within the desired realm of national form. Although Huang was concerned more with theater than with dramaturgy, the implications for drama are clear. Whatever exception might be taken to his statements, Huang's discussion on the whole represents the best-formulated proposal for the development of spoken drama in China.[15] Of course, the choice of Brecht as a model could only be problematic for several reasons. Brecht was more interested in challenging and confronting the emotions of his audience than in gratifying them. This, his very controversial theory of "alienation," has had no counterpart (intentionally) in China, where quite the opposite effect has always been sought. Brecht wrote largely for what he contemptuously regarded as a bourgeois audience and focused on what he considered the failures of their society and vision, rather than portraying the achievements of Communist society and its heroes, a mandatory feature for much of drama in the People's Republic of China. And last but not least, despite Brecht's preeminence among Communist modernists, he ended his lifelong preoccupation with theater as a means of instruction by concluding that the theater is "a place of entertainment."[16] This was and is not a view seen fit to publish in China with any approval.

In 1966 the well-known outcome of all the discussion on the role and form of drama was the sacking of the theatrical establishment in the Cultural Revolution period, lasting through 1976. So stunning was the purge of both traditional opera and much spoken drama that it will always be regarded more in terms of overarching power struggles than of the merits of any esthetic arguments. Party writers and artists were charged with ideological heresies, promoting feudalism, capitalism, or fascism, and failing to produce or deliberately blocking the development of a literature for the workers, soldiers, and peasants that supported class struggle in their interests. The earlier call of Republican-era critics to close down the old theater to make room for the new came back to haunt writers in ways never envisioned. The new drama promoted the theme of class struggle waged by the workers, soldiers, and peasants. Spoken drama, though never entirely abandoned, was given low priority next to the development of new "model revolutionary works" (ko-ming yang-pan hsi) under the guidance of Chiang Ch'ing, Mao's wife, who saw to ensuring a lively blend of Chinese and Western music and movement that, taken as a whole, was assuredly neither ancient nor foreign and brought ceremonial drama to a sheer panegyric.

With the arrest of Chiang Ch'ing, Yao Wen-yuan, and others of the Maoist cultural establishment, a non-Maoist drama began to reemerge in the late 1970s. The key note sounded by authorities was that literature and art were once again to serve the "whole of the people," thus broadening the audience to include those whose class status had not been defined as worker, soldier, or peasant.[17] While in general reaffirming Mao's "Yenan Talks," the Party leadership took a step back from direct esthetic prescriptions but retained authority to judge works on ideological grounds. Certainly this did not remove Party control from esthetics, so that on several occasions the manner in which a Party figure was portrayed in a work or the degree of emphasis given to an antisocial or individualistic character was grounds for censoring the work. However, in addition to the kinds of positive sentiments and ideas called for by socialist realism, writers also placed more emphasis on aspects of psychology and social criticism that are the territory of realism, and experimented lightly with nonrealistic modernism. The plays by Tsung Fu-hsien, Sha Yeh-hsin, and Chou Wei-po et al. exemplify these trends in varying degrees.

The influence of modernism has been more apparent in the drama of Taiwan, where existentialism and absurdism as well as social criticism have been explored by dramatists, along with a large quantity of realistic plays, many devoted to patriotic themes supporting Nationalist Party goals and ideals.[18] By the 1970s writers of Taiwan, too, were searching for something "national" in their form and debating how they should identify with social problems in Taiwan as opposed to a more cosmopolitan world. Yang Mu's verse drama *Wu Feng* is very much a product of this period of debate.

This brief account of theoretical concerns in twentieth-century Chinese drama, however essential to an anthology, only goes part of the distance to recommending the works themselves to the reader. There are as well the writers, the recurring themes and motifs, character types, the attention given to various social settings and periods of time all to be considered as part of forming a representative view of the development of drama. Ultimately, it is the recognized historical significance of some works and the sometimes less recognized esthetic merit of other individual plays that most deserve further introduction.

Short, topical, and educative, Hu Shih's comedy *The Greatest Event in Life* was inspired by Ibsen's *A Doll's House*. The realistically appointed box-set parlor, the action commencing close to the climax, which involves unexpected turns of action, are elements of well-made drama appearing in Ibsen's work. And as in Ibsen's work, such techniques serve the presentation of arguments in ordered, logical fashion, exposing inferior views and providing a platform for the ultimate gestures of the protagonist, who storms out of the house like Ibsen's Nora, but in this case to a more promising independent life. Hu Shih's themes of feminism (albeit mild compared to Ibsen's) and free love (understood in the Chinese context as the right to choose one's partner in marriage) are thus neatly and entertainingly presented. Unfortunately, in 1919 no respectable young woman would act the part of such a rebel and several years passed before the play was performed. By that time other young men interested in spoken drama had a much stronger vision of the sort of spectacle which may be achieved in drama and which Hu Shih's lacked.

One such writer was Hung Shen, who upon returning to China from study in the United States was struck by the oppression and devastation created by the warlords then vying for control of his homeland. This prompted him to write the play *Yama Chao*, Yama (or Yen-wang) being the name of the King of Hell in traditional Chinese legends. The play is closely modeled on Eugene O'Neill's *The Emperor Jones*, imitating its structure and its expressionist techniques, and also permitting the central character a share of both good and evil tendencies. Yet critics have found *Yama Chao* significantly different from *The Emperor*

Jones in its exclusive concern with the central character of Chao Ta as a social being, the product of hellish social forces, rather than a representation of man in the more universal context of nature.[19] Hung Shen's concern with exposing the roots of an unjust, benighted society in *Yama Chao* is representative of a strong trend in twentieth-century Chinese adaptations of Western drama toward emphasizing themes of social injustice and social identity over and above other themes. *Yama Chao* is also important to the development of dramatic form in China, for while Hung Shen was not the only playwright to experiment with expressionistic techniques,[20] his work was the most fully developed, and the bewildered rejection with which it was greeted by so much of its Chinese audience served as a warning to other writers against any presentation of the grotesque that strayed too far from realism or the nonrealistic conventions of tradition.

By contrast, the plays of Ting Hsi-lin, such as his well-known one-act comedy *Oppression*, had more success with audiences as well as with critics.[21] In his work one finds a renewed concern with the craft of the well-made play, first essayed by Hu Shih. But in the hands of Ting Hsi-lin, the form has, in addition to the restrained note of reason, greater subtlety and a characteristic moment of astonishment, so that even critics disappointed with Ting's refusal to intellectualize his characters agreed that his control of his craft was superior to that of most other artists. Ting's plays do in fact deal with social concerns of the times. In *Oppression* there is the exploration of free love in a dull, moralizing society. The characters display the triumph of wit over obtuseness, where that obtuseness leads to oppression and the mind is the chief instrument to overcome submission.

Yet, despite the success of Ting's work, it is little concerned with strong portrayals of passion, commitment, and assertiveness. There were writers who felt a need for these qualities to overcome stultifying social roles and rules, and who wrote about them often with greater emotionalism than wit. These were the "romantic" writers of the 1920s, whose most important contribution to dramatic literature perhaps was their reinterpretation of traditional Chinese tales. Kuo Mo-jo's *Cho Wen-chun*, the best known of these costume dramas, was a hit with schoolchildren who loved the defiant young heroine.[22] Yet, if the point was to overturn tradition, the most daring and imaginative play in this vein was Ou-yang Yü-ch'ien's *P'an Chin-lien*. A hybrid work, *P'an Chin-lien* is neither a one-act nor yet a full-length play, its series of short scenes suggesting the organization of traditional operas. Written and published as a spoken drama, it was revised and performed as an opera with traditional musical arrangements, costumes, and settings, and featured Ou-yang himself, a noted performer of female roles in opera, in the part of P'an Chin-lien. The play had been based on the traditional tales of the nymphomaniacal villainess P'an Chin-lien, particularly the novel *Shui-hu chuan* (All Men Are Brothers, or The Water Margin). In the play what is most significant is Ou-yang's treatment of P'an Chin-lien, his transformation of her from the psychopathic, self-destructive figure of tradition into a woman who, however wanton, is an intelligent, passionate rebel against the harsh, conventional morality represented at its best and worst by the famous warrior hero Wu Sung, ultimately confounded as well as outraged by P'an. P'an Chin-lien is drawn to Wu Sung as a powerful hero who stands above convention. Yet he does so only to reinforce convention, whereas she aspires to destroy it. Once doomed to failure, she would rather meet destruction at the hands of this superman than be buried by the conventional society she so despises. Here is something approaching the full-fledged romantic transvaluation of a classic example of evil, whose vision is now seen to transcend the conventional moral context.[23]

Ou-yang wrote and staged *P'an Chin-lien* when he was on the verge of devoting himself to Communist themes, including a production of the Soviet writer Sergei Tretiakov's *Roar China!* Indeed, during the 1930s theater in Shanghai and elsewhere was largely aligned with Communist Party programs and experiments. Even so, it was the work of the young college graduate Ts'ao Yü which stole much of the public's attention. His plays such as *Thunderstorm* (1934) and *Sunrise* (1936)[24] were in sympathy with certain Communist themes, the collapse of traditional, "feudalistic" society and its capitalist heirs, but were not coordinated with Party propaganda programs and helped establish drama companies which were not under the direction of the Party.

Yet, given the importance of the development of Communist drama, the first significant breakthrough came with the plays of Hsia Yen. *Under Shanghai Eaves* (1937) is among the most substantial representations of two major themes in the drama of the mid and late 1930s: patriotism in the face of Japanese aggression from without and determination in the face of misery brought on by class exploitation and oppression from within and without. It should be noted also that Hsia Yen sets his play not among the lowest rungs of society, but among the petit-bourgeoisie, whose expectations are only frustrated by the status quo. Hsia Yen aims at the panoramic, the sociological schematization, and with a certain logic avoids creating a central protagonist and subordinates plot to concern with the situation, the oppressive atmosphere and its ingredients. Such elements it shares with a range of works from Elmer Rice's *Street Scene* (1929) to Fujimori Seikichi's *Light and Dark*, which one critic has observed is the immediate source for *Under Shanghai Eaves*.[25] Still, these plays are in turn indebted to Gorky, whose *The Lower Depths*, written under the influence of Chekhov and Zola, has always been the centerpiece of "dust-bin," "slice-of-life" realism. Critics have argued forcefully that in such panoramic works the fundamental human observations (such as the theme of man and wife versus economic necessity in *Under Shanghai Eaves*), are never developed, and there is a tendency to rely on the exposure of deprivation as being inherently dramatic when it is not.[26] In any case, the kind of play which Hsia Yen produced was to be repeated with variations throughout the period of the War of Resistance, Yü Ling's *Shanghai Night*, Sung Chih-ti's *Chungking Fog*, and finally an adaptation of Gorky's *The Lower Depths* by Shih T'o and K'o Ling, entitled *The Night Inn (Yeh tien)*, which does examine the lowest rung of society, being the best known.

Indeed, Russian writing exerted a stronger influence on modern Chinese drama than any other single foreign source, be it in the form of Soviet-inspired theories of Mao Tse-tung, the translations and productions of Soviet and prerevolutionary plays, or the influence of Chekhov, Ostrovsky, Gorky, and Gogol. Among those influenced by Gogol, the works of Ch'en Pai-ch'en during the War of Resistance include some of the liveliest social satire in modern China. Gogol's most famous play, *The Inspector General*, is known for its use of the device of a nonentity impersonating a high-level official; Ch'en Pai-ch'en's best-known work, *The Promotion Plan (Sheng-kuan t'u*, 1945), also employs this device. More important is Ch'en's readiness to use the grotesque, which was wonderfully elaborated on the stage by the visual effects in the 1946 production directed by Huang Tso-lin in Shanghai. But Ch'en's employment of the grotesque is even more fully apparent to the reader of his 1939 play *Men and Women in Wild Times*, filled with the outrageous behavior and speech of his unscrupulous and unpatriotic characters. Here, as in Hsia Yen's play, the themes are patriotism and social inequity, although unlike Hsia Yen's work, the examples in *Men and Women in Wild Times* are nearly all negative, as they should be in satire. The fact that so many self-appointed guardians of patriotism in the arts during the war were appalled at Ch'en's satires could only have gratified him, since the exposure of sham is central to his work. In fact, devotees of satire might well argue that Ch'en's portrayal of the positive messages in his work is too obtrusive, yet the purer forms of satire have never been appreciated by the Chinese Communist Party or middlebrow critics, and positive characters and gestures have always been considered appropriate by them. Yet even such issues cannot detract from the appreciation of Ch'en's masterful orchestration of manners and moods and his breaking away from static scenes to fluid, dynamic ones. Disorder is his trademark: be it an official's home invaded by an indignant mob, an office filled with slovenly bureaucrats, an apartment being rented to a couple just after the former tenant has deserted it, or, as in *Men and Women in Wild Times*, a train packed to overflowing with refugees and their possessions. And so this play remains among the most memorable of the war period.

Though neither Yang Chiang's *Windswept Blossoms* nor Li Chien-wu's *Springtime* ostensibly concerns itself with war, each is representative of the war period because of its quality. Written in the mid-1940s, a time when audiences were less concerned than heretofore about the fighting, and in Shanghai, a place where the theater was thriving but unresponsive to authority in the form of the Japanese military's puppet government, they were not published until 1946, when the war was over. *Springtime* does not lack a social theme or references to events that took place in China around the turn of the century in the closing years of the Ch'ing dynasty, when the play is set. But its art is bent toward the creation of typical characters in a well-worn situation of frustrated courtship, freshened by Li's comic approach. At a time when the social order was breaking down, Li—much like Thornton Wilder in the West— presented himself as a sophisticated man of letters nostalgically turning back to the comfortable features of a Chinese mental landscape. Yet— again like Thornton Wilder—Li portrays real pain and pushes the action to the brink of disaster, only to arrest it with the reassertion of that which is familiar and reassuring. In such a world authority always has its limits; anarchy is benign. If this seems an inadequately serious view of Chinese society at the time, it is nevertheless the nature of farcical comedy to rescue action from grim consequences. And if it seems out of place as the work of a French-educated admirer of Flaubert like Li, he has actually offered an authentic style, not simply pastoral imitation, loading the dialogue with the language of his native Hopei-Peking region, and spicing it with the patter of folk-style oral recitation and the derisive jingles of urchins. For readers accustomed to American English, David Pollard's rendering of the play in colloquial British English enhances the effect of the original Chinese dialogue.[27]

Yang Chiang's *Windswept Blossoms* is also set in rural north China, and its title too contains a reference to spring; the blossoms are fallen flowers of the willow tree that cover the earth in that season. But here the similarity to Li's play ends, for the title is also symbolic of the play's unsparing protrayal of a handful of educated Chinese, dominated by a consuming determination to be architects of a new China, as they confront not only the ample injustices of their society but the self-inflicted failure of their own ideals. As often as this theme has been treated in its social context, *Windswept Blossoms* is unusual for its concentration on the psychology of its characters. The play is no less unusual as an exercise in irony, from the sarcastic tone that permeates so much of the dialogue to the action of the principal characters, doggedly pursuing their ideals and crushed instead into the opposite of what they intended to become. There is in this more than an echo of the Ibsen of *Hedda Gabler* and *The Wild Duck*. On the other hand, Yang Chiang once commented that *Windswept Blossoms* is a potboiler. The play includes a tense love triangle and a suicide, both of which were very common ingredients in the Chinese potboilers of the Republican era, and one may question whether Yang maintained the same high degree of control over the conclusion of the play that she showed in its development. But whether or not the handling of the conclusion is flawed, it is meticulously prepared for and the ironic vision of the action to the end distinguishes *Windswept Blossoms* from the potboilers of its time as surely as Ibsen's problem plays are distinguished from their source, the well-made play.

Developments in dramatic literature and theater arts during the war period were substantial, including a wave of historical costume dramas which were particularly popular, such as Yao K'e's *Malice of Empire (Ch'ing kung yuan)* and Kuo Mo-jo's *Ch'u Yuan*.[28] But with the establishment of the People's Republic of China in 1949 and the spread of Mao Tse-tung's theoretical authority in literature and the arts, the kind of work undertaken outside Yenan in the 1940s had only a limited role to play, or none at all. The new works that emerged were more specifically designed "to coordinate with the current political tasks," as the phrase went, and thereby emerged new tensions in drama. Yang Lü-fang's *Cuckoo Sings Again* (1957) and T'ien Han's *Kuan Han-ch'ing* (1958-61) are representative of the achievements and concerns of the first decade of modern drama in the People's Republic.

Cuckoo Sings Again was an exceptionally popular play of the 1950s, and in many ways it is exemplary of contemporary prescriptions for writing, well thought of by a number of Party critics at the time. The play portrays a proper segment of society—the poor peasants—under the leadership of Party members. The characters and situations for the most part faithfully reflect the official document *Model Regulations for Advanced Agricultural Producers' Coopera-tives*.[29] The author is thoroughly familiar with the speech and manners of the hill folk of central China whom he portrays, and he incorporates into his realistic scenes several peasant songs which helped inspire regional operatic versions of the play, as well as a film for national distribution. There is plenty of love for labor and enthusiasm for the cooperative movement among the characters, though it is not altogether of the selfless variety. And though the aridity of so much Soviet and Soviet-inspired literature has been derided by the phrase "boy meets tractor," Yang Lü-fang actually managed to breathe life and charm into his version of this very theme—a young girl named Cuckoo's ambition to become a tractor driver.

The play also embraces two important developments of the 1950s. The first was the evolution of women's liberation among the workers, soldiers, and peasants, which was treated in numerous plays of the early 1950s. The second was the process of rural collectivization prior to the formation of communes during the Great Leap Forward of 1958. In its treatment of this latter theme, it ran afoul of powerful critics. Whatever its other flaws, it is an irreverent play, gently but persistently poking fun at proper ideological terminology, the melodrama of thought reform, the bureaucratic mentality, the all-important reminders of past bitterness in the old society, and other familiar topics normally treated with sobriety if not reverence. And there are more disturbing episodes, when members of the Party auxiliary—the Youth League—use their position to read other people's diaries, rig meetings, manipulate document flow and decision-making, and we see other various darker aspects of life dominated by powerful organizations. These elements and the action they attend serve to pose the question whether Communist programs exist to further the needs, rights, and goals of individuals or to foster the creation of a selfless, ideologically correct member of a mass organization. For all its *Oklahoma* lightness, *Cuckoo Sings Again* goes as far as any play of the era in asking, Given that the individual is for the sake of society, what then is society for? And given the increasing importance of ideological orthodoxy to Maoist critics during and after the Great Leap Forward, such writers as Yao Wen-yuan took an increasingly hard line against the play, to the point that after more than three years of debate Yao concluded that there was not a single character in the play who understood socialism.[30] Yang Lü-fang's name went back into the obscurity whence it had come.

Indeed, by the late 1950s many of the established writers were turning away from contemporary situations to portray the historical past. In this endeavor they were not only reconstructing a vision of the tradition as a process culminating in the People's Republic and what it stood for, but also indirectly raising questions about the new socialist state. T'ien Han's *Kuan Han-ch'ing* is an occasional piece, written to coincide with a commemoration of the great Yuan dynasty playwright of that name. Such a play gave T'ien Han full opportunity to use traditional operatic materials and techniques, as was the trend. And he took ample artistic license to assemble fragments of history into a unified dramatic piece that conveys the requisite themes of past bitterness under a "feudal" system and foreign domination (in this case by the Mongols, now considered a national minority), a heroic tradition of defense of the common people, and an unswerving faith in history as leading toward ultimate social justice. In particular, this play, not surprisingly yet notably, turns out to be about artists and their art—its genesis, its form, its social function and influence, and its place in cultural history—all as seen by one of the deans of modern drama at the height of his abilities in the late 1950s. Central to this motif is the duty of the writer to speak out against social injustice. While there is no firm reason to believe that T'ien intended the audience to infer anything but praise for con- temporary society, his interpretation of Kuan Han-ch'ing's own play *The Injustice to Tou Ngo* as the use of a story from the ancient Han dynasty to criticize the later Yuan dynasty of Kuan Han-ch'ing's own time inevitably raises the question of interpreting T'ien's own play as in turn an injunction through history to speak out against contemporary injustice.

There seems to have been no shortage of plays in the late 1950s and early 1960s that were straightforward panegyrics on themes of the Party and the new society.[31] But plays precisely aimed at borrowing from the past to criticize the present, or to leave open the inference of such criticism, did appear. T'ien Han's own *Hsieh Yao-huan* (1961), Lao She's *Teahouse* (Ch'a-kuan, 1957), and finally Wu Han's opera *Hai Jui Dismissed from Office* (1961) have all been seen in this light. As politics would have it, Yao Wen-yuan's attack on Wu Han's play signaled the opening of the political upheaval known as the Cultural Revolution and made *Hai Jui Dismissed from Office* the most conspicuous piece of dramatic social and political criticism. The opera dramatizes the actions of an upright Ming dynasty official who is dismissed by the throne owing to the calumnies of influential gentry whom he is determined to punish for their abuse of the peasants and their lands. Through this opera Wu Han sought to defend Party officials sacked for criticizing the failure of Mao Tse-tung's economic policies. Instead, the critic Yao Wen-yuan rose to prominence and power as the chief spokesman for the Maoist faction denouncing it for, as they put it, championing an historical figure like Hai Jui whose actions really only served to justify and perpetuate a corrupt, "feudal" social system.

Hai Jui Dismissed from Office is written in traditional Peking Opera style, and even its presentation of a mistrial set right by a proper trial follows traditional operatic form. Although this anthology is almost exclusively devoted to modern spoken drama and its accommodations with traditional forms, it is helpful as well to give some indication of its competition. Wu Han's work, because it is typical of a major form of opera, is an appropriate choice. Unfortunately, if no work written for the stage can be adequately presented in print alone, opera is even less well served by it. This holds true also for those spectacular operas and ballets termed "model revolutionary works" which, under the tutelage of Chiang Ch'ing, dominated the performing arts from 1966 through 1976. Model revolutionary works were born out of practical frustration with the limitations of spoken drama as a popular entertainment, and ideological rage at the inherent resistance of traditional operas to Maoist thought; the genre began in 1963 with *The Red Lantern*, whose martial music, traditional gestures, and spectacular acrobatics hardly come through in the stage directions, but whose stern message of firm class loyalty and selfless devotion to the Party is driven home in aria and dialogue. The positive characters, who by formula command prominence in the work, are all members of the class of workers, soldiers, and poor or lower-middle peasants. Despite the fervent Maoism of the pieces, neither Mao nor any other major historical figure was ever represented on stage (until after their deaths). Nor did the model operas and ballets directly portray the volatile and complex times whose reigning ideology they promoted. Rather, they largely reinterpreted earlier tales about previous decades, purifying the outdated or erroneous literature fostered by the Party in the past.

More directly concerned with portraying immediate conflicts of the day were a number of spoken dramas that appeared from time to time at local or regional levels.[32] But these plays failed to be accepted as models, and spoken drama did not rise to national prominence again until the late 1970s. When it did, younger writers moved immediately to deal directly with current social issues, and just as quickly created controversy, first with the literature of the "wounded," those types of persons victimized by the Cultural Revolution, and then with the literature of "exposure," concentrating on corruption in the Party.

If at a general level a comparison with Soviet works is inevitable, dramatic works from *Kuan Han-ch'ing* on through *Hai Jui Dismissed from Office* and *The Red Lantern* represented an increasing rejection of any *specific* Soviet influence. So, too, the young writers of the late 1970s looked to sources antedating Soviet influence. Tsung Fu-hsien's "wounded" piece, *In a Land of Silence*, looks back on Ts'ao Yü's plays of the 1930s in particular with their stifling, gloomy corruption in a "respectable" household and also on Ts'ao Yü's sources, such as Ibsen. In a broader sense, *In a Land of Silence* is a very straightforward reprise of staple themes in twentieth-century Chinese drama. The value of family solidarity is challenged by higher commitments and an authoritarian parent is overthrown; an exile returns not to the situation she expected to find but to shocking revelations that alter or ruin her vision in exile; a physician is challenged to extend his ideals of dedication and commitment to the amelioration of the sickness of society; a kind, aged person devotes her attention to restoring the failed courtship of two younger people; martyrs staunchly face their demise to render their causes with unambiguous clarity and provide flawless personifications of *das Prinzip Hoffnung*, the principle of hope. So *In a Land of Silence* offers its tribute to those who suffered and struggled against the forces that dominated the era of the Cultural Revolution in terms that have recurred again and again since the 1920s, both in the plays included in this anthology and in dozens of others. In contrast to this sense of continuity, the bold topicality of the play results in frequent reference to events and public figures very fresh in the minds of its original audiences. The ensuing danger of this approach, so carefully avoided in the model revolutionary operas, is exemplified by the fact that within three years the Party, which had promoted this play, was to decide officially that Mao Tse-tung and his successor Hua Kuo-feng were not so blameless as they are made to appear in the play.

With the open discussion and admission by the Party of its failures and the relaxation of the most stringent censorship, young writers took to ridiculing targets of opportunity, never challenging the national leadership, but striking at the image of rank and file Party bureaucrats. *The Artillery Commander's Son* and *If I Were Real* established the furthest limits for a kind of satiric literature that was popular with the new crop of university students, but decidedly less so with the Party. *The Artillery Commander's Son* is in many ways the comic counterpart of the more melodramatic *In a Land of Silence* and, too, after sixty years of dramatic experiment still irresistibly invited comparison as much as contrast with Hu Shih's *The Greatest Event in Life*. What was "new" about it in the context of the times is the reemergence of Gogol as an inspiration both for the device of an impersonator manipulating a social-climbing official and the light experiment with the grotesque at the start of the play. Just as startling at the time were the renewed allusions to classical Chinese and Western culture that fall from the educated lips of the university student, a new hero in the era of national commitment to the "four modernizations." Youth has its day in this play: sons and daughters of the Party and the workers unite as workers and intellectuals to build a new China, and in all this the only thing left to inference is the question of what the role of the Party is.

This question is more ominously confronted in the satire *If I Were Real.* In such works as *In a Land of Silence* and *The Artillery Commander's Son* there is little question as to which characters are perfectly in the right, or will prove to be so, and precisely what the mood of each scene is. *If I Were Real* evinces a more complex attitude. Concerned with social disparities in individual privileges and the quality of life in the countryside versus the city, the fifth scene of this play goes further than ever, not only in portraying social ills and demoralization among the Party and youth, but also in charging the scene with shifting tones of moral, emotional, and political significance. Against this background, in a play largely devoted to lampooning Party bureaucrats, the authors have yet provided a Party cadre in this scene with one of the simplest and most memorable gestures of personal integrity in recent Chinese drama. The youth who initiates these displays of folly and moral courage among Party cadre is not only an impersonator of the son of a high-ranking cadre in the mold of Gogol's *The Inspector General* but is made to conceive the idea of the impersonation through going to a performance of the play. It is the departure from Gogol which is evident in the fifth scene offered here, and further in the concluding scene of the play in which the audience, far from being challenged by Gogol's line, "Who are you laughing at but yourselves," is not laughing but called upon to render a verdict in the trial of the youth for his impersonation. The originality of these scenes on the Chinese stage also shows an unwillingness to treat the audiences as anything other than the masses whose judgment is the ultimate in probity and wisdom, a more standard role for the audience assumed by playwrights. Other formal innovations, such as a scene played before the curtain and in the audience, exemplify the trend to experiment beyond the conventions of naturalistic realism.

Drama in Taiwan has also undergone some important experiments. As the course of Taiwan has been separate from that of the Mainland, so the literature that has developed there has been in very significant ways distinct from that of the People's Republic.

Uncertainty has always been a prominent feature of the life of Taiwan, whether in its prodigious economic development or its often painful relationships with other nations. Yang Mu (one pen name of C. H. Wang) wrote *Wu Feng* (1979) after a decade of cultural debate on the role of writers and artists of Taiwan and in the midst of complex social and political ferment. In response the play recalls a period of stress some two centuries before in the far simpler, but much starker, circumstances of a community of Taiwan aborigines inhabiting the region of Taiwan's central landmark, Mount A-li, or A-li shan. Here the natives of Taiwan and their mentor Wu Feng, son of a Chinese trader who emigrated to the island, struggle with the question of their threatened extinction, what it signifies, whether they have any control over their fate, and how, whatever their fate be, they should face it.

Although modern drama in Taiwan has received neither the attention nor the status of other genres, there has been considerable experiment in it. Yang Mu's *Wu Feng* is distinguished by its author's ambitious use of verse in a style of his own creation. Schooled in both Chinese and comparative literature, Yang Mu as a modernist poet renders the past of his native Taiwan, its actions, images, and symbols, with a sense of irony and tension, as have his counterparts, like Robert Lowell in his trilogy *The Old Glory.* And of course the motif of martyrdom cannot fail to recall T. S. Eliot's *Murder in the Cathedral.* Yet Yang Mu's creation, for all its modernism, is not at all seeking to adapt the insights of a

Lowell or an Eliot, but to evoke the significance of an event distinctly rooted in the cultures of Taiwan and China and their point of mutual contact. *Wu Feng* thus may be taken as representative of the strong currents, cosmopolitan and provincial, which have exercised a complex influence on writers of Taiwan.

The story of the development of the drama and theater in twentieth-century China is both interesting and, often enough, dramatic in itself—in fact, it was once the subject of a play. And like so many plays it was not included in this volume, nor were the works of several prominent playwrights, such as Ts'ao Yü, Lao She, Kuo Mo-jo, and Yao K'e. They might well have been included were they not already available in translation elsewhere, and no slighting of their contributions was intended. Neither, though, is an apology: with work of the calibre of Ch'en Pai-ch'en's, Li Chien-wu's, or Yang Chiang's the foundations of a modern Chinese drama are well laid, and with playwrights as promising as Sha Yeh-hsin there should be much to look forward to. This volume, then, intended to fill the basic need for an anthology of twentieth-century Chinese drama based on a systematic appreciation of its development and representative concerns, also renews the questions of a fuller evaluation of individual works as well as introduces the subject.

Apologies are offered here for the abridgement of some of these plays. Given that some abridgement is a practical necessity, the results reflect less the tastes of the editor than a judgment as to which abridgments do the least damage to appreciation of the text remaining. And we have followed the principle of presenting scenes and acts in their entirety or deleting them altogether and substituting a synopsis of the contents omitted. Authorial prefaces have also been deleted, to await a presentation of their contents in critical works designed for fuller discussion. In the same vein, biographical notes have been kept to a minimum.

To those who have joined in this project as translators to make these plays readable and even performable, I am most grateful. Special thanks are due to the late Kai-yu Hsu and to Leo Lee, as well as to many others, for proposing this project, offering suggestions, and sharing their expertise, including Bi Shuo-wang, Cyril Birch, Roger Howard, C. T. Hsia, Joseph S.M. Lau, Bonnie S. McDougall, Tsu-lin Mei, Harold Shadick, Stephen Soong, and Constantine Tung. I would like also to acknowledge the financial support provided by Cornell University toward the preparation of the manuscript and the Universities Service Center, Hong Kong, in providing certain materials, as well as the National Endowment for the Humanities for generously helping to underwrite the publication costs.

Notes

1. Hu Shih's views were most succinctly expressed in "Wen-hsüeh chin-hua kuan-nien yü hsi-chü kai-liang" [The concept of literary evolution and dramatic reform] in Chao Chia-pi, ed., *Chung-kuo hsin wen-hsüeh ta-hsi* [A comprehensive anthology of modern Chinese literature: 1917-27]. 10 vols: vol. 1, *Chien-she li-lun* [Toward a constructive literary theory], pp. 376-86. Hu Shih's other essays on this subject are included in vol. 2, *Wen-hsüeh lun-cheng* [Literary debates].

2. Herbert Lindenberger in his *Historical Drama: The Relation of Literature and Reality* (Chicago, 1975) briefly discusses this on page 91 in a footnote: "Ibsen would much rather have been known as the author of *Emperor and Galilean* than of *Hedda Gabler.*"

3. Li Chien-wu under the pseudonym Liu Hsi-wei discusses the belief in "contemporary realism" as a confusion over the term for realism, *hsien-shih chu-i*, and a homophone for "actuality," as well as the result of theoretical statements by Zola and others, in *Chü-hua erh-chi* [Ruminations II] (Shanghai, 1942; 2d. ed., 1947):69-109.

4. See T'ien Han in Chung-kuo hsi-chü-chia hsieh-hui [Chinese Dramatist's Associa-tion], *Hsin-ko-chü wen-t'i t'ao-lun chi* [Discussion of the issue of new opera] (Peking, 1958):4.

5. Heralding Rolland's proposals for a theater of "joy," "energy," and "intelligence," and echoing his scorn for "bourgeois" and "aristocratic" drama, the Peking People's Dramatic Association also sought a popular form for a new theater. Rolland's own vision, however, was vitiated when Richard Wagner's operas, his model for Europe, were taken up by the Nazis. Rolland thought their music was their chief flaw, whereas the operas have survived their association with Nazism chiefly because of the music.

6. The famous seventeenth-century dramatist K'ung Shang-jen wrote: "The function of the plays is to correct society and awaken the world. . . . The songs and dances on the stage are nothing but guiding posts and mirrors for the spectators" (cited in Hung Shen, "What is the Chinese Drama," in *The China Journal of Science and Arts*, 1:3 [May 1923]:221). In 1905 a Chinese reformer concluded that "theater indeed is a great school for everyone in the country; the actors actually are the people's teachers throughout the country" (cited in A Ying [Ch'ien Hsing-ts'un], *Wan Ch'ing wen-hsüeh ts'ung-ch'ao.* Shanghai, 1960:52). The concept of "literature as a vehicle of the Way" (wen i tsai tao) is of course a broad phenomenon in China and has its theatrical aspects despite the repeated protests that young theater artists in the Republican era felt compelled to make that *they* were turning a form for entertainment into a vehicle for education and that theater artists needed more respect. For the above references I am indebted to Bernd Eberstein's paper "Music Theatre and Spoken Theatre" delivered at the Berlin Conference on Modern Chinese Literature, 1978.

7. The term ceremonial drama and the characteristics of it are taken from Lindenberger, *Historical Drama*, pp. 78-86.

8. See Hung Shen, "Tao-yen" [Introduction] in *Chung-kuo hsin wen-hsüeh ta-hsi*, vol. 9: *Hsi-chü chi* [Plays]:21-22.

9. For a discussion of the development of these concepts, see Lars Ragvald, *Yao Wen-yuan as a Literary Critic and Theorist: The Emergence of a Chinese Zhdanovism* (Stockholm, 1978). The quintessential example of Yao in debate with other critics in the field of drama is found in the exchange of views over Yang Lü-fang's comedy *Pu-ku-niao yu chiao-le* [Cuckoo sings again] in Chü-pen and *Hsi-chü pao* during 1958-60. See Ragvald, p. 146.

10. See, for example, the article by Yao Wen-yuan's old adversary, Ch'en Kung-min, "Kung-chü-lun hai-shih fan-ying lun" [The theory of utility or the theory of reflection], *Hsi-chü i-shu* [Dramatic Arts] (Shanghai), no. 1 (1979):1-4.

11. For example, the question of what form should be the "base" for "new opera" (hsin ko-chü) on a national scale has inevitably led to discussion of various regional forms or possible combinations of them. See *Hsin-ko-chü wen-t'i t'ao-lun chi*:3.

12. "When our modern drama troupes go to perform 'spoken' dramas instead of the traditional operas in the villages, they often come up against an embarrassing situation. The curtain has risen and the play is on, but the peasants stay outside the hall, smoking or chatting; when asked to take their seats they may retort, 'What's the hurry? The music hasn't started. Those fellows on the stage are just having a chat like ourselves! We shall go in when they begin to sing!'" See Tso-lin (Huang Tso-lin), "The Chinese and Western Theatres: A Study in Contrasting Techniques," *Chinese Literature*, no. 8 (1962):109. See also Chin Chien, "Man-t'an nung-min k'an hua-chü" [About the peasants watching spoken drama], *Hsi-chü pao*, no. 2 (1963):17-19: "Some people say that peasants like opera and are unwilling to watch spoken drama. . . . How to facilitate peasant acceptance of spoken drama is the vital problem to be solved at present." This lack of acceptance among a large portion of the population became increasingly critical as the criterion for esthetic judgment was pronounced to be the appreciation of the workers, soldiers, and peasants. (See *I-chiu-liu-san nien hua-tung-ch'u hua-chü kuan-mo yen-ch'u wen-chi* [Essays on the 1963 East China spoken drama festival] [Shanghai, 1965]:77.) Fifteen years later the same problem of peasant acceptance was alluded to by Arthur Miller. After watching the 1978 play celebrating Chou En-lai, *Loyal Hearts (Tan-hsin p'u)*, Miller recounts having met an intellectual during a train journey who discussed it with him: "The physics professor we

met on the long train ride felt that the play, which he had watched on its nation-wide telecast, was way over the average man's head and much too sophisticated. 'I don't think the peasants had the slightest notion what the play was all about,' he said surprisingly." Arthur Miller and Inge Morath, *Chinese Encounters* (New York, 1979), p. 93.

13. See T'ien Han in *Hsin-ko-chü wen-t'i t'ao-lun chi*:4; see also Chao Ming-i, "Hua-chü yun-tung san-shih nien kai-kuan" [Survey of thirty years of the spoken drama movement] in *Chung-kuo hua-chü yun-tung wu-shih nien shih-liao chi: ti erh chi* [Historical materials of fifty years of the Chinese spoken drama movement] (Macao, 1976):16-23.

14. *I-chiu-liu-san nien hua-tung-ch'ü hua-chü kuan-mo yen-ch'u wen-chi* [Essays on the 1963 East China spoken drama festival] (Shanghai, 1965):77.

⫽ 15. See Tso-lin (Huang Tso-lin), "The Chinese and Western Theatres: A Study in Contrasting Techniques," *Chinese Literature*, no. 8 (1962):101-11.

16. John Willet, *The Theatre of Bertolt Brecht* (London, 1959):181. Shaw's work, too, was haunted by the comment attributed to Egon Friedell that one could suck off.the sugar coating of his entertainment and put the bitter pill of the message back on the plate unconsumed. Cited in Eric Bentley, *Theater of War* (abridged edition, New York, 1973), p. 205. In China, however, Shaw was introduced to audiences by a production of *Mrs. Warren's Profession* at a time when it was still banned in England. The expressions of shock and dismay by members of the Chinese audience were equally decisive.

17. The shift in defining the nature of the audience was apparent in the addresses at the Fourth Congress of Delegates of Literary and Art Workers (Wen-hsüeh i-shu kung-tso-che ti-szu-tz'u tai-piao ta-hui) from 31 October 1979 to 16 November 1979, including speeches by Teng Hsiao-p'ing and Mao Tun (*Jen-min jih-pao* 31 October 1979:1-2), Hsia Yen and Hu Yao-pang (*Jen-min jih-pao*, 17 November 1979:1), and Chou Yang (*Kuang-ming jih-pao* 2 November 1979:1). In Teng Hsiao-p'ing's speech, for example, the phrase "workers, soldiers, and peasants" was used only once, while "the people" (jen-min) and the "mass of the people" (jen-min ch'un-chung) were characteristic terms, and in discussing the people Teng placed emphasis on variations in age, ethnicity, employment, and levels of education and economic status.

18. Translations of two representative plays in Taiwan by well-established writers are included in Joseph Chen-ying Yen, *Two Modern Chinese Dramas* (Ph.D. dissertation, Brigham Young University, 1973): Chang Yung-hsiang, *A Stormy Night Visitor (Feng-yü ku-jen lai*, 1960) and Wu Jo, *As Eternal as Heaven and Earth (T'ien-ch'ang ti-chiu*, 1965). Plays of the later sixties and seventies, reflecting more modernist influence, have been translated, including Shih Shu-ch'ing, *The Barren Years and Other Stories and Plays* (San Francisco, 1975), Yao I-wei, *Suitcase*, tr. Chou Shan (Taipei, 1974), and Chang Hsiao-feng, "The Man of Wu-ling," tr. Nathan Mao, *The Denver Quarterly* (summer 1977):139-67.

19. See David Y. Chen, "Two Chinese Adaptations of Eugene O'Neill's *The Emperor Jones*," *Modern Drama* vol. 9, no. 4 (February 1967): 431-39; and Marian Galik, "Chao—The King of Hell and The Emperor Jones: Two Plays by Hung Shen and O'Neill," *Asian and African Studies* (Bratislava) vol. 12 (1976):123-31.

20. See David Roy's discussion of expressionistic influence on Kuo Mo-jo's early work in *Kuo Mo-jo: The Early Years* (Cambridge, 1971):96-98. David Y. Chen, among others, also discusses the influence of O'Neill's early expressionism on Ts'ao Yü's play *The Wilderness (Yuan-yeh)* in "Two Chinese Adaptations of Eugene O'Neill's *The Emperor Jones*" cited in note 19.

21. Joseph S.M. Lau provides a critical study of Ting Hsi-lin's work in "'Oppression' as a Situation Comedy: A Note on the Stagecraft of Ting Hsi-lin" in William H. Nienhauser, ed., *Critical Essays on Chinese Literature* (Hong Kong, 1976).

22. A translation of part of Kuo Mo-jo's *Cho Wen-chun* appears in Harold Isaacs, ed., *Straw Sandals* (Cambridge, 1974), pp. 45-67.

23. There is apparently no discussion of P'an Chin-lien in English. A brief Chinese commentary may be found in T'ien Han, et al., *Chung-kuo hua-chü yun-tung wu-shih*

nien shih-liao chi, pp. 121-22. For a general observation on romantic transvaluation in literature, see Robert Scholes, *Structuralism in Literature* (New Haven, 1974), p. 44.

24. There are several translations of Ts'ao Yü's plays. The most available rendition of *Thunderstorm* is translated by Wang Tso-liang and A. C. Barnes (Peking, 1960).

25. Liu Hsi-wei (Li Chien-wu), *Chü-hua erh-chi* [Ruminations, II] (Shanghai, 1942):92. Unfortunately the original Japanese title of Fujimori's play is not given and cannot be confirmed.

26. For a general discussion of such views, see Henry Adler, "To Hell with Society" in Richard Corrigan, ed., *Theater in the Twentieth Century* (New York, 1963), pp. 245-72.

27. Students of Li Chien-wu should see David E. Pollard's unpublished paper, "Li Chien-wu and Modern Drama Standards" (presented at the conference on "The Role of the Writer in Modern China," Dedham, Massachusetts, August 1974). More recent biographical information on Li appears in *Chü-pen* [Playscripts], no. 5 (May 1980).

28. Both plays are available in translation as *Ch'u Yuan* (Peking, 1955; reprint ed. 1978) and Yao Hsin-nung, *The Malice of Empire*, tr. Jeremy Ingalls (London, 1970).

29. I am indebted to Daniel Talmadge for pointing out the relationship of the play to the *Model Regulations*.

30. See Yao Wen-yuan, "Lun Ch'en Kung-min ti 'szu-hsiang yuan-tse' ho 'mei-hsüeh yuan-tse'" [On Ch'en Kung-min's 'principles of thought' and 'principles of esthetics'], *Chü-pen* [Playscripts], no. 6 (June 1960):81-91. The date of this article, some three and a half years after the publication of *Cuckoo Sings Again*, is evidence of the protracted debate over the play, which involved a number of critics and theorists. Ch'en Kung-min, referred to in the title of this article, was a defender of the play. In 1979 he was teaching at the Shanghai Drama College, editing the journal *Hsi-chü i-shu* [Dramatic Arts].

Several other plays aroused controversy for their unorthodox treatment of their subjects, including Yüeh Yeh's *Together through Thick and Thin* (*T'ung-kan kung-k'u*, 1956) and Chao Hsün's *Homecoming* (*Huan-hsiang chi*, 1960), portions of each appearing in translation in Kai-yu Hsu, ed., *Literature of the People's Republic of China* (Bloomington, Indiana, 1980).

31. Several such plays have appeared in translation as book editions, in addition to works offered in the monthly *Chinese Literature* (Peking). See, for example, such well-known works as Tuan Ch'eng-pin and Tu Shih-chun, *Taming the Dragon and the Tiger* (Peking, 1961); Chin Shan, *Red Storm* (Peking, 1965); and Shen Hsi-meng, *On Guard beneath the Neon Lights* (Peking, 1966). A portion of the much-discussed 1963 play *The Young Generation* by Ch'en Yun and others appears in a translation by Kevin O'Connor and Constantine Tung in Kai-yu Hsu, ed., *Literature of the People's Republic of China*, pp. 628-41.

32. A discussion of spoken dramas during the Cultural Revolution period may be found in Roger Howard, *Contemporary Chinese Theatre* (London, 1978). However, scripts for such plays as *Madman of the Modern Age* and *In the Bloom of Youth* do not appear to be available. Background information on the play *Madman of the Modern Age* (1967) may be found in William Hinton, *Hundred Days War* (New York and London, 1972), pp. 135-36. I am indebted to Roger Howard for indicating this source.

TWENTIETH-CENTURY
Chinese Drama

Hu Shih

The Greatest Event in Life

Translated by Edward M. Gunn

Cast of Characters

MRS. T'IEN
FORTUNE-TELLER
LI MA
MISS T'IEN YA-MEI
MR. T'IEN

Setting

The parlor of the T'ien home. There is a door on the left leading to the front door, and a door on the right leading to the dining room. Upstage is a sofa, flanked by two armchairs. At center stage there is a small round table with a flower vase on it, flanked by two chairs. There is a small writing desk against the left wall.

The walls are hung with scrolls of Chinese paintings and calligraphy, along with two Dutch-style landscape paintings. This East-meets-West arrangement on the walls strongly indicates an atmosphere of a family in transition from tradition to the modern age. It is 1919.

The curtain rises slowly so that the audience can hear from onstage the final notes played by the FORTUNE-TELLER on his stringed instrument. MRS. T'IEN is seated in one of the armchairs, while the FORTUNE-TELLER, who is blind, sits on a chair next to the table.

MRS. T'IEN I don't understand very well what it is you're saying. Don't you think this match will work out?

FORTUNE-TELLER Mrs. T'ien, I tell it exactly according to the book of horoscopes. All of us fortune-tellers tell it exactly according to the book of horoscopes. You understand that—

MRS. T'IEN And according to the book how is it going to be?

FORTUNE-TELLER This match can't work. If the young lady in your family marries this man, then no good will come of it in the future, that is certain.

Mrs. T'ien Why?

Fortune-teller You understand, I'm merely telling it just as it is. Now the calculations for the year and day of the man's birth and the year and hour of the young lady's birth work out to coincide exactly with the entry in the book that reads:

> If snake and tiger marry and mate,
> The male will the female then dominate.
> If pig and monkey you try to blend,
> There's certain to be an untimely end.

These are birth calculations which constitute the strongest taboo against marriage. The signs of snake and tiger by themselves spell mutual destruction—and when you add the day and hour signs on top of that, with the pig and the monkey jinxing each other, then these are two most unpleasant fortunes. If these two people become man and wife, they are certain not to survive together into old age. To be specific, the man will emerge as the stronger, the fate of the husband overtaking that of his wife. Probably the woman will die an early death. Mrs. T'ien, you mustn't be offended. I'm telling fortune just as it is.

Mrs. T'ien I'm not offended, not at all. I like it when people are straightforward. And what you said is definitely correct. It's what the Goddess Kuan Yin said yesterday, too.

Fortune-teller Oh! The Bodhisattva Kuan Yin also said so?

Mrs. T'ien Yes. Over at the temple I got a slip of paper from her with a verse that read—oh, let me get it out and read it to you. [*She walks to the writing desk, opens a drawer, takes out a slip of paper, and reads*] This is fortune tally number seventy-eight. Most inauspicious.

> Spouses are chosen before we are born.
> The course that this takes we must not seek to bend.
> Those who scorn heaven will find life most forlorn.
> Their marriage will suffer an untimely end.

Fortune-teller "Their marriage will suffer an untimely end." Why, that's exactly what I just said.

Mrs. T'ien Of course, what the Goddess Kuan Yin says can't be wrong, but this is the greatest event in our daughter's life, and it's up to us as her parents to take the utmost care in our arrangements. So yesterday when I drew this fortune tally I was a little bit uneasy about it, and so I invited you over today to see if there was anything in their birthdate calculations that indicated a match.

Fortune-teller No, nothing at all.

Mrs. T'ien Since there are only a few phrases on the goddess's fortune tally it's not easy to interpret the message. Now that your calculations today coincide with the verse on the tally, then of course that settles it. [*Producing money to pay the* Fortune-teller] I'm much obliged to you, and here is your payment for calculating birthdates.

FORTUNE-TELLER [*Taking the money*] That's not at all necessary, not at all. Thank you. Thank you so much. I never imagined that what I said would match the verse on the tally! [*He rises*]

MRS. T'IEN [*Calling out*] Li Ma! [LI MA *enters from the door to the left*] Show him out. [LI MA *exits, leading the* FORTUNE-TELLER *off through the door to the right*]

MRS. T'IEN [*Gathers up the slips of red paper with the birthdates of her daughter and the young man on them, folds them and puts them in a drawer of the writing desk. She then puts the yellow tally with the verse on it in with them, and says to herself*] What a shame! Such a shame that these two can't be married!

[MISS T'IEN YA-MEI *enters from the outside through the door to the right. She is twenty-three or twenty-four, dressed for outdoors in an overcoat. Her face has the look of a woman with something on her mind. Upon entering, she takes off her coat as she speaks*]

YA-MEI Mother, what's got you telling fortunes again? I bumped into one of those fortune-tellers at the door as he was going out. Have you forgotten that father doesn't allow them in the house?

MRS. T'IEN Just this once, my child. I won't do it again.

YA-MEI But you promised father you wouldn't have anything to do with fortune-telling.

MRS. T'IEN I know, I know, but this time I *had* to ask a fortune-teller. I had him come over to check horoscopes for you and Mr. Ch'en.

YA-MEI Oh! Oh!

MRS. T'IEN You must understand: this is the biggest event in your life. And you are my only child. I can't just blindly let you marry a man with whom you're not compatible.

YA-MEI Who says we're not compatible? We've been friends for years. We certainly are compatible.

MRS. T'IEN You certainly are not. The fortune-teller said you're not.

YA-MEI What does he know?

MRS. T'IEN It's not just the fortune-teller who says so. The Goddess Kuan Yin says so, too.

YA-MEI What? You went to ask Kuan Yin? Father's really going to have something to say about that.

MRS. T'IEN I know your father opposes me in this, just as he opposes me no matter what I do. But think of how we older people presume to decide upon your marriage. No matter how careful we are we can't insure against error. But the Bodhisattva Kuan Yin never deceives people. And then, too, when it gets to the point that both Kuan Yin and the fortune-teller are saying the same thing, that's even more reason to believe it. [*She stands and walks to the desk, opening a drawer*] Read the verse from Kuan Yin for yourself.

YA-MEI I don't want to.

MRS. T'IEN [*Left with no choice but to close the drawer*] Don't be so obstinate, child. I like that Mr. Ch'en very much. He looks to me like a very dependable person. You've known him all these years since you met in Japan, and you say you know very well what kind of man he is. Still, you're young and inexperienced yet, and your judgment could very well be mistaken. Even those of us who are in their fifties and sixties don't presume to put complete faith in their own judgment. It was because I didn't dare put such faith in myself that I went to consult Bodhisattva Kuan Yin and the fortune-teller. Kuan Yin said it wouldn't work out. And then the fortune-teller said that it wouldn't work out. They can't both be mistaken! The fortune-teller said that the calculations for your birthdates were precisely those under the strongest taboo in the book of horoscopes. It's called something like, "If pig and monkey try to blend/There's sure to be an untimely end." Since your year and hour of birth and his—

YA-MEI That's enough, mother, I don't want to hear it. [*Both hands over her face, she sobs*] I can't stand listening to you talk that way! I know father won't agree with you. I'm sure he won't.

MRS. T'IEN I don't care what he thinks. My own daughter is not going to get married to someone if I don't agree to it. [*Walking up to her daughter*, MRS. T'IEN *daubs at her tears for her with a handkerchief*] Don't cry. I'll leave you to think it over carefully. We're only thinking of you, and want what's best for you. I'll go see if lunch is ready. Your father will be back soon. Don't cry, that's a good girl. [MRS. T'IEN *exits through the door to the dining room*]

YA-MEI [*Wiping her tears and looking up, she sees* LI MA *enter.* YA-MEI *beckons to her to come closer and speaks to her quietly*] Li Ma, I need your help. My mother won't approve of my marrying Mr. Ch'en—

LI MA What a pity! What a pity! Mr. Ch'en is such a polite gentleman. Why, I ran into him on the street this morning and he nodded and spoke to me, oh my.

YA-MEI Yes, he saw you bringing the fortune-teller to this house, and he was afraid our plans might take a turn for the worse. So he telephoned me at school right away to let me know. When I came back he followed behind me in his car. He should still be at the corner waiting to hear from me. Go and tell him. Say my mother won't let us marry, but father is coming home, and he's bound to help us out. Have him move the car to the back street and wait for my message. So go ahead. [LI MA *turns to go*] Oh, come back! [LI MA *turns and comes back*] Tell him—tell him—tell him not to worry! [LI MA *smiles and exits*]

YA-MEI [*Walks over to the writing desk and opens the drawer for a surreptitious peek at the contents, and then looks at her watch*] Father ought to be back soon. It's almost twelve o'clock.

[MR. T'IEN, *by appearance a man of fifty, enters*]

YA-MEI [*Quickly closes the drawer and stands to greet her father*] Father, you're back! Mother is saying—Mother has something important to discuss with you—something very important.

MR. T'IEN What's so important? Tell me first.

YA-MEI Mother will tell you. [*She walks toward the dining room and calls out*]Mother. Mother. Father's back!

MR. T'IEN Who knows what you two are up to now. [*He sits on a chair by the table as* MRS. T'IEN *enters from the direction of the dining room*] Ya-mei says you have something important to tell me— something urgent you want to talk over with me.

MRS. T'IEN Yes, it's very important. [*She sits on the left-hand chair*] I'm talking about this marriage with the Ch'en family.

MR. T'IEN Fine. I've been giving this matter some thought for several days now.

MRS. T'IEN Good. We all ought to give it some thought. For Ya-mei this is the greatest event in life. And once I think of how important this matter is, I get so upset that I can't sleep or eat, either. Now as for this Mr. Ch'en, we've gotten together a lot, but even so I'm still a little uneasy about him. The way things used to be, you got one look at your proposed son-in-law for the sake of principle and that was it. The way it is now, the more we see him the harder our responsibility is to bear. His family may be wealthy, but then children from wealthy families more often turn out bad than good, a lot more often. He's gone overseas to study, too, but then a lot of overseas students no sooner get back than they get rid of the wives they were matched with in the first place.

MR. T'IEN That's quite a speech. So after all what is on your mind?

MRS. T'IEN My point is this: that in arranging this important matter for our daughter, we can't just stick to our own judgment alone. I wouldn't presume to trust my judgment alone, so yesterday I went to ask advice at the Temple of Kuan Yin.

MR. T'IEN You what? Didn't you promise me you wouldn't go burning incense and praying to Buddha any more?

MRS. T'IEN I did it for the sake of our daughter.

MR. T'IEN Humph! Humph! All right, enough of this. Go on.

MRS. T'IEN I went to the temple and drew one tally. The verse on the tally said that this marriage wouldn't work. I'll show you the verse. [*She starts to open the drawer*]

MR. T'IEN Phooey! I don't want to see it. I don't believe in these things! You said yourself that this is the most important event in our daughter's life, and that you didn't presume to trust yourself. You don't mean to tell me that you trust some wood and plaster bodhisattva, do you?

YA-MEI [*Joyfully*] I said that father doesn't believe in that stuff. [*Walking over to her father*] Thank you. We ought to trust our own judgment, isn't that so?

MRS. T'IEN It wasn't only Kuan Yin who said so.

MR. T'IEN Oh! Who else?

MRS. T'IEN I still wasn't satisfied after I saw the verse. I still had some doubts. So I had someone go and invite in the most renowned fortune-teller in the city, Blind Chang, to come and make birthdate calculations.

MR. T'IEN Humph! Humph! There you go again forgetting what you promised me.

MRS. T'IEN I know, but for our daughter's sake I've been so unsettled, so uncertain of how to handle things, that I had to go find him to settle on a decision.

MR. T'IEN Who told you to go to Kuan Yin and stir up doubts about it in the first place? You shouldn't have asked Kuan Yin to begin with—you should have come to me first.

MRS. T'IEN Blasphemy. Blasphemy, oh, Amida Buddha— That fortune-teller said the same thing as Kuan Yin. Now isn't that most unusual?

MR. T'IEN Enough! Enough! No more of this nonsense. You have eyes, but you won't use them. Instead you take the word of a blind man with no eyes. If that isn't a joke.

YA-MEI Father, you are perfectly right. I knew you'd help us.

MRS. T'IEN [*Turning her wrath on her daughter*] Why, of all the cheeky things, to say "help us"! "Us" is supposed to be who? You're so crass! [*Covering her face with her handkerchief, she weeps*] You're all in it together against me! My own daughter's biggest event in life—can't I as a mother have anything to do with it?

MR. T'IEN It's precisely because it is the greatest event in our daughter's life that we as parents must be particularly thoughtful and sober. This business of plaster bodhisattvas and fortune-telling is all just a swindle. You can't believe it. Ya-mei, is that so or isn't it?

YA-MEI You bet that's so. I knew you couldn't believe in that stuff.

MR. T'IEN From now on, I'm not going to allow any more of this superstitious talk. We're finished with plaster bodhisattvas and blind fortune-tellers once and for all. And we're going to discuss this marriage properly. [*To* MRS. T'IEN] Now don't cry. [*To* YA-MEI] You sit down, too. [YA-MEI *sits on the sofa*] Ya-mai, I don't want you to marry Mr. Ch'en.

YA-MEI [*Startled and upset*] Father, are you joking or is this for real?

MR. T'IEN For real. This marriage definitely can't work. It hurts me to say so, but I have to say it.

YA-MEI Is it that you've discovered something bad about him?

MR. T'IEN No. I like him very much. He's as fine a son-in-law as one could choose. And that bothers me all the more.

YA-MEI [*Bewildered*] Do you now believe in bodhisattvas and fortune-tellers?

MR. T'IEN No. Absolutely not.

MRS. T'IEN *and* YA-MEI [*Simultaneously*] Then what is it?

MR. T'IEN You were overseas for so long that you have forgotten all our customs and rules. You've even failed to keep in mind the laws laid down by our own clan ancestors.

YA-MEI Just what law am I breaking by marrying Mr. Ch'en?

MR. T'IEN I'll go get it and show you. [*He stands and exits toward the dining room*]

MRS. T'IEN I have no idea what it is. Amida Buddha, it's just as well this way, just so long as he doesn't permit the marriage.

YA-MEI [*Her head bowed in thought, she suddenly looks up showing an air of determination*] I know how to handle this.

MR. T'IEN [*Enters carrying a large set of clan records in both hands*] Look, here are the records of our clan. [*He opens the books, stacking them in an untidy pile on the table*] Look, 2,500 years of our ancestors in the T'ien clan, and is there one single marriage of a T'ien to a Ch'en?

YA-MEI Why can't someone named T'ien marry someone named Ch'en?

MR. T'IEN Because Chinese custom forbids persons of the same family to marry.

YA-MEI But we don't have the same family name. His family is named Ch'en and ours is named T'ien.

MR. T'IEN We do have the same family name. Long ago the ancients pronounced the word Ch'en and the word T'ien in the same way. So sometimes our family name was written T'ien and sometimes it was written Ch'en.[1] Actually, they're the same. Didn't you read the Confucian *Analects* when you were a little girl?

YA-MEI Yes, I did, but I can't remember much about it.

MR. T'IEN In the *Analects* there appears a fellow named Ch'en Ch'eng-tzu. But in the commentaries his name is written as T'ien Ch'eng-tzu, and the reason for that is what I just told you: 2,500 years ago the Ch'ens and the T'iens were all one family. It was only in later ages that the people who used the character "t'ien" concluded that their surname was T'ien and the people who used the character "ch'en" concluded that their surname was Ch'en. To look at them, you'd think that they are two different family names. Actually, they are one family. So descendents with these two names are not permitted to marry.

YA-MEI You don't mean to tell me that a man and a woman whose family names were the same 2,000 years ago can't get married?

MR. T'IEN They can't.

YA-MEI Father, you're someone who understands reason. You certainly don't accept a law as unreasonable as this.

MR. T'IEN It makes little difference that I don't accept it. Society accepts it. Those clan elders accept it. What would you have me do? This doesn't only apply to people named T'ien and Ch'en, you know. There's a Mr. Kao working at the local magistrate's *yamen* who told me that his ancestors with the name Kao were originally grandsons of Ch'en Yu-liang at the end of the Yuan dynasty. Later they changed their family name to Kao.[2] So because 600 years ago these people named Kao had the name Ch'en, they won't marry someone named Ch'en. On top of that, since 2,500 years ago people named Ch'en were also named T'ien, these Kaos won't marry anyone named T'ien, either.

YA-MEI That's even more unreasonable!

MR. T'IEN Reasonable or not, it makes no difference. This is a law of the clan ancestral shrine. If we break the clan shrine law, we lose our place in it. A few decades ago there was a merchant family in the south named T'ien, and they married a daughter to someone named Ch'en. Later, the girl died, but the head of the Ch'en clan would not allow her spirit a place in the Ch'en clan ancestral shrine. Before she was allowed a place, her own family had to donate a substantial sum of money to the Ch'en clan shrine as a fine for their mistake, and change her name from T'ien to Shen by lengthening the middle vertical stroke.[3]

YA-MEI That's easy enough. I'm willing to extend the mid-vertical stroke and change my name to Shen.

MR. T'IEN It's easy enough to say. You may be willing. I am *not* willing! I will not for the sake of your marriage suffer the ridicule and scorn of our clan elders.

YA-MEI [*Upset to the point of tears*] But we do not have the same name!

MR. T'IEN The clan records say the names are the same, and the clan elders also say the names are the same. I've asked a number of the elders and they all say this. You must understand that as parents arranging a daughter's wedding, while we shouldn't listen to plaster bodhisattvas and blind fortune-tellers, we *have* to listen to those elders.

YA-MEI [*Beseechingly*] Father!

MR. T'IEN Let me finish. There's one more difficulty. If your friend Ch'en were not wealthy, that would be fine. Unfortunately, he is a very wealthy man, and if I give you to him in marriage, the clan elders are certainly going to say that out of greed for his money, I would ignore even our ancestors and sell my daughter off to him.

YA-MEI [*In despair*] Your whole life you've wanted to break free of superstitious practices, and now finally you can't break with a superstitious clan law. I never dreamed this could happen.

MR. T'IEN Are you angry with me? I can't blame you. It's only natural for you to be upset. I don't blame you at all for being so angry with me—I don't blame you at all.

LI MA [*Entering through the door to the left*] Lunch is ready.

MR. T'IEN Come. Come on. We'll have something to eat and then talk it over. I'm starved. [*Goes into the dining room*]

MRS. T'IEN [*Walking over to her daughter*] Don't cry. You must understand for yourself. We only want what's best for you. Pull yourself together and have lunch with us.

YA-MEI I don't want to eat.

MRS. T'IEN Don't be so stubborn. Go and calm yourself first, then come. We'll wait for you. [MRS. T'IEN *also goes into the dining room. After closing the door,* LI MA *stands motionless*]

YA-MEI [*Looking up and seeing* LI MA] Is Mr. Ch'en still waiting in his car?

LI MA Yes. Here's a note he wrote for you. [*She produces a sheet of paper and passes it to* YA-MEI]

YA-MEI [*Reads*] "This matter concerns the two of us and no one else. You should make your own decision." [*She repeats the final sentence*] "You should make your own decision!" Yes, I should make my own decision. [*Speaking to* LI MA] Go in and tell my father and mother to go ahead and eat. There's no point waiting for me. I'll eat after a while.

[LI MA *nods and goes into the dining room.* YA-MEI *stands, puts on her overcoat, hastily jots down a note at the writing desk, and places it underneath the flower vase on the table. With one look back, she hurries out the door to the right. There is a pause*]

MRS. T'IEN [*Offstage*] Ya-mei, come on and have lunch now. Your food will get cold. [*Enters*] Where did you go? Ya-mei?

MR. T'IEN [*Offstage*] Leave her alone. She's angry. Let her calm down and she'll be all right. [*Enters*] Did she go out?

MRS. T'IEN Her overcoat's not here. Maybe she's gone back to the school.

MR. T'IEN [*Seeing the note under the flower vase*] What's this? [*He reads the note*] "This is the greatest event in your daughter's life. Your daughter ought to make a decision for herself. She has left in Mr. Ch'en's car. Goodbye for now." [*Hearing this,* MRS. T'IEN *staggers backward and sits in an armchair*]

[MR. T'IEN *dashes to the right-hand door, but as he reaches it he looks back with a wide-eyed, helpless look of hesitation and uncertainty*]

[*Curtain*]

Notes

1. The character for T'ien is written 田; the character for Ch'en is written 陳.

2. Ch'en Yu-liang (1320-1363) was a powerful military leader in rebellion against the Mongol Yuan dynasty. His chief rival in rebellion was Chu Yuan-chang, who succeeded in killing Ch'en, destroying his army, and becoming the founding emperor of the Ming dynasty. Ch'en Yu-liang's surviving relatives changed their names to avoid being associated with their ill-fated kin.

3. The character for Shen is written 申.

Hung Shen

Yama Chao

Translated by Carolyn T. Brown

Cast of Characters

CHAO TA (YAMA CHAO), a soldier, orderly of the Battalion Commander
LAO LI, a soldier
HSIAO MA, a guard
BATTALION COMMANDER
OTHERS: soldiers; several black figures; a County Magistrate of the
  Ch'ing Dynasty; several guards; an old man; a woman; a foreigner;
  the foreigner's lackey; bandits

PART I

Scene 1

The action occurs in a military camp located in a deserted village in the early 1920s. The village is not far from a crowded, bustling town with thousands of inhabitants. Aside from a small grocery and five hundred soldiers, the village is empty. Since the weather is cold, everyone is asleep. Only in a few of the officers' quarters are the lamps and braziers still lit.

The scene is the bedroom of the Battalion Commander. Against the rear wall on the extreme left is a metal, military folding cot, and on it a white wolfskin rug with a Western style pillow and a pink silk comforter on top. Against the left wall is a low dresser with an attached mirror above and storage for clothes below. Piled in a disorderly heap on top are a pistol, an army sword, a military hat and unbuckled belt which have been casually tossed there, plus a face-powder compact, perfumed soap, a mirrored case, and a perfume bottle. On the right wall hangs a scroll painting of a traditional beauty, and to its right a door leads to the courtyard. To the left of the painting several of the Battalion Commander's uniforms hang from nails. The small square window with paper window panes located on the back wall toward the left is closed. In front of the window are piled two wooden trunks sealed with slips of paper by order of the quartermaster. On the left side of the room, in front of the bed, a small charcoal brazier contains the remnants of a fire. A small square table with four chairs is placed on the right side of the room. Two kerosene lamps sit on the table, one unlit and the other burning very faintly, as if the oil were nearly used up.

The door on the right opens violently and CHAO TA *comes in. He is wearing an old and dirty gray uniform. Many of the jacket's buttons are missing. He is not wearing leggings, but only regular trousers. His cotton padded shoes, which have done many days' service, are beginning to gape at the toes. The man is stooped, with hunched shoulders, a face full of wrinkles, and a touch of gray at the temples. He is dispirited and very tired. He is only in his early forties, but because he has led a hard life he appears to be over fifty. He is holding a china teapot gingerly, as if very hot.*

After coming in, he turns to close the door, takes a cup from the table, pours it half full of tea, and sips slowly. Then he warms his hands by holding the pot between them. Having finished drinking, he places the teapot on the brazier to keep it warm, and stirs up the charcoal, then pulls a chair over, intending to warm himself beside the brazier, but instead suddenly walks to the window, looks out, shakes his head, and talks to himself.

CHAO TA What time is it? It must be past midnight. But that's still early for him! He won't be back for a while. [*Looking toward the door*] Suppose I slip out, return to my tent, look for something to eat, and then take a long nap. He never finishes playing those sixteen rounds of mah jong before the fourth watch. Damn, it's cold. [*He walks toward the door but changes his mind suddenly again*] Forget it. I'd better do what I'm supposed to. These last few days the Commander has lost a lot of money. And that means tough luck for me. Everything always goes wrong. Later when he finds the room isn't warm and there's no hot tea—*what* have I been doing? [*He sits beside the brazier*] The more plain tea I drink, the hungrier I get. [*He stares vacantly at the fire awhile, feels colder, and shudders from head to toe. He drags the pink silk comforter from the bed, wraps it around himself, and sits down again. He is just about to doze off when he hears a sound outside. He stands up quickly and replaces the comforter. Not hearing anything more, he grumbles*] He's not back. I'm hearing things!
[*Someone stealthily opens the door, sticks his head in, and in a low voice says*] Hey, Brother Chao Ta.
CHAO TA [*Turning, in a low voice*] So it was you outside, you joker! You're letting the heat out. If you're coming in, Lao Li, hurry up and come in.
[*LI is also a soldier, just a little over twenty. Although his uniform is old and tattered, the man himself is vigorous. He enters tiptoeing, and carefully closes the door*]
LAO LI This is heaven. If you could sleep in my tent and not freeze to death, I'd be surprised! [*He points to the bed*] The stakes will probably be high tonight.
CHAO TA I know.

LAO LI If Platoon Leader Wang is winning, he probably won't dare stop playing until dawn.

CHAO TA Don't they always play until dawn! [*He points to the kerosene lamp*] We always use two lamps full of oil every night.

LAO LI [*Takes a bottle of liquor from inside his jacket*] Let's have a cup.

CHAO TA [*Takes two teacups from the table, pours the liquor, and drinks*] This is good Kaoliang liquor!

LAO LI When the grocery manager came to town, he brought along two bottles. He sold me one for half a dollar, which really is outrageous. But what can I do?

CHAO TA Doesn't he give credit? [*As he listens, he extinguishes the lamp which has been lit and lights the other*]

LAO LI He does. But I've heard that they're going to pay us soon.

CHAO TA Who says so?

LAO LI Hsiao Ma.

CHAO TA How could Hsiao Ma know that?

LAO LI Eh! [*He takes two gulps of liquor, glances at the wooden trunk, feeling slightly embarrassed about giving his reason for coming*] Brother Chao Ta, since you work for the Battalion Commander, you must know more than Hsiao Ma. So, brother, how about lending me some money?

CHAO TA [*Laughs*] When a bonze bumps into a baldy, both heads are bare.[1]

LAO LI Don't say that. You're better off than we are.

CHAO TA How could I be? All of us soldiers depend on our pay. And in this camp we haven't been paid for months. Who isn't hard up!

LAO LI You're really broke?

CHAO TA [*Sarcastically*] I've got money. I haven't seen any pay in over five months. What bastard has any money? But Lao Li, we still have a little good luck. We still get fed every day, so wait and see what happens.

LAO LI [*Stands up angrily*] Wait! Isn't this waiting? Our job is a damn hard one. Those motherfuckers buy our lives for a few stinking ounces of silver. Our lives are worth only eight ounces of silver a month, and even then we don't get paid for over five months. What are we doing it for?

CHAO TA You certainly are right.

LAO LI Every poor bastard in the world has to eat. Even a horse has to have food. We haven't been paid in half a year, and we haven't had any job to do either. If they sent us out to fight, even if the motherfuckers didn't pay us double-rate, we could always find something to make it worthwhile. If we got killed, what would it matter? Brother, am I right?

CHAO TA You're right. You're right. [*Thinks silently*] I think every man has his fate, and we're stuck with a bad one.

LAO LI Some soldiers have good luck. Have you heard about the newly formed 89th Division? Originally it was a brigade. Now it's been changed, and they're recruiting. They're not behind in paying salaries: they pay cash.

CHAO TA So I've heard.

LAO LI A lot of our comrades feel they don't want to serve here; they don't want to wait for their back pay; and they'd go wherever cash is being paid just like that. Well, if you don't get rich when you're young, when you're old you just wait to be discharged.

CHAO TA [*Sadly pensive*] Should I go somewhere else again?

LAO LI Brother, have you also been thinking about it?

CHAO TA [*Smiles slightly*] Lao Li, sit down. [LAO LI *is perplexed, but sits*] Each bag of flesh and bones has his fortune, his fate. When I was eighteen, my father died. I set out to make a living and became a soldier in my early twenties. I've been to Kwangtung and Kwangsi. I've been beyond the Great Wall. In Szechwan I fought the Miao; in Nanking I fought the revolutionaries. In Honan I captured the White Wolves.[2] There's no place I haven't been, nothing I haven't eaten, and nothing I haven't seen. [*As he talks, he picks up the gun on the dresser and glances at it*] See this gun I'm holding? It holds six bullets. I would kill seven men, never five. My comrades said that I was as vicious as Yama, the King of Hell. In his whole life this man named Chao has never suffered at anyone's hands. Now Yama Chao is over forty years old. Look! Look what I've become! [*Laughs bitterly*] Yama Chao is not someone who's never been rich. [*He sighs*] Good food, good drink, gold watches, money! Don't you think I wanted them when I had them? But fate wasn't with me. They came and went like water. Get rich, indeed! Chao doesn't think that way any more!

LAO LI Brother, here you're happy to go on being hungry?

CHAO TA I'm not happy, but I'm not complaining either.

LAO LI You fill his wash basin, empty his chamber pot, boil water, wipe the table, on very cold nights stand watch, get cursed and slapped; you're a slave, a pig, a dog, and that isn't enough to make you happy!

CHAO TA Lecture me, and I'll kill you!

[*The two men glare at each other*]

LAO LI [*Unwilling to ruin his plan, he restrains his anger*] I was just thinking how unfairly you've been treated. But there is a way to get rich, and I can't keep from telling you about it. In lots of places, north and south, troops are being recruited. Why don't we go? It would be better for us.

CHAO TA [*From experience*] It's always the same, north or south.

LAO LI No. Listen to me. Our Battalion Commander has a superior, doesn't he? And even his superior is not that big. He only commands a brigade of a few thousand men. Above him is the Division Commander who commands over 10,000 men. And above him is the general. Now he has money and power. Even the president in the capital doesn't have as much as he does. For example . . .

CHAO TA I know all of that.

LAO LI Even though the leader who I said was recruiting soldiers is a

Division Commander, he's in charge of the troops for a whole province. And there's one advantage. [*He comes close, speaks cautiously*] He's our general's enemy.

CHAO TA What do you mean?

LAO LI He's willing to take anyone, whoever they are. If someone has been a soldier, he may make him a Company Commander. If someone under our general deserts, he'll rate him highly.

CHAO TA I don't believe it.

LAO LI It's something new. It wasn't this way the first few years. It must be because their hatred has grown. [*Pauses*] But we don't really need to worry about that, do we? They hate each other; it works to our advantage. If we go, how can we not be rated highly?

CHAO TA [*Shakes his head*] You make it sound so easy.

LAO LI We'll slip away!

CHAO TA Can we do that?

LAO LI Sure. When we leave camp, we won't go west. About forty *li* west is the town, crowded with people. We might be spotted and that could be awkward. But if we run to the north, in less than 20 *li* there is a pine forest which is twenty to thirty *li* around, stretching from level ground up into the mountains, forming a solid mass. In that forest during the day it's pitch black. There isn't even a path through it. The ground is covered with decaying leaves, rotting tree branches, and dead rodents. No bullet can hit its target, and no one can see a thing. A large party of men and horses would be useless. They'd get confused and lose their way. And maybe they wouldn't be able to get in or out. But since we'd be only two in number and would know the way, we could thread our way through the forest, cross the mountains, and get far away from them. How could we fail to slip away!

CHAO TA Couldn't they bypass the forest to get over the mountain? If they caught us . . .

LAO LI By the time they get over the mountain, we'll already have been gone three days. They wouldn't be able to catch us.

CHAO TA If they did capture us, we would be shot.

LAO LI [*With real fear*] You're saying "shot" to scare me!

CHAO TA Getting caught after deserting is worse than getting drunk, or gambling, injuring someone in a fight, or fooling around with young girls. If you do any of those sorts of things, you can still plead and save yourself. But if you desert . . . all right! Our commanders pay us so that when something happens and they say "fight," we go all out and risk our lives. When we uphold their honor it's called loyalty. But if you eat their food now and then because you're annoyed go somewhere else, that's not appreciating their generosity. If this general who's been spending his money on you doesn't shoot you, who else will he shoot?

LAO LI You're right, *if* we are captured. [*Not conceding and speaking defiantly*] But Heaven sees everything. We eat their food but we also work for them, why do you call it their generosity? What favor have they done me!

CHAO TA When you reach that other place, will it really be much better? [*Patiently*] Will it be any better than here? Will you really get anything out of it?

LAO LI There you get cash when you enlist.

CHAO TA Right! They give ready cash so they don't owe you money. [*Ironically*] But how long will that last?

[LAO LI *doesn't know how to respond. He drinks two cups of liquor in succession and sits down to reflect*]

CHAO TA They'll pay for a few days and then the money will be gone. [LAO LI *drinks and doesn't reply*] Furthermore, your new comrades may not be as good as the old ones here. We've gone through thick and thin together. And as for the new general, suppose his temper is worse than our Commander's. If your service is not satisfactory, you'll suffer. [LAO LI *turns his head, not wanting to hear*] Besides, what camp today doesn't have money trouble? What officer doesn't rely on scheming against others, harming them, and treating his men cold-heartedly, all so he can get rich! It's the same everywhere. Why not stay here and make the best of it! [LAO LI *gives him a vicious look*] If your own intentions aren't good, then will your superiors do you any favors? You still think that respect will come of it and that you will be made a company commander. That's just dreaming!

LAO LI [*Stands up, apparently quite tipsy, his body swaying, and his words slurred*] Basically my leaving has nothing to do with becoming a "loyal official" and a "filial son." [*He is not really very drunk but is putting on an act as an excuse to speak his mind freely*] When someone has a high post, he has a lot of money, and the world is his. Those who commit large crimes have high positions and get rich. Those who commit small crimes take the blame and get killed. Virtuous intentions and good deeds get you nowhere. [*Pounding the table*] What I want is fame and money. To hell with "principle" and "morality." [*He raises his foot to give a kick, but stumbles into the chair*]

CHAO TA Are you drunk?

LAO LI I'm speaking the truth.

CHAO TA Go, go, go. Get some sleep.

LAO LI I'm giving you good advice. [*Stands up unsteadily.* CHAO TA *goes over to support him but is pushed away. Slowly* LAO LI *goes to the door, and groping for the knob, opens it. When the cold wind hits his face, he stops, straightens up, and breathes deeply twice. Then becoming clearheaded, as if he's just waking up from a dream, he glances around the room. Almost but not quite smiling,* LAO LI *clears his throat and turns to close the door again. He walks back toward* CHAO TA] Brother, look at me. How could I be so mixed up? I've forgotten the real thing I came for.

CHAO TA There's something else?

LAO LI I want to borrow several months' pay to live on for the rest of my life.

CHAO TA [*Finds this extremely strange*] Borrow pay . . . ?

LAO LI Exactly! Exactly!

CHAO TA Where are you going to borrow it from?

LAO LI From this very room!

CHAO TA Don't talk nonsense.

LAO LI There's a lot of money in this room. Brother, I want to talk to you, and don't tell anyone else about this. The Battalion Commander is really rich.

CHAO TA Ha, ha! Rich!

LAO LI This is a secret. Brother, I'm not drunk. Hsiao Ma, he said that he knows, that he's seen it. It was by coincidence. Hsiao Ma says our pay has already been sent down from above, two months' worth. There's eight or nine thousand dollars.

CHAO TA [*Impatiently*] It can't be. How can the pay be sent down and not issued?

LAO LI Couldn't he do that? The Battalion Commander certainly has some reason for it. [CHAO TA *suddenly stands still. He contemplates this but doesn't reply*] Brother, that nine thousand, the Commander is hiding it; it's all here in this room. [CHAO TA *shakes his head*] It's true. This is our chance. In two days the pay may be distributed and then it will be too late.

CHAO TA [*With calm confidence*] The pay has definitely not been received.

LAO LI [*Not giving in*] You are not going to listen!

CHAO TA [*With absolute certainty*] I know!

LAO LI None of our five hundred comrades in camp knows about it. Hsiao Ma asked the Platoon Leader, and he didn't know either. You . . .

CHAO TA [*Calmly*] I know!

LAO LI How do you know?

CHAO TA The Commander's business is my business. He tells me everything that's on his mind; all of it. If the pay had been received already, he certainly would have mentioned it to me. But since he didn't say anything about it, it definitely hasn't been received.

LAO LI Brother. I'm not drunk. You're the one who's drunk.

CHAO TA Then you don't believe that the Commander respects me?

LAO LI Certainly he respects you a great deal, and calls you a bastard and slaps your face.

CHAO TA That's true. [*Passionately*] But he also treats me as a man. He makes use of me; he has faith in me. [*Speaking slowly now, and with pain*] In the beginning I got into bad trouble and ran east and west with nowhere to stay. I said to myself, how can you have no conscience at all? If someone were willing to take me in and help me to change my ways, I would behave from then on as a decent and upright man. Then I came to this camp and started serving the Battalion Commander day and night for almost four years. And here I am now. The Commander has made me his trusted assistant. He trusts me with everything, whether big or small, good or bad. Things that he can't tell others, he tells me. Things that he hides from others, he doesn't hide from me. Why is this? Although he doesn't say, don't I know why in my heart? Because the Commander understands my loyalty and good will, and my gratitude toward him. He needs me, trusts me. So what if he curses me and hits me. He doesn't hold anything against me, and I don't hate him. Don't talk about nine thousand dollars. Even if there were ninety thousand involved, he wouldn't deceive me, Chao Ta.

LAO LI [*Not willing to give up*] Brother, your words are straight-forward. The Commander wouldn't deceive you because he remembers Chao's good points. Brother, that Chao is really lucky. [CHAO TA *glances at him*] Hu Chin-piao got sick from nearly freezing and couldn't go to drill. Because he didn't get enough medicine, he slept in his tent feeling miserable. But the Commander didn't care. Chang Te-shen bought food on credit, and when the pay wasn't issued, he couldn't pay it back. So he quarrelled and had a fight with those people. And when he got back to camp, they recorded it, and he was put in prison for three days. And the Commander didn't care. If somebody orders our comrades around, throws them out, pushes them away, curses them as if they were four-footed beasts who can't talk, and when dissatisfied with their answers beats them thirty or fifty strokes, afterwards they still have to bear the pain of the wounds, act grateful, and go on serving. And the Commander doesn't care. Never mind that we deal in lead, despised everywhere we go, and still do a good job. When things go bad, no matter what, it's on our heads, we're cursed for eight generations, and that Commander couldn't care less. In the fighting north of the capital, our comrades were thrown into confusion and were wounded and killed. What really was the point of it? Several hundred men were buried in a pit with no separate grave mounds and no coffins. And the Commander didn't care. And he treats us like human beings! [CHAO TA *wrinkles his brow and says nothing*] What I've discovered about this money being sent here must be absolutely true, and I have been planning this for a long time. Besides, it isn't the Commander's own money. Since he's stashing it away and not issuing it, he probably plans to keep it himself. His own background is questionable. We are thieves stealing from a thief, and there's no crime in that. When we get the money in our hands, we'll immediately go to that other camp and enlist. He may even be afraid of hearing other people talk about it and not dare to let anyone know. And if he does try to catch us, we will have found our way through the woods, and been long gone. [CHAO TA *still isn't completely convinced*] Brother, you're the only one who knows about the money in this room. If someone else turned the room upside down, he still might not be able to find it. Besides, you're an insider and I'm on the outside. How could I do anything without you? I came tonight to invite you to come along with me. Really that's the only reason I talk to you about the money.

CHAO TA It doesn't matter whether there's money or not. Even if the room were piled with money and the Commander specifically asked me to guard it, I couldn't do anything against my conscience.

LAO LI Why are you sticking to him like that? It can't be that you're still hoping for something, that you still hope to get promoted, or get rich? Why don't you take advantage of the fact that your hair is still black and that you still have white teeth to spend a few days in happiness. You said that the Battalion Commander thinks well of you, has confidence in you. Don't you remember Wang Kou-tzu? He and our [*Lowers his voice*] Brigade Commander were friends for many years, had such great affection for one another. How is it that later on Wang Kou-tzu died at the hands of that Brigade Commander!

[*Hearing him bring up the Wang Kou-tzu affair,* CHAO TA *suddenly becomes very angry, the expression on his face changes, and his eyes become red*]

LAO LI Whatever you say goes. So we won't run away and enlist elsewhere. A person who hangs his life on the muzzle of his gun to look for a buyer never knows for certain what day he'll die. If you had these few thousand dollars, wouldn't it be enough for you to go back home and live on for the rest of your life? Brother? [*No response*] Brother? [*No response.* LAO LI *becomes anxious*] Where is the money hidden? Show me! [*No response. Now both angry and agitated*] I must have this money. I want to borrow a few thousand, and I won't leave without it. Even if I have to kill you.

CHAO TA What lawless and godless stuff you are talking. You may not be afraid of men, or of ghosts, but aren't you afraid [*Pointing to the sky*] of the Old Lord Heaven above? [*Raises his head and shudders*] The gods are right above our heads looking down. You'll pay for it in good time. No one can escape it; no one can run away from it. If you kill someone, you will pay with your life. If you get somebody, someone else will surely get you!

LAO LI [*Ruthlessly*] What motherfucker doesn't want to get rich! Don't interfere with other people's business. My knife goes in white and comes out red, and it will send any motherfucking bastard into the next world.

CHAO TA [*Determined*] Yama Chao may be old but his fists aren't. Don't even mention money. I won't let you touch the dirt on the floor.

LAO LI You really are loyal and patriotic. [*As he talks, his eyes are searching the four corners of the room*]

CHAO TA What are you doing?

LAO LI [*Rushing toward the dresser*] Looking for something.

CHAO TA [*Moving forward to block his way*] You can't do that.

LAO LI Bastard! [*Punches him.* CHAO TA *is knocked unconscious to the ground and for some time can't make a sound. Meanwhile,* LAO LI *searches the room in great agitation. First he rifles the bedding, then quickly dumps out the contents of the top dresser drawer onto the floor. It contains only old books and papers, bits of cloth, and tattered shoes. Quickly he opens the lower drawer and finds it filled with*

*clothing, some loose, some in bundles. He feels these, thinking that
something may be hidden among them. He can't see clearly, so he
drags the drawer over to the table and examines it carefully under the
light: everyday clothing. He throws these on the floor and picks out a
bundle. He rips it open but there's no money, only clothes. Furious, he
throws the package aside, squats down, bends over, and is about to feel
through the other things]*

CHAO TA [*By this time, he's come to. He props himself against the wall
to help himself stand up and grabs the gun from the table*] Put those
things down!

LAO LI Damn you! [*He stands up quickly and turns to strike* CHAO TA]

CHAO TA You! [*Points the gun at* LAO LI]

LAO LI [*Changes his tone*] We're old pals, aren't we? Look. What's the
point of this? [*As soon as he says "this," he viciously attacks* CHAO TA
*and, grabbing his right arm, twists and turns it until he knocks the
gun to the ground and kicks it away*]

CHAO TA [*Holds* LAO LI, *yells*] Thief! Thief!

[LAO LI *struggles to get away, but* CHAO TA *would rather die than
let go. The two struggle with each other all over the room, upsetting the
bed and overturning the table and chairs. In the midst of their fighting, a
great commotion is heard outside—confused voices, feet running back
and forth, police whistles being blown.*

[LAO LI *punches* CHAO TA *brutally several times and presses him to
the floor.* CHAO TA *still manages to hold his legs and refuses to let go.
Step by step* LAO LI *retreats toward the door, dragging* CHAO TA *along
the floor.*

[*Several men in military uniform push open the door, rush in, and
grab* LAO LI. *As for the last man to come in, although he is wearing
military trousers and leather shoes, he has on a fur-lined black brocade
jacket with fastenings in the middle of the front. Instead of a military
hat, he's wearing a small, round skull-cap topped with a red button.
Although his clothes are such a medley of styles as to be ludicrous, he has
an air of authority. The whistles have stopped, and the soldiers inside
and outside the room are all waiting for his commands.*]

LAO LI [*Struggling*] Comrades . . . let go . . . this is none of your
business.

SOLDIER The Battalion Commander wants you.

BATTALION COMMANDER [*Kicking Chao*] Get up! Talk!

[*Two soldiers half drag, half pick him up and stand him to the side*]

COMMANDER What's going on?

CHAO TA [*Gasping*] In answer to the Battalion Commander's question,
Li Lien-ch'eng attempted murder and robbery. . . . He was going to
kill me. He wanted to rob . . . he was searching the room for the pay.
He wanted it for himself.

COMMANDER Who said there was pay in the room?

CHAO TA Ask him . . . he's outrageous. He came in to drink and talk, but
everything he said was nonsense.

COMMANDER [*Seeing the room turned upside down and the liquor bottle still on the table, he becomes furious. He smashes the bottle*] Bastards! You're trying to get yourselves killed. Everyone in the camp has been disturbed. If I don't punish you severely, then I might as well give up being the Battalion Commander. You collect your pay. So can't you behave yourselves and do as you are told? And now you want to revolt! All right. All right. [*To the guards*] Take him out. Lock him in the courtyard and let him sober up. [*To* LAO LI] I'm too busy for you today, but tomorrow I'll take my time and question you under military law. Shooting you will be easy.

LAO LI You, Chao. Listen. Injustice is repaid in kind, and hatred is repaid in kind. I won't see you again in my lifetime, but when I become a ghost, we'll meet again. Remember that.

[*The guards pull* LAO LI *out*]

COMMANDER [*Calls out*] Hsiao Ma.

HSIAO MA [*From outside*] Yes, sir.

COMMANDER Go back to Platoon Leader Wang and tell him it's nothing to worry about. We can go on playing. Tell them not to leave. I still want to recover the money I've lost. I'll be right back.

HSIAO MA [*From outside*] Yes, sir.

CHAO TA [*Picking up the clothes and folding them slowly*] Everything's okay. Nothing's been lost.

COMMANDER [*Doesn't really believe him. He closes the door, drags a leather case out from under the bed, opens it, and examines it. On top are a few old clothes; hidden underneath are bundles of bank notes. Hurriedly he counts them, and seeing that they are all still there he relaxes. Then he becomes angry again*] Damn him! If he really had stolen the money, all my work would have been for nothing. How quick and easy it would have been to do. [*Takes a roll of bank notes, closes the case again, and hides it under the bed while* CHAO TA *watches, dumbfounded, realizing that* LAO LI *was right.* COMMANDER *suddenly becomes aware of him and turns, furious*] You dog! [*Putting the money in his jacket, he moves toward the door.* CHAO TA *opens the door and stands waiting for him to go out. The* COMMANDER *stops suddenly, glances at* CHAO TA, *and slaps his face several times*] Bastard! Where do you think this is that you let just anybody come in here? Eh? Just whose room do you think you're taking care of?

CHAO TA [*Doesn't dare to make excuses or dodge the blows*] Yes, sir. Yes, sir. Yes, sir.

COMMANDER You really do just as you please, letting Li Lien-ch'eng come in here to drink and talk. You've got some nerve! If any money is missing tomorrow, you'll have to answer to me, you bastard. I'll take care of you when I get to it. [*He leaves. The door clicks closed, and his footsteps recede into the distance*]

[*For a while* CHAO TA *is immobile. Slowly he turns his head and stares at the leather case under the bed as if he's found an enemy at which to direct all of his resentment. He charges across the room violently, stops suddenly, and, calming himself with a great effort, forces out a laugh*]

CHAO TA Ha, ha! Did you see that, Bodhisattva? [*Shaking his fists and addressing the heavens*] Any man who tries to be good, or has a conscience, who is honest, who cares about being loyal—that man is an imbecile! [*He's first furious, then shakes his head and waves his hand in a gesture of resignation*] It's better to act like an imbecile. [*He goes over to pick up the clothes again, and one by one brushes away the dirt and puts them back in the drawer*] So there really was a lot of money, over nine thousand dollars. If it's getting rich and living well that you want, why with this much, you'd have no worries about being able to buy a few acres, build a big house, and keep some good horses. It would be nice to have lots of money; I can't blame Lao Li for wanting that. [*Finds the gun and puts it on the dresser*] This is the end for Lao Li. If the questioning at tomorrow's military trial doesn't go well, they'll shoot him for sure. He doesn't deserve that, and he will hate my guts. He certainly won't forget all this. I'd better avoid him. Why not run away? [*Absently, he rearranges some old books*] What a poor nothing I am. I haven't one single cent. No money, and no way out! [*Suddenly looks speculatively at the case of money*] I . . . it's only petty thievery, which is a small, limited crime. And we suffered a great deal, didn't we? And I have to say that there's nothing shameful about taking it! [*He mulls it over. Stands up, then squats again*] No. No. Up till now has the Commander taken advantage of me in any way? He has been good to me. [*Put the two drawers back in place and goes to make the bed*] His temper is terrible, fiery. I've never seen anyone that unreasonable before. [*Stands up straight, stamps his foot*] What's the point of doing this work? Since I am not an officer, how can I hope to have a future? Since I'm just a lowly soldier, can I look forward to happiness, or peace, or fame, or wealth? Yama Chao, how can you be so stupid! [*Greed begins to surface*] I'll just borrow a few hundred dollars. The Commander probably won't care about that little bit. It's not enough to do him any harm. [*He glances at the case and folds his hands in prayer*] I swear to Heaven. Dear gods, I've no other way. I just want to borrow a few hundred dollars as traveling expenses to go somewhere else so I can escape his revenge and avoid disaster. If I have this money, I can go settle down somewhere else. And afterwards I really will be good. [*Kneeling*] Dear gods, just this once, and I'll never commit a crime again. And if I break my promise, may I be struck down dead by a random bullet. [*He stands up and looks around, approaches the bed, when unexpectedly he hears the door open, and turns guiltily*]

CHAO TA [*Nervously*] Hsiao Ma!

HSIAO MA [*As he enters*] Did I startle you?

CHAO TA Do you think you can come into the Commander's room any time you want? You're disgusting.

HSIAO MA Don't fuss. Don't fuss. The Commander sent me on official business. The Commander has lost again and told me to come get a few hundred dollars.

CHAO TA I know. I'll take it to him. You may go.

HSIAO MA [*Seeing that* CHAO TA *is so distracted, he guesses eighty to ninety percent of what is going on*] Say, Yama Chao, when there's good rice everyone should taste it. No one man should eat it all by himself. As the saying goes, whoever sees it should get some of it. You've found a way to get rich. I'm begging you to take care of me. Think of poor Hsiao Ma.

CHAO TA What are you talking about?

HSIAO MA There's no point in spelling it out. We both understand. The Commander is keeping the pay. You work for him. "When there's a river at the front door, it's very easy to carry water." [*He winks*] True?

CHAO TA I don't understand.

HSIAO MA You really don't understand? Let me speak plainly. The pay is everybody's property. The Commander can use it; I can use it too. To say nothing of you.

CHAO TA [*Guiltily*] Okay. Be dishonest. But you shouldn't listen to nonsense.

HSIAO MA Nonsense?

CHAO TA [*Forcing himself*] There's nothing to all of this.

HSIAO MA Do you mean to say there's no money in this room?

CHAO TA There isn't!

HSIAO MA [*Looks* CHAO TA *dead in the eye, not shifting his gaze*] Humph! [CHAO TA *turns his head away*] Okay. [*Laughs coldly*] It's not here. Okay, it's not here. [*He leaves*]

CHAO TA [*With animosity*] You laugh? What are you laughing at? Am I afraid of you? You try to take too much advantage of me. [*While he utters reproaches, he pushes the chairs close to the table*] I haven't been caught at anything. [*Stands still, addressing the door*] I couldn't stand it if I tumbled into his clutches.. It's perfectly clear [*Sits down, his face worried*]that as old as I am, I've lost face by letting Hsiao Ma humiliate me with his laughter. [*He can't stand thinking about it, quickly buries his head in his hands, and covers his eyes*] To be stomped on by that bastard makes me less than dirt. [*He lowers his hands slowly and thinks vacantly. He shakes his head, moves his feet slowly, and then paces for awhile*] Since Hsiao Ma had just come in, how could he have seen anything in so short a time? [*More forcefully*] "If the tiger doesn't eat men, he gets his bad name for nothing." There's money in this room. There's an escape route in the forest beyond the mountains. If I take some, why not take three or five thousand and live it up right now! [*Vehemently*] I haven't had a good day in my whole life. [*Resolutely*] So be it! If I get killed, I get killed. It's worth it. [*He goes to open the case under the bed. The door slowly creaks open and closes again with a faint thud. It's only the wind*]

CHAO TA [*Startled, kicking the case under the bed*] Who's there? [*No response. He becomes more suspicious*] Who's there? [*Still no answer*]

[*On tiptoe, he goes stealthily to the door, stands still, and listens. Then he pulls it open violently. Outside he doesn't see a trace of anyone. It's a bad winter, and the dead of night. Although there are some scattered stars and a moon, their light is hidden by the black clouds blown by the north wind. It's bitter cold and pitch black everywhere. He can't see what's in front of him, but can only hear what seems like a thousand different sounds in the sky—sounds of men wailing, animals crying, metal clanging, sand whirling, all terrifying]*

CHAO TA [*Quickly closing the door, he shrinks back into the room*] Ghosts! [*His courage fading, he feels guilty; he addresses himself angrily*] Yama Chao, how can you let your conscience be hidden and think of doing such bad deeds? I was born to be nothing, but I must learn to be good; won't you let me be a good man all the way through!

HSIAO MA [*Enters and slouches in a chair*] The Commander wants you!

CHAO TA [*Surprised*] Wants me?

HSIAO MA Go right away. The Commander lost quickly and wants you to send over five hundred dollars. Why don't you take it!

CHAO TA Terrible! I forgot! [*Quickly takes several rolls of bank notes from the case, stands up, and sees HSIAO MA smiling, covetously and enviously looking on. He is suddenly afraid that HSIAO MA is lying*] Can I bother you to please take it to him for me?

HSIAO MA [*Not moving*] Take it yourself. The Commander has some instructions to give you.

CHAO TA Would you please go back and say that I can't leave. [*He gives a sideways glance at the case, his thoughts apparent*] There are things in this room.

HSIAO MA Turn the room over to me. I'll watch it for you.

CHAO TA [*Increasingly suspicious*] You dog. Don't pull the trick of "luring the tiger out of the mountain." You better be telling the truth about this five hundred dollars.

HSIAO MA You are so careful with the Commander's money. You protect it this carefully and nothing can go wrong. Even the Commander himself won't be able to get to it. [*Standing up*] Don't hurry. The Commander will reward you! [*Viciously*] And don't be afraid of having difficulty explaining yourself. I'll speak up for you. [*walks out*]

CHAO TA [*Gradually understands that things are going badly. If the Commander believes HSIAO MA, even if he doesn't steal, he will be accused of stealing anyway, and there will be no chance to explain*] So be it! So be it! [*He might as well take lots of bank notes. He stuffs them on his person and gets ready to leave. Just as he's about to go, he suddenly hears someone at the door. He snatches the gun up at once and points it at the man entering—the COMMANDER. Both men are startled. Neither speaks. The COMMANDER backs toward the door, intending to block the way. CHAO TA shoots. The COMMANDER is hit and hesitates slightly. CHAO TA has already charged out the door.*]

[*Curtain*]

PART II

Scene 2

The scene is the place where the road ends. Ahead is a forest of large trees which screen the sky and block off the ground. The forest is thick with interconnected vines forming a vague black mass. There's no way to tell what it's like inside. Outside of the forest are several straight, old trees and piles of squat, rough rocks, all evil-looking. The night has become deeper. A tiny bit of starlight shines on the frozen ground. The cold is bone-chilling. Off in the distance can be heard the sound of bugles and drums.

CHAO TA [*Dashes onstage. As soon as he sees the forest, he looks for a stone and sits down*] So this must be the pine forest. I've finally gotten here. Good. Let me give my feet a rest. [*Rubbing them with his hands, he offers them consolation*] My poor feet! Today I've worked you very hard. When we get home, I'll give you hot water and warm wine, and wash off the dirt. But now I can't let you relax. You still have more work to do to take me through the forest. [*Looking back at the road he's come along*] This trip hasn't been easy. I've run for twenty *li* without stopping in only about two hours. [*Resting against a tree, he can't help being troubled by the intermittent beating of the drums*] Dum-de-de. Dum-de-de. Why don't the damn drums ever stop? Lift your legs. How can you catch me just by beating the drums? [*He can't see his pursuers*] It doesn't matter how far behind they are. I wouldn't be able to see them if they were only one hundred paces away. [*He lifts his head*] The whole sky is filled with black clouds. [*He laughs for no reason*] Tonight it is really black, blacker than the Commander's heart. [*As he turns toward the forest, his smile suddenly disappears*] Look at this forest. What kind of place is it? Has any living person in all of history ever gotten through it? [*Again the drums beat, and the wind blows the sound to his ears*] Dum-de-de. Go ahead and beat the fucking drums forever! Yama Chao doesn't have enough time to do anything about it. [*He gives a cold nasal laugh*] They've sent the troops out just for me—two hundred, three hundred, the whole battalion. But can they follow me into the woods? [*Pointing*] You see that tree, and that one, and that one, all sizes, growing every which way so that you can't tell north, south, east, or west. If several hundred men blindly, wildly stumble around in there, how could they be anything but baffled? It's easy to get in but hard to get out. In this forest, over ten *li* around, you'll go around in circles. You can go around for twenty-five years, and don't think you'll get out alive! [*He makes a calculation, and feeling that he is not worried or afraid, decides he might as well use a stone as a pillow and go to sleep on the ground*] [*A strange rustling is heard in the forest*]

CHAO TA [*turning over and sitting up, shouts*] What is it? Who's there! Who's there? [*Jumps up, takes the gun from his waist, and faces into the darkness*] I'm going to shoot. [*But the woods are absolutely still*]

What? No one's there? It must be a squirrel. [*Sees a squirrel climbing up a branch*] So it was a squirrel, stupid thing. And you're making fun of me. [*Stretches his arm upward and shakes the pistol twice*] If you dare to scare me again I'll kill you. [*But instead he relaxes*] Yama Chao's eyes can see one hundred paces at night, and I can even hit mice in the dark. [*He starts to put the pistol in his pocket, but because he has walked too much for one night with the leather belt and the jacket tied around his body, he is not very comfortable. He undoes the belt to rearrange everything. He digs the bundles of bank notes out of his pockets and spreads them on the ground*] I hadn't intended to take so many. [*He counts them carelessly*] This pile has three thousand dollars. Chao, you are going to have some new experiences real soon. Then you'll know that you haven't lived your life for nothing! [*He hurries to hide the money in his pockets again. A few bundles are left over, and these he wraps in his handkerchief and ties at his waist*] Tomorrow when I get to the other side of the forest, all of this money will be mine. Let me get going.

[*In an instant, black clouds cover the stars and moon*]

CHAO TA [*Afraid*] Oh, my god, how can it be so dark! I can't tell where the road is. [*He nods his head*] That's natural. If I go north, I will be able to get out. [*Again he looks for the path*] But there's no path. I can't find any sign of it. How will I know whether I'm going north or south! [*Thinks*] Right. I heard someone say that at the place where you enter the forest, there's a tree with torn bark. That's the marker. Let me take a look. [*He strikes a match, goes to the side of a tree, and looks up and down*] Wrong one! [*He moves to another tree, lights a dried twig, and looks carefully.*] Why can't I find that tree? Don't tell me I've come to the wrong forest! [*Again he moves to another tree, and suddenly blows out his light*] What a lunatic I am! Yama Chao, usually you are intelligent and clever, more so than a fox, but today you're all confused. On a pitch black night you let a light give you away, let everyone see you and aim at you! [*He quickly hurls the twig and matches to the ground, scrapes up some dirt, and covers up the remaining fire*]

[*The night becomes even darker. Squatting down, CHAO TA is like a dark shadow, his features indistinguishable*]

CHAO TA [*Stands up, moves backwards. His expression changes; his eyes bulge. Terrified, he cries out*] You! You! What are you doing here! Blood! Blood! Blood! Bloody face and head! [*Identifying the object more clearly, he is even more terrified*] Commander! Commander! You! You've come to get me! No! No! Not this time! Chao doesn't work for you any more. I want to go. I have to go. Even if I have to strangle you! [*All alone, he throws his hands around wildly, fighting with thin air*] I can't get my hands on you. [*He opens his eyes and is relieved*] Everything's disappeared. [*Sighs*] The Commander's at the camp. I just shot him. Even his shadow couldn't get here! [*Gasping*] I've walked until I'm too tired. I've walked so much I'm feverish. Because my mind is drained and I'm all upset, I'm seeing ghosts and phantoms. Actually there's nothing to worry about. If I only relax, in a little while I'll be okay. [*Before he finishes speaking, he leaps up again*] Hsiao Ma, you've come too! What right do you have to share my take? You can't do this to me. [*He wards off something in the air*] Get out of here! Get out! [*Puts his hands down*] He's gone. Chao's nickname is Yama; he's not afraid even of real ghosts. And certainly not afraid of fake ghosts! [*He gives a forced laugh*]

[*A gust of wind passes by, making the beating of the drum louder*]

CHAO TA That drum sounds closer. [*Feeling for the gun*] This gun never misses. Don't you know that, comrades? There's no feud between us. Why should you have to chase me! [*Suddenly he becomes cruel*] If you turn against me, for every bullet I have, I'll take one life. There are still five bullets. That's five lives. Those five who come to get me will find that Chao's life doesn't come cheaply. [*He yells wildly in the direction of the soldiers who are pursuing him*] Come and get me! Come and get me! Five of you will die first before you can expect to catch Chao. I'm going! And you? Get lost, you motherfuckers. [*Gathering his resolve, he enters the forest*]

[*Curtain*]

Scene 3

Inside the forest. The night is dark and still. The moon is faint and gloomy. Ancient trees, thickly spaced, stand straight and towering. Drums can be heard vaguely in the distance. Something at the base of a tree rustles.

CHAO TA [*Enters, treading on broken twigs and fallen leaves, threading his way through, looking carefully for the path. He trips on a tree root, pulls himself up, and leans against a tree to catch his breath*] It's really different in here from outside. What's wrong with Chao? Can't I even run along a path? [*Rubbing his knees*] I'm always knocking against trees and falling down on stumps. My clothes are ripped and I'm bruised in various places. [*He looks at the trees and sighs*] In this black place on this dark night, the trees look very peculiar. No beginning and no end. I've passed tall trees and short trees, walked through one area and then another. It always looks the same, and I never finish walking. [*He sighs and sits down*] If I don't rest a little, I really won't be able to go on. [*He pats the ground, feeling pressured by anxiety*] And there's nothing to eat anywhere!

[*Suddenly a strange sound comes up from the rock by the roots of a tree—a tragic sound like that of seven or eight people weeping and crying*]

CHAO TA [*Seems to see several people coming out from behind a tree. Apparently he recognizes them; he stands right up and starts smiling*] So! More than ten of you have come! [*He folds his hands in salute to them and waits for them to sit*] Good! Good! Not bad. I'm fine, thank you. [*The following speech is delivered as if he were talking to someone, with pauses between phrases as if he were listening to their replies*] What do you have to say, second brother? . . . You're thinking of going back! . . . Back home. . . . Yes. With all those mountains and streams in between it's so far! . . . Your old mother at home is concerned about you. . . . Yes. You've been gone over ten years. And should have gone back long ago. . . . Your wife waits for you all day long. Everyone feels like that. Every wife expects her husband to come home soon. . . . You can't go back! Why not? . . . Oh! You've been wounded. . . . When one fights, one can't avoid being wounded! . . . This time the fighting was savage. . . . You saw me, no doubt. I was on the battlefield too. . . . Three days and three nights. No break in the shooting. . . . And it rained hard. And afterwards you were shot. . . . You waited, waited for someone to carry you back to a tent, to give you medicine and heal you. . . . What did you say? They ignored you! . . . Second Brother, they buried you alive! . . . You hadn't died, yet they went ahead and buried you! [*He stands up indignantly*] What inhuman bastards to do such a cruel thing! Really? Really? . . . They're animals with wolves' hearts and dogs' lungs. Those brutal, inhuman little bastards. [*Gnashes his teeth*] Just wait. There's always time for retribution. Thunder will strike them and fire will burn them; heaven will punish them and earth will destroy them! [*Yells*] You who were so unjustly killed, were you so helpless that you didn't seek revenge? [*The weeping and crying is heard again. The sound is desolate. After a short time, it stops*]

CHAO TA [*His face showing terror*] Second Brother! . . . I . . . are you blaming me? [*Without conviction*] I really did do that, but it was the general's orders—take all those seriously wounded with next to no hope and throw them in a pit. [*Turns his head away, looking ashamed*] I remember everything you said to me then. [*Speaks slowly*] You saw thirty to fifty bodies all together in a pit. Don't mention coffins. There weren't even straw mats! You had tears in your eyes. You kowtowed and begged. You said you had three bullet wounds and were losing so much blood, you didn't know whether you would recover or not. You thought chances were you'd die, but you just might live. Because you could still breathe, in your heart you hoped just a bit that perhaps you would heal and your life would be spared. You wanted me to set you aside and not bury you in the pit, to let you test your own luck. If you were going to die, then you wouldn't worry about your corpse being exposed in the field, the rain beating down on it and the winds blowing, the dogs dragging you around and the wolves gnawing at you. You absolutely wouldn't blame me. And if by chance you were saved, when you got home, all their lives your whole family would remember Chao's mercy in saving your life. Because we served the same leader together and ate together in the same camp, you wanted me to remember our previous friendship, leave you there, so that way we wouldn't have been friends for nothing. Second Brother, when

Chao heard what you said, his heart was grieved, and he could hardly bear to do what he did. [*Argues earnestly, trying hard to be convincing*] Second Brother, everyone knows that the General's rules are stringent. No matter who it is, you aren't allowed to have personal feelings. Even if it's your own comrades who were severely wounded, they are to be treated the same as the enemy. All must be buried quickly. There was nothing Chao could do about it. [*His hands warding the other off, he bends to the side as if to dodge a blow*] Second Brother, don't be so quick to start something. Listen to me. Don't you understand yet? Even if you had healed, you would never have been able to carry a gun or fight again. If I had taken the trouble to save your life, it would have been wasted. The General had it figured out. You were useless, finished. Anyway, you were going to die. Isn't it better quick and easy, to get it over with sooner? Second Brother, you're blaming others for your fate. Chao was just a bystander. [*Nervously*] You say I had already agreed to save you, but because I saw that you had over eighty dollars on you, I got the wicked idea of burying you alive? You say that was outright murder for greed? What kind of talk is that? [*His shame turns to anger*] Get out of here! If I listened to you instead of the General, wouldn't I have lost my own head? Yama Chao is going. What can you do to me? [*Laughs coldly*] This is Yama Chao's temper. And if he gets angry he doesn't give a damn even for a friend.

[*The only sound anywhere is that of weeping and crying. It's constant, as if the grief were endless*]

CHAO TA [*Extremely angry*] Shut up! Shut up! I'll teach you a lesson! [*He shoots the pistol at the tree. Immediately all the sounds are silenced. Satisfied, he laughs foolishly*] A cheap sacks of bones! This pistol stopped them. [*He calms down. The drumming has become louder*] Why have I delayed so much? They're beating drums and chasing me. But instead of pushing along here I am shooting at nothing and wasting my bullets. I don't know what I'm doing. [*Quickly he starts to move, but seeing the forest, can't help losing his courage*] Hey! What am I afraid of! There are only trees in the forest. How can there be anything else there! [*He enters the forest*]

Ch'anghsintien, Hopei—1922

[*Curtain*]

Scene 4

Now the moon is showing through the dark clouds, providing some illumination. In this section of the forest, there are no large trees. Nearby are one or two which have fallen on the ground. In the distance is a thicket of low trees. Rushing and stumbling in, CHAO TA leans against a fallen tree, lies down, and pants loudly. He forces himself to sit up, and groans.

CHAO TA Ah, my feet! [*With his hands, he moves his feet closer to his body*] I can't take another step in these shoes. [*Taking his time, he *removes his cotton shoes*] My feet have swelled up so much. Look how swollen they are! [*He stretches his feet out straight*] Aiya! [*He looks at the forest and sighs*] How can I still be in the forest? I should have left it already. [*Worried*] I've walked and walked. I must have been walking for hours. [*The drumming seems to be louder*] Listen! The damn drum is beating again. [*Shakes his head*] The sound is a little closer. No, it's still far away. I can't tell. [*Again he consoles himself*] What are you afraid of? They're a long way off. How can they catch up with you anytime soon? [*He leans backwards, and raises his head to look at the moonlight*] Good. When the moon comes out, I can look for the path and not have to go blindly bumping and banging around again, stumbling and staggering. But how can one night be so long? The sky won't get light. [*Looks all around*] When there's sun, at last I'll know which direction is east, which is north. [*Smiles bitterly*] Before, when Yama Chao was in camp, he just went about doing his job. Now suddenly I'm running for my life in a wild forest! [*He lowers his head and is silent*]

[*A greenish and mysterious will-o-the-wisp appears from inside a clump of low trees and flickers*]

CHAO TA [*Feeling his pockets*] The money! Good, it's still there. [*He's satisfied*] This money was meant to be mine. It will always be mine! [*He pulls it out*] If it weren't for you! [*He is choked with sobs and cannot make a sound. After a while he speaks again*] Okay. Since I can enjoy being rich and finding happiness, having risked my life once is worth it. [*He thinks about having shot the Commander and is apprehensive*] I've got to remember how I got this money. If I do some good deeds, then it will be all right! [*Points to one roll of bank notes*] First I'll take a few hundred to buy a very small wheat field, and in exchange for my own labor I'll get food and clothing from it. Then afterwards, with a clear conscience, I'll do everything I'm supposed to do and be a good man! [*Points to another roll*] Then I'll spend a few hundred to repair the temple of the Bodhisattva. I'll hang a new tablet, and on the first and fifteenth of each month I'll make offerings and burn incense. If I've committed a crime, the crime will be forgiven; if I've done something wrong, the wrong will be excused. And I will be guaranteed peace and comfort. [*Points to another roll*] These few hundred are for relatives, friends, the poor, the old, for victims of natural disaster or human catastrophe. I've met with all kinds of pain in my life. How could I just stand and watch with my hands in my pockets? [*Points to another roll*] With these few hundred I'll repair bridges and build roads. In the summer I'll give out medicine and in the winter provide rice gruel. Then the twenty-some years that Chao has been away from home will not have been wasted.

[*A rattling sound is heard. A dark shadow drifts forward with the will-o-the-wisp. As it approaches, it is seen to be a man's shadow. Its left hand holds a bowl, and its right is tossing dice into it*]

CHAO TA [*Raises his head to look*] I wonder who it is? It's Wang

Kou-tzu! I haven't seen you in a long time. I've missed you. They said you were a spy for a revolutionary party, and the General shot you. How happy I am to see you! Why don't you speak?

[WANG KOU-TZU *puts the bowl on the ground and just throws the dice. Then he makes a gesture as if to invite* CHAO TA *to join him*]

CHAO TA [*Immediately becoming furious*] You vile, shameless dog. From the first Chao Ta was always basically a decent man. From the first I was always careful about spending money for food and clothing. I saved my money, planning to go back home after my discharge and take up different work as soon as possible. It was you, Wang Kou-tzu, who tricked me, who invited me to gamble with you and won all my money. What could I do? So I started all over again and became a soldier, asking only to be fed. When I thought about the past and the future, it was you, you stinking bastard, who was responsible for me drifting down this low road, on and on and on down to today. [*Grabbing the money, he waves it in* WANG KOU-TZU's *face, and then quickly stuffs it away*] Today Chao has gotten rich again, and once again he plans to return home and make good. And are you, Wang Kou-tzu, with your black, cheating heart, again inviting me to gamble with you? [*Pulls out the gun*] Kou-tzu, I've already taken your life once. And now aren't you forcing me to take it again!

[*The rattle of the dice is heard*]

CHAO TA Go to hell! [*There's a gun shot, and then the entire scene disappears*]

Spring, 1916

[*Curtain*]

Scene 5

A mountain which rises steeply to form a small ridge. Beyond the ridge stretch endless mountains and peaks densely covered with trees. On the ridge is a patch of level, bare area approximately one hundred feet around. It is still nighttime.

CHAO TA [*Shouts as he walks along*] It's so hot! So hot! So hot! [*When he reaches the top of the ridge, he looks in all directions. Suddenly his limbs become rigid; he closes his eyes tightly; he turns back and forth moving stiffly, all as if he were not in control of himself. After a while he stops to open his eyes and keep a lookout off in the distance. Gesturing a good deal, he keeps talking as if in his sleep*] Smoke! [*Pointing to one spot*] Black smoke rising straight up. [*He shrinks backwards*] Something's on fire. . . . What a large fire! It's not far away! Not far away! [*Inclines his ear*] What? . . . Weeping. . . . The sound of women . . . several women weeping. [*He stands on a stone and looks around. He's alarmed*] Aiya! So many girls and women running in all directions. [*Gulps*] Soldiers chasing them. [*Not able to turn his eyes away*] Oh! . . . Oh! . . . Oh! [*There is sound of weeping*] A young girl, rushing down the road. They've grabbed her.

[*Looking carefully*] Isn't that Third Sister Wang, the younger sister of Wang the barber? [*Worried*] They're laying her on the ground. . . . Three soldiers all piled on top of her. [*Covers his eyes with his hands*] Ah! . . . Ah! . . . Ah!

[*The drum beats with great agitation*]

CHAO TA [*Still in a trance*] Terrible! The soldiers are coming, coming toward our house! [*Waves his hand*] No! No! This is my house! I don't want to go! [*Dry laugh*] I'm so old, so ugly. What am I afraid of? [*Entreatingly*] Sister Yü. You! Run quickly, quickly! Run quickly! [*Alarmed*] That won't work. The soldiers are at the door. You can't run away. [*Agitated*] Sister Yü, hide, quickly. Hide, hide! It would be better to die! [*Sighs*] A young virgin, so pretty. [*Stamps his foot*] Hurry, hurry! . . . Jump out the window! Isn't that a window! [*Holding his breath*] Good! Good! [*But consoles himself*] My daughter! She's safe after all . . . she's dead. [*Hides his face and sobs*]

[*The drums sound again*]

CHAO TA Honorable soldiers, what do you want in here? . . . Why are you opening the chest? . . . We're a poor family. We don't have anything valuable . . . [*Shouts sternly*] Leave that fur-lined gown! . . . Soldiers, I wouldn't have the nerve. [*Changes his tone of voice*] Leave the clothes here, for pity's sake . . . There's only one piece of silk clothing. It was made for a wedding. My mother-in-law gave it to me. . . . Don't get it dirty . . . I hid it for Sister Yü's dowry. . . . Don't take it away . . . listen to what this old lady says . . . a person of over sixty years . . . what she says can't be wrong! . . . Get out of here. Get out of here! Go to a rich man's house. Have pity on poor people. Let them go! . . . Are you starting a fire? . . . You're not going to burn the house . . . oh God! . . . The white smoke goes straight up. In a moment it's making its way through the roof . . . why are you so cruel? Are we poor people standing in your way! Honorable soldiers! There's no one, no one is hidden under the bed . . . [*A placating smile*] I only have this one son. . . . He's terrified. This child can't hurt anyone. . . . Spare him! Don't hit him. The butt of the gun is so heavy. . . . [*Agitated*] Don't point the gun at him. This way is not good . . . [*Kneels*] I beg you. I beg you on my knees! . . . Oh broad-minded, prosperous soldiers . . . kill me instead . . . gentlemen, don't . . . [*Loud cry*] Oh! . . . Oh! . . . Oh! . . . My son is dead too! Dead! Dead! . . . [*Laughs*] . . . How hot it is! . . . [*Takes off his clothes*] The fire is getting bigger and bigger. So be it! . . . Fiery Goddess Bodhisattva, take this old woman too! What do I have to live for? [*Hugs his body, leaps, falls to the ground, and wildly rolls around crying*]

[*Again the drums sound*]

CHAO TA [*Gradually calming down and lying still. He suddenly sits up, not comprehending*] What have I been doing! [*Looks around*] Am I still in the forest? [*Pointing to the clothing that he has taken off*] Look. My clothes and money are scatterd all over the ground! [*Puts his clothes back on*]

[*Again the drums sound. Blackened human figures appear one by one until there are several dozens of them*]

CHAO TA Who are you? . . . All are wronged ghosts who burned to death. Aren't those three pretty young girls? Why are their bodies black all over and their eyes and noses missing? . . . And here are the old . . . and the young. [*Shocked, he steps back*] Thousands of my comrades set the fires too. Why have you only come looking for me? [*Pulls out the gun*] You think I'm the easiest one to handle! [*He fires two shots in succession and everything disappears*]

Nanking—1910

[*Curtain*]

Scene 6

The same as Scene 5

CHAO TA [*Prostrate on the ground, praying*] Old Lord Heaven, save me. In my lifetime I've committed every sin there is. I know I should have paid for them long ago and should have died long ago. But please remember that I never purposely planned to hurt anyone. Old Lord Heaven, I never meant to do those bad things.

[*Continuous drumming is heard*]

CHAO TA [*Kneeling and pleading*] That time I saw the men and women, the old and the young, in the flames, rolling about and screaming, I asked my comrades to spare them. They said that if we didn't burn them, we couldn't rob them, that you have to pull weeds up by the roots. I couldn't stand it and I wanted to go back to camp, but my comrades held a knife to my throat and said that we would cross rivers together and go down to the water together, would share wealth together and share misfortune together, and that no one was going to be allowed to go off all by himself to be a good fellow. Whoever turned against the group would be killed first. There wasn't anything I could do. I had to go along with them. Later I stopped thinking about what I was doing and just did whatever I pleased.

[*The drums sound*]

CHAO TA [*Kowtows*] That Kou-tzu and I were from the same village. When we drifted around the country, I got the money to cure him when he was sick, and also found him a job. But that bastard repaid me with spite. He used loaded dice to cheat me out of my money. What redblooded man can put up with that! So I just reported that he was a revolutionary. I intended to make him suffer a little and to get my revenge. How could I have known that the investigation would find solid evidence that he really was a spy and that he would be killed by the Battalion Commander. When the Battalion Commander was promoted, I felt extremely sorry for what I'd done. That five-hundred-dollar reward—I didn't take a penny of it. Old Lord Heaven, you saw it too! [*Kowtows*] Don't take Chao Ta for a terribly evil man. Mostly I've been falsely accused. Old Lord Heaven, have pity on me and be merciful.

[*Gradually it grows lighter. A yamen appears with an official inside. He's wearing a plumed hat and a long robe with a jacket. He sits at an elevated table. Ten attendants with angry expressions stand on either side. A pen holder, container of bamboo tokens, instruments of torture, and bamboo paddles are all in readiness. This is a court of the old Ch'ing dynasty.*

[*A woman is kneeling facing the official. The official intently questions her. The woman only shakes her head. The official thinks a while, a contented expression on his face, and then pointing to* CHAO TA *questions her again. The woman still shakes her head. The official pounds the table and questions her angrily, but she only shakes her head. There's nothing he can do, so he asks the attendants to take the woman to one side.*

[*Now an old man comes forward and kneels in the court. As before, the official questions him. He shakes his head. The official earnestly explains the situation, but the old man stubbornly refuses to go along. He just shakes his head. The official's countenance is severe. He takes out a bundle of bamboo tokens and points to* CHAO TA. *The old man performs one kowtow, kneels, and shakes his head. The official is furious and orders the attendants to torture the old man. The man becomes unconscious from the pain*]

CHAO TA [*Not knowing what to do, he keeps calling*] Old Lord Heaven!

[*Someone spits a mouthful of cold water on the man and he gradually comes to. The official points to* CHAO TA *and asks again. The old man turns his head, glances at him, sighs, and as if he has no choice, gives a slight nod. The official is greatly pleased*]

CHAO TA Just and Honorable Lord, the accusations are unjust!

[*They bring the woman forward and question her again. Still she shakes her head. The official is furious. He throws down a token, and the attendants hold her down and whip her*]

CHAO TA Aiya! Honorable Lord!

[*When the woman has been beaten nearly to death, the official points to* CHAO TA *and asks once again. Immediately she nods agreement. The official is greatly pleased*]

CHAO TA Just and Honorable Lord, the accusations are unjust!

[*The yamen attendants get the bamboo paddles and instruments of torture and look at him savagely*]

CHAO TA [*Crawls forward and kneels, then kowtows and pleads*] Just and Honorable Lord, the accusations are unjust! [*He says this several times, but the official refuses to listen*] Your Honor, don't take me for a murderer. I never killed anyone. Your Honor, they are dazed from the beatings and so they point blindly and make wild accusations. The accusations are unjust!

[*The yamen attendants throw the instruments of torture on the ground*]

CHAO TA Your Honor, be merciful. Please don't beat me. My legs have already been broken in the press, Just and Honorable Lord.

[*The attendants rub their hands, eager to begin*]

CHAO TA [*Lifts his head and addresses Heaven*] Old Lord Heaven, is this fair? Is this reasonable? When ordinary people like us who don't have money and don't have power meet a pack of [*He is filled with resentment*] ravenous wolves, how can we hope to survive! [*Heatedly*] But Chao will not die easily. I'll kill some of them first. [*Swears*] Honorable Spirits, Old Lord Heaven, only this once and then I'll never commit another crime. Chao Ta will go away to avoid revenge and escape catastrophe. And from now on I'll be a good man. [*Pulls out his gun and points it at the official*] Listen, you cur! Now under the Republic we have laws. Do you still think that you can make unjust accusations! [*He fires one shot and the scene disappears*]

1905

[*Curtain*]

PART III

Scene 7

Same as Scene 3. The drumming sound is nearer.

CHAO TA [*Exhausted, he is having difficulty walking*] But how can this be? [*Stumbles to the ground*] I've used up five bullets, and the sky's not light yet! [*Drags himself up to go and falls down again*] Let them catch me. I really don't care. [*His head buried in his arms, he cries*] How could I come to this! From the beginning— [*He sits and thinks of the past, miserable beyond measure*] We were a law-abiding family. We farmed for a living. When the old man died, he left a house and a piece of land. I took care of my mother. And as for Hsiao Chin-tzu, the young daughter of our neighbors the Liu family, across the river . . . [*As he thinks of her, his expression grows tender*] We grew up together from the time we were little. Hsiao Chin-tzu consented to be my wife, and we hoped to be married before long. And we hoped that the three of us, mother, son, and wife, would have food and clothing, that we would live in peace and have many happy days together. [*Long sigh*] How could we have known that that year a foreigner would come and say that worshipping the ancestors and respecting the spirits was completely wrong and that when we died we would still be punished in hell. The foreigner came especially to teach the villagers to accept the foreign religion, to speak the foreigner's language, and to worship the foreign Bodhisattva. The motherfucker also wanted to build a foreign church, and that was terrible. I asked how could they keep me from planting my own land. The real reason was that Wang the Tiger of our village took advantage of the fact that mother was a widow and I was an orphan. No one helped us. He appropriated our land to sell to the foreigner, who built a church and a large red brick house. Wang the Tiger made several hundred strings of cash, and we didn't get a cent of it. The foreigner was powerful, so how could we get our rights? Mother became sick with anger and died.

And my Hsiao Chin-tzu, she . . . also . . . died! Damn foreigner! Damn foreigner! [*Buries his head and cries again*]

[*Two men come out from behind a tree. One has deep-set eyes and a yellow beard, foreign clothes, and a walking stick. The other has a fat face and large belly, and wears a broad-sleeved long gown. The foreigner points haughtily in all directions, and the other, the foreigner's lackey, fawns on him, smiling in an ingratiating manner as they walk along.*]

[*In jest, the foreigner beats* CHAO TA *lightly over the head with a stick*]

CHAO TA [*Jumps up, cursing*] You bastard!

[*The foreigner raises his head and peers down his nose at* CHAO TA. *Now it is he who is angry*]

CHAO TA [*Suddenly getting scared, does not know what to do with himself, and so quickly kneels down*] Honorable Foreigner, Great Foreigner, don't beat me. Don't beat me! Great Foreigner! [*Kowtows*]

[*Satisfied, the foreigner slowly walks away*]

CHAO TA So! We're not human beings! [*Pulls himself up and speaks with hatred*] Such a savage foreigner! The county heads are afraid of him; the heads of the prefectures are afraid of him. The regional heads and the provincial governors are all afraid of him. Everyone is afraid of him, even the emperor in Peking. Well, that's the way it is. [*Weeps loudly and bitterly*] But the poor aren't afraid of him. Don't drive us poor people to the wall. Sooner or later, we'll rebel and kill the foreigners one by one and get our revenge. [*Stands on a stone and looks sideways at the foreigner and his lackey. Suddenly he laughs wildly, his eyes fiery, and his voice ruthless*] I wonder who it is! So it's Wang the Tiger. You ruined me, ruined me. So. But now the time has come when I've got my hands on you. [*Laughs wildly*] Today those you've killed will get their revenge, and will take back the money you owe.

[*The lackey bows to the foreigner; then the foreigner walks forward to protect him*]

CHAO TA [*About to grab his enemy, but the foreigner impudently blocks him off. He is angry beyond control*] What's this? Just because Wang the Tiger has kowtowed to the foreign Bodhisattva he gets away with bullying others?

[*The foreigner's lackey ridicules him from behind the foreigner's back*]

CHAO TA [*Slowly, speaking with pain shared by all his compatriots*] Foreign Devil! Listen to me! You came to our village with honeyed words and a smile on your face and said that your purpose was to do good deeds and save us from suffering. We are too trusting. We were fooled, and we treated you politely as friends. How could we have known that you bastards said the opposite of what you meant, that you would associate with scoundrels and thugs and take advantage of good people, all to benefit yourselves at the expense of others and to do as you pleased. You are powerful; we were no match for you. Now you've become rich and taken away our land. Everything is done according to your rules; everything works to your advantage. And we've become a laughingstock. We aren't even human beings! We deserve our bad luck! We'll never be as good as the foreigners! We're not even as good as pigs and dogs. The Chaos had land. Mother and son lived in peace and happiness. Damn foreign devil! You ruined our family and killed us. Did you think that Chaos were bastards without pride, without conscience, afraid to die, too timid to do anything to the foreign devil! I . . . I . . . I . . . [*He raises his hand and is just about to commit murder*]

[*The foreigner quickly raises his stick straight up in the air*]

CHAO TA [*Threatened by the foreigner's customary powerful status, in the end* CHAO TA *does not dare do anything and is completely frustrated. He can only swallow his feelings. And the hand that he has raised, he puts down slowly*] What . . . can . . . I . . . do . . . the foreigner has the stick. [*He feels helpless, but his fury increases*]

[*The foreigner also is somewhat worried and guards himself with his stick*]

CHAO TA [*Suddenly, not caring whether he lives or dies, he jumps up and yells*] If it weren't for you pack of hairy barbarians, how could the Chaos ever have come to this. Give me back my piece of land, give me back my Hsiao Chin-tzu. I won't die content until I've killed you. [*Taking out the gun, he fires three times, but there's no sound*] Even the gun cheats me. [*Hurls it to the ground*] I don't need it. Even if you have a gun, I'm not afraid. I have a special talisman. Your bullets can't get me. Give me a wooden rod. Give me a stick! [*Picks up a tree branch*] Chao has never been a loser in all his life. I'll kill the big hairy barbarian; I'll kill the number two hairy barbarian; I'll kill the number three hairy barbarian![3] [*He strikes wildly with the stick; the scene disappears*]

The Boxer Rebellion—1900

[*Curtain*]

Scene 8

Same as Scene 4. The drums are even closer.

Standing close together in a group are many men, most of them dressed in tatters; they look like beggars. Several have red cloth wrapped around their heads, wearing makeup and clothing embroidered with patterns. They are dressed as the traditional stage characters Erh-lang, San T'ai-tzu, the Monkey King, Pigsy, Ch'in Sh-pao, Wu Sung, Huang T'ien-pa, etc.[4] Some are holding weapons, some picks and shovels and carrying poles. There are red flags with the trigram for "heaven" written on them. In addition there are several pennons with such slogans as "Support the Ch'ing and Destroy the Foreigners," "Heavenly Spirits and Heavenly Fighters of the Boxers," "Kill the Big Hairy Barbarian, Kill the Number Two Hairy Barbarian, Kill the Number Three Hairy Barbarian," "Chiang T'ai-kung is Here," "Master Yüeh Kuang is Here."[5]

CHAO TA [*Prostrate on the ground, intones a spell*]

> Spirits of Heaven,
> Spirits of Earth,
> I respectfully ask the patron saint
> To display his spiritual powers.

[*He kowtows thirty-six times*]

> On the left is the green dragon,
> On the right is the white tiger.
> Buddha of the Cold Clouds in front,
> Spirit of Dark Fire behind.
> First I invite the Heavenly King's General.
> Then I invite the Black Terror God.

[*He lies prostrate on the ground without moving. In a short while, white foam oozes from his mouth. He leaps up and commands the group. Holding a stick, he dances and leaps, shouting in time to the drums*][6]

[*Curtain*]

Scene 9

Same as Scene 2. The drumming has blended into a steady rumble. Then it stops.

HSIAO MA, *leading a company with* LAO LI *serving as guide, has arrived at the place where* CHAO TA *entered the forest.*

HSIAO MA *and* LAO LI *peer into the forest while the men hide behind trees and rocks, their guns in readiness, as if a great enemy were near.*

LAO LI This is the forest!
HSIAO MA [*Very unhappy*] Good grief. We've walked over thirty
    li on foot. [*Wipes away the sweat*]
LAO LI [*With satisfaction, examining the ground*] He went in here.
    There's no mistake about that.
HSIAO MA [*Not believing him*] That's your opinion!
LAO LI [*Picking up a dry twig*] See this twig? Someone had to light it,
    or do you think it could burn by itself?
    [*The men all turn to look*]
HSIAO MA [*Still unwilling to concede anything*] But you can't say
    that he's still inside!
LAO LI [*Coldly*] He couldn't run away!
HSIAO MA He got here six hours ahead of us. By now he's probably
    on the far side of the forest.
LAO LI [*Coldly*] Not necessarily. He didn't know the path. Since he
    wouldn't be able to get out and would bump and push his way
    through blindly, he probably could spend his whole life inside going
    around in circles.

HSIAO MA This is a hell of a job! In the dead of winter when we're even cold sleeping all wrapped up in bed, here we are out in the wilds swallowing up the northwest wind. If we catch Chao Ta and return with the stolen goods, tomorrow all of our comrades in camp will get paid. But we won't get anything out of all this misery.

LAO LI Didn't the Commander say that if we don't catch Chao Ta, he'll figure that he doesn't owe us any money this month.

HSIAO MA If it weren't for this money, I wouldn't have come!

LAO LI We'll get him.

HSIAO MA He's long gone, far and fast.

LAO LI He's in there.

HSIAO MA Okay. So he's in there. He's in a dark place and we're in the light. He's lying in wait with his gun. Everybody knows that Chao Ta never misses.

[*Lao Li has nothing to say. The men, hearing* HSIAO MA, *hide quickly*]

LAO LI Wait! Wait! Wait! The sun's about to come up. The sky's getting light.

[*Suddenly they hear a loud noise inside the forest*]

HSIAO MA Careful! Careful!

[*Now they hear* CHAO TA *inside the woods, shouting wildly at the top of his lungs*]

HSIAO MA It's him! It's him! It really is Chao Ta. All by himself. Dancing and leaping like a madman. [*Very happy*] He's not holding the gun. He's dancing with a tree branch in his hand. [*He signals with the hand and the soldiers follow him and rush into the forest*]

LAO LI [*Goes to the edge of the trees with them. He suddenly changes his mind and does not go in*] So that's the way it was! The Commander put the whole blame on Chao Ta. And Hsiao Ma and these bastards believed him! [*Laughs to himself*] What I don't understand is why Chao Ta missed that time. How was a slight wound in the leg supposed to have killed him?

[*From the forest comes a burst of gunfire*]

LAO LI [*He is silent. After a while he heaves a long sigh*] It's done. All because you didn't understand people. You wanted to be totally loyal and patriotic toward evil tigers and vicious wolves. Now you're finished.

HSIAO MA [*Comes out*] We caught him! We caught him!

[*The soldiers return triumphantly. Some of them carry in the body of* CHAO TA *and put it down*]

LAO LI [*Unfastens* CHAO TA's *clothing, feels his chest, and shakes his head*] So! [*As he does this, he picks up a roll of bank notes*] So much money! There's sure to be several thousand dollars here.

HSIAO MA Here. Give it to me. I'll take it back.

[*Lao Li hands it to him, pack by pack. The men watch greedily*]

LAO LI [*He feels a pack of something around* CHAO TA's *waist. It seems* to be several rolls of bank notes. He is surprised] Oh! [As he wrinkles his brow, a plan comes to mind. He quickly turns CHAO TA's body over and takes off his uniform jacket] There's more. It's all in his pockets. [To HSIAO MA] Take the jacket with you!

HSIAO MA [Takes the jacket happily] Lao Li! I've relied on you completely. If it weren't for you, we couldn't have known that Chao Ta took this path into the woods. When you get back to camp, the Commander will certainly be lenient and let your success here make up for your crimes.

LAO LI [Hearing this makes him uncomfortable. He knows that even though the Commander released him to serve as guide, stealing the pay originally was his idea, and it will be hard to avoid being punished for it. Fortunately he already has a plan. So he nods his head, then deliberately looks at CHAO TA and sighs] But we were friends for many years. We fought alongside together three times. That was a sad way to die.

HSIAO MA [Apparently moved] Just bad luck for him, wouldn't you say?

LAO LI You gentlemen go on ahead. [Pointing to the body] Let me dig a pit and bury poor Chao Ta.

[The men are sad.]

LAO LI [Emotionally] Perhaps we all may end that way some day.

[The men listen in silence]

HSIAO MA Let's go. The Commander is waiting!

[He leads the men off, to the beating of the drum]

LAO LI [Can't help really feeling emotional] Brother Chao Ta! Brother! [Grieving] Dear Yama, in the end your death didn't go unnoticed. Your comrades in orderly formation are sending you off with drums beating. [Bends down and adjusts his clothing] Did the Commander treat you well? Of all the men in camp, you're the only one really sincere, and really foolish. [Pointing out his weaknesses, he both blames and pities him] You! Your heart was too bad for you to be a good man, and too good for you to be a bad one. But good or bad, you weren't at home being either. I watched you running helter-skelter. Wherever you went, you found trouble. In your whole life, you never had a single good day. [Tears in his eyes] Today only Lao Li is here to bury you. [Pause] Lao Li is begging you to help him. Is it okay if I borrow the money around your waist for my traveling expenses? [He cannot bear to act, stops a moment, but ends by untying the knotted handkerchief around CHAO TA's waist. He takes out the money, puts all of it around his own waist, and then wraps the handkerchief around CHAO TA's head] Brother Chao Ta, if you don't turn into a ghost, then that's that. But if you do have a spirit, then protect me as I cross the forest to go home! [Dragging the body, he turns his head and glances at the sky] It's getting light. [He walks into the forest]

[Curtain]

Notes

1. Bonze—a slang term for monks, who traditionally shaved their heads.

2. During 1913-14 in Honan and surrounding provinces, there was a White Wolf Rebellion, so named for its leader, known as "White Wolf."

3. The Boxer Rebels classified "Hairy Barbarians" in three categories: the "big" or "number one" barbarians were foreigners; the secondary barbarians were Chinese Christians under the patronage of foreign missionaries; the tertiary barbarians included all those Chinese who used foreign articles.

4. These are names of famous warriors, often possessed of magical skills, appearing in popular fiction and drama of the Ming and Ch'ing dynasties. Erh-lang (Yang Erh-lang or Erh-lang shen), the Monkey King (Sun Wu-k'ung, or Monkey Aware of Vacuity), and Pigsy (Chu Pa-chieh, Pig of the Eight Vows) are all fabulous characters appearing in the novel *Hsi-yu chi* (Journey to the West, or Monkey). Erh-lang also appears in the novel *Feng-shen yen-i* (The Investiture of the Gods) along with San T'ai-tzu, better known as No-ch'a. Ch'in Shu-pao, a hero of the Sui-T'ang period, is portrayed in many paintings as one of the two "door gods" of popular mythology and appears in the novel *Shuo T'ang yen-i* (Romance of the T'ang dynasty). Wu Sung is a heroic outlaw in the novel *Shui-hu chuan* (The Water Margin, or All Men Are Brothers). Huang T'ien-pa was a leader of the Yellow Turban rebels at the end of the Han dynasty, and appears in the novel *Shih-kung an* (Cases of Lord Shih).

5. Chiang T'ai-kung (Chiang Tzu-ya) is described in history, drama, and fiction (notably in *Feng-shen yen-i*) as the strategist who helped King Wen destroy the decadent Shang or Yin dynasty and found the celebrated Chou dynasty. Yüeh Kuang is a messianic figure common to folk Taoism and Buddhism, especially millenarian Maitreyan sects.

6. The chants and actions that conclude this scene, as well as the allusions to popular heroes above, follow closely the description of Boxer rites found in Lo Tun-yung, "Ch'üan pien yü-wen" [A further account of the Boxer incident] in A Ying, ed., *Keng-tzu shih-pien wen-hsüeh chi* [Literature on the incident of 1900], 2 vols., Shanghai, 1959: II, 960ff.

Ting Hsi-lin

Oppression

Translated by Joseph S. M. Lau

Cast of Characters

WANG MA
MALE VISITOR
LANDLADY
FEMALE VISITOR
POLICEMAN

Scene

A room in an old-fashioned Chinese house. A door in back opens to the courtyard, and doors to left and right lead to side rooms in the wings. In right center of the room stands a square table surrounded by a few chairs. There is a white tablecloth, and in the middle are placed a kerosene lamp and a tea set. Toward the left, against the wall, is a tea table with two chairs. A raincoat is flung over the back of one of the chairs and a leather suitcase stands by its side. At rear left can be seen a small table with a mirror that looks something like a washstand; on top of it are a clock and a vase. There are other furnishings in the room, and some painting and calligraphy scrolls on the walls, all simple and unpretentious.

When the curtain rises, a man in a Western-style worsted suit and leather boots is seated in one of the chairs by the tea table, smoking a pipe. WANG MA, the maid, is standing outside the door, reaching her hand beyond the eaves to see if it is raining.

The mock-serious title is explained by the dedication, which is to a friend of Ting's whose unsuccessful search during the previous winter for an apartment of his own provided the inspiration for the play. By the time it was written, the friend was dead of cholera; Ting's dedication reads in part: ". . . the thought came to me that if you had had the same good fortune as the protagonist of this play, to run into such a sympathetic person [as the female visitor] while you were earnestly looking for an apartment, to resist 'hand in hand' with you not only the 'oppression of the landed class' but also all sorts of bullying and oppressions in our society—I am sure you wouldn't have died."—EMG

Wang [*Entering*] The rain has stopped. Why isn't *t'ai-t'ai*[1] back yet? [*She takes the teapot from the table and pours some tea for* Male Visitor]

Male [*Getting impatient, standing up*] Would you fix me something to eat?

Wang Well, we do have something in the house, but again we'll have to wait for *t'ai-t'ai* to come back.

Male Even for something to eat?

Wang [*Heaving a sigh*] Yes, for something to eat and about the apartment, too.

Male All right, so I'll wait till your *t'ai-t'ai* is back. It makes no difference after all whether she comes back or not. [*Sits down again*]

Wang [*Shaking her head*] Looks as if *t'ai-t'ai* isn't going to rent you this place.

Male Not going to rent me this place? They why did she accept my deposit?

Wang True, but *hsiao-chieh*[2] is to blame for this. In fact—um—our *t'ai-t'ai* is a bit strange. What's wrong with a gentleman like you? It would be safer to have a man around the house in the middle of the night in case something happens.

Male Has this place been rented before?

Wang It's been vacant for more than a year now.

Male It isn't a bad place, why is it that nobody wants it?

Wang Noboby wants it? Everyone who has looked at it would like to have it. It's clean and bright and it has such a nice garden in front.

Male Then why hasn't it been rented for more than a year?

Wang Since you're no longer a stranger, I guess there's no harm in telling you this. Well, you know, our *t'ai-t'ai* loves nothing more than a game of mah-jong. So she's out all the time, only *hsiao-chieh* and I stay at home. Whenever someone came to see the apartment, it was *hsiao-chieh* who answered the door and she turned down anyone with a family. She'd accept only bachelors, but as soon as *t'ai-t'ai* returned and found out it was a bachelor she'd turn him down. If they keep on doing this, I wouldn't be surprised this place is not rented for ten years!

Male Isn't that interesting! Has something like this happened before?

Wang I don't know how many times! Every time *t'ai-t'ai* and *hsiao-chieh* would have a fight over renting the place. But up to now *hsiao-chieh* hasn't gone so far as to make a decision on her own. The trouble this time is that she has accepted your deposit without consulting her mother.

Male You mean if she had her way, this place would have been taken long ago?

Wang Yes, but normally people wouldn't say another word once they were told that the apartment was not available. They weren't like you, sir, so . . .

Male Strange, you mean. Yes, your *t'ai-tai*'s temperament is a bit strange and mine is too, so when we two run into each other there won't be any easy way out. Really, I find this a nice apartment, especially with that little garden in front.

WANG I can see that you love quiet; day in and day out you wouldn't hear any racket in this place. It's close to your office too, so . . . so I've been thinking. . . .

MALE Yes?

WANG Just tell *t'ai-t'ai* that you have a family, and that they're coming to join you in a few days. If you say that, *t'ai-t'ai* wouldn't have any objection to renting this place to you.

MALE Fine, but what if after a few days I don't have a family to join me?

WANG By that time *t'ai-t'ai* should have found out that you're all right. She wouldn't bother you then.

MALE That's no good. An unmarried man isn't a criminal. Why can't I even rent a place to live?

WANG Well, I only thought that since you love this place so much you'd feel bad if you can't have it, so I thought of this wild plan, sorry if I said anything improper. Ah, that must be *t'ai-t'ai* now. [*Moving toward the door, aloud*] T'ai-t'ai? [*An answer from outside*] Yes, in here.

[*The maid goes out:* MALE VISITOR *also stands up. After a while, the* LANDLADY *enters from the back door followed by* WANG MA]

LANDLADY Sorry to have kept you waiting.

MALE I should apologize for disturbing you. I asked Wang Ma not to trouble you, but she wouldn't listen.

LANDLADY That's all right. [*Taking a bill from her purse*] Here, it's your deposit, please take it back.

MALE I'm sorry, but I've come to stay, not to take my deposit.

LANDLADY What? Didn't I make myself clear to you yesterday that I couldn't rent this apartment to you?

MALE Oh yes, you did.

LANDLADY Then why did you still have your baggage sent here?

MALE [*Happily*] It was you who asked me not to come; I didn't promise you that I wouldn't come, did I?

LANDLADY [*Gradually becoming more resentful*] I don't quite follow you. You seem to be saying that you're the one to decide whether this apartment should be rented or not. Is that what you mean?

MALE Oh, no! It's naturally up to you to decide whether this apartment should be rented or not, but since you've accepted my deposit, it becomes my decision to accept your return of the deposit or not. You know, the question is no longer to rent or not to rent, but to accept the deposit or not to accept the deposit.

LANDLADY [*Getting angry*] When did I rent this apartment to you?

MALE When you took my deposit.

LANDLADY The devil! Just when did I take your deposit? It was my daughter who took it, and she didn't know what she was doing.

MALE Didn't know what she was doing? She's not a child, is she?

LANDLADY Well, there's no point in going over all this, I do want to rent this apartment, but I want to rent it to someone with a family. Now if you have a family to stay with you, then I wouldn't mind renting it to you.

MALE You're being unreasonable. Did you say anything about a family when you advertised for the apartment? And did I lie to you?

LANDLADY [*Taking a conciliatory approach*] No, it's true I didn't mention it, but as I told you yesterday, we don't have a man in the family. . . .

MALE [*Stopping her*] Eh! Eh! Let me ask you. Did you have a man in the family when you put this apartment up for rent? Why hasn't this occurred to you until now?

LANDLADY You're just being unreasonable! I don't have time to argue with you any longer.

WANG [*Trying to be a peacemaker*] T'ai-t'ai, it's too late for this gentleman to go out and look for a place to stay now. Besides, it's raining. Wouldn't it be all right if you let him stay for the night and try to find a way out tomorrow?

MALE [*Stubbornly*] No, it wouldn't do. If this isn't my apartment, I'll be leaving this minute, but since my deposit has been accepted, this place has to be rented to me.

LANDLADY Then I'm telling you: you've got to leave tonight.

MALE [*With a sneer on his face*] Huh! [*Sits down*]

LANDLADY [*Confronting him*] Are you leaving?

MALE No.

LANDLADY Wang Ma, go and call a policeman.

WANG Uh, *t'ai-t'ai*.

LANDLADY I'm telling you to call a policeman!

MALE What if a policeman comes? He has got to listen to reason too.

WANG *T'ai-t'ai*, I think . . .

LANDLADY Call the police! Did you hear me? Are you going?

WANG All right. [*Leaves by the back door*]

LANDLADY Tell him to come right away. [*Goes out the back door and slams it shut*]

MALE [*Feeling helpless; fishes out a pipe and a tobacco pouch from his pocket. Finding the pouch empty, he takes out a can from the suitcase, fills up the pouch first and then the pipe. Just when he is about to light the pipe, there is a knock on the door. He hollers*] Come in! [*Remains standing with his back to the door*]

FEMALE VISITOR [*Pushes the door open, enters in light steps. She is wearing a raincoat and carrying an umbrella in one hand, a small handbag in the other. She begins to speak as soon as she enters and once she has opened her mouth it seems nothing can stop her from talking*] Oh, I'm sorry. Do forgive me. [MALE VISITOR *makes a swift turn and only now does he realize that the one who has just entered is such a person*] This is very impolite, I know, but I can't help it. Your front door is open, I knocked on it several times, no one answered, so I just came in.

MALE [*Though still angry, he does not forget to remove the pipe from his mouth and put it on the table*] What do you want?

FEMALE Me? I've come to work for the Ta Cheng Company. In fact, I just arrived from Peking today. I took the 3 p.m. train and got here at 6, only ninety miles and it took three hours, just think! Now I'm looking for a place to stay. I jotted down several addresses at the train station and I've looked over several places but I couldn't find one that suits me. I was told that there's an apartment here. . . .

MALE [*Taking her to be a rival*] So you've come to rent an apartment.

FEMALE Yes, I wonder if it's still available.

MALE [*Heartlessly*] You're out of luck, the rooms have just been rented.

FEMALE It's just like what you said, I'm indeed out of luck. The country roads have been hard on my feet, especially in this kind of weather. Look, I'm soaked all over and my feet are sore. [*Heaves a sigh*] Ah, can I sit on your chair for a while?

MALE Sorry, please do. [*All his anger has vanished*]

FEMALE [*Puts down her handbag and umbrella*] Thanks. [*She sits on a chair by the tea table and looks around*]

MALE [*Beginning to feel an interest; takes a seat on a chair by the square table*] Just now you said you've come to work for Ta Cheng Company; what will you be doing there? Oh, perhaps I shouldn't ask.

FEMALE Shouldn't ask. Why not? There isn't anything to hide about this. Two weeks ago they advertised in the newspaper for a secretary. That advertisement appeared in all newspapers; I'm sure you have seen it.

MALE [*Nods*]

FEMALE Last Friday, an announcement by the same company appeared in the newspapers saying: "Notice is hereby given that the post for a secretary earlier advertised in this paper has now been filled. No more applications will be received." Did you see that?

MALE [*Nods again*]

FEMALE The one who filled that post is me. Are you surprised? Did it ever occur to you that the one who got that job might be a woman?

MALE No, it didn't.

FEMALE [*Quite proud of herself*] But what am I going to do now? Just think, I shall have to report for duty day after tomorrow and I still haven't found a place to stay! I haven't had any rest since I started walking at half past six today. To tell you the truth, I haven't even eaten. [*Stands up to adjust her dress and walks to the mirror to take a look at herself*]

MALE [*Seemingly sympathetic*] You haven't eaten? That won't do! Maybe I can be of some help in this matter. [*Stands up to pour her some tea*]

FEMALE Thanks. I merely wanted to tell you the truth. I didn't mean to ask you to feed me.

MALE Oh, I'm sorry. Anyway, have a cup of tea first.

FEMALE Thanks. [*Returns to her seat*]

MALE [*Fishes out a cigarette case*] Do you smoke?

FEMALE No, I don't, but I don't mind if others smoke. [*Sips her tea*]

MALE Thanks. [*Replaces his cigarette case and pipe; turns his back and lights a cigarette*]

FEMALE [*Touches her feet*] Good Heavens! Look at my feet! What a sight they make!

MALE [*Turns toward her*] What's the matter?

FEMALE They're not only soaking wet, but also muddy.

MALE [*Attentively*] That's too bad. Do you want to change socks? If you want, I can go out.

FEMALE No, thank you. Even if I want to, there's no need for you to go out.

MALE No matter. If you don't have socks with you, I can loan you a pair.

FEMALE Many thanks. I really appreciate your kindness, but what's the use of changing since I'll soon be walking in the water again?

MALE Walking in the water? Why?

FEMALE How can I help it? It's so dark, how can I tell where there's water and where it's dry once I step outside?

MALE [*As if lost in thought*]

FEMALE [*Takes another sip of tea; heaves a sigh and stands up to take leave*] Oh well, sorry for troubling you. [*Holding her umbrella and handbag, she is ready to go*]

MALE [*Stopping her*] No need to rush, stay another minute. A while ago you said you want to rent an apartment, didn't you?

FEMALE [*Facing him*] What? You still haven't understood me after all I've said?

MALE Well . . . yes, I have. But . . . ah, what do you think of these rooms?

FEMALE But didn't you say they have been rented?

MALE They're indeed rented, but perhaps they can be released to you.

FEMALE [*Happily*] Released to me? Do you mean it? [*Puts down her umbrella*]

MALE Of course I mean it. [*Pours another cup of tea for her*]

FEMALE [*Sits down, taking the teacup from him*] Thank you. How can they be released to me? Do you mean that if I'm willing to take them you can get out of renting it to the other person?

MALE [*Shakes his head*]

FEMALE Or perhaps you were just kidding me. This place has never been rented in the first place. Is that it?

MALE No, I told the truth. This apartment has been rented and it isn't being taken back. When I said it could be released to you, I meant that the one who rented it is willing to release it to you.

FEMALE This I don't understand. Why would he want to release it to me?

MALE That you don't have to know.

FEMALE Is this house haunted?

MALE Are you afraid of ghosts?

FEMALE Oh no. I mean perhaps that person is afraid of ghosts.

MALE He isn't, but ghost or no ghost, let's take a look at the rooms, shall we? [*He takes a lamp to lead the way. This is a bedroom. He opens the door at the right and lets her in*] Matted ceiling, cement floor, foreign-style bed with sheets and blanket. Outside the window is a little garden and you can hear the chirping of the birds early in the morning. In the daytime the sunlight will flood in as soon as you draw the window curtains. [*She comes out. He takes her to the side room on the right*] This is also a bedroom with bedding and furniture. It's the same size as the one you've just seen, only not as bright. If you stay here by yourself, you can use this one as a bedroom and the other as study. [*She walks out*] This space in between can be used as dining room and sitting room. [*Puts the lamp down*] The house is bright and clean, day and night you wouldn't hear any noise. Besides, it's close to your office; I don't think you can find a better place.

FEMALE What is the rent?

MALE Very reasonable. These three rooms for only five dollars a month.

FEMALE It's really a nice place and the rent is reasonable. [*Pauses*] Are you sure I can take it?

MALE Of course I am. Why should I lie to you?

FEMALE But I can't possibly move in tonight, can I?

MALE Why not? [*Pauses, as if something suddenly comes to mind*] But, eh, are you married?

FEMALE [*Jumps up, stiffens herself with raised eyebrows*] What?

MALE [*Repeats*] Are you married?

FEMALE [*Angry*] Your question is ridiculous!

MALE Ridiculous?

FEMALE It's an insult!

MALE [*Happily*] An "insult," yes, that's right, that's exactly what I said, but the first thing the landlords or landladies ask nowadays is if you're married or not.

FEMALE What has it got to do with you if I'm married or not?

MALE Yes, you're right there. What business is it of theirs if I'm married or not? But that's what they keep asking you, isn't it strange?

FEMALE I don't understand.

MALE Who expects you to? Of course you don't. But be patient, let me tell you and you'll understand—you said a while ago that you've come to work for Ta Cheng Company, right?

FEMALE You really have a short memory, how can you forget so easily what I told you just a minute ago?

MALE Don't get mad. I only want to tell you that I also have come to work for Ta Cheng.

FEMALE You also work for Ta Cheng?

MALE Yes, that never occured to you, did it?

FEMALE What do you do there?

MALE I'm an engineer.

FEMALE Then you're not the landlord.

MALE Who told you I was? Did I say that? Do I look like a landlord?

FEMALE [*Interrupting him*] Oh, I get it now! You're the tenant of these three rooms, and you don't like them, so you want to give them up!

MALE Want to give them up? Who said I wanted to give them up?

FEMALE Didn't you just say that these rooms could be released to me?

MALE I did, but I only said "release," not "give up."

FEMALE You've got me completely confused. If you don't want to give them up, why release them?

MALE You really don't understand?

FEMALE I really don't. [*Sits down*]

MALE Because—when I saw you—oh, well, because the landlady wouldn't rent them to me.

FEMALE Why not?

MALE Because it's a question of marriage. Now we're getting to the point. A week ago, I came here to take a look at this apartment and I ran into the landlady's daughter. As soon as she saw me, she cross-examined me, asking me if I'm married, if my mother is with me, whether I've children and brothers and sisters, etc. She was not satisfied until I told her in so many words that I'm single, then she agreed to let me have this apartment without even bothering to talk much about the rent.

FEMALE Don't you understand? It must be that she knew you're an engineer and wants to marry you.

MALE Really? Why didn't I think of that? Anyway, when I came yesterday afternoon, the old lady told me if I don't have a family with me, she wouldn't rent this place to me. Outrageous, wouldn't you say? She knew that I'm single and she used this excuse to keep me out.

FEMALE Why wouldn't she rent it to you if you were single?

MALE I don't know. She said they don't have a man in the house.

FEMALE Nonsense.

MALE It's an insult, isn't it?

FEMALE Yes—but what happened afterwards?

MALE I gave her a good talking-to.

FEMALE And did she see the logic in it?

MALE The logic in it? I tell you, there isn't any room for any logic in the mind of a person over forty, only old-fashioned ideas.

FEMALE What are you going to do now?

MALE Now? I'm not leaving.

FEMALE What about her?

MALE Her? She has sent for a policeman.

FEMALE Sent for a policeman? What for?

MALE To throw me out.

FEMALE Really?

MALE Why should I lie to you? If you don't believe me, see for yourself. The police should be here any minute.

FEMALE This is really interesting, but what would you do if the policeman really wants to throw you out?

MALE I didn't have any idea before you came, but I've got one now.

FEMALE What is it?

MALE I'll beat him up, so he'll have to take me to the police station. Then I'll ask the landlady to release my apartment to you so that you and I both have a place to stay.

FEMALE That won't do. [*Appears to be thinking*]

MALE Why not?

FEMALE Because you wouldn't have a chance to get even with the landlady—oh, I've got an idea.

MALE Yes?

FEMALE [*Pauses*] How about taking me as your wife?

MALE What?

FEMALE You needn't be so frightened. I'm not asking you to marry me.

MALE You've misunderstood me. I . . . I . . . I really haven't thought about this as a way out.

FEMALE This is the best way out. She said she wouldn't rent the apartment to you because you aren't married. Now you can tell her you have a family and see what she can say.

MALE She can't possibly have anything to say. But do you really want to do this?

FEMALE Why not? What would I lose, since I'm not your real wife?

MALE Oh, thank you, thank you.

FEMALE Please don't misunderstand me. I don't mean that there's something to lose in being your wife. That's an entirely different question.

MALE Yes, that's an entirely different question, but I want to thank you nevertheless. After all, you've helped me solve my housing problem.

FEMALE Thank me? Why? Since neither of us is qualified to rent this place, it is only logical that we unite together to fight them. [*Cocks her ears to listen*]

MALE You're right, yes, you're right.

FEMALE I hear someone talking outside.

MALE Then it must be the policeman. [*Hastily*] What shall I say now, since I already told them that I'm single?

FEMALE Just tell them we've had a fight, you ran away and you don't want people to know . . .

MALE [*The policeman is already at the door outside; he gives a nod and signals her not to speak any more*] Shh! [*He sits by the square table, pretending to be angry.* FEMALE VISITOR *sits by the tea table. The back door is pushed open from outside, a policeman enters carrying a hurricane lamp, followed by* WANG MA *and the* LANDLADY. *They are surprised to see a woman in the room. No sooner have they entered than* FEMALE VISITOR *stands up to greet them. The policeman puts the hurricane lamp on the table and makes a bow to the angry* MALE VISITOR]

POLICE May I have your name, please?

MALE [*Rudely*] Wu.

POLICE [*Nods*] Thank you. And your address?

MALE Address? I have no address.

FEMALE [*Begins to play the role of an abused wife*] So you've decided to disown your family?

POLICE [*Beginning to take notice of the interrupter; turns to* MALE VISITOR] This lady is . . . What's her name?

MALE [*Not being able to answer, throws a glance at* FEMALE, *who is fully aware of his embarrassment; he can only resume his role as a sulky husband*] I don't know. Ask her yourself.

POLICE [*Following his suggestion*] What's your name please?

FEMALE [*Cheerfully*] Me? My name is also Wu.

POLICE Oh, also Wu.

FEMALE Yes.

POLICE [*Can't think of anything to say*] And your address?

FEMALE My address? I live in Peking, No. 375, Taiping Alley, West Four Memorial Arches opposite the Kuan-ti Temple, telephone W 4692. . . . Oh, you'd better take it down because you might forget it afterwards.

POLICE [*Pulls out a notebook as told*] Peking . . . [*Writes*]

FEMALE Taiping Alley, West Four Memorial Arches [*Pauses for the policeman to write*], opposite the Kuan-ti Temple.

POLICE House number?

FEMALE 375, telephone number is W 4692.

POLICE [*Finishes writing*] Thank you. [*Replacing the notebook, turns to* MALE VISITOR] You're here to rent the apartment, right?

MALE Wrong! I've come to take up residence here. I rented this apartment some time ago.

POLICE [*Stumped; finding no way out, turns to* FEMALE VISITOR] And you're here to . . . ?

FEMALE Me? I've come to look for someone.

LANDLADY [*Cannot control herself any more*] Who're you looking for?

FEMALE [*Nods to her very politely*] I've come to look for my husband.

LANDLADY Look for your husband? Who's your husband?

FEMALE I think you should have known, since you've rented the rooms to him.

LANDLADY What? So he's your husband?

FEMALE I don't know. You ask him. See if he admits it.

WANG [*She too cannot control herself any longer*] T'ai-t'ai, see what I mean? Didn't I tell you in the beginning this gentleman must have a family and you didn't believe me.

POLICE [*Confusedly*] What? Just now you told me this gentleman didn't have a family, why is he all of a sudden a married man?

WANG Don't be foolish. This lady was not here a while ago, so how could we know? If she had come earlier, it would have saved me a trip in the rain.

FEMALE I'm sorry, but really I can't be blamed for this. My train was late and I arrived here only at six.

WANG No, I didn't mean you. I only want to say that the policeman should have known better.

POLICE Now, this must be made perfectly clear. It was *t'ai-t'ai* who asked me to come, saying that this gentleman has rented three rooms and is staying here all by himself. She said that since only womenfolk live here, it would be quite inconvenient to have a male tenant around. Now that Mrs. Wu has arrived, then there shouldn't be any more problems, because if Mr. and Mrs. Wu are staying here together, I don't have any more business. But in case Mrs. Wu is not staying, then I . . .

WANG Don't talk such nonsense. Of course Mrs. Wu is staying, can't you see a thing as simple as that? Mr. and Mrs. Wu are just having a quarrel over some small matter, and you're talking nonsense when you should be helping them to make up. Where is Mrs. Wu to stay if not here? All right now, no more business for you, you can go back to your mah-jong game. [*Hands over the hurricane lamp to him*] Go! Go!

POLICE Well, if that's what it is, I really don't have any more business here. Goodbye! Goodbye!

FEMALE Goodbye! and don't you worry. I'll let you know when I'm not staying here any more.

POLICE I'm sorry for the disturbance. [*Exit.* WANG MA *cheerfully follows him with the teapot. The* LANDLADY *is now reconciled to her defeat, takes a look at her tenants and retreats with a long face*]

MALE [*Closes the door, then it occurs to him that he has not asked a question, which should have been asked at the beginning; he suddenly turns around*] Er, what's your name?

FEMALE I . . . oh . . . I . . .

[*Curtain*]

Notes

1. Servants' term of address for mistress of the house; also, when following surname, used as "Mrs."

2. Young Mistress; also used as "Miss."

Ou-yang Yü-ch'ien

P'an Chin-lien

Translated by Catherine Swatek

Cast of Characters

CHANG TA-HU, a corrupt member of the gentry; rich and powerful, but old and ugly

KAO SHENG, his servant

HO CHIU, a coroner, about 50 years old

WANG P'O, in her fifties, a teahouse owner and go-between for illicit affairs

P'AN CHIN-LIEN, an intelligent young woman with a strong personality

HSI-MEN CH'ING, a young, conceited local boss, eager to pick a fight and equally eager in pursuing women

WU SUNG, a brave and high-minded young captain, whose outlook is steeped in the old Confucian morality

YÜN KO, a young peddler

OTHERS: Chang Ta-hu's concubines, maidservants, and manservant; two orderlies; two waiters; a beggar; the neighbors

Period The Northern Sung dynasty (A.D. 960-1127)[1]

SCENE 1

Chang Ta-hu's summerhouse. The house is at stage left–only the veranda and a section of some stone steps are in view. At stage right is a bamboo fence, with a door leading to the garden beyond. Climbing roses, just at their peak of bloom, spread over the top of the fence, beyond which one can glimpse several flowering shrubs and what appears to be the corner of a small building in the shade of a willow tree. In front of the steps is a clump of bamboo. In addition, several potted plants and goldfish cisterns have been set out in a row. One can tell at a glance that this place belongs to a rich and pleasure-loving man. CHANG TA-HU is reclining in a folding chair, before a small stone table. One maid-servant gives him a massage; another holds a spittoon, while a third is stationed behind him holding a fly whisk. A teapot, teacups, and a wine service have been placed on the table; a light feast has just concluded. The concubines are seated here and there; each holds a musical instrument (a Chinese lute, reed pipes, bamboo flutes, and the like). As the curtain call sounds music strikes up behind the curtain, and as the short melody is about to end a gale of female laughter is heard. The curtain opens. The concubines are all beaming with seductive good looks. As they tune their instruments they steal glances at CHANG, *attentive to his every whim.* CHANG's *air is one of complete ennui. He makes a noise indicating that he wants to spit, and the maid proffers the spittoon. A concubine quickly offers some tea;* CHANG *averts his head, indicating that he doesn't want any.*

CONCUBINE #1 Why are you so peevish lately? What's bothering you?

CHANG The trouble is that in this entire household there isn't anyone who can satisfy me or do what I want. [*As he speaks, he waves the masseuse away, a funny smile on his face*]

CONCUBINE #1 My! My! Aren't you hard to please—you live in a great mansion, employ lots of servants, and run a whole herd of pack-mules.

CHANG A clumsy bunch—all of them.

CONCUBINE #4 [*Pointing at* #1] But there's big sister to fix you up in silks and satins the whole year round—and with her own clever hands! [CONCUBINE #1 *purses her lips and affects an air of disgust*]

CHANG I'm worn out.[2]

CONCUBINE #4 Second sister goes to the kitchen herself to fix you delicacies and treats—day after day. [CONCUBINE #2 *smirks*]

CHANG I'm fed up.

CONCUBINE #4 Then there's third sister, whose hand with the lute can thrill your soul. [CONCUBINE #3 *laughs and points a finger at* CONCUBINE #4]

CONCUBINE #2 It's fourth sister who has the talent—she can sing, she can dance, she can turn any way you want.[3] [*She makes a face at* CONCUBINE #4, *who takes a piece of fruit from the table and throws it at her*]

CHANG Enough—what else are you peddling? I've heard it all. What I can't understand is how other men's women get prettier and younger looking all the time. Look at you dumbheads—the older you get the worse you look.

CONCUBINE #3 I know that I'm not good-looking, but it doesn't necessarily follow that all of us are ugly.

CONCUBINE #1 Except for "Old Three," it's we who are really the ugly ones.

CONCUBINE #4 Even if we are ugly, old Master, your face isn't much to look at either, is it?

CHANG Keeping women is like raising goldfish: you want the fish to be pretty but what's the use of a pretty fish keeper? It's only for fun.

CONCUBINE #2 Listen to him—treating us as if we're goldfish!

CHANG As long as a man has money and power, there isn't a woman he can't have. A woman without a man to love her is finished, so if I take care of you it's like doing a good deed.

CONCUBINE #4 Stop blowing your own horn. There's someone right under your nose that you couldn't bring down.

CHANG Who?

CONCUBINE #4 I won't say—I'm afraid I'd embarrass you.

CHANG You little bitch! Watch me skin you alive. It's P'an Chin-lien you're talking about, isn't it?

CONCUBINE #4 A maid that no amount of your money could buy. It wasn't for lack of money or power—you just weren't cute enough. [*Laughs*]

CHANG You can't argue with Fate. Didn't Chin-lien turn me down only to end up married to that ugly, short, filthy, good-for-nothing Wu Ta?

CONCUBINE #1 You said it!

CHANG People said that marrying Chin-lien to Wu Ta was like sticking a flower on a cow pie. But with a temper like hers he was the only man fit to marry her to. Served her right!

CONCUBINE #4 Enough of this. You got angry because Chin-lien wouldn't get into your bed, so you married her to that penniless "three inch nail"[4] on purpose, just to break her spirit. But she . . .

CONCUBINE #2 I hear that it was Chin-lien who murdered Wu Ta. I wonder if it's true.

CHANG That's just what I'm going to find out.

CONCUBINE #1 It's lucky that you didn't take a vicious woman like that as a concubine.

CONCUBINE #4 As they say, "A good woman is a stupid one." Take dummies like us—we do anything that our old man puts us up to.

CHANG I may put up, but you don't put out.[5]

CONCUBINE #4 Oooh . . . Aah! [*The concubines all laugh, the maidservants giggling as well*]

CHANG With a woman like Chin-lien, the day will come when I'll get her to come begging to me. Otherwise, it would be an outrage for her to run wild like this.

[*The concubines look at each other without a word. A servant, KAO SHENG, approaches the fence from offstage and looks over it*]

CHANG Kao Sheng!

KAO SHENG Yes, sir! [*He enters very respectfully, facing the audience, eyes fixed forward. His behavior is dictated by the strict rules that segregate the "inner" and "outer" areas in wealthy households*]

CHANG Have you summoned Ho Chiu?

KAO SHENG He's been waiting for hours. Since your Excellency hasn't called, I haven't dared report.

CHANG Scatterbrain!

KAO SHENG Yes, sir!

CHANG Call him in.

KAO SHENG Yes, sir.

CHANG [*To the concubines*] There's someone coming. Go inside.

CONCUBINES Yes . . . hide . . . let's go inside! [*They exit through the door to the garden as* HO CHIU *enters via the stone steps at stage left*]

HO CHIU I hope that Your Honor is in good health? [*Exit* KAO SHENG]

CHANG Ho Chiu—when P'an Chin-lien murdered Wu Ta, how big a bribe did you take from Hsi-men Ch'ing?

HO CHIU Your Honor, no one knows how Wu Ta died. The talk that's going around isn't necessarily reliable, and as for saying that I took bribes, that's unfair. You can check it out for yourself.

CHANG Everybody knows that P'an Chin-lien and Hsi-men Ch'ing are lovers.

HO CHIU [*Hurriedly*] But *I* didn't know about it. I only heard some sort of talk like that.

CHANG You say you don't know. Wu Ta died suddenly. Who went to certify it for burial?

HO CHIU I did.

CHANG You saw Wu Ta's corpse. Did he die of natural causes or was there foul play?

HO CHIU When Wu Ta died his wife, P'an Chin-lien, told Old Lady Wang to ask me to come for an autopsy. I went right away. Who could have known that as soon as I entered the house, I'd have a seizure, fall to the floor and pass out? So I didn't get a good look at the condition of the corpse.

CHANG You've covered yourself pretty well. I give you three days to clear the matter up. If you don't, I'll have the magistrate come down hard on you. There is a murder case here. We'll see how many more meals you'll eat at public expense.

HO CHIU In answer to that, Your Honor, even if Wu died under suspicious circumstances, since no plaintiff has come forward it isn't up to the coroner to interfere.

CHANG When I tell you to do something you do it. As one of the local gentry I naturally have a responsibility to keep up the standards of the community. You may go.

HO CHIU Yes, sir. [*Exit* HO CHIU. CHANG *looks very pleased with himself. Two concubines come out, thinking to eavesdrop.* CHANG *catches a glimpse of them and scolds*]

CHANG Get back. [*The concubines hide themselves away. Enter again* KAO SHENG]

KAO SHENG Sir, Old Lady Wang has come.

CHANG She didn't meet Ho Chiu?

KAO SHENG No. She came by the back door and Ho Chiu left by the front.

CHANG Good. Tell her to come in. [KAO SHENG *goes over to the fence and beckons.* WANG P'O *enters*]

KAO SHENG [*To* WANG P'O] The Master's asking for you, watch your tongue. [WANG P'O *nods her head as she passes him*]

WANG P'O Master Chang—how are you? I've come especially to ask after you. What is it you want me to do?

CHANG You and P'an Chin-lien have done a fine thing!

WANG P'O What do you mean, sir?

CHANG How did Wu Ta die?

WANG P'O He died of a heart ailment.

CHANG Didn't you set Hsi-men Ch'ing up to commit adultery with P'an Chin-lien and murder Wu Ta?

WANG P'O Heavens! That's a serious accusation!

CHANG That's what all of Yang-ku city is saying—that P'an Chin-lien murdered her own husband.

WANG P'O There's always idle talk. Wu Ta's wife is nice looking. The playboys and bachelors[6] see her and who doesn't get ideas? When they realize they can't have her, they have to manufacture these rumors. As they say: "Fresh gossip every day; pay no heed, it goes away."

CHANG Doesn't Hsi-men Ch'ing hang around there a lot?

WANG P'O Master Hsi-men Ch'ing only goes to my place to have tea. I don't know how he spends the rest of his time.

CHANG Just now Ho Chiu was here and he says that Wu Ta died under suspicious circumstances. That puts the burden of proof on you, old woman.

WANG P'O Damned old fool! I'm going to find him. [*Turns to leave*]

CHANG Come back here! What's your hurry?

WANG P'O I'm going to find that old fool and have it out with him. Really—where did he come up with that?

CHANG Hmmm, you really are something. I have this to say: I have a score to settle with all of you. Chin-lien was a maidservant in my household. She didn't know her place and wouldn't accept favors from me. All I could do was marry her off. Even then her refusal to do her duty as a wife caused some ugly talk. My idea is to take her back and straighten her out. Go tell her that if she's willing to turn over a new leaf, I'll take care of everything for her. If not, then one of these days the whole affair will get out and her number will be up. If she has any sense, you'll come with her reply and I'll send someone to fetch her. Understand?

WANG P'O More or less. Your Honor would like to take her back. But, as they say, "A daughter married is like water thrown out the door." Is it any less true of the maidservant that's been sold? Miss Chin-lien has already been Wu Ta's wife. Now that her husband is dead, do you really think that if you let her come back and be your maidservant she'll be willing? Forget about straightening her out; when a person is grown her mind is made up—who can change it? Be forgiving, Your Honor—let her go and be done with it.

CHANG What? Nonsense! With a nuisance like her, people start talking. On top of that, they'll say that the maidservants in my household don't behave themselves. If I order her back she has to come; if I want to straighten her out, nobody can stop me. She has to be made to understand Right and Wrong. If she's willing to listen to me, I may give her some encouragement. If she isn't, I'm afraid that even you won't have long to live.

WANG P'O Yes—yes, Your Honor. Someone like you with money and power—not old, either, kind, and gentle to people too. You have no need to fear that a woman won't do whatever you want her to. But . . .

CHANG Nonsense! Kao Sheng!

KAO SHENG Yes, sir.

CHANG Throw the old woman out. This is outrageous! I can handle them. . . . [*As he speaks he enters the house by way of the garden*] [WANG P'O, *at a loss for words, watches him go inside.* KAO SHENG *goes over to her and claps her on the shoulder*]

KAO SHENG Mother Wang—you've been around; still going to play dumb?

WANG P'O Things couldn't be more clear. Men crave, women love, and that's what makes the world go 'round. However in this case, he feels a craving, but she isn't loving. How can you spar without a partner?

KAO SHENG That's pretty good. But that Chin-lien is too headstrong. She forgets who she is and wants to take things into her own hands. She used to be our maidservant. The Master wanted to take her as a concubine. She wouldn't go along, then on top of that she fell for one of the servants. That was wrong of her, and you can't blame our Master for getting even by marrying her to Wu Ta. That was to take the wind out of her sails. Considering that our Master is a little on the old side [*Whispers*] and not all that good-looking, he's a whole lot better than the likes of Wu Ta: not even five feet tall, with a big head and flat feet, a red, runny nose, bleary eyes, a sooty face and a snotty mouth. He'd talk and it would be like a broken gong banging; he'd walk and it would be funnier than a wobbling watermelon. Now people are saying that P'an Chin-lien is having an affair with Hsi-men Ch'ing and that she murdered her own husband. You know, don't you, how awful the penalty is for those crimes? Lingering death by slow mutilation. But as long as she goes along with our Master, he'll take care of everything for her. She could murder her own husband and several others to boot and there would be no problem. You tell her that as long as she comes around in her thinking, gives the Master a kiss or two around the whiskers and says some nice things to him, then I guarantee that he won't even fool around with the other concubines. Isn't that a pretty good deal? The Master would give you a big reward, too.

WANG P'O Uh-huh. I'll go and speak with her, but there's no telling whether she'll listen or not. But "to catch a thief, get him with the loot." Hsi-men Ch'ing is a big shot and no pushover, either.

KAO SHENG Nonsense. Do you think you can stick up for him? I'll tell it to you straight—my Master is a man of his word, and he isn't about to let some stinking maidservant run wild. I'll come for your answer tomorrow. You'd better get going. That's all I have to say.

WANG P'O [*Forcing a smile*] All right, all right—you're higher and mightier than your Master. [*She exits*]

KAO SHENG [*Contemptuously*] Humph! The old hag doesn't know a good thing when she sees it. We'll see. [*He smiles malignantly*]

[*Curtain*]

SCENE 2

The interior of the rear courtyard of the Wu household. To the right, aslant the rear corner, a door leads to the outside. Further to the right, a small door leads to Wang P'o's house. In the center is a low window; its wooden shutters are closed. A door on the left leads to the rooms. Beside the door is a scrawny tree, and underneath the window are a broken-down mortar and pestle and a bamboo broom. There is a plank bench beside the tree. In the center of the stage, and slightly to the right, is a well encircled by an old railing. Atop the wall is a windlass on a wooden frame. WANG P'O is seated on the mortar taking a nap. As the curtain rises there are no signs of life. P'AN CHIN-LIEN emerges from the doorway and leans dispiritedly against it.

CHIN-LIEN I'm bored to death.

WANG P'O [*Yawning as she speaks*] The weather's really awful; I haven't any energy at all.

CHIN-LIEN When you want to die you can't blame it on the weather.

WANG P'O What kind of talk is that?

CHIN-LIEN I really want to die.

WANG P'O You needn't take what I said to you about Chang so hard. With a big shot like Hsi-Men Ch'ing around what are you afraid of?

CHIN-LIEN Who cares about that old dog? I want to die; it's none of his business.

WANG P'O Now that a big shot likes you, you have food to eat and money to spend—and you're still not satisfied?

CHIN-LIEN [*Contemptuously*] Humph! Who could get along with him for long? You are always thrown together with your enemy in the past life.[7] He relies on his money and influence to come around here looking for a good time—where does he have any real feelings? I only keep him around to relieve my boredom and pass the time. The minute I can't take him anymore the whole thing will be off. What's there to like about men? All they do is bully us. Even if you had all the talent in the world they wouldn't let you do anything with it. All you can do is dance on their strings.

WANG P'O Men get the respect, women the contempt—it's always been that way. What's the use of getting all worked up about it? Just take things one day at a time.

CHIN-LIEN And so I want to die. As long as I'm young I can still depend on my looks to get men to fall in love with me. But once I show the slightest sign of age, I won't be worth a cent. It doesn't matter who you are—if some man doesn't have some feeling for you you won't be able to live. Mother, haven't you had enough?

WANG P'O Me?

CHIN-LIEN When you were young, didn't a crowd of men follow you around? How many tender speeches and vows of undying love did you listen to then? Now you're hard up for coarse tea and plain rice. Don't you prove my point? [*She sighs regretfully*] Ai! Better that a girl die sooner, while she's young, and be spared a living hell. Ah! Why don't I just throw myself into the well! [*Smiling, she walks over to the well, as if to throw herself in.* WANG P'O *stands up quickly*]

WANG P'O Oh! Don't frighten me! Surely the worst of lives is better than the best of deaths.

CHIN-LIEN A good death is better than a bad life. Best of all would be for women to die off completely.

WANG P'O If the women all died, what would happen to the men?

CHIN-LIEN So great are their crimes—let them suffer.

WANG P'O Not bad. The women die off and let the men go hang. See if they wouldn't find that hard to take!

CHIN-LIEN [*Smiles and sighs*] I'm bored to death. The only thing to do is chatter and laugh and let off some steam.

[*Enter a blind and lame* BEGGAR, *through the door on the right*]

BEGGAR [*Calling out to either side*] Kind ladies—have pity on this cripple—please help me!

WANG P'O Poor wretch—come, here's a couple of coins.

BEGGAR Bless you, merciful lady!

CHIN-LIEN [*Holds* WANG P'O *back, keeping her from giving the money*] Don't—mother! What are you doing giving him that? This is the sort of man I despise the most!

WANG P'O This is the only sort of man I can have any feeling for.

CHIN-LIEN Look at him—blind, crippled, unfit for anything—isn't he hopeless? He's hopeless and still he doesn't die—in fact he'd rather suffer. There are plenty of ablebodied men who haven't anything to eat; where is there rice to spare for this sort of creature? Give him money? The best thing would be to kill him!

BEGGAR Don't talk like that. Be careful—you may be blind and crippled some day. I was good-looking once, too.

CHIN-LIEN Don't worry. Before I half resemble you I'll be dead. You won't catch me eating other people's scraps.

BEGGAR You're the one who's blind. And you think I'm blind? [*He opens his eyes wide*] Look—aren't these perfectly good eyes? [*Stamps his foot*] Look—isn't this a perfectly good leg? The world loves cripples. I have no choice. If I want to eat I've got to put on an act.

CHIN-LIEN [*Looks at him with astonishment*] Oh! You even had me fooled. It's quite a trick. Good—considering that you do have a little bit of talent, you can have the money. [*She gives him the money*] But I found you out. [*Laughs*] I win! I win!

BEGGAR This lady's a little crazy. I'm getting out of here.

WANG P'O [*To* CHIN-LIEN] He's right, you *are* crazy. It's horrid to lie and cheat, but you go and give him money for it!

CHIN-LIEN I'd rather be hated than pitied. [*As she talks she returns to the bench underneath the tree and sits down*]

[KAO SHENG *stands in front of the door and calls*]

KAO SHENG Mother Wang! Mother Wang!

[WANG P'O, *who has been pondering the meaning of* CHIN-LIEN'S *speech, turns her head to look*]

WANG P'O Oh! Kao Sheng! I was wondering who it could be. [*She hurries over to him*]

KAO SHENG I've come for your answer. How about it?

[WANG P'O *whispers to* KAO SHENG, *indicating to him that things aren't going well.* KAO SHENG *replies in a loud voice, to show that he isn't backing down*]

KAO SHENG What's that you're saying? Tell me how I'm going to explain that to the Master. Who ever heard of a maid acting so stuck-up?

CHIN-LIEN [*Stands up*] Who's that? What's causing all the racket?

KAO SHENG [*Quickly all smiles*] Miss Chin-lien. It's me.

CHIN-LIEN Sonny boy—running over here to show off your bad manners?

KAO SHENG Well, well! You should be a little more hospitable. You're no better than me. When you were a maid and I was a servant it was me, after all, who escorted you to Wu Ta's house when you were married. This time you—[*Laughs*] Who's kidding who? You ought to be nice to me, but all you do is curse at me. Hah! You've really got nerve.

CHIN-LIEN I'm asking you. What have you come here for?

KAO SHENG Me? I've come to ask a favor.

CHIN-LIEN Ah—you want a favor? I have a favor. Come here—[*She opens her arms as if to embrace him.* KAO SHENG *goes over to her and she slaps him on the face*]

KAO SHENG Aiya! What was that for?

CHIN-LIEN Take that, you dog! Coming over here to run wild. Haven't you heard that I'm a hard mama who can lift a man on one fist and shoulder a horse?[8] [*As she is speaking she takes up the broken broom at the foot of the wall and commences beating him.* WANG P'O, *while pretending to break up the fight, holds* KAO SHENG *down*]

KAO SHENG [*Shouting as he wards off the blows*] Aiya! You're killing me! You're killing me! You murdered your own husband—now you want to do it again!

CHIN-LIEN Wretch—dead cur! I'm not afraid of your bawling. [*She strikes even harder.* WANG P'O *makes a token effort to break up the fight. At which moment, enter* HSI-MEN CH'ING. *Taking stock of the situation, he steps between them to break up the fight.* CHIN-LIEN *stands back, keeping a grip on the broom and still cursing at* KAO SHENG]

KAO SHENG Boy! You really are something!

CHIN-LIEN What are you going to do about it, you stinking swine! [*She looks as if she still wants to fight.* HSI-MEN CH'ING *stops her and turns to question* KAO SHENG. CHIN-LIEN *backs up*]

HSI-MEN What are you doing here?

KAO SHENG You can come and I can't?

HSI-MEN She's a widow; you're a man. What business have you got with her?

KAO SHENG You say that she's a woman? Well well, as if we didn't know. Stop your playacting, you mother— . . .

HSI-MEN My business is no business of yours. I come if I like; no one can do anything about it. Beat it. Don't look for trouble.

KAO SHENG [*Laughs*] I can't tell whether you really *do* have something up your sleeve.[9] My Master will be looking for you . . .

HSI-MEN Fuck your bastard Master! Beat it, I said. [*He grabs one of* KAO SHENG*'s legs, throws him down easily and drags him over to the well*]

KAO SHENG Aiya! Aiya!

HSI-MEN Do you want to live or die?

KAO SHENG Let me go! Let me go!

HSI-MEN Get the hell out of here! [*He gives a shove.* KAO SHENG *rolls over and gets up*]

KAO SHENG We'll meet again. [*Exits, running*]

CHIN-LIEN [*Laughing*] I love it! What an odious little man. If Wu Ta had been here, he would have bowed and scraped. "It looks like you really do have something up your sleeve." I love it! I love it! [WANG P'O *takes a jug, and, gesturing to* CHIN-LIEN *that she is going to get some wine, exits*]

HSI-MEN That was nothing—even the strongest men don't dare take me on, much less runts like him. Do you think I need you to sweet-talk me?

CHIN-LIEN If you talk like that, you must figure to be second to no one.

HSI-MEN Of course.

CHIN-LIEN Are you so sure?

HSI-MEN Have you seen anyone stronger?

CHIN-LIEN If you were to meet up with that tiger-killer Wu Sung,[10] you might be out of luck.

HSI-MEN [*Laughs*] You really do have the mind of a woman. And Wu Sung—you can talk about money, you can talk about influence, you can talk about looks, or you can talk about fighting skill: where does he compare with me?

CHIN-LIEN Granted he can't compare with you when it comes to influence, let alone money. But if you're talking about looks or fighting skill he has it over you a hundred times.

HSI-MEN You think he's so hot—if he and I were standing here who would you love, him or me?

CHIN-LIEN Him, naturally.

HSI-MEN [*Very surprised*] Oh? You have the nerve to say so! You know that you love him but he doesn't love you. You killed his brother. When he comes back I'm afraid he'll want to kill you!

CHIN-LIEN You know enought to fear his coming back, too. That's for sure. But he doesn't love me and my loving him is all my doing. I tried all kinds of ways to tempt him, but from the first to last he stuck to his principles—he really is a man of iron. At the same time you were on your knees to me begging, and I still wasn't making any promises. And so I respect him; I only feel pity for you.

HSI-MEN You say these things to me just to make me angry. You know that I can kill you with my bare hands!

CHIN-LIEN Save yourself the strain. You know perfectly well that I can't fight you; why do you have to get rough? Save your strength for someone your own size and try it out on him. I'll match wits with you, not strength.

HSI-MEN [*With an angry laugh*] It's only today that I'm beginning to make you out. You really don't have a heart. [*Enter* WANG P'O, *who is perplexed at their quarrel*] I haven't been mean to you, why are you making me angry like this? Okay, you won't see me here anymore. [*He turns to leave.* CHIN-LIEN *sulks.* WANG P'O *advances to block* HSI-MEN*'s retreat, overturning the wine jug. She holds onto him as if her life depended on it, urging him to come back*]

CHIN-LIEN Mother, let him go. We wouldn't want him to get into trouble with Chang Ta-hu.

[HSI-MEN *pauses, puzzled, but doesn't say anything*]

CHIN-LIEN He can't take responsibility for me. It's better to let him go away angry. If there's trouble, I'll face it myself.

HSI-MEN I'm not going to listen to any more of your fast talk.

CHIN-LIEN If you think I talk fast, why do you take it so seriously? Let me tell it to you straight. Chang Ta-hu wants to take me back and make me his concubine. Supposing I go—I wouldn't be able to give you up. Supposing I don't go—then I'm afraid that you'd be no match for him. [*Sighs*] You'd better go. Every party has to end sometime. [*During this speech she sits down with her head turned away from* HSI-MEN CH'ING, *her back shaking almost imperceptibly. Her delivery has been most affecting*]

WANG P'O Your Honor, can you show me a lady with as much goodness?

HSI-MEN [*Seeing the light*] Ah! So that's your reason for sending me away. This is too stupid. How can that old dog Chang stand even one blow from me? Now, I am not going; I'd like to see how he'd have the guts to come and get you. If I can't beat that old dog, my name isn't Hsi-men Ch'ing.

CHIN-LIEN I didn't know you, too, could be jealous. And you do have a heart after all. But if I tell you a little joke, you're ready to kill me with your bare hands. I wouldn't dare get involved with you anymore as long as I live. [*These last words are spoken most ingratiatingly; she then fixes* HSI-MEN *with a mock-angry look and turns toward the door. He grabs her by the sleeve*]

CHIN-LIEN How would it look if someone were to see? [*As she talks she tugs her sleeve away and goes inside.* WANG P'O *looks at* HSI-MEN *and points a finger after* CHIN-LIEN]

HSI-MEN [*To* CHIN-LIEN] I want to see what kind of tricks you've got up *your* sleeve! [*Pursues her inside.* WANG P'O *shrugs her shoulders and smiles*]

[*Curtain*]

SCENE 3

A small sitting room in the Wu household. A table with Wu Ta's spirit tablet on it has been placed to stage left. Two orderlies are sleeping on the floor beside it. At stage right is a staircase. Several chairs and benches have been arranged haphazardly. At both sides of the sitting room and on the altar are pairs of guttered candles. It is extremely gloomy. Outside one can hear the sound of the wind. WU SUNG *is seated to the right of the altar, clasping a wine jug in one hand, as the curtain opens.*

WU SUNG [*Stands up and sits down again; stands up again and walks several steps, deep in thought. He looks upstairs and comes to a halt, facing the altar*] Brother, my sister-in-law says that you died of some heart ailment, but I'm afraid that you died mysteriously. You have a spirit; I want you to tell me in a dream what really happened. If there was any foul play, Wu Sung will certainly avenge you. [*He sighs, glances upstairs, then looks again at the spirit tablet. He pours a bowl of wine and drains it with one gulp. He hears* CHIN-LIEN'S *footsteps descending the stairs and sits down, looking both angered and grieved*]

CHIN-LIEN [*Appears on the stairway. She takes a look in the direction of the spirit tablet, then descends, carrying a teatray*] Brother-in-law.

WU SUNG [*Stands up and greets her formally*] Sister-in-law.

CHIN-LIEN I thought that you would be pleased to be back; I never thought that it would make you so sad. [*Sighs*] Men die and cannot come back to life. Brother-in-law, you must watch your health; you shouldn't grieve too much. [*Very respectfully*]

WU SUNG When I think how bitterly my brother died, and that he and I were brothers born of the same mother, how can I not grieve? How can I not be angry?

CHIN-LIEN [*Sighs*] Hai! When he was alive your brother didn't get very far on his own, and he often caused you a great deal of worry and trouble. Now that he's dead he's causing you to grieve like this; it makes me feel very bad.

WU SUNG This is a matter of my duty to my brother. It has nothing to do with you.

CHIN-LIEN Will you have some tea?

WU SUNG Please put it on the table.

CHIN-LIEN Yes. [*The second watch—about 9 o'clock in the evening— sounds backstage*]

WU SUNG You said that my brother died of a heart ailment?

CHIN-LIEN Didn't I explain that to you the moment you arrived back here?

WU SUNG When the body was placed in the coffin, who besides Ho Chiu was present?

CHIN-LIEN The neighbors were all present.

WU SUNG Why did you have the body cremated?

CHIN-LIEN You weren't here and I wasn't able to go out and look for a burial site. I didn't have the money anyway. I could think of nothing better than cremation.

WU SUNG I see. [*Very respectfully and firmly*] It's getting late. Please go get some rest.

CHIN-LIEN Yes. [*She slowly takes two steps in the direction of the stairs, then glances fleetingly in* WU SUNG*'s direction, thinks something over, sighs, and resumes her slow pace, looking very disappointed*]

WU SUNG Sister-in-law—come back!

CHIN-LIEN [*Quickly turns her head and retraces her steps*] Yes? [*At the sight of* WU SUNG*'s face, she stops cold*]

WU SUNG [*Stiffly*] What did my brother really die of?

CHIN-LIEN Haven't I told you several times? [*Sighs*] There is one more thing I could say. Your brother was too much of a weakling. He let people walk all over him. For a man like him, simply to be alive was to suffer hardship. Truly, life wasn't worth living. The way I see it he's better off dead.

WU SUNG What kind of talk is that? Does that mean that people who are weak deserve to be bullied and that people with power have the right to bully them? All my life I've taken satisfaction in fighting these injustices; my only thought has been to help the weak and oppose the strong. Above all else I hate people who use force to bully the weak.

CHIN-LIEN Hai! If your brother had been half the man you are, would he have left me alone like this, without a lord and master? Brother-in-law, how could you know my heart?

WU SUNG Hunh—you're clever and able and have always been able to have things your way. When my brother was alive, he never could have been your lord and master.

CHIN-LIEN [*sighing*] Hai—really, your brother caused me hardship enough! You say I'm clever. I really can't be considered clever, but I'm not stupid either. You say I'm able. I'm really not able enough but I'm not an incompetent either. But "fishes in ponds don't swim far; a bird in a cage doesn't fly high." What can I do? [*Sighs*] You still don't know my heart.

WU SUNG What's the point of all this talk? You'd better go upstairs.

CHIN-LIEN I hear that you'll be going to the Eastern Capital. Is it true?

WU SUNG No such thing.

CHIN-LIEN I hear that you'll be going to the Eastern Capital to look for a job with Kao Ch'iu. Is it true?

WU SUNG [*With contempt*] Hunh! Kao Ch'iu, T'ung Kuan and that crew—they're all a pack of traitors.[11] I'm a man of principle. Do you think that I'd go looking for work at the gate of those traitors? What kind of man do you take me for?

CHIN-LIEN If His Excellency the magistrate were to recommend that you go be houseboy to those traitors—be their errand boy—would you do it?

WU SUNG Throw pearls before those swine? I'd die first!

CHIN-LIEN Ah, you feel the same way—that it's better to die than to throw away one's jewel. So men and women feel the same way!

[*At this moment, the sound of clappers striking the second hour of the second watch is heard in the distance.* WU SUNG *is silent, as if thinking about something. Outside, the sound of the wind]*

CHIN-LIEN It's late. Please—why don't you go upstairs and get some sleep?

WU SUNG [*Shocked*] Uh?

CHIN-LIEN Don't misunderstand me. What I mean is that it's dirty downstairs and a little cleaner up above. Please—you go rest upstairs. I'll come down here and keep watch for you. Isn't that all right?

WU SUNG It doesn't look very dirty to me here—and the upstairs isn't necessarily any cleaner, either. Don't concern yourself so much about my affairs. Please—go quickly and get some rest!

CHIN-LIEN Yes, I shouldn't have put it that way. What is there that's clean and what is there that's dirty? What does clean or dirty mean anyway? As long as you trust in yourself things will be all right.

WU SUNG My only fear is that other people won't trust you.

CHIN-LIEN Ah, so you only worry about what other people think, not about yourself?

WU SUNG The thief who kills a man, and the whore who ruins a man—people don't trust them, do you think that I, alone, should trust them?

CHIN-LIEN Whenever a man wants to abuse a woman there are lots of men to back him up. Only women who meekly allow men to torture them to death are "chaste and exemplary."[12] Anyone who survives the ordeal is a whore, and the woman who isn't willing to put up with a man's abuse is a criminal. No wonder you work for the magistrate, you're just like him. You only preach one-sided truths.

WU SUNG I fail utterly to comprehend your ravings.

CHIN-LIEN You're better off a little confused. If you were in less of a muddle you couldn't be such a good follower of Confucius.

WU SUNG Standards of integrity and morality never change. Will you die without understanding that?

CHIN-LIEN I understand it too well. If I were more mixed up I could live long and grow rich. I long to be confused to the point that I forget even who I am. But it won't happen in this life. . . . [*Sighs*] Hai! It's late—let's get some rest. It's too late for me to wait with you for the dawn. [*Gathers up the tea bowls, scatters the tea on the ground, and starts to leave, then turns her head and softly and suggestively utters one sentence*] May you live long and grow rich! [*She goes straight upstairs, her feet beating a rhythm on the steps. Outside the sound of the wind grows louder*]

WU SUNG [*Watches her go in stunned silence*] I didn't think such women existed! [*He takes the wine jug from the table opposite and empties it in one gulp. In a whisper*] Hai! How could my brother not die? [*He thinks for a moment*] Orderly!

[*The orderlies wake up, then doze off again*]

WU SUNG Orderly! Orderly!

ORDERLIES Sir, is it morning?

WU SUNG It's still the middle of the night.

ORDERLIES What's the matter?

WU SUNG Let's go.

[*From behind the curtain the third hour of the second watch sounds in the distance*]

ORDERLY #1 Sir, where are we going at this hour of the night?

ORDERLY #2 Won't we be violating the curfew?

WU SUNG We're going on patrol.

ORDERLIES [*Yawning, they gather up their things, looking very unhappy*] Sir, what's your hurry?

WU SUNG I can't stay here. . . . Sister-in-law! Bar the door. I'm going.

[CHIN-LIEN *slowly descends and stands silently on the stairs*]

WU SUNG Are you ready?

ORDERLIES Ready.

WU SUNG Go!

ORDERLIES [*Open the door and the wind blows in*] Aiya!

[WU SUNG *and the orderlies exit.* CHIN-LIEN *descends several more steps, cranes her head and watches the door at stage left, motionless. Her air is one of great disappointment, anger, and resignation. Suddenly a gust of wind extinguishes the lamp, and the stage becomes pitch black*]

[*Curtain*]

SCENE 4

A small wineshop. In the center rear of the stage is a portable screen; the right side is set off by a wooden partition; on the left side are two windows. Adjacent to the partition is a doorway, a blue curtain hanging over it. Two tables have been placed side by side, and several benches have been arranged around them. There are two waiters. One is wiping tables, the other is leaning against the window watching the street as the curtain opens.

WAITER #1 [*Singing a tune as he wipes the table*] Hey! All you do is watch the street all day. P'an Chin-lien isn't going to pass this way.

WAITER #2 Foul mouth! All you've got on your mind is P'an Chin-lien. Thinking of eating the swan's flesh? You toad!

WAITER #1 You're not much of an improvement on Wu Ta. Don't ask for it, you mother— . . . !

WAITER #2 Hey! Come have a look.

WAITER #1 What d'ya see, a ghost?

WAITER #2 Really—come look at him.

WAITER #1 Who?

WAITER #2 Come see if it isn't that tiger-killer, Captain Wu.

WAITER #1 Is he back?

WAITER #2 It sure looks like him.

WAITER #1 [*Moves to the window*] It's him, it's him. Who's the old man talking with him?

WAITER #2 Isn't that Ho Chiu?

WAITER #1 It looks like they're coming here.

WAITER #2 Wu Sung's back; I'm afraid that means trouble. [*As they talk they move away from the window*]

WAITER #1 What trouble? Not long after Wu Ta died P'an Chin-lien took up with Hsi-men Ch'ing. What do you take Wu Sung for, some kind of superman? Even if he figures that Wu Ta was done in, he hasn't any proof.

WAITER #2 Let's knock off that talk! "Sweep the snow on your own doorstep," that way you don't talk too much and stir up trouble. Let's hurry up and sweep the place cleaner—don't spend all your time gossiping. [*The two men resume wiping tables.* WU SUNG *and* HO CHIU *can be heard talking offstage*]

WU SUNG Uncle Ho, don't be so polite. Please, have a seat. [*The two men enter the shop, and the waiters quickly show them to a table*]

HO CHIU Here you've just come back, and before I have a chance to welcome you with a meal you're playing the host. How does that make me feel?

WU SUNG Please, sit down! [*They sit down*]

HO CHIU Yes, all right.

WU SUNG Waiter, bring wine and a couple of things to go with it. [*Exit waiter.* WU SUNG *lapses into silence;* HO CHIU *looks uncomfortable*]

HO CHIU It's been more than two months since you went to the capital. [WU SUNG *nods*]

HO CHIU And everything went to your satisfaction. [WU SUNG *smiles disdainfully*]

HO CHIU We've all been looking forward to your coming back. [*The waiter brings the wine and food*]

WU SUNG You may go. [*The waiter exits*] Uncle Ho, have some wine.

HO CHIU Young Master, your health! [*He looks very uncomfortable.* WU SUNG *remains intent on his drinking and doesn't say anything*]

HO CHIU [*Looking at* WU SUNG, *he raises his wine cup and drinks. At a loss, he tries to test* WU SUNG *with conversation*] When His Excellency the magistrate saw how well you managed your assignment, he must have been very pleased. [WU SUNG *grimaces and doesn't reply*]

HO CHIU What I can't figure out is how your brother could just up and die. It's really true that "a man's life is as uncertain as the weather."

WU SUNG [*Coldly*] What illness did my brother die of?

HO CHIU I heard something to the effect that he died of a heart ailment.

WU SUNG Were you there when they laid him out?

HO CHIU I was there.

WU SUNG Were there any suspicious signs?

HO CHIU There didn't appear to be.

WU SUNG Did you go to the funeral?

HO CHIU I was at the cremation as well.

WU SUNG Were there any suspicious signs?

HO CHIU There didn't appear to be anything there, either. [WU SUNG *stands up, whips out a dagger from inside his coat, and jabs it into the table. Ho* CHIU, *frightened, lets the wine cup fall onto the table and jumps back, nearly falling down. A waiter, who has been eavesdropping behind the door curtain, withdraws quickly in fright]*

WU SUNG Uncle Ho, "Every crime has a culprit and every debt has a lender." Don't be afraid; just tell the truth. Tell me the cause of my brother's death, then you won't have anything more to do with it. If I harm you, I'm not a man, but if you utter so much as one false word, I'll fill you so full of holes that the light will shine through! *[He glares]*

HO CHIU Young Master, don't get angry. I've got important evidence right here. *[He removes a bag from his sleeve as he talks]*

WU SUNG What important evidence? *[He takes the bag and opens it. Inside are a piece of silver and two bones]*

HO CHIU I don't know how and why it happened. Maybe she murdered him because she had a lover—it's hard to say for sure. It was the 22nd of the first month. I was at home that day, when Old Lady Wang who runs the teashop came and asked me to go and lay out Wu Ta's corpse—

WU SUNG *[Interrupting him]* So you saw my brother's corpse? How was it?

HO CHIU Don't be in such a hurry, young Master. Let me tell you at my own pace.

WU SUNG Have a seat and go on. *[They sit down again]*

HO CHIU I heard Old Lady Wang calling me, and I promised her that I'd go right away. No sooner did I get to the corner of Amethyst Street than I looked up and who did I see but Master Hsi-men Ch'ing himself. He collared me and dragged me off with him to a wineshop for a drink. He took this piece of silver and gave it to me and told me, in his words, to "keep a lid on" anything I saw when I went to Wu's house for the laying out. You know what an evil character that Hsi-men Ch'ing is. He gave me money; who was I to refuse? I accepted the money, drank the wine, left the shop and went straight to Wu Ta's house. The first thing I saw when I lifted the burial shroud was that the orifices of the body were clotted with blood and there were teeth marks on the lips. It was obvious that he had been poisoned.

WU SUNG Why didn't you file a report?

HO CHIU The thought crossed my mind. But for one thing, there was no one to bring charges—his own wife said that he died of a heart ailment; what good would it do for me to speak up? For another thing I really couldn't risk provoking Hsi-men Ch'ing. Under the circumstances all I could do was to fake a seizure and collapse. They carried me home and got somebody else to take care of the body. Three days later I heard that they were taking the body off to be cremated, so I bought a packet of paper money and acted as if I was one of the mourners. I gathered up these two bones on the sly and kept them wrapped up in my house. You can see for yourself that they're blackened; that's further evidence of poisoning. And then there's this piece of paper with the date, the time, and the names of the mourners written on it. I was waiting for you to come back so I could tell you this, too. When you went looking for me just now I guessed what it was you had in mind and made a point of bringing these things along to save you another trip.

WU SUNG Who's her lover?

HO CHIU I don't really know and I wouldn't care to guess. I did hear that there's a young fellow who sells pears named Yün Ko, who went once with Wu Ta to the teashop to catch them together. Everybody on the whole street knows about it. If you want to know the details, you'd better go ask Yün Ko.

WU SUNG All right. As long as we have him, we'll go look for him together. Waiter—the bill, please.

WAITER Yes, sir.

[*As WU SUNG is paying, the sound of a quarrel is heard downstairs.*]

VOICE #1 You little brat—are you blind? Do you know you ran into somebody?

VOICE #2 I'm loaded down, couldn't you get out of my way?

VOICE #1 Yün Ko, you little bastard, pigheaded as ever. You only take it when Old Lady Wang is dishing it out! [*More bickering*]

HO CHIU We're in luck—from the sound of things it must be Yün Ko. [*He runs to the window to take a look*]

WU SUNG If it's him, tell him to come up.

HO CHIU [*Nodding*] Yün Ko! Yün Ko! Be quiet, be quiet! Come on up, I have something to say to you.

YÜN KO I'm not coming.

HO CHIU Come on—my treat—hurry up!

WU SUNG Is he coming?

HO CHIU He's coming.

[*A flurry of footsteps on the stairs. A waiter calls from inside the partition*]

WAITER Here—in here. [YÜ KO *enters*]

HO CHIU Yün Ko—do you know Captain Wu?

YÜN KO I've known of him ever since he killed the tiger on Ching-yang Ridge and brought it here. What do you want me for?

HO CHIU The captain has some questions he wants to ask you.

YÜN KO Before you say anything, I can guess some. But there is one thing: I have a sixty-year-old father and no one to look after him. So I can't go off with you and fool around with any lawsuit. What do you say?

WU SUNG Good brother, [*Taking out a piece of silver*] take these five ounces of silver for the time being and give them to your father to live on. You may be young, but you're a dutiful son. I need you. After this business is over with I'll give you another fourteen or fifteen ounces as capital. Now, tell me exactly, how did you and my brother go to catch P'an Chin-lien with her lover?

YÜN KO I'll tell you, but don't get upset. On the thirteen of the first month I was carrying a basket of snow pears over to Hsi-men Ch'ing's, hoping to sell them to him. But I never could find him. When I asked around people said that he was at Old Lady Wang's teashop on Amethyst Street, keeping company with the cake vendor Wu Ta's wife. She was his latest find, so he was spending all his time over there. When I heard that, I ran straight there to look for him, but to my surprise my way was blocked by that old bitch Wang; she wouldn't let me in. When I said something that touched her sore spot, the old hag beat me with her own hands, pitched me out, and dumped my pears in the street. I was really worked up, and went looking for your brother and told him the whole story from beginning to end. He got mad and wanted to go right away and catch them in the act. I told him that wouldn't solve anything. I said that Hsi-men Ch'ing was rough and tough, and that he just might get hurt. I discussed a plan with your brother right then and there. My idea was to have your brother make fewer cakes the next morning. We would agree to meet at the head of the street and wait until we saw Hsi-men Ch'ing go into Old Lady Wang's shop, then I would go in first. I was to throw my basket into the street as a signal, then Wu Ta would go in and catch them together. The next day came and we did things according to plan. When I saw Hsi-men Ch'ing go through Old Lady Wang's door I went straight over and cursed out the old bitch. When that old woman came at me, I rammed my head into her chest and threw the basket into the street. Wu Ta saw it and came forcing his way in after me. Old Lady Wang wanted to stop him, but I had her pinned so she couldn't move. All she could do was scream that Wu Ta had come. Hsi-men Ch'ing and your sister-in-law were in the back room and barricaded the door—I don't know what they were up to in there—Wu Ta started hollering and screaming outside the door, but that didn't stop Hsi-men Ch'ing from coming out and kicking him to the ground. I saw your sister-in-law come out to help your brother up, but I slipped away before he was on his feet. Not many days after that I heard that Wu Ta was dead. How he died I don't know.

WU SUNG Is what you say true? Don't lie to me.

YÜN KO If I told it to the judge, it would be the same story.

WU SUNG Good brother, today I'm going to file a complaint, and I'll have to trouble you two to go with me to act as witnesses. [*As he talks he wraps up the silver and the bones*]

YÜN KO I'll go! I'll go!

HO CHIU I—I'll go too.

WU SUNG Let's go then! [*He makes way for* HO CHIU *and* YÜN KO, *bringing up the rear, like an escort.* HO CHIU *has a helpless expression and coughs several times.* WU SUNG *pats* YÜN KO *on the back*]

[*Curtain*]

SCENE 5

Several days later. The setting is the same as Scene 3. Incense and candles are burning on the table where the spirit tablet rests. At center stage a table is set for a formal banquet.

In the interval between Scenes 4 and 5 WU SUNG *has filed a complaint before the local magistrate who, having been bribed by* HSI-MEN CH'ING, *throws it out.* WU SUNG, *under the pretense of holding a service for Wu Ta's spirit, then coerces* P'AN CHIN-LIEN, WANG P'O, *and several neighbors into attending the funeral banquet (see* Shui-hu chuan, *ch. 26).*

WANG P'O *and* YAO WEN-CH'ING, *by virtue of their age, are seated at the places of honor.* WU SUNG *is standing near the corner of the table, attended by two soldiers.*

WU SUNG [*Holds up the wine cup with both hands in a formal toast*] Honored neighbors—when my brother died I, Wu Sung, was not at home. You have been kind enough to look after my affairs. I am a simple man, and haven't any good things with which to entertain you. One glass of port wine cannot convey my thanks. But please don't laught at me. [*He drains his cup with one gulp and sits down*]

OLD CHANG Before we've had a chance to welcome you back with a feast we come breaking in on you like this. Really—it's not right.

GUESTS Yes—we'll come another time!

HU CHENG-CH'ING [*Stands up, intending to leave*] I'm sorry, but I'm very busy today. Please excuse me.

WU SUNG You can't go! Since you've come, keep your seat for a minute— even if you are busy. [HU CHENG-CH'ING *sits down*]

YAO WEN-CH'ING [*Stands up*] I really do have some business to attend to.

WU SUNG I'm right in the middle of what I have to say—wait a little while longer. Orderlies—take away the cups and plates for the time being; we'll have something more to eat in a moment. [*The guests leave their places and the orderlies clear away the dishes.* WU SUNG *wipes the table while the guests say their goodbyes.* CHIN-LIEN, *not the least bit flustered, pulls up a bench and sits down without a word*]

A NEIGHBOR Captain Wu—many thanks.

WU SUNG You can't go! Orderlies—guard the doors! [*The orderlies comply. The neighbors look at each other apprehensively*]

A NEIGHBOR The captain has something he wants to say.

WU SUNG Does anyone here know how to write?

A NEIGHBOR [*Pushes* HU CHENG-CH'ING *forward*] Hu Cheng-ch'ing knows how.

WU SUNG Good. I'll trouble you to write this down. Orderly! Bring some paper and a brush.

ORDERLY Yes sir. [*He gives the paper and brush to* HU CHENG-CH'ING, *who sits down, shaking all over*]

WU SUNG [*Takes a dagger out of his coat*] Good neighbors. Although

I am a simple man, I do know that "Every crime has a culprit and every debt has a lender." Today all I'm doing is asking each one of you to act as a witness. I'm not going to harm you in any way, but if anyone tries to leave before we are through I won't be so nice. I'll let him be the first one to taste this knife. Even if I have to pay for his life with my own I don't care.

[*Sounds of nervous agreement from the neighbors*]

Wu Sung [*Points the knife at* Wang P'o] Old bitch—my brother's death is on your head. I'll get back to you later.[13] [*He turns and faces* Chin-lien, *pointing a finger at her*] You tell me—how did my brother die?

Chin-lien He was murdered.

Wu Sung By you, of course.

Chin-lien No.

Wu Sung Hsi-men Ch'ing!

Chin-lien No again.

Wu Sung [*Emphatically*] Ah?

Chin-lien To go to the root of the matter—the man who killed your brother was Chang Ta-hu.

Wu Sung That's absurd! Chang Ta-hu had nothing against my brother—why on earth would he kill him? [*He waves the dagger in* Chin-lien'*s face*] You're talking like a fool!

Chin-lien Brother—you've staked your life in exchange for mine; I'm staking my life for the chance to have my say. Would I lie to you? What's your hurry? If you're in a hurry, go ahead and kill me; I won't say anything. I just wanted to tell you my side of the matter. If you won't listen, then that's the end of it!

A neighbor Captain—let her have her say.

Wu Sung Fine—have your say.

Chin-lien I was a maidservant in Chang Ta-hu's household. Chang saw that I was quite good-looking, so he became determined to make me his concubine. When I wouldn't go along he was humiliated and got angry. He said to me, "All right, since you're not willing to be a concubine, I'll make a married woman out of you." He used his position as a rich and powerful member of the local gentry to marry me, without my consent, to that ugly, short, dirty, good-for-nothing and revolting Wu Ta—the number one freak of Yang-ku county. I'm made of flesh and blood; how could I take that kind of injustice? But I knew very well there isn't a man on earth who will speak up for a woman. So, like they say, "marry a cock, follow a cock; marry a dog, follow a dog." But I didn't think that someone else would come on the scene to do your brother harm.

Wu Sung Who was he?

Chin-lien You. [*Consternation among the neighbors.* Hu Cheng-ch'ing *stops writing and watches*]

Wu Sung Huh! [*Flustered*] Don't you smear me!

Chin-lien [*Sighs*] Hai! Don't worry. To think that you are brothers born of the same mother! How could your brother be so ugly and you be so handsome? How could he be so deformed and useless when you can kill a tiger with your bare hands? I was in hell, and seeing you was like seeing the sun. I thought, if a man and wife are a bad match what difference does it make if they part and remarry? If you and I could be together, wouldn't it be the perfect match? We'd be loving companions and grow old together. Do you remember that day—it was snowing—you came home and I heated a jug of wine for you to throw off the cold? And then I tried to draw you out with talk and tell you my thoughts. You not only didn't respond to me, you got angry as well and wanted to hit me. Then I really hated you . . . hated you as much as it is possible to hate someone. [*Sighs*] Hai! But as my hatred for you reached an extreme so did my love. You want people to admire you as some kind of hero, sage, and superior man and for this you've cut off your youth in its prime. And how can I be so unfeeling that I blame you for it? [Hu CHENG-CH'ING *is amazed. Looking at* WU SUNG, *he starts writing again*]

WU SUNG [*Interrupting*] Don't beat around the bush. Just explain how you murdered my brother.

CHIN-LIEN After you got angry and left, it was as if I had lost my soul. I was alive, but everything was meaningless. Then your brother took the tack of playing the master-husband, which added to my troubles a thousand times over. Just when I was thinking of killing myself I met Hsi-men Ch'ing by accident. On the whole, he was gentle with me so I took him as my lover. Yes—I committed adultery. That's all it was, because there was no real love between us. [*Sighs*] Hai! I was going crazy; I was sick; I had already lost hope. Why should I play it safe? Besides, he was like you in some ways. [*With emotion*] I willingly became his plaything. In my whole life, before meeting him, I hadn't even had the good fortune to be someone's plaything. [*Hurt and angry*] Don't ask what I did. In my husband's eyes I had committed a crime punishable by death, but I wasn't willing to die at the hands of a man like him. So I poisoned him.

WU SUNG You thought that no one would find out that you had murdered my brother. This just goes to show that there is justice in Heaven. I'm going to kill you right now.

CHIN-LIEN Everyone has to die. Better to commit the crime, face disaster, and die forthright than be tortured to death bit by bit. To be able to die at the hands of the man I love—even to die—is something I'll do gladly. Brother—is it my head you want, or my heart?

WU SUNG I want to cut out your heart.

CHIN-LIEN Ah, you want my heart. That's very good. I've already given you my heart. It was here, but you didn't take it. Come and see— [*She tears open her clothing*] inside this snow white breast is a very red, very warm, very true heart. Take it! [*As the neighbors, nerves drawn taut, watch with amazement,* WU SUNG *drags* CHIN-LIEN *to him with one arm; she half reclines on the ground*]

Wu Sung Who said you could talk so much? All I want now is to avenge my brother's murder. I'll tell you the truth: I've already killed Hsi-men Ch'ing. [*He takes a cloth bundle from an orderly and throws it down in front of* Chin-lien. *A man's head rolls out*] As for a woman like you—even when you've died and gone below to the nine springs my brother won't be willing to see you. Better that you go with Hsi-men Ch'ing. [*He raises the knife*]

Chin-lien [*Raises both hands*] Ah! You've killed Hsi-men Ch'ing. That shows that I was right all along. But, brother, you just said that I'd better go with Hsi-men Ch'ing. Those words really hurt me. I can't be together with you in this life; in my next life I'll be reborn as an ox and flay my hide to make boots for you. I'll be reborn as a silkworm and spin silk to make clothes for you. Even if you kill me, I will still love you. [*She opens wide her arms, wanting to get up and embrace* Wu Sung *and fixing him with a look of passionate feeling*]

Wu Sung [*Steps backward, his left hand grasping* Chin-lien*'s right hand, eyes open wide*] You love me? I . . . I . . . [*With one thrust of the knife* Chin-lien *falls.* Wu Sung *stares at the corpse and lets the knife drop to the ground. All are struck dumb*]

[*Curtain*]

Notes

1. Ou-yang Yü-ch'ien's play is a reinterpretation of a famous episode in the traditional novel *Shui-hu chuan*, translated into English by J. H. Jackson as *The Water Margin* (Shanghai: The Commercial Press, 1937) and by Pearl Buck as *All Men Are Brothers* (New York: Grosset & Dunlap, 1933). See chapters 24-26. The story of P'an Chin-lien and Hsi-men Ch'ing also formed the basis for several novels, notably *Chin-p'ing-mei*, and traditional operas.

I would like to acknowledge the assistance of Mr. Li Yao-chung in preparing this translation.

2. "I'm worn out" is a translation of "ch'uan kuo le" which literally means "I've had enough of wearing them (the clothes)" but in the context of the repartee also suggests the meaning offered in the translation.

3. "She can turn any way you want" (sui-che ni chuan) is, more literally, "follow you about anywhere you go," but with a nuance in the context suggested by the translation.

4. The Chinese text contains a sexual nuance of the sort suggested in the translation.

5. The sexual puns are impossible to capture accurately in English, which in Chinese derives from two such double entendres: *hua* (flower, a woman's vagina) and *hsing* (enthusiasm or appetite, erection).

6. The Chinese slang expressions are a good deal more vivid: "oily head" (playboy, "slick dick"); "bald stick" (bachelor).

7. The sense of P'an Chin-lien's remarks is "Don't people who meet all end up enemies?" As is the case with much of Chin'lien's language, the remark can

be taken in more than one way. Referring to Hsi-men Ch'ing, it indicates Chin-lien's contemptuous estimate of her lover; referring to Wu Sung, the same remark suggests her realization that her brother-in-law will never be her lover.

8. See *Shui-hu chuan*, ch. 24.

9. It is highly likely that in this context Kao Sheng's remark could be taken to mean, as well, "I can't tell whether you really do have something up your pants."

10. In the episode of the novel which immediately precedes this one, Wu Sung encounters a maneating tiger on Chin-yang Ridge and kills it with his bare hands, for which he is made a captain of the local militia by a grateful magistrate. See *Shui-hu chuan*, ch. 23.

11. The men referred to are all historical figures that hover in the background of the novel. All achieved notoreity in their day as the corrupt and despotic officials who contributed to the fall of the Northern Sung dynasty under the weak Emperor Hui-tsung (r. 1101-25). Kao Ch'iu became an imperial favorite after attracting Hui-tsung's notice by sending him a gift of a football. He rose to become commander of the army. The Prime Minister Ts'ai Ching (1047-1126) was popularly regarded as "the wickedest of the six villains" who dominated Hui-tsung's court. T'ung Kuan (d. 1126) was a general.

12. Chin-lien is making scathing reference to the practice of honoring dead women, in some cases women driven to suicide by the harsh treatment of their families or communities, with memorial arches erected to commemorate their "chaste and exemplary" conduct.

13. "I'll get back to you later": In the novel, Wu Sung takes Wang P'o to court where she is implicated in the murder of Wu Sung's brother through the testimony of the neighbors, and for her complicity in the crime is condemned and executed by being sliced to death. See *Shui-hu chuan*, ch. 27.

Hsia Yen

Under Shanghai Eaves

Translated by George Hayden

Cast of Characters

YANG TS'AI-YÜ, Lin Chih-ch'eng's wife, aged 32
PAO-CHEN, Ts'ai-yü's daughter by K'uang Fu, aged 12
CHAO'S WIFE, aged 42
AH-HSIANG, the Chaos' daughter, aged 5
CHAO CHEN-YÜ, tenant of the scullery, aged 48
AH-NIU, the Chaos' son, aged 13
LIN CHIH-CH'ENG, sublessor of the lane house, aged 36
KUEI-FEN, wife of Huang Chia-mei, aged 24
SHIH HSIAO-PAO, tenant of the front room upstairs, about 27
HUANG CHIA-MEI, garret tenant, aged 28
HUANG'S FATHER, aged 58
"LITTLE TIENTSIN," Shih's pimp, about 30
K'UANG FU, Ts'ai-yü's former husband
LI LING-PEI, tenant of the rear room upstairs, aged 54
OTHERS: second-hand goods vendor, vegetable peddler, restaurant delivery boy, etc.

ACT I

The time is April 1937, on a day during the rainy season. The setting is the same throughout the play.

The curtain rises on a cross-section of a "lane house" typical of Shanghai's east side. On the right is an open back gate through which people can be seen walking along the lane. Adjoining the gate is the scullery, with a water faucet and a cement water basin downstage. Slightly beneath the open window of the garret above the scullery is a galvanized steel awning which on rainy days shelters the women washing clothes and rice around the basin. At this window hang flat baskets used for washing rice, steaming racks, and laundered diapers, left there to dry. To the left of the scullery is a steep staircase, its edges worn down in the middle through constant use and its bottom steps patched with boards. A door to the garret is to the right of the stairway landing, and over the landing

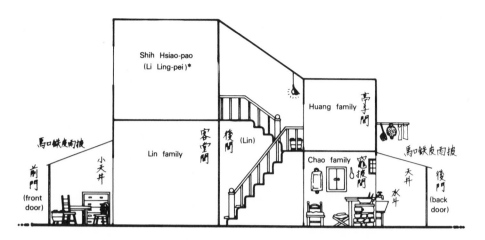

hangs a five-watt light bulb, with only half of its shade remaining. A banister leading to the front room upstairs is visible to the left of the landing. Slats partition off a "rear room" to the right of the stairs, and when no light is on, nothing can be seen in it. Further to the left on the ground floor and separated by a wall of boards is the parlor with its long and narrow French windows. Furthest left is a small courtyard and half of the front gate. This courtyard, like the one in the back, is covered by a galvanized steel awning, and beneath it, dilapidated furniture, a small cookstove, plank tables, and such are piled every which way.

In all, five households occupy this two-story house. The sublessor, Lin Chih-ch'eng, and his family occupy the parlor. The scullery makes up the room of the primary school teacher Chao Chen-yü. Through the window and doorway of the scullery can be seen an iron bed at a right angle to the window and, close to the window, a square table and a small cot across from it. On the wall are hung a cabinet, hamper, and other items, and by the entrance a coal cookstove set on a pedestal built of broken bricks, a wok, and other cooking utensils. Huang Chia-mei, once an employee of a foreign-owned company but now unemployed, lives in the garret. A kerosene stove is on the stair landing; here his family does their cooking. The upstairs front room is where Shih Hsiao-pao lives alone; she does no cooking but has lunch and dinner sent over from a caterer. The attic, not visible to the audience, is the home of an old newspaper vendor who drinks heavily from time to time and is a bit eccentric. His fondness for singing the line from the traditional play Li Ling pei (Li Ling's Monument), "When I gaze on the lovely child, I can hold back no longer . . ." has earned him the name of the play as his sobriquet.

The parlor, as the residence of the sublessor, is furnished with somewhat more care than the other rooms. A desk and a glass bookshelf, now converted to a clothes cabinet, show that Lin Chih-ch'eng was once, perhaps, a writer.

It is the rainy season, and uncomfortably stuffy. From the opening curtain to closing curtain the fine rain rarely stops. Heavier rain can be heard occasionally, gurgling in the drainpipes and pouring off the eaves, but then, a minute later *perhaps, a pallid sun may thread its way through the clouds. The barometer is low and the air is very heavy, which has its effect on the emotions of the tenants. Their actions and speech reveal the depression, irritability, and anxiety they all share, so that the slightest provocation can at any moment trigger an outburst of excessive pent-up anger.*

The time is shortly before eight o'clock in the morning. Since it is raining, the rooms are very dark. YANG TS'AI-YÜ *is in the process of tidying up the apartment and the breakfast dishes.* PAO-CHEN *sits alone at the table, playing a toy piano and singing softly, her eyes intent on some books.*

At the back gate, CHAO CHEN-YÜ's *wife,* AH-HSIANG *close by her side, is buying vegetables.* CHAO CHEN-YÜ, *wearing his eyeglasses, is concentrating on his newspaper, and* AH-NIU, *about to leave for school, is gathering up his schoolbooks.*

The constant noise of peddlers and their loud chatter comes from the front and back lanes.

PAO-CHEN [*Sings*] ". . . But let me ask you this:
　　　　　From one bolt of cloth, how much can
　　　　　　　you earn . . ."
　[*The melody is not quite right, and so she starts over*]
　　　　　". . . But let me ask you this:
　　　　　From one bolt of cloth, how much can
　　　　　　　you earn?
　　　　　Once they have your money,
　　　　　Once they have your money . . .
　　　　　They'll turn it into bullets right
　　　　　　　away . . ."

TS'AI-YÜ Pao-chen! It's getting late!

PAO-CHEN [*Wrinkles up her mouth and pays no attention*]
　　　　　". . . Once they have your money,
　　　　　They'll turn it into bullets right
　　　　　　　away,
　　　　　And one by one, one by one—
　　　　　They'll get you right in the heart . . ."

TS'AI-YÜ Listen to me; it's getting late!

PAO-CHEN But I haven't learned the song right yet, and I have to teach it after school.

TS'AI-YÜ You're going to teach something when you don't even know it yourself? [*Picks up a piece of clothing from the bed*] When you take off your clothes, you wouldn't dream of hanging them up nicely, oh no, you just toss them on the bed. Twelve years old now, and you can't even take care of yourself, much less teach anyone else. What kind of a "little teacher" are you going to make?

PAO-CHEN [*Puts her books in a stack*] That's for the laundry!

TS'AI-YÜ Laundry? Well, you have all the answers, don't you? It would never get dry with all this rain, even if I did launder it. [*Hangs up the clothing*]

PAO-CHEN [*Runs over and quickly takes it off the hook, and then throws it into the leftover water in the washbasin*] It's unsanitary to wear dirty clothes!

TS'AI-YÜ [*Both amused and angry*] I need *you* to tell me that, do I? [*Goes to the courtyard with the washbasin*]

PAO-CHEN [*Packs her book bag*] Ah-niu! [*Picks up the book bag and walks toward the scullery*]

CHAO'S WIFE [*Offstage*] If it's for sale, then sell it and be done with it; if it isn't, then haul it away! [*She enters in a huff, carrying a grocery basket. A vegetable peddler, counting the coins in his hands and wearing an expression of enormous grievance, forces his way through the gate and speaks with a tone of desperation*]

PEDDLER All right, have it your way, two and a half cents an ounce; even that's three cents off. With the basket it's one pound two ounces; without the seven-ounce basket it's eleven ounces, twenty-seven and a half . . .

CHAO'S WIFE Seven ounces? What are you talking about? [*Dumps the Indian rice stalks out of the basket and weighs the basket on the scales*] Looks like eight and a half to me . . .

PEDDLER Hey, look . . .

CHAO'S WIFE [*Goes through the motions of weighing the basket, considers her point made, then heads indoors*] If you're going to sell it, sell it; if you're not, then take it out of here!

PEDDLER All right, all right, two cents more . . .

CHAO'S WIFE [*Turns around and feels in her pocket, hesitates on purpose, then grudgingly hands him two coins; when he picks up his carrying basket and is just leaving, quickly snatches a stalk from the basket*] One more!

PEDDLER [*Flustered*] Oh no you don't . . .

CHAO'S WIFE [*Slams the gate, AH-HSIANG trying to help by propping the gate closed with her body*] You vegetable peddlers never stop arguing! [*Turns her head and says to herself*] After half a month or so of rain, it's getting so you can't even afford spinach or rice stalks any more!

PEDDLER [*Offstage*] Hey! Hey! [*Pushes on the gate a few times, then gives up and, with a long, quavering voice*] Ehhh . . . rice stalks, oh, cabbage for sale— [*CHAO CHEN-YÜ gives his wife a glance, and a slight smile, then quickly turns back to the newspaper*]

PAO-CHEN [*Loudly*] Ah-niu, have you learned the song I taught you yesterday?

AH-NIU [*Sticks his head out of the scullery*] You're not supposed to call me that; you have to call me Chao Ch'en!

PAO-CHEN I'll call you that if I want to. Ah-niu, Ah-niu, Niu—[1]

AH-NIU So, you're really going to call me that, are you?

PAO-CHEN Well, weren't you born in the year of the ox?

AH-NIU Then I'll call *you* something! I'll call you Ah-t'o, for stepchild![2]

PAO-CHEN [*Urgently*] Chao Ch'en!

AH-NIU Ha, ha, ha! [*Ducks back inside and grabs his book bag*] [TS'AI-YÜ *is just coming out with her grocery basket;* PAO-CHEN *pouts and gives her mother a look*]

TS'AI-YÜ What are you—

PAO-CHEN [*Pointing to* AH-NIU] Ah-niu said it again; he called me—

TS'AI-YÜ [*Softly but with force, as a shadow passes across her face*] Don't pay any attention to him. Go to school! Do you have your snack money?

[PAO-CHEN *shakes her head.* TS'AI-YÜ *goes back inside, gets some money, and gives it to her. At this moment* LIN CHIH-CH'ENG *enters through the front gate. His face wooden, as if beset with countless injuries, without a sound he crams the door key of a spring lock into his pocket. He takes a glass of water from the table and gulps it down, then flops down on the bed.*]

TS'AI-YÜ [*A bit surprised*] What's wrong, aren't you feeling well? [*Silence*] You aren't even changing your clothes . . . [*Hands the house robe to him, but* LIN *says nothing. Angrily*] What is it? You, always taking your anger out on me; well, I won't have it!

[*On seeing that* TS'AI-YÜ *is upset,* LIN CHIH-CH'ENG *sits up in order to change his clothes. He is about to say something but stops short.* TS'AI-YÜ *ignores him, picks up the grocery basket, and leaves with* PAO-CHEN, *closing the door between the parlor and the back room on the way out.* LIN CHIH-CH'ENG, *after changing, plunks himself down and goes to sleep*]

AH-NIU [*Seeing that* PAO-CHEN *is leaving for school, shouts*] Wait up, Pao-chen! [*Turns back to his mother*] Mom, five cents for pencils.

CHAO'S WIFE Don't have it!

AH-NIU The teacher says I have to have it!

CHAO'S WIFE That may be what *he* says, but *I* say you don't!

[CHAO CHEN-YÜ, *laughing, hands* AH-NIU *some money from his pocket*]

AH-NIU [*To* PAO-CHEN] I still don't know the last two lines . . .

PAO-CHEN The last part . . . [*Sings*] "One by one, one by one . . ."

AH-NIU Okay, one more time . . . [*Both start to leave*]

TS'AI-YÜ [*After them*] Pao-chen! Come right home after school. If you run around like crazy outside and your dad finds out, you'll . . .

PAO-CHEN [*Irritated*] What "dad"? [*Exits*]

[KUEI-FEN, *on her way back from buying groceries, comes face to face with* TS'AI-YÜ; CHAO'S WIFE *steals a glance at* TS'AI-YÜ]

TS'AI-YÜ [*To* KUEI-FEN, *trying to cover up*] Oh, good morning! [*She leaves through the gate*]

CHAO'S WIFE [*Quickly, to* KUEI-FEN] Did you hear that?

KUEI-FEN What?

CHAO'S WIFE [*She purses up her mouth in the direction of the gate, then says softly*] When they started talking about her dad, Pao-chen got angry and started pouting, [*Imitating* PAO-CHEN] "What 'dad'?" Hm, times have certainly changed. Children are getting so they understand grownup things early now; you can't get the slightest thing past them anymore!

KUEI-FEN [Smiling] She's twelve or thirteen now; why shouldn't she understand? [She takes her vegetables out one by one near the water basin]

CHAO'S WIFE [Cocks her ear toward the parlor, then says softly] But I hear that when Lin married her mother she was still very small.

KUEI-FEN To be fair about it, Lin treats her very well indeed. I always say, a stepfather like him is pretty hard to come by these days.

CHAO'S WIFE [Breaking in] You're so right. It's been almost a year since we moved here, and I've never heard him spank her or bawl her out. Sometimes, when Lin is having a fight with her mother and gets in a fit of temper, all he has to do is look at the young girl and he won't have anything more to say at all.

KUEI-FEN Hm, I suppose that's human nature, to treat someone who's not your own child a little differently. What's more, her playmates like to tease her about being a stepdaughter. . . . [Laughs] Children are always trying to best each other.

CHAO'S WIFE [After a pause] Well, let me tell you, when she's talking with our Ah-niu and the conversation gets around to Lin, it's always "Uncle Lin"; I've never heard her refer to him as "Dad."

KUEI-FEN Isn't that because they knew each other before?

CHAO'S WIFE More than that; Lin and her own father were good friends, no less, from what I hear.

KUEI-FEN Oh, then why . . .

[Suddenly the rain, as if a thundershower, comes down in large drops]

CHAO'S WIFE Ugh, the rainy season is such a nuisance, wet and stifling; you feel you're being suffocated!

KUEI-FEN Yes, with the rain never stopping, it even gets through your rubbers!

CHAO'S WIFE [Sees the fish and meat that KUEI-FEN is washing] Oh, you bought all that today?

[In the garret, HUANG'S FATHER coughs loudly]

KUEI-FEN [Gives a strained smile] Our dad's here from the country, so we have to buy a little extra!

CHAO'S WIFE Oh, that's right, I forgot—his first time in Shanghai? [Peels a rice stalk]

KUEI-FEN Uh huh, actually he was supposed to come last fall—

CHAO'S WIFE Oh, [As if recalling something] he's here to see the new grandson, right?

KUEI-FEN [Smiles in a forced manner] He—it's been five or six years now since we've visited him!

CHAO'S WIFE Well, he looks in good health! The Three Companies, Nanking Road,[3] I suppose you've taken him to see everything?

KUEI-FEN Almost everything; you know, the usual things for somebody in Shanghai for the first time.

CHAO'S WIFE He got back late last night. Did your husband take him to the Great World Theater?

KUEI-FEN No, to somewhere close by, the movies at Eastern Sea. [Laughs spontaneously] But once the money was spent on the tickets, he didn't like it, said people's heads were big one minute and small the next, and as soon as he was getting the hang of what was going on, poof, everything would jump away.

CHAO'S WIFE [*Agreeing*] I don't like movies either; all that flashing makes me dizzy. Older people always like the theater; take him to *The Burning of Red Lotus Temple*. The end of last year, my brother took me once, and oh, it was wonderful! The costumes were fine, and the scenery was all new. When they turned the lights off, everything on stage was suddenly completely different. Right, let him have a look before he goes back to the farm, and [*Laughs*] he may never stop talking about it for days on end.

KUEI-FEN Yes, that's what Chia-mei says.

CHAO'S WIFE Will he be staying a few more days in Shanghai?

KUEI-FEN [*Lowers her eyes*] I can't say for sure; a few more days, I suppose.

CHAO'S WIFE Lucky for him! His son getting established in Shanghai, and a grandson . . .

KUEI-FEN But . . . if only Chia-mei had a job . . . [*Glances at the garret, then softly*] It's what they mean when they say you don't always know what's going on in a family. In my father-in-law's eyes, a life like ours must be pretty disappointing. A farming family sweats blood to raise a son and put him through college. Country people have such a narrow way of looking at things; they're thinking, Chia-mei has become a success in Shanghai and is doing something important, but . . . [*Becoming somewhat despondent in spite of herself*] now that he's come to Shanghai and seen for himself, a whole family living in a garret . . . [*Finishes washing the vegetables and stands up*]

CHAO'S WIFE Does your husband have any brothers in the country?

KUEI-FEN Well, it would be nice if he did; he is the only son.

CHAO'S WIFE [*Tries to offer some kind of consolation*] But your husband has a lot of spirit, and the day will come when—

KUEI-FEN [*Breaks in*] What good is it, when in this godforsaken Shanghai the ones without it seem to get by all right, and he, he has that bad attitude of his, won't settle halfway on anything!

CHAO [*Puts down his paper and, removing his glasses with one hand, rubs his eyes with the back of the other*] No, no, to take it easy and settle halfway, *that's* a bad attitude. Society goes bad because people go bad, and a good man starts with himself. If everyone were as serious and uncompromising as your husband—

KUEI-FEN [*About to leave*] Taking things seriously entitles you to live in a garret, is that what you mean?

CHAO No, no, that's not what I'm getting at. All you need is a clear conscience; for example—

CHAO'S WIFE [*In exasperation*] Spare us your "for examples"! If you don't get going, you'll miss class, that precious class of yours that's worth a few cents an hour, and they'll deduct something from your salary too . . .

CHAO Not at all. It's quarter to eight now, and four and a half minutes is all it takes to get to school. [*Turns back to* KUEI-FEN, *then earnestly*] For example— [*When he looks up, he finds that* KUEI-FEN *has already gone upstairs*]

CHAO'S WIFE [*Smiling scornfully*] Do you think anybody wants to listen to what you have to say? If you want to talk like that, go to the classroom and give a lecture, go hoodwink the children!

CHAO [*Undisturbed*] They can listen or not, as they choose, but whether I speak or not is my business! I, I—

CHAO'S WIFE Fine, fine, now get going or Lin will come by soon, and you'll never stop talking, you and your verbal diarrhea . . .

CHAO [*Looks toward the parlor*] Has he been on the night shift the past few days?

CHAO'S WIFE Day shift, night shift, what do you care? [*Outside the gate the sweet rice peddler is heard*]

AH-HSIANG Mom, I want some sweet rice!

CHAO'S WIFE [*Searches her pocket, apparently finds no money, and so changes her tone*] Didn't you just have some porridge?

AH-HSIANG Uh-huh! I want—

CHAO'S WIFE [*Exasperated*] Wait till your dad gets rich! [AH-HSIANG *enviously looks out the gate*]

[*In the front room upstairs,* SHIH HSIAO-PAO *has just gotten up. Her room is very dark, and, after stretching herself, she lets in some light by jerking aside the window curtain. She lights a cigarette, then opens the window, frowns, and makes a face at the rain. Taking a thermos bottle along with her, she ambles downstairs. When she reaches the garret landing, she glances through the crack in the garret door and, as if having seen something amusing, smiles to herself with pursed lips.*

[*She is a so-called "cheap" modern young woman. Her hair is fashionably curled, and some makeup from the previous day remains on her sleep-filled eyes. The mandarin collar on her deep red flower-print dress is loose, and she scuffs along in her slippers. She is not really very pretty, but her eyes hold a certain charm, and there is a kind of languid grace to her walk.*

[*She goes to the scullery entrance and casually throws away her cigarette, not yet half smoked. When* CHAO'S WIFE *hears her coming down, she gives her a scathing look, then purposely averts her eyes, meanwhile energetically fanning the coal brazier and producing a straight column of white smoke*]

SHIH [*Gives* CHAO'S WIFE *a glance*] Oh, you're all up so early! [*Yawns*] Raining again. The sound of the raindrops makes me want to stay in bed . . . [*Yawns*]

CHAO'S WIFE [*Maliciously*] Well, aren't you the lucky one!

SHIH [*Gives her a smile*] Oh, aren't you going to school today, Mr. Chao? [CHAO CHEN-YÜ *concentrates on his newspaper*]

SHIH [*A bit taken aback*] What's the matter with you today? Even when people don't speak to you, you usually have plenty to talk and laugh about anyway. Now, when I speak to you, you don't pay any attention to me.

CHAO [*Quickly puts down his newspaper*] Ah ah, it's you; look at this, the paper says . . .

SHIH [*Casually pours the left-over water out of the thermos*] What does the paper say?

[*The water splashes onto* CHAO'S WIFE, *who shoots her a murderous glare*] Ah, sorry! [*Leisurely opens the rear gate and goes out to get some boiled water*] [LIN CHIH-CH'ENG, *unable to sleep, tosses and turns, finally sits up*]

CHAO [*On seeing his wife's furious expression, cannot hold back*] Ha, ha . . .

CHAO'S WIFE [*Suddenly turns around*] What are you laughing at?

CHAO Why can't you ever get along with her? Here you are, living in the same house, and you start bickering the minute you lay eyes on her. It's disgraceful!

CHAO'S WIFE It's the way she acts that I can't stand: a streetwalker pretending to be something else. The witch, her husband never around, and bringing all kinds of trashy men home with her . . .

[*In the garret,* HUANG CHIA-MEI *coughs violently and leans halfway out of the window. He is pale and emaciated, with a melancholy expression. He fans away the coal smoke with his hand and closes the window. From within comes the sound of a baby crying*]

CHAO Eh, what business is that of yours? You can't exactly blame her, either. Haven't I told you? She has to eat, what with her husband roaming all over the world on a ship, Japan today, the South Seas tomorrow, America the day after that, able to come home less than three or four times a year; no resources, no ability, no way to earn a living, and you want her to be a paragon of fidelity. Now, aren't you being a little too . . . too . . .

CHAO'S WIFE If you're going to give a sermon, go to church and do it! No matter what it is, out you come with one of your long sermons. But I know you're just sounding off. You for one have some talent and education; how are *you* at earning a living? Huh! Suppose I can't get along with her; what does that have to do with you? When I talk with other people, I don't want you butting in!

CHAO What? I . . . ridiculous . . .

[*Gesticulating, he walks up to his wife and is about to make some kind of pronouncement when, at the call of a cake seller outside the gate,* AH-HSIANG *runs back and interrupts*]

AH-HSIANG Mom, I want to buy some cake!

CHAO'S WIFE Are you ever full? You just . . .

[SHIH HSIAO-PAO, *back from getting hot water, pushes the gate open with one hand*]

SHIH [*Toward the lane*] Cake, hey! [*Buys several pieces, turns her head and catches sight of* AH-HSIANG's *expression, then back to the cake seller*] Hey, another piece! [*To* AH-HSIANG] Come on, come on!

[AH-HSIANG *walks over to take it*]

CHAO'S WIFE [*Loudly*] Don't take it.

SHIH [*Laughs*] What's the harm? Children love it.

CHAO'S WIFE Don't take it! Listen to what I tell you! [AH-HSIANG *watches her mother but still has her hand outstretched*]

SHIH It doesn't matter; go ahead.

CHAO'S WIFE [*Jerks* AH-HSIANG *away*] Spineless little brat! Haven't you ever had cake before? [*Face suffused with anger, looks at* SHIH]

SHIH [*Raises her eyebrows*] Oh, for heaven's sake!

CHAO'S WIFE For heaven's sake what?

SHIH It's just a child; why take it so seriously?

CHAO'S WIFE The child happens to be mine, so even if you don't care to take it seriously, I do! I'll tell you this: we may be poor, but we're not about to let our children eat anything bought with dirty money!

SHIH [*Also angry now*] What do you mean? Whose money is dirty?

CHAO'S WIFE [*Laughs scornfully*] You have to ask *me* that?

SHIH Oh, why are you so unreasonable? You don't even know what's good for you, and when someone with the best of intentions—

CHAO'S WIFE [*As if spitting it out*] Who needs your "best of intentions"?

SHIH All right then, forget it! [*Laughs*] Unreasonable—[*Starts upstairs*] idiot!

CHAO'S WIFE [*Mounts one step*] Who are you calling an idiot?

SHIH [*Turns back from the staircase with a look of disdain, but still smiling*] You! [*Skips upstairs*]

CHAO'S WIFE [*Just when she is about to say something further,* HUANG CHIA-MEI'S FATHER *comes down the stairs with a two-year-old child in his arms.* KUEI-FEN, *carrying dirty clothes, follows. All* CHAO'S WIFE *can do at this point is spit*] Shameless!

[HUANG'S FATHER *is very much a man of the countryside; over his rough demin robe of faded blue he wears an apron. His hair and beard are grizzled. Holding his grandson with an air of satisfaction, he descends cautiously, step by step, as if unfamiliar with the narrow staircase. With a glance of curiosity toward* SHIH HSIAO-PAO, KUEI-FEN *speaks to her father-in-law in a loud voice*]

KUEI-FEN You can take a walk in the lane, but don't let him near the entrance to the street. There are cars out there.

HUANG'S FATHER [*Waves eagerly to* CHAO CHEN-YÜ *and points to the child*] He wants me to carry him out on the street. Ha, ha, Shanghai does not let you walk anywhere you please; now, if we were in the country—

CHAO [*Joining in the conversation*] Do you find Shanghai more interesting than the countryside?

HUANG'S FATHER [*Not having heard* CHAO'*s question*] A few days ago he was bewildered by seeing me, but after a while he started to get used to me around here! Look, how he always wants me to carry him. Heh . . .

CHAO [*At a loss*] Hm?

KUEI-FEN [*To* CHAO] He's hard of hearing; he didn't hear you.

CHAO [*Nods, then loudly*] Do you find Shanghai more interesting than the countryside?

HUANG'S FATHER The countryside? Oh, oh, I'll be staying a few more days; Chia-mei and she [*Points to* KUEI-FEN] won't let me leave. It's all right, though; the silkworms have been taken care of. We don't make silk ourselves, so once we've sold off the cocoons, we don't have anything more to do. . . .

CHAO Hm, how interesting. [*To* KUEI-FEN] How do you carry on a conversation with him? Can't he hear anything at all?

KUEI-FEN [*Laughing*] You shout or make hand signals! [HUANG'S FATHER, *carrying the boy, pushes open the gate and steps through, and* AH-HSIANG, *seizing this opportunity, follows along behind*]

KUEI-FEN [*Runs up*] Hey, [*Loudly*] don't buy him anything to eat! He'll get a stomachache. [*Turns back in, speaking to herself*] He loves him so, he'll give him anything at all to eat, and I just can't get it across to him. [*To* CHAO'S WIFE] Still, there's something to be said for his being hard of hearing! We can keep unpleasant things from him; even now he has no inkling whatever that Chia-mei is out of a job. We've told him that it's examination time at school and classes have been out these past few days. He doesn't understand anyway, so . . .

CHAO You've told him your husband teaches school? So we're colleagues, are we?

KUEI-FEN [*With a forlorn laugh*] Chia-mei told him he teaches at a YMCA night school, and he believed every word of it. The other day when we were on a streetcar going by the front gate of the YMCA, he started shouting, "Ah! that's Ah-mei's school," as if he owned the whole building. That gave everybody on the streetcar a good laugh! [*Starts washing the clothing*]

CHAO Ha, ha, ha, that's the way to look at it: I own the whole building! Ha . . . [*The sun suddenly appears.* LIN CHIH-CH'ENG *paces back and forth, then pushes open the French windows*]

CHAO'S WIFE [*Hearing these sounds, very quickly*] It's time now, get going. Lin's up; in a little while he'll be here, and once you start talking to him, you'll never get away.

CHAO It's all right.

CHAO'S WIFE What do you mean, "all right"? Hurry, he's already up.

CHAO What're you afraid of? He's not a tiger, and he's hardly going to ask you for the rent right now.

CHAO'S WIFE I just don't like his manner, cold as ice, as if you've done him some kind of a wrong, and when you say hello to him, the air catches near his throat, "Mm." Even the children are scared of him, [*Solicits agreement from* KUEI-FEN] isn't that right? [KUEI-FEN *nods*]

CHAO [*With a self-satisfied expression*] But he gets along well enough with me; whenever he sees me, he—

CHAO'S WIFE [*Interrupting angrily*] God, I'm sick of hearing it: verbal diarrhea; he can't even manage his own affairs, yet he still talks about the nation, soc-, soc-, society. [*To* KUEI-FEN] I could never learn all that blather, even if I wanted to! [KUEI-FEN *smiles*]

SHIH [*Comes to the edge of the stairs, softly*] Mr. Huang! Mr. Huang!

HUANG [*Steps out of the garret*] What is it? [*Somewhat embarrassed as they approach each other*] I . . . these past few days . . . your money . . .

SHIH [*With a charming smile*] No, don't mention it; what does such a little amount matter. . . . Uh, Mr. Huang, I wonder if you would do me a favor?

HUANG What? [KUEI-FEN *is listening to this*]

SHIH [*Takes a letter out of her pocket*] Please read this to me!

HUANG [*Looks the letter over*] This is from your father. Hm, . . . he says everything's fine at home. . . .

SHIH [*Before he can finish*] But he wants some money, doesn't he?

HUANG Hm . . . a windstorm blew down the wall, so he'd like . . .

SHIH It's always the same. Don't read any more, Mr. Huang; just tell me how much he wants.

HUANG . . . Mm, at least fifteen dollars. Plus . . .

SHIH [*Suddenly takes the letter back*] Fifteen again; well, his daughter's rich, isn't she, a lady of the house and everything. . . . [*about to leave*]

HUANG Oh, about the five dollars I owe you; at the end of the month . . .

SHIH [*Gives him an arch look*] You—take everything too seriously; what does it matter? [*Laughs*] The world doesn't have enough honest men like you! [*Gives his chin a gentle tap with a magenta-polished fingernail, then blithely walks off. Somewhat embarrassed,* HUANG *feels the spot where she touched him and returns slowly to the garret*]

LIN [*Walks to the faucet and rinses his mouth, muttering*] Buying groceries, huh? What's taking her so long?

CHAO [*Beaming*] Good morning. Were you on the night shift?

LIN [*Without a trace of a smile*] Mm . . .

CHAO [*As if speaking to himself*] You must be very busy, with business so good at the silk factory. . . .

LIN Huh! It's all the same with us, no matter what business is like. When business if off, we worry every day about a shutdown or a layoff, and when business finally gets going again, then it's three shifts a day and work all night. They don't care whether you live or die; they can always get another workhorse!

CHAO Still, it's surely better for business to be good than bad! For example—

LIN No such thing. Right now the factory's driving us day and night, and the goods have been ordered all the way up to March of next year. Our boss was having a rough time for a few years and got ten million or so into debt, but now he's paid every penny of it back in one year. Altogether he's got five factories now. He must be taking in an average of thirty-five thousand dollars a day, and in a month, let's see, three times five is fifteen, three times three makes nine—over a million a month, and of course that makes twelve million a year. We're the ones who suffer, though. If the workers can't take it, they can always cut a shift or two, but an office worker doesn't have that privilege. For thirty to fifty dollars a month, you've brought yourself a manager, who'll do your arithmetic and your paperwork, your cuffing and your bawling out for you. . . .

CHAO Hm, thirty-five thousand a day, twelve million a year; why, in ten years that comes to a hundred and twenty million . . .

LIN Everything else aside, take payday, several thousand dollars every half month; all that bright-colored paper slipping through my fingers. Everybody thinks paying the wages is a fat job, but I can't get used to that sort of monkey business. And yet, if you act in good conscience, they make you pay for any little discrepancy. Just today I failed to deduct thirty-five cents for savings[4] and got a "reprimand" from the head of the Labor Department. Reprimand! He joined the plant two years after I did, but he's good at kissing up to the top men, so now he's head of a department. Ah, none of it makes any sense at all!

CHAO [*Nods*] Mm, one is never happy with one's own job, as the saying goes. But there's another way of looking at it: to be with a factory for five or six years, as you have, why, there's something to be said for that, at least. A life like ours naturally seems bad when you compare it with those on top, but we're still better off than the ones on the bottom. . . . [*Points to a newspaper article*] Scads of people in Shanghai are destitute. Now when you put yourself alongside them—

LIN [*Before he can finish*] No, the way I see it, when you're on top or on the bottom, at least you know where you are; the worst-off are people like us. If you're rich, all right, you live in a big foreign-style house and ride around in a car, and everything's just fine. And if you're poor, then you might as well be like Li Ling-pei up there in the attic, and that's that. He eats when he can, and when he can't, well, he just cinches up his belt, climbs up to the attic, and goes off to sleep. He doesn't have to worry about appearances or reputation; no wife or children, no social obligations; and when his clothes get tattered, he gives a stitching woman a few pennies to fix them up. He goes out on the street, just the same as you or I, and nobody laughs at him, but we, now, do you suppose we could get away with going to work with patches in our clothes? Goddamned office types, we'll put on a show even if we have to go into debt to do it!

[KUEI-FEN *glances at him surreptitiously*]

CHAO But from Li Ling-pei's point of view, our life just might seem better than his! A person can never be satisfied, and when he's dissatisfied, he starts to complain. The complaining makes him pessimistic, and the pessimism ruins his health. Now, tell me, since my health is all I have, why should I want to do it any harm? So, here's the way I handle it: whenever I'm dissatisfied about something, I compare my lot with people worse off, and then I calm down. For example . . .

CHAO'S WIFE [*Interrupts in an explosive tone*] "For example, for example"! You'll never amount to anything, the way you're always stooping beneath you! Why don't you try comparing yourself with the people with money and power sometime?

CHAO [*Paying no attention to her but settling down for a long conversation*] For example—

CHAO'S WIFE No more "for examples," please! Aren't you going to school today?

CHAO [*As if he hadn't heard*] For example, we had an opportunity to be educated and find out about things. And we can observe this bustling world we live in, even come out with an opinion from time to time. This, after all, is a privilege. [*Loudly*] Ha, ha, ha—

LIN [*In sharp disagreement*] Oh no, I don't feel I'm entitled to privileges like that at all!

CHAO But, Mr. Lin, looking at it dispassionately, you'll have to agree that society has been pretty good to us educated people. After all, how many people are there in China who can read, who can, as we do—

CHAO'S WIFE [*Sarcastically*] Oh, yes, pretty good, all right! Hah, so you can go out begging for a living!

CHAO I say that nowadays everyone in the whole world is equally miserable; everybody has his own particular suffering. Look at this news item. [*Offers him the newspaper*] When we see them on the street, they look fierce and proud, sitting in their armored cars. There's such a vicious expression on their faces; those hard, glinting eyes under their helmets look as if they'd like to gobble us up. But take off their tiger skins and they're no different from us!

LIN [*Takes the paper and looks at it, then, with an expression of pain*] What— [HUANG CHIA-MEI *pushes the window open and looks down*]

CHAO'S WIFE [*Her curiosity piqued*] What's the matter?

CHAO It's all beyond you!

CHAO'S WIFE So that's why I'm asking in the first place!

CHAO All right, then I'll explain it to you. [*Unconsciously assuming the tone he uses in telling stories to his grade school students*] It says in the paper, in . . . a country right next to our China, there was a soldier who had been in combat and had earned a medal—do you know what I mean? a medal you wear on your chest—but when he got his discharge, he found he couldn't support his wife and parents, and one evening he sneaked off to a room he'd taken for the purpose and swallowed opium. . . . No, no, [*Takes a quick look at the newspaper*] he swallowed poison and killed himself! In his suicide note he said, "I've sold what I can, and now I have nothing left but the body my mother and father gave me. I've heard that medical schools buy corpses; if that's so, then sell my corpse so that my family can eat. . . ." The upshot of it was that they did sell the corpse as he'd requested, for thirty-six dollars, minus the hotel bill of a dollar twenty, and with tears in his eyes, his father took away an estate of thirty-four dollars

and eighty cents! The newspaper reporter gave the story a headline—
you know what a headline is, don't you? it means title—"Hero for
Sale: $34.80"!

LIN [*Vehemently*] Goddamn it, [*Throws the newspaper away*] the
bastard who took away the dollar twenty is nothing but a robber!

CHAO You're so right. Just for money, for such a piddling amount
too— [*Turns and deliberately teases his wife*] So you see, I hate the
sight of money.

HUANG [*In an aggrieved tone*] Kuei-fen! [KUEI-FEN *is absorbed in the
conversation and does not reply*]

LIN Huh . . . with corpses floating all over this China of ours, I
wonder if anyone of them could get a price like that![5]

CHAO [*Off on a new topic*] Say, speaking of floating corpses, it says
in today's paper . . .

["LITTLE TIENTSIN," *a young Shanghai street type, pushes his way
through the gate, eyes everyone, and goes straight up the stairs. With
an expression of disgust mixed with some self-satisfaction,* CHAO'S WIFE
whispers in KUEI-FEN'S *ear*]

KUEI-FEN [*Eyes alight with interest*] Really?

CHAO'S WIFE [*Points to her own eyes*] I saw it with my own eyes. He snuck
out with her night before last, and they didn't get back till daylight
yesterday. Right here last night [*Points to the water basin*] I saw him
get his cut from her!

KUEI-FEN [*Covering her mouth*] Disgraceful!

LIN Damn it, the men are thieves and the women whores in this
world, and it's all for money. There's nothing they don't do for it!
[*Upstairs,* SHIH HSIAO-PAO *catches sight of* "LITTLE TIENTSIN" *and
yells,* "Get out of here!" *Everyone looks up*] There will come a day
when I'll have some power, and then I'll [*Viciously*] get those—

CHAO [*Interrupts loudly*] Oh my god! [*Jumps up*] I've got only
three minutes! [*Picks up his book from the table and dashes out*]

CHAO'S WIFE [*Staring angrily after him*] Won't you ever change?

HUANG [*From upstairs*] Kuei-fen! Kuei-fen!

KUEI-FEN [*Raises her head*] What?

CHAO [*Pushes through the gate violently*] Forgot my hat! [*Rushes
into the house, gets his hat, stuffs it on his head, and rushes out again*]

CHAO'S WIFE [*Chasing after him and shouting at the gate*] Hey,
why haven't you put your rubbers on? [*Sees that he is well on his way
and so turns around and mumbles something.* KUEI-FEN *is wringing
out the laundry*]

LIN [*Returns to his room, now that his companion in complaining
and conversation has left*] Shopping for groceries, huh? Nine o'clock,
and not back yet.

HUANG [*Descends from the garret, while* KUEI-FEN, *wiping her hands,
is on her way up*] Come here!

KUEI-FEN What is it? I haven't finished all the laundry yet.

[CHAO'S WIFE *cleans up her room, and* LIN CHIH-CH'ENG, *alone, pours out some water and washes his face]*

HUANG [*Standing in the middle of the stairs*] What's the rush? With the weather the way it is, it'll rain in a little while anyway, and it'll never get dry.

KUEI-FEN [*Looking at him*] What's the matter?

HUANG [*Hesitates for an instant*] Do you have anything left?

KUEI-FEN [*Uncomprehending*] What do you mean?

HUANG Yesterday's— [*Swallows the rest*]

KUEI-FEN [*Understands his meaning now, lowers her head*] I have a few dimes left over from groceries.

HUANG Then, today . . .

KUEI-FEN [*Looks up at him*] Today?

HUANG [*Falls silent a moment, then, as if searching for another topic, puts on a wry smile*] Kuei-fen! Do you think Dad—do you think Dad is disappointed in me? From his expression . . .

KUEI-FEN Why? I can't tell.

HUANG [*Painfully*] Why? He sold his land, mortgaged his house, borrowed money at a blood-sucking rate just to raise his son, but now . . .

KUEI-FEN [*Cutting him short*] There you go again; what's the good of all that? You haven't done anything wrong; you're not too lazy to look for work. If you can't find some little job or other in a place as big as Shanghai, well, it's not your fault.

HUANG [*Runs his fingers through his hair, becoming more and more excited*] It's all because of the bad advice of that elementary school teacher, Mr. Yao. He told my dad, "This boy is a genius. Our school has never had such a gifted student, and he's really going to amount to something. It would be a shame to keep him buried out here in the country!" But if he were alive today, I'd like to invite him here for a good look at his genius, living in a garret! [*Coughs*]

KUEI-FEN Oh, for heaven's sake, you're . . . [*Worried that others will hear, tries to calm him down*]

HUANG [*After a pause, exhales and lowers his voice*] Now that Dad's finally gotten to Shanghai, to have him stay in the room all day looking after the baby is a damned shame!

KUEI-FEN I know, but—

HUANG Doesn't the baby still have his locket? [*Averts his eyes*]

KUEI-FEN [*Raising her eyebrows*] The three dollars or so I gave you last time, wasn't that from the gold locket?

HUANG That's right! [*In despair*] Poor little child, even an insignificant thing like that. . . .

[KUEI-FEN *looks at him and says nothing*]

HUANG Then, you— [*Breaks off*]

KUEI-FEN What? [*Looks at him*]

[HUANG CHIA-MEI *lowers his head and says nothing*]

KUEI-FEN [*Slowly*] Actually, I suppose, when you're rich, you should live like a rich man, and when you're poor, you should live like the

poor. Perhaps—your dad isn't going to be here for very long. . . .
[HUANG *says nothing*]

KUEI-FEN [*In a spontaneous outpouring*] But what I'm worried about
is the future. If we keep on borrowing three dollars here, five dollars
there, and living hand to mouth from one day to the next, the day will
come when—

HUANG [*Suddenly raises his head and as if exploding*] You think
I'm never going to find a job, is that it? [*Stops abruptly and looks
down*]

KUEI-FEN [*In consternation*] No, no, that's not what I mean. Oh, you,
[*Shifts to a pleading tone*] Chia-mei, I just didn't put it the right way!
[*Silently,* HUANG CHIA-MEI *caresses her shoulder, turns, and goes
toward the stairs*]

[*At this moment, the back gate creaks open, and* HUANG'S FATHER
*enters holding his grandson. He seems to be very happy. The boy has
a piece of cake in one hand and a string of water chestnuts in the other.*
AH-HSIANG, *her hands behind her back, follows along behind, stealthily,
her eyes glued to her mother*]

HUANG'S FATHER Ha, ha, that's right, that's right, this is the place,
all right; say, you're pretty clever!

HUANG Ah, you're back, Dad! [*About to go up to him, but suddenly
is seized with a fit of coughing*]

KUEI-FEN Go upstairs; it's windy here.

CHAO'S WIFE [*Looking at her daughter's hands*] What in the world?
Who gave you . . .

AH-HSIANG [*Also has a string of water chestnuts; pouts*] I told him I
didn't want any, but he [*Points to* HUANG'S FATHER] insisted on giving
me some.

CHAO'S WIFE Idiot, you just don't have an ounce of manners! [*About to
say something to* HUANG'S FATHER, *then suddenly remembers his
deafness and shows her thanks with gestures*]

HUANG'S FATHER [*Loudly*] I'm much obliged to her. The houses in
Shanghai all look alike, and as soon as I was out the door, I couldn't
tell which one it was! Ha, ha, ha! [*Goes to the stairs*]

CHAO'S WIFE [*Takes three water chestnuts from* AH-HSIANG'*s string*]
You can have half! [*Puts her apron to* AH-HSIANG'*s nose*] Blow! [*AH-
HSIANG gives a hefty and very noisy blow*] Five years old, and can't even
blow your own nose! [*Takes* AH-HSIANG *into their room*]

HUANG [*Holding back a cough and forcing a smile, takes the boy
in his arms*] Little rascal, just have to have your grandpa hold you,
don't you? [*To his father*] Dad, go on up and lie down for a while.
We're going to the theater tonight, *The Burning of Red Lotus
Temple!* [KUEI-FEN *stares at the water chestnuts in her son's hand*]

HUANG'S FATHER [*Has not understood*] Ai, that's all right, that's all
right, it doesn't matter! Kids in the country eat thirty or fifty or so at a
single sitting. The more you eat, the more you get used to them! Ha,
ha . . .

[*With a downcast expression,* KUEI-FEN *goes back to the water basin, but when it suddenly pours down rain, she retreats to the scullery door.* HUANG *comes out of the garret and coughs violently, holding a handkerchief to his mouth, as if to prevent his father from seeing him.* KUEI-FEN *is listening to him*]

CHAO'S WIFE [*In an admonishing tone*] You'd better have a doctor come and see what's wrong with your husband! Early in the morning his coughing sounds really terrible!

KUEI-FEN But he . . .

CHAO'S WIFE Oh, while we're on the subject, I have a prescription that's done the trick for quite a few people. At noon of the fifth day of the fifth month, you take forty-nine large cloves of garlic, and when nobody is around . . .

[*All of a sudden, from* SHIH HSIAO-PAO*'s room comes an earsplitting noise as if something has been pushed over.* CHAO'S WIFE, KUEI-FEN, *and* LIN CHIH-CH'ENG *simultaneously look up, listening. Immediately afterwards,* "LITTLE TIENTSIN" *comes out with a nonchalant air. He is whistling—probably the latest dance hall tune—and* SHIH HSIAO-PAO *is close on his heels, shouting*]

SHIH I'm not going, I'm not, I'll be damned if I will! [*"*LITTLE TIENTSIN*" stops on the stairs, turns his head, and looks at her. He keeps on whistling and says nothing.* SHIH *walks down to the landing*] Go tell him it's not my fault. He wants me to apologize to him, does he? Forget it! If I hit him, he had it coming. Hah! What a pig, asks me out to eat, then starts to get ideas! I told him Johnnie's coming back, and if he has anything he wants to say, he can say it to him! [*Turns and is about to go off.* "LITTLE TIENTSIN" *beckons her with his chin*]

SHIH [*Descends a few steps*] What? [*Raises her eyebrows*]

"LITTLE TIENTSIN" [*Casually grabs a banister rail, gives it a light twist or two, breaks it off, and brushes the wood chips from his hand, then coldly to* SHIH HSIAO-PAO] You'll still have to walk in the Shanghai Bund perhaps. If you don't listen to me . . . well, your legs aren't any stronger than that wood, are they? [*He resumes his whistling, continues downstairs under the fixed stare of several pairs of eyes, and saunters out the gate.* CHAO'S WIFE *hurriedly follows him out and watches him leave, then slams the gate closed*]

SHIH [*A little shaken, but feels compelled to put up a bold front*] Thieving son of a bitch! [*Goes back upstairs and throws herself on the bed*]

LIN [*Hearing the quarrel, he has run out from the parlor and stood watching* "LITTLE TIENTSIN'S" *departure. Finally he goes over to the stairway and picks up the banister rail, then angrily*] I must have been blind! What a splendid bunch of tenants I've got! [*He is about to turn around and go back when there is a knocking at the back gate. Since* CHAO'S WIFE *doesn't dare to answer it but stands watching* LIN CHIH-CH'ENG *instead, he gathers his courage and pulls the gate open. The person at the gate is a middle-aged man with dishevelled hair and a beard, in ill-fitting Western clothes which are soaked through at the shoulders. His eyes, long and narrow at the corners, are kind. He has a high-bridged nose. From his bearing it is clear that at this moment a surfeit of hardship has left him physically and spiritually exhausted. This is* Ts'ai-yü's *former husband,* Lin's *close friend, and* Pao-chen's *father—*K'uang Fu]

K'uang I wonder if a certain Mr. Lin— [*Sees* Lin *and looks him up and down*] Ah, there you are, Chih-ch'eng! I've been looking all over for you!

Lin [*Taken aback; stares with bloodshot eyes and steps back a few paces*] You . . . you . . .

K'uang You don't recognize me any more, eh? I . . .

Lin [*After close scrutiny, turns pale*] Ah, Fu-sheng! What . . .

K'uang [*Warmly extends his hands*] Oh, I've changed, all right! I'll bet if you'd run into me on the street, you wouldn't have known me, would you? [*Smiles sadly*]

Lin [*Almost as if struck by lightning, speechless and utterly bewildered*] Ah—

K'uang [*Grabs* Lin's *hand in great enthusiasm*] Chih-ch'eng!

Lin [*After the shock of recognition, seized now with the emotion of seeing an old friend*] Fu-sheng! You've come back! It's you! [*Starts to embrace him, but stops and assumes a bleak expression*]

K'uang [*Looks around him, sees the others staring at him, and politely greets them, then to* Lin] Are these people all your family?

Lin [*As if waking from a reverie*] Ah, no, no. Come on in and sit down!

[*He leads* K'uang Fu *to the parlor while the others look on in astonishment. As soon as they are inside,* Lin *closes the door*]

K'uang [*Walking along*] This area's changed entirely; you've got a trolley bus through here now, and most of the houses are new. When I lived here seven or eight years ago . . . [Lin Chih-ch'eng *looks at him as if in despair*] What's the matter, Chih-ch'eng? You see the way I look . .

Lin [*Trying to mask his confusion*] Mm mm, sit down, sit down. Have a smoke? [*Searches a drawer for cigarettes*]

K'uang Hm? Have you forgotten I don't smoke?

Lin Oh, oh, then . . . [*Tries to pour some boiled water from the thermos but is unaware that it is empty and that he is merely going through a pantomime of pouring*] Have some water! [*His hands are shaking*]

K'uang [*Watching* Lin's *hands and beginning to be alarmed at his distraught expression*] What's the matter, Chih-ch'eng? Did I come here too unexpectedly? Is it too much of a shock? How have you been feeling? There's nothing wrong, I hope.

Lin [*Even more distressed*] No, no . . .

K'uang Then, my old friend, why aren't you happy over my new-found freedom? If you count the year and a half before I went in, it's been ten whole years since we last saw each other!

Lin Mm mm, Fu-sheng, I—I'm very happy, but, it—it must be a dream!

K'uang [*Laughing*] No, squeeze my hand. It isn't a dream, it's real!

[LIN CHIH-CH'ENG *grips his hand, glances at him, then lowers his head in silence*]

K'UANG [*Emotionally*] I dreamt for eight years in that pigeon cage, and now, by god, it's all come true! Whenever we'd get out into the yard and I'd breathe the fresh air, or when the wind would blow in from far off, I'd think of you right away, Chih-ch'eng. And when my time was up, I had to find you first of all, so that I could see my Ts'ai-yü and my Pao-chen! Chih-ch'eng, they, they . . .

LIN [*With a gleam of terror in his eyes*] They, uh, they . . .

K'UANG Are they all right? They . . . [*Grips* LIN*'s hand tightly*] Oh, Chih-ch'eng, I don't know how to thank you. Tell me how they've been for the past few years. [LIN *is unable to reply*] Are they all right? Chih-ch'eng, say something!

LIN [*His throat constricted*] They—

K'UANG [*Alarmed*] What's happened to them? [LIN *cannot speak.* K'UANG *jumps up*] Chih-ch'eng, tell me, how are they? They . . . no use trying to fool me, they've— [*Grief-stricken*]

LIN No, no, they're all right. . . . In a little while—

K'UANG [*Relieved*] Oh, they're all right, are they? Chih-ch'eng! If I hadn't had a friend like you, they might have been dead by now, or drifting around in the streets. I don't know how many terrible dreams I've had, of Ts'ai-yü and Pao-chen begging for food in the streets. My god . . .

[*While they are talking,* AH-HSIANG *goes on tiptoe to the door and peeks in, listening.* CHAO'S WIFE *is frying vegetables on a small stove, and when she sees that* AH-HSIANG *has run off to eavesdrop, she immediately rushes over and pulls her away, threatening her with her fist. Helplessly* AH-HSIANG *walks away. But when* CHAO'S WIFE *hears* K'UANG *mention* TS'AI-YÜ, *she stops short and in spite of herself assumes* AH-HSIANG*'s identical stance, eavesdropping through the crack in the door.* AH-HSIANG *stands by the stairs and, pouting, glares at her mother.*

[*Before* K'UANG FU *has finished speaking, there is a sudden knock at the front gate.* LIN CHIH-CH'ENG, *in embarrassment, stands up but does not go to answer it. He finally makes a decision*]

LIN She . . .

VOICE [*Interrupting from outside the gate*] Ma'am, do you have any bottles or old newspapers?

LIN [*Furiously*] No!

VOICE [*Monotonously*] Got any used-up pots and pans, old clothes, old shoes to trade in, anybody? [*His cries drift away*]

K'UANG [*After this interruption, he picks up the glass, notices that it has no water in it, and puts it down again. He looks the room over for the first time, and his gaze falls upon a dress hanging on the wall*] Oh, Chih-ch'eng, [*With forced enthusiasm*] I had no idea; are you married?

LIN [*With increased anguish*] Mm . . .

K'UANG For how many years, and who is she? [*Again* LIN *can't speak*] I don't know why it is, but when I was inside, the days seemed to crawl by. Actually, now that I think about it, the time went pretty fast, and now my old opponents in the dining hall fights at school are all already middle-aged men! Chih-ch'eng, you're thirty-five now?

LIN [*Can hold off no longer*] Fu-sheng! Why haven't you written in the last few years? You might at least have sent me a letter saying you were all right! It wouldn't have been impossible, would it?

K'UANG What do you mean?

LIN Ever since I got that one letter from you when you were in the Lunghwa prison, not a word—and at that time your case was so serious!

K'UANG My friend, I'm sorry. I had no idea what the situation was like outside, and it might have been dangerous for you if I'd sent you a letter.

LIN [*On the brink of tears*] But, but, Fu-sheng! In that way, in that way you made me commit a crime, a crime so horrible I can't even face you, my friend! Fu-sheng, spit on me, curse me, I beg you to do it! I'm vile, I've done a terrible thing to you . . .

K'UANG [*Shocked*] What is it? Tell me—

LIN I'm unspeakable, I can't face you, I . . . [*Holds his head in his hands*]

K'UANG What are you talking about? I don't understand; tell me! Tell me!

LIN Fu-sheng!

K'UANG What?

LIN I— [*Stops*]

K'UANG What's the matter? Go on.

LIN Ts'ai-yü and I . . . [*Between clenched teeth*] Ts'ai-yü and I have been living together!

K'UANG [*Confused and unconscious of his actions*] Uhh— [*Collapses onto his chair; as if by rote*] living—together!

KUEI-FEN [*Loudly*] Oh dear! Mrs. Chao, your vegetables are getting burnt! [CHAO'S WIFE *runs back awkwardly.* KUEI-FEN *takes some laundry upstairs*]

LIN [*Softly but emphatically*] Once I got the letter you'd had relayed to me from Lunghwa, I went to Ts'ai-yü, and as you had feared they were living in poverty in an attic, almost everything you owned having been taken away when you were in trouble. I . . . [*takes a deep breath*] I looked out for them as well as I could, but a year went by, then two, and I didn't get any news at all from you. Some of the ones sentenced along with you died, others changed completely. I waited for you three full years, [*In gradually increasing excitement and louder voice*] and I just didn't know if you were alive or dead. [*Quickly changes his tone*] But no, no, I can't use that as expiation; I did a criminal act, and I'm ashamed to face you. But, Fu-sheng! I'm a human being, I have feelings, and because I wanted them to be happy, I . . .

K'UANG [*Excitedly*] You wanted them to be happy! [*With great effort brings his confused emotions under control*] Mm ... wait, I ... let me think ...

LIN I understand now that the cause of my misery was a worthless thing called devotion. I wanted to help a friend, help a friend's family. Every time I'd see Pao-chen, I would think to myself that I had to protect her and make sure she got an education, so that she could follow in your footsteps. ... But that made me commit my crime, and I ...

K'UANG [*As if lost in thought and oblivious to what* LIN CHIH-CH'ENG *has just said*] Wanted them to be happy—

LIN [*With a touch of hysteria*] I'm a man, and I have some education. You used to treat me like your own brother, and so when you were up against it, do you suppose I would do anything to hurt you? After a month or two, I felt the danger, and I made up my mind several times to leave. I planned to gather up a good amount of money and give it to Ts'ai-yü. In that way I wouldn't have to look after them all the time, but—

K'UANG [*Has finally recovered his equilibrium*] So, what about Ts'ai-yü?

LIN I suppose you could say the same thing happened to her; fate covered both our eyes, and the more we struggled, the worse the danger became, until finally—

K'UANG Wait, so now ...

LIN [*Before he can finish*] Now? Isn't everything clear enough already? I've committed a crime, and I'm waiting for your sentence. No, before you pronounce sentence, I must tell you I've already suffered the inquisition of my conscience. Whenever I would feel even the slightest degree of happiness, something of the warmth that a family can bring, at that very instant, some invisible instrument of torture would clamp down on my heart. But it's all right now, you're here, and I've confessed to you, held nothing back. ... I acknowledge my crime before you and await your verdict! [*After all this in one stream, takes a long breath, exhausted but seemingly content*]

K'UANG No, I don't care about that. What I want to know is whether you and Ts'ai-yü are happy.

LIN [*Curtly*] Do you think happiness can be built on misery?

K'UANG [*Sadly*] Mm—

[*After an interval of silence,* KUEI-FEN *comes out of the garret with a bottle*]

HUANG'S FATHER [*Offstage*] Don't buy anything to drink; I'm not having anything.

[KUEI-FEN *goes to the back gate just as* LI LING-PEI, *the attic tenant, comes in with several unsold newspapers under his arm. He has already had a bit to drink, and, unmindful of the others, is singing to himself as he goes up the stairs*]

LI [*Sings*] "When I gaze on the lovely child, I can hold back no longer; the tears fall like pearls from my eyes. ... [*Plaintively*] My son, my seventh son, gone back to Wild Swan Gate for more troops to come in aid, why, oh why, now that you are gone, do you not come back . . ."

K'UANG [*Following with his eyes* LI LING-PEI*'s voice as it proceeds to the roof, then despondently*] I should never have come to see you; I'm just stepping in where I'm not wanted. . . .

LIN What do you mean? [K'UANG *is silent. Someone knocks at the gate, and* LIN CHIH-CH'ENG *gets up without the slightest hesitation. He has clearly come to a decision*] Good, she's back. I—I'm going out now, so you two can talk, and I'll agree to anything you decide. My friend, I'll be waiting for your decision. . . . [*He opens the gate, but the person who enters is a young man in working clothes*]

YOUNG MAN [*Excitedly*] Mr. Lin, hurry, the head of the Labor Department wants to see you right away; there's trouble at the factory. Hurry . . .

LIN [*With indifference*] It's the day shift; it's none of my affair.

YOUNG MAN No, no, it's really a mess. Hurry, everybody's waiting! [*Tugging, at the point of coercion*]

LIN No, no, I'm busy. . . . [*Under pressure, finally changes his clothes and leaves*]

[K'UANG FU *once again examines the room closely; he walks over to the desk, picks up a songbook left by* PAO-CHEN, *and gives it a glance*]

K'UANG [*To himself*] Lin Pao-chen; hm, Lin! [*Puts the book down and counts on his fingers*] She was five then . . . [*Absentmindedly plays a few notes on* PAO-CHEN*'s toy piano*]

[*At this moment there is a flash of sunlight.* HUANG'S FATHER, *holding his grandson, leans out of the garret window and looks at the sky.* HUANG CHIA-MEI *hurries down the stairs with a package and, when he reaches the water basin, comes upon* KUEI-FEN, *back from buying some liquor*]

KUEI-FEN [*Noticing his package*] What's that?

HUANG [*Somewhat ashamed*] Some clothes . . .

KUEI-FEN [*Pulls out part of a piece of clothing sticking out from the package, looks at him, then*] Chia-mei, that's all I have to wear when we go out. [HUANG'S FATHER *is watching from the window*]

HUANG [*As if in self-justification*] Well, you don't have any social life anyway, and it's so hot now you don't need it. In a few days . . . [*Sees* KUEI-FEN*'s reluctance to part with it, and so, with forced indifference, walks away*]

KUEI-FEN Chia—

[HUANG *walks on without turning his head. Her eyes fixed on his retreating form,* KUEI-FEN *suddenly covers her face with her hands and bursts into tears.* HUANG'S FATHER, *watching from upstairs, turns solemn and comes rapidly downstairs. When the two come face to face by the stairway,* KUEI-FEN *greets him with a strained attempt at a smile*]

KUEI-FEN Dad . . .

HUANG'S FATHER [*Looking at her*] Mm . . .

[*At the back gate,* TS'AI-YÜ, *holding a grocery basket, directs a curious glance at them.*

[*The rain increases, as does the shouting of children in the lane*]
[*Curtain*]

ACT II

It is the afternoon of the same day.

In the parlor, TS'AI-YÜ *is slumped over the table in tears.* K'UANG FU *paces back and forth aimlessly, his hands behind his back. Both are silent.*

Above the parlor, "LITTLE TIENTSIN" *is lying on* SHIH HSIAO-PAO'S *bed, smoking a cigarette and smiling maliciously.* SHIH HSIAO-PAO *is sitting at her dressing table and applying makeup to her sad face. They too are silent.*

In the garret, amidst the sound of a child's crying, HUANG CHIA-MEI *is talking loudly to his father, but the words are muffled.* KUEI-FEN, *her expression distraught, slowly descends the stairs with a thermos. As she opens the rear gate and steps out, she listens to the conversation.*

In the scullery, CHAO'S WIFE *is silently mending clothes.*

A minute passes. The sun appears and casts a dazzling beam of light into the house, long soaked with humidity. CHAO'S WIFE *quickly gets to her feet and opens a soggy umbrella outside to dry, then puts a bamboo pole with wet clothing on it into the sunlight.*

HUANG'S FATHER [*Offstage*] Look, isn't that the sun shining? [*He opens the window*]

HUANG [*Offstage*] Stay a few more days, Dad. When it clears up tonight we'll go see *The Burning of Red*— [*coughs*]

HUANG'S FATHER [*Offstage*] After a half month's rain, I'm afraid the lower land has been flooded over by now, and if I don't get back and replant, what're we going to eat this year?

[*After finally putting all the clothes out to dry,* CHAO'S WIFE *goes back inside, gets herself settled comfortably, and picks up her sewing. The sunlight disappears, and it showers heavily again. She gets up immediately and retrieves the clothes*]

CHAO'S WIFE [*Peevishly*] Damn!

K'UANG [*Paces up to* TS'AI-YÜ *and stops*] So you mean . . . you've been living with Chih-ch'eng . . . You've been living with Chih-ch'eng just to stay alive, not on account of any feeling . . .

[*Without making a reply or raising her head,* TS'AI-YÜ *reaches automatically for her handkerchief with her right hand.* K'UANG FU *picks her handkerchief up from the floor and hands it to her without speaking. There is a moment of silence. From the back gate comes the voice of a peddler.* AH-HSIANG *quietly opens the back gate but, apparently worried about her shoes, which are thoroughly wet, is afraid to step inside*]

K'UANG Hm, to stay alive, just to stay alive! [*Nods and sits down in dejection, then after a moment, as if in both ridicule and release of pent-up resentment*] Ten short years have changed us completely! Ten years ago, for the sake of love you forsook your family; ten years ago, for the sake of love you risked everything and married a man without roots like me, but now after those ten years . . . the courageous disciple of love triumphant over all has finally turned into a timid little housewife!

[Ts'AI-YÜ *makes no reply but wipes her eyes and looks at him*]

K'UANG Ts'ai'yü! I doubt if anybody would have thought you could . . . [*Breaks off*]

Ts'AI-YÜ [*Softly*] You still hate me, don't you?

K'UANG No, I don't hate anybody!

Ts'AI-YÜ Then you must be laughing at me . . . you must despise me. While my own husband, whom I loved, was suffering in prison, I was thinking of marriage as just an occupation and was confusing sympathy with love, and so, very cautious and circumspect about everything, I've been keeping house for someone else.

K'UANG Ts'ai-yü!

Ts'AI-YÜ [*On a slightly higher pitch*] But before you blame me, you have to try to imagine what it's been like for the last ten years! After we got married, we didn't spend a day in peace: poverty-stricken, on the run, separated from all our friends and family. At that time, I suppose you could say I was just barely hanging on, hanging on for the sake of your ideals and for everyone else's future. But once you went to prison, I couldn't locate a single one of your friends. Oh, the ones I did find might not have said so in so many words, but I could tell from the way they acted they were afraid I'd get them involved. All right, I was K'uang Fu's wife and I'd have to get by on my own, so I made up my mind to look for a job. But I had Pao-chen tied to me, she was only five then; I tried everywhere, thought of everything, but do you think anybody would spend his money to hire a woman with a child? On days so hot the asphalt on the streets would stick to the soles of our shoes, Pao-chen would go along with me. At first, before she could get very far, she would cry out that her feet were sore, but as the days went by, when I would ask her, "Pao-chen, can you keep going?" she would smile and say, "I'm used to it now, Mommy; I'm not a bit tired." [*Tries to fight back her tears but fails*] That was—how we lived!

K'UANG [*Painfully, walks over to her and puts a hand on her shoulder*] Ts'ai-yü, I haven't the slightest intention of blaming you; I just think . . .

Ts'AI-YÜ Do you think there's a chance at all in this world for us women to find any job? They use every trick they can think of—sarcastic smiles, contempt, pressure, insults, anything to force you into marriage, to force you into the role of the nice, sweet housewife!

K'UANG Ts'ai'yü It's no good talking about the past; you can't bring it back anyway. You've got to calm yourself; we can talk about other problems, after all.

Ts'AI-YÜ [*After a pause*] Other problems? [*Turns around*]

K'UANG Yes . . . [*Falls silent and resumes pacing*]

[KUEI-FEN *comes in with boiled water and several biscuits*, AH-HSIANG *enviously following along*. KUEI-FEN *goes upstairs and, after a moment, comes out onto the stairs again with* HUANG, *who is furious*]

HUANG What did you say to Dad the minute I stepped out? [KUEI-FEN *shakes her head*] Nothing? Then why was he on top of the world this morning and now all set to go back home? He said he's going back tonight!

KUEI-FEN Tonight? [*In surprise*] Didn't you tell me we were going to the theater?

HUANG [*Viciously*] He's already packing his things, as if you didn't know.

KUEI-FEN As if I didn't know? What do you mean?

HUANG I mean you forced him to go!

KUEI-FEN I . . . forced . . . him . . . to go! Chia-mei! You can't just say everything that comes into your head like that; why would I want to force him to go? How could I?

HUANG [*Coldly*] As for why, because I've pawned your clothes, and as for how, with your tears, that's how, with that frowning look you carry around with you all day. He may be deaf, but he isn't blind yet, and your intentional worrying and sighing over our poverty have kept him . . . kept him from staying on.

KUEI-FEN My intentional—

HUANG My dad is getting old, and you, you—

KUEI-FEN [*Finally goaded to a retort*] You can't be so unreasonable! Don't try to get the idea from somebody else around here that you can use your wife as a whipping boy. You'd like your dad to stay on a few days, I understand that, it's a natural thing to want. But let me ask you this: what good would it do for him to stay a few days more under these circumstances, for him, and for you? You keep on this way and you'll drive us all to our deaths, all of us together. Why, [*Begins to weep*] why would I ever want to force him . . . to go . . .

[HUANG CHIA-MEI *says nothing but savagely runs his hand through his hair*]

KUEI-FEN [*Tenderly*] Chia-mei! Your health . . .

[*From the garret comes the sound of a child's crying*]

HUANG'S FATHER Oh, don't cry, don't cry. I'll hold you. It's all right, it's all right . . .

[KUEI-FEN *wipes her tears with her sleeve, and* HUANG *quickly wipes her eyes with his own handkerchief. He steps back to allow* KUEI-FEN *into the room, then with head bowed follows her inside*]

K'UANG [*After listening to the Huangs' conversation*] So—your life now . . .

TS'AI-YÜ [*With a sad smile*] See for yourself!

K'UANG I see that Chih-ch'eng has aged a lot. I suppose my coming today was too much of a shock, but the moment I laid eyes on him, I had the feeling that, on top of the melancholy he's had ever since childhood, there's anxiety too. . . . . How is he getting along at the factory? [Ts'ai-yü *shakes her head*] He still can't get along with anybody, is that it?

Ts'ai-yü [*Nods, then after a pause*] What about me? I've aged, haven't I?

K'uang [*Has some difficulty in answering this*] Uh . . .

Ts'ai-yü Haven't I? [K'uang Fu *looks at her*] Go ahead and say it, I— [*He is still silent. She gives a forced laugh*] You won't say it, all right, I will. I'm no longer the Ts'ai-yü of ten years ago!

K'uang [*Nervously*] No, no, I was just thinking. . . . [*Silence*]

Ts'ai-yü You were thinking, were you? Well then, do you think I've been happy?

K'uang I hope so!

Ts'ai-yü Tell me the truth! Do you think he's been able to make me happy?

K'uang I hope he has.

Ts'ai-yü [*Smiles sarcastically and avoids his eyes*] You say I've changed, but I think you have too. You're not as natural as you used to be, or as candid.

K'uang What do you mean?

Ts'ai-yü [*Quickly continues*] Suppose I told you that Chih-ch'eng has been unable to make me happy, that I've been miserable, that Pao-chen, along with me, has been treated badly? He can't get along with people at the factory; he takes all kinds of abuse, he's the target of jokes, and his juniors climb on past him, one after the other. He worries all day about losing his job, and by the time he gets home, he's ready to let out all his frustrations on me with a vengeance. At the slightest provocation he pouts and refuses to say anything, plays dumb for three days or even more . . . Fu-sheng! Can you possibly consider a life like that happy? .

K'uang [*In anguish*] Ts'ai-yü, I'm ashamed of the way I've treated you— [*The back gate opens, and* Pao-chen *enters in a rush. When* Chao's wife *sees her, she quickly beckons to her, but* Pao-chen *seems not to notice and strides directly into the parlor. The conversation thus interrupted,* K'uang Fu *in a reflexive action gets to his feet*]

Ts'ai-yü Pao-chen, come here; this is— [*Hesitates*]

K'uang [*Breaks in*] Is this Pao-chen? [*Looks at her tenderly*]

Pao-chen [*Startled*] Do you know me? May I ask your name, sir?

Ts'ai-yü Pao-chen— [*Finds it impossible to go on*]

K'uang [*Laughing*] My name is K'uang.

Pao-chen [*Innocently*] How do you write "K'uang"?

K'uang [*Writes on the table with his finger*] Like this: the "king" character inside a box.

Pao-chen K'uang? I didn't know there was such a strange name! What does the character mean?

K'uang [*Caught short*] Well, let me think—

Pao-chen [*Quickly goes to the table and finds a tiny dictionary, which she leafs through*] "Box" radical, one, two, three, four strokes . . . here it is; hm, "*k'uang, to reform, to correct.*" But, Mr. K'uang, do people still use a character like this?

K'UANG [*Never taking his gaze, amazed yet loving, from her*] Well, yes, but pretty seldom now.

PAO-CHEN My teacher says useless characters should be done away with, isn't that right?

TS'AI-YÜ Pao-chen!

K'UANG Mm! You're right! [*Laughing*] From now on I'll do without it.

PAO-CHEN Oh good! Mom, why are you staring at me that way? Come on, give me something to eat; I'm off to school.

K'UANG How's that? Didn't you just get through with school?

PAO-CHEN No, [*Proudly*] what the teacher just got through teaching me, I'm going to go teach somebody else. I'm a "little teacher"; I teach singing and reading.

K'UANG "Little teacher"?

[TS'AI-YÜ *gives her a few crackers; she takes them and eats while she talks*]

PAO-CHEN You don't know what "little teacher" means? The idea is "once you find out, pass it on"; once we learn something, we tell it to other people. . . . Oh, it's getting late; bye-bye! [*Bounds off, singing*] "It's bootleg, dirt cheap!"

CHAO'S WIFE [*Softly but with force*] Pao-chen . . . [PAO-CHEN, *paying no attention, exits*]

K'UANG [*Unconsciously follows her for a few steps, then, after watching her leave, turns around*] Hmm, where have all the days gone?

TS'AI-YÜ [*Nostalgically*] Don't you think she acts just the way you did when you were young? When you were a student, wouldn't you stay up for several nights on end and get sick, just on account of an algebra problem? She's the same way; she just has to get to the bottom of everything!

K'UANG But I don't have that attitude any more. . . . [*Ponders, then, as if remembering something*] Ts'ai'yü! I'm content now, because when I was in prison and the beriberi was bad, I'd already given up hope of ever seeing you both again, but now, now that I've seen Pao-chen with my own eyes and find she's just like me when I was young—

TS'AI-YÜ Content? Do you think Pao-chen is happy?

K'UANG No, that's not what I mean. . . .

TS'AI-YÜ [*Despondent*] Her memories used to be so unclouded, but a stain is on them now that can never be washed away. The other children call her . . . [*Looks at* K'UANG FU]

K'UANG What do you mean, that even she has—

[*At this instant, the sound of children fighting comes from the rear gate.* CHAO'S WIFE *looks out the gate*]

AH-NIU'S VOICE Give it back! Give it back!

AH-HSIANG'S VOICE It's mine! Mommy! [*Screams*]

CHAO [*Apparently just back from school; enters holding the two children apart*] Go on inside! Go on! [AH-NIU *and* AH-HSIANG *wrestle*] Ha, ha . . .

AH-NIU Give it back! [*Turns to his father*] It's my "work project," and she took it. Give it back!

AH-HSIANG Mommy gave it to me to play with! It's mine! [*The two wrestle and hit each other.* CHAO *makes no attempt to interfere but looks on, smiling.* CHAO'S WIFE *immediately sets her sewing down and steps outside*]

CHAO'S WIFE Ah-niu! [*Sees* CHAO*'s expression, then furiously*] Hope you're enjoying the show! They could be beating each other to death, for all you care! [*Pulls on Ah-niu*]

CHAO [*Calmly*] No chance, no chance of that at all. It's the rainy season, and they need all the exercise they can get!

CHAO'S WIFE No hitting, Ah-niu! You brat! [AH-NIU *hits* AH-HSIANG, *who cries*]

CHAO Ha, ha, ha . . .

CHAO'S WIFE [*Jerks* AH-NIU *away*] Have a good laugh. [*With mocking obedience,* CHAO *stops laughing. At this instant,* AH-NIU *charges by and grabs a cardboard model from* AH-HSIANG*'s hands*] What are you doing, stealing that! [*Pulls* AH-NIU *into the room*]

CHAO [*Squats down and wipes* AH-HSIANG*'s tears with a handkerchief, meanwhile, in a tone that only a teacher could perfect*] Don't cry now. I've told you, don't laugh when you win and don't cry when you lose. Only crybabies cry! [*Softly, for fear his wife will hear*] You can fight again tomorrow! [*Takes* AH-HSIANG *into the apartment*] You've heard the story I've told your brother; now, when Napoleon was banished to Elba, what did he say? Hm? Hm? . . . Ah, look! There's Ah-niu laughing already. [*Loudly*] Ha, ha, ha . . .

[*In the front room,* SHIH HSIAO-PAO, *her makeup completed, hears* CHAO CHEN-YÜ*'s laughter and heads downstairs, as if remembering something she had forgotten*]

"LITTLE TIENTSIN" [*Angrily*] Where do you think you're going?

SHIH [*Raising a slippered foot*] What are you getting so excited about? I can't exactly run away. [*Descends the stairs and goes to the scullery door, where she surreptitiously beckons to* CHAO] Mr. Chao!

CHAO Oh, you're home, are you? [*Walks over, while his wife glares angrily*]

SHIH [*Softly*] Would you mind looking something up in the last few issues of the newspaper for me?

CHAO What is it? [*His wife gets to her feet and stands at the scullery door*]

SHIH If you would try to find out about Johnnie—when his ship is due back in Shanghai.

CHAO Oh, oh, [*Turns back in to get the newspapers, then, seeming to recall something*] what's the name of the ship?

SHIH Well, let's see. . . . Uh, it's got a *maru* on it.

CHAO Ha, ha . . . a lot of ships have a *maru* in their names; for example—

SHIH Then—

CHAO'S WIFE [*Making it a point to be heard by* SHIH] Shameless!

CHAO Your husband is coming home soon, is he?

SHIH [*Turns away and becomes despondent*] If only he could! [*She climbs partway up the stairs, thinks of something, and comes back down again. She goes to the parlor, sees that there is a visitor, and hesitates*] Oh, sorry. Is Mr. Lin out?

TS'AI-YÜ Mm hm, is there anything I can do?

SHIH [*Has difficulty in broaching the subject*] Mrs. Lin! I'd like to talk to you about something.

TS'AI-YÜ [*Walks to the doorway*] What is it?

SHIH Is Mr. Lin coming back right away?

TS'AI-YÜ Do you have some kind of problem? You can tell me.

SHIH [*Falters for a moment, then decisively but softly*] Is there any way you can get rid of that thug in my room for me?

TS'AI-YÜ What do you mean, thug? [K'UANG FU *stands up*]

SHIH He, he wants me to— I don't want to go, and if that man of mine comes back in a day or two, there could be trouble.

TS'AI-YÜ I don't understand; who is your—

"LITTLE TIENTSIN" [*Somewhat suspicious; gets up and goes to the head of the stairs*] Hsiao-pao!

SHIH [*In alarm, quickly*] He's a gangster, and he's trying to make me go to—

"LITTLE TIENTSIN" [*Loudly*] Hsiao-pao!

SHIH [*Turns around and mounts the stairs; in a pleading tone*] When Mr. Lin gets back, would you tell him to . . . [*Goes upstairs*]

K'UANG [*Once she has left*] What's the matter?

TS'AI-YÜ I have no idea! [*They look upstairs*]

SHIH What are you getting so excited about? We're not rushing to a coroner's office!

"LITTLE TIENTSIN" He's waiting; let's go!

SHIH [*Against her will, sits down and puts on high-heeled shoes*] Cigarette. ["LITTLE TIENTSIN" *pulls out his cigarette case, sees that it is empty, and hands her the cigarette he is smoking.* SHIH *takes a long drag, then flips the cigarette away; with an intentionally nonchalant air*] Johnnie's coming back tomorrow, you know. ["LITTLE TIENTSIN" *seems unconcerned*] Aren't you afraid he'll raise hell?

"LITTLE TIENTSIN" [*Ignores this; suddenly stands up*] Let's go!

SHIH [*Smiles archly*] But let's get something settled before we do! [*Approaches him suggestively*]

"LITTLE TIENTSIN" You want me to get rough? [*Pulls her sharply*]

SHIH [*Concealing her distress*] Then tomorrow I'm going to tell him; the whole story, since you're not afraid of anything anyway. [*Starts off, with* "LITTLE TIENTSIN" *following her downstairs in a coercive manner*]

"LITTLE TIENTSIN" [*On the stairs*] Let me tell you something. Johnnie's in the States right now, got that?

[SHIH *says nothing. As they leave,* CHAO'S WIFE's *angry eyes follow them out. She looks back, about to make a remark, but stops when she finds she has no one to make it to.*]

[*A peddler is calling his wares outside the gate. The sky darkens suddenly.* KUEI-FEN *steps out to the landing and shouts.*]

KUEI-FEN Mrs. Lin, would you turn the main light switch on, please?

[*When* TS'AI-YÜ *without a word turns on the main switch, the garret is suddenly filled with light. Thunder sounds in the distance, and while* K'UANG FU *and* TS'AI-YÜ *are talking, the tenants of the garret and the scullery begin to prepare dinner*]

TS'AI-YÜ You still haven't answered my question just now; do you think our life now is a happy one? [*He does not reply*] If, tell me the truth now, if you thought Pao-chen and I were unhappy, then . . . [*There is a pause*] Could your conscience be at peace? [K'UANG, *distressed, makes no reply*]

TS'AI-YÜ [*Takes a step toward him*] Why don't you say something? Didn't you used to tell me you would do anything to make me happy?

K'UANG [*Painfully*] Don't press me, Ts'ai'yü! My mind is all confused, and I don't know what to do. I—I . . . [*Gets to his feet and paces aimlessly*]

TS'AI-YÜ [*After a moment of silence*] Oh, Fu-sheng! Do you remember about Dasha?

K'UANG [*Stands still*] Dasha?

TS'AI-YÜ Mm hm, when we were living at Little Sandbar Lane and I had the flu, you sat by my bed and told me stories. Wasn't there a woman in a novel who was called Dasha?

K'UANG Ah, ah . . .

TS'AI-YÜ You said then that I was too weak, and when you told about Dasha, you would say, "Ts'ai-yü! You should try to be brave like Dasha!" What book was that? I can't remember!

K'UANG Hm, it was . . . the name of the book was *Cement* by Gladkov, wasn't it?

TS'AI-YÜ That's right, *Cement*. How do you feel about a woman like Dasha now? [K'UANG *makes no reply*] Out of all the stories you told me, I don't know why but I've never forgotten Dasha. Maybe—

K'UANG [*Interrupting*] Don't say anything more, Ts'ai-yü; I understand what you mean, but—

TS'AI-YÜ I know I can't compare myself to Dasha, but didn't you used to say you always, always wanted me to be happy? As long as you lived. Do you think I can't be like Dasha? Just as in the novel, when her husband comes home—

K'UANG [*Despairingly*] But although you could be Dasha, I'm no longer a Gleb. When Dasha saw her husband again, he was a hero back from victory, while I [*Softly*] am just a casualty from life's battlefield.

TS'AI-YÜ Fu-sheng!

K'UANG Just now you said I'd changed too. You're right, I'm aware of it myself, I have changed. I used to look at everything so simply, as if everyone were just like me, and with determination anything at all could be accomplished. But in the past few years I've seen too much, and things just aren't that simple. Pettiness, deceit, self-seeking, hurting others for no purpose, like wild animals, these are the things men do. . . . [*Seems to remember something suddenly*] Oh, but don't misunderstand. I don't mean Chih-ch'eng; he's like me, he's one of the weaklings too!

Ts'AI-YÜ [*Shocked*] Is this you talking, Fu-sheng? Weakling, you're admitting you're a weakling? Didn't you used to say time after time—

K'UANG So, I admit openly that I've changed. Look at me. These past few years have ruined my health and destroyed my courage, and when I think about going on with life, I have no more confidence in myself. Do you think a casualty like me could still make anybody happy?

Ts'AI-YÜ Then you think . . . our . . .

K'UANG [*In despair*] I just got through saying to Chih-ch'eng, I regret coming here to see you; I'm just making things worse!

Ts'AI-YÜ Fu-sheng! Is that what you really think? You never used to lie! [*There is a pause. She continues, with a trace of anger*] Then you're too selfish; you've tricked me! All the time we've been married.

K'UANG What do you mean? [*Takes a step toward her*]

Ts'AI-YÜ Ask yourself!

K'UANG Ts'ai-yü! That's not what I meant. I was only saying that as far as going on living is concerned, I've lost faith in myself and have no guarantee that I can make you and Pao-chen more—

Ts'AI-YÜ Then let me ask you this, very simply: suppose for these eight and a half years you hadn't had a friend like Chih-ch'eng and he and I hadn't had the relationship we now have, then as a matter of course, suppose Pao-chen and I had been in the streets, destitute, and, perhaps, one of us dead by now. Suppose, in a situation like that, you had found me and I had asked you for help. Could you have said then, as you just did, "I no longer have the self-confidence to make you happy; I can only let you starve to death in the streets"?

K'UANG [*Stymied*] I— I—

Ts'AI-YÜ Then I can only say that you're either cruel, or jealous!

K'UANG [*At a complete loss*] Ts'ai-yü!

Ts'AI-YÜ If the situation were different, you would not doubt say to me, "Ts'ai-yü, I'm home now. Don't be afraid; we'll make a new start." But now—you, you're casting me aside—because I wanted to stay alive. . . .

K'UANG Don't say things like that, Ts'ai-yü. What, what should I do? I just can't think of any other solution! [*In anxiety and pain*]

[*At the impatient cry of "Evening paper!" in the lane,* CHAO CHEN-YÜ *hurries to buy a newspaper*]

Ts'AI-YÜ [*In a tone of supplication*] Fu-sheng! You can't leave me again; you can't leave Pao-chen, who everybody thinks has no father. For Pao-chen's sake, for our only . . .

K'UANG [*After a moment of reflection*] Wouldn't—wouldn't that make Chih-ch'eng . . . make Chih-ch'eng even more miserable?

Ts'AI-YÜ [*Pauses*] But I told you before, it was only for survival. . . .

K'UANG [*Hangs his head, then listlessly*] Ts'ai-yü . . .

TS'AI-YÜ [*Gripping his hand*] Be brave. . . . It's my turn now to tell you what you used to say to me. [*Laughs and raises his head*] You're still young. [*Feels his chin*] Now then, shave off that beard of yours. . . . [*While speaking, gets* LIN*'s safety razor and various other articles from a drawer*] Fu-sheng! Don't think any more about it. Today we're supposed to be happy, aren't we?

K'UANG [*As if all of his pent-up affection is bursting forth*] Ts'ai-yü! [*Leans his head on her breast*]

TS'AI-YÜ [*Stroking his head*] Fu-sheng! You, you . . . [*Overcome with emotion, she weeps; they embrace*]

[*The sky gradually darkens. A hoarse, tired voice calling "Evening News, Evening Gazette, radio programs, . . ." passes by outside the front gate, along with the piercing voice of a woman crying "Evening paper" and so forth. A light comes on in the scullery.*]

[*Suddenly there is a sharp knock at the front gate. In reflex,* K'UANG FU *and* TS'AI-YÜ *break apart*]

TS'AI-YÜ Who is it? [*Opens the gate*]

[*A young employee of the factory, leading someone who looks like a foreman, enters, his face covered with perspiration*]

YOUNG MAN Hurry, they want Mr. Lin right away!

TS'AI-YÜ He isn't back yet.

YOUNG MAN [*As if wanting to charge in and conduct a search*] Mrs. Lin, I need your help. The head of the Labor Department is already in a fit, and it's none of my responsibility. [*Loudly*] Mr. Lin!

TS'AI-YÜ [*Startled*] It's true, he hasn't come back. He left this morning and hasn't been back since! Is anything the matter?

YOUNG MAN [*Impatiently*] I'll say there is. . . . Mrs. Lin, did he really— Then, do you know where he went?

TS'AI-YÜ [*Worried*] How should I know? When did he leave the factory? Is anything the matter . . .

YOUNG MAN [*Does not reply but turns to the foreman*] All right, hurry over to Number Two Plant and take a look. [*The foreman looks* K'UANG *over, then exits*] Mrs. Lin, this is serious. If he doesn't come . . . [*Wipes the perspiration from his forehead*] Well, when he does get back, ask him to come over right away. The boss is waiting for him too. [*Hurries off*]

TS'AI-YÜ All right . . . [*Shuts the gate, and looks anxiously at* K'UANG]

K'UANG [*Worried*] What's the matter?

TS'AI-YÜ There's been a lot of trouble at the factory lately, but . . .

K'UANG Where did he go? [*Uneasily*] He wouldn't do anything . . .

TS'AI-YÜ [*Lowers her head*] No, I'm sure he wouldn't, but . . . [*Also feels uneasy*]

[*Amidst the sounds of laughter and cursing, the back gate swings open, and* LI LING-PEI *staggers in drunk, singing to himself. A crowd of women and children, apparently enjoying the scene he is making, follows along behind,* AH-HSIANG *among them.* K'UANG *perks up his ears, but* TS'AI-YÜ *is accustomed to such performances. She glances at the safety razor and pours some water*]

LI [*drunkenly*] You want a song, all right, you'll get one, that's nothing to me . . . [*Sings*] "The sun is sinking, the moon is rising, it is twilight. . . . When I gaze on the lovely child, I can hold back no longer, the tears fall like pearls from my eyes. . . ."

VOICE [*Outside the gate*]Great! About as good as the master Ma Lien-liang![6]

SECOND VOICE One more verse!

THIRD VOICE Hey, Li Ling-pei! Your "lovely child" is dead! Dead!

LI [*Suddenly turns around*] Goddamn it, who says so, who says so? Our Ah-ch'ing is a general; he may be a division commander, or a commissioner, or maybe . . . maybe . . .

FIRST VOICE Or maybe he's cannon fodder by now!

SECOND VOICE Don't interrupt him; let him sing!

LI [*Threatening a child by the gate with his fist*] Goddamn it, even you dare to treat me bad too, huh? [*The children give a yell and scatter, then with a sound of laughter begin to gather again*] When Ah-ch'ing comes back a general, I'll be . . . [*Speech thickening*] the Patriarch, goddamn it . . . [*Walks up to* CHAO CHEN-YÜ *and rudely snatches his newspaper away, then points to it*] Mr. . . . Mr. . . . Mr. Chao, is there anything in the paper about General Li, General Li Ah-ch'ing coming to Shanghai? [CHAO *smiles at him*] When there is, you . . .you tell me, and I . . . I'll buy you a drink! [*Returns the newspaper*] Goddamn it, one fine day Ah-ch'ing'll come home . . . [*Lurches upstairs, singing plaintively*] "With tears of sorrow, I enter the camp. My brows are knit in worry; I am hungry and cold, trembling . . ."

CHAO [*Gets to his feet and disperses the onlookers*] Nothing to see here. . . . [*Turns his head and spots* AH-HSIANG, *grabs her*] So you're enjoying the show too. I've told you before, when Li Ling-pei comes around, you're not to laugh. You . . . you . . . [*Unconcerned whether or not she understands him*] You just exult in another person's pain, don't you? That, that . . . [*The sky grows even darker.* TS'AI-YÜ *turns on a lamp and, after pouring out some water for* K'UANG, *watches him*]

K'UANG What was that all about?

TS'AI-YÜ The roomer in the attic, a strange man. He had an only son, who joined the army during the January 28 Campaign against the Japanese and was killed.[7] They never found the body. He insists that his son is still alive, and is a general. He's not quite right in the head.

K'UANG Mm . . . [*Is affected by this; begins to shave*]

LI'S VOICE [*Plaintively*] ". . . I can hold back no longer, the tears fall like pearls from my eyes. . . ."

[HUANG'S FATHER *comes down the stairs holding the boy. There is distant thunder*]

KUEI-FEN [*From the garret door*] Dad, it's late, don't take him out!

[HUANG'S FATHER *has not heard this; he sees* CHAO *and waves to him eagerly*]

CHAO Mr. Huang! It's going to rain!

HUANG'S FATHER [*Has not heard this either*] I'm going back home tonight, so I'm holding him a little extra, ha, ha . . . [*With a touch of sadness*]

CHAO What's that, going back to the country? Didn't you say they were [*Turns to ask his wife*] going to the theater tonight? [HUANG *leans out the window*]

HUANG'S FATHER Too much rain this year; I've got to replant the spring shoots in the lower fields.

CHAO Enjoy yourself a few more days. There are a lot more places to see in Shanghai.

HUANG'S FATHER [*Playing with the child; to himself*] All right, all right, let's go out and I'll get you something to eat. . . . [*Just as he is about to step out the gate, there is a flash of lightning and a clap of thunder. He turns around and looks at the sky; to* CHAO] That's why I say the world has changed. When we were young, there would always be thunder with the lightning, but now that it's the Republic, the lightning doesn't make a sound any more, right? They say, "The thunder god's drum is broken."

CHAO What do you mean? Wasn't that thunder just now? [*After a moment of consideration, understands*] Ha, ha . . . [*Loudly*] Mr. Huang! The thunder god's drum isn't broken; it still makes a noise. You're hard of hearing, so you just can't hear it, ha, ha, ha . . .

HUANG'S FATHER What's that? What I say is if there isn't any thunder, the spring flowers will . . .

CHAO [*Suppresses his laughter with some effort; to his wife*] Did you hear that? He said now that it's the Republic, there's no thunder any more, ha, ha, ha— [*Earnestly to* HUANG'S FATHER] The thunder in the sky is electricity, and it makes a noise even with a change of rule. . . . [*Another roll of distant thunder*] Yes, yes, there it goes again.

HUANG'S FATHER [*Puzzled*] What's that? In the sky . . .

CHAO [*Loudly*] The thunder in the sky isn't a bodhisattva, it's electricity, [*Into his ear*] electricity!

HUANG'S FATHER [*Still uncomprehending*] City? What about the city?

CHAO [*Loudly*] Electricity, like in an electric light . . .

CHAO'S WIFE We're out of soy sauce, go get some!

CHAO [*Loudly*] The clouds in the sky have a kind of electricity in them, elec—

CHAO'S WIFE [*Holds the soy sauce bottle under his nose*] Go buy some soy sauce!

CHAO [*Without thinking, to his wife in an even louder voice*] Have Ah-niu go buy it!

CHAO'S WIFE [*Startled, then angrily*] I'm not deaf! [*The usually melancholy* HUANG *finds himself smiling at this*]

CHAO [*With sudden realization*] Ah, right you are. [*Softly*] Have Ah-niu go buy it, all right? [*Turns back to* HUANG'S FATHER; *softly*] There's a kind of electricity in the sky. . . .

CHAO'S WIFE [*Angrily*] Ah-niu's studying. [*Stuffs the soy sauce bottle into his hand*]

CHAO [*Out of excuses; to* HUANG'S FATHER, *loudly*] Wait, I'll be right back. [*Exit*]

HUANG'S FATHER [*Confused; to* CHAO'S WIFE] What was he talking about? Hm, my bad ears . . . [*Turns and goes upstairs*]

KUEI-FEN [*Just coming down with a pail; on the stairs*] Be careful, Dad. [*Turns on the stairway light*]

HUANG'S FATHER [*Startled*] Mm . . . [*Looks at the light, then continues upstairs*]

CHAO'S WIFE [*Notices* KUEI-FEN *coming down*] Say, why is your father-in-law going back tonight? [KUEI-FEN *nods but makes no reply*] Is there something urgent? At home?

KUEI-FEN Older people sometimes act a little funny! He just upped and said he wanted to go, and off he's going tonight.

CHAO'S WIFE [*Surreptitiously*] You know, [*Points to the parlor, softly*] Mrs. Lin's former husband . . .

CHAO [*Re-enters and sees his wife's expression*] Incorrigible! I keep telling you not to meddle in other people's business, and that goes for other people's husbands too.

CHAO'S WIFE [*Interrupting angrily*] Pah! [*In a low voice*] Then what are you doing meddling in mine?

CHAO [*Scratches his head; suddenly remembers something*] Ah, where's old Mr. Huang from upstairs? We haven't finished our conversation.

CHAO'S WIFE [*To* KUEI-FEN, *surreptitiously as before*] Just now I heard Lin tell him such and such about Pao-chen. . . . [*When* AH-HSIANG *comes over to listen in, angrily*] What are you listening for? Little brat! [*Again to* KUEI-FEN] Lin ran off, and I just now heard her crying. Good heavens, it's really a mess! Have you seen him?

KUEI-FEN [*Shaking her head*] Is he still here?

CHAO'S WIFE [*Nodding*] Mm hm, with rags on his back, like Hsüeh P'ing-kuei in the play . . .[8]

[*She is about to go on, but* LIN CHIH-CH'ENG, *exuberant, enters through the back gate. She quickly swallows what she was going to say and assumes a bland expression. He has a bottle of liquor and some snacks; as usual, he ignores everyone as he walks in*]

CHAO [*Noticing him*] Oh, Mr. Lin! [*Stands and points to a newspaper item*] Today your factory— [*When* LIN *walks on past, seemingly oblivious,* CHAO *sits down again.* CHAO'S WIFE *excitedly watches* LIN *walk away*]

TS'AI-YÜ [*Looks at* K'UANG, *now clean shaven*] Now, don't you feel a lot younger?

[*When* LIN *enters without saying a word,* TS'AI-YÜ *and* K'UANG *step away from each other, the latter feeling somewhat ill at ease*]

TS'AI-YÜ Young Ch'en from the factory was here just now; he said they want you.

LIN [*Morosely*] I know. [*Hands* TS'AI-YÜ *the bottle and the food*]

TS'AI-YÜ Is there something the matter at the factory? He said they want you to come right away.

LIN I know. We were out of food, so I went to the little place on the corner and ordered a few dishes. [*To* K'UANG] I thought we'd do a little drinking tonight.

K'UANG Chih-ch'eng, you—

LIN [*With unnatural joviality*] Fu-sheng! It's been a long time since we've had a meal together. You don't drink, I know, but you've got to have a glass tonight. I haven't had a drink in a long time myself, but I feel very good today. You'll be glad to know I've been liberated.

K'UANG [*Pained*] Chih-ch'eng, don't talk like that.

LIN No, no, I feel so relieved now. I've been freed from the life I've been living: taking it from one side and dishing it out to the other. [*Loudly*] I'm out of a job, but from now on I don't have to act against my own conscience toward anyone.

K'UANG and TS'AI-YÜ [*Almost simultaneously*] What have you . . .

LIN Ridiculous, wanting me to go out and hire gangsters to beat somebody up. Hah! Why should I do a filthy job like that? I quit instead! Hah, what a relief! Head of the Labor Section, always so high and mighty, [*Gets increasingly excited*] well, I saw through him today! [*To* TS'AI-YÜ] How about fixing something to eat?

K'UANG [*Concerned*] Relax a little, Chih-ch'eng; you look exhausted!

LIN No, no, I feel just fine. A big stone that's been pressing down on my mind has finally been taken away! Fu-sheng! It's strange, isn't it? I was always afraid of losing my job. Whenever they were making noises at the factory about letting people go, I'd always go in and take a look at the head man's expression. And whenever he'd send for me, I could feel all the blood in my body rushing to my face. But today when he got blue in the face, pounded on the desk, and said, "Get out!" I wasn't frightened a bit, I was very calm. I can hardly believe it myself.

TS'AI-YÜ [*Carrying a basin of water to him*] You . . .

LIN [*Still in a state of excitement*] Plant manager isn't a job for a human being at all. The ones over you treat you like an ox, and to the ones under you you're a dog. From morning to night, nobody, top or bottom, will give you the time of day. But now I don't have to take the rap for anybody; I don't have to be treated like a dog by anybody. [*Hysterically*] Ha, ha, ha.

K'UANG Don't get too excited now, Chih-ch'eng—

LIN But first of all, you've got to be happy for me, that I got out of that kind of life!

TS'AI-YÜ [*Unable to keep from asking*] Then from now on you—

LIN From now on. Hm. [*Washes his face*]

[*At this moment* CHAO'S WIFE *seizes an opportunity to peer in; meanwhile* AH-HSIANG, *seeing that her mother is absent, makes a beeline out the gate*]

CHAO Ah-hsiang, Ah-hsiang!

[CHAO'S WIFE *glances back. A restaurant delivery boy enters through*

the back gate with a food basket and heads upstairs. He knocks at SHIH
HSIAO-PAO *'s door and, when there is no answer, peeks through the crack
in the door. He puts the basket down before the door and leaves*]

LIN [*Finished washing his face; with* TS'AI-YÜ *gone to prepare dinner,
    walks up to* K'UANG *and is about to say something, then hesitates*] Uh,
    Fu-sheng!

K'UANG Yes?

LIN Can we still be friends . . . the way we were before?

K'UANG Of course . . . but about this matter, I still have to . . . no, ahh,
    I just don't know what to say. . . .

[LIN *sits down dejectedly.* CHAO'S WIFE *returns to her room, finds*
AH-HSIANG *gone, and runs to the gate*]

CHAO'S WIFE Ah-hsiang, Ah-hsiang! [*Goes out the gate, then comes in
    dragging* AH-HSIANG] Twerp! Fooling around outside all day, don't
    you want to eat anything?

[*On the landing,* KUEI-FEN *is cooking on the kerosene stove.* TS'AI-YÜ
goes out to buy groceries]

LIN [*Routinely*] Isn't Pao-chen back yet? Ts'ai-yü, go look for Pao-chen!

[*Outside the gate, the sounds of peddlers as usual*]

[*Curtain*]

ACT III

The evening of the same day. In the parlor, after dinner, LIN CHIH-CH'ENG
has had a little too much to drink and is slumped in a chair. TS'AI-YÜ *is silently
gathering up the dishes.* K'UANG FU *is engrossed in a conversation with*
PAO-CHEN, *while* AH-HSIANG *sits beside them, staring at* K'UANG.

The room above the parlor is dark and empty.

In the garret, KUEI-FEN *is busy packing her father-in-law's things.*

In the scullery, CHAO CHEN-YÜ *is contentedly reading a book; he frequently
waves his head back and forth while reciting a passage. In one hand he holds
a rush fan, with which he mechanically drives off the mosquitoes.* CHAO'S WIFE
is wiping her hands after having finished washing the dishes. AH-NIU *is bent
over his homework at the table.*

*There is the sound of rain. In the distance, a popular Cantonese song can
be heard on a radio. When the curtain rises,* K'UANG FU *and* PAO-CHEN *are
laughing.*

K'UANG Now that's interesting.

PAO-CHEN [*With a touch of self-satisfaction*] That kind of thing happens
    a lot. When a "little teacher" holds class, the grownups sometimes like
    to make trouble. For example, we would ask, "Do you understand
    that? Those who do raise your hands." At that point they would stick
    their feet up, just to have fun with us. So I told everybody, "Don't pay
    any attention to them. Grownups who don't know how to behave are
    worse than we children." The children ignored them and studied as
    usual, and later on they stopped trying to fight me.

K'UANG Hm . . .

PAO-CHEN The "middle teacher" who teaches us said to me that they must have been thinking how humiliating it was for a child to know something they didn't.

K'UANG Are there a lot of those "big students"?

PAO-CHEN I teach five: a fruit seller, a laborer— There's an old man whose grandson is as tall as I am.

K'UANG Then you . . .

AH-HSIANG Pao-chen, teach me a song.

PAO-CHEN Wait a minute for your brother to get here. I'm teaching him a really good one.

AH-HSIANG I still haven't learned the one you taught me yesterday.

PAO-CHEN Yesterday's? Hm . . . [*As she goes through the song on the piano,* K'UANG *avidly watches them*]

AH-NIU [*Taking his schoolbook over to his father*] Dad, "'A' saves sixty-five dollars a month; after three years and eight months, what do his total savings come to?" What's the answer?

CHAO [*Assuming a strict attitude*] Ah-niu! If you bother me again when I'm reading, you can forget about hearing any more of my stories.

AH-NIU [*Goes to his mother*] Mom, somebody saves sixty-five dollars every month; after three years and eight months, how much does he have altogether?

CHAO'S WIFE Saves money? Who is that, pray tell? If we don't run into debt we're doing all right. Think we have anything left over? Sixty-five dollars every month! Are you dreaming?

AH-NIU It's in the book.

CHAO'S WIFE What does something in a book have to do with us? Sixty-five dollars, hah! If your dad has six dollars and fifty cents left every month, it's a miracle!

AH-NIU [*Can do nothing now but go back to the table*] Three years and eight months, three years, thirty-six months . . .

[HUANG, *holding an umbrella, returns with bananas, apples, and biscuits; he hurries upstairs.*

[LIN CHIH-CH'ENG *tries to stand up, but his legs give way, and he sits down again*]

LIN Hm, I have such a feeling of relief tonight!

HUANG [*Loudly*] I told you before not to buy anything; take it back to the store, go on, take it back!

KUEI-FEN [*Loudly*] It's nothing much, just a snack for the trip.

HUANG'S FATHER I don't want anything! Chia-mei, I can't eat that foreign stuff. . . .

TS'AI-YÜ [*Helps* LIN *to his feet*] You've had too much; go to bed.

LIN No, no, just a drop or two . . .

K'UANG Go take a rest, Chih-ch'eng! I—I—

LIN No, no, I want to have a talk with you. [TS'AI-YÜ *helps him into the back room*]

AH-NIU [*Once again takes the book to his mother*] Mom, a man named Wang gets paid three hundred and fifty dollars a month, and a man named Li get two hundred and eighty. After three years, what's—

CHAO'S WIFE [*Before he can finish; as if exploding*] I don't want to hear any more of that business! Your dad doesn't even make thirty-five dollars a month!

CHAO [*Startled*] What's that?

AH-NIU [*Pleading*] Tell me! The teacher's going to ask me tomorrow. It's something in the book. A man named Wang gets three hundred and fifty dollars a month . . .

CHAO'S WIFE [*Irritably*] Go ask somebody who's rich; I've never laid eyes on three hundred and fifty dollars in my whole life!

AH-NIU [*In resignation goes to his father*] Dad, after three years, what's the difference between the amount of money each one has?

CHAO Mm, mm, three hundred and fifty and two hundred and what?

AH-NIU Two hundred and eighty . . .

CHAO What you have to do first is find out the difference between the two men's salaries of one month, do you get that? [*Does some calculations with his pen*]

CHAO'S WIFE [*Still incensed*] Three hundred and fifty dollars a month salary, saves sixty-five dollars a month, fantastic!

AH-NIU [*Turns around in rebuttal*] It's in the book!

CHAO'S WIFE In the book, huh? This kind of book is for the rich people!

CHAO [*To* AH-NIU] Hey, hey, look, look at what I'm doing here.

[TS'AI-YÜ *waits for* LIN *to get into bed, then pours a cup of tea and places it on the bedside table*]

TS'AI-YÜ Would you like some tea?

[LIN *mumbles a reply, as if already asleep. She puts a small quilt over him. Carefully opening a chest with a key, she takes out a large quilt and spreads it over a smaller bed. She then takes the pillow from the small bed into the parlor.*

[PAO-CHEN *has finished teaching her song*]

K'UANG [*With great enthusiasm*] Hm, then on rainy days like these, don't your students skip class? They're all . . .

PAO-CHEN [*Proudly*] Not a bit. Not only on rainy days, they come even when it's snowing, and they're not a minute late. They're more on time even than the students at school assembly. A few days ago a fruit seller's kid—

TS'AI-YÜ [*Interrupts*] Calling the others kids makes you an adult, I suppose? [*Laughs*]

PAO-CHEN A fruit seller's daughter was coming to learn how to read. When somebody outside yelled, "Anybody have any bananas for sale?" she didn't even answer but ran straight over to us with basket and everything.

K'UANG Hm, that's a good story. But I'll tell you something: when we were little, we'd always pretend to have a stomachache and ask the teacher to let us stay home.

PAO-CHEN [*Innocently*] Then you weren't a very good student!

Ts'AI-YÜ Pao-chen!

PAO-CHEN If one of our students gets lazy and doesn't come to class, the next time he has to write on the board! "So and so is a lazybones and doesn't work"!

K'UANG [*Unable to keep from laughing; then off guard*] But when you were little, you used to be lazy too!

PAO-CHEN I was? How did you know that? [Ts'AI-YÜ *gives* K'UANG FU *a warning glance*]

K'UANG Ah, that's not right; I was talking about my own daughter. She's the same age as you. . . .

PAO-CHEN [*Looks at* K'UANG FU *closely, then at* Ts'AI-YÜ] Mom! [*Steps away*] I have a question to ask you.

Ts'AI-YÜ What? [*Follows her*]

PAO-CHEN [*Softly, so that* K'UANG FU *cannot hear*] Just now Mrs. Chao told me— [*Whispers in her ear*] . . . is that right? [*Glances at* K'UANG FU]

Ts'AI-YÜ [*Somewhat embarrassed*] Nonsense! Oh, don't bother about it—that's something that concerns grownups; just don't bother about that.

PAO-CHEN [*Pouting*] I'm a grownup now. Tell me, come on, tell me, is it the truth? Hey . . . [*Leans up so that her ear is close to her mother's mouth*]

Ts'AI-YÜ What a nuisance; you're such a busybody!

PAO-CHEN Is it true? Nod your head if it is!

Ts'AI-YÜ Busybody! [*Nods*]

PAO-CHEN Ah! [*Jumps up and looks at* K'UANG FU *without blinking*] [LIN CHIH-CH'ENG *turns over, listening*]

K'UANG [*Unmindful now of anything else; walks toward her*] Pao-chen! Say it to me! Say it to me!

PAO-CHEN [*Faltering*] Da— [*Runs away bashfully*] . . . Ah-niu! Ah-niu!

K'UANG [*Breaking out in fresh, spontaneous laughter, in sharp contrast to his previous melancholy and taciturnity*] Ha, ha . . . [*The laughter arouses* LIN CHIH-CH'ENG; *he sits up and listens*]

AH-NIU I'm busy! You come over here!

Ts'AI-YÜ [*Joyfully*] Do you think she . . .

K'UANG There's a saying from overseas, "We live through our issue"! The spirit I had ten years ago still survives in Pao-chen. She has taught me so much!

Ts'AI-YÜ [*Gripping his hand*] That's right, and you're still young. For her sake, you should try all the harder now! [*Picks up a mirror from the table and holds it up to him*] See? [*Laughs*]

K'UANG Oh, I'm so grateful to you. And you too should—

Ts'AI-YÜ Fu-sheng! [*They embrace*]

PAO-CHEN [*At the door of the back room*] Ah-niu, come on, I'll teach you a song!

AH-NIU Wait a minute. Figure it out for me; "A" gets a salary of three hundred and fifty dollars a month, and "B" gets . . .

CHAO'S WIFE [*Furiously*] I don't want to hear any more about it! If you have to do your arithmetic, go to the front room. [*Muttering*] Three hundred and fifty indeed. . . .

CHAO Ha, ha . . .

[*Making a face,* AH-NIU *tiptoes to the parlor. On hearing his approach,* TS'AI-YÜ *steps away*]

TS'AI-YÜ [*Pointing to* K'UANG FU*'s shirt*] Oh, it's torn here. Take it off and I'll mend it for you. You won't get too cold, will you?

K'UANG [*Taking off his shirt*] No, no, it's so hot and humid.

TS'AI-YÜ [*Hands him his jacket, now dried*] You're not very strong. If you're not careful, you'll catch a chill. . . .

PAO-CHEN [*To* AH-NIU] Where's your dad? Go get him to tell a story.

AH-NIU Let's sing first, then he'll come over.

[PAO-CHEN *brings out her toy piano and a song book.*]

[*After mulling things over for a long while,* LIN CHIH-CH'ENG *gets up in a determined manner, then holds his head in his hands, thinking.*]

[HUANG CHIA-MEI *glumly comes downstairs carrying a net basket*]

KUEI-FEN [*At the garret door*] Chia-mei, we need three rickshaws.

HUANG [*Turns his head*] What's that?

KUEI-FEN I'm going too.

HUANG Then the baby will wake up. . . .

KUEI-FEN It won't matter if he does. I've arranged with Mrs. Chao to look after him. [HUANG CHIA-MEI *puts the basket under the stairs and leaves to get the rickshaws.* AH-HSIANG *sneaks out in the direction of the parlor*]

CHAO [*To his wife*] Huh, is he really leaving? [*She pays no attention.* CHAO *stretches*] Ah, ah . . . Where's Ah-niu? Ah-hsiang! [*Stealthily gets to his feet and glances at his wife, thinks about sneaking away as well, but just as he is about to move*]

CHAO'S WIFE Where are you going?

CHAO Nowhere; I'm going to look for Ah-hsiang!

CHAO'S WIFE No you don't! Forgetting your own age and learning songs from children; aren't you ashamed?

CHAO What's the matter with that? Confucius said that to feel no shame—

CHAO'S WIFE [*In swift counterattack*] I don't want to hear about your precious Confucius!

[*From outside the gate come sounds of rickshaws and voices*]

HUANG'S VOICE Come in and get the luggage! [*Enters and shouts upstairs*] The rickshaws are here!

KUEI-FEN'S VOICE You come up! Papa won't let me carry the luggage!

VOICE OF HUANG'S FATHER It's not heavy, not heavy at all. . . .

HUANG [*Calling to a rickshaw man*] The net basket goes. [*Turns to* CHAO]Mr. Chao, sorry, but would you mind keeping an eye on things?

CHAO Fine, fine.

HUANG [*Going upstairs*] I'll get it, Dad!

HUANG'S FATHER [*Comes down carrying an old-fashioned chest*] If

I can't even manage this little thing, how am I supposed to do any planting? Have to haul a load of rice too. . . . [*Refuses* CHIA-MEI's offer of help]

HUANG Dad, let the rickshaw man . . .

KUEI-FEN [*Comes down holding the boy*] Heavens, older people are really— [*Turns the light off in the garret*]

CHAO [*Sticks up his thumb toward* HUANG'S FATHER]Bravo! Bravo!

HUANG'S FATHER [*Proudly*] That's nothing; when I was young, I used to haul two hundred pounds of grain and still . . . [*When a drop of rain from the eaves falls on his neck, looks up at the sky*] Still raining? Damn! The lord in heaven never gives poor people a break! Got to get back right away! The land by Hsia's Pond must be washed away by now! [*When a rickshaw man comes up to take the luggage, he is refused firmly, but to* HUANG, *as if suddenly remembering something*] Keep an eye on this! I . . .

KUEI-FEN Mrs. Chao, I'm really sorry to trouble you with the baby. He's sleeping right now. . . .

CHAO'S WIFE Fine, I'll hold him. . . .

HUANG'S FATHER [*Comes back in*] Let me hold him one more time. [*Takes the baby*] Mm, sound asleep. [*Leans down and nuzzles him*] Mm, mm, I'm not getting any younger, and I never know what the next day is going to bring. [*Half to* HUANG, *half to himself*] You never come out to the farm, and I can't come to see you very often. Maybe . . . I won't be able to hold him too many more times. Mm, one more time. [*To* KUEI-FEN] Take good care of him now. Let him eat all he wants, and whatever he wants. None of this foreign business about several hours between meals; you'll starve him to skin and bones that way! [*When no one is looking, stuffs a paper envelope into the child's clothing*] Ha, ha, ha . . . [*To* CHAO] Once you've held your own grandson, you've lived a full life. Ha, ha . . .

CHAO [*Loudly into his ear*] Fortune has been good to you!

HUANG'S FATHER [*Joyfully*] Thank you! Goodbye! [*Gives the child to* KUEI-FEN, *who puts him on the Chaos' bed*]

HUANG Mr. Chao, I'm sorry to trouble you like this!

CHAO Not at all.

HUANG'S FATHER [*At the gate, turns back once more to* CHAO CHEN-YÜ *and the others*] Come on down to the country and see us some time! Ha, ha . . .

[HUANG CHIA-MEI *and his wife exit with* HUANG'S FATHER. *The sound of rickshaw men shouting is heard*]

CHAO'S WIFE Ah-niu! Ah-hsiang! [*The steadily increasing rain pours through the drainspouts*] Damn, it just keeps on raining; for most of the month, drip drip drip!

CHAO What are you upset about? So it keeps on raining; it'll clear up some day.

CHAO'S WIFE It'll clear up, huh? Take a look for yourself!

CHAO [*Placidly*] Even so, do you say the rain will last all year?

CHAO'S WIFE [*Angrily*] I'm through talking to you! [*Sees* CHAO *timidly sneaking out*] Where do you think you're going?

CHAO Uh, I'm going to check on Ah-niu. . . .

CHAO'S WIFE To check on Ah-niu! We don't even have any money for groceries tomorrow, and it seems it's up to me alone to run this household; as soon as you get home, it's read your newspaper, read your books, blather on about God knows what, and sing songs with the children, not giving a damn about anything to do with household . . .

[CHAO CHEN-YÜ *is aware that she is off on another of her tirades and quickens his steps in the direction of the parlor. In the back room,* LIN CHIH-CH'ENG, *after a siege of agonized reflection, gets to his feet, as if he has settled on a plan of action. He stands in the dark, absorbed in thought and listening to the conversation in the front room*]

PAO-CHEN When I raise my hand, [*To* AH-NIU *and* AH-HSIANG] sing in unison, and when I drop my hand, listen to me sing the solo, got that?

AH-HSIANG [*Shaking her head*] I don't know it!

PAO-CHEN Listen to me play it through first!

TS'AI-YÜ [*Finished with the mending*] Finished. Now put it on; it's going to cool off soon. [*Puts it on him*]

CHAO [*Steps in, mistakes* K'UANG, *whose back is toward him, for* LIN CHIH-CH'ENG] Ah, Mr. Lin, didn't your factory have a big— [*When* K'UANG *turns his head in* CHAO'*s direction*] Ah, I'm sorry, uh, uh . . . [*To* TS'AI-YÜ] Where is Mr. Lin? Has he gone out? I—I was—

K'UANG [*A bit ill at ease*] Your name, sir?

CHAO [*Searches a long time for a name card but cannot find one*] Ah, ah, I'm Chao Chen-yü. May I ask . . .

TS'AI-YÜ [*Speaking for* K'UANG] Mr. K'uang, Chih-ch'eng's old classmate . . .

CHAO Oh, [*Offers his hand*] it's a pleasure. . . . ha, ha . . . Mr. Lin and I really get along very very well—

AH-NIU [*Before he can finish*] Come on, Dad, tell us a story!

CHAO What, a story? Haven't I finished telling it?

AH-NIU [*Pushing him*] Tell us one!

CHAO Ha, ha . . . We have a visitor today, and we're talking. Uh, sing some songs, why don't you?

PAO-CHEN No, no, tell us a story first, and after you get through, I'll teach you a fine song, one I just learned today!

CHAO [*To* K'UANG] Will you look at them, always wanting me to tell . . . ha, ha, what'll I tell this time? Say, how about an old favorite, one about Napoleon . . .

AH-HSIANG No, you've told us about Napoleon ten times already.

CHAO But you've forgotten what I just asked you, haven't you? When Napoleon was sent in exile to Elba, what did he say?

AH-HSIANG No, no!

CHAO Well . . . well then, you sing your songs now and let me think of something. . . . [*Turns back and glances into the room, then to* Ts'AI-YÜ] Has Mr. Lin gone out?

Ts'AI-YÜ No, he had a little too much to drink and is sleeping in back. . . .

CHAO Hm? Mr. Lin, drinking? That's strange, I thought he never used to touch it.

AH-NIU Dad, listen to this, "Brave little children . . ."

[PAO-CHEN *plays the piano. Meanwhile,* LIN *quietly packs some things together in the back room, as if preparing to leave.* Ts'AI-YÜ, *reminded by* CHAO, *goes to the back room to look in on him and is astonished to see him standing in the dark*]

Ts'AI-YÜ Oh dear, you're up? [K'UANG *listens to this intently, while* CHAO *and his children are listening to* PAO-CHEN *teaching her song.* LIN *gestures to her to be quiet*] What's the matter with you? [*Turns on the light*] Aren't you feeling well? [*Sees that he is packing and stops in surprise*] What are you doing?

[*In the lane, a wonton peddler shouts*]

CHAO Who taught it to you?

PAO-CHEN Never mind about that. I'll teach it to you now. [*Plays the piano*]

Ts'AI-YÜ [*Alarmed, but softly*] Chih-ch'eng! What are you doing? You—

LIN [*Looks at her without replying, then, as if having made up his mind, stretches out his hand to her*] I have to be going now, Ts'ai-yü.

Ts'AI-YÜ [*Going?* [*Grips his hand*]

LIN [*Nods*] I've nothing to worry about now, and it's time for me to leave.

Ts'AI-YÜ But . . . [*Turns and is about to call to* K'UANG *but is pulled back by* LIN]

LIN [*Softly*] Don't let Fu-sheng find out; let me go quietly! [*Grips* Ts'AI-YÜ*'s hand again*] I wish you both well.

Ts'AI-YÜ No, no, Chih-ch'eng, where are you going?

LIN [*Shakes his head*] Right now I don't know myself, but no matter what . . .

Ts'AI-YÜ [*Panicky*] What do you mean? Are you going to—

LIN [*Stops her*] No, I'm free now, and content. Just as long as you and Fu-sheng can forgive me, I'll have peace of mind. [K'UANG *is listening closely, his expression troubled*]

Ts'AI-YÜ [*Weeping*] But you . . .

LIN Don't cry! No matter what, the world has a lot of room in it, and there has to be one place where I won't be the odd man out. All right then! Ts'ai-yü! Forget about me, forget all about me. Look on these past eight years as a dream.

Ts'AI-YÜ No, no, you can't go, I— I can't let you go— I know, [*Weeping*] I know you don't want to leave us—

LIN [*In a burst of emotion*] Ts'ai-yü! [*Holds her tightly as she sobs*] [K'UANG *is standing, lost in thought*]

PAO-CHEN Good, now watch my hand, one, two, three . . . [*Sings*]
            "Little children, little children,
              Everyone clasp hands and join in the game!"

ALL [*In unison*]   "Little children, little children,
                    Everyone clasp hands and join in the game!"
PAO-CHEN [*Sings*] "Who is a brave little child?"
ALL [*In unison*]   "I am, I am!"
PAO-CHEN [*Sings*] "Let me ask you this."
ALL [*In unison*]   "Go ahead and ask, go ahead and ask!"
PAO-CHEN [*Sings*] "If the bandits come, will you fight?"
ALL [*In unison*]   "We'll fight, we'll fight!
                    If one's not enough, everybody help!"
PAO-CHEN [*Sings*] "Right! If one's not enough, everybody help!
                    When you walk in the dark, are you afraid?"
ALL [*In unison*]   "I'm not afraid, I'm not afraid!
                    If I fall, I can pick myself up!"
PAO-CHEN [*Sings*] "Right! If I fall, I can pick myself up!"
[K'UANG FU *becomes absorbed in their song*]
PAO-CHEN [*Sings*] "When you cry, are you foolish or not?"
ALL [*In unison*]   "You're foolish, you're foolish,
                    You're a good-for-nothing fool!"
PAO-CHEN [*Sings*] "Right! You're a good-for-nothing fool!
                    When the going is rough, are you afraid?"
ALL [*In unison*]   "I'm not afraid, I'm not afraid!
                    The rougher it gets, the braver I am!"
PAO-CHEN [*Sings*] "Right! The rougher it gets, the braver I am!
                    Good! We're all brave little children!
                    All uniting to save our country!"
ALL [*In unison*]   "Save our country!"
{PAO-CHEN
{ALL [*In unison*]} "Good! We're all brave little children!
                    All uniting to save our country! Save our country!"
[*The children and* CHAO *applaud enthusiastically*]
CHAO That was wonderful! "When you cry, are you foolish or not?"
    That's in the story about Napoleon too. Napoleon had never cried
    before, so—
AH-NIU Pao-chen, sing the first few lines again by yourself!
PAO-CHEN You still don't get it? You really are an ox— [*Looks at*
    CHAO *and laughs*] Then listen! [*Softly sings again, everyone joining
    in*]
[K'UANG *comes to a decision, and his expression is no longer
as forlorn as before. As if to keep* PAO-CHEN *and the others from
noticing, he takes up a pen, leans over the desk, and writes something.
He then stands and walks over to* PAO-CHEN]
K'UANG Pao-chen! Come here! Let me look at you!
PAO-CHEN [*Stops singing; surprised*] What's the matter? Don't you think
    we sing well?
K'UANG [*Nods emphatically*] You sing very well, Pao-chen. You deserve
    to be a "little teacher"; you've certainly taught me a lot!
[*Upon hearing* K'UANG's *voice*, LIN *and* TS'AI-YÜ *fall silent*]
PAO-CHEN [*Innocently*] You sing too, okay?

K'UANG No, no, it's all clear in my mind now, Pao-chen! Let me have another look at you! [*Is overcome with emotion; kisses her tenderly*] You be a brave little child now! My blessings go with you, through the rest of your life! Goodbye!

PAO-CHEN [*Changes from shyness to surprise*] What do you mean? Are you going? Da—

K'UANG [*Stops her*] Goodbye! [*Holds her tightly, then, taking his hat and stepping out into the rain, quickly pulls the gate open and is gone*]

PAO-CHEN [*Puzzled, as she watches him leave*] Mom! Daddy—is going away! [AH-NIU, AH-HSIANG, *and* CHAO *are at a loss.* LIN *and* TS'AI-YÜ *run out,* TS'AI-YÜ *wiping her eyes with her sleeve*]

LIN What's happened?

TS'AI-YÜ Going away?! [*Sees the note on the table*]

LIN [*Snatches up the note*] He . . .

TS'AI-YÜ What does it say?

LIN [*Reading aloud in a puzzled tone*] "It makes me very happy to know now that your life together means more than just survival! I realize that by staying on, I would be disturbing the peace you share. . . . I shall always love you both. . . ."

TS'AI-YÜ [*Half crazed*]Fu-sheng! [*Rushes out into the rain without waiting for* LIN] Fu-sheng!

LIN [*Comes to his senses*] Yes, I've got to get him back! [*Rushes out*]

CHAO What is going on?

[PAO-CHEN, *shocked, looks at the others.* AH-HSIANG *runs out to look but shrinks back immediately when the cold rain hits her. Amidst the sound of rain and the shouts of the wonton peddler, the back gate squeaks open, and* SHIH HSIAO-PAO *enters. Her clothes are torn, and her hair is awry. Her face is streaked with tears. She almost hurls a handful of coins at a rickshaw man, and half of them fall onto the ground. As the rickshaw man picks up the coins, he stares at her in surprise.* CHAO'S WIFE, *startled from her nap by the noise, looks up, glaring, and sees* SHIH's *sorry condition, then, curious, gets up. While* SHIH *is running straight upstairs,* CHAO'S WIFE *follows her to the staircase and stares upward.* SHIH *runs into her room, turns on the light, and collapses onto the bed, weeping*]

SHIH Johnnie, Johnnie . . . [*sobs*]

CHAO'S WIFE [*With a disgusted expression*] Pah! [*Looks toward the parlor*] Ah-niu! Ah-hsiang! It's late! [*On hearing his wife's shouts,* CHAO *returns on tiptoe*]

CHAO'S WIFE [*Angrily*] You're hopeless, always with those children. . . . Ah-niu! Ah-hsiang!

AH-NIU [*Makes a face*] We're singing. . . .

[*There is a knock at the back gate, and when* CHAO *opens it,* HUANG *and* KUEI-FEN *enter, their clothes drenched*]

HUANG [*Notices* CHAO] Sorry! In all this rain! [*To his wife resentfully*] I said to take a rickshaw, but no, you wanted to walk. . . .

KUEI-FEN [*To* CHAO'S WIFE] Thank you, Mrs. Chao. Did he wake up?

CHAO'S WIFE No, he's been sleeping nicely.

KUEI-FEN [*Holding the child*] Thank you. It's late; see you tomorrow! [*Goes to the staircase, then to* HUANG] Yes, we could have taken a rickshaw, and there would have gone tomorrow's grocery money.... [*Climbs a couple of steps, then turns around, as if having made a sudden discovery*] Chia-mei!

HUANG What?

KUEI-FEN Look! It's . . .[*Takes a red envelope from the child's pocket*] Your father must have left it for him.

HUANG [*His eyes wide with astonishment*] Huh? Let me see! [*As he grabs the envelope, one or two silver dollars roll onto the ground*]

KUEI-FEN [*Snatches them up*] What in the world . . .

HUANG [*Counts out several bills and three silver dollars, then stands stock-still on the stairs, a grief-stricken expression on his pale face*] Probably the only money Dad has left after all the sweat and pain he's been through! [*Bitterly*] We tried to deceive him! We tried to deceive him, but he knew all the time! [KUEI-FEN *suddenly breaks out in tears*]

HUANG [*In sorrow, to the baby*] You must never forget, your grandfather's hopes in me have come to nothing, and now they lie in you!

KUEI-FEN [*Stops him*] Sh, don't wake him up. . . .

[*With her head bent down, she carries her son upstairs, followed by* HUANG. *The garret light comes on, and* KUEI-FEN*'s sobs can be heard faintly. The front gate opens, and* LIN *enters holding* TS'AI-YÜ; *both are soaked by the rain. As if in a daze, they walk into their room and forget to close the door, the children watching them in amazement.* LIN *stands with his head bowed*]

PAO-CHEN Mom, what's the matter?

TS'AI-YÜ [*Paying no attention; after a moment, suddenly to* LIN] He wouldn't . . . he wouldn't take his own life, would he?

LIN [*Startled*] What?

TS'AI-YÜ What if something should happen . . . [*Gives a choked sob*]

LIN [*Gravely*] I think you can rest assured on that score. Look, he says, "Pao-chen has taught me so very much. In leaving you, I am not running in flight, and I will never disappoint you. Live your lives in courage, my friends. Goodbye!" [TS'AI-YÜ *reads the letter*] He will hold onto his courage, for all of us who suffer . . .

TS'AI-YÜ [*Bursts out in bitter weeping*] Fu-sheng!

[*Without a word* LIN *steps up and puts his arm around her heaving shoulders. There is the sound of rain.* PAO-CHEN *walks over and tugs at her mother's dress.*

[LI LING-PEI *comes down from the attic, one step at a time, singing sadly to himself*]

LI [*Sings*] "Day after day, burning oil pours onto my heart . . ."

AH-NIU [*Frowns toward* PAO-CHEN *and* AH-HSIANG] Oh, there goes Li Ling-pei again. Don't listen to him; let's sing! [*Sings*] "When you cry, are you foolish or not?"

AH-NIU and AH-HSIANG [*In unison*] "You're foolish, you're foolish,
You're a good-for-nothing fool!"

PAO-CHEN [*Joins in*]
"Right! You're a good-for-nothing fool!
When the going gets rough, are you afraid?"

AH-NIU and AH-HSIANG [*In unison*]
"You're foolish, you're foolish,
You're a good-for-nothing fool!"

PAO-CHEN [*Sings*] "Right! The rougher it gets, the braver I am!"

[LIN *and* TS'AI-YÜ *realize what the children are singing and look up. While his wife is turned the other way,* CHAO *comes in again on tiptoe and listens to the children sing*]

ALL [*In unison*] "Good! We're all brave little children,
All uniting to save our country! Save our country!"

[*During the song, the curtain slowly falls*]

[*Final curtain*]

Notes

1. "Niu" means "ox." Along with the southern familiar prefix "ah" it makes up the boy's childhood name; on formal occasions he would be called by his legal given name, "Ch'en." In the same way, "Ah-hsiang" is his sister's childhood name or "milk name."

2. "Ah-t'o" is a derisive term for "stepchild."

3. The Three Companies refers to three leading department stores, Sincere (Hsien-shih), Wing-on (Yung-an), and Hsin-hsin, since taken over in Shanghai by the state and redesignated by numbers (although in Hong Kong the companies have remained in business under their old names). In Shanghai these stores are located on or adjacent to Nanking Road (Ta-ma lu), one of two major commercial thoroughfares in the former International Settlement.

4. "Savings" is a euphemism for a mandatory deduction from a worker's wages.

5. "Floating corpses" were those of miners and factory workers tossed into rivers after they had been beaten or collapsed from exhaustion under abusive labor conditions. During the 1930s such incidents were familiar enough to inspire the play "Floating corpse" (*Fu-shih*) by Yü Ling, another Communist playwright, written at the same time as *Under Shanghai Eaves*. For the text of this play, see Yü Ling, *Yü Ling chü-tso hsüan* (Selected plays of Yü Ling) (Peking, 1958), pp. 136-77.

6. Ma Lien-liang (1902-67) was a leading actor of "old man" (lao-sheng) roles in opera, whose very successful career lasted until the Cultural Revolution in the mid-1960s.

7. The January 28 Campaign, or Shanghai Incident of 1932, involved Japanese ground and air attacks on the city of Shanghai to break a boycott there of Japanese goods. Chinese troops assisted by civilians resisted until the Chinese

government reached an accommodation with Japan in May of that year.

8. Hsüeh P'ing-kuei is the name of a character in various local traditional operas, a warrior from an impoverished background.

Ch'en Pai-ch'en

Men and Women in Wild Times

Translated by Edward M. Gunn

Cast of Characters

CH'IN FAN, a member of the Resistance
HSÜ SHAO-CH'ING, an important official and businessman
MRS. HSÜ, his wife (née Fang Mei-hua)
WANG YIN-FENG, a nightclub entertainer
P'U SHIH-CHIN, an *au-courant* youth
WU CH'IU-P'ING, an editor
MADAME BUREAU CHIEF
MISS VIOLET WAVE, a writer
MIAO I-OU, a translator
WANG HAO-JAN, a writer
LI MAN-SHU, a mysterious woman
OTHERS: assorted refugees, passengers, workers, children, a hotel steward, etc.
(Acts I and III are translated in full. Act II is omitted.)

ACT I

Scene 1

A railroad station in Nanking in November 1937, two weeks before the Chinese army was forced to abandon the city to advancing Japanese forces.

A bell is clanging. A train engine whistle shrieks. People's voices clamor.

As the curtain opens a train is stopped at a station platform. The side of a coach has been removed—for this you mustn't blame me, since it has been pulled off in accordance with the conventions of the "fourth wall"—revealing a second-class passenger coach. The train car and the proscenium are not parallel, but slightly at an angle to each other, so that those of the characters in this crowded coach seated in the seats along the upstage side cannot be seen by the audience. This is of no consequence, for if a given character must be seen, the director can have him stand up.

The seats are already filled with people, and from time to time a head pokes out. People have also been sleeping there all along. The baggage racks are crammed with sleepers too. And of course people are sitting on the suitcases, trunks, and baskets piled in the center aisle, where in addition a few people are standing who are probably the overflow from the third-class coaches, packed to bursting.

Among all these people there are some persons of refinement who must be introduced to the audience first. They are: P'u Shih-chin, Violet Wave, Miao I-ou, Wang Hao-jan, Ch'in Fan, Wu Ch'iu-p'ing, Wang Yin-feng, and Li Man-shu. Naturally there are many others besides these, but it is unnecessary to know them. On the stage these others are called the crowd, and a character in the crowd is a part that even a fifth-rate star wouldn't act. So it will do to call them Person A, Person B, Person C, and so forth. And lastly there are some customers of the "fifth-class" coach—these comprise the group riding on the roofs of the coaches. Naturally the members of this group have names, but they are merely sounds like Hairy, Doggie, Chang the Third, and Li the Fourth—not very refined. So we'll just call them refugees, and label them A, B, C, D, and so on.

As to blocking the stage positions of these characters, forgive me for not explaining in more detail. Even if I went into particulars here, an intelligent director could probably arrange them in more suitable places. However, that character CH'IN FAN, *wearing a gray-green cotton coat, is quite clearly asleep up in the luggage rack.*

Through the coach windows we can see the station and the platform. People on the platform are moving back and forth like a swarm of ants locked in battle, wildly shouting and yelling. Baggage has been piled into such a mountain that even the station is not altogether clearly visible.

The interior of the train coach is chaotic: chatting, arguing, sighing, cursing, and groaning are interspersed with sobbing and weeping, and also with wild laughter, singing, and the ruckus of a poker game, as well. People are squeezing and boring their way in and out, so that the assemblage is in a constant wave of motion. As the train appears on the verge of moving out, the whistle blows, and outside the window there is pandemonium. People inside the coach next to the window suddenly start crying out.

CROWD [*In a babble of raised voices*] Hey! Hey! You can't do that! You can't do that! . . . How can you climb through the window? Isn't there a door over that way? Get down. Get down. . . . Can you believe that person? Trying to climb through the window?

[*The climber gropes his way in after all. He turns out to be* HSÜ SHAO-CH'ING, *manager of a certain factory for a certain large business and also committee member of some official commission or other. He is slightly plump, but not like the image of the capitalist as usually portrayed with an obligatory outsized stomach. He has a pale complexion, which is flushed from exertion. Like a large beast he crawls in through the window and plows through people, addressing them loudly but without actual courtesy*]

HSÜ Oh! Ahem. Excuse me! Pardon me! Beg your pardon! [*Spoken in a constant stream as he enters. He raises himself to a standing position amid the splutterings of the other passengers*] Excuse me, everybody! We're all refugees. The train will be pulling out right away!

PERSON A [*Offering only token dissent*] Isn't there a door over there?

HSÜ Sir, there were so many people blocking it I could hardly get on.

[*Outside the window a woman is crying out shrilly on the platform. It is* MRS. HSÜ SHAO-CH'ING, *or* MS. FANG MEI-HUA *by maiden name, the model of the "modern wife"*]

MRS. HSÜ Quick! The train is about to start! How can I get on?

HSÜ [*In a voice of command*] Climb up! Climb up! I'll give you a hand.

MRS. HSÜ Now how can I climb up? [*With both hands she grasps the window but cannot pull herself up*] Oh, no! Oh, no!

HSÜ Pull up with all you've got. Pull! Pull! . . . Oh, it's hopeless. [*He holds out his hand to pull her up*]

PERSON A She can't climb up here, sir! [*He deliberately leans into the woman next to him,* WANG YIN-FENG, *a Nanking entertainer. She exhales a cloud of cigarette smoke with disgust and brushes ashes from her clothes, giving ground slightly*]

WANG YIN-FENG Ugh! Ugh!

HSÜ [*To the other passengers*] Oh, oh, I'm sorry. Very sorry. We're all refugees. Let's have a bit more consideration for each other. Hey, come on! Pull hard!

MRS. HSÜ Ah! Oh! Whew! [*Entering through the window, as* HSÜ SHAO-CH'ING *supports her, she makes every effort to avoid brushing against anyone*]

P'U SHIH-CHIN [*He is one of the oft-seen au-courant youth, looking like one of the current crop of university students, also like a movie actor, and also like a writer. Then, too, he looks a bit like a journalist. But he is none of the above. He gazes at* HSÜ SHAO-CH'ING, *and suddenly turns to* WU CH'IU-P'ING] Do you recognize him? That's Hsü Shao-ch'ing! Commissioner Hsü! Also Director Hsü at the Great China Plant of the China Redevelopment Company! Now *that's* a "bourgeois."

WU CH'IU-P'ING [*He is short and sleazy, with a self-important air*] Oh— that's him all right.

HSÜ Move, move! Quick, go that way! First class is that way. This place is a madhouse.

MRS. HSÜ Oh, this is second class? No wonder—how do we get through?

HSÜ Never mind! Just come with me! [*Shoving and pushing, he squeezes his way toward the first-class coach*] Ah, oh! Pardon me! Excuse me!

P'U [*Addressing* HSÜ] Ah, are you—

HSÜ [*Ignoring him as he continues on his fixed course*] Excuse me! Excuse me!

P'U Yeee, I wonder if that guy is Hsü What's-his-name after all? Whew, we've had a little *confusion of consciousness** lately. What a supreme

---

*P'u's dialogue is larded with "trendy," often incorrectly used, Chinese terms of Western derivation. We have italicized these in the translation.—EMG.

mess! That just *absolutely* can't be Hsü Shao-ch'ing. Why, we're old friends.

WU I should say so! Actually doesn't look like him!

[*There is another uproar at the window as a toilet and a suitcase are pushed in*]

CROWD [*Calling out in indignation*] Hey! What's that? A toilet! . . . That's not allowed! You can't put that in here! You can't do that!

[*Other people are laughing. The toilet is withdrawn outside the window and in its place a woman appears.* MADAME BUREAU CHIEF, *the wife of a government bureau chief, thin, angular, and still well preserved in middle age*]

MADAME BUREAU CHIEF What's this? I can't carry on my own things?

PERSON A [*Squeezing against* WANG YIN-FENG] Look around! It's impossible to pack anything more in here. How can you bring on a toilet? Turn it over to the baggage coach!

MADAME The baggage coach! They won't take it there! They want me to carry it myself. [*The toilet again emerges through the window*]

CROWD [*Clamoring once more*] Hey! Hey! Hey!—You can't. You can't do that!

[*Someone pushes the toilet out on the platform with a loud clunk*]

MADAME [*Furious*] Why did you push my things out? Why did you push my things out? [*As she chatters away she herself climbs in carrying a suitcase. But halfway in she gets stuck, unable to go forward or back, and sets up a howl*] Hey! Hey! I'm sorry, but someone give me a hand! Give me a hand!

[*They all look at one another and smile, but no one does anything.* MADAME BUREAU CHIEF *screeches at the top of her lungs.* WANG YIN-FENG *tries to pull her in, but she won't budge*]

MADAME Pull some more! . . . Hey, you on the platform! Come on and give me a push. Push!

[*No one on the platform pays any attention to her. Only the train whistle screams even louder*]

MADAME [*Panicking*] Hey! Quick! Quick! The train is going to pull out! Hey, someone! You! Come here, come here! Push me in. I'll give you forty cents. Come on! I'll make it fifty cents! . . . A dollar, a dollar! . . . A dollar! *Two* dollars!

WORKER [*Only his head is visible through the window*] Don't yell, ma'am. I'll give you a hand. Forget about the money.

MADAME Oh, good. Thank you. Put your hand here . . . put your hand on my rear and push up! . . . Ai, ai, great! [*She enters the carriage*] Ah! Oh! . . . Heavens! . . . [*Again addresses the worker*] There's the toilet, too! The toilet! [*The toilet is hoisted up once more, to the consternation of everyone, but it is finally brought in.* MADAME BUREAU CHIEF *fishes out a dollar*]

MADAME Now, now! Here is a dollar for you—I only have a dollar and some change.

WORKER There's no need for that. I don't want any money.

MADAME [*Having tossed it down*] That's no way to talk. A deal is a deal, isn't it? [*Turning around, she begins brushing off her clothes furiously*] Oh, no. I'm so filthy I could die! Just die of all this filth! [*To* WANG YIN-FENG] I'm sorry, but will you look and see if there are any lice on me? . . . Ah, ugh. I'll die of this filth.

YIN-FENG [*Smiling*] There aren't any. None at all!

MADAME [*Hugging her suitcase, she is unable to find a seat. Finally she sits on the toilet next to* WANG YIN-FENG] Whew . . . Permit me the honor of making your acquaintance, madame.

YIN-FENG How kind of you. My name is Wang. . . . May I know your name, madame?

MADAME My maiden name is Liu. My married name is Chou. But at home the servants don't use my surname; they call me Madame Bureau Chief.

YIN-FENG Oh, Madame Bureau Chief. Now that you're trying to get away from the war, why did you bring a toilet?

MADAME [*Astonished*] And if I didn't bring a toilet—then what would I do? How can you use the toilets on these trains? Ah, ugh. Just filthy. I tell you: I've carried this suitcase and the toilet around Nanking ever since the evacuation alert. The suitcase, well, naturally has some important things in it. It's my life! But as for this toilet, I simply couldn't get through a single day without it!

[*Another group of people is setting up an outcry*]

PERSON B This is a second-class coach. Go on, move out!

PERSON C That way! That way! It's absolutely crammed in here. Get yourself over to the third-class coach!

PERSON D There's no room in here! No room! Go over to third class.

[*An elderly man leading a young girl of thirteen or fourteen squeezes in through the crowd, carrying a large satchel and holding up a carrying pole. He calls out as he moves forward*]

ELDERLY MAN Pardon me! Pardon me! . . . Folks, just stay as you are! I only want to stand wherever there's a place. Just stand for a while. Pardon me! Pardon me!

CROWD [*In a babble*] There's no room! No space!—Go up front. Up front!—You can't stand here!—Go, go!

ELDERLY MAN [*Arriving in front of* P'U SHIH-CHIN, *he sees a bit of space he can stand in and puts down his satchel*] Pardon me, pardon me! Everybody . . . we'll just be standing.

P'U [*In great heat*] Not here you won't! You're blocking our *line* here, do you understand?

ELDERLY MAN Sir, please have some consideration for this poor child, that's all. She simply can't move through all this! We looked through two cars, and they were so packed we couldn't fit in. It's really awful how her mother died, ripped to shreds by a bomb! I must take the child away for her own sake. We only want this space to stand in, just for a while. We won't get in your way.

P'U What do you mean you won't get in our way? I told you, the *line* is blocked! Now move on! Move on. Go up front.

WU It's really disgusting! These people running away—where are they running to? Why aren't they defending their own homeland to the death?

ELDERLY MAN Please have some consideration. It's so wretched for this child. She really—

P'U I'm telling you, you are *mistaken!* This is a second-class coach! Go on to third class! Move! Move! Move!

ELDERLY MAN [*Vacantly picking up his bundle*] Where can we go? . . . Where can we go? [*He looks around*]

[*Next to them seethes a woman,* MISS VIOLET WAVE, *a poetess, amateur actress, women's liberation activist, and sometime participant in film productions. Her expression is filled with sympathy; her body melting with feeling. Although she is wearing work clothes, the material is fine serge. At first glance her face is very pretty. Upon closer inspection she appears unhappy and her face seems to show the traces of human endeavor. She stands up to intervene*]

VIOLET WAVE [*In a melodious voice*] Now, now. If this gentleman isn't altogether in your way then let him pause here, all right?

P'U [*Taken by surprise, he mumbles*] Oh.

VIOLET [*Declaiming*] How sad the lot of this father and daughter! They are among our unfortunate compatriots. Just to see them brings to mind those struggling comrades in the war zone who by the tens of thousands have fallen into such tragic circumstances. . . . We must offer them our deepest sympathies.

P'U [*Somewhat embarrassed*] Yes, indeed. I was simply thinking that it's so crowded in here, and I was afraid that such an elderly man and such a young girl might not be able to stand it. Of course I reasoned that they should move up front because I heard that there was still space up there. So, ah, you two just rest right here! Put your things down and seat yourselves on top of them. Just sit down and make yourselves comfortable.

ELDERLY MAN [*Deeply moved*] Oh, I'm so sorry! Pardon me! Thank you, sir. This is so very, very kind of you. Very, very kind.

[*The* ELDERLY MAN *arranges his things and sits down.* P'U SHIH-CHIN *and* WU CH'IU-P'ING *whisper to each other with sidelong looks at* VIOLET WAVE. *A worker is now climbing onto the roof of the train, and the roof stirs with commotion*]

WOMAN REFUGEE A [*One child in her arms and one child seated in front of her*] Hey! Hey! Don't crowd me! My child is here. [*The child stand up*] San-tzu, don't get up. Be careful, the train is going to pull out!

WOMAN REFUGEE B Aiya! Don't bump my feet!

WORKER [*Unperturbed*] Ha, so what if I bump into your feet? [*Pointing below*] That good-looking woman in the coach let me have a good handful of ass and finally gave me a dollar for it.

WOMAN REFUGEE B That's just 'cause she's got so much money on her it makes her itch. If it makes you so happy, then why don't you go spend your life patting rich women's asses! Don't bother leaving Nanking!

WORKER Don't leave Nanking? I don't figure on being a traitor! That's nonsense.

WOMAN REFUGEE B Well if you don't want to talk nonsense, then lie down! Watch out when the train starts you don't fall off!

WORKER [*Sitting down*] Okay. We won't talk! Just keep quiet. Fine! [*The roof again grows quiet*]

P'U [*His whispered conference with* WU *has reached a conclusion, and he addresses* VIOLET WAVE] Excuse my being so forward, but may I know your name? I've absolutely seen you somewhere before—are you Miss Violet Wave?

VIOLET [*With a smile of pride and satisfaction*] Why yes, I am Violet Wave.

P'U [*Looking at* WU, *with a start*] Oh, sure! [*Extending his hand*] I am P'u Shih-chin.

VIOLET P'u-hsi-chin?

P'U Right, right—ah, no, well, almost just like the sound of the name of the great Russian poet. Pushkin. P'u-shih-chin. [*He produces a name card*]

VIOLET [*Enthusiastically*] Oh, it's Mr. P'u! Very pleased to meet you! [*A woman wails, "Oh, my little one!" Other people are trying to quiet her*]

P'U Oh, let me introduce you [*Indicating* WU]. This is my old friend, Mr. Wu Ch'iu-p'ing. He's well known in Nanking as the editor of *China Monthly*. And this is the poetess Miss Violet Wave.

VIOLET [*As though meeting an old acquaintance*] Oh, so this is Mr. Wu Ch'iu-p'ing—my! Your magazine is really well edited! I'm one of your faithful readers. [*Firmly extends her hand*]

WU [*Shaking her hand*] You're too kind! Too kind! I've read quite a bit of your work and seen a number of your plays. You really are a genius! I'm always in Nanking, so I don't meet many people, but I remember you came to Nanking about a year ago, it seems. Isn't that right? It seems to me I've seen you here.

VIOLET Yes, it's very kind of you to say such things. I'm really not very talented at anything.

WU Not at all! Not at all! Since you've been in Shanghai we haven't had any real contact! But *now* you simply must write something for our magazine—make it long or short, it doesn't matter—whatever you write will do! We'll be putting out *China Monthly* again once we get to Hankow.

VIOLET Fine. Fine. Let me introduce you. [*Indicating* MIAO I-OU, *who is sitting next to her*] This is the well-known translator Mr. Miao I-ou. Mr. Miao, this is the editor of *China Monthly*, Mr. Wu Ch'iu-p'ing.

MIAO I-OU [*He is neatly dressed in a Western suit, with snowy bright shoes, hair shiny with pomade, and the face of a handsome barracuda. He rises gracefully*] Pleased to meet you, indeed.

P'U [*Holding his card in readiness, waiting for an introduction*] I, eh . . .

VIOLET And this is, eh, P'u Hsi-chin.

P'U [*Quickly offering his card*] It's P'u *Shih*-chin!

MIAO [*Without enthusiasm*] Oh, Mr. P'u. [*Etiquette dictates that he accept Mr. P'u's card and offer one of his own in exchange.* P'U *is on the verge of saying something to* MIAO, *but* WU *breaks in first*]

WU We've been in Nanking, while all this time you two have been in Shanghai, so we've had little contact. It's really a shame we haven't met until today—but from now on, no matter what, I ask you both to offer some of your work to help us out.

[*Nearby another gentleman rises from his seat. This is* WANG HAO-JAN. *Though his clothing is rumpled, he looks distinguished; his manner is graceful and refined*]

WANG HAO-JAN [*With a cry of surprise*] Oh! I-ou? You're leaving town, too?

MIAO [*Turning to him*] Oh, Hao-jan! So you're here! Great! Violet Wave, have you two met?

VIOLET WAVE [*Affecting astonishment*] Oh, no! Don't rush me. Let me think: aren't you Wang—Mr. Wang Hao-jan?

WANG [*Looking at* MIAO] And this must be the Miss Violet Wave you've told me so much about.

VIOLET [*With renewed enthusiasm, even more vigorously extending her hand*] Oh! [*After half a minute of oohing and aahing*] I'm simply at a loss for words.

P'U [*Offering a card, and extending his hand at the same time*] So this is Mr. Wang Hao-jan? P'u Shih-chin!

WANG [*With a slight nod to* P'U] Yes, I am. [*To* VIOLET WAVE] Miss Violet Wave, where are you traveling?

VIOLET To Hankow. There are no boats. Haven't you been at the battlefields up north to do relief work?

WANG Yes. General Liu asked me to have a look at the front lines. I just got back, and now I'm headed for Hankow, too.

MIAO Oh, Wang, old man, this is Mr. Wu Ch'iu-p'ing, editor of *China Monthly*. Mr. Wu, this is Mr. Wang Hao-jan.

WANG [*In a perfunctory manner*] Oh. So it's Mr. Wu.

WU Pleased to meet you! Pleased to meet you! Mr. Wang, you've been in Shanghai, while all this time we've been in Nanking, so we haven't had much contact! But from today on, *China Monthly* will definitely be asking you to contribute! Lots of contributions!

[P'U *has just thought of something to say when a group of poker players breaks into uproarious laughter. Then some other people argue over a seat. A din arises from the train platform.* WANG HAO-JAN *is talking with* VIOLET WAVE, *while* WU CH'IU-P'ING *is chatting with* MIAO I-OU. P'U *is still unable to get a word in when* HSÜ SHAO-CH'ING *and his wife return, still searching for seats*]

HSÜ We'll just have to sit in the second-class coach.

MRS. HSÜ It's all because of you! You had to climb into second class, and then we couldn't get through. Here we bought first-class tickets, and we can't even get a second-class seat.

Hsü Stop squawking. [*His wife desists and resumes searching for a seat*]

Mrs. Hsü First-class tickets, and we're scurrying around in second-class. This is really the limit.

Hsü [*Commanding*] Stop your nonsense.

P'u [*Rising to greet him*] Aren't you, eh, Commissioner Hsü? Are you looking for a seat?

Hsü [*Caught by surprise*] Uh, uh . . .

P'u [*Producing his card*] P'u Shih-chin! Last February we met during the reception at Minister Wang's.

Hsü [*Perfunctorily, wanting to get by him*] Oh, ah, oh.

P'u Are you looking for a seat?

Hsü Why, yes. I bought first-class tickets, but I can't get through.

Elderly man [*Kindly*] Sir, you're in the wrong place. This is second class!

P'u Don't talk so much! [*To Hsü*] So why don't you squeeze in here?

Hsü [*With growing politeness*] Oh, oh! That's very kind of you. I don't think we could!

P'u [*Making way*] Sure you can. It's all right. I'll give up this seat, and you and your wife can crowd in together.

Hsü Now, now. How could we do that? Oh, ah, this is my wife, Fang Mei-hua. And this, my dear, is Mr. P'u.

[*Up in the luggage rack,* Ch'in Fan, *startled, observes* Mrs. Hsü]

Hsü This is too much to ask of you.

P'u No, it's nothing. Nothing at all. Please, have a seat! Please, sit down!

Hsü This, eh, well . . . I really must thank you.

P'u Ah, let me make the introductions. This is Mr. Hsü Shao-ch'ing, or Commissioner Hsü, also Director Hsü. And this is Mrs. Hsü. Here is Mr. Wang Hao-jan, Mr. Miao I-ou, Miss Violet Wave, and Mr. Wu Ch'iu-p'ing—all old friends! All old friends. Mr. Hsü is one of our *brilliant national capitalists!*

[Mrs. Hsü *brushes the seat, while* P'u *urges her to sit*]

P'u [*With unflagging persistence*] Please, have a seat! Please, have a seat!

Hsü [*Seeing that* Mrs. Hsü *is about to sit next to* Wu, *hastily inserts himself in the middle and sits down*] Many thanks, many thanks. . . . And what about you?

P'u Oh, don't worry about me. Don't give it a thought! You are *absolutely* not to worry. I can stand!

Elderly man [*Quickly rising*] You, sir, you can sit here. I can still stand allright on these legs of mine. Please, have a seat. Please.

P'u [*Not standing on ceremony*] Fine, fine. Everyone is a refugee now. [*He sits down, quickly addressing* Hsü] Commissioner Hsü, you recently . . . [*He is interrupted by an old peasant woman wailing, "My little one"*] How obnoxious! That woman is simply *hysterical!* Director Hsü, recently—[*He is interrupted by an argument breaking out among the poker players*] They're simply addlebrained *quasi-capitulationists!* Ah, Mr. Hsü, you recently—[*Suddenly there is a thump, as a bag kicked off the rack by* CH'IN FAN *tumbles down*]

CROWD [*Crying out in alarm*] Aiya! What's going on! Who did that? Who? Who?

PERSON A Friend, what are you doing? That bag hasn't done anything to you.

CH'IN FAN I'm sorry. I was just careless and knocked it off.

MRS. HSÜ [*With a startled look at* CH'IN FAN] Aiya!

CH'IN [*Makes an effort to conceal the emotion he is feeling*] Sorry. Sorry. [*He puts back the fallen bag*]

HSÜ [*Startled*] What . . . ? [*Looks around*]

MRS. HSÜ It's nothing. [*The train whistle blows*] Listen! The train is pulling out!

CROWD [*In a chorus of welcome*] Good, good! The train is pulling out! We're leaving Nanking right away! Damn, we've been waiting for this all day! Amida Buddha, at last!

[*Outside the window a cluster of people surge forward, clamoring to enter through the coach window*]

CROWD [*Alarmed*] You can't! You can't! No, no, you can't get on! Over that way! Get over to the third class.

MADAME [*In an angry, commanding voice*] Don't you get on, you rotten eggs! Close the windows!

CROWD Right, right! Close the windows! Don't let them on!

MADAME That's it! Close the windows! Don't let them get on! . . . Ah, oh! They scare me to death!

[*The people at the window succeed in shutting it completely while the people outside yell curses and pound the window with their fists. But before long the commotion subsides, and they hurry to take their places in "fifth class"*]

VIOLET [*Stands up, intending to say something, but seeing the window has been closed, sighs*] Ah, those poor people. Where will they go? [*Dejected*]

MIAO [*Gently seating her*] Violet Wave, don't be so downcast! The War of Resistance is a hard and bitter struggle!

WU They shouldn't be running away to the rear! Why aren't they out there defending their land?

[*There is a burst of raucous laughter at one end of the coach, with everyone joining in a barrage of commentary*]

CROWD [*Question-and-answer style*] What happened?—A woman just gave birth!—Wow, how did it happen? Gave birth?—The kid is already out!—Where did she have it?—In the WC!—Oh, ah. How vile!—Listen! [*Everyone smiles at the strong wail of the baby*]

MIAO Listen! A newborn protagonist for China has entered the world! Thanks to the new army of resistance!

WU We must fight for our sons and grandsons!

[*So many refugees have climbed onto the roof that it is overcrowded, and arguments break out*]

WOMAN A Aiya! It's too crowded to fit anybody else on! There are too many people! . . . Aiya, don't crowd my child!

WOMAN B Why is everybody crowding around up here? This is really dangerous! Isn't there any space left in the coaches?

REFUGEES No more people! Nobody else comes up!

[*Just as they are arguing, the steam whistle screams savagely and the coaches give a jolt. Everyone on the roof quiets down again*]

CROWD [*Cheers go up inside the coach*] The train is pulling out! Here we go!—Good! Good!—Let the alerts keep coming! Who cares? We're really leaving Nanking!

[*The whistle blows. As the train moves forward, the electric power poles on the platform move back, while all is commotion inside the coach*]

Hsü [*Mournfully*] Ai, it's over. Finished. Everything is finished! Half a lifetime's work gone like water over the dam. Whew!

MADAME Ai. We're starting. We're starting. Who knows how our Bureau Chief will survive? Our Bureau Chief . . .

VIOLET [*Leaning against the window and sighing*] Nanking! Beautiful Nanking! Heroic Tz'u-chin Hill! Entrancing Hsüan-wu Lake! Until we meet again—oh, [*Tears well up in her eyes*] sayonara, Nanking!

MIAO [*Comforting* VIOLET WAVE] We'll return to Nanking someday. Just as long as we give our all to the Resistance!

P'U [*To* WU] What does "sayonara" mean? Is that some foreign language?

WANG [*To* VIOLET WAVE] Put your mind to rest. The final victory will belong to us! This beautiful land will forever be ours!

WU [*Enthusiastically*] That's right! Don't be pessimistic! Don't despair! We must believe that Nanking will be our enemy's grave! We must counterattack! We must see our foe exterminated at the foot of Tz'u-chin Hill!

[*At the same moment, the train cars bump each other and the people on the roof are tossed about violently. The child in front of the refugee Woman A is thrown off*]

CHILD REFUGEE A [*Crying out in distress*] Ya!

REFUGEES [*Shocked*] Aiya!

WOMAN A [*Her scream like an explosion*] Ya! Hsiao San-erh! [*Leaps up*] Hsiao San-erh! [*Wanting to jump down*] San-erh! [*Wailing madly, on the verge of jumping*] San-erh!

WORKER [*Leaping up and grabbing her*] Wu Ta-sao, you can't do it!

REFUGEES You can't do it! You can't . . . sit down! Sit down!

WOMAN A [*Moaning with grief*] San-erh . . . San-erh . . . [*As the train picks up speed, she wrests free of the worker's hand and throws the baby in her arms off the train. The crowd reacts with shock. Then she herself leaps screaming from the train*] I can't live! San-erh!

[*The cries of distress fade out. Greatly startled, people down in the coach are peering out to investigate*]

VIOLET [*Looking out*] Aiya! What's going on? [*A gust of wind blows away her handkerchief*] Oh, no! My handkerchief! My handkerchief!

MADAME [*Clutching her suitcase, suddenly cries out*] Aiya, my suitcase? My suitcase? Oh, oh!

[*Lights dim. The train roars on. Gradually it stops again*]

Scene 2

It is the middle of the night. The train is stopped for no apparent reason at a small rural station. Some passengers wait anxiously. Some have gone to sleep. Others are chattering away, while still others sob or silently play poker. But on the roof they are moaning with cold and hunger.

[PERSON A's *head is tilted; he is snoring. He deliberately allows his head to droop onto the shoulder of his neighbor,* WANG YIN-FENG.]

YIN-FENG [*Has been entertaining herself by blowing smoke rings, and now pushes away* PERSON A's *head with disgust*] Whew! Yuck!

PERSON B This is really aggravating. Why don't we move? First they say we were waiting for a troop train, so a whole bunch of troop trains go by. Then they say we're waiting for a special train, and the special train goes by. *Now* what are we waiting for?

PERSON C Humph. With the moon as bright as it is, all we can be waiting for is an air-raid alert.

PERSON B [*Shaking his head*] Damn. There's not even one cloud in the sky.

PERSON D If I'd known we'd still be here now, I would have taken the time to pack a couple more suitcases.

MADAME Yes, indeed. I should have brought a few more things, too. Look at it: this suitcase simply can't hold anything.

PERSON B Never mind suitcases! I've lost two plots of land and a house! If only this train had left a little sooner! If we get bombed again it won't be any joke! Oh, good heavens—listen! Is that an air-raid alert?

[*Most people are startled. They listen quietly—but the poker players are still chortling*]

PERSON B [*Cursing loudly*] Be quiet! Be quiet! The siren is sounding!

[*Everyone listens anxiously, but there is no sound*]

PERSON E [*One of the poker players*] What siren?

PERSON B [*Angrily*] You still talking? What are you, a traitor?

PERSON E What a joke! So no matter what somebody says, if he just talks he's a traitor, huh?

MADAME Aiya! [*Clinging for dear life to her suitcase*] Stop arguing! Are the planes coming or *aren't* they? Stop frightening me to death!

PERSON E Relax, Madame Bureau Chief. If there's an alert on the rail line, then the train will ring its bell.

CROWD Sure, they'll ring the bell, not blow the siren.

[*Now the atmosphere of conversational babble is restored*]

YIN-FENG [*Pushing off* PERSON A] Ugh, uh! This guy—

PERSON A [*Half-awake*] Huh, huh. [*Again letting his head droop*]

PERSON C Anything is better than spending another day in Nanking! Aiya! Those bombings in late August ruined my nerves! And the sound those enemy bombers make—whew!

PERSON B Don't talk about them! You want them to come around again?

PERSON C What a laugh! Are you trying to tell me that if we don't talk about them they won't come back?

YOUNG GIRL Papa, I'm hungry!

ELDERLY MAN Child, you'll just have to bear it with a little patience. We're refugees!

PERSON B Okay, okay. Go ahead and talk about it! Go ahead! I want to see if you can talk your stomach into being full!

PERSON C Do you mean to tell me that if I don't talk I won't be hungry?

PERSON D Will you two stop talking about being hungry, okay? Can't get anything to eat for a whole day—where do you two get the energy?

P'U [*To* HSÜ] Ah, speaking of the bombings, where were you during that big raid, Commissioner Hsü?

HSÜ Oh, in Nanking.

P'U Well, during that raid I really had a close call! That was absolutely a supreme *crisis!* Do you know where *I* was when the final alert sounded?

HSÜ [*Who is watching his wife*] Oh, uh, where?

[*Mrs. Hsü has been planning to signal to* CH'IN FAN, *but now stops*]

P'U There I was on Chung-shan Road—I had a journalist's permit— and suddenly I heard up in the sky, "eeeow—woom!" I knew it was bad news—airplanes! With quick inspiration I took the fastest *step*—in one bound I leaped to the side of the street. By now the bombs were already falling, "harrump!" As they went off I thought to myself, "You've been sacrificed!" Before I knew it, half a minute passed. My eyes slowly focused, and when I took a look—aiya! Can you guess what *phenomenon* was there?

HSÜ [*Has simply turned away, not listening*] Eh, eh—Mei-hua, what's on your mind?

MRS. HSÜ Nothing—why are you always inspecting me like a police-man?

YIN-FENG Hey, hey—you! Sit up!

PERSON A Uh, uh. [*Continues to pretend he's sleeping*]

P'U [*Turning toward* VIOLET WAVE] Do you know—do you know what it was? Well, a bomb had burst right next to me—just three feet away! Just three feet away!

VIOLET [*Turning toward* WANG HAO-JAN] Eh, Mr. Wang, are you hungry?

WANG [*Head lowered, writing*] What difference does it make. If you're hungry, then you're hungry.

P'U All around me—left and right, in front and behind—people were lying there, every single one of them dead! *But*—and this is really an unbelievable *coincidence*—I wasn't even scratched!

VIOLET Oh, yeah, that really was a coincidence.

HSÜ [*Abruptly stands up and orders his wife to change places with him*] You sit in the middle.

[MRS. HSÜ *indignantly changes places with him, her face averted from* CH'IN FAN]

MIAO Talk about coincidences. I have an even bigger coincidence for you! I was at the Sung-chiang train station when the siren started. There was this refugee who didn't have enough for his train fare and was hanging around on the platform. When the bombs fell he was so scared that he fainted. But by the time he woke up then—wow—what do you know! There, wrapped in his arms, was this leg blown off a woman! It was all covered with blood, but it was still neatly dressed in a silk stocking. And there were over five hundred dollars in bills stuck inside the stocking! So the refugee took that money right away and made his getaway inland! That's what you call a "War of Resistance Windfall"!

P'U [*Getting even more worked up*] Say, speaking of that, I was in another bombing where there was a coincidence to end all co-incidences—

VIOLET [*Wanting to cut him short*] Mr. P'u, look at you, so worked up. You don't mean to tell me you're not hungry?

P'U [*Smiling*] I can't do anything about being hungry. My stomach was already *devoid of content* some time ago! Anyway, that bombing—

MIAO [*Has been talking about something confidential to* HSÜ SHAO-CH'ING] That report has been verified. It's from reliable sources. But don't under any circumstances spread it around! For the war effort, you must never, ever repeat it!

HSÜ [*Nodding*] We can't go on fighting this way with what we have for weapons. It was no good from the beginning. Only if Germany and Italy can step in and mediate, then I think we might scrape through somehow. We might just as well hang on to some shred of our national vitality.

MRS. HSÜ [*Defiantly*] Hasn't the vitality of our nation already been damaged? If we sue for peace, how will that preserve it?

HSÜ [*Scolding her*] What do you women understand?

MIAO But, Commissioner Hsü, aren't we committed to all-out resistance?

HSÜ All-out resistance: that depends on what strength we really have! And if you look at our actual strength, haven't we already resisted all-out?

MRS. HSÜ Isn't our real strength still intact? Take us, for instance, we haven't done a thing for the resistance!

HSÜ What do you know!

YIN-FENG [*Pushing away* PERSON A, *she rises indignantly*] Ai! You're really incredible!

PERSON A [*Intimidated*] Oh, oh, I'm sorry. I was just sleeping.

YIN-FENG What do you mean "sleeping"? You're really—incredible!

PERSON A [*His shame turning to anger*] Well, everyone here is a refugee. Why do you have to act that way?

YIN-FENG Since you're so aware that everyone's a refugee, why are you still trying to take advantage of people?

PERSON A [*Stubbornly*] Who's taking advantage of people?

YIN-FENG Everybody is on the run. Whoever is taking advantage of people knows it perfectly well. [*Sits down angrily*]

[PERSON A *turns his face away. The others look at each other, smiling*]

P'U [*Making a funny face*] She's Wang Yin-feng, the singer over at that night spot, "The Temple of Confucius."

MADAME [*Nervously*] Aiya! So she's a prostitute?

P'U A singer at The Temple of Confucius.

MADAME Isn't that the same thing? Aiya! [*Rising hastily, she brushes off her clothing and moves away slightly from* WANG YIN-FENG] No wonder! She has a loose look about her! Flies don't get at uncracked eggs, they say—small wonder that man was acting the way he did! Hmm.

HSÜ You'd better watch out with that woman! She's really out to do business!

P'U Yes, this woman is absolutely up to no good.

VIOLET A woman without a soul!

P'U For sure, a woman *absolutely* without a soul!

MIAO But we still can't talk about her that way. It's really something admirable to see a prostitute in the middle of the War of Resistance who knows enough to move back to the rear area! In viewing everything, we ought to look at it from the perspective of the War of Resistance!

VIOLET Whew, you can't say anything without bringing up the Resistance this and the Resistance that, as though it's just you doing all the resisting, just you headed for the front! Now that unclean woman—

MIAO Okay, okay. No need to get upset. My mistake, okay?

MADAME Oh, my. I don't want an unclean woman like that passing her diseases on to me!

P'U I say that kind of woman is absolutely—[*Suddenly clutches his stomach*] Oh, my god!

ELDERLY MAN [*Alarmed*] Sir, what is it? Is it a stomach ache?

P'U [*Silently shaking his head, he addresses the others*] I've had it! It's, it's—[*His empty stomach gurgles loudly*] Oh, ah!

HSÜ Aiya! The stinkers! Not one person has come from the dining car. [*Clutches his stomach*]

MIAO It's really too much! Not a thing to eat all day! In this War of Resistance—

VIOLET What are you doing bringing that up again? Don't mention it, forget it, and we'll be a little better off, okay?

MIAO But I'm hungry!

VIOLET You still want to say "I'm hungry"—"hungry"—It's really obnoxious of you to use that word.

MIAO Uh-oh, I'm wrong again.

YOUNG GIRL Papa, I'm hungry!

ELDERLY MAN Hush, now! Look at how hungry all these people are and they're putting up with it.

WU All right, everybody. No more talking about hunger! It's the same as our long-term War of Resistance: a long, hard struggle. Now the train has to start sometime. If we'll only bear with it, bear with it until

we get to a big station, then we'll have something to eat! As for now,
. . . now . . . [*He too clutches his stomach*]

WANG [*Taking out a bottle of wine*] Here's some wine! Miss Violet
Wave, wine is something even more precious than bread! [*He drinks thirstily*] This is the best of French grape wines! Take its color—just like your name. It's a bottle of Violet Wave! [*He passes the bottle*]

VIOLET Thank you. That is wonderful! I believe that wine can make people forget everything. [*Drinks*] Good wine! . . . Still, when I drink this wine [*Sanctimoniously*] I can't help thinking of our fighting men at the front, and of the comrades suffering in the war zone! [*Tearfully*] And red wine like this especially calls to mind the blood they've shed! . . . However hungry we may be here . . . whatever small injustices we suffer here, we still can have a drink of Mr. Wang's good wine, while for them it's probably hard to get so much as a glass of water, no?

MIAO [*Drinking*] But that doesn't mean this bottle is being wasted on us! One may say that we here are all pillars in the work of the Resistance! And as much strength as this wine gives us, so it gives that much strength to the War of Resistance!

WU [*With deep emotion*] How right you are! Think of this red wine not as the fruit of the vine, but as the blood of the Japs! We must gorge ourselves on the blood of the Japs! [*Drinks*]

HSÜ [*Looking at the label*] Hmm! It's good wine! The real thing from France! Too bad we can't get it these days! Ai—thank you!

[MRS. HSÜ *passes the bottle to* MADAME BUREAU CHIEF *without drinking*]

MADAME [*Repeatedly wiping the mouth of the bottle with her handkerchief*] Oh, my. How can I drink it like this? [*Wiping it some more*] Our Bureau Chief and I never use the same glass! This—[*In the end she doesn't drink*]

P'U This really is a bottle of "Violet Wave." [*Drinks*] Oh, Miss Violet Wave, may I ask you to explain something to me?

VIOLET I have no idea what you want me to explain—by all means ask.

P'U You use the pen-name Violet Wave. Now, strictly speaking, naturally no one can have the surname "Violet." So then, what is your real surname?

VIOLET [*With a sudden tragic air*] Oh! [*She takes a look at* WANG HAO-JAN *and continues in a theatrically tragic tone*] I have no family name. Even I myself don't know just what my family name is. But it doesn't matter. A name is nothing more than a label. It doesn't matter what we call ourselves, does it? [*Bleakly*] You—

P'U [*Changing tone*] Sure. When I was in Shanghai I saw an article on you in the tabloids. The rumor was that your mother was—

VIOLET [*Blushing*] Does it matter what sort of person she is? Let them suspect all they want to! Let them say she's Japanese, or that she's White Russian! Let them go ahead and say she's American, too! [*Firmly*] But, Mr. Wang, just look. I myself am Chinese, isn't that so? [*Everyone is silent*] Everyone, [*With feeling*] just as long as I'm a citizen of the Republic of China, that's what counts! *And*, on top of that, I am a citizen of China in the War of Resistance! My only fatherland is the Republic of China! [*She daubs tears, pretending to conceal them from others*]

WANG [*Enthusiastically*] Violet Wave! [*Offering his hand*] You are one of us! You are our Amazon! Come on! Have another good drink of this wine! [*He drinks deeply. Then* VIOLET WAVE *drinks the wine, while everyone applauds*]

P'U Preserve and protect Miss Violet Wave!

[*Suddenly at one end of the car, someplace we can't see, there arrives a hawker selling things to eat. Instantly the coach is thrown into a turmoil*]

VOICE Bread! Spiced beef! Tea eggs!

CROWD [*Buzzing like a hive of hornets*] Bread! Bread!—He's selling eggs!—He's selling beef!

[*While many struggle to buy and seize items, still more are yelling and cursing. Hsü turns his head and cries out, raising his arm and stretching his neck*]

HSÜ Bread vendor! Bread vendor! Over here. Over here! The dolt!

CROWD Over here! Over here! Come over here and sell!

YOUNG GIRL Bread! Bread! I want some!

VOICE No more! We're sold out. Sold out!

HSÜ Stinker! How could you sell out? Go get some more!

VOICE No more! There's nothing left! All sold out!

HSÜ Stinker! How can you be all sold out? Stinker! Go get some more! Go get more!

[*There is no reply. The vendor has obviously left. Now the sound of munching begins. Hsü and others hang their heads in dismay and sit down, cursing. On top of the coach the refugees are also getting restless. Some are weeping, some moaning*]

REFUGEES Oh, god. I'm freezing to death. . . . I'm starving to death! Oh, god. Oh, god. . . .

[*Hsü SHAO-CH'ING and the others are as deflated as a punctured soccer ball. Listening to the din on the roof and the rumbling in their stomachs, they sit facing each other in silence*]

YOUNG GIRL [*Crying as before*] I'm hungry! I'm hungry!

WANG [*Pulling himself together he takes out a piece of verse he has composed*] Miss Violet Wave, would you offer some criticism of my verse? These are some of the poems I just wrote, the harvest from the battlefields up north. These two poems here I gave to General Liu. And these are some odes on the battlefield. And these are—

VIOLET [*Unable to summon any interest*] Eh, very good, very good. It's a shame I don't have any feel for classical-style poetry. These— [*Clutches her stomach*] these—

WANG [*Watching in alarm*] What's the matter, Miss Violet Wave? [*He also holds his stomach. Moaning is still heard from the roof, and the young girl is still crying*]

MIAO [*Comforting her*] How's that? Hungry? Oh, don't feel good, eh?

VIOLET [*Angrily*] Who told you to start talking about being hungry again? [*Her stomach rumbles again*]

MIAO [*Intimidated*] Oh, oh!

[*Everyone is now reduced to silence, although their stomachs are gurgling and rumbling loudly, while the refugees on the roof moan, and the young girl cries that she's hungry. Now* PERSON B *and the others resume arguing*]

PERSON C Humph, with the moon as bright as it is, just when we're facing hunger and cold, if those bombers come again we'll really be in a fix.

PERSON B Hey, just why do you have to talk about being bombed?

PERSON C What's it to you if I do talk about being bombed?

PERSON B I don't want to hear it!

PERSON C Well I want to talk about it! Just because you don't have anything to eat you start taking your hunger out on me. That's going too far!

PERSON B You stinker! You say I'm hungry—you mean to tell me you're not?

PERSON D As I see it, everybody's hungry! So what are you arguing about?

[*Everyone lapses into silence. But now* WANG YIN-FENG *opens a paper bag and takes out bread, biscuits, and other food. This draws the attention of the whole coach. The others follow her movements with their eyes, but once she raises her head they all resume sitting straight and stiff*]

YOUNG GIRL [*Eyeing* YIN-FENG *greedily*] I'm hungry!

ELDERLY MAN [*Covering her mouth*] Be quiet!

MADAME [*Moving away slightly, with disdain*] Why, the greed of that woman! Look at how much she eats!

[*Everyone peers at her through lowered eyes, listlessly searching for a topic of conversation*]

P'U Well, this is . . . this, ah . . . it's getting pretty late now, isn't it?

HSÜ Eh, oh, is it past nine?

WU Hmm. Since we got on the train this morning it's been twenty or thirty hours!

MIAO Over a day now, and not a thing to . . . [*Looks at* VIOLET WAVE *and swallows the rest of his sentence*]

VIOLET Why haven't we moved? . . . It's really aggravating!

WANG Ah, now even the wine is gone!

[WANG YIN-FENG *is not only eating, but also drinking water from a thermos bottle she has opened.* PERSON A *is now reclining against the seat pretending to sleep. The young girl is crying that she's hungry*]

P'U It would be so nice if we had another bottle of wine.

WANG It sure would—it would be so nice if we could get drunk!

P'U Actually, at this point if I could buy a bottle of drinking water, that would satisfy my *inner needs*.

MIAO Water is really secondary. If everyone could just have half a— [*Looks at the bread*]

HSÜ Those stinking waiters! They stink!

P'U Actually, I'm ready to buy what can be bought. But—[*He looks at* YIN-FENG]

[LI MAN-SHU, *a woman who apparently is in government service, has been looking sympathetic and suddenly speaks up*]

LI MAN-SHU I think she might sell. She can't eat all of it, anyway. And it will just go bad otherwise.

MADAME The only thing that sort of person wants is money! For a little extra money is there anything she wouldn't sell?

P'U [*Summoning his courage*] Yes, that's what I was thinking.

HSÜ Buy from her? Oh, forget it. She won't sell . . . still . . .

LI I think she might. Try and see. Go ahead.

MIAO Yes, you can always try.

VIOLET Forget it. Why do you want to buy something from her? It's not worth being refused by her.

MIAO Why are you afraid of buying something from her? It's not as though we weren't paying! And it's for the war effort!

MADAME Sure! If you have money you can put the devil to work! Give her something more than this dollar. Another eighty cents, say. At most, two dollars, Won't that do it? Ha, I can see right through that kind of woman!

P'U Don't people who have been thrown together on the same boat help each other? Now, when everyone's a refugee, she *should* sell.

HSÜ If she won't sell, then we'll *make* her sell!

P'U Sure, we can force her to do it! But who'll go first?

MIAO You're just the one to take a crack at it—it's for all of us.

HSÜ Oh, yes, great! Mr. P'u is skilled in communications.

SEVERAL OTHERS Right! That's right. Mr. P'u!

P'U But what can I say? What can I say? Can't we find some sort of *theoretical basis*?

LI Everyone is a refugee. Why can't we bend the rules a bit to take care of things?

MIAO It's simple. You just say that it's for the war effort.

MADAME Aiya. I say if you have money that's enough right there. What are you afraid of? Here, I have money—now you go on over!

P'U [*Bracing himself, he squeezes his way over to* YIN-FENG *and assumes an expression of surprise*] Oh—Aren't you Miss Wang Yin-feng?

YIN-FENG [*Startled*] Oh! How kind of you. Why, may I know your name?

[HSÜ SHAO-CH'ING *and the others all sit rigidly with bated breath, appearing not to listen*]

P'U My name is P'u—P'u Shih-chin. [*Offers his card*]

YIN-FENG [*Reading the card*] Miao I-ou. Oh, Mr. Miao!

P'U [*Startled*] What? Oh, that's someone else's card. I, eh—[*Feels about for another card but finds none*] I, ah, my name is P'u—P'u Shih-chin!

YIN-FENG Oh, Mr. P'u. It seems I've met you somewhere. But I have a poor memory. I'm awfully sorry.

P'U Now, now. Not really . . . I've heard you perform at the Temple of Confucius.

YIN-FENG I'm so flattered that you recognize me. But it's a pretty awful show. Must give you quite a laugh.

P'U That's really too modest of you! [*Unable to find the next words*] You, ah, ah—you—

YIN-FENG [*Puzzled*] Oh, well, you look quite successful. Where have you found your success, Mr. P'u?

P'U [*At a loss for words*] Well, ah, I certainly haven't found any on this train.

YIN-FENG [*Taken aback*] Mr. P'u, what do you—

P'U [*Spluttering*] I mean, that is—we're all refugees on this train.

YIN-FENG You don't have a seat?

P'U Oh, no, no. That's not it. . . . Eh, are you going to Hankow?

YIN-FENG Yes. I can't stay on in Nanking, so I just have to push on from city to city. And you?

P'U I, I, I, I'm also going to Hankow.

MIAO That jerk is just talking rubbish.

MADAME Where does he dig up all that nonsense?

YIN-FENG [*At a loss for words*] Sure, sure.

P'U [*Turning and looking at everyone*] It's just that . . . it's . . .

YIN-FENG Oh, you . . . don't have anything to eat? [*Smiles*]
[*The others slowly raise their heads*]

P'U [*Embarrassed*] Oh, uh, no, uh, it's ah . . .

YOUNG GIRL Papa! I'm hungry!

P'U Your deduction is quite *correct*. It's quite simply *absolutely* correct.

YIN-FENG [*Bewildered*] Er, what?

P'U Yes, yes, indeed. You're quite right.

YIN-FENG Well, don't stand on ceremony. Here are some snacks. Help yourself! Please excuse me for not serving you.

P'U No, no! You have so much. I would like to offer to pay for them!

YIN-FENG You're joking! You must be joking. These things aren't worth anything. Don't put yourself out so. Have some!

P'U I'm not putting myself out, because—because there are quite a few of us! [*Indicating everyone, while they again turn away sheepishly. However,* WANG HAO-JAN *and* MIAO I-OU *do not turn in time*]

MIAO Miss Wang, please don't stand on ceremony with us. Actually, we haven't been able to buy anything. Now, with the War of Resistance on—

WANG If you could let us have something. Already we are moved to the bottom of our hearts.

YIN-FENG Why, it's nothing. All of you, be my guests. [*She offers all the bread and biscuits*]

MADAME [*Forcing herself to speak first*] So good of you. Thank you. Thank you.

CROWD Thank you very much! Many thanks!

P'U [*While taking the food*] No! No! We must settle up with money! We must pay what we owe! [*Handing it out to everyone*] Everybody, [*Making a face and smiling*] please now.

LI [*First taking a roll*] Please let me have a roll!

MADAME [*Taking a roll*] Mine. [*Clutching her suitcase and furiously brushing ashes from the paper wrapper, with great loathing she peels away the bread crust*] Agh! Yuch! Filthy! How can I eat this . . . oh, agh, yuck!

HSÜ [*Vigorously grasping two rolls*] Everybody share! Share!

[*Each person takes a piece.* HSÜ SHAO-CH'ING *eats immediately.*
MRS. HSÜ *looks at the man in the luggage rack*]

YOUNG GIRL Papa, I want some!

ELDERLY MAN [*Scolding*] That belongs to other people! Stop yelling!

YOUNG GIRL [*Wailing as she watches the others*] I'm hungry!

WANG [*To* VIOLET WAVE] This Miss Wang is really a pretty unusual woman.

VIOLET [*Not pleased at this remark, but decides it's best to agree*] Yes, there is greatness in her sympathy for her fellow human beings.

P'U [*With his mouth full*] Well, and sympathy itself is great.

[*Everyone is in high spirits. But suddenly a bell clangs*]

PERSON B Oh, no! Listen! What is that sound?

[*Everyone is silent as the bell sounds loud and clear*]

PERSON D [*Alarmed*] Aiya! Air-raid alert!

[*For a moment the coach is as silent as a ghost ship*]

MADAME [*Screaming as she dashes off panic-stricken, her suitcase falling to the floor*] Aiya!

CROWD [*Suddenly pandemonium breaks out. Those who are stronger climb over the others, rushing for doors and windows*] Quick! Quick! The planes are coming! Off the train fast! Move! Move!

[*Most of the women are so crowded together they cannot move.* WANG YIN-FENG *is trampled under* P'U SHIH-CHIN *and others.* MRS. HSÜ *is abandoned by her husband. Children wail. The people on the roof of the coach leap down*]

CH'IN FAN [*Calling from the luggage rack*] Don't run! Don't panic! Women and children off first! Calm down a little. Calm down and let the women and children go first!

[*No one pays any attention to him. People crowd into each other as before.* MRS. HSÜ *is so hemmed in that she cannot move.* CH'IN FAN *jumps down from the luggage rack to help her, and carries her off*]

MRS. HSÜ [*Embracing him, weeping*] Ah! Fan!

CH'IN FAN [*Hugging her*] Ah! Mei-hua!

[*Chaos. Fast curtain*]

ACT II (SUMMARY)

Act II takes place several months later, during the summer of 1938, in the city of Hankow.

Ch'in Fan tells Mrs. Hsü that he has always loved her, and that he was crushed, several years before, while a student in Shanghai, when she broke off their relationship to marry the wealthy and powerful man her family had chosen for her. Mrs. Hsü then expresses her dissatisfaction with the marriage; Hsü has kept her a virtual prisoner wherever they live, and not allowed her to participate actively in society. She implores Ch'in Fan to help her run away so that, despite her delicate health, she can make a new life for herself devoted to genuine work in the Resistance.

However, the two are spotted together by P'u Shih-chin and Violet Wave, who are currying favor with Hsü, and with their help he is able to prevent his wife from carrying out her plans, threatening violence to Ch'in Fan if she does not obey him.

Meanwhile, Li Man-shu has emerged as a hostess of dubious reputation, conducting dancing parties at her residence which feature an assortment of easily available young women. As for the other characters, Wu is still predicting the resumption of *China Monthly*; P'u is embellishing the same anecdotes; Madame Bureau Chief is obsessed with finding her husband; Violet Wave is attending a ceaseless round of cultural conferences; Miao is still leading them all in their rhetorical support for the Resistance while ignoring the pleas of the poor and desperate. But their stay in Hankow is to be ended by the continued advance of Japanese forces.

ACT III

Act three finds them in January 1939 at a hotel in some city further in the interior of China, such as Chungking, Chengtu, or Kunming.

In this act the rear area of the stage represents a suite in a luxury hotel. Adjoining the main room is a smaller room, allowing people to converse in some privacy. The furnishings and decoration should be appropriately elegant. In particular what is necessary is a large bed. A terrace is also indispensable. It is about 11:00 a.m. MIAO I-OU, P'U SHIH-CHIN, WU CH'IU-P'ING, and LI MAN-SHU have gathered in the room. Having surrounded a newspaper, they are engaged in animated discussion.

P'U [*Savoring the thought*] So it was like this: last summer in Hankow, Mrs. Hsü created a scene.

WU In Hankow?

P'U Sure! One evening last summer, six months ago—it was the same day that our air force made that long distance raid on Tokyo. Weren't we all at an evening garden party? Don't you remember seeing a young guy with a sort of military look about him?

LI Oh, I remember. Just when Mrs. Hsü and that fellow were coming out of the garden they ran into Mr. Hsü.

MIAO [*Now echoing* LI] Right! Old Hsü suddenly stood up and this guy bolted.

P'U Right. That joker's name is Ch'in Fan! He was dressed like a *proletarian*; he may not look like anything special, but he is Mrs. Hsü's old admirer.

MIAO Oh, *that* guy! He wouldn't have the nerve to run off with Mrs. Hsü.

P'U Oh, he wouldn't, eh? He absolutely did have the nerve! That very night in Hankow they were getting ready to go. But old Hsü got my report, so when he saw her he made a few *threats*, and she folded—capitulated. Since they didn't succeed in getting away that night, Ch'in Fan went back to North China to join his guerrilla unit. [*With a start*] Aiya, someone's coming.

[*As everyone turns to look,* MADAME BUREAU CHIEF *enters*]

MADAME [*Opening a newspaper*] Oh, good. You're all here! Oh, Mr. P'u, please read this for me. Our Bureau Chief's name is in this paper. You see it, don't you? Those three characters: "Chou Tzu-liang." I can't read the others, but I'd recognize those if they were burned to ashes! Oh, for over six months I've been scanning the papers day in and day out, day in and day out.

MIAO Really, Madame Bureau Chief, have you been reading them every day?

MADAME Oh yes. Every day I go over the paper from front to back, looking for my notice that I lost my money and for the name of our Bureau Chief. Maybe today you'll read it for me! Oh, please read it to me, Mr. P'u! Aiya, all of you read the newspapers, too! What do you see?

P'U [*In his customary bossy manner*] Now look, Madame Bureau Chief, we're talking! We don't have the time for this!

MADAME Well, what's so important about talking? Miss Li, you read it for me. There, right there.

LI [*With an air of resignation*] "Chou Tzu-liang and Lo Yü-ying are to be ma—ma—" [*Stunned*] Ah! [*Everyone crowds around her to look*] Madame Bureau Chief, there's nothing at all in this paper. [*The others exchange looks*]

MIAO [*Mumbling*] Oh no, nothing at all.

MADAME It doesn't say anything? Then why is there a notice about him! Has he arrived in that other city?

LI Oh, ah, he's arrived here. He just arrived. There's a special notice in the newspaper.

MADAME [*Delighted*] He's really here? Where is he staying?

LI Hmm. It doesn't say. [*The others take the paper and pass it around*] Oh, he's probably in some hotel.

MADAME [*Snatching back the newspaper*] Don't get it dirty—Let me go find out if he's—[*Rushes off*]

LI So, coincidences really do happen in this world! He's even getting married right here in this hotel, and she doesn't know it yet.

MIAO Wow! The wedding is right downstairs?

WU Ah, men and women in wild times like these, they dump each other and find new partners all the time; there's nothing special about it. But P'u, old boy, go on about Mrs. Hsü.

P'U Afterwards, Mrs. Hsü went with Old Hsü to that other town, and everything went back to normal. I know this for sure, because Old Hsü never lies to me about what's going on in his household. And whenever anything comes up, then he absolutely wants me to "review and discuss" the matter with him.

MIAO Stop trying to impress us with your connections and get on with the story!

P'U [*Solemnly*] Don't get upset. Recently Ch'in Fan came back, and when Mrs. Hsü got word of it, right away she began *vacillating*, and started thinking of running away with him again. Yesterday morning I ran into Ch'in Fan on the street, so then I went to find Old Hsü. I found out he'd just come back from relaxing at the Hot Springs, and so I said to him: "Commissioner Hsü, you absolutely have to watch out. I think there may be another sudden change in events!" And sure enough, when he went home last night, he found that his wife had already skipped out.

LI Do you know where they went? Have they left the city?

MIAO Haven't they left yet? Are they still here now?

WU I bet they've already left the city, eh?

P'U [*With firm assurance*] No, they haven't. Absolutely not. She can't get out of my *grasp*. Since he had me *review and discuss* the situation and *analyze* the problem, I've put a notice in the papers for him, urging her to reconsider and come home immediately. That's the carrot. Now on the other hand, I went and put out a bulletin for old Hsü with the Security Bureau, the Police Department, and the Military Police Command so that all the stations and steamboat terminals are covered, and every *line* is *blocked*. They'll never get away. That's the stick. She absolutely can't get out. Within three days we'll have her back—oh, is that old Hsü coming?

[*The door opens and* MADAME BUREAU CHIEF *dashes in*]

MADAME Aiya! Did I leave my newspaper in here? Oh, ah, isn't this a fine fix? Why, before I could find our Bureau Chief, downstairs some creatures from I don't know where were getting married, in the middle of times like these, too, and they took the newspapers I had and crumpled them all up!—Ai-ai, have you seen that newspaper of mine? [*To* P'U] Oh, is that my newspaper?

P'U Well, well! [*He draws a newspaper out from under her armpit*] Madame Bureau Chief, isn't this your newspaper here?

MADAME Uh—oh, this lousy thing! What a nuisance! [*Seizes the paper and dashes off*] What a nuisance. . . .

[*Everyone laughs*]

MIAO But about Mrs. Hsü: you can't get her back. Even if you get her to come back, you can't keep a hold on her feelings!

P'U I wouldn't say that. Old Hsü is more than good to his wife. With all he can do to keep her well-fed and entertained, won't that satisfy her? Don't give me any of that nonsense. Why, every years she spends a good eighteen thousand dollars—and that's absolutely one-hundred percent true! I swear.

MIAO But a person still has to have some inner happiness, and Mrs.

Hsü just doesn't have any freedom. Director Hsü looks on her as he looks on a convict. He's always busy being an official, busy speculating in foreign currency, while his wife is simply locked up in the house. She won't put up with that—not while he's going around with other women, and even chasing after Violet Wave!

Wu That's right! Mrs. Hsü ought to take a lesson from Ibsen's Nora![1]

P'U You are all *absolutely* wrong—

Li Well, I find it a little hard to believe that Mrs. Hsü really wants to go off and be a guerrilla fighter with Ch'in Fan!

Miao Indeed, Miss Li has a point. Can she really take the hard life of a guerrilla unit?

P'U Exactly! Miss Li's reasoning is correct: Mrs. Hsü can't endure combat experience. If she goes that route, she won't get far.

Miao But Old Hsü is such a stinker! He's still chasing Violet Wave!

P'U That's most insulting of you—and it isn't worth a fart. You've not only insulted Commissioner Hsü, but you're insulting Miss Violet Wave as well!

Miao Violet Wave? Humph! What a zero! I tell you everything about her is phony. Everything she's ever published I wrote for her. Now she's trying to get Wang Hao-jan to write for her. What is there about her that I don't know? Humph!

P'U [*Changing color*] Miao, old boy, I'm warning you never to insult them again to my face. Otherwise, I'll grind you up so fine there won't be anything left of you.

Miao What? Are you—

Li What's gotten into you two? Old friends joke around, it doesn't mean anything—come on, let's not talk about these obnoxious things, okay? Miao, how about dancing with me?

Miao [*As though receiving an imperial edict*] Splendid! Marvelous! [*He prepares to dance*]

Wu Ai-ya-ya! Dancing again! Dancing again! We still haven't even talked about what we came here for, and it's already dancing time again! You've forgotten all the trouble we got into last time! Now this is what they mean when they say that "merchants and women are oblivious to the agonies of a defeated nation."

Li Mr. Wu, you have all the courage of a mouse. A Szechwan rat has more guts than you do! What about the last dance? Who's got the nerve to do anything to me? If I, Li Man-shu, want to throw a party, don't I go ahead and throw one? And if I feel like having one tonight, let's just see who's going to do anything to stop me.

Wu But hasn't a newspaper printed an article about you?

P'U No need to worry about the papers. I've already settled it with Old Hsü. He's putting up the capital right away, so my *Rear Area Evening News* will start publishing next month. Once I get control of things, there's no fear of any interference. If they say you were dancing, I can prove you weren't dancing. Just let them pick a fight and whoever they are, their paper is *sunk* for sure.

MIAO Great! Great! What were we going to talk about?

WU What we are doing about the play for the Charity Performance.

MIAO We've been waiting for Wang Hao-jan to bring the script over. It's past eleven now, and he still hasn't come.

WU Past eleven? Wow, I have to get to a meeting right away. But what about our expenses for the performance? Now that Old Hsü's wife has run away, can we still count on the thousand-dollar advance he promised us?

P'U I can absolutely guarantee the thousand dollars. There's absolutely no connection with his marital problems. Anyway, I'll absolutely have her back in three days! Then that thousand is absolutely in our hands. You can absolutely relax and go ahead with things. We can be absolutely optimistic about the future. Except we absolutely have to give Old Hsü some title of recognition for the performance—such as "distinguished director" or "noted performer" or something. These things are all absolutely no problem.

WU [*Applauding*] Fine! Just as long as Old Hsü is willing to put up the thousand dollars, our Charity Performance will be a success.

LI But this problem with Mrs. Hsü won't be settled right away! It's going to have an effect on our play for certain.

MIAO And how! If Mrs. Hsü has made up her mind to go, she won't come back.

P'U No! Absolutely not! If she won't come back voluntarily, I'll have to drag her back.

[*The door opens, and* MRS. HSÜ *appears in the doorway, pale and downcast, and a bit nervous*]

CROWD Oh! Mrs. Hsü.

MRS. HSÜ Oh! May I ask you—hasn't Hsü Shao-ch'ing come?

P'U [*With severe politeness*] Why, Mrs. Hsü, have you come back? That's marvelous! Mr. Hsü is on his way. He'll be here soon. Why have you come here instead of going home? Oh, and please have a seat.

CROWD Please, sit down, Mrs. Hsü.

MRS. HSÜ [*Fatigued by stress*] I will never return to his home. It frightens me. It's a prison!

P'U Mrs. Hsü, you musn't talk that way. Ever since you left yesterday Commissioner Hsü's grief has deepened to a *pinnacle*. It would be best if you returned now. I knew you would have a change of heart.

MRS. HSÜ Mr. P'u? Don't misunderstand my intentions. The reason I came here looking for Mr. Hsü was to explain some things to him. I have no intention of returning. I've already said it: I will never go back to his home! [*Weeps*]

LI Mrs. Hsü, you musn't be too obstinate. Since Mr. Hsü wants you back and has published a notice besides, let it go at that and go back home!

MIAO Yes, Mrs. Hsü. We very much sympathize with your situation. But during this era of the War of Resistance, in all things we must compromise our own interests for the sake of the general good.

WU We all sacrifice so much for the war effort.

MRS. HSÜ No, Miss Li. Since you read the newspapers, you should be aware of how he has disgraced me. He has said that I absconded with his property and eloped. This is an utterly malicious insult. My leaving was open and aboveboard. In the past I've raised the subject of divorce, but he refused. I asked to get out to do something to help our country. This he also refused. What course was left open to me? For my own freedom, for my desire to join in the Resistance, I could only leave. But before I went, I left a note to inform him. I said that when the war was over I'd return to him and, further, that I had taken nothing of his. Can this be called absconding? Ch'in Fan was my classmate in middle school. I asked him to take me to a guerrilla unit. He saw himself simply as someone who could introduce me to people. Can anyone say that going with him is eloping? I won't accept this humiliation from him. To show that I have been forthright I decided to come back and make him take back what he said—to my face. [*Weeping*] As for his ruining my reputation in the newspapers, I mean to have him correct his errors.

P'U Oh, Mrs. Hsü, you musn't get too carried away. Commissioner Hsü will be here shortly. You just rest here for now.

MRS. HSÜ [*Rising*] Since he isn't here yet, I'll go. We're starting out at one o'clock, and I still have some arrangements to make. Mr. P'u, now that you're Mr. Hsü's close friend, will you please tell him what I've said.

P'U What! You can't leave. Commissioner Hsü will be here any minute now. You absolutely musn't leave.

MRS. HSÜ [*Angered*] Mr. P'u, you may cease concerning yourself with my actions! I give my word that I am returning and still you are afraid that I won't?

P'U Ah! Oh! [*Embarrassed*] I didn't say that. It's just that being Old Hsü's close friend, I'm naturally most concerned when it comes to the happiness you share as husband and wife. So I . . .

MRS. HSÜ Fine. I thank you—oh, Mr. Miao, Mr. Wu, Miss Li, see you all shortly. [*Exits dejectedly*]

[*Everyone exchanges glances and sighs*]

P'U I've got to call Old Hsü right away. [*Exits in haste*]

WU Calling Old Hsü? While you're talking to him, you might mention that thousand dollars for the performance and find out when we can get it. Oh, no! It's almost noon, I have to get to a meeting. [*As he exits*] Aiya, meetings, meetings! I don't know how I'll make it through all these meetings. They'll be the death of me yet!

MIAO [*Looking after P'U*] P'u Shih-chin, that little creep. This whole ostentatious show of success and importance of his he owes to Old Hsü, as though he were Old Hsü's adopted son.

LI Oh, you can talk!

MIAO [*Moving close to LI*] That's right. I can't very well talk about others—we still haven't worked out our own plans.

LI Our own plans? [*Slips away*]

MIAO [*In pursuit*] Man-shu! Why do you always play dumb with me?

LI [*Retreating to the door of the adjoining room*] Play dumb? But I couldn't.

MIAO [*Overcome with emotion*] Oh, Man-shu, don't go giving me a hard time again! [*He seizes her hand and nudges her into the adjoining room*] Please forgive me for putting it so awkwardly, Man-shu, but I must say it: you love me!

LI [*Pursing her lips to hold back her laughter*] You want me to love you? What a laugh! How did you come up with that idea?

MIAO Oh, Man-shu, don't lie to me. I know you don't love any of those men who come by your house, because all they want is to chase after those girls who stay with you. But you have saved all your love for one man, and I know that man, and even more I have the nerve to take the liberty to admit to you now: it is I!

LI [*Bursts out laughing*] Ah-ha! So it's you—how come I never knew?

MIAO Oh, Man-shu, you musn't make fun of me. Answer me straight out. [*Kneels*]

LI Very well, only stand up first. I can't stand the sight of you doing that.

MIAO [*Leaps up joyfully*] So, you—

LI [*Stepping back*] I'll tell you straight out: as long as you tell me, I'll set you up with any of the girls in my house you like. But as for me, whew—I'm a bit too old, little boy!

MIAO Man-shu, how can you think that's what I meant? If that's how you feel, then there's nothing left for me but suicide, to prove my feelings! . . . Man-shu, it's you I love, and only you.

LI What? So now you want to kill yourself. Well, I'm not going to take the responsibility for that . . . .

MIAO Right. Of course I can't kill myself! I must still work for the Resistance, for the nation, for our people! But if you reject my love, [*Sorrowfully*] Man-shu, then how will I find the courage to go out and live and work? [*In great agitation*] And so, Man-shu, for the sake of the Resistance, for the sake of the nation, for the sake of our people, you *must* love me!

LI So, to love you is to serve the Resistance and the nation?

MIAO Of course it is.

LI [*Laughing*] So I might as well go to war myself, and go love our people myself.

MIAO [*Indignant*] Man-shu, now you're joking with me!

LI [*Smiling*] It's you who's joking with me! You simply think you can talk nonsense to me as if I were a child.

MIAO [*Misunderstanding*] Man-shu, oh, if I was talking nonsense to you, I'll kill myself! I love you—

LI Aiya! That isn't what I meant. Just listen to me—

MIAO But I really am in love with you. I'll simply go mad. And I have figured out a plan for our future—oh, Man-shu! I have some hush-hush news. Did you know, there's a certain VIP who skipped off to Hanoi and then moved to Hong Kong! And he's promoting peace![2]

LI Yes, I know—have you seen how little there's been for me to do these last two days? All those visitors to my house have started getting busy, very busy.

MIAO Exactly. Think about it, if a peace movement starts growing, what are we going to do? I am committed to serving only the Resistance. So I've gotten Hsü Shao-ch'ing to buy for me twenty thousand dollars' worth of foreign currency. That way, when the time comes we can take a trip to the Soviet Union.

LI The Soviet Union!

MIAO Sure, go for a trip to Russia.

LI Well, you really do think ahead. I haven't even thought of what I'm going to do this evening!

MIAO From now on maybe you'll believe I haven't been fooling you— Oh, Man-shu, believe in my love for you. [*Starts to kneel again*]

LI [*Rising quickly*] Oh, I'm not kidding you: you've seen all those gentlemen who go in and out of my house. Once they've asked me to introduce them to a girl friend, there's not one that's been turned down. So if you're determined to find a girl friend, then you come to the party tomorrow night and I'll introduce you to whichever one you want—do you understand, little boy?

MIAO Oh, Man-shu, I love only you. I love only you! [*He suddenly rushes toward her. She stops him*]

LI Listen! Someone's coming!

[MIAO *stops still. The hall door opens and* VIOLET WAVE *enters, followed by* P'U SHIH-CHIN *carrying a bunch of flowers.* LI *checks* MIAO *with a gesture of her hand and peeks stealthily through the crack in the door of their adjoining room.* VIOLET WAVE*'s attire is rather outlandish, a bit like a woman soldier's, and then again a bit like an aviator's, consisting of a short leather jacket, riding boots, baggy trousers, and an American style military cap. She enters whistling "Happy People" (a popular Soviet tune), and starts to offer a greeting in English*]

VIOLET *Hello!* [*Finding no one about*] Hey! Anyone here?

P'U They've probably stepped out—a few haven't come yet—please have a seat, Violet Wave.

VIOLET Old Wang hasn't come yet? Still hasn't brought the script for the play?

P'U Nope—oh, Violet Wave, just now when I saw you coming I went right out and bought these: white camellias. This is absolutely a beauty surpassing matchless beauty. [*Presents the flowers*]

VIOLET [*Routinely*] How nice. Thank you. Isn't this the eighth time you've given me flowers? [*She takes them and then sets them aside with indifference*]

P'U Why, yes. You really have a good memory to remember so clearly the number of times I've brought you flowers. It's most gratifying to me. [*He moves closer to sit shoulder to shoulder with her*]

VIOLET [*Rising to avoid him*] Thank you so much—oh! Is the play Old Wang was looking for someone to write finished yet?

P'U I hear the first couple of acts are finished. Old Wang is bringing it over right now. I'll certainly insist that you be allowed to take the female lead— this is a *responsibility* which I must assume.

VIOLET Thank you. [*Again moving a little farther away*] I can't act.

MIAO [*Inside the adjoining room*] What's that? Allow *her* to act the lead? That role is certainly yours, Man-shu!

LI [*Cutting him off*] Good! Thank you—be quiet.

P'U [*Rising to follow her*] Don't be modest. The female lead is absolutely made for you. I can absolutely guarantee it, guarantee it. But, I can tell you— [*He tries to take her hand*]

VIOLET [*Slipping away*] Eee! Why isn't Old Hsü here, either?

P'U Oh, Shao-ch'ing will be here in a minute. Not only is he lending us a thousand to do the play, but he's also bringing another five thousand for me to set up the *Rear Area Evening News*—oh, Violet! I absolutely want you to edit the supplements section of the paper—

VIOLET Where would I find the time to do it? Right now I've got several key jobs in women's organizations, plus I manage the women's departments for several other groups. Where would I find the time to put together the ass-end of a newspaper? I'm supposed to be in the Northwest and down in Southeast Asia at the same time, and now it's always meetings, meetings! It'll be the death of me yet.

P'U But you absolutely have to do it, for me. This is for you what a front-line position is for a soldier. It's where you must be— Oh, Violet, can I tell you? [*He stretches out his hand*] My heart—

[*A worker opens the door, holding a stack of newspapers and a bamboo tube collection box*]

WORKER Buy a paper, sir! It's for charity today.

P'U [*Furious*] Go on! Beat it! [*Kicks the door closed*]

[*Li and Miao laugh, and Miao pulls her over to sit with him and talk. Li gestures to him to stop*]

P'U [*Turning back again to* VIOLET WAVE] Oh, Violet Wave, did that give you a start?

VIOLET Not at all. [*Walking away*] Just what is happening with this play? They still aren't here. This is getting to be annoying.

P'U Indeed, Chinese have no *concept of time*. Very annoying. But Violet Wave, this play is absolutely the one you must act in. This supplement is absolutely the one you must edit. And, my love, too, you must absolutely—

VIOLET What's that?

[*Again the door opens and a child enters carrying a selection of toilet articles*]

CHILD Sir, ma'am. Buy a little something! These are on sale today for the refugee charity drive.

P'U You little fiend! Scram! [*He drives her out the door*] Steward! Steward! Throw that kid out! Steward! This place must hire dead men for stewards!

MIAO [*Tugging at* LI] Oh, Man-shu, don't bother with them. Please, listen to me, I—

[*Now as* MIAO *walks toward* LI, P'U *also walks toward* VIOLET WAVE;

they move and speak simultaneously]

{MIAO Oh, Man-shu, [*Kneels*] I love you—
{P'U Oh, Violet Wave, I love you—

{LI [*Rising*] Ai, what a pain! [*Hurries toward the outer room*]
{VIOLET [*Rising*] Ai, how obnoxious— [*Hurries out of the room*]

MIAO [*Seizes his head in agony and sinks into a chair*] Huh—

P'U [*Simultaneously seizes the flowers to heave them after* VIOLET WAVE. *But when* LI MAN-SHU *emerges from the adjoining room,* P'U *with sudden inspiration pretends to be sprinkling water on the flowers with his hands and turns toward* LI] Oh, Miss Li, I just now bought these flowers outside to give to you—they're camellias, truly a beauty surpassing matchless beauty!

LI [*Startled*] Oh—isn't this the fifth time you've brought me flowers? [*She sets them aside indifferently*] You've really got nerve!

P'U You've really got a good memory. Most gratifying . . .

MIAO [*Bursting in to pursue Li*] Man-shu, Man-shu— [*Stops, thunderstruck*]

P'U [*Startled*] So, you two were in there all along.

[HSÜ SHAO-CH'ING *enters through the hall door, followed by* MADAME BUREAU CHIEF]

P'U Oh, Old Hsü, you've come—have a seat in here [*Leads* HSÜ *to the adjoining room*]

HSÜ Oh, oh. [*Shaking hands with everyone*] Please sit. Miss Li, don't leave. I was just going to ask you something. [*He enters the adjoining room*]

[P'U *and* HSÜ *talk quietly inside, their expressions tense*]

MADAME [*Holding a large batch of newspapers*] Aiya! It's just terrible! What sort of a person is it who has to go and get married in times like these!

LI [*Avoiding* MIAO] Madame Bureau Chief, where did you get all those newspapers?

MADAME Ai, don't bring that up. Today the streets are full of people selling newspapers—adults, children, women everybody crowding around you to sell newspapers! To sell newspapers! They were saying something about a "charity sale," a "charity sale." I don't know what's going on.

LI Oh, so that's why you bought those newspapers, is it—but they're all the same!

MADAME Yes! At first I wouldn't buy. But then I bought these just because they're all the same—our Bureau Chief's name across the top of every front page! But those people, ugh! Each and every one of them so filthy I could just die; and all around me so that I couldn't get away. What could I do! If I didn't buy some newspapers then all those lice on everyone would crawl onto me!

LI [*Laughing*] There aren't any. Don't worry.

MADAME Oh, it was so awful. And these newspapers, why each copy was a dime! So I bought a dollar's worth—oh, no! Miss Li, I'm going to faint again. Look at the paper again for me, and see if it mentions a place.

LI Hmmm, no, no place is given.

MADAME [*Unconvinced*] Mr. Miao, you look at them for me, please. Is there or isn't there a place? The rickshaw puller told me that up top here [*Indicating the newspaper*] it says something about a hotel! Is it possible that it's none other than the very Continental Hotel we're standing in right now?

MIAO Oh, no, no. It doesn't say anything about a location. Really, doesn't say a thing.

MADAME [*Heartbroken*] Now where will I look? Where will I look? I've already been to every other hotel [*She whimpers, her head bowed*] [LI *pretends to offer* MADAME BUREAU CHIEF *some encouragement so to forestall further conversation with* MIAO]

HSÜ [*With an air of command*] Good! You go arrange things according to my instructions. And be quick about it so that everything's arranged before she comes back.

P'U Fine! I'll go take care of it right away. But Commissioner Hsü, what about the plans for the *Rear Area Evening News*?

HSÜ I've said what I have to say. There's no problem with the five thousand dollars. When I have this domestic problem cleared up, I'll issue it to you. You go start making the preparations first—ask Miss Li to come in.

P'U Sure. I'll be right back. [*Hurriedly enters the main room*] Miss Li, Old Hsü would like to have a word with you, inside. [*Exits*]

[LI *enters the adjoining room.* MIAO *eavesdrops suspiciously*]

HSÜ Miss Li, may I ask you to do something for me? Hasn't Miss Violet Wave come yet?

LI Don't worry, Commissioner Hsü. She's an odd one, hard to figure out. But give it some time, and I can get the upper hand for you. Right now she's pretty cozy with Wang Hao-jan. Pretty soon I may turn into—but anyway why do you want to get involved now, with a wife on the loose?

HSÜ My wife—I'm about to rein her in. You see if she can get loose—but I have to rely on you when it comes to Violet Wave. That vixen is too slippery, and I just can't handle her by myself. [*He turns to go out*] Good, then, I'll be counting on you. And in the future there's certain to be a substantial reward, heh-heh! [*Going out, he collides with* MIAO] Oh!

MIAO Oh, ah! . . . Commissioner Hsü, I was just coming to report some urgent news. [MIAO *draws* HSÜ *back into the adjoining room.* LI *goes out smiling.* MIAO *reports his secret in a low voice*]

LI All right, I'll let you two discuss your urgent news. . . . [WANG HAO-JAN *enters, cuddling* VIOLET WAVE. WANG *is still living as loosely as ever*] Oh, Mr. Wang is here. Violet Wave, did you just arrive?

VIOLET Whew, I've been running myself ragged! We were just at the Public Stadium to see off the new recruits going to the front. I could just die from exhaustion. All those people!

LI You! Take better care of yourself. Oh, Mr. Wang, did you bring the play script?

WANG Only the first two acts. The third isn't done yet. [*He produces copies of the script*] Everyone first take a look—what, no one's here yet?

LI Old Hsü and Old Miao are in the next room. Wu Ch'iu-p'ing and P'u Shih-chin went out, but they'll be right back. What's this? This play is called "Men and Women in Wild Times"? What sort of a title is that? I don't suppose there could be a decent character in a play like this, could there?

VIOLET That's not necessarily so. Have you seen "Heroic Deeds in Wild Times," or "Loyal Service in Wild Times," or "Orphaned in Wild Times"?

MADAME [*Suddenly standing up*] Oh, lord, it's just too much! What am I doing just sitting around in here? I've got to go out and find him. [*Exits*]

LI Ai, it's pitiful. By the time she finds her husband the Bureau Chief he'll already be married to someone else.

WANG and VIOLET What? Her husband is marrying someone else?

LI Getting married right downstairs in this hotel, and she doesn't know yet.

WANG Now that's really a case of "men and women in wild times."

[WANG, VIOLET *and* LI *sigh and read their scripts as the conversation in the adjoining room continues*]

MIAO This is completely reliable news. It came in this morning: this certain VIP is probably in Hong Kong at this very moment and is probably about to issue some kind of statement.

HSÜ [*His expression grave*] The bastard! The bastard! The day before yesterday I go to relax at the Hot Springs. I get back to find myself up against a surprise there, spend a whole day coping with it, and now this incident comes up. I don't know; I just don't know—as it stands now, I suppose things are looking hopeful for a peace settlement.

MIAO Not necessarily! I don't think the resistance will end. But Mr. Hsü, why don't you move your factory out here to restore your business? Now there are plenty of industrialists opening up the Northwest and the Southwest, aren't there?

HSÜ My losses have been too large! Half a lifetime's work completely ruined. [*With determination*] But I have to find a way to recover.

MIAO There's still the Northwest to open up and exploit—

HSÜ No, first I've got to revive my old industrial base! [*Suddenly realizes his indiscretion*] Oh, but that's just talk, of course—my factory has already been seized by the Japanese, so I can't restore it—oh, has Hao-jan come?

MIAO [*Suddenly seized by a thought as he is about to leave*] Ah, this news shouldn't be repeated to anyone else!

HSÜ [*Smiling*] Of course not! Of course not.

[MIAO *and* HSÜ *start to walk out as* P'U *and* WU *enter. They greet each other, everyone churning around like a roulette wheel*]

P'U [*To* HSÜ] The order of battle is all drawn up. You may rest assured—

VIOLET Oh, *hello*. Why, Old Hsü, you're already here. Why that's marvelous, marvelous. Did you know that a group has just been formed to go do international propaganda work in Southeast Asia? They've asked me to be group leader. I haven't agreed yet, but I still have to give this group my help. How can I deal with it? Old Hsü, you've just got to help me out!

WU [*Simultaneously joining in the babble*] Oh, Old Wang, marvelous to see you! First of all, *China Monthly* is coming out again here, and no matter what, you've got to write an article—besides that, I'm also editing *Vigor Weekly* and I need you to write something for that, too—oh, Commissioner Hsü, I want you no matter what to put a few words in our publications for me. It's a must, a must! And you, too, Old Miao, you certainly have to translate a couple of things!

P'U [*Simultaneously joining in the babble*] Oh, Old Wang, my newspaper will start publishing soon. I absolutely have to have your help, all the help you can give. Hey, Violet Wave [*As though nothing had occurred between them*] In the future you absolutely must edit the supplement section for us. [VIOLET WAVE *laughs*] Old Wu, we'll have to swap manuscripts, eh! Absolutely! Absolutely!

VIOLET Oh, Old Wang, pretty soon I'll probably have to lead some young friends of mine into the Northwest. But transportation is a real headache of a problem. You have to come up with an idea for me, okay? Don't forget, now!

LI [*Shouting*] Aiya! What *is* all this business, all this chit-chat! All right! I have an announcement for you! Tonight, at nine o'clock, at my house—

VIOLET You'll have a party with dancing, right?

LI Clever child! Everybody: whoever doesn't come has no guts.

EVERYONE Okay! We'll be there! We'll be there!

WANG Fine! I'll go! But now that everyone is together, we can discuss performing this play. Everyone, take a seat and we'll talk. The script was written for us by Mr. T'ang. T'ang is a friend of mine. You all know him, so there's no need for any introduction. But now that the first two acts are written, according to him, he'll wait until we've started our rehearsals, and then have the third act for us. [*Distributing the remaining copies of the script*] Here is the script. Everyone read it. Today we have to discuss some questions. The first is that of the parts. Besides those of us here who can act, such as Violet Wave and Manshu, which stars should we try to get to help us with the other parts? Secondly, whom should we ask to direct it? Thirdly, there's the question of finances—

WU [*Unwilling to miss an opportunity to say something*] These last two days the charity sale drive has really stirred up this city. We shouldn't lag behind on this. If we stage this play as soon as possible, then we may well have the largest possible take at the box office to give as a contribution to our government. The significance of this performance is unusually great. Through it we can express our support for the charity sale [*Applause*], our support for the Resistance [*Applause*], and strike down Japanese imperialism! [*Strong applause*]

P'U But as for this script, I think that first of all it doesn't sound quite *right*. I mean, how can you use a title like "Men and Women in Wild Times"? This absolutely has to be a satirical comedy. And do we have any intention right now of putting on a *comedy*?

MIAO I think this phrase "wild times" contains more than a touch of reactionary skepticism! Now is the era of the War of Resistance, so how can somebody say it's "wild times"? And this phrase "men and women" is none too refined. So I say we change the title to "Sons and Daughters of the Resistance"—what do you all think?

P'U I think "Sons and Daughters of the Resistance" still needs clarification—let's just go ahead and call it "Heroic Sons and Daughters."

EVERYONE Good! Good!

WANG I think we can leave that question alone for a while. Why don't we hold our comments until we've all had a look at the script.

P'U However, I do think that several of the important roles should be decided on first. For instance, the female lead in this can be taken by Violet Wave. And the male lead, for instance, I'll go ahead and take. This way it'll be easier for us later on when we start reading the script together.

MIAO But I'm afraid I don't quite agree. There's no one better suited for the female lead than Violet Wave, of course. However, this is a Resistance play, and I still think that if the female lead were taken by Miss Li, then the social experience would be even more enriched, since Miss Li has been a civil servant.

P'U Your *theoretical foundation* is insufficient. Miss Violet Wave has grown up in the Resistance. She herself is a figure of the Resistance! How can you say she couldn't act it out? Although Miss Li, too, can act out this play.

MIAO You don't understand artistic creativity. Taking part in the Resistance doesn't necessarily mean one can act out a Resistance character.

P'U [*Furious*] Then you're a total *mechanist*! What do you mean by saying that Violet Wave necessarily can't act?

MIAO [*Furious*] You're twisting my words. I never said Violet Wave couldn't act. I only said that Miss Li could do it better!

P'U [*Leaping up in a rage*] Now you're absolutely twisting the facts. Violet Wave *can* act. Why won't you let her act?

LI [*Laughing*] Aiya! You two are really a riot! I can't act at all. This play is for Violet Wave, that's all.

VIOLET [*Laughing*] Nonsense. I may have acted in a few plays, but of course Man-shu should do this one.

P'U Did you hear what Miss Li said? She admitted herself that this is Violet Wave's play!

MIAO Well, did you hear what Violet Wave said? This is Miss Li's play! Miss Li was just being polite, that's all.

P'U You couldn't be more correct. Miss Violet Wave was just being polite too!

[*The hall steward rushes in panic-stricken*]

STEWARD Everybody! Ladies and gentlemen! The air-raid siren is blowing, please be quiet!

[*The sound of the air-raid siren is heard. Everyone is momentarily silent*]

WU [*Collecting himself*] Go on! Get out! We're not intimidated by air-raid warnings!

EVERYONE Go on. Leave. Don't bother about us.

[*The steward leaves. P'U and MIAO resume quarreling*]

P'U I say this is Violet Wave's play.

MIAO And I say this is Man-shu's play.

WU Hey, hold on for a minute! Do you know how many women's roles there are in this play?

EVERYONE How many? How many?

WU In all there are five important female roles, all equal! So what are you fighting about? Everyone has a part.

EVERYONE Ha ha!

WANG So I say, let's read the play first and then talk.

[*Everyone starts flipping through the script. HSÜ draws P'U into the adjoining room to talk*]

MIAO [*Suddenly recalling something, he puts down the script and draws WANG aside, speaking privately*] Old Wang, come over here. Come over. Have you heard the news?

WANG What news?

MIAO This is classified news. If you won't tell anyone else I can fill you in. [*Tensely*] More news about the peace movement! A certain person has already found out.

WANG Oh, I know about it already.

MIAO [*Disappointed*] Ah, you know already? What do you think?

WANG I don't think anything, since it won't have any effect on the Resistance. The Resistance will hold on to the finish. However, I figure I can't go on with my plans, you know?

MIAO [*Startled*] You won't—why?

WANG Not enough freedom in it, so I can't do it. If I could have a freer hand then I could do a lot more.

MIAO Isn't that the truth. But how else can you handle this work?

WANG "Work"? Anyone can handle this bureaucratic mumbo-jumbo. [*He continues to read the play*]

MIAO Sure, sure. So I was planning to go soon to the Soviet Union for a while and do some propaganda work for the nation, as long as I'm there.

HSÜ [*In the inner room*] When my wife comes back, you keep an eye on them. Don't let them listen in on my conversation with her—and whatever I tell you, just agree to it. Do you understand?

P'U I understand fully. I absolutely won't let them listen in. [*He starts to leave*]

Hsü And then I want you to take my card to the airline office and reserve two seats for me—to Hong Kong.

P'U [*Surprised*] What? Are you going to Hong Kong?

Hsü Never mind. I have a use for them—for the time being be sure not to tell them.

P'U Fine. I understand. I understand.

Wu [*Suddenly raising his voice*] Aiya! Who is this supposed to be? [*Calling over*] P'u Shih-chin! P'u Shih-chin, isn't this character you? [P'U *and the others murmur, "What? What?"*]

P'U [*Picks up a script and reads*] Ridiculous! You can't tell me I can be some "typical character."

Wu Ha, ha! The young man in this script is just exactly you. Look at how he's got a mouthful of jargon and wears those crazy suits. If it isn't you then who is it? Ha, ha!

MIAO You're right! Here it shows him doing nothing but mingling with famous people. And then it shows him on the train passing around his cards to everyone. Ha, ha—

EVERYONE That's right! It fits him exactly!

P'U Ridiculous! Ridiculous! You're twisting the facts again! When did I ever mingle with famous people? [*To* MIAO] Are you trying to tell me you think you're famous? Look, before that—who is it who wears evening clothes and goes around barking about the Resistance, the Resistance, and spends all day chasing women? Isn't that absolutely you, Your Excellency? Ha, ha!

VIOLET That's right! And here it shows him going around everywhere blabbing secret, classified news reports! [*All laugh*]

MIAO That, that, that . . . that's not like me at all. When was I like that? It's simply absurd! I see there's a woman writer in this, some poetess or whatever. It must be you! Look how every time she opens her mouth it's "dosvidania," or "hello." And always talking about work, work, work. Yes, and here it says you got your eyelids fixed—

VIOLET [*Leaping up*] That bastard T'ang! Why did he pick on me! But still, you can't say that's me just because of some foreign phrases, can you? There are lots of people who speak foreign languages!

Wu But all this shouting here every day about "Meetings! Meetings!" and "I'm so busy it will be the death of me"—that's *you* and nobody else.

VIOLET Nonsense! Don't you go yelling everyday, too, "meetings! Meetings! I'm so busy it'll be the death of me!" That isn't you?

P'U Be quiet. After all, this is Violet Wave in this play. But then, Old Wu—there's an editor here, too! Sorry about that! You're in it, too! Ha, ha . . .

Wu [*Furious*] Bastard! He's even had the nerve to say I'm the editor of *China Monthly*!

Hsü This guy is a bastard! How could he write such a play about all the people right here before my eyes?

LI Heh-heh. You musn't get angry, Commissioner Hsü. Have a look!
You're here, too!

Hsü [*Furious*] What! Did he dare to write about me? The bastard,
bastard, bastard! . . . This T'ang is simply a bastard!

LI Here it has the truth—Didn't you keep your wife inside your home
and not let her go out?

Hsü Never mind my wife. It's my right as head of the household! It's
none of his business! I won't permit this play of his on the stage. I
won't permit this script to be published. We'll see if he dares to write
about me again.

LI Commissioner Hsü! He still hasn't shown where you go dancing. If
he put that in it would really be a mess.

Wu Humph! Take a look at the second act! Who do you think it is
who's getting people over to her house for a dance?

LI Ah, so it's true! He's put me in? All right! Let him write! Let him
advertise my parties for me!

WANG Whew, Old T'ang does carry his joke a bit too far—still, he's
an old friend of mine. He wouldn't put me in this.

LI Wouldn't put you in, eh—see if this character pulling some chippie
onto the dance floor isn't you? Ha, ha! Your old friend! I'll say.
Theater people have no respect for feelings. On no account should we
have anything more to do with these theater people! No matter whose
old friend he is—

P'U Hush now. Mrs. Hsü is coming back.

[Hsü *walks to the door. Everyone is silent. The door opens and
in walks* MADAME BUREAU CHIEF. *Everyone bursts out laughing*]

VIOLET Well, if this character in the play who carries around a toilet
isn't our very own Madame Bureau Chief! [*All laugh*]

MADAME Well! What are you all laughing at? Poor me, I'm tired to
death! As soon as I left, the air-raid alert sounded and the police
wouldn't let me go look for our Bureau Chief—oh, how exasperating!
[*She heaves with soundless weeping*]

MIAO We shouldn't be laughing. I say this play doesn't amount to
anything. It simply isn't a play, is it? We ought to—

P'U It absolutely comes down to this: that there's some *friction* between
T'ang and us.

Wu It's sheer, deliberate libel, and we should sue him in court.

MIAO We have to get even with the guy who wrote this, that's what we
have to do. It's no use suing him.

VIOLET We can all write articles tearing this play apart; say it's—

MIAO Say it's "irrelevant to the Resistance," or "damaging to the
Resistance"!

LI I know! I'll get him to come to one of my parties and have him dance.
Then we'll see if he still writes this kind of play or not.

WANG But maybe I could persuade him to revise it.

VIOLET [*Accusingly*] That's right! You and T'ang are such good friends!
It's all your fault I ever met him! Now he goes and puts me in his play.
Why does he have only me speaking foreign languages? Here I am,

about to go off into the Northwest. Why doesn't he put that in? This is all your good friend's doing. We owe this all to your good friend!

WANG Violet Wave, don't get so carried away. The third act isn't written yet. After all, he may make everyone turn out to be good in the third act. [*To all*] Besides, we musn't be so suspicious. What he wrote may bear some resemblance to us, but it isn't altogether like us!

P'U Old Wang, you're trying to stick up for your friend after he's sold you out and betrayed you like this?

VIOLET Think of it! If we let somebody stage this play and put us up there one after the other to be disgraced and made a laughingstock of in front of an audience, then, then . . . [*Weeps with rage*] Old Wang, I demand to know what you're going to do about this!

HSÜ Miss Violet Wave, don't worry. I'm going to see to it that this play will never be allowed on stage, never. And never published, either.

P'U That's it! We stand behind Old Hsü's proposal. [*Gestures at* HSÜ. *A worker enters carrying newspapers*] Ah, who is that?

WORKER Ladies and gentlemen, buy a newspaper! It's for charity today. All proceeds from the newspaper sales go for the nation. Buy a copy!

HSÜ Get out, get out. Nobody's buying.

P'U You stinking punk, you're back again! Beat it! Some charity sale! I know that money is going right into your pockets, isn't it?

WORKER [*Stung*] Don't swear at me, sir! If I keep this money for myself let heaven strike me dead with lightning and burn me to a cinder and let all my ancestors rot!

P'U Just what do you think you're doing here! Scram!

WORKER There's no law against selling things for charity! What's got you so worked up?

MADAME [*Leaping to her feet*] Charity sale! Charity sale! And still more charity sale! You sold me a dollar's worth and still there wasn't a thing about where my Bureau Chief is. What lousy newspaper are you selling, anyway! Get out! Now! Get out!

WORKER [*Studying her*] Oh, so it's you again, Ma'am—I know you!

MADAME That's absurd! You animal! Who knows you, you filthy animal! [STEWARD *enters*]

STEWARD Move on! Let's go! Beat it. You're just stirring up trouble. We've got an emergency alert now. Any more trouble from you and I'll have you taken out. [*He hustles the worker out*] Gentlemen! Ladies! Downstairs, please. Emergency alert. We won't have anyone up here to take care of you.

[*The whine of the alert siren is heard. They all look at one another for a moment*]

WU Go on, get out! We're not worried.

EVERYONE We're not worried! You go on! Go! [*The steward exits*]

WU The planes won't come here.

P'U That's right. It's next to impossible to fly through all the mountains and fog around here. When they get to those mountains every one of those planes will be absolutely wiped out.

MIAO If we go by experience, then not once has a plane entered the air space over the city.

VIOLET Oh, for heaven's sake, what are you all going to do about this play? You're just going to let it go like this?

P'U What do you mean just let it go—this play is not to be performed no matter what!

[*The door opens abruptly and* MRS. HSÜ *appears in the doorway. Everyone is startled into momentary silence*]

HSÜ [*With an expression of surprise and delight*] Why, Mei-hua, you're back. [*Takes her by the hand and moves toward the inner room*]

MRS. HSÜ [*Icily*] I've just now returned. [*Nods slightly to the others*]

MADAME Oh, Mrs. Hsü, how are you—you didn't play cards, after all?—Aiya! It's so upsetting! Our Bureau Chief has come back, but—

HSÜ [*Lightly brushing her aside*] Madame Bureau Chief, I'm so sorry, but my wife has just now returned and needs to rest— [*Enters the adjoining room with* MRS. HSÜ]

P'U [*Pulling* MADAME BUREAU CHIEF *back*] Can't you see you're interrupting! Go on out and look for your husband!

[*He follows* HSÜ *into the adjoining room*]

[*The others at first watch dumbly, their eyes following* P'U *as he walks in. Then they crowd around the door to listen in.* HSÜ *escorts his wife to a chair, then speaks in a deliberately loud voice to* P'U]

HSÜ Go tell the Police Department, the Security Bureau, and the Military Police that as of two o'clock they can withdraw their detectives from the steamship docks, the train station and the airport. Tell them my wife has returned.

[P'U *voices agreement and starts to go, while* MRS. HSÜ *gasps with surprise. Seeing* P'U *moving toward the door, everyone there quickly withdraws*]

MADAME Just what is happening?

P'U Nothing. Nothing at all. Everyone please be seated and I will continue to develop our discussion of this play.

[*The others casually grunt yes while listening to the action in the next room. Closing the door,* HSÜ *moves back to his wife, taking her hand with an air of warm affection*]

HSÜ Mei-hua, I knew you would come back. And sure enough that's exactly what you did. Marvelous. And after all, moving around from one place to the other is no way to live.

MRS. HSÜ [*Flinging his hand away*] Shao-ch'ing! Hasn't Mr. P'u told you yet? I'm not coming home. I'm calling you to account for what you've done.

P'U Okay, everybody. Let's talk about the play. [*But no one speaks*]

HSÜ [*Considerately*] Call me to account? There's nothing to it, really. The notice carried in the newspapers wasn't genuine; it was nothing more than a deliberate ploy to get you to come back. Mei-hua, can you believe I would actually resort to that kind of underhandedness toward you?

MRS. HSÜ Then how could you humiliate me and say that I'd eloped and absconded with your property? I absolutely won't put up with these accusations! I absolutely won't put up with them!

HSÜ [*Meekly*] Very well! I should not have brought these charges against you. I am at fault. I will go correct them. Will that be all right?

MRS. HSÜ [*Rising*] Good. Write a notice of apology right now, and let me take it over to the newspaper offices.

HSÜ Done. I'll send it over to the newspapers this evening, and they'll be sure to publish it tomorrow.

MRS. HSÜ [*Firmly*] No. I want you to write it immediately and then deliver to the newspapers immediately.

HSÜ Oh, Mei-hua! Why get so anxious about it? [*As though appeasing a child*] Very well, since we've made up, why wouldn't I put things right? Wouldn't that be ruining my own reputation?

MRS. HSÜ Shao-ch'ing, don't play dumb. I won't be coming back to your home—I have to leave by one o'clock.

HSÜ [*His tone unchanged*] Very well, Mei-hua. Why must you be so deadly serious? I know this is·one of your moods and you'll get over it.

MRS. HSÜ Shao-ch'ing, why must you be so unctuous? I'm leaving today for certain.

[HSÜ SHAO-CH'ING *is silent for several moments. Then he breaks into a mirthless laugh that sends a shudder through everyone outside*]

P'U [*Interrupting*] Now, everyone, as I was saying, this play must absolutely not be performed. [*Everyone ignores him*] Everyone, I say, ah—

HSÜ [*Abruptly turning serious*] Mei-hua! You, too, can drop your act. Go ahead—can you leave?

MRS. HSÜ [*Indignantly*] Why couldn't I leave? I haven't taken a thing of yours. I'm not eloping with anyone. I'm simply going with a friend to do some work at the front. You can't say that's illegal, can you? No one would dare stop me!

HSÜ [*Coldly*] Of course someone will stop you.

MRS. HSÜ I'm not afraid of these detectives or police or whatever. My cause is just, and I am in the right! I haven't committed any crimes.

HSÜ [*Cruelly*] It won't get as far as train stations and detectives. You can't get out the front door of this hotel.

MRS. HSÜ Can't get out, huh! Don't bother trying to intimidate me. I'm not a three-year-old. [*She starts to leave*]

HSÜ [*Coldly*] Didn't you see the two men in long black gowns when you came in? They're waiting for you! You can try dealing with them if you want. It's all up to you. [*He pushes the door open slightly to allow her to leave*]

MRS. HSÜ [*Startled, she halts*] Hsü Shao-ch'ing! So you'd pull a cheap trick like that! That's it. You *bet* I'm going. [*She starts out*]

Hsü [*Grasping her hand firmly, with renewed mildness*] Mei-hua,
    we're in the middle of an air-raid alert. The all clear hasn't sounded
    yet.

P'u All right now, everybody, we still have a play to put on! Now,
    as for this play script . . .

Hsü [*Returning her to her chair and speaking gently*] Mei-hua, what's
    the problem? You want to go out and do something constructive,
    don't you? [MRS. HSÜ *weeps*] Actually, I never prevented you from
    going out. It's just that your health has been so poor. Loving you the
    way I do, how could I be unconcerned? So now, it'll be all right. Since
    you want to go out and work, I won't stand in your way!

MRS. HSÜ [*Exasperated*] Stop trying to fool me.

Hsü What's the point of fooling you? This is something you *should* do!
    Nowadays all the wives of ranking members in the civil service go out
    and put a lot of their energy into Resistance work. Why shouldn't you?

MRS. HSÜ Humph! You're not going to trick me again.

Hsü Mei-hua! How can you think of me that way? I have only love for
    you, that's all. However, if you want to get involved in some work,
    then of course it's all right with me if you stay here or go off to a
    guerrilla base. But what about your health? Will it hold up? When I
    think of your stomach and your insomnia, I'm afraid that once you go
    to the guerrilla base areas you won't last three days. There won't be
    any decent hospitals or doctors out there. In the end you'll be ill, you
    won't get any work done, and you'll just be a burden on other people
    doing Resistance work. Now isn't that exactly the opposite of what
    you intended? Where is the benefit to the Resistance, or to yourself?

MRS. HSÜ You needn't bother yourself about me . . .

P'u Everybody, let's not bother ourselves with them. . . . Hey, what's
    there to listen to anyway?

MIAO What's it to do with you?

P'u This is a case of individual ethics.

Hsü Ah, it's not that I'm bothering about you; it's that I'm looking
    after you. I can't just watch you go off and make yourself miserable!
    It's not that you're unwilling to endure this kind of misery, but that
    your body *can't* endure it. Let's say you do go: can you give up your
    fine bedroom? Can you give up all those things you love? And can you
    give up your dearest friends? However, I won't use force, if you're
    determined to go. Because I love you, I could tell those men at the door
    to let you go. But you must know that public opinion will deal with
    you harshly. Far more harshly than those two men at the door! Society
    will put a judgment on you for the rest of your life, condemn you for
    the rest of your life!

MRS. HSÜ [*Weeping*] Fine. Why not just kill me outright and be done
    with it? . . .

Hsü [*Taking advantage of the situation to comfort her, he strokes
    her head*] Hua, I can't bear to let you do this. I truly love you—it's

just because I've loved you too much that I've been too strict with you!
Yet, I realize that I've been wrong. . . .

[MRS. HSÜ *weeps softly, and* HSÜ *comforts her. The eavesdroppers
exchange disappointed glances. Outside is heard the sound of a child,
screaming and crying as though beside itself. Everyone now rushes out
asking, "What's the matter?" and bringing the little girl inside*]

VIOLET   Oh, poor thing! Haven't I seen this child somewhere before?

LI   Yes! In Hankow—the little refugee we saw that night at the Yeh-hua
Gardens.

VIOLET   Oh, that's right. Poor child—but here, now, who was bullying
you?

CHILD   [*Still crying*] There's a guest in that room down there. I went
to sell him something for the charity sale, but he wouldn't buy
anything and then he wouldn't let me go. He tried to do things with
me, and he tried to kiss my mouth—

MIAO   The son-of-a-bitch! So there are creatures as perverted as that!

P'U   This is absolutely the work of an animal!

WANG   What kind of man is this—we ought to report him to the police.

MADAME   Ai, it's really sad! This child— [*Giving her a second look*]
but how could anyone get so filthy?

WU   Child, now tell us, what happened next?

CHILD   I started to run and he grabbed me and I bit his hand and so he
got me and started beating me and saying I stole his things! [*Cries*]

VIOLET   Ah, just looking at this child makes me think of so many
homeless, wandering children! Child, do you still have a home?
Where are your mama and papa?

CHILD   [*Shaking her head*] I don't have any—Didn't I tell you? My
parents were blown up by the Japs. [*Weeps softly*] Mister, ma'am,
thank you. [*She starts to go*]

VIOLET   Ah, Old Wang, you've been saying how important the problem
of child care is! If I weren't going up to the Northwest I'd do
something about this sadly neglected task. [WANG *nods and sighs. All
sigh*]

MADAME   Oh, when I look at that child I start thinking of our Bureau
Chief. Who knows where he is? [*Weeps*]

MRS. HSÜ   [*Kindly*] Ai, child, don't go. I have something I want to
ask you—don't you have any family? Any relatives?

CHILD   [*Weeping*] No one—just me.

MRS. HSÜ   [*Sighing deeply*] Ah . . . don't you have a hard time? Child,
can you get along by yourself with no one else?

[*The child is choked by tears*]

MRS. HSÜ   [*Comforting her*] Don't cry, little sister . . . don't cry. Let's
talk. We'll go to my house, okay? You go with me, and we'll be like
sisters, okay?

CHILD   [*Startled*] Ma'am, what—

MRS. HSÜ   Come home with me and be my kid sister. You won't be going around selling things on the street anymore, all right?

CHILD [*Naively*] Really?

MRS. HSÜ Really. Just as long as it's what you want to do. Come back with me right now. [*To* HSÜ] What do you say?

HSÜ Sure you can, just as long as you're happy.

CHILD [*Delighted*] I'll come! I'll come! I can get things done for you, you know. I know all these streets like the palm of my hand.

MRS. HSÜ [*Embracing her*] What a fine sister you are! I like you already.

P'U This is wonderful! Mrs. Hsü has really brought happiness to someone. This is "greatness in action."

EVERYONE Wonderful! Marvelous! Great!

CHILD [*Suddenly pulling away*] I'm going out to give Mr. Chou the money I took in today from the charity sale. I'll be right back.

MRS. HSÜ Don't go! The all clear hasn't sounded yet. Sister, come back!

CHILD I'll be right back! He's just at the door [*Pulling away and running out*] Nothing to worry about! Don't worry! [*Skips out*]

VIOLET [*Taking* MRS. HSÜ's *hand*] Mrs. Hsü, I'm simply so impressed by you. What you have shown is genuine concern.

[*Suddenly the sound of aircraft is heard, startling everyone*]

P'U Aiya! Enemy planes!

MADAME [*A cry of panic*] Aiya! . . . [*She scurries madly for cover*]

[WANG HAO-JAN, P'U SHIH-CHIN, and MIAO I-OU *dash onto the terrace to get a look.* HSÜ SHAO-CH'ING *scrambles to hide behind a chair.* WU CH'IU-P'ING *burrows under the bed.* VIOLET WAVE *wraps herself in the cotton quilt.* LI MAN-SHU, *on the other hand, burrows under the desk.* MRS. HSÜ *freezes. Finally* MADAME BUREAU CHIEF *also settles on a spot beneath the bed. Now several bombs whistle down and as they explode antiaircraft machine guns open fire. The people in the room all burrow into their chosen spots.* MADAME BUREAU CHIEF's *rear end protrudes outside the bed, while* VIOLET WAVE *has buried her head in the quilt. Those on the terrace pour back in panic.* MIAO *drops down and crawls along the floor.* P'U *has flattened out on the terrace with only the upper half of his body inside the room. Only* WANG *still stands there gazing out*]

WANG Not to worry. It's nothing serious. Don't panic.

[*Planes again roar overhead, their sound gradually fading*]

WU [*Poking his head out from beneath the bed*] Have they . . . have they . . . gone?

HSÜ [*Poking his head out above the back of the chair*] Did they . . . did they . . . bomb us?

MRS. HSÜ [*Woodenly*] They bombed.

MADAME Amida Buddha! Amida Buddha!

LI Were we . . . were we bombed?

P'U [*Shrieking about nothing*] Ah, ah! What is this! [*Each person's head retracts into hiding*] I'm on fire!

WANG Where are you on fire?

P'U My ass is hot! I'm on fire for sure! Don't just stand there! Help me put it out!

WANG What are you raving about? Your ass got baked from being in the sun!

P'U Oh! Oh. [*He rolls over and stands up, rubbing his rear end*] Oh— it's nothing.

[*Everyone gradually crawls out and gets up. HSÜ SHAO-CH'ING sags exhausted into the chair. Others look timidly out on the terrace*]

WANG They bombed along the river. There's a modern highrise building and a row of thatched houses on fire over that way. [*Sitting down dejectedly*] Ah, a cruel bombardment. . . . [*His head is sunk in deep thought. Then he calls out*] Steward! Steward! Let's have some wine!

MRS. HSÜ Aiya! Who is that dead person down in the street?

P'U Oh, it's that little girl who just went out.

MRS. HSÜ [*A startled cry*] Oh! [*Drops into a chair, weeping*] Poor kid sister. . . .

MADAME [*Pulling out a newspaper*] Just where is our Bureau Chief? Just where is he?

[*Sighing, Hsü props himself up and walks over to his wife. The bleak sound of horns is heard as fire trucks drive past on the street*]

HSÜ Mei-hua, let's go. My car is at the door of the hotel.

MRS. HSÜ [*Weeping*] The kid . . . my kid sister . . .

HSÜ She is dead. What can you do? Let's go home and figure things out. [*To P'U*] Wait a little while, please, and then go over to the airline office and reserve two seats for Hong Kong.

P'U What? Are you both going to Hong Kong?

HSÜ Just for a while, and then we'll come back—all right, Mei-hua! Come on.

MRS. HSÜ No. [*On the verge of tears*] Ch'in Fan will be here looking for me any minute now. I have to see him.

HSÜ [*Dejected*] You still want to see him?

MRS. HSÜ No. I'm adamant about seeing him! If I'm going with you, I must see him. I've let him down. [*Weeps*]

HSÜ All right. Where does he live? It's best if we go meet him. We'll go together. [*He takes his wife by the arm and starts to leave*]

P'U Commissioner Hsü! If you're going to Hong Kong, then what about my plans for the newspaper?

HSÜ [*Turning back*] The newspaper? When I get to Hong Kong I'll let you know.

P'U Then, I can go to Hong Kong, too?

HSÜ Wait until after I'm in Hong Kong, and then I'll let you know.

WANG What's this? Old Hsü, are you off to Hong Kong? Then what are we going to do about the Charity Performance?

HSÜ This play "Men and Women In Wild Times" cannot and will not be performed under any circumstances.

Wu So then, ah, what do you say about the thousand-dollar advance? Mr. Hsü?

Hsü That . . . that will also have to wait until after I'm in Hong Kong. [*Again the* Hsüs *start to leave*]

Li Mr. Hsü, what about the business you wanted me to take care of for you? [*She works her mouth in mimicry of* Violet Wave]

Hsü After I'm in Hong Kong!

Madame What's this? You are going away, Mrs. Hsü. . . . Oh! How pitiful not to know where our Bureau Chief is living! Would you please tell me what the newspaper says about him?

Mrs. Hsü [*Reading*] Oh! This is the wedding of Chou Tzu-liang and Lo Yü-ying at the Continental Hotel.

Madame [*Shrieking*] What? Chou Tzu-liang married someone in the Continental Hotel? Isn't that the hotel we're in?

Mrs. Hsü Yes, it is!

Madame [*Sobbing*] Ah-ah! Chou Tzu-liang! Chou Tzu-liang! [*She runs out to go downstairs. The sound of her sobbing fades*]

Li Oh, Mrs. Hsü, Chou Tzu-liang is her husband, the Bureau Chief! How could you tell her?

Mrs. Hsü [*Nonplussed*] Oh! . . . Ah, what pathetic people, all of them. [*She walks out slowly with* Hsü]

P'u The fink! That guy is absolutely a fink! He'll "let us know" about everything once he's in Hong Kong— Fink! Fink! He's absolutely a "bourgeois"! [*He is so upset that he collapses into a chair*]

Wang People like him can never be relied on. So if he wants to go to Hong Kong, let him go! We'll redo the play ourselves!

Violet But I've decided to go down to Southeast Asia to be the leader of the International Propaganda Group. Look at the savagery of this bombing! This sadistic butchery! It makes my blood boil! My feelings will explode! I really can't put up with it! I'm going, for sure I'm going abroad to call for international sympathy, to seek out international aid—but, Old Wang, while I'm away you must help out with communications as a liaison.

Wang Just as long as you go, I'll be certain to help out. Oh, the all clear is sounding. [*He starts to leave, and as the all clear sounds,* Wang Yin-feng *enters*]

Yin-feng Oh, Mr. Wang, here you are. Wonderful! I was just looking for you to help me with something.

Wang What's that?

Yin-feng [*Drawing out several bank notes from her silk stockings*] Yesterday at the restaurant the audience had me sing twenty-four numbers. And here's twenty-four dollars. Everyone's involved in some sort of charity sale, so I've marked these twenty-four dollars for charity. But I don't know where to take them. Mr. Wang, you're always in touch with those official people, so I'm giving this to you to deliver for me! Thanks so much— The police held me up for hours on the street. I'd better get back right now while the all clear is holding. Sorry. [*Starts to exit*]

WANG [*In ecstasy*] Oh, Yin-feng, wait! I'll go with you and turn the money over to the Rear Area Relief Association. I'm so moved by what you've done! When I see you, I know that China won't be lost. I especially want to introduce you to the people at the Association— Come on, Violet Wave! [*Taking* VIOLET WAVE *and* YIN-FENG *each by the arm*] Let's go together. [*They exit together*]

VIOLET [*Looking back at the others*] Okay! *Dosvidania!*

MIAO Well, so you're all going . . . Man-shu! How about our plan to go to the Soviet Union?

LI [*Laughs*] What? Haven't you given up on that? [*She starts to leave*]

MIAO How could I give up? I'll never forget you through eternity!

LI [*On her way out*] I'm telling you straight out: if you want me to introduce you to a girl friend, I can guarantee you success. Just come to the dance at my house tonight. Old Wu, Old P'u, I'll be seeing you there tonight! [*Exits*]

MIAO No, Man-shu [*Following her out*], it's you alone I love! Only you. . . . [*Exits*]

WU They've all gone! All gone! What selfish, cowardly creatures they are: Hong Kong, Southeast Asia, the Soviet Union! Okay, do as you please! I'll never ever leave this place. We should defend—oh! It's past twelve! Old P'u, I have to go to a luncheon meeting. See you later! [*Exits quickly*]

P'U [*Stands up listlessly, then with a single motion sweeps the assorted articles off the table*] Damn! Go to Hong Kong! Go to hell! [*Seeing the flowers, he hurls them down*]

[*The door opens.* CH'IN FAN *rushes in, still wearing his gray-green cotton overcoat*]

CH'IN Mei-hua! Mei-hua! [*Looks around*] What's happened? No one's here?

P'U Oh, you're Ch'in Fan, aren't you? [*He produces a name card*] I am P'u Shih-chin.

CH'IN Oh . . . is Miss Fang Mei-hua—that is, Mrs. Hsü—here?

P'U [*Obsequiously*] You are looking for her to accompany you in an automobile?

CH'IN Yes. She agreed that we would go together to a guerrilla base in North China.

P'U She has now once again been "converted." She's not going. She just went back home with her Mr. Hsü. They're getting ready to take a plane to Hong Kong tomorrow morning. But they left just now, so if you want to, you could still catch up with her. [*Looks out the window*] Oh, look, aren't they getting into a car down there right now? You'd better get going if you want to catch her!

CH'IN [*Becoming calmer, he too looks out the window*] I don't really want to catch up with her. If I did it wouldn't do any good. She just plain can't go with us. [*He sits down*]

P'U [*Sitting down*] Aaah. Mr. Ch'in, I hear all sorts of good things about what's going on in the North China guerrilla units. I think this is absolutely right—but can one go and join them now?

CH'IN Join up? Who wants to go join up?

P'U [*Standing erect*] Ah, I've been in the rear area too long. I want to go and join in the Resistance myself! I want to go to the guerrilla zone! I want to take my place out there at the front—

[*From beneath the window are heard the sound of marching feet, battle songs, and shouted slogans*]

CH'IN [*Looking at* P'U] You want to join the Resistance!

P'U [*Swelling with emotion*] Yes—I!

CH'IN [*Gravely*] If you want to join the Resistance, then practice what you preach. Empty shouting is useless. If you want to fight, you can join up anywhere. It doesn't have to be North China! Any unit will do. It doesn't have to be guerrilla unit. Look! Aren't those recruits marching out—they are going to fight!

[*The sounds of marching, singing, and chanting swell. The curtain falls*]

Notes

1. Ibsen's Nora: The allusion is, of course, to Henrik Ibsen's play *A Doll's House*, commonly referred to in Chinese by the name of the heroine, Nora.

2. The allusion is to Wang Ching-wei, a prominent leader of the Nationalist Party and rival of Chiang Kai-shek. In December 1938 Wang Ching-wei flew to Hanoi, contacted the Japanese and set up a peace movement with headquarters in Hong Kong. This led to the announcement of a Nanking regime headed by Wang Ching-wei under Japanese sponsorship in March 1940.

Li Chien-wu

Springtime

Translated by David Pollard

Cast of Characters

LITTLE BLACKY, aged 9 *sui*
TIGERCUB, his older brother, 12
T'IEN HSI-ERH, a boy of 18
HSIANG-TS'AO, the mayor's elder daughter, 17
SCHOOLMASTER CHENG
WIDOW T'IEN, mother of Hsi-erh
MAYOR YANG, 40
NUMBER TWO, a farm laborer
ANOTHER FARM LABORER
REDNOSE, a watchman
MRS. YANG. wife of the mayor, 45
HSIANG-CHÜ, the mayor's younger daughter
DR. LUO, an important person
MASTER LUO, his 11-*sui*-old son

Setting

A village in rural North China, in the closing years of the Ch'ing dynasty.

ACT I

In front of the temple to Kuan Ti. A day in early summer 1908, about noon.
The building is both a temple to Kuan Ti (variously God of War, of Letters, and of Wealth), and a school; almost all villages you might come across in North China have a similar arrangement. Presented to the audience's view is just half a temple door, rickety and worm-eaten; like the Great Ch'ing dynasty–or what remains of it—it is merely an empty shell. The door is pushed to. The ring knocker, due to its antiquity, can be turned right around. The stone beasts guarding the door are now maimed, but from years of grownups sitting and children standing on them, they have been polished as shiny as jade. As the other leaf of the door almost falls outside the stage, only one stone beast can be seen,

and of the lettering above the door only the character "Kuan" and half a "Ti" are visible.

The temple wall is of no great height. It allows sight of the clear blue sky of early summer and of the temple roof tiles and trees, on which the noonday sun pours down. A low flat bench has been moved from the porch of the temple to under the temple wall. A locust tree, creaking with age, occupies the center of the stage, which is the edge of the road.

BLACKY *stands beside the trunk of the tree,* TIGERCUB *beside the bench. They are looking up admiringly and encouragingly at* T'IEN HSI-ERH, *who is straddling the wall.*

BLACKY Hope to die if I tell a lie, Hsi-erh, I've never tasted anything so sweet as the one Rednose let me have then!

TIGERCUB I had one too!

HSI-ERH You two lads stand lookout for me outside. If anybody comes give me a shout. What peaches I get we'll split three ways.

BLACKY I'll keep watch on this side, brother Hsi-erh.

TIGERCUB I'll keep watch on this side, brother Hsi-erh.

HSI-ERH If the schoolmaster catches me, you'd better not leave me in the lurch.

TIGERCUB The schoolmaster's having his nap, he'll never find out.

BLACKY If he comes out, you'll see him first, being as you're on the wall.

[HSI-ERH *stands on the wall, and, as if he were walking a tightrope, is about to raise his foot when he sees* HSIANG-TS'AO *approaching from the right, carrying a big pitcher of water. It is quite a weight, and a bit of strain for her. As she starts to change hands, she catches sight of the daredevil on the wall*]

HSIANG-TS'AO [*Exclaims aloud*] It's Hsi-erh!

HSI-ERH [*Startled, he nearly loses his balance*] Hsiang-ts'ao!

HSIANG-TS'AO You—! Come down, you scared me to death!

HSI-ERH [*Grinning*] If I break my neck I'll get you a new me!

HSIANG-TS'AO Wherever have you been these last few days? Your mum's been looking for you everywhere.

HSI-ERH Don't take any notice of her. She still looks for me everywhere even when I'm at home.

HSIANG-TS'AO What are you doing standing on the wall with the sun beating down like this? Mind the schoolmaster doesn't see you and take his stick to you.

TIGERCUB Brother Hsi-erh is picking peaches for us.

HSIANG-TS'AO Oh, very nice! I'll tell the schoolmaster!

BLACKY It's nothing to do with me! It's Hsi-erh.

HSI-ERH [*Mimicking*] "It's nothing to do with me! It's Hsi-erh"— that's rich, that is! You turn me in even before they give you the third degree! Right, then! Seeing you've come out with that, if you think I'm pinching peaches for you you can think again! [*Sits on the wall with his back to the temple garden, his legs dangling*] In any case it's always me, nobody else, who gets it in the neck!

TIGERCUB [*Currying favor*] Brother Hsi-erh, I didn't say anything like that.

HSI-ERH As for you, you haven't got what it takes either!

HSIANG-TS'AO [*To the young brothers*] Don't you two hang around with him; when I passed your house just now I heard your old grandad shouting his lungs out for you.

TIGERCUB Granddad's having his nap!

HSI-ERH Be off! If your granddad sees you two with me he'll give you a mouthful you won't forget!

BLACKY I'm going. Tigercub!

TIGERCUB [*Looking at Hsi-erh*] Now I come to think of it, granddad says you're always meddling with things that don't concern you—

HSI-ERH You tell your granddad your brother Hsiao-lung doesn't meddle with things that don't concern him, oh no, he lets his wife have a fancy man!

HSIANG-TS'AO [*Pushes* TIGERCUB] Hurry and catch up with Blacky! Don't pay any mind to Hsi-erh's loose talk!

[TIGERCUB *goes off, right, with* BLACKY. HSIANG-TS'AO*'s and* HSI-ERH*'s eyes meet.* HSIANG-TS'AO *lowers her head, sighs, and picks up her pitcher to leave*]

HSI-ERH [*Calls out and stops her*] Hsiang-ts'ao! [*She shivers*] I'm back!

HSIANG-TS'AO Mm. So I see.

HSI-ERH I've been staying a couple of weeks at Mr. Ching's house in town. He's that chap who came down from the provincial capital who studied in Japan. Your dad invited him for dinner, you remember.

HSIANG-TS'AO What did you go for?

HSI-ERH He wants to set up a new foreign school, I went— [*Feels the need to brag*] No, that's not for your ears! You ought to see that Mr. Ching's house: there's a great big courtyard as you go in, then more courtyards leading off, each one stretching back farther than the last, and rising higher all the time. He himself lives in the fifth. As soon as he saw me he said, young man, you're going right to the top, and nothing will stand in your way; we've nothing on here quite up to your mark, but stay for a few days and we'll see what turns up. He had me put up in the fourth courtyard. They were all heroes to the last man staying with me. I slept in a bed of gleaming white ivory, under a light and warm eiderdown. We fed on gourmet delicacies from the ocean and drank Dragon Well scented tea from Yueh Fei's tomb.[1] I had a grand time!

HSIANG-TS'AO [*Envious*] Was it really as good as that!

HSI-ERH They put on plays for us as well!

HSIANG-TS'AO Were they nice?

HSI-ERH Great! I was in tears as soon as they started to sing. And I cried again the next time I saw them.

HSIANG-TS'AO So what's so good about crying? People cry without going to plays.

HSI-ERH Um . . . that's because you're naturally weepy! Me, I have a good laugh.

HSIANG-TS'AO You're in a class of your own—head in the clouds all day, your feet never touching the ground, always gallivanting about!

HSI-ERH Doesn't my ma keep on belting me?

HSIANG-TS'AO Do you call that belting? Now if it was my dad—

HSI-ERH He's never laid a finger on you.

HSIANG-TS'AO [Sighs] I only wish he had! [Picks up the pitcher] How nice it would be if everybody could be like you! To take off whenever you feel like it, what freedom! And not a second thought for mum or dad!

HSI-ERH Where'd you get that idea? My ma's the last person I'd run out on. There's another person in this village I couldn't run out on either! Guess who it is? . . . Go on, who is it?

HSIANG-TS'AO I don't know!

HSI-ERH Have a guess!

HSIANG-TS'AO If I don't know, I don't know, and that's flat!

HSI-ERH If you don't know what have you gone red for? Come on, what have you gone red for? [HSIANG-TS'AO turns to go] Where are you off to?

HSIANG-TS'AO Down to the fields.

HSI-ERH Sit down for a while.

HSIANG-TS'AO I can't! I'm taking them some water.

HSI-ERH I've got a thirst, as it happens. Give me a drink first.

HSIANG-TS'AO There's no water for you! Go to your Mr. Ching's house for something to drink! Dragon Well scented tea!

HSI-ERH I want to get a drink from you.

HSIANG-TS'AO Don't be so brazen! I haven't been to any newfangled school, you know!

HSI-ERH Leave me to die of thirst if you like! Your dad can't wait to see me dead, and you too—

HSIANG-TS'AO [Pouting, goes over to the wall, stands on the bench, and with a struggle lifts the pitcher up to him] Be my guest! Drink!

HSI-ERH [Lies prostrate on the wall, and, mouth to the lip of the pitcher, gulps down some big mouthfuls] This water is good!

HSIANG-TS'AO Drink your fill!

HSI-ERH [Wipes his mouth] I'm done!

HSIANG-TS'AO [Puts the pitcher on the bench and sits beside it] All right!

HSI-ERH All right!

HSIANG-TS'AO Ah!

HSI-ERH Ah!

HSIANG-TS'AO Hsi-erh!

HSI-ERH Mm, I'm listening.

HSIANG-TS'AO I— I know why you went away from the village. Someone made a proposal for me to my dad.

HSI-ERH [Looks sullen] If you know that's all right then.

HSIANG-TS'AO In that case you shouldn't have come back!

HSI-ERH Why not? I missed you.

HSIANG-TS'AO Didn't you say in the country town you had . . .

HSI-ERH Don't pay any attention to my tall stories! Mr. Ching's new school didn't get off the ground; the county court stuck its seal on the door and put it out of bounds.

HSIANG-TS'AO What happened to Mr. Ching?

HSI-ERH He's gone, looking for something elsewhere.

HSIANG-TS'AO So you . . .

HSI-ERH I played doorkeeper for ten days, then slipped back home.

HSIANG-TS'AO Then you didn't come back because you missed me.

HSI-ERH Hsiang-ts'ao, if I hadn't missed you I wouldn't have come back to the village.

HSIANG-TS'AO But what was the point of coming back?

HSI-ERH To see you.

HSIANG-TS'AO Pooh! You don't expect me to go off with you, I hope.

HSI-ERH I've got a plan. I'll come and fetch you tonight after supper.

HSIANG-TS'AO [*Horrified*] You—

HSI-ERH You go to bed early—that is, pretend to go to bed. Come out as soon as I knock on the window—

HSIANG-TS'AO You'll get yourself hanged!

HSI-ERH I can't think of any other idea.

HSIANG-TS'AO You can count me out!

HSI-ERH If you can't get something by fair means you get it by foul. As I can't get you by asking for you, I'll make off with you. [HSIANG-TS'AO *is silent*] Are you going with me? If you say no, I'll never show my face in this village again. I'll be as true as my word.

HSIANG-TS'AO There's another person in this village, your mum.

HSI-ERH One day when I've made good elsewhere I'll send for her.

HSIANG-TS'AO In that case I . . . [*She cries*]

HSI-ERH I've had just about as much of this village as I can take. Your dad first and foremost can't stand the sight of me. He's against me because I'm poor; he's against me because I'm thick with you. One day, you'll see, I'll set a torch to this village and burn it to the ground, so you'll never know it existed. Then I'll have got my own back.

HSIANG-TS'AO My dad is a good man.

HSI-ERH [*Picks up some broken tiles in his irritation and throws them away*] I know, I know. If he wasn't good, people wouldn't have elected him mayor. [*Carried away*] It's the good people who ought to be killed! I just feel like committing murder, Hsiang-ts'ao! Come on, tell me, are you going with me or not?

HSIANG-TS'AO Tonight?

HSI-ERH [*Threateningly*] If you don't go with me . . .

HSIANG-TS'AO [*After a pause*] I can't leave mum . . .

HSI-ERH [*Disdainfully*] *I* can!

HSIANG-TS'AO As for you, your mum is looking for you, if you did but realize it . . .

HSI-ERH Let her look, I won't get lost.

HSIANG-TS'AO [*Still shakes her head*] No, it won't work.

HSI-ERH Won't work?

HSIANG-TS'AO [*Definitely*] Won't work. [*Both of them fall silent*]

HSI-ERH [*Looking left into the far distance*] From what Mr. Ching says, there are more than a hundred really humming places in the provincial capital—the county town hasn't got one to compare with them. As for Peking, that's even more fabulous, the playhouses alone run into tens and hundreds . . . [HSIANG-TS'AO *stands up and picks up the water pitcher*] What are you doing?

HSIANG-TS'AO If dad saw me with you he'd get into a rage.

HSI-ERH [*Makes a dismissive gesture, as if brushing away a fly*] Pay him no heed! He's of no consequence! [*Stands on the wall, carried away with enthusiasm*] Sweet Hsiang-ts'ao! My Hsiang-ts'ao! Come away with me! Go to the provincial capital with me! Just you and me, wouldn't that be lovely! Wouldn't that be lovely! I can't leave you behind by yourself, we grew up together, you're the only one I care about. . . . You and me together, forever together, that would be great! What a time we'd have!

[*While the one gets carried away making the speech and the other gets carried away listening to it, the temple door opens quietly and there emerges first the sanctimonious* SCHOOLMASTER CHENG, *then behind him the weeping and wailing* WIDOW T'IEN]

CHENG This divination of mine works every time . . . it's called the King Wen divination,[2] set your mind entirely at rest, ma'am . . . [*Discovers the bench isn't there*] Eh? The bench that was here . . . ? [*Steps out beyond the doorway and sees at a glance the person on the wall*] What's this!

[HSIANG-TS'AO *gives a shriek and makes herself scarce.* HSI-ERH *turns to face the temple door*]

CHENG So! It's you! [*To* WIDOW T'IEN] You can stop crying, your son has come back! [*With a burst of speed, he makes for the bench*] Fine goings on! I was wondering how come I was missing a dozen peaches out the back. It turns out it was you good-for-nothings stealing them! Let's see how you're going to get down when I move the bench away! [*He picks up the bench in his arms and takes it away*]

WIDOW My boy Hsi-erh! Hsi-erh, my boy! You broke my heart going off and leaving me like that! You're right! Let him fall and kill himself! Let him fall and half kill himself! Let him smash himself black and blue! Let him fall flat on his face!

HSI-ERH Ma! Did I hear you right? Fall and half kill myself—!

WIDOW You heard right! You'll see what I'll do to you, you pest—!

HSI-ERH [*To* CHENG]] Schoolmaster, if I fall to my death you'll have to help my mum buy a coffin for me!

[*Before the words are out of his mouth, he takes a leap into midair, but doesn't come down to earth: he grasps hold of a branch in front of him and as if on a swing, sways back and forth*]

WIDOW [*Startled out of her wits*] Oh saints above! Come down quickly! You frightened me to death!

CHENG [*Hastily drops the bench*] Come down at once! Mind you don't break your leg!

HSI-ERH Stand aside, both of you, I'm going to crash to my death to show you!

WIDOW [*Imploring*] Dear son, darling boy! Come down! Come down and don't frighten your ma!

CHENG I won't tell you off if you come down!

HSI-ERH Stand where you are, schoolmaster, and I'll drop on top of you!

CHENG No, don't. Don't!

HSI-ERH It's no good, I'm losing my grip!

CHENG [*Makes haste to pick up the bench again*] I'll get the bench for you to step down on. . . .

WIDOW Yes, yes! Run and get help!

[*They have hardly turned away before* HSI-ERH, *with an easy bound, comes to rest between the two old people*]

HSI-ERH I'm down! [*They look at him, startled and relieved. He grins all over his face*] Ma! Your son is back. Schoolmaster! Your pupil is back!

WIDOW You haven't injured yourself anywhere?

HSI-ERH No.

CHENG You didn't sprain your back?

HSI-ERH No.

WIDOW [*Suddenly lets fly*] So! Do you call yourself a dutiful son? All you do is torment your ma! Your ma has struggled as a good widow woman for ten years to bring you up. What wrong have I done you that you make my life a misery from one year's end to the next? How could I have faced your dead father if you'd fallen and broken something?

CHENG [*Similarly rebukes him*] You never gave a thought to where you are! This is not the place for your antics! The temple to Kuan Ti! The Cheng Private Academy! [*As if something has struck him*] Ah, yes! What were you standing on the wall for, if not to steal peaches?

HSI-ERH I didn't steal any.

CHENG You say you didn't steal any when you've actually eaten some? Your word is not to be trusted, my boy.

HSI-ERH Smell my breath and see, schoolmaster.

CHENG I will and all. [*He goes up and smells his breath*] No, you haven't eaten any.

WIDOW There, what did I say in the temple, schoolmaster, Hsi-erh leads us a merry dance all right, but as to his heart—I'm his mother, I should know—he's got a heart of gold.

CHENG I'm blessed if I don't go and count the peaches on the trees. [*Indeed he does retrace his steps to the temple to go and count his peaches*]

WIDOW [*Sits on the bench*] Just listen to that! Just listen to that! You hear how the schoolmaster reprimands you: your word isn't to be trusted. All the thanks I get for staying faithful to your father's memory! [*She is about to weep, but checks herself*] I'd like you to tell me something. You're eighteen now, you're as strong as an ox, you've had a good few years' schooling, you must have read nearly a dozen books, but you've not a certificate or a degree to your name. I'd like to know in what way you've been a good son to me?

HSI-ERH [*Leaning against the tree*] One of these days, ma . . .

WIDOW "One of these days"! For the past five or six years that's all I've heard from you—"one of these days"! "One of these days" your ma's bones will have rotted under the sod, and you'll still be saying "one of these days"! [*Starts to cry*] O my dead husband! What kind of widowhood have I condemned myself to! This son you left me is driving me to an early grave!

HSI-ERH Ma, if there's nothing you want this precious son of yours for, he's off.

WIDOW [*Grabs hold of him*] Where are you going?

HSI-ERH Let go of me first, ma. . . .

WIDOW Not on your life! From now on I'm going to keep you on a rope at the window where I can see you, like we tether the animals in their stall. You won't find it that easy to walk out on me again! I've been searching for you up hill and down dale! Just now I even got the schoolmaster to read the signs for me! You spineless wonder, before when you used to disappear for a day or two I'd be a bag of nerves, but this time you did yourself proud, when you lit out it was for a fortnight, and you didn't even drop me a line to tell me where you were. Such callousness might come easy to you, but your ma's hair turned white with worry!

HSI-ERH It's not as if I'm a baby still taking milk . . .

WIDOW Since you stopped taking milk you stopped being my child, is that it? Very nice! That you can bring yourself to say such a thing . . .

HSI-ERH Ma, all this pushing and shoving will make us a laughingstock.

WIDOW Who's to laugh? I have a right to push my own son. Are you telling me you're not my son? [*Beats the air with her free hand*] How terrible! He doesn't even acknowledge me as his mother any more! What a wretched lot is mine, poor old woman!

HSI-ERH [*Puts his arm round her and lifts her up*] I can see you're tired off your feet, ma . . .

WIDOW [*Yells*] Oy! How dare you! Put me down at once!

HSI-ERH What's there to be afraid of? Isn't it my dearest darling mother I'm holding? [*Looks her in the face*] Do you mean to say you're not my mother? [*Holding her securely, he deposits her correctly on the bench*] Very nice! The old lady doesn't even acknowledge me as her son any more!

WIDOW [*Laughs*] Just wait, you beast. . . .

HSI-ERH When you smile, ma, you look lovely, like the Amida Buddha.

WIDOW [*Suddenly jumps up*] Enough of your humbug! You've got a whipping coming to you from the mayor! If it hadn't been for me that Mr. Yang would have beaten you to a pulp the last time. I ask you, what got into you? What did you want to pick that young maid up for while she was picking mulberry leaves and sit her up in a tree and leave her to squeal and screech?

HSI-ERH She enjoyed it.

WIDOW If she enjoyed it would you have got a beating?

HSI-ERH It was her father who didn't enjoy it.

WIDOW There's nothing wrong with that young maid—comely, sensible, polite to everybody, and there's not another maid in the villages around who can touch her for needlework and embroidery, for cutting a shoe pattern, for sewing a long gown . . . what have you got to offer her? If you expect she'd take you in the clothes you stand up in . . . Have you got fields? Have you got land? Have you got a sackful of money and a barnful of grain? Have you got a daddy with a mandarin button in his hat?[3]

HSI-ERH [*Grinning cheekily*] I've got a question to ask in return.

WIDOW [*Stopped in her tracks*] What question?

HSI-ERH It's this: where are your fields, where is your land, where's your sackful of money and barnful of grain, where's your daddy with a mandarin button in his hat?!

WIDOW [*At a loss for words for a long time*] I . . . just you wait, you jackanapes! You make my blood boil! For my sake, make the best of a bad job, take my advice and settle on another bride. . . .

HSI-ERH I don't want another bride.

WIDOW You can't very well turn down somebody your ma has picked out for you, can you?

HSI-ERH If that's what you've been up to you've bothered your head for nothing. [WIDOW T'IEN *glares at him, then starts searching around*] What are you looking for, ma?

WIDOW [*In high dudgeon*] Never you mind! You're determined to cross me. I'll . . .

HSI-ERH You wouldn't be looking for a stick to beat me with? There's a branch over here as it happens. [*Indeed there is a branch up against the wall; he goes over and picks it up*] Will this do a turn, ma? [WIDOW T'IEN *snatches it from him*] Don't be too heavy handed, ma.

WIDOW [*Wades into him*] You take off for a fortnight . . . when you come back you just get my goat . . . I'll beat the life out of you, you unfilial brute.

HSI-ERH [*Letting out wild shrieks and howls*] Ma, I won't dare do it again! . . . I'll turn over a new leaf! . . . Spare me!

WIDOW That's just what I won't do! What does a body raise a son for . . .

[*He trots ahead of her, she totters behind. Without receiving any blows to speak of, he raises the most awful din. They go round and round the tree in this fashion.* CHENG *comes out of the temple, his anger now subsided*]

CHENG You needn't beat him any more, ma'am; he didn't steal any peaches.

WIDOW [*Panting*] It wasn't about the peaches. . . . You don't realize, schoolmaster . . .

HSI-ERH My ma is going to beat me to death, schoolmaster!

CHENG [*Meditating*] You deserve it! [*Then*] Mrs. T'ien, ma'am! You may desist! Actually what are peaches for if not for people to eat? Since he didn't steal them, the matter might as well be dropped.

[*He coaxes her to sit down over by the stone beast.* HSIANG-TS'AO, *empty-handed, reenters from the left, and looks on, staying in the shadow of the wall*]

HSI-ERH [*Espies* HSIANG-TS'AO, *winks at her, and at the same time says in a loud voice to* CHENG] Schoolmaster, put yourself in my position: my ma has lined up a match for me, the party is neat and trim, her family is passable, . . . but my ma, oh she's so pigheaded . . .

WIDOW Me pigheaded! You've got no conscience! You'll drive me round the bend! [*Rushes across to hit him;* CHENG *has his work cut out to hold her back*] I'll kill you, you rebel! I'll have you up before the magistrate! I'll have you charged with flagrant disobedience!

CHENG Leave him to me. I'll put him in his place.

HSI-ERH Not only that, ma has fixed up a match for me here . . . and Mr. Ching has arranged a match for me in the county town as well.

WIDOW Mr. Ching! That globe-trotter! No wonder you've picked up bad habits! I don't want to know about any match he proposes!

CHENG I'll make him see the error of his ways! Leave me to show him the error of his ways by and by! [*He persuades her to go into the doorway, where she leans on her branch and cries in fits and starts*]

HSI-ERH [*Speeds like an arrow over to* HSIANG-TS'AO] Sweet Hsiang-ts'ao, listen to me.

HSIANG-TS'AO [*Pushes him away*] I hate you!

HSI-ERH Getting on to the second watch tonight . . .

HSIANG-TS'AO Keep away from me!

HSI-ERH I'll be there, you can count on it!

HSIANG-TS'AO Leave me out of it!

HSI-ERH [*Angry*] All right! If you're going to be heartless I'm not going to play fair! [*He turns abruptly to go*]

HSIANG-TS'AO [*Hurriedly grabs hold of the front of his jacket, cries out*] You— [*Quietly*] Hsi-erh!

HSI-ERH [*Eying her*] You agree?

HSIANG-TS'AO But that girl in the county town—

HSI-ERH [*Hugging her*] That was to annoy my ma. I made it up.

HSIANG-TS'AO Your mum has found you a bride—

HSI-ERH That's only an idea of hers.

HSIANG-TS'AO Are you really not afraid then—

HSI-ERH Afraid of what?

HSIANG-TS'AO I can't say it. I feel—

HSI-ERH [*Embracing her*] You feel—

HSIANG-TS'AO [*Tenderly*] Dear Hsi-erh!

HSI-ERH Dear Hsiang-ts'ao, tell me.

[*She can't come out with it. All bashful, she gives him a look. Sticking close to the wall, the one hugs and the other lets herself be hugged, lost to the world. But a bolt from the blue:* MAYOR YANG *comes to an unsteady halt by the roadside; following him are* NUMBER TWO *and* ANOTHER FARM LABORER, *carrying ropes, sickles, and other farm gear*]

YANG [*His face livid*] Hsiang-ts'ao! Hsiang-ts'ao!

[HSIANG-TS'AO *looks up and discovers it is her stern father, utters a cry of* "Dad," *blushes to the roots, and exits right as if on winged feet*]

HSI-ERH [*Putting on a bold face*] Uncle Yang, I hope you're keeping well.

YANG "Uncle Yang"! Sod your "Uncle Yang"! I couldn't have given you a good enough licking last time, you're at it again, taking liberties with a respectable girl! I'll have to teach you a sound lesson, you've got no respect for the law of the land, you unruly brat! [*To the laborers*] Tie him to the tree!

HSI-ERH [*Does not back down in the face of the two stalwart laborers*] This time you won't find me such a pushover!

[*The two farm laborers rush at him. He dodges behind the tree;* NUMBER TWO *bumps into the trunk. But* CHENG, *hearing the sound of voices, steps out of the doorway and as luck would have it blocks* HSI-ERH's *escape route. The other laborer makes a grab for him and hauls him round, pushing him up against the tree.* NUMBER TWO *shakes out the rope and binds him*]

CHENG [*Paying his respects to Yang*] You're back from the fields, Mr. Mayor?

YANG Good day to you, schoolmaster. [*Pointing to* HSI-ERH] This boy is too blackguardly for words!

CHENG Quite so; actually his mother was giving him a beating only just now. [*Calls out*] Mrs. T'ien! Mrs. T'ien! Good news, the mayor is teaching your son his manners for you!

WIDOW Hsi-erh! My precious son! [*To the laborers*] Let my Hsi-erh loose!

CHENG [*Flabbergasted*] Just now didn't you—

WIDOW Just now was just now! [*To* HSI-ERH] My darling son! Your ma can't look on while other people bully you! [*To* YANG] Uncle Yang, you can't take it out on Hsi-erh without just cause!

YANG Me? Without just cause?

WIDOW Are you telling me you have cause?

YANG Haven't you got eyes in your head? Just now my daughter—

WIDOW Your daughter! [*Snorts*] It seems to me you've got a hundred daughters! Whenever you open your mouth it's your daughter! [*To the laborers*] Let my son go! If you dare to lay a finger on him . . .

HSI-ERH Let them tie me up and be done with it, ma; one of these days . . .

WIDOW [*Gives him a backhander*] Shut up about "one of these days"! [*To* YANG] If you dare to touch my son, Uncle Yang, there'll be a showdown between us!

YANG It's as plain as a pikestaff you've been hitting him yourself . . .

WIDOW He's my son, that's why! I'll hit him if I feel like it, I'll give him a dressing down if I feel like it, but that doesn't go for other people!

YANG [*To* CHENG] Is there another woman in the world as unreasonable as this one?

WIDOW Since when have you been reasonable as mayor? Who is it who at every turn was set on brazenly fleecing people of their money? [*To* CHENG] Schoolmaster, you're an educated man, you can be the judge of who is in the right. I've kept myself as a chaste widow these ten years, I've only got this one son left to me . . .

CHENG [*In an awkward position*] True, very true . . .

YANG I saw him take liberties with my daughter with my own eyes.

CHENG True, very true . . .

WIDOW But what about your daughter? In just the wink of an eyelid, while I was standing in the porch of the temple, my son so quickly took liberties with your daughter?

CHENG True . . .

YANG T'ien Hsi-erh, this moment . . .

WIDOW Most likely it was your daughter took liberties with my son!

YANG What! My daughter took liberties with your— Teacher, I ask you!

CHENG That couldn't be . . .

WIDOW If you're afraid your daughter will go astray, why don't you have a gold chain made for her and chain her up?

YANG Chain her up with a gold chain?

WIDOW So that my son won't be bewitched by her!

YANG The world can be my witness! T'ien Hsi-erh now . . .

CHENG Ask him and see.

WIDOW What't the good of asking him, a kid still wet behind the ears, and only just back from town? Uncle Yang, don't you take it out on Hsi-erh on account of his having no father. You've made trouble for him all along! As for me, I may be poor but I've got my pride! Even if your daughter came to us in a big sedan chair carried by eight men I'd still send her packing with a flea in her ear! [*To* HSI-ERH] Stand up for yourself, let ma find another one for you! [*To* CHENG] The world can be my witness, that young miss of the Yangs' is not the only wonder of the world! I was a young miss myself in my time! I don't give a fig for her! I don't give a tinker's cuss! [*To* HSI-ERH] You say it! Don't give a fig! Say it after me! If you don't I'll pinch you!

HSI-ERH Yes, ma, I don't give a fig.

[*The laborers have by now put away the rope*]

YANG [*Stumped for words*] Deaf to reason! [*To* CHENG] I ask you, schoolmaster, how can you get through to her? [*To the laborers*] Don't stand there gaping! Let's go! Go back and harness the cart.

[YANG *goes off right, fuming. The two laborers grimace at each other, and follow*]

WIDOW [*Upbraiding* HSI-ERH] You'll be the death of me! To think that in the twinkling of an eye you could stop Hsiang-ts'ao and make up to her! They didn't give you enough stick last time in the mulberry orchard!

HSI-ERH Ma, you're really something!

WIDOW Bugger off! Watch out I don't give you another clip round the ear! [*As if shooing hens*] Shoo, shoo! Get off home! Anything more can be said at home! [*They exit right, the one after the other*]

CHENG [*Lifts up the bench and carries it to the porch, shaking his head*] This mother and son . . .

[*Curtain*]

ACT II

The Yangs' back garden. Seven to nine o'clock, the evening of the same day.

The Yangs' back garden adjoins the threshing ground. It is said to be a riot of color, full of rare shrubs and flowers, but the corner visible to us is stocked with ordinary plants, like pomegranates in full bloom, and roses of Sharon and Chinese roses, growing as if wild, in five- or six-foot high clumps; at the same time the sunflowers and hollyhocks are not daunted: they stand up as straight as arrows alongside the garden wall. There is a gap in the wall with a heap of bricks beside it, and not far off a willow tree, whose switches and slender leaves sway in the wind. Now this is a world ruled by the stars. Everything merges indistinctly in the shifting, flickering dimness, while overhead hang the azure hue and luminescence of sky peculiar to summer nights. In the distance there is the sound of dogs barking and the watch being struck. The watchman seems to have had more than his share of drink—you can't make out which watch it is he is striking.

A breeze rustles the stillness of the evening; the flowers and leaves seem to converse. A head peeps out of the gap. Very soon it becomes two. From their voices, the two are TIGERCUB *and* BLACKY. *They look furtively round the garden.*

TIGERCUB [*Young as he is, he knows how to keep his voice lowered*] It was in here, I saw them with my own eyes.

BLACKY Go on and pick them.

TIGERCUB Don't hang on to me.

BLACKY I'm scared.

TIGERCUB Then come in with me.

BLACKY I'm scared.

TIGERCUB I told you not to come, but you wouldn't listen.

BLACKY That was because you were coming!

TIGERCUB Don't make such a racket! The pomegranates are just huge, I saw them. . . . [*Jumps through the gap*] Are you coming across or not?

BLACKY I'm afraid of the dog biting me.

TIGERCUB There's no dog here. [*Helps* BLACKY *in*] Stick close to me. The pomegranate tree is over . . .

BLACKY I can hear somebody walking about!

TIGERCUB That's the branches making that sound.

BLACKY [*Yells*] A ghost! A ghost!

[T'IEN HSI-ERH *stands in the gap*]

TIGERCUB I told you not to come . . .

HSI-ERH [*Cocks his ear*] So it's you two little bastards kicking up a row here!

TIGERCUB [*His terror abates*] T'ien Hsi-erh!

BLACKY Brother Hsi-erh, it wasn't my idea. Tigercub said the pomegranates were ripe in the Yangs' garden . . .

HSI-ERH Oh, I see, you've turned up at the Yangs' to pinch pomegranates. They're like marbles, they're no good to eat. You'd better buzz off, and quick!

TIGERCUB [*Hesitates*] But I saw them, they're just over—

BLACKY Go on and snaffle some!

HSI-ERH [*Cocks his ear*] Here comes Rednose striking the watch!

[*The sound of the clapper had died away, but suddenly it starts up from near at hand.* T'IEN HSI-ERH *turns and vanishes*]

TIGERCUB [*His support gone*] Brother Hsi-erh!

BLACKY [*In abject terror*] Rednose will have us for breakfast!

[TIGERCUB *makes for the gap.* BLACKY *breaks into shrieks: "Tigercub! T'ien Hsi-erh! Rednose!"* REDNOSE *does indeed appear on the threshing ground side of the wall*]

REDNOSE [*Stops at a distance*] Who's there? [*The sound of crying and shouting suddenly ceases*] What's all that caterwauling going on there? [*Trying to dominate by bluster*] Who's there? [*To himself*] Only three jugs, and drunk already? [*Barks*] Who's there? [*To himself*] I swear I heard . . . it was a high-pitched voice . . . like some bit of skirt . . . somebody wouldn't be trying to do themselves in, would they? [*Barks*] Who's there? [*To himself*] Maybe it's ghosts haunting the place? . . . I swear I heard . . . I thought they even called my name, Rednose! . . . what would they want to call me for? [*Can't help getting goose-pimples*] Who's there? [*Plucks up courage*] Nobody! What did I say, nobody! . . . I wish I'd brought a lantern out with me tonight! [*For the last time*] Who's there? [*Relaxes*] It's my imagination, I'm a bit nervy tonight, my ears are playing tricks on me.

[*He goes forward two steps, and strikes his watch clapper.* BLACKY *comes out with a great wail*]

REDNOSE The lord help us! [*He turns and runs*]

TIGERCUB [*Hisses*] Blacky! Blacky!

BLACKY Tigercub! Tigercub!

[T'IEN HSI-ERH *appears in the gap again*]

HSI-ERH Mind you stay out of the way, Tigercub! [*He jumps down lightly and goes over to* BLACKY] Don't cry! It's all right, Blacky, I'll lift you out. [*He picks* BLACKY *up and swings him through the gap*] Off you go! [*Turns to* TIGERCUB] Take care and see he gets back all right! In future don't be so greedy!

[TIGERCUB *steps through the gap and vanishes with* BLACKY]

HSI-ERH [*Somewhat uneasy*] I hope all the noise they made won't foul things up. Then my luck *would* be out! [*Listens*] Not a sound. How quiet the night is, and the sky all full of stars. [*Pause*] There's no going back now. [*Takes a few steps, then stops*] What if they catch me and take me for a thief, what then? [*Makes up his mind*] Nothing worse than a beating . . . [*Listens*] Somebody coming! And I can hear people talking! I . . . I . . .

[*He looks around, and hides behind a dark clump of shrubbery.*
REDNOSE*'s voice, as before. He stands gingerly at the boundary with* NUMBER TWO, *peering in*]

REDNOSE [*In hushed tones*] It was as black as pitch, I couldn't make out what it was like. As soon as I yelled out it let loose an almighty howl—I couldn't tell whether it was male or female. Most likely it was a female ghost.

NUMBER TWO Imitate the sound it made for me.

REDNOSE No thanks! It will come out again if I imitate it.

NUMBER TWO All to the good! Then we'll get a proper go at it.

REDNOSE No need for any rough stuff, it was definitely a female ghost.

NUMBER TWO If you didn't see it how do you know the ghost was female?

REDNOSE Ah, well—humph! I know. Last night when I wobbled my way up to here, a shiver went through me. I felt a gust of cold air go right up my nose—just as I expected, tonight . . . You don't realize, there's a temple to a goddess not far away, and there have always been funny goings-on there . . . It was a bad day this wall fell down, it let the vapors out of the garden. Now there are messes of flowers everywhere, and that's just what the sprites and goblins go for. Take a sniff, the scent is enough to knock you over!

NUMBER TWO [*Goes forward*] I can't see anything. [*Jumps onto the breach in the wall*] There's nothing here at all.

REDNOSE Have another listen! [*A breeze brushes past*] There, you see! [*He cowers back*]

NUMBER TWO [*Derisively*] That's the wind! You've had one over the eight tonight, Rednose! [*Pause*] I'm off, Rednose!

REDNOSE Where to, Number Two?

NUMBER TWO Ah, me, I've got something nice lined up!

[*As they stand by the wall,* T'IEN HSI-ERH *takes the opportunity to edge further into the garden. Inadvertently he bumps into something*]

REDNOSE Listen!

NUMBER TWO There *was* something made a noise!

REDNOSE What was it?

NUMBER TWO Most likely a hedgehog.

REDNOSE Blast! I seem to have got off on the wrong foot tonight. There's no two ways about it, I didn't get enough grog down me tonight.

NUMBER TWO What watch is it now?

REDNOSE Lord knows! It went clean out of my mind a long time ago! [*Tugs at his trouser leg*] Don't go, Number Two, take a dram with me.

NUMBER TWO You've got some drink with you?

REDNOSE [*Pulls a hip flask out of the front of his coat*] What do you call this?

NUMBER TWO There's only just enough for you there. See you tomorrow, I'm going to have a good time! [*He jumps out of the garden and makes tracks*]

REDNOSE [*Calls after him*] Number Two! Just a word! Blast! What kind of a friend is that!

[T'IEN HSI-ERH *dodges away, and is out of sight*]

REDNOSE [*Sits in the gap, his back against the broken wall*] Sod it! Well, I'll drink by myself! And I'll get well and truly sozzled! [*Puts his clapper in the front of his coat*] Mother Chang's booze is as strong as you could wish it! [*Drinks a mouthful*] Got a scent, got a bite! [*Another mouthful*] You won't find another drop like this the length and breadth of the land! [*Another mouthful*] Well, it's good I've got the flask of drink. [*Another mouthful*] Now, if only I could find a bit of something to go with it! [*Heaves a sigh*] Forget it! These days if you can get hold of a drop of Mother Chang's drink you're not doing too badly! [*One mouthful after another*] Cheers! Cheers! Cheers! [*The flask is emptied*] A lovely drop of drink! [*Sings*] "The third watch—dum—the midnight hour—di—the young bride all alone—di dum dong—all alone keeps vigil—dum—in her boudoir . . ."

YANG'S VOICE [*From the direction of the threshing ground*] Who's that roistering in the dead of night?

REDNOSE [*Tipsy*] Little old me!

YANG'S VOICE Damn your "old me"!

REDNOSE Swear at people, would you, you blighter! Come out and show yourself!

YANG'S VOICE Why don't you sound the watch as you're supposed to, instead of droning some soppy tune? If there's any trouble I'll have your hide, see if I don't!

REDNOSE Have your mother's hide! I want to keep my hide to see me through the winter! [*Stuffs his flask in his chest*] Fair enough, the moon's coming out now, I've had a good rest, now I ought to see to me duties. [*Thinks*] Let's see, the time now—yesterday was the 18th, today is the 19th, the moon is only just out, it must be about the third watch. Let's strike up "the third watch—dum—the midnight hour—di—the young bride all alone—di . . ." [*Studies the inside and outside of the garden*] Which side is the garden? It makes no odds, I'll follow wherever my feet take me. If I keep along the wall I can't be far wrong!

[*He jumps down out of the garden, and moves off along the outer side of the wall sounding his clapper. A dim light suddenly approaches from the threshing ground*]

YANG'S VOICE Where's that son of a bitch clapped off to with that clapper of his?

[YANG *enters, holding up an oil-paper lantern, followed by the other laborer*]

YANG Slobs! Absolute slobs! [*To the laborer*] Slaphappy, every man jack
of you! You only think of your bellies. "Is everything neat and tidy?"
"Yes, all neat and tidy!" There's a big coil of rope left by the coach
gate, and nobody thinks of putting it away!

LABORER That was Number Two's doing. I was feeding the livestock.

YANG Where's Number Two got to? He's got a good day's work in
the fields ahead of him tomorrow, and instead of bedding down nice
and early in the byre, he's gone prancing off in the middle of the night.

LABORER He was still here just now.

YANG Here? If he was still here, how come there's no sight nor smell of
him? [*Comes to the gap, is taken aback*] What! This gap hasn't been
filled in? [*Stamps his foot*] Devil take him! What if we get burgled? I
told Number Two first thing this morning as soon as he came back
from the fields he mustn't forget to bring some bricks and fill it in—

LABORER The bricks are here.

YANG But why haven't they been shifted over and laid? It's only a
matter of a few steps; if they can be moved to there why can't they be
moved to here? Just a lot of shirkers who only think of their bellies—I
don't take back a word of it!

LABORER Number Two said he could fix the wall first thing tomorrow.

YANG Why did it have to be first thing tomorrow?

LABORER It would be handy for him to get back in this way, it would
save him having to call somebody to open the carriage gate.

YANG [*His eyes pop*] Where can he get to this time of night, with it so
dark?

LABORER [*Gives a twisted smile*] He . . .

YANG If you don't give it to me straight you'll be out on your neck
tomorrow!

LABORER I tried more than once to get him to see reason . . .

YANG He goes gambling?

LABORER He hankers after some sport . . .

YANG What sport?

LABORER [*Embarrassed*] Women . . .

YANG Women! [*Steps onto the broken wall*] Disgraceful! You lead the
way!

LABORER Where to, boss?

YANG To put a rope round that randy bastard and his whore! It's
an outrage!

LABORER [*With simple directness*] That woman is a real handful,
even her old man has no control over her; and you're not her old
man, boss. . . .

YANG What do you say, then?

LABORER Let it lie! It's not as if he's having it off with your old woman.

YANG Get stuffed! [*But having sworn at him, he sees the sense of
it*] P'raps you're right! It won't look too good if I interfere! [*As if
alarmed*] What's that noise over there?

LABORER [*Blankly*] Over where?

YANG [*Pointing to the threshing ground*] Over there! Go and take a look.

LABORER [*Takes a few token steps forward and looks around*] Nothing, it was the wind.

YANG [*Listen*] That's all right, then. But if there's any trouble I won't let you lot of craphounds off lightly! Where's Rednose wandered off to sounding his clapper?

LABORER He's inside the wall, by the sound of it.

YANG Any fool can tell he's outside the wall. He's had one too many for sure, and got squiffy. He's gone sounding his watch off into the fields. Go and fetch him back. [*He steps out of the breach, allowing the laborer to pass*] A load of shits! Every man jack of them a useless layabout!

[*Lighting his way with the lantern, he takes the opposite direction along the line of the wall. A solitary wild goose honks in the sky. Over by the threshing ground a clump of shrubbery rustles and shakes. From it there come suppressed whispers*]

HSI-ERH He's gone.

HSIANG-TS'AO'S VOICE He hasn't.

HSI-ERH'S VOICE Take a look if you don't believe me.

HSIANG-TS'AO'S VOICE Wait a bit longer!

[*The sky is now a lot paler. A sliver of waning moon moves remotely against the branches of the crests of the trees. The wind seems to have picked up; it bends the branches back and forward, like a sweep of black waves; at the same time they seem to be engaged in whispered debate, and panicky disarray.* T'IEN HSI-ERH *is the first to emerge*]

HSI-ERH [*Looks around, turns back to the shrubbery*] Not a soul about.

HSIANG-TS'AO'S VOICE Take a good look.

HSI-ERH Your dad has gone back. There's no light from his paper lantern.

[*He stretches out his hand and draws* HSIANG-TS'AO *from the shrubbery. She is carrying a bundle in the other hand*]

HSIANG-TS'AO I'm shaking in my shoes!

HSI-ERH Hold my hand tight.

HSIANG-TS'AO Dad heard you talking just now.

HSI-ERH He didn't, I'm telling you, he didn't.

HSIANG-TS'AO Listen! People keep calling out after me.

HSI-ERH No, that's a wild goose passing.

HSIANG-TS'AO The moon is out now.

HSI-ERH That's good, it'll light our way for us.

HSIANG-TS'AO People will see me.

HSI-ERH There's no need to be afraid with me with you.

HSIANG-TS'AO If dad saw me he'd flay me.

HSI-ERH He won't be able to see you, he's gone back.

HSIANG-TS'AO If mum misses me she'll be worried to death.

HSI-ERH Your old lady is asleep, like my ma. [*Draws her onward*] I'll take you somewhere far, far away. Just you and me. There won't be anyone who knows us. [*Bumps into a shrub*] Ouch!

Hsiang-ts'ao Do be careful!

Hsi-erh What's this? It's all thorns!

Hsiang-ts'ao That's a Chinese rose, it's in bloom now.

Hsi-erh I wondered what that queer smell was!

Hsiang-ts'ao The pomegranates have blossomed as well, and their little fruits have formed.

Hsi-erh Get a move on! Don't keep gassing!

Hsiang-ts'ao My legs are all trembling! Listen! There's a dog barking. It's our Brownie.

Hsi-erh Let it bark.

Hsiang-ts'ao I don't seem to be able to leave anything behind . . .

Hsi-erh You'll feel all right when you get used to it.

Hsiang-ts'ao The trees keep moving.

Hsi-erh The wind has got up.

Hsiang-ts'ao I feel cold.

Hsi-erh You'll warm up when you get moving.

Hsiang-ts'ao [*Shrieks*] Agh!

Hsi-erh [*Impatient*] What is it now?

Hsiang-ts'ao Somebody's got hold of my pigtail!

Hsi-erh There's nobody there.

Hsiang-ts'ao I can't get free. My hair! There *is* someone holding it, Hsi-erh!

Hsi-erh Just don't panic. Let me have a look. Turn round and see for yourself, there really isn't anybody there.

Hsiang-ts'ao I don't dare look round.

Hsi-erh As I thought! A branch has got tangled in the end of your pigtail! Stand still and let me free it.

Hsiang-ts'ao Hurry up. There are heaps and heaps of black things all moving about, as if they're going to come at us.

Hsi-erh It's the wind blowing them. [*Pause*] I can't get it undone. [*Pause*] Stay still. [*Pause*] All the hairs are knotted in the branch. [*Suddenly*] I've got it!

Hsiang-ts'ao Got what?

Hsi-erh I'll just break off the branch. [*With a cracking sound the branch breaks*] I got it!

Hsiang-ts'ao Hsi-erh!

Hsi-erh My nerves won't stand it any more! [*He takes her hand and makes for the gap*]

Hsiang-ts'ao [*Stumbling along*] Hsi-erh!

Hsi-erh What?

Hsiang-ts'ao [*Crying*] I . . . I . . .

Hsi-erh [*Lets go of her hand, looks at her*] What are you crying about?

Hsiang-ts'ao I can't abandon . . . I can't part with . . .

Hsi-erh You'll drive me crazy!

Hsiang-ts'ao I can't . . . I grew up here . . .

Hsi-erh That dog keeps barking!

Hsiang-ts'ao [*Frightened*] They're out looking for me!

[*Calls come from the direction of the threshing ground*]

HSI-ERH [*Jumps onto the broken wall*] We'll be safe once we're over this wall!

HSIANG-TS'AO [*Listens closely*] It's mum calling me!

HSI-ERH Come on up! I'll give you a hand!

MRS. YANG'S VOICE Hsiang-ts'ao!

HSIANG-TS'AO It *is* mum!

HSI-ERH Pass me the bundle!

HSIANG-TS'AO [*Hands him the bundle*] Mum will go out of her mind if she can't find me!

HSI-ERH If you keep on chattering we'll never get away!

MRS. YANG'S CALL Hsiang-ts'ao! Hsiang-ts'ao! [*Gets nearer and nearer*] Hsiang-ts'ao!

HSIANG-TS'AO Hsi-erh! Mum is here!

HSI-ERH [*Blurts out*] I'll take your mum along too!

[MRS. YANG *arrives at the edge of the threshing ground*]

MRS. YANG [*Calling out very loudly*] Hsiang-ts'ao!

HSIANG-TS'AO [*Instinctively*] I'm coming, mum!

HSI-ERH [*Softly*] Hsiang-ts'ao!

MRS. YANG Hsiang-ts'ao, where are you?

HSI-ERH [*Pleading*] Dear Hsiang-ts'ao, come with me!

MRS. YANG My Hsiang-ts'ao, where are you?

HSI-ERH [*Loses his head*] She's not here, Mrs. Yang!

MRS. YANG [*Turns toward the sound*] Who are you?

HSIANG-TS'AO [*Quietly*] It's you mum is asking! [*Briskly*] I'm off. Don't let mum and the others see you!

MRS. YANG [*Demanding from a safe distance*] Who's that standing in the gap in the wall?

HSIANG-TS'AO It's nobody, mum, it's only me! [*She runs across and falls into her mother's arms*]

MRS. YANG [*Reproving*] Hsiang-ts'ao!

HSIANG-TS'AO [*Sobbing*] Mum!

[T'IEN HSI-ERH *jumps down from the wall. He has taken a few steps in pursuit of her when a voice suddenly speaks behind him*]

YANG'S VOICE [*Sharply*] Who's that? Stand where you are!

[HSI-ERH *dives for cover behind a shrub. The moon slides behind a ragged canvas of clouds.* YANG*'s dark figure emerges*]

YANG Who is it? [*Looks around*] Who's that over there?

MRS. YANG Me! Hsiang-ts'ao's mother!

HSIANG-TS'AO [*Tremulously*] Dear mum!

YANG Who else?

MRS. YANG Hsiang-ts'ao!

YANG [*Emphatically*] I asked who else?

MRS. YANG I don't know.

YANG I'll flush him out! [*He makes for where* HSI-ERH *is hiding*] I'll get you, you swine! You won't get away!

[*He and* HSI-ERH *circle round the bush, moving in step. But mother and daughter, looking on, are thrown into a panic*]

Hsiang-ts'ao Mum!

Yang Wife! Go round behind and help me get him!

Hsiang-ts'ao Oh! Mum! [*She faints*]

Mrs. Yang [*At her wits' end*] Help!

[Hsi-erh *throws his bundle smack into* Yang's *face*]

Yang [*Cries out in alarm at the same time as his wife*] O dear, O lor', I've been hit!

[*He falls on his back beside the bush. From beyond the wall the rattle of a watchman's clapper draws nearer and nearer.* Hsi-erh *jumps up into the gap, is outside with a bound, and disappears*]

[*Curtain*]

ACT III

The Yangs' garden, next day, early morning.

The wind has died, day has dawned. Feeble sunbeams slant through the clumps of trees, falling on this leafy nook. The shrubs revel in their finery, unmoved by the disturbances of yesternight. The cock's last crows can still be heard. The magpies chatter from their hiding places. From the distance comes the complacent braying of an ass. All the while humankind is up in arms.

Yang *is holding that fateful bundle and recounting to* Cheng *the events of last night, complete with all the actions.*

Yang . . . As soon as I shouted, he dived behind here . . . I went after him, and he was off like a shot . . . another step and I would have caught him . . . I thought to myself, I've got him this time, I'll grab him and haul him up before the county magistrate on a charge that would put him away for good. . . . then he let fly with this bundle in my face . . . you couldn't see your hand in front of your face, it was so dark a night . . . I . . . took a tumble . . . just missed falling here . . . where it's all thorns . . . it was a close one, all right . . .

Cheng [*As if supplying end-rhyme, to show his concern*] Ooh! . . . Ah? . . . Ooh! . . . Ah? . . . Ooh! . . . Ah? . . . [*Finally*] An outrage, I call it!

Yang My backside ached the rest of the night . . . and there's the back of my pate . . . [*Rubs it*] a lump as big as an egg! [*Clenching his fist*] He won't get away . . . Number Two has taken some others to look for him at home . . . he won't get away!

Cheng How do you intend to deal with him, mayor?

Yang I . . . I . . . I'll put him to death! [*His mind made up*] That's right, I'll put him to death!

Cheng There's one thing, though, his mother is a virtuous widow . . .

Yang I can't be bothered about all that . . . he came to my house at black of night to steal . . . this bundle is his loot to prove it.

Cheng Ah! What a waste!

Yang What?

Cheng A fine monument to chasteness, ruined in front of our eyes through the work of this no-count son!

YANG Well, these things are written in a person's stars, there's no going against them! [*Suddenly*] Who has she got to blame? She spoiled the boy, so he behaved that way.

CHENG That lad Hsi-erh was full of mischief from the start. . . .

YANG [*Emphatically*] Absolutely, a good-for-nothing!

CHENG To be sure. . . . I remember years ago there was a bird's nest in the very top branches of the cypress tree in the temple yard. He climbed up and dismantled every last twig of it, and when the two crows came back at nightfall they just flew around the tree in circles, cawing so pitifully they sounded human!

YANG He's gone too far this time! He'll wish he'd left my house alone!

CHENG If it was as dark as all that last night, how could you tell it was him?

YANG This village has been quiet and peaceful for over a fortnight . . . the first day he comes back I get trouble at home . . . work it out for yourself, schoolmaster, what son-of-a-bitch would have the infernal gall . . .

[HSIANG-CHÜ *runs in from the threshing ground, unwashed and unkempt: clearly no one has attended to her morning toilet*]

HSIANG-CHÜ [*Shouting as she runs*] Daddy! Daddy! Daddy!

YANG [*Gives her a glare*] Why aren't you in the fields?

HSIANG-CHÜ [*Falteringly*] Sister . . . sister . . .

YANG [*Gives her another glare*] There's nothing wrong with your sister!

HSIANG-CHÜ Sister has passed out again!

YANG [*Irritably*] Let her drop dead altogether! That would be one less to worry about!

CHENG You're talking about Hsiang-ts'ao?

YANG [*Covering up*] The silly girl caught a chill last night. . . . [*To* HSIANG-CHÜ] Is that what all the hurry was about?

HSIANG-CHÜ They say T'ien Hsi-erh is coming . . .

YANG [*Blows his top*] So what!? Get off to the fields with you!

HSIANG-CHÜ There's no one to plait my pigtail for me.

YANG Ask your mother to plait it for you!

HSIANG-CHÜ Mum is busy looking after my sister.

YANG A big girl like you, you can get down three or four steamed rolls at a sitting, yet you don't know what those things at the end of your arms are for?

CHENG She's only a child, you have to make some allowances.

YANG [*Remembers his manners*] Come over and pay your respects to Schoolmaster Cheng.

HSIANG-CHÜ [*Timidly*] Good morning, Schoolmaster Cheng.

YANG Be off with you. [*In fact she doesn't leave; she retreats behind a bush to stay and watch the fun*]

YANG [*Returns to the subject*] Never mind about the rest of it, for him to dare to make this throw in these times when everybody's got the jitters makes me think he's teamed up with some unsavory persons on the outside . . . if this keeps on, what chance has the village got of staying peaceful?

CHENG After all, you're the mayor. . . .

YANG [*Even more solemn*] That's just what I was getting at. . . .

CHENG [*Shakes his head*] Really preposterous!

YANG So I've made up my mind . . . that's what I'm going to do . . . you can be my witness, schoolmaster. . . .

HSIANG-CHÜ [*Claps her hands and shouts*] Brother T'ien Hsi-erh! Brother T'ien Hsi-erh!

[REDNOSE *can be heard shouting in the distance*]

REDNOSE The guv'nor is over the gap in the wall! Don't let him get away!

[*In fact,* T'IEN HSI-ERH *has no chance of escaping. He seems half-asleep still, his eyes lacklustre, his arms hanging down, all limp; he is quite simply a different person.* REDNOSE *leads the way,* T'IEN HSI-ERH *is in the middle, and the two farm laborers bring up the rear. The escort is not exactly full of pep either*]

YANG [*Disgruntled*] How come you didn't tie him up?

REDNOSE He was asleep on his feet . . . his two legs are like strings of noodles . . . he'd never raise a gallop . . . he's been yawning all the way . . . [*While he is explaining, he yawns himself*] What a rotten night it's been!

[T'IEN HSI-ERH *bears out his story by yawning in his wake. The two farm laborers make no bones about yawning too*]

HSI-ERH [*As if he were a spectator in the affair*] I feel worn out! I . . . I . . . You haven't even got a seat here! Uncle Yang, Schoolmaster Cheng, excuse me if I stretch out on the ground! [*He goes to sit on the ground. The laborers hurry forward and hold him upright*]

HSI-ERH [*To the laborers*] What are you up to?

REDNOSE [*Brusquely*] Up to? The mayor has some questions for you!

YANG [*To* CHENG] You see, schoolmaster, the very picture of a rascal. [*To* HSI-ERH] That's rich, that is! You keep everybody else on the go all night, and now you want to sleep? You guttersnipe, you don't give a damn for authority. Well, I'll give you something to think about, right now!

HSI-ERH [*Discovers* HSIANG-CHÜ] Hsiang-chü, what's your sister Hsiang-ts'ao been doing all this time?

HSIANG-CHÜ [*Not knowing she is speaking out of place*] Hsiang-ts'ao does nothing but cry.

YANG [*Erupts*] Rebellion! Barefaced rebellion! Ignore me, would you? Give him a slap in the mouth! Give him a slap in the mouth! [*No one responds*] I told you to slap him in the mouth, you lily-livered buggers!

REDNOSE His ma said she is a chaste widow, and this is her only son . . .

YANG I— I—

CHENG Question him first . . . question him first.

[TIGERCUB *and* BLACKY *can be descried intermittently, peeking through the gap in the wall*]

YANG Just as you wish, schoolmaster. I'll question him first, then. [*Turns to* HSI-ERH] Can you explain what you were doing at dead of night scaling walls and entering my property?

[TIGERCUB *has not come to see the fun. While the attention of the others is diverted he steps across the gap, slips into the garden, and searches for something on the ground*]

YANG [*Not receiving an answer*] You won't speak up, eh? Not past feeling ashamed of yourself, then. Come on, don't be shy. Who would credit it that a bit of a kid like you would cause more trouble than all the rest of them put together!

[TIGERCUB *picks up a little slipper and waves it at* BLACKY. *From his delight it is clear that this is what he was looking for*]

BLACKY [*Innocently*] Give it to me!

YANG [*Turns around*] What's that?

HSI-ERH [*Chortles*] That's right! Ask Tigercub, he knows!

[*Everyone looks toward the two young brothers.* TIGERCUB *hurriedly hides the slipper behind his back*]

YANG [*Glowering, walks toward* TIGERCUB, *his steps punctuating his words*] Let me see it! What have you got? What's that you're hiding? Bring it out and give it to me, quick!

BLACKY [*Shouts wildly*] Tigercub, give it to me, quick!

YANG [*Turns to* BLACKY] Give you what?

BLACKY My slipper! The slipper I left behind!

YANG Slipper! [*Lifts* TIGERCUB's *arm, finds it is indeed a slipper*] Well, I never . . . how did that get in my garden?

[TIGERCUB *stays dumb*]

HSI-ERH [*Being helpful*] Tell him, Tigercub. Mind Uncle Yang doesn't bash you if you keep him waiting.

YANG [*Putting him in his place*] You hold your tongue!

TIGERCUB [*Stuttering*] Pome . . . granates . . .

YANG Pome—granates?

HSI-ERH [*Amused*] That's right! They came to pinch pomegranates! I ran into them while they were at it.

YANG Pinching pomegranates? [*His eye sweeps over the shrubs*] Where are the pomegranates?

TIGERCUB [*Pointing away in the distance*] There . . . there . . .

[YANG *goes over to investigate*]

CHENG [*Suddenly an idea occurs to him*] Ah! So it was you two! [*Comes over to stand between the two young brothers*] Out with it! Which of you stole the peaches in my temple? My beautiful peaches, just about to get ripe, then dozens of them disappeared. Which of you stole them?

[REDNOSE *is understandably uneasy. He looks away*]

BLACKY Rednose once—

REDNOSE [*Frantic*] Blacky! You mind what you say!

TIGERCUB [*Confirming*] Rednose once . . .

REDNOSE The little bastards!

YANG [*His inspection complete, to the laborers*] There are five fruits there, and one missing. What about it?

REDNOSE [*To the young brothers*] You see, Uncle Yang trusts me!

YANG [*Abuses him*] Trust you, my arse! You're the biggest blighter of the bunch! Who told you to go sounding your watch off into the fields outside the wall? You'll end up roasting in hell! [*Turns to* TIGERCUB] Did you see T'ien Hsi-erh?

TIGERCUB Blacky couldn't climb out, so Hsi-erh lifted him over.

HSI-ERH See, Uncle Yang. I'm a decent sort of chap.

YANG [*Stamping in anger*] Decent my foot! You don't know what decency is! [*Pause*] Tell us for that matter what you were doing on my property.

HSI-ERH [*Languidly, propping himself against the willow tree*] You know the score, Uncle Yang.

YANG I'm damned if I do!

HSIANG-CHÜ [*Chips in*] He came for my sister!

YANG [*Goes over and boxes her ears*] You speak when you're spoken to!

HSIANG-CHÜ [*Cries*] He did . . . he did come for my sister!

YANG [*Glaring at her*] Be off! Get out of my sight!

[HSIANG-CHÜ *goes out of view, sniveling*]

YANG [*Pointing at* HSI-ERH]You cur! You have the cheek to come stealing from me, the mayor! Years ago when your dad was on his deathbed he bound me to take special care of you as the last of his line, saying he would rest in peace if one day you got yourself a mandarin button or such like. Now look at you! You're eighteen now, and what have you done that your dad could be proud of? You're a misfit, you've turned thief, you steal— steal—

TIGERCUB [*All good intentions*] He didn't steal. He fancies sister Hsiang-ts'ao. . . .

YANG [*Threateningly*] If I clap eyes on you two again I'll have your guts for garters!

REDNOSE [*Blustering*] On your way! Or are you looking for a bashing? [*He hustles them through the wall, then waves his fist after them intimidatingly, but when he comes down from the breach in the wall he has to avoid* CHENG*'s eye, as the latter is still glaring at him*]

YANG [*Turns to* HSI-ERH] I ask you, is there another one like you in the village? You're the oldest among the youngsters: if you go to the bad that's not important, the thing is that all the other kids follow your lead. Even if I had it in mind to let you off, the other parents wouldn't go along with it. [*To* CHENG] If he's so impossible as a mere stripling, what will he be like when he grows up? [*To* HSI-ERH] Yes, I've got to teach you an honest lesson. I'm not going to tell you off, I'm not going to give you a hiding. To tell the truth I haven't got that kind of time to spend on you! I've hit on a good idea: I'm going to string you up till you croak! I'll hang you up in the cowstall, and for three days on end I'll give you no food or water. I'll starve you, I'll parch you, and in the end I'll hang you!

[WIDOW T'IEN *appears in the breach, supporting herself on that knobbly, crooked, but sturdy tree branch. She comes in looking radiant as spring*]

WIDOW There you are! Schoolmaster as well! Good morning.

CHENG [*Uneasy*] Morning, ma'am.

WIDOW [*To* YANG] Good day, Uncle Yang.

YANG [*Shortly*] Good day.

WIDOW [*To* HSI-ERH] Look at the way you're slouching! [*To* REDNOSE] You stand by my Hsi-erh and you won't lose by it later on.

YANG [*Misunderstands*] Leave Hsi-erh in my hands. Don't worry about a thing, ma'am.

WIDOW Yes, indeed! As his father said when he gave up the ghost, he's just shot up in front of your eyes, and he eats enough for two, so by rights he ought to do two people's work. He'd always been worried over him ever since he missed out in the county examination. He never got down to his books properly, and wild! He's wilder than the grasshopper in the fields! If you don't put him to a trade to keep him in order, there's no hope of him growing up, Uncle.

YANG You're too soft on him, being his mother—

WIDOW Isn't that what I've always thought myself? I keep at him to mend his ways.

YANG Just giving him a talking to isn't enough . . .

WIDOW But he's got two legs, and he's a boy as well. He'll have to make his own way in the world.

YANG That's very sensible of you, ma'am! Not like that crabby old woman of mine . . .

WIDOW [*More and more sure of herself*] So here I've come chasing after them! Hsi-erh has no tact, and he's still very green. I was afraid he would offend you now that you want to do him a good turn. Nowdays, even since the Longhairs[4] went on the rampage, people have changed: you've got a long way to go to find a gentleman of the old school. Hsi-erh's dad was a good man, but he never had a break in his short life! But there's no need to bring that up now. Ever since the Longhairs went on the rampage, people have only been leaving the village; I've never seen any coming back. . . .

YANG [*Cutting her short*] If you approve, ma'am, that's all right.

WIDOW What could I have against it? After all it's for the boy's own good. And it won't end there, I know . . . [*Sees* MRS. YANG *approaching, and calls out in warm welcome*] Good day, Aunt.

[MRS. YANG *totally ignores her; she comes across from the threshing ground*]

MRS. YANG Good morning, Schoolmaster.

CHENG Good morning, Mrs. Yang.

MRS. YANG [*To* YANG] Breakfast is ready, get on and send the workmen off to eat so that they can get to work in the fields. They're all late today.

[REDNOSE *and the laborers have been winking and grimacing all the time, making a bit of a joke of the affair; but hearing the mention of food makes them realize they are hungry, and they look toward* YANG, *waiting for the signal to go*]

YANG You must be hungry after all this time, Schoolmaster . . .

CHENG [*Politely*] I'll go back home for breakfast.

YANG Since you're here you can eat with us. [*To* REDNOSE *and the laborers*] String him up in the cowstall, and don't go in for breakfast until you've finished the job.

WIDOW [*Confused*] String up who?

REDNOSE Who? That precious son of yours!

WIDOW My son! T'ien Hsi-erh! Didn't you just say when you came to my house that his uncle wanted him to come for breakfast to talk over some business?

REDNOSE That was to kid him into coming quietly.

HSI-ERH Don't waste your breath on them, ma, they're out to settle a score with me. [*To* YANG] Uncle Yang, let me have a lousy little nap in the cowstall first of all, and then you can hang me up for three days. There can't be anything wrong with that?

WIDOW Hang up my son? Hang him up for three days? [*Lands him a blow on the backside with her branch*] You keep quiet! [*Turns to* YANG] What for? You can't hang somebody up like an animal for nothing, it's never been heard of!

YANG Just now you were telling me to give him a good and proper . . .

WIDOW Good and proper! Is that the word you use for hanging my son, "good and proper"? [*To* CHENG] Stringing up somebody else's son without rhyme or reason, when has the law ever allowed that?

YANG You tell me what you would do yourself; that precious son of yours kept us on the go all night with his ructions . . .

WIDOW I saw him go to bed with my own eyes, and he slept right through till full light this morning, how could he go climbing over walls and getting into a scrap with you? You can't go around saying such preposterous things, you know!

YANG Look at the way he's drooping about, does he look like a young lad who's had a good night's sleep?

WIDOW He was born that way; this isn't the first day he's drooped about!

YANG [*To all*] Did you hear that? It's his own mother that says so.

WIDOW Yes, I say so, I say so. When I find fault with my son I speak as I find. I carried him for ten months, and if I say he's this or that, that's what he is, 'cause I'm his mother!

YANG Yet when other people say a word against him . . .

WIDOW It depends on who it is.

YANG He turns up at dead of night at my house to steal—

WIDOW Steal what?

YANG Goods and chattels!

WIDOW Tripe! You've got some brass, goods and chattels indeed! [*Loudly*] A petticoat, maybe!

[*Everyone is shocked*]

HSI-ERH Mum, go easy, leave me some face!

WIDOW [*Lets him have another taste of her branch*] There's some face for you!

YANG It was burglary as plain as a pikestaff . . .

WIDOW "To take a thief, you need the loot; to prove adultery, you have to catch the two of them at it." You can't just make accusations without something to back them up.

YANG [*Discovers the bundle*] I don't know, all this time I'd forgotten about this! [*To* WIDOW T'IEN] Look! Take a good look at this!

WIDOW [*Snatches the bundle and throws it on the ground*] We haven't got fancy wrapping cloth like this in our house!

YANG That's just what I mean, it belongs to us!

WIDOW If it belongs to you, and was in your house, how can you use it to trump up a charge of thieving against my son?

YANG [*Explains*] I chased him . . . I chased him like this . . . I wasn't on guard against him having something in his hand . . . then he tossed the bundle in my face and knocked me over, head over heels . . .

WIDOW You didn't break your neck?

YANG You don't break your neck as easy as that!

WIDOW Why shouldn't it be easy?

YANG Take a gander at this lump as big as an egg on the back of my pate . . .

WIDOW [*Zanily*] I know what that is—you got that from your smallpox!

YANG What?

WIDOW You were born with it!

YANG [*Exasperated, to* CHENG] There's no way of getting any sense out of her. [*Picks up the bundle*] This bundle . . .

WIDOW [*Quick off the mark*] As a matter of fact I *would* like to see what things were stolen from your house, whether of gold, of silver, bricks or tiles.

HSI-ERH Don't look, ma, those are other people's things!

WIDOW Are you afraid I'll knock off something in front of all these people? [*Loosens the slipknot*] Ah!

[*Everyone crowds around.* T'IEN HSI-ERH, *striking a casual pose, is alone in his indifference*]

MRS. YANG [*Concerned for her daughter, keeps saying at* YANG'*s side*] Don't look! Don't look!

WIDOW A pair of bracelets!

YANG Gold!

WIDOW A pair of eardrops!

YANG Gold!

WIDOW A packet of money!

YANG Silver!

MRS. YANG Don't look, don't look, I say!

WIDOW A skirt!

YANG Satin!

WIDOW A pair of trousers!

YANG Cotton cloth!

MRS. YANG Don't look, don't look, I say!

WIDOW A red jacket!

YANG More than one!

WIDOW Another patterned one!

YANG For visiting!

WIDOW Another sky-blue one!

YANG For wearing at home!

MRS. YANG Don't look, don't look!

WIDOW [*Shakes the wrapping cloth*] Nothing else!

YANG Nothing else!

[*As* WIDOW T'IEN *retrieves each item,* YANG *takes it from her and passes it on separately for* MRS. YANG *to hold.* MRS. YANG *is apprehensive and bitter at the same time. The three employees exchange looks; their mouths drop open, as if they had before them a dazzling hoard of treasure.* CHENG *looks from the things to* HSI-ERH, *shaking his head*]

WIDOW [*Spreads the bundle wrapper flat on the ground*] What a terrible shame! Hurry and wrap them up again!

YANG [*Takes one item from* MRS. YANG, *who is standing there like a dummy*] Here!

WIDOW [*Folds it up*] For wearing at home!

YANG [*Another item*] Here!

WIDOW [*Folds it up*] For visiting!

MRS. YANG How could you! How could you!

YANG [*Another item*] Here!

WIDOW [*Folds it up*] Red!

YANG [*Another item*] Here!

WIDOW Cotton cloth!

MRS. YANG How could you! How could you!

YANG [*Another item*] Here!

WIDOW Satin!

YANG [*The packet of money*] Here! [*On second thought*] No! [*He puts it away in his pocket*]

WIDOW There's more to come!

YANG Isn't that enough! [*The bracelets and eardrops he puts in another pocket*] It's the sum total of my valuables.

MRS. YANG [*Empty-handed*] How could you! I told you not to look, but you would insist! [*She sits down, beats the ground, starts to cry*] I want to die! I don't want to go on living!

[*Everyone sympathizes*]

WIDOW [*Ties the bundle and throws it to her*] You can keep it! No one wants it! [*Stands up straight, suddenly puts the question*] Who is it that wears these fancy colored things, this gold and silver? You're not going to tell us that you, Aunt, who won't see forty again, that you would get yourself rigged out in them?

MRS. YANG Wait till I get hold of you, Hsiang-ts'ao, you little bitch! To think you'd have the heart to make off with all the belongings I gave you on the quiet! I've been so good to you! And you, without so much as a word . . .

YANG [*With great disgust*] You're mad! In front of all these people . . .

[MRS. YANG's *commotion does indeed subside, but* WIDOW T'IEN *bursts out*]

WIDOW [*Brings her branch right down on* HSI-ERH's *head*] You'll drive your ma to an early grave with your tricks, you want to be rid of her! [*Lashing out at him*] What have I tried to drum into you all the time, and still you let me down like this! Fancy trying to carry off a respectable young girl! You'll come to a sticky end, you brute!

[T'IEN HSI-ERH *howls and shrieks, covers his head and scampers off; he jumps through the gap and puts a safe distance between himself and his mother*]

CHENG [*Trying to get her to desist*] Ma'am . . . ma'am . . .

YANG [*Appeased*] He had it coming to him, he had it coming!

WIDOW [*Hears the last part, turns round at the gap, looks at him*] I'm hitting *my son*!

YANG I'm all for it!

WIDOW Why don't you two get together and produce one, if you're up to it!

YANG [*Touched on a sore spot*] Who might you be referring to, you old hag?

WIDOW I'm referring to whoever has brought up his wench to lead young lads astray!

YANG [*Rolls up his sleeves*] That does it, the bitch!

CHENG [*Hurriedly intervening*] She's a widow!

YANG What if she is? This is one widow that's going to get a good beating!

[*They hardly succeed in restraining him before* WIDOW T'IEN, *in great ire, returns to the attack*]

WIDOW Daughters are two a penny! Whatever faults my Hsi-erh might have, he's still a male!

CHENG [*Intervening*] He's the mayor . . . ma'am . . . do restrain yourself!

WIDOW [*Leans against the tree trunk, starts to cry*] You've no idea what I have to put up with, not having a husband!

YANG [*To his employees*] Listen to that! She's fallen back on the old sob-story again! [*To* MRS. YANG, *in great irritation*] And not a peep out of you all this time!

MRS. YANG You can't get the better of that widow so you take it out on your own old woman!

YANG [*Stamps his foot*] I spit on her, and all her ancestors!

WIDOW [*Stops crying, gets hold of* CHENG's *sleeve, analyses her insights*] There's human nature for you. If you can't produce a son yourself, other people's sons are a thorn in your flesh. You would understand that, schoolmaster. People always covet the things they haven't got themselves. Other people's flowers are nicer. . . .

CHENG It's time to go, ma'am . . . I'll see you on your way.

WIDOW [*Stands in the breach and delivers a parting shot*] You can marry your precious Hsiang-ts'ao to the first bloke that comes along, us T'iens don't give a monkey's!

[CHENG *accompanies her out through the gap, then suddenly stops and turns*]

CHENG [*Looking at* REDNOSE, *significantly*] Rednose! Watch out! [*He makes a dignified exit*]

YANG [CHENG*'s final touch fans the ashes of his anger, to his men*] Get out of my sight, the lot of you! Stealing peaches from the temple—

NUMBER TWO [*To* REDNOSE, *mockingly*] He means you.

YANG [*Continues*] Climb over others' walls . . .

REDNOSE [*Gets his revenge, to* NUMBER TWO] This time he means you.

YANG [*Concludes*] All a lot of blackguards!

LABORER [*Not having been personally rebuked, with an air of rectitude*] Come on! Let's go and have some breakfast!

[*They head toward the threshing ground*]

YANG [*Shouts after them*] Remember to fill in the gap in the wall!

[MRS. YANG, *holding the bundle in her arms, wipes her nose*]

YANG [*Still fuming, fixes his eyes on her; after some time*] It's all your fault!

MRS. YANG [*Countering*] I couldn't have a son, is that it? Am I supposed to get children by myself?

YANG I might ask you the same question. If you remember, for the first five years we were married your belly never looked like swelling. Are you going to blame me for that?

MRS. YANG Be fair now, I was nineteen when I married into your family. At that time you were only a little shrimp. All day long I had to be wiping your bottom and fetching your stool for you. Where was I supposed to conjure up a baby from?

YANG [*Stands at the edge of the stage*] Well, this is final: we can't keep Hsiang-ts'ao at home any longer. I've already decided on Dr. Luo's son for her. He's entered for the Civil Service exams. We'll get schoolmaster Cheng to be go-between, and she'll be off our hands before the year's out!

MRS. YANG How old is he?

YANG He was born in the year of the ox, that makes him eleven!

[MRS. YANG *sits on the ground, looking stunned. It had never occurred to her that her daughter in her turn would be married to a child-husband*]

[*Curtain*]

ACT IV

In front of the temple to Kuan Ti, early summer 1909, mid-afternoon.
Time has sped by; now another summer has come round. All is as before

*in front of the temple to Kuan Ti. The temple door is pulled to. The green
leaves afford shade as the sun beams down from the southwest. The bench
has been moved over to the tree, and the children play around it. Rednose has
awakened from a sleep—as he is a night watchman, he has the right to sleep in
the daytime—and sits on the bench nursing his strength, a short pipe stuck
in his mouth.* TIGERCUB, BLACKY, *and* HSIANG-CHÜ *clamor for a story.*

REDNOSE [*Knocks out his pipe on the sole of his shoe*] We won't tell of
the Longhairs today; we'll have something new. Tigercub, Blacky,
come over here. [*Stands up, sits them down shoulder to shoulder*] You
two little 'uns can be mum and dad. Hsiang-chü, you stand at the side
and listen to this song I'm going to sing for you, "Little Black Girl."
CHILDREN "Little Black Girl"?
REDNOSE The little black girl is supposed to be you, Hsiang-chü. I'm
going to be Little Black Boy in a minute. [*Stands at an angle from
the children, and, stabbing with his pipe, sings his ballad in uncertain
imitation of stage recitative*] Ready?

> I spin a silly yarn,
> You've never heard the like:
> There was an old couple shelling black beans,
> A pile of black beans, some left undone,
> Off they went home and Black Girl was born.

BLACKY [*Interrupts*] That's you, Hsiang-chü.
REDNOSE [*Nodding*] That's right.

> Dad was fretting,
> Mum did frown,
> Young Black Maid was letting her hair down.

TIGERCUB [*Interrupts*] She's going to get wed!
REDNOSE [*Grumpily*] You sing it if you know so much!
HSIANG-CHÜ [*Resentful at* TIGERCUB*'s intervention*] You shouldn't be so
mouthy!
REDNOSE I'll act the part of Little Black Girl for you:

> Black Maid fancied some wild salad,
> Hooked a black basket over her arm,
> Took a black sickle in her hand,
> Went to a black spot at the south end of town.
> Whom should she meet coming her way
> But Little Black Boy,

BLACKY Little Black Boy, that's you yourself.
REDNOSE And here I come!

> Little Black Boy led a big black ox,
> Black whipstock
> Black whiskers
> Black halter
> Black headstall.
> Black Boy cocked his eye at her.
> Black Maid cocked her eye at him.

Black Boy said:
"I've no need to goggle,
You've no need to stare.
Us two will make a fine pair."
Black Boy wrote a black marriage contract
To take Black Maid to wife.
Along came a crow-black sedan chair,
Eight black bearers helping to bear;
Four black bandsmen bringing up the rear.
When they got to the house they kowtowed their black heads.
Black windows,
Black archway
Black room
Black bed
Black pillows
Black table
Black chopsticks
Black bowls
Black cookpot.
When they'd been married for five years plus two,
[REDNOSE *playfully ruffles* BLACKY'S *hair*]
They had a little chappie
Black as black can be.
Named him Little Blacky,
Sent him round selling black bean oil.
[*Wipes the dribble from his mouth with the back of his hand*] That's
the end!

HSIANG-CHÜ [*To* BLACKY] So there, Blacky, you're Rednose's son now!

BLACKY Poo! That's not me, that's you!

TIGERCUB No, she's Little Black Girl, she's our ma!

REDNOSE [*Laughs*] Do you think you could have a son as big as him,
Hsiang-chü? [*As he has his back to the temple door, he does not see*
CHENG *come sauntering out, carrying a hookah before him*]

HSIANG-CHÜ I'll tell my Dad if you say rude things.

REDNOSE No, don't. I was only joking. [*To the young brothers*] Was
that long enough for you just now?

CHILDREN I'll say!

REDNOSE Did you keep a count? How many black things were there?

CHILDREN Sing it again.

REDNOSE Sing it again! Huh! Let's see the color of your money.

HSIANG-CHÜ I don't want to hear it again—all black and dingy, never
an end to all that blackness.

REDNOSE Do you call that black? Think of me. I'm asleep in the daytime,
I don't see the daylight, I only move about after dark—I'm your man
for blackness! Everything you can think of is black. Black shoes, black
socks, black trousers, black coat, black hat. And on a night when

there's no moon or stars, it really is black and no kidding, as black as ink—you're black, I'm black, everybody's black . . .

HSIANG-CHÜ It gives me the creeps!

TIGERCUB I bet there's ghosts!

REDNOSE Ah, now . . .

CHENG [*His voice is calm, but to the four hearers, it is like a roll of spring thunder*] Rednose, none of your tall stories!

CHILDREN [*Flinching, with extreme deference*] Schoolmaster!

REDNOSE [*Adds his piece*] Schoolmaster! Nice weather we're having!

CHENG Hmm. [*Pulls on his hookah*] Rednose, you're always up to some monkey-business; if you're not leading the children up the garden path, you're stealing the temple peaches—

REDNOSE I haven't touched the temple peaches this year!

CHENG I'll give you that; you gambled away all your money and haven't been able to buy any drink. But when you've had a drink, what a performance. You can't do anything right.

HSIANG-CHÜ [*Catches sight of movement over to the left, in surprise and delight*] Ey! Look!

CHENG What is it?

HSIANG-CHÜ It's my sister! [*She goes out to meet her, calling "Sister, sister!"*]

CHENG There seems to be someone with her.

REDNOSE Hsiang-ts'ao's father-in-law, and her husband following behind.

CHENG [*Excited*] Dr. Luo! Just the man I wanted to see! [*Steps out to meet him*] Look at me, I'm still in my shirtsleeves! I'll be a laughingstock! [*Enjoins* REDNOSE] Beg pardon of the old gentleman; impress on him that he should pause a moment at the temple. I must consult him about something. I'm going in to put on my gown. [*Hurries toward the porch*] The old gentleman is a doctor of letters, take care! [*He bolts into the temple*]

REDNOSE [*To the young brothers*] You saw the old schoolmaster there, how he was all of a dither. You can imagine how he would pat the old doctor gent's arse if he was here in person! Now stand aside and watch me do my stuff!

TIGERCUB It's not as if Dr. Luo had grown two heads!

REDNOSE He's easily got seven, eight, nine, ten heads! It's just that you common jerks can't see 'em!

TIGERCUB I saw Dr. Luo last year, when Sister Hsiang-ts'ao got wed!

BLACKY Her husband can't be more than a couple of years older than me. I bet I could beat him in a fight!

REDNOSE Cheeky little bugger! Our guv'nor's new son-in-law is very highbrow. Next year he's going to take his bachelor's. A little ragamuffin like you had better not think of mixing it up with the likes of him! [*Bellows*] Get over there! [*He chases the brothers out of the way and goes to accost Dr. Luo*]

LUO [*To his son, behind him*] We'll soon be at our father-in-law's! Be on your best behavior now!

[*Young* MASTER LUO *appears, very seemly, older than his years*]

REDNOSE [*With great ceremony*] Your worship!

LUO [*Looks him over cursorily*] You are—?

REDNOSE I work for Mayor Yang.

MASTER LUO [*Butts in*] Red—nose, the watchman. I've heard my wife speak of him.

REDNOSE [*Gratefully*] At last this nose of mine has come in useful! [*Returns to his welcoming*] Good day, your worship! Good day, young master! Our guv'nor is in the fields. I'll go and tell him you've come.

[HSIANG-TS'AO *and* HSIANG-CHÜ *enter at this moment, hand in hand*]

REDNOSE Good day, Young Mistress.

HSIANG-TS'AO How are you, Rednose?

LUO [*To* HSIANG-TS'AO] Your father is in the fields.

HSIANG-TS'AO [*Bows her head*] Yes, father-in-law.

REDNOSE There's nobody at home. The missus is in the fields, too. I'm just on my way. When the missus knows that her daughter has come home she'll be thrilled to bits. [*He starts to leave, then stops*] Oh, yes! [*To* LUO] I nearly forgot! Schoolmaster Cheng saw you coming and has gone in to put on his gown. He wants a word with you.

LUO Very well. I'll stop at the temple for a rest.

REDNOSE [*To* HSIANG-TS'AO] Haven't seen you for the best part of a year, Miss. Now you've put your hair up you look thinner, it's true, but a lot handsomer.

[HSIANG-TS'AO*'s head sinks even lower.* LUO *gives him a dirty look.* TIGERCUB *and his brother twit him from behind the tree.* REDNOSE *is off like a shot*]

MASTER LUO I'm hot, pa.

LUO You've been moaning about being hot all the way.

MASTER LUO My clothes—

LUO Aren't I in gown and jacket as well? I don't feel hot. [*To* HSIANG-TS'AO] Go and mop your husband's brow for him.

HSIANG-TS'AO Yes, father-in-law. [*She has in her palm a handkerchief that is already soaked with sweat. She goes across, bends over, and mops young* LUO*'s sweat away*]

MASTER LUO Look at you!

LUO What's wrong?

MASTER LUO She rubs your face so it hurts.

LUO [*To* HSIANG-TS'AO] Can't even trust you to wipe a face! You— [*Notices* HSIANG-CHÜ, *changes his tune, to* MASTER LUO] Come with me and pay your respects to Schoolmaster Cheng.

MASTER LUO I—

LUO You what?

MASTER LUO I don't want Hsiang-chü to go away.

Luo Stupid boy! Conduct yourself in a proper manner! [*Moves off*] Come with me!

[*Just at this moment* CHENG *comes rushing out of the temple*]

CHENG [*With an effusiveness mingled with deference*] It's been a long time, good sir!

Luo [*Returns the compliment*] You are too polite. How are you, Schoolmaster Cheng?

CHENG Our young friend is with you, I see.

Luo [*Reminds his son*] Come over and pay your respects to School-master Cheng.

MASTER Luo [*Awkwardly*] Good day, Schoolmaster Cheng.

CHENG Too kind. How are you, young friend? [*To* Luo] Your son lives up to Confucius' description: "genteel the man, genteel the manner."

Luo I intend to put him in for the county examination next year. As he is so young it doesn't matter if he passes or not, but the experience will be useful.

CHENG A child prodigy, sir, I'm sure he will carry off the honors.

Luo [*To his son*] Did you hear? [*Grumbling*] You shouldn't keep staring at Hsiang-chü. She is your sister-in-law, it's only proper to keep a respectable distance.

CHENG "True it is, he who is learned in ritual is close to righteousness." You teach your son wisely, good sir. [*Comes closer*] Someone brought word from the county seat that an educational society has been set up recently to bring about two major changes, the abolition of the civil service examinations and the founding of modern schools.

Luo The man behind it is that Ching fellow; he's in favor of reform and constitutional change . . .

CHENG It's the height of absurdity!

Luo Would it were only absurd! To add lustre to the family name is a glorious duty laid upon a son. To abolish the examination system, to destroy the ladder of success for the scholar, is the surest way to plunge the Empire into chaos.

CHENG Even more so if they set up modern schools and throw out Confucius and Mencius like so much trash . . .

Luo Teaching a mishmash of heresies . . .

CHENG A human being without his deep-rooted heritage . . .

Luo Would you still be able to call him human?

CHENG If you have a mind to, good sir, we could retire to my humble abode and discuss this at length . . .

Luo My relatives are in the field . . .

CHENG All the better for you to step into my abode and rest, good sir.

Luo In that case I will trespass on your hospitality. [*To his son*] Sit with your wife under the tree. I'll be out very shortly.

MASTER Luo Yes, pa.

Luo Don't go away. [*More severely*] And don't loll about.

MASTER LUO [*Sitting upright*] Yes, pa.

LUO [*To* HSIANG-TS'AO] You keep an eye on him, daughter-in-law, and don't be remiss. If he gets hot, mop his brow for him.

HSIANG-TS'AO Yes, father-in-law.

LUO You sit down as well.

HSIANG-TS'AO [*Likewise sits on the bench*] Yes, father-in-law.

LUO Keep your sister away from your husband.

HSIANG-TS'AO Yes, father-in-law.

[CHENG *clicks his tongue in admiration.* LUO *shows satisfaction. He and* CHENG *bow each other into the temple*]

HSIANG-CHÜ [*Pointing after* LUO, *quietly*] Your father-in-law has a funny way of talking.

HSIANG-TS'AO You're too young to understand. Tell me, how has mother been?

HSIANG-CHÜ Mum talks about you all the time. She's afraid that in your husband's house you . . .

HSIANG-TS'AO [*Stops her*] You're too young to understand.

MASTER LUO [*Still looking straight ahead*] Has pa gone?

HSIANG-TS'AO Um.

MASTER LUO [*Bounds up*] Great! [*Pulls* HSIANG-CHÜ *to her feet*] Let's go to the pond, you and me, to see the frogs and the tadpoles!

HSIANG-TS'AO Your pa won't allow it.

MASTER LUO [*Showing off*] I want to!

HSIANG-TS'AO Ask pa first.

MASTER LUO You ask him!

HSIANG-TS'AO [*Fed up with him*] Mind you don't make your clothes dirty!

MASTER LUO I'm hot, you help me off with them.

HSIANG-TS'AO Your pa won't allow it.

MASTER LUO [*Acting up*] But I'm hot!

[HSIANG-TS'AO *has no choice but to start helping him off with his clothes. Now* TIGERCUB *and his brother show their faces*]

TIGERCUB Hsiang-chü, look at the pair of them:

> "There was a big girl of ten years and seven,
> Four years later she was one and twenty.
> She found a husband who was only ten,
> That means she was older than him by eleven."

HSIANG-CHÜ If you're rude to my sister I won't play with you.

MASTER LUO [*Has already taken off his jacket, to* TIGERCUB] Right, that's an insult!

TIGERCUB No it isn't!

MASTER LUO Yes it is!

TIGERCUB Take it whichever way you want.

> "Took a walk to mother-in-law's place
> To see how tall the new husband was.
> The sight I saw when I got to the door

Made me see red:
A long gown one foot one,
Split-seat trousers seven inches seven."

MASTER LUO [*Takes off his gown; every bit as mischievous as* TIGERCUB]
If anybody wears split-seat trousers it's your mum! You say I wear
them! Have a look! [*Spreads his legs*] See! Am I wearing them?

HSIANG-TS'AO Tigercub, you're not to sing that. [*Folds up gown and
jacket and puts them on her knees*] Tell me, how's your granddad?

TIGERCUB He's taken to his bed the last few days.

MASTER LUO [*Pulling* HSIANG-CHÜ] Let's go to the pond and skim
stones! Let's see who can skim them the farthest!

HSIANG-CHÜ You'll win, you'll win! Shall we go now? [*All eagerness,
he runs off right, pulling her after*]

HSIANG-TS'AO [*Continues*] Is everyone in the village all right?

TIGERCUB Ts'ao San's mother died. Chao Ssu has had another son.
T'ien Hsi-erh went down with a long illness.

HSIANG-TS'AO A long illness?

TIGERCUB It wasn't serious.

HSIANG-TS'AO You mean it?

TIGERCUB He kept calling your name when he was sick—that's what
my mum said. My mum told my dad, too, that T'ien Hsi-erh is a lost
cause, he just moons over some girl.

HSIANG-TS'AO [*Dazed*] He's stayed in the village all this time?

TIGERCUB He's only been back a few days. He's been in the county town.
They're short of hands in the fields, so his mum wrote to him to come
back. His mum still rows with him all day.

MASTER LUO'S VOICE Come on, all of you! Let's have a competition to
see who can skim the farthest!

BLACKY Show him what you can do, Tigercub!

TIGERCUB Right! I'm coming!

[*The two run off.* HSIANG-TS'AO *does not seem to have heard any
of this. A sadness she could not describe assails her. She sighs a faint
sigh. She has no words to express her desolation. She seems to be
numbed, to be in a dream.*

[WIDOW T'IEN *enters right, supported by her tree branch*]

WIDOW [*Approaches, spits*] Bah! I wondered who it was; it turns out
to be you, Hsiang-ts'ao!

HSIANG-TS'AO Good afternoon, ma'am.

WIDOW On easy street now, aren't you? Got your nose in the air! I'm
surprised you stoop to notice a poor old woman like me! [*Spits
again*] Bah! I don't give a damn!

[*She exits left forthwith.* HSIANG-TS'AO *is stupefied. She feels weak,
sits down, and in spite of herself, starts to sob. A breeze gently ruffles her
hair. From afar an ox lows.* HSIANG-CHÜ *slips back*]

HSIANG-CHÜ Sister, you're crying?

HSIANG-TS'AO It's nothing.

HSIANG-CHÜ You were crying, sister!

HSIANG-TS'AO I was crying because I was happy. You don't know how I've missed you all these months—and mum, and all the family!

HSIANG-CHÜ [*Enigmatically*] I know what you mean!

HSIANG-TS'AO What do you know?

HSIANG-CHÜ I know you miss T'ien Hsi-erh too.

HSIANG-TS'AO [*Stops her*] Sister! Don't be ridiculous!

[YOUNG LUO *runs back, calling* HSIANG-CHÜ. *He stands beside the temple door*]

MASTER LUO [*In the brief moment he has been away, his face has become streaked with mud; the state of his hands can be imagined*] Hsiang-chü, come on!

HSIANG-TS'AO [*Alarmed*] Oy! What have you been up to? Don't play with mud!

MASTER LUO I haven't been.

HSIANG-TS'AO Look at your face!

MASTER LUO They threw it at me.

HSIANG-TS'AO Look at your hands!

[*Young* LUO *makes a face*]

HSIANG-CHÜ I know what's been going on. He wanted to scoop up tadpoles, but Tigercub wouldn't let him!

MASTER LUO Hsiang-chü, come!

HSIANG-TS'AO Don't get into any fights.

[*She watches* HSIANG-CHÜ *move away. Suddenly the sound of* T'IEN HSI-ERH *calling her name breaks the silence—"Hsiang-ts'ao!" The first sound produces a remarkable reaction in* HSIANG-TS'AO: *her lonely soul thrills; her whole being is instinctively drawn toward the source of the sound; her wan face takes a flush. Her initial feeling is delight. But the second call, louder, seems to have the opposite effect. She takes fright. She checks the stride she had already started and casts around desperately for somewhere to hide. The third call seems to come from beside her. She decides to hide behind the locust tree. But the pressure of this eerie call, which promises ill and also happiness, constrains her. She feels herself drained of initiative and bows her head helplessly.* T'IEN HSI-ERH *runs in, a rake over his shoulder*]

HSI-ERH [*Excited*] Hey! You don't know how much I've been looking forward to your coming back! I thought of going to the Luo village to see you. I couldn't quite screw myself up to it, but I wanted to know, I wanted to see with my own eyes how you were getting on with the Luos. Still, it's all right now, my waiting has been rewarded at least!

MASTER LUO [*To* HSIANG-TS'AO, *from the distance*] You two have a chat, we're off.

HSI-ERH Who's that?

HSIANG-CHÜ This is my sister's husband, brother Hsi-erh! [*Explains to young* LUO] Brother T'ien Hsi-erh, he's sweet on my sister!

LUO [*Naively*] T'ien Hsi-erh, you have a nice talk with my wife! We're off to play!

HSI-ERH [*Doubting his ears, instinctively takes a few steps after him*]

It's him! It's this bit of a kid! . . . The blighter I've been planning to do in all this time, even in my dreams, turns out to be you, a pissy little kid still wet behind the ears! It's you who took my Hsiang-ts'ao! . . . Why should you have all the luck! . . . If I just bring my rake down on your head, your life won't be worth a light!

HSIANG-TS'AO [*Remonstrating gently*] T'ien Hsi-erh!

HSI-ERH He even told us to have a nice talk! [*Laughs*] It wouldn't do to show ourselves ungrateful for the favor! [*Returns to* HSIANG-TS'AO*'s side, but suddenly is depressed and has nothing to say*] Hsiang-ts'ao!

[*The two of them are silent.* T'IEN HSI-ERH *sits on the bench and leans his rake beside him*]

HSIANG-TS'AO [*With a wry smile, she speaks first*] Hello, Hsi-erh. [*He nods and sighs*] I hear you've been ill. [*He nods, looks at her; she does not know how to continue*] I . . . I . . . since I got married . . .

HSI-ERH [*Jeering*] You've been in clover?

[HSIANG-TS'AO *sits down, does not reply, begins to cry quietly*]

HSI-ERH [*Moves closer to her*] I shouldn't have said that . . . you must be miserable . . . we are both miserable. I know you went to them to be a drudge, not a wife . . . you've never been out of my mind. . . . Whenever anybody mentioned you, my heart missed a beat—and I cleared off out of the way . . . but then I was sorry I hadn't stayed to listen. . . . It's been practically a year . . . I haven't set eyes on you since that night. . . . They said you were ill . . . they said Schoolmaster Cheng had been called in to make a match for you. . . . They said you had married into a good family, with lots of money and plenty of pull . . . I was in the county town all the while, doing the rounds for Mr. Ching. . . .,

HSIANG-TS'AO I wish I had died!

HSI-ERH While there's life . . . things are bound to look up one day.

HSIANG-TS'AO I'm afraid if things go on much longer like this . . . I won't be able to last out . . .

HSI-ERH If only you'd come away with me that night!

[HSIANG-TS'AO *just lowers her head and moans.* HSI-ERH *does not speak either. The sun sinks further in the west. From the distance comes the sound of a donkey braying*]

HSI-ERH [*Sits down on one end of the bench, facing her*] Sometimes I get to thinking, you know . . . taking my cue from others— I think that one of us must be wrong, if not both of us. . . . Otherwise how come it just happens that everything seems to be against us? . . . When I heard you were married . . . I hid myself away in the Temple of the City God from first thing in the morning, not wanting to see a soul. . . . All I felt was hate! I hated you, I hated your whole family, I hated all the people in the village, I hated everybody on earth, I hated myself . . . the whole world seemed black, I had no one to tell my troubles to, life was just a torment . . . then bit by bit, little by little, I calmed down . . . one by one I took in the Ten Kings of

Purgatory around me . . . they all seemd to want to tell me something
. . . they seemed to say, this world doesn't belong to young people—
but neither does it belong to the grownups: the truth is, it belongs
to *us* . . . you can't go against fate! It was written in the book of fate
that Hsiang-ts'ao should be my childhood sweetheart, it was written
in the book of fate that Hsiang-ts'ao should part company with me
when she grew up . . . When it got dark I went back to the school,
and took straight to my bed . . . I was sick for a full month and more . . .
I got my back up: if she could up and marry someone else why
couldn't I carry on as before without her? That was the answer!
I told myself I would carry on as if nothing had happened, to show
them, to show her, to show Hsiang-ts'ao, to show all her family! . . .
[*Shakes his head*] No use! No use getting my back up! When ma told
me she was in front of the temple, nobody could have stood in my
way; I, I came running. [*Turns around to face* HSIANG-TS'AO] Sweet
Hsiang-ts'ao, how hard it would be for me to forget you!

HSIANG-TS'AO [*Overcome*] Dear Hsi-erh! . . . I knew you were miserable
. . .

HSI-ERH You were miserable too!

HSIANG-TS'AO You and I were miserable both!

[*The two are speechless; hand is laid over hand; only their souls are
in play in the silence.* WIDOW T'IEN *reenters from the left, and rudely
wakens them from their painful, beautiful dream*]

WIDOW [*Thumps her branch as she enters*] So, my fine fellow! I
was wondering how come you disappeared as soon as my back was
turned! This is where you waltzed off to! [*Wades into him*] You young
reprobate! You think it right to snuggle up to a young married
woman! In this public place!

HSI-ERH [*Taking evasive action*] Ma! It was you who said you'd seen
Hsiang-ts'ao in front of the temple!

WIDOW Did I tell you to beetle off to the temple and make up to this
brazen hussy?

HSI-ERH Don't talk so coarse, ma.

WIDOW Since when have you been so prissy?

HSI-ERH She hasn't caused you any—

WIDOW She offends my sight!

HSI-ERH She's feeling very low—

WIDOW It's her own doing!

HSI-ERH [*Stands his ground*] Ma, if you say another word . . .

WIDOW [*Her temper flaring*] You can't tell me to shut up, not if
you're my son!

HSI-ERH [*Turns on her*] From now on, then, ma, I'm not your son.

WIDOW Balls!

HSI-ERH [*Unexpectedly gives her a vigorous push*] I can get angry,
too, ma!

WIDOW [*Panicky*] You blackguard! [*The branch waves uselessly in the
air*] What are you going to do with me?

HSI-ERH I'm going to push and shove like this until I push you right into the pond . . .

HSIANG-TS'AO [*Puts down the gown and jacket and wrings her hands in desperation*] Hsi-erh, you mustn't!

WIDOW [*Simultaneously*] Then I'll be done for, I'll drown! Dear Hsiang-ts'ao, he listens to you . . .

HSI-ERH This is the end for you, ma!

WIDOW [*Squawks like a chicken having its neck wrung*] Help, save me! . . . Hsiang-ts'ao, for pity's sake . . . he's going to kill me!

HSIANG-TS'AO [*Goes over to hold him*] Hsi-erh, you've gone mad! She's your mother!

HSI-ERH [*Carries* WIDOW T'IEN *toward the temple door*] I *am* mad! I'll kill anybody that stands in the way! [*He carries her in through the temple door and ever so carefully deposits her within*]

WIDOW What are you going to do with your mother? You . . . you . . .

HSI-ERH Dearest mama, have a lie-down here! [*He jumps back out the door, pulls it to with both hands, notices* WIDOW T'IEN*'s branch lying on the porch, picks it up, and sticks it through the door rings that turn on their own axis*] You stay there and have a good, long rest. [*He looks at the stunned* HSIANG-TS'AO *and laughs*] What's the matter with you?

HSIANG-TS'AO I . . . I . . . what's the matter with *you*?

HSI-ERH [*Comes over to her side*] Ma will be all right in a tick.

WIDOW'S VOICE Open the door, you pest of humanity! [*Batters on the door*] Wait till I get you, you brute!

HSIANG-TS'AO You've barred the door from this side?

HSI-ERH The old lady's got no chance of getting out.

HSIANG-TS'AO But my father-in-law—

HSI-ERH Your father-in-law?

HSIANG-TS'AO He's inside having a conference with Schoolmaster Cheng.

HSI-ERH [*Tickled pink*] I couldn't ask for anything better! Our schoolmaster, your doctor of letters father-in-law, my widowed mother, all in the same boat!

CHENG'S VOICE T'ien Hsi-erh, open the temple door! [*Bangs on the door*] Do you want to land in prison? [*Bangs on the door*] Open the door for your schoolmaster!

WIDOW'S VOICE Open the door for your ma!

[*The battering on the door is thunderous*]

HSI-ERH [*Sticks out his tongue in alarm, quietly*] They'll break the door off its hinges!

HSIANG-TS'AO For heaven's sake, open the door for my father-in-law!

HSI-ERH He's not in there. I didn't hear any shouts from him.

HSIANG-TS'AO He'll get in the most terrible temper, and once he loses his temper . . .

HSI-ERH Let him lose his temper; in the meantime we'll go over by the pond and have a good time!

HSIANG-TS'AO You're not afraid—

HSI-ERH For your sake I'd take arson, looting, and bloody murder all in my stride—and be tried and topped, too. [*Presses close*] Hsiang-ts'ao!

HSIANG-TS'AO [*Tempted*] Hsi-erh!

HSI-ERH Have you really changed toward me?

HSIANG-TS'AO [*Lowers her head*] One day I know I'll just die.

HSI-ERH You won't die, Hsiang-ts'ao. You married a child, that doesn't count as marrying. One of these days, if I get power . . . [*Lowers his voice*] Mr. Ching says there's a change of rule coming, and everything will change along with it. . . .

HSIANG-TS'AO You're always looking on the bright side.

HSI-ERH One of these days—Tush! That's two "one of these days" in the space of a few seconds!

HSIANG-TS'AO Dear Hsi-erh, I can't last out till that day comes.

HSI-ERH Yes you can, and it won't be long either—That racket they're making is getting on my nerves. Let's go and talk around in back of the temple.

HSIANG-TS'AO I'm not going.

HSI-ERH Why not?

WIDOW'S VOICE So you're really not going to open the door, eh, you devil! That's a respectable young married woman you're with. Don't bring calamity down on your mother's head!

HSIANG-TS'AO Pay heed to your mother!

HSI-ERH Take no notice of her!

CHENG'S VOICE Open the door! Open the door!

[*The door is being banged on all the while*]

HSIANG-TS'AO Look out for my husband—

HSI-ERH That's him! He's fighting with Tigercub! [*Points*] See!

HSIANG-TS'AO Stop him, quick! I'll get it in the neck from father-in-law!

[*Suddenly a head pops over the top of the temple wall. As it comes into full view it is seen to be that of* DR. LUO. *He is standing on a ladder, peering around. Seeing the young couple below he almost faints from shock*]

HSI-ERH Let him get on with it!

HSIANG-TS'AO How can you be so unreasonable?

HSI-ERH [*Persisting*] Come with me round the back of the temple. There's no one about, and I've got something to say to you.

LUO [*Lets out a cry*] Daughter-in-law!

HSIANG-TS'AO [*Terrified, looks around*] My father-in-law!

HSI-ERH [*Looks round*] Can't see him.

LUO [*Sternly*] Daughter-in-law!

HSIANG-TS'AO It *is* my father-in-law!

HSI-ERH He's inside the temple.

LUO [*Brandishes his fist threateningly*] Daughter-in-law!

HSI-ERH [*Snatches her up in his arms*] You're going right now!

HSIANG-TS'AO [*Pushes, panics, pummels*] Let go! My father-in-law! Let go!

HSI-ERH He won't see us!

HSIANG-TS'AO [*Cannot get free*] You'll be the ruin of me, Hsi-erh!

[HSI-ERH *gallops off right, carrying her in his arms*]

LUO [*Desperate*] Come back! Come back! [*One hand holding onto the wall, the other hand waving in the air*] That's the limit! I'll never live this down! What price my degree now! [*He is struck rigid with anger on the wall*]

[*Curtain*]

ACT V

In front of the Kuan Li Temple, some minutes later.

DR. LUO, *consumed with anger, has gone limp. He still teeters on the ladder. As the setting sun lays its coating over the scene, it strikes right on his skull cap. He has gone into a swoon, and is prostrate over the top of the wall; looking down over the gown and jacket on the bench, he just groans.*

The temple door is still barred. The children are gathered before it, shouting, laughing, even jumping up and knocking at the door rings, but despite their best devising, they haven't found a way of withdrawing the stout branch.

CHENG'S VOICE Have you got it open?

TIGERCUB No, we can't get it open.

WIDOW'S VOICE What about Hsi-erh?

BLACKY Don't know where he is.

WIDOW'S VOICE Is Hsiang-ts'ao there?

MASTER LUO No.

WIDOW'S VOICE Who are you?

MASTER LUO I'm her husband!

WIDOW'S VOICE Oh luv! Now we're in a pickle and no mistake! How did I come to give birth to this pox on mankind!

CHENG'S VOICE Don't cry, ma'am! [*Pauses*] Is there anyone passing by?

MASTER LUO No, there's only my pa. He's climbed up on top of the wall, and he's not moving a muscle.

HSIANG-CHÜ Here comes Rednose!

[*The children run over to him; each stretches out a hand, and pushing and pulling form a procession for the saviour*]

REDNOSE What's up? What's going on?

CHILDREN Go and open the temple door! It's been jammed by T'ien Hsi-erh! The schoolmaster is in a stew inside, and T'ien Hsi-erh's mum is in there too.

MASTER LUO Don't forget my pa! He tried to get out, but couldn't, and has been stuck up on the wall shaking like a jelly.

REDNOSE [*Looks up at the wall*] Lord a' mercy! I've hardly been gone a minute, and all hell breaks loose!

CHENG'S VOICE Rednose, open the door! [REDNOSE, *at the door, withdraws his stretched-out hand*] Rednose, get a move on!

CHILDREN Get a move on!

REDNOSE [*Makes a sign to the children*] Be quiet! [*All are quiet*] Schoolmaster, your peaches haven't been stolen?

CHENG'S VOICE   What's that got to do with it? You're supposed to be opening the door!

REDNOSE I'm trying! I can't shift it! [*Pauses*] This year's peaches must be ripe now?

CHENG'S VOICE [*Impatiently*] You open the door, Rednose, and later on I'll pick out some of the juiciest ones for you to feed on.

REDNOSE [*Wrinkles his nose at the children*] Yes sir, Schoolmaster! [*Pulls away the branch with a mighty tug*] Stand aside, I'm pushing open the door!

[*The double door opens wide, making a rending sound.* WIDOW T'IEN *charges out first*]

WIDOW [*Snatches the tree branch from Rednose's hand*] We'll see if you can find a bolt hole now! [*Looks all round*] He's really not here! [*Calls*] T'ien Hsi-erh, T'ien Hsi-erh!

[*She exits left, calling.* CHENG *comes out hard on her heels. He is likewise irate, and likewise seeking* HSI-ERH]

CHENG Wait till I get hold of you, you swine! . . . No respect for your teacher, no respect for the old! . . .

MASTER LUO [*Draws his attention to the top of the wall*] Look, Schoolmaster Cheng, my pa!

CHENG [*Greatly shocked*] Dr. Luo! [*Calls up to him*] Good sir!

LUO [*Gasps*] I . . . I . . .

CHENG Good sir!

LUO I . . . I've never been so vexed in all my life!

CHENG Good sir! Come down!

LUO Can't . . . can't come down! . . . My legs . . .shaking . . . I'm afraid I'll fall—and kill myself!

CHENG [*Turns to Rednose*] Quick! To the rescue of the mayor's kinsman! . . .

[*Pushing* REDNOSE *ahead, he charges into the temple with the children.* HSIANG-CHÜ *stays outside, hesitates, then pulls her hand free from* YOUNG LUO*'s and peers all round*]

HSIANG-CHÜ [*Warily*] Sister! Sister! [*Discovers someone approaching from the left*] Mum! Dad! [*She runs up to meet* MAYOR YANG *and* MRS. YANG *as they enter*]

YANG Are you all on your own?

MRS. YANG Where's your sister?

HSIANG-CHÜ She was here just now, she's just this moment left. [*Points to top of wall*] Look!

MRS. YANG Isn't that our kinsman!

YANG Too true it is! [*Calling to him*] Kinsman!

LUO [*Addressing the helpers inside, he does not hear*] Hold the ladder properly! I can feel it swaying!

CHENG'S VOICE Don't worry! It's quite firm!

LUO Then . . . then . . . I'll come down . . . no, I can't do it—someone help me down!

CHENG'S VOICE Rednose! Go up and give him a hand!

[YANG *loses patience, runs into the temple to see what is going on.*
LUO *eventually disappears down the other side of the wall*]

HSIANG-CHÜ [*Quietly*] Mum!

MRS. YANG What is it, scallywag?

HSIANG-CHÜ [*Holding something back*] Sister . . .

MRS. YANG What about your sister?

HSIANG-CHÜ She and T'ien Hsi-erh—

MRS. YANG [*Anxiously*] What about T'ien Hsi-erh?

HSIANG-CHÜ They've gone off!

MRS. YANG [*Incredulous*] None of your nonsense, you silly child! [*On second thought*] Isn't your sister in the temple too?

HSIANG-CHÜ No. She was with me to begin with, sitting on the bench here. Look aren't these her husband's clothes?

MRS. YANG [*Panics*] And where is she herself?

HSIANG-CHÜ I didn't see.

MRS. YANG Inside the temple?

HSIANG-CHÜ No, outside the temple! [*Adds*] And she wasn't accompanied!

MRS. YANG Her husband—?

HSIANG-CHÜ He's in the temple with the others.

MRS. YANG How terrible! Go and call your sister, hurry, hurry! [*Calls* HSIANG-CHÜ *back*] Tell T'ien Hsi-erh to make himself scarce! Tell your sister to come by herself! [HSIANG-CHÜ *runs off to the right*]

MRS. YANG If her father-in-law saw these goings-on her goose is cooked!

[LUO *comes out of the temple, with* REDNOSE *supporting him.* YANG *and* CHENG *follow. The children bring up the rear*]

YANG What's it all about, kinsman? I simply don't understand.

LUO [*Head on one side, brusquely*] It's about—what it's about! You didn't witness it in person, of course you don't understand! But I, I did witness it in person! It was there for *all* to witness! A public spectacle!

YANG [*Asks* CHENG] What is he saying?

CHENG He's saying he saw it.

YANG Saw what?

CHENG He didn't say.

LUO [*Sits down on the bench*] In broad daylight—such audacity!— It makes me seethe!

MRS. YANG [*To Yang*] Our kinsman is angry.

YANG Do I need you to tell me that? He made that plain enough himself! [*To Luo, solicitously*] Kinsman!

LUO [*Turns a deaf ear*] The man's a bandit, the woman's a whore, such infamous behavior— Abhorrent to nature, anathema to god and man . . . it's monstrous! [*Calls out*] Young man!

[MASTER LUO *hides behind the others, not daring to show his face*]

LUO [*Looks around*] Young man! [*Discovers him*] Wretch! Come here, you!

MASTER LUO [*Dillydallying*] Yes, pa.

Luo [*With a mixture of shock and horror*] Mud all over your face! Your forehead black and blue! Hands all muddy! What have you been up to while you've been on the loose? And what's happened to that sweet little wife you were keeping an eye on?

MASTER Luo [*Casting about for an answer*] Pa . . . you told my wife to keep an eye on me, you didn't tell me to keep—keep an eye on my wife . . .

Luo [*Stamps his foot*] Get stuffed! You're a craphound! [*Sits down again*] You say she was keeping an eye on you, well, what sort of job did she make of it? . . . Where's your gown? Where's your jacket? [*Everyone searches*]

MASTER Luo I . . . I don't know.

Luo Where did you take them off?

MASTER Luo I handed them to my wife.

Luo I won't hear mention of her!

REDNOSE [*Pointing*] What is that under your worship's backside?

Luo [*Whips them out smartly*] Isn't this them, nitwit? Put them on!

MASTER Luo I . . . I . . . I'm hot!

Luo [*Stands up*] Put them on! And get off home when you've put them on!

[MRS. YANG *comes up to help*]

Luo [*Repulses her*] Don't bother!

YANG Since you have come, kinsman . . .

Luo A good thing I did come! . . . If I hadn't come I'd still be in the dark! [*To young* Luo] Put them on.

[*In dead silence he helps his son to dress*]

CHENG Old sir, as regards the setting up of these modern schools—

Luo [*To son*] See to the buttons yourself! [*To* CHENG] When you arrange a match in future, sir, look to it that your inquiries are thorough!

YANG Kinsman, what you are saying . . .

Luo Please desist from addressing me as "kinsman," sir. In the presence of the go-between, I will state my position plainly: I am disowning that precious daughter of yours! [*To son*] That's it! We'll go!

MRS. YANG [*Stops him*] Kinsman, even if my daughter and T'ien Hsi-erh—

Luo As you know about that, that's all the better! [*Prods his son*] Move!

MASTER Luo My wife . . .

Luo [*Loudly*] She's finished!

MASTER Luo [*Shrilly*] I want her!

Luo Want her, my arse! Do you want to be a cuckold? You're not afraid of dragging my name as a Doctor of Letters in the dirt? Do as you're told, and be on your way! [*Then, from the edge of the stage, to the assembly*] when I get back I will send a bill of divorce! I don't care what becomes of that precious daughter of yours, as far as my house is concerned she doesn't exist! [*He jerks up his sniveling son, and, elongating his stately gait, he goes on his way without a backward glance. The tension is released*]

YANG [*Like thunder*] Where's that little hussy Hsiang-ts'ao? [*No answer*] Bit of muck! I'll never be able to hold up my head again.

TIGERCUB [*Pointing to the left*] There she is!

[*All eyes turn as* HSIANG-TS'AO *enters, followed by her younger sister. They approach in fear and trembling*]

MRS. YANG [*Thinking to get a preemptive strike*] You'll see what I'll do to you, Hsiang-ts'ao . . .

YANG [*Shoves her out of the way*] A fine daughter you bore me! [*Looking at* HSIANG-TS'AO, *his face livid*] You've fouled things up good and proper for me, haven't you?

HSIANG-TS'AO [*Lowers her head*] Dad!

YANG [*Steadies himself*] What about T'ien Hsi-erh? [HSIANG-TS'AO *doesn't dare open her mouth*] Where is he? [*Growing more intimidating with every question*] Run away? So now you've had your tryst with him? You didn't even disguise it from your father-in-law? Lord almighty, who do you think you are? Have you any regard for your elders? You're seventeen or eighteen years old, haven't you got a sense of shame yet? [HSIANG-TS'AO *is deathly pale; she kneels*] Do you know what your father-in-law has done with you? [*No answer*] He's cast you off! And him, he just upped stakes and left! He's sending the divorce papers through straight away! You're banished from his house! [*Picks up the rake*] I . . . I . . . I'll have your life!

REDNOSE [*Intervening*] Guv'nor!

YANG Get lost! I'll beat her to death this time, I *will*! [*To* HSIANG-TS'AO] You shameless trollop! This is the last day you'll ever see! If your husband's family doesn't want you, your own family wants you even less!

REDNOSE Guv'nor! That tool belongs to somebody else.

YANG [*Hands him the rake*] Take it away!

[REDNOSE *puts the rake back where it came from, makes a sign to* MRS. YANG]

MRS. YANG [*Kneels at* YANG's *side, sobbing*] Spare your daughter Hsiang-ts'ao—hand her over to me!

YANG Hand her over to you! To go on living? To go on disgracing my name?

HSIANG-CHÜ [*Likewise kneeling*] Daddy! Daddy!

YANG [*To wife*] Get up! Take Hsiang-chü back home first! I don't want her to watch all this! Get up! Do you hear? I'm asking you to get up!

MRS. YANG [*Gets up*] Promise me you won't . . .

YANG I don't promise you anything! [*To* HSIANG-CHÜ] Go back with your mother! I won't be long! [*To* REDNOSE] Drag her back home!

CHENG Mr. Mayor, you have to admit . . .

YANG Schoolmaster, what would you do if this happened to you?

[CHENG *has no choice but to stand aside.* YANG *sits on the bench*]

MRS. YANG [*Goes up to* HSIANG-TS'AO] My child!

HSIANG-TS'AO [*Crying soundlessly*] Mum!

MRS. YANG How could you . . .

HSIANG-TS'AO I didn't do anything, Mum. . . . I lost interest in living a long time ago. I'll make my final kowtow now.

[Mrs. Yang *lets out a wail*]

Cheng [*Pacifying*] You mustn't take it to heart so, ma'am—

Mrs. Yang [*Imploring as she leaves*] You can't be so cruel . . .don't take my daughter from me! [Cheng *accompanies her off left*]

Rednose [*Drying his tears and at the same time coaxing* Hsiang-chü] Your mamma has gone—we'll leave too, shall we?

Hsiang-chü [*Resists*] I want my sister! . . . I want my sister!

Rednose Your dad will bring her [*half dragging, half carrying her, he shoos away* Tigercub *and his brother at the same time*] Get going! You can't stay here and gawp! Be off, the both of you!

[*Only father and daughter are left in front of the temple.* Hsiang-ts'ao *stops sobbing. She is as still as death*]

Yang [*Looking at* Hsiang-ts'ao, *after a while*] Ah! It's all over, then! [*Stamps his foot, then*] Do you still want to live?

Hsiang-ts'ao Dad!

Yang Do you still want to live? Speak!

Hsiang-ts'ao No.

Yang You know there's only one course open to you—death. Is that right?

Hsiang-ts'ao Yes, dad.

Yang Let me make this plain first. It's not that I've no feelings for you as a father. You knew yourself, if you got up to such shameful behavior . . .

Hsiang-ts'ao I didn't . . .

Yang You didn't?

Hsiang-ts'ao Well it was only . . .

Yang Well it was only . . .

Hsiang-ts'ao [*She can't continue*] Dad!

Yang It won't cross your lips, is that it? [*Falls silent*] In that case, do as I tell you: come into the temple with me.

[Widow T'ien *reenters left. She sees the situation and stops automatically*]

Hsiang-ts'ao Into the temple?

Yang Yes, into the temple. [*Stands up*] I'll take you through to the main hall, and there you'll make three kowtows to Kuan Ti, and pray that he will watch over you in the life to come and keep you on the straight and narrow.

[T'ien Hsi-erh *appears on the right and takes cover in the porch*]

Hsiang-ts'ao Yes, dad.

Yang If you had been as obedient before as you are now, you wouldn't have come to such a sorry end. [*Pained*] I'm not the only father who's been put on this spot. I'm not the only one either who's hardened his heart. [*At her side*] You realize that when a daughter is cast off by her husband's family and comes back home, the disgrace is harder for the father to live with than the daughter.

Hsiang-ts'ao It's my fault . . .

Yang No point in regrets . . . I feel just as bad about it. [*Wipes away his tears*] Get up and go inside and make your three kowtows to Kuan Ti. I'll give you a belt. You go on your own with it to the rear yard; and pick out one of the lower peach trees . . . I can't go on, you know the rest.

[*He cries.* HSIANG-TS'AO *cries.* WIDOW T'IEN *cries too*]

YANG [*Hears the third person*] Who is it? [*Discovers* WIDOW T'IEN] Damn it! It's you! [*To* HSIANG-TS'AO] Get up! If you don't make an end of yourself, I'll never hold up my head again in this village.

[HSIANG-TS'AO *nods; sobbing, she prepares to stand up. But her legs have turned to jelly, her soul seems to have left her body; for a long time she cannot stand up*]

WIDOW [*Suddenly bangs on the wall and starts inveighing, apparently goaded by conscience*] Wait till I catch you, Hsi-erh, you brute! . . . You've ruined this young lady, driven her to her death! . . . With this sin on your ledger you've got no hope of getting on in this life . . . the young lady's ghost will surely come back and haunt you at night! I . . . I . . . my life is in ruins!

YANG [*At first he is impatient, but then is moved by the tone and import of her words. In spite of himself, he goes across to comfort her*] Don't distress yourself, ma'am . . . your husband's been dead all these years; to raise a son by yourself . . .

WIDOW How could he? . . . I've worn myself out trying to be a good mother, and what reward have I got? . . .

[*It is at this moment that* HSI-ERH, *reckless of the consequences, goes up behind* HSIANG-TS'AO. *She raises her head, sees him, is about to exclaim in surprise, but stops herself*]

HSI-ERH [*Quietly*] I'll help you up.

HSIANG-TS'AO [*Stands up herself, under the shock, and holds onto the locust tree for support*] Watch out for my dad!

YANG [*Turns round and discovers* HSI-ERH. *His face hardens*] What are you up to?

HSI-ERH [*Calmly*] I came to fetch my rake! [*Pointing to it*] I dropped it here just now and forgot to take it.

YANG [*Harshly*] You came just at the right time. I need you as a witness so that when she's dead, people will know it wasn't me, her father, who forced her into it.

WIDOW [*Lifts up her tree branch to hit* HSI-ERH, *but, weakened from weeping, can only make it half way, and sits down on the bench*] I'll teach you, you demon! . . . Through your interfering you've signed this young lady's death warrant! . . .

HSI-ERH [*Goes over to her*] Listen to my side of it, ma.

WIDOW I don't want to listen to your side of it! [HSI-ERH *picks up the rake*]

YANG [*To* HSIANG-TS'AO] You go ahead, into the temple.

[HSIANG-TS'AO*'s eyes fall on* HSI-ERH; *she wavers, lowers her head, and sobs*]

YANG [*Urging*] Go on!

HSI-ERH Uncle Yang, just a word.

YANG [*Coldly*] I'm listening.

HSI-ERH You really want to be rid of your daughter?

YANG A daughter who leaves the house in marriage is water tipped down the drain. Her father-in-law washed his hands of her to my face. There's no way I can take her back.

HSI-ERH It was me who got her into this mess.

YANG You won't go scot free, don't worry!

HSI-ERH I'm not trying to.

YANG Good for you!

HSI-ERH Then you truly don't want Hsiang-ts'ao any more?

YANG [*Nods*] That's the size of it.

WIDOW [*Interrupts*] And she such a fine girl . . .

HSI-ERH Don't go on, ma. [*To* YANG] Ma is right, she is a fine girl. It can't be right to stand by and see her die. Hsiang-ts'ao and I are both young and thoughtless . . .

WIDOW That's just it, you should have stopped to think . . .

HSI-ERH [*Shoots her a glance, continues*] That's at the bottom of scrapes we have got into. And that's the root of our troubles too. Take my mother, Uncle Yang: she's the person in this world who loves me most, and I dote on her too, but, Uncle Yang, every day she's in a stew on my account . . .

WIDOW That's because you're not an obedient son . . .

HSI-ERH [*Loses his temper, bangs the rake on the ground*] Saints above! Will you kindly let me finish? [*Continues*] Mum couldn't live without me, Uncle Yang . . . if I got had up for murder, mum still wouldn't turn me away as long as I had breath in my body . . .

WIDOW [*Begins to cry quietly*] You've never spoken a truer word, my darling boy . . .

HSI-ERH Uncle Yang, when you rich people have food you can't eat, things you can't use, things that have gone mouldy or rotten, you throw them away, tip them away, chuck them away, and that's a terrible waste whatever you say. . . . But you always do the right thing, and throw the leftovers from your table to the beggars at your gate . . .

YANG What you're getting at is . . .

HSI-ERH [*Kneels*] Uncle Yang, I knock my head on the ground to you: do a kindness, and throw the thing you don't want to this beggar . . . good Uncle Yang, before you wouldn't let Hsiang-ts'ao marry me, and you were right, because I was poor . . . I knew myself I wasn't in a position to marry . . . but now none of you want her, and I'm kneeling here asking for her, imploring you to cast her off on me, as you would send a beggar on his way with a thing of no use to you. . . . And it would be one less sin to pay for in the underworld. . . . Good Uncle Yang, I've always been a hard nut, but look, now I'm blabbing . . . I could be in your debt the rest of my life . . .

[HSIANG-TS'AO *joins him in crying.* WIDOW T'IEN *is also moved by her son that she also starts crying again*]

WIDOW Wait till I get you, you big-hearted little brute! . . .

HSI-ERH Good Uncle Yang, I wouldn't be the only one who'd be grateful to you . . . Hsiang-ts'ao . . . my kind old mother . . .

WIDOW [*Abruptly stops crying, stands up*] Uncle Yang, don't listen to him . . .

YANG That I won't! Hsiang-ts'ao is my daughter and I'll dispose of her as I please.

HSI-ERH If you let her live, Uncle Yang, I, Hsi-erh, will buckle to and lead a respectable life. If I let you down in any way, I'm a son of a bitch . . .

WIDOW [*Objecting to his last words*] If you're a son of a bitch, what does that make me, I'd like to know? [*Turns abruptly to* YANG, *to support her son's previously expressed sentiments*] Hsi-erh is quite right, Uncle Yang, better hang on to a miserable life than die a glorious death—

YANG [*Firmly*] She can forget about any kind of life! [*Turns to* HSIANG-TS'AO] Speak for yourself, have you got the face to keep on living? Is it your wish to live?

[HSIANG-TS'AO *just sobs*]

HSI-ERH She's a human being, what's wrong with her living? Uncle Yang, if I make another kowtow to you, then let me take her away with me.

WIDOW I can't take in a daughter-in-law somebody else has sent away!

HSI-ERH She hasn't done anything wrong. Why make a big thing about being sent away? What's more, it was me who got her into this mess.

WIDOW Let's have less of your lip! [*To* YANG] Uncle Yang, don't let Hsi-erh take her away.

YANG I wouldn't think of it. [*To* HSIANG-TS'AO] It'll be dark any minute, off you go to the temple!

[HSIANG-TS'AO *is just about to move when* WIDOW T'IEN *gives voice again*]

WIDOW You, Uncle Yang, should spare her life, and let her go to a convent. Hsi-erh is right, she's still a human being. Everybody has been doing the dirty on me, an old widow woman, all these years that my man has been dead, but look at me, for every day this diabolical Hsi-erh of mine is alive I want to be alive and kicking too, and that's the truth!

YANG You speak for yourself.

WIDOW Are you, Uncle Yang, not made of flesh and blood also? No matter how badly the girl has behaved, she still is part of her parents' flesh and blood.

YANG I can never get it straightened out with you. The Yang family's girl is Yang family business, you don't have to bother about it.

WIDOW Now, that's what you said yourself.

YANG Yes, that's what I said.

WIDOW It has nothing to do with the T'ien family.

YANG You needn't trouble yourself.

WIDOW That's fine. [*Goes to stand between father and daughter*] I want to make this clear now, Uncle Yang: if your daughter kills hersef, it's not my son that's driven her to death.

YANG [*Challenges*] You mean to say that it's me?

WIDOW What? You the father drive your daughter to death and you want to make other people pay for it?

YANG Nobody has to pay for it!

WIDOW [*Thumps her branch*] Aha! So that's your little game! [*To* HSIANG-TS'AO] Dear Hsiang-ts'ao—you stay alive just to show your dad! [*Goes over and grabs her*] We'll see if he does do anything to you while this poor old woman is around! [*To* YANG, *venemously*] Try and see! Try and see!

YANG [*Choking with anger*] You! . . . You!

WIDOW [*To* HSIANG-TS'AO] Don't cry, child, you've been through enough already. [*To* YANG] Nobody wants her, is that right? Then I'll adopt her as my daughter!

HSI-ERH [*Weeps for joy*] Ma! Good old ma! Your son kowtows to you!

WIDOW As if I cared!

HSI-ERH [*Counts as he knocks his head on the ground*] One, two, three, . . . [*Rises up*] You've earned your place in heaven, ma!

WIDOW It's for your sake I'm doing it, you good-for-nothing.

HSI-ERH You call me all the names you like, ma: from now on I'll take it all lying down!

YANG [*Explodes*] You're up the pole! Don't kid yourself that you're going to take her away!

HSI-ERH Uncle Yang, do you understand what it is to be human? Supposing Hsiang-ts'ao had already gone to her death at your hands, she'd be dead to you anyway, so what harm is there in letting her go?

YANG Just let her move and see what will happen! [*Sternly*] Hsiang-ts'ao! Into the temple with you!

[HSIANG-TS'AO *trembles and actually takes a step*]

WIDOW [*Grabs hold of her*] Hsiang-ts'ao, my dear, what will become of my Hsi-erh if you die? What will become of him?

HSIANG-TS'AO [*The shaft strikes home; her face streaked with tears, she glances at* HSI-ERH *and falls into* WIDOW T'IEN*'s arms*] Ma'am!

WIDOW [*Patting her just like a child at the breast*] There, there! I knew you didn't want to die!

YANG [*Sternly*] Hsiang-ts'ao! Are you going to disobey your father?

WIDOW You claim to be her father? You're simply not human! [*To* HSIANG-TS'AO] Pay him no heed! Come home with me!

YANG [*Sternly*] Hsiang-ts'ao! You dare!

WIDOW [*Loudly*] How can you be so pigheaded? When all's said and done, she's still your flesh and blood; what's all this whooping and hollering about?

YANG Am I to let you do whatever you please?

HSI-ERH Ma! We—

WIDOW [*Gives him a crack with the branch*] Don't you start! Pick up your rake! Lead the way!

HSI-ERH Yes, ma!

WIDOW [*With her arm around* HSIANG-TS'AO, *walks slowly toward the left*] Hsiang-ts'ao, my dear, I don't want to speak ill of my son, but Hsi-erh isn't good enough for you, and that's flat—

YANG [*Watches them, indignant, abashed, at odds with himself, distressed, lonely; but he says with vitriolic hatred*] I won't let you get away with this! I'll go to the county seat and lay a charge against you! That's it! I'm set on it! [*With this resolution, he exits left, unsteadily*]

WIDOW [*Stops, and says to* HSIANG-TS'AO *with the authority of experience*] Don't be afraid, my dear. "Trees have bark, people have face": the last thing your dad will do will be to go to the county court and wash his dirty linen in public! [*To* HSI-ERH, *as if calling in the hens*] Anything else can wait till we get home. Cluck, cluck! Off you go!

[*A low shaft of sunlight falls on their retreating figures, as the evening draws in. The farmers have finished their work in the fields and their sounds are carried from the distance–their singing, their commands to their animals; at the same time the lowing of oxen and the braying of asses, and the cawing of crows as darkness falls, weave together to make the music of the countryside*]

[*Curtain*]

Notes

1. Dragon Well (Lung-ching) is a famous spring in the province of Chekiang that gives its name to the tea of the region. It is situated near the grave of the famous Sung dynasty patriot Yüeh Fei.

2. King Wen's divination refers to an arrangement of the traditional eight trigrams used in fortune-telling.

3. The "Mandarin button" refers to insignia worn on caps identifying those men who passed certain stages of the civil service examinations that qualified them for privileged legal status as gentry and possible appointment to official posts.

4. "Longhairs" was a popular term for participants in the mid-nineteenth-century Taiping Rebellion, who let their hair hang freely in defiance of ordinances imposed by the ruling Manchus prescribing a braided queue.

Yang Chiang

Windswept Blossoms

Translated by Edward M. Gunn

Cast of Characters

NANNY WANG (WANG NAI-MA)
SHEN HUI-LIEN, a young wife
TANG SHU-YUA, an attorney
YEH SAN, a local landowner
FANG CHING-SHAN, husband of Shen
OLD CHIN, Yeh San's servant
FANG'S COUSIN
FANG'S UNCLE
VILLAGERS —women, children, men

ACT I

The setting is rural Republican China. A dilapidated temple in the countryside, its statue of Buddha discarded, has been repaired, whitewashed, and converted into a hall. Along one side are arranged several low benches. Beside them lie a number of unfinished rattan baskets and bamboo implements. At the foot of the benches are piled strips of rattan and bamboo. Along another side are frames for embroidery, while in the far corner on a table covered with clean white cotton cloth are gauze bandages, cotton dressings, and the like. To the right hangs a memorial photograph of Fang Ching-shan's mother, above an altar set up in her memory. In front of the temple is an ancient locust tree, casting the interior in deep shade. As a balmy breeze blows, willow blossoms float about, filling the air and covering the ground.

Within the temple hall an apartment can be seen at the rear, newly tiled, above which is written: "Yeh Shih Primary School." Next to the temple, beyond a low wall, budding peach blossoms reach halfway along the outstretched limbs of a peach tree. Beyond the wall are neat, green rice paddies, their length and breadth inlaid with plots of golden rapeseed blossoms. At the furthest edge of the fields are railroad tracks. The remains of white smoke from a train that has passed have formed clumps of white clouds, pressing down heavily along the horizon. Dogs are barking nearby and in the distance.

As the curtain rises, NANNY WANG *is standing on the stone steps at the front of the temple, chasing the willow blossoms with sweeps of her broom. Two village women stick their heads through the half-open gates to the courtyard and enter.*

FIRST WOMAN Nanny Wang!

SECOND WOMAN [*Chuckling and nudging* FIRST WOMAN] Just look at that. If Nanny Wang gets any happier she'll go crazy.

NANNY WANG What's with these willow blossoms! It's like they've gone mad, dancing and tumbling all over the place. It's nearly impossible to sweep the place clean. And in a little bit our young gentleman will be back—

FIRST WOMAN Did your young gentleman really get out?

WANG [*Annoyed*] What do you mean "really"? Are they going to keep him locked up the rest of his life? What law did he actually break?

SECOND WOMAN Ai, Nanny Wang, we were just asking. When did he get out?

WANG [*With great satisfaction*] Look— [*Pointing into the distance beyond the wall*] the next train after the one that just went by without stopping, that will be his.

[THIRD *and* FOURTH WOMAN *enter carrying strings of firecrackers*]

THIRD WOMAN Nanny Wang, is Mr. Fang going to come back?

WANG Ai, Heaven isn't blind. There was Fat P'an to wrong him. And then there was a good man to help our young lady free him.

FOURTH WOMAN [*Presenting the firecrackers*] Little Fish's father had me bring these over to you. We can really celebrate and drive out the filthy bad luck.

WANG Aiya, thank you very much—ya, I'm so rattled. Please have a seat.

[*Two small boys enter together, and seeing the ground covered with willow blossoms, begin to swipe at them*]

WANG Hey, Ah Lung, you came at just the right time. You can set off these firecrackers for us in a little while!

FIRST CHILD I'll do it!

SECOND CHILD I'll do it!

THIRD WOMAN Don't argue!—Ah Lung, you'll get a good swat from me. What did you do to our younger brother yesterday?

FOURTH WOMAN [*Nudging* THIRD] Let it go—

[*Two village men enter*]

FIRST MAN [*Presenting firecrackers*] Nanny Wang, celebrate! Make it good and loud!

WANG Oh, Chao Lao-ta, you shouldn't have gone to so much trouble.

SECOND MAN This is a happy occasion, Nanny Wang! When will Mr. Fang be back?

[ELDERLY MATRON *enters*]

ELDERLY MATRON Nanny Wang, your young gentleman was released?

VILLAGERS Madame Mu!

WANG Sit, sit, please, Madame Mu. Our young man is on his way back now.

[*Five or six children stick their heads through the gate*]

A CHILD [*Beyond the gate*] Has Mr. Fang come?

VOICES OF CHILDREN [*Offstage*] Oh wow! Mr. Fang's back! Mr. Fang's back! Hurray!

WANG [*Loudly calling beyond the gate*] What are you up to? Why, you are supposed to put on a homecoming party as your teacher said!

[*Distant rumbling, a train whistle sounds*]

SECOND WOMAN It's here! [*Stretching her neck, looking beyond the wall*]

WANG That's the train! [*All necks are stretched looking beyond the wall*]

FIRST CHILD Set them off?

THIRD WOMAN Outside. Set them off outside.

[*The two boys exit with the firecrackers*]

[*Offstage*] Now? Nanny Wang?

WANG Now? Wait!

[*Childen's voices offstage*] Now! Now! Now! [*Fireworks explode. Offstage children clap their hands and shriek*] They're shooting way up high!

VILLAGERS [*Onstage*] It's good luck for everyone!

[*Offstage children clap their hands and shriek*] They're shooting far!

VILLAGERS [*Onstage*] It's in with the good and out with the bad, forever!

[*Offstage children cry out*] Oh, wow! It's good luck! Our luck has changed! [*Fireworks explode*]

FIRST WOMAN Eh, your young lady?

WANG She must have gone to meet him. I haven't seen her.

SECOND MAN We'll go meet him, too!

SECOND, THIRD, AND FOURTH WOMEN [*Shading their eyes with their hands as they look beyond the wall into the distance*] He's coming! He's coming!

WANG Do you see him?

SECOND WOMAN The train has stopped.

SECOND MAN Let's go meet him!

FIRST MAN Shall we go?

WANG Let's go!

FIRST, SECOND, THIRD WOMAN Let's go, let's go!

ELDERLY MATRON Let's all go!

[*They all exit through the gate in an uproar. Outside dogs bark wildly. Children shriek "Mr. Fang's back! Mr. Fang's back!" The voices gradually subside into the distance in a vague clatter*]

[*SHEN HUI-LIEN enters listlessly from the rear apartment, and stands for a while on the stone steps. She slowly strolls under the locust tree. With one arm embracing the tree trunk, she rests her head against it, and gazes absently at the swirling willow blossoms. NANNY WANG hastily enters through the front gate*]

WANG Eeeee! Miss, you're *here*!

[SHEN, *as though startled from a dream, looks blankly at* NANNY WANG]

WANG [*Stamping her foot*] Your husband is here, and everyone's gone to meet him, and I said you'd already gone! I just thought there was nobody here, and I'd forgotten to close the gate—what's this? You're here alone!

SHEN He isn't coming.

WANG The train is here. Look, look! [*On tiptoe, she shades her eyes with her hand*]

SHEN It won't be that train.

WANG You said the young gentleman would be on that train.

SHEN I said that? I'm afraid he couldn't catch that train.

WANG If we'd known he wasn't coming, we should have rushed into town to meet him.

SHEN Unless you happen to love crossing one another en route. Mr. T'ang wrote in his letter that we should wait for him at home.

WANG So you never went out? Just now you were in the back rooms. Didn't you hear the firecrackers when we set them off? Everyone was celebrating and calling for good luck.

SHEN I'm much obliged.

WANG It was, after all, very nice of them, wasn't it? We have to get some good luck to offset the bad luck. Such a decent man to be locked up in prison for over a year. He hadn't even been married to you a year, then he was locked up for over twelve months.

SHEN I'm grateful for their kindness.

WANG [*Moving closer to look at* SHEN*'s face*] What is it?

SHEN When he is returning, they put on a noisy celebration. Did they miss Ching-shan when he was not here?

WANG You can't blame them for—

SHEN Fat P'an framed him. Now if Fat P'an himself went and did the things Ching-shan has done for them, wouldn't they say *he* was so good and capable! Such a grand fellow!

WANG That bastard!

SHEN Take a look. Wasn't it Fat P'an who came and renovated this dilapidated temple! That tiled room, wasn't it Fat P'an who built it! So what if this village is minus one Fang Ching-shan!

WANG How right you are. How many time I've told you both: if you want to teach, you could teach anywhere. If you want to open a school, you could do it anywhere. But you had to go find this brokendown old temple in the countryside. I can remember when you first came here as a new bride. It was pouring rain. Here it was leaking, there it was leaking. You, the daughter of a fine family, in a crummy old hovel!

SHEN Nanny, I didn't ask you to come with us.

WANG It's not that I resent it. I'm angry for your sake! You stuffed yourself with book learning, and for what? To come here and teach village girls how to make wicker baskets, bamboo baskets, do embroidery. Which one of them isn't a lot better at it than you! They hide out here to play around and save themselves from scrubbing pots and cooking and doing the laundry at home. Who wants your this and that reforms, your this and that service? You spent your whole dowry for wrapping up their chilblains and daubing iodine on them. And when the sores get bigger you get so worried you just call on Nanny for help.

SHEN [*With resentment*] Ai, when will the day come that I'll be rid of this hopeless work!

WANG Ya! That's odder yet! Once your husband was arrested, I talked till I was blue in the face to get you to go back to your own family. But would you listen? And Mr. T'ang also urged you not to live here but go to the city. And would you listen?

SHEN Sure, and just give in to Fat P'an! He wrecked Ching-shan, so I'll leave everything else up to him to take care of just as he pleases!

WANG Well, you ought to be satisfied. Fat P'an was no match for you! It didn't matter that he had a headful of schemes and a town full of connections. Master Yeh San came on swaggering like a hero and he bought up this public land as real estate! Huh, Fat P'an could only get out! This is Yen San's land, Yeh San's rooms, Yeh San wanted *you* in place of Ching-shan, not P'an. [*Picks up her broom and sweeps the ground*]

SHEN I wouldn't let him! I wouldn't let P'an get together with Yeh San. You're all afraid of Fat P'an, the local boss of every thug in the region. But not me!

WANG Enough. Men fear ghosts and ghosts fear men. I saw how you put Fat P'an to work when you came down to the countryside. Without him, you wouldn't have gotten anywhere. With him, why one day he'd set about taking people's money to buy things for them, and then make a profit for himself by buying at a discount; and then the next day he'd take public funds and build himself a new pigsty in his own home—

SHEN Ai, Nanny, and that was Fang Ching-shan's great mission! His highest ideal! And so it was for this great noble undertaking that I wouldn't listen to my parents, but came here to help him carry it out—to take care of some pig pen of Fat P'an's! Look how much we've accomplished! We've exchanged the best years of our lives for such an achievement. Fat P'an has gone. Ching-shan is coming back, and everyone is out shooting off fireworks for him and saying nice things! Ai, Nanny, I should be pleased, too! I should be ecstatic!

WANG [*Perplexed*] Are you joking?

SHEN Look at how happy I am! I'm full of jokes!

WANG [*Carefully observing* SHEN] You must be sarcastic, right? I don't understand it. I'm for laying things wide open and speaking straight to the point. I tell you, earthworms eat the dirt of their own territory. If you break somebody's rice bowl, if you block somebody's way, they won't have any regrets about chewing you up. If you're not careful, it won't stop with just Fat P'an setting fires and accusing Ching-shan of being in some lawless, godless party or group. You mark my words—

SHEN Oh, so if we don't go back to the city, we'll be arrested?

WANG [*Anxiously pressing her hand against* SHEN's *mouth*] What are you doing, miss, saying things that will bring bad luck.

SHEN Isn't that what you want to say? You're afraid of bad luck, so now we must scurry off and hide. A man getting out of prison is nothing but bad luck.

WANG [*Spitting several times to avoid bad luck*] What do I fear? Didn't I go into the prison with you to see him? He won't bring back any filthy bad luck. When he gets out he gets his head shaved, takes a bath, and comes out shiny as a goldpiece!

SHEN You think he has the time to spend on all that?

WANG Mr. T'ang can take care of him! With Mr. T'ang around you can just let him take care of your problems.

SHEN Are you saying that Mr. T'ang met him and is coming back with him?

WANG They should be coming back together. Why, for your man's sake Mr. T'ang had to run back and forth into the city a hundred times. How much concern he showed, not to mention how much money he spent, or how much trouble he went to dashing around here and there in winds and rains. You figure it out! I reckon Ching-shan still has two friends. In the city it's Mr. T'ang, and there's a lawyer for him, right there. In the countryside it's Yeh San, and there he's got his wealthy patron, ready made.

SHEN What does Yeh San count? He doesn't amount to anything worth calling a friend.

WANG If he hadn't bought up this public land, and helped you get rid of Fat P'an, would you have been able to stay on here at all? Who in this fleabag town doesn't think he's a bigshot? Over the last two years haven't you relied on him to look after you? He's always been sending fish, meat, and what all.

SHEN Did I take anything from him?

WANG So you were too polite to eat it, but he had the kindness to offer it—am I wrong?

SHEN You've never been wrong.

WANG What are you doing, acting prickly as a porcupine? [*Closing in on* SHEN *to look carefully at her face*] If Ching-shan isn't back yet, it isn't me that's holding him up. I'm waiting for him, too. Look, I've gotten out his clothes and fixed up the bed. I killed the chicken this morning, and got it all ready cooking on the fire. Ai, I've gotten so worked up waiting for him that I feel I'm starting to run a fever!

SHEN You go ahead and run a fever. My temperature is normal.

WANG Ho, ho. So now we're putting on airs! Of course—you're not waiting for him to get back, at all.

SHEN Whew, Nanny, you've really put your finger on it that time.

WANG Heh, heh, heh. Cook the egg long enough and it will get tender for sure! Before you were married you were so shameless you didn't care a bit how you acted. Your father despised Ching-shan for being so poor, but you went ahead and insisted on him and didn't care what anybody said. And yet now you're ready to act like you don't care at all! You think I believe it? Afraid old Nanny will laugh at you?

SHEN I'm not worried whether you laugh at me, and I'm not worried whether you believe me! Am I saying things to make you believe me? I can't go on pretending, I'm so ready to explode. I'm spitting things out to try to make myself feel better.

WANG Who are you upset with?

SHEN Myself.

WANG You haven't had a man at home to keep you in your place for over a year. But then we've spoiled your temper.

SHEN "We"? Who's "we"?

WANG Hasn't Master Yeh San tried to please you?

SHEN Who wants him to try to please me? He's been taking advantage of the fact that Ching-shan's not at home to try to please me.

WANG Haven't I spoiled you? And what about Mr. T'ang—

SHEN [*With a slight smile*] How has Mr. T'ang indulged me?

WANG Oh, he's so polite to you—

SHEN Polite? Heh, polite. [*Sighs*]

WANG We've pampered you, and now, when Ching-shan is back, you go and throw a fit over him. That's just— [*Shakes her head*]

SHEN Did I throw a fit with him after our marriage?

WANG Oh yes. But it's only proper that you should get along better together.

SHEN Okay, Nanny. If he says this table is round, then I'll say it's round. If he says it has corners, then I'll say it has corners. If he says he's the greatest thing on earth, then I'll say he's the greatest thing in heaven as well.

WANG What's wrong with that? You know that it's happiness and good fortune for a husband and wife to be reunited.

SHEN He's my cross, and I have to go on carrying it on my back.

WANG What?

SHEN To carry the burden I chose for myself, and take the road I myself chose to take. That is my lot.

WANG What sort of nonsense is that?

SHEN [*Stamping her foot resentfully*] Now I know how much I hate him!

WANG Now what is there to hate? Ching-shan will be here in a little while.

[T'ANG SHU-YUAN *opens the gate and enters*]

SHEN Mr. T'ang.

WANG Where's our young master?

T'ANG He's been abducted by them. Listen!

[*In the distance a large number of children are yelling*, "Wow! Hurray! Mr. Fang is back! Mr. Fang is back!"]

T'ANG I couldn't even get through on the road. I had to take a detour to get here. They've taken Ching-shan off to a homecoming celebration.

WANG Come on, young lady, let's get out there and have a look at the homecoming celebration!

SHEN With all those people all around him? What's the point? If you want to go, go ahead.

WANG [*Opening the gate and shouting*] Young master! [*Dashes through the gate in great haste*]

T'ANG You'll have to blame me for botching his homecoming—they were on top of us like a wave and swept him away. There simply wasn't anything I could do.

SHEN [*Turning her face away*] It's so disappointing.

T'ANG [*Earnestly*] I really apologize—but, at any rate he's back! Even if you have to wait till dusk, it's only an hour off! Mrs. Fang, we ought to celebrate our success!

SHEN If success is worth celebrating.

T'ANG [*Surprised*] How's that?

SHEN Is there anything less interesting than success? When you've succeeded at anything interesting, anything worthwhile, then it's finished, over. You've hit a wall, and you can't go further.

T'ANG [*Looking at* SHEN *with surprise*] Well, fortunately the projects you two are involved in are still a long way from success.

SHEN Oh, our projects! They're not *mine*.

T'ANG Don't you work together and share the same hopes?

SHEN United in our work and dreams! [*Smiling, points to the fluttering willow blossoms*] Mr. T'ang, take a look at that one willow blossom. Its dream is to reach heaven!

T'ANG [*Smiling*] And can a person be so pathetic?

SHEN The same as the grass and trees. In the spring the flower blooms in the sun, the spring breeze blows it away where it will—ideals, love: they're nothing more than spring sunlight and spring breeze. Tomorrow that blossom will fall to earth, sprout, grow roots, nothing more than a seed—if the environment lets it live.

T'ANG [*With a forced smile*] When did you think up this "botanical philosophy"? When you were scrapping with Fat P'an the year before last you didn't seem much like a botanical specimen.

SHEN There are botanical types that don't know their place. Here they fly, there they fly, thinking they have so much strength, that they're in charge! The law-abiding ones, like rice and wheat, have already quietly let themselves rot in the soil and turn into fertilizer for the next generation.

T'ANG Still, I respect Ching-shan for being able to see himself as his own master. I love that blind determination of his.

SHEN He can have his blind determination. What he ought to realize is that he's not the world's indispensable great man, shouldering some great mission to save the people.

T'ANG It's only because of his self-confidence that he has that blind determination.

SHEN He only believes in himself. He's never been able to look at himself through other people's eyes! He's never acknowledged what his self is like in the mind and the eyes of anyone else.

T'ANG Why does he have to look through the eyes of someone else? In other people's eyes he's nothing more than a naive, unrealistic fool. He ought to go back to the city, take up something ordinary, and settle down. Oh, I almost forgot, when I went to meet Ching-shan, I ran into his cousin—Ching-yuan, right? When I told him the news, he said he didn't have any time today, but he'd be out here to see you both tomorrow or the next day.

SHEN Who wants him to come here?

T'ANG Probably he's going to urge Ching-shan to go back to the city.

SHEN They can mind their own business! What do they understand! So what if Ching-shan *is* inexperienced, undereducated, naive, if he is some young Turk that people can't stand. It doesn't matter: they still don't have any right to come and lecture him. The only things they understand are making money and raising families, raising children to be good, obedient animals. How can he have the nerve to come here! I'll ask Yeh San for that pack of police dogs he keeps to come over and sink their teeth into him—we'll see if he dares come!

T'ANG [*Smiling*] Why are you getting so worked up? Weren't you just saying that Ching-shan wasn't able to see himself through other people's eyes?

SHEN [*Unswayed*] I'm not in any mood for logic today. I just can't stand anything today. Can't stand anything.

T'ANG Because it's all happened so suddenly?—I myself feel—feel— it was Old Ch'iu's secretary who called on the telephone and said he was released. I never thought it would happen so fast. To have hoped for it for so long, and to have it all of a sudden be so easy, it seemed as if all our concern over the last year was missing the point. Had I known—

SHEN But who is that smart? Who could have known beforehand? I shouldn't have let Ching-shan be taken away by the police in the first place. I wanted to have it out with those two bastards all the way to the death—

T'ANG You couldn't have won. They have guns.

SHEN So I don't? [*Removes a brick from the wall, and draws out an automatic pistol from the hole*] Take a look!

T'ANG Where did you get this pistol?

SHEN It's a souvenir. [*Puts the pistol back in the hole*] A souvenir. Having it here fortifies me. It's all because Nanny held me back with her arms around me. I should have used it then and not let Ching-shan be arrested here in the countryside. Why, the *city* isn't as lawless as this place. In the city they wouldn't have poured vinegar through his nose and burned holes in him with lighted incense sticks to get a confession out of him.

T'ANG If you'd fought it out with them, you yourself would have lost out—

SHEN Ai! It would have been better to die then. It would have spared me this day— [*She suddenly breaks off, looks at* T'ANG, *startled to have said this, and lowers her voice*] I've longed for nothing else but this day, waiting for him to come back. But now, I wish he hadn't come at all. I'm afraid of his coming back. I don't want him to come back! [*Choked with emotion*] Mr. T'ang, I'm talking nonsense. I'm talking nonsense.

T'ANG Because you're too happy, so you feel strange and uneasy. Just rest for a little while. Ching-shan will be back very soon. [*Takes his hat*] I'm going.

SHEN Going? You're not waiting for Ching-shan?

T'ANG I came especially to say goodbye.

SHEN Goodbye?

T'ANG I have some business to attend to. I'm going up north for a while.

SHEN In such a rush? Can't you wait until Ching-shan returns?

T'ANG I already spoke to him.

SHEN Oh—what important matter is this? I haven't heard you mention it, have I?

T'ANG It's something that came up all off a sudden.

SHEN Oh. All of a sudden! When will you return?

T'ANG I don't know—perhaps—I don't know . . .

SHEN "You won't be back for a while."

T'ANG I won't be back for a while.

SHEN I knew it! I knew it! [*Raises her head, gazes challengingly at* T'ANG, *who slowly averts his eyes and lowers his head.* SHEN *extends her hand to him and says quietly*] Mr. T'ang, goodbye. [*They shake hands*] I'll tell you why I feel so distraught today. It's because I knew you were leaving.

T'ANG You knew?

SHEN I've known for some time. I've known that there would be a day like this, when you would suddenly have some business and move on.

T'ANG How did you already know—?

SHEN How! How! I should have known. Of course I've known. All along I've known.

T'ANG I hope I haven't told you.

SHEN With everything but your mouth.

T'ANG I never knew I was such a pathetically transparent person.

SHEN No, you're not transparent. I was just taking a wild guess, saying wild things— What nonsense have I been talking?

T'ANG You haven't been talking nonsense— Goodbye, Mrs. Fang—

SHEN Goodbye, Mr. T'ang. What you remember of me, think of it as a bundle of waste-paper and put it away somewhere. Bury it deep and never open it up to look at it again.

T'ANG If I can.

SHEN Because I've never liked looking at my past self. It always makes me dislike her, look down on her, break out in a sweat with shame for her. Since you are going, taking along what you remember of me, promise me now, and bury it like a deep, dark secret. Don't open it up and look again on what I entrust to you.

T'ANG All right. As secure as a gem buried in a mountain. Don't worry.

SHEN I've felt you are about as stable as a mountain; and I'm no more than a small tree tossing about in a storm. For a year now I've been sheltered by your mountain, but from today on, once again I'll have to— [*Smiles*] It's just that you've taken too good care of me—we'll see each other again—if we will see each other again.

T'ANG If.

SHEN Also—

T'ANG Eh?

SHEN Nothing—I forgot—

[*They look at each other silently. T'ANG exits abruptly. SHEN stands woodenly, dully looking at his retreating figure. YEH SAN enters, dragging T'ANG back onstage with him*]

YEH Come on, come on—wait up a bit. As long as I have you here, Mr. T'ang, then Mrs. Fang will favor me with her presence.

T'ANG But Mr. Yeh, I have to go take care of something.

YEH Hold on, hold on— [*Toward offstage*] Old Chin, where have you gone? Bring it in! [OLD CHIN *brings on a full load of chicken, meat, and fish on a carrying pole. SHEN stands on the stone steps, looking dubiously at this load of gifts. OLD CHIN stops and sets down his load, sitting on the pole*]

SHEN Mr. Yeh, this—

YEH Say no more, say no more—if you go on being so stiff I'll say you have no respect for me.

SHEN Nothing of the kind—Mr. Yeh—

YEH Don't say it, don't say it—I know, I don't have enough face, I don't deserve the honor—but coming in the gate I ran into Mr. T'ang here! Fine, I said! As long as Mr. T'ang is here, then there'll be someone here with face. I can't say a thing; but he's got a silver tongue.

T'ANG [*Smiling*] It can't match your iron arm—

YEH What use is that! People like me are just countryfolk, that's all. We may have a temple full of ancestors who were big officials, but in the end we're just country hicks. Can't talk like Mr. T'ang—he is the one Mrs. Fang would favor with conversation!

SHEN You favor *me*, coming to this dilapidated temple.

YEH Please don't treat me like a stranger, Mrs. Fang—this is my birthday feast. I knew I couldn't get you to come over for dinner, so I brought it over here instead—Mr. T'ang, put in a good word for me, don't let her keep on with that polite talk, never giving me a chance. You just say the word, and Mrs. Fang will agree to it—oh, but there's one condition appended: Mr. T'ang cannot leave today. He has to stay and drink with us, all right?

T'ANG [*Angry*] Yeh San—

SHEN [*Smiling placatingly*] Mr. Yeh, you didn't give me a chance to speak. I didn't know it was your birthday. I thought this was all to welcome Ching-shan home.

YEH Ching-shan what?

SHEN Ching-shan's back, so in a little while we'll celebrate your birthday and have wine with you. Mr. T'ang has a previous engagement.

[T'ANG *waves to* SHEN *and exits.* SHEN*'s eyes follow him out.* YEH SAN *is oblivious to their exchange*]

YEH What's this? What's this? Fang Ching-shan has returned?

SHEN He's back.

YEH How did that happen?

SHEN T'ang Shu-yuan got him out.

YEH T'ang Shu-yuan? He really meant to get him out? Heh, heh. Now that such a friend is back they can see each other more often. It's a little more convenient!

SHEN He's going on a long trip. He won't be coming.

YEH [*Surprised*] Oh? Say—does T'ang Shu-yuan have a woman? They say he's never married.

SHEN That's not our business.

YEH They say his mother likes to gamble, and that he has a flock of sisters who can spend money like water. Whatever he makes, they spend. So he hasn't taken a wife.

SHEN Where did you hear all this, Mr. Yeh?

YEH Old Chin's brother is a chauffeur, lives right next door to them. I know everything that goes on in that family.

SHEN His mother loves to gamble?

YEH Nasty-tempered.

SHEN He has a lot of sisters?

YEH All made up like temptresses. Some of them have married into rich families. Hey, he's probably got used to looking at city women—and has gotten someone in mind.

SHEN That's his affair.

YEH Heh, heh, heh—He's really good friends with Mr. Fang, is he?

SHEN They were schoolmates. When he learned what had happened to Ching-shan this time, he went on his own to find him and help him out—he's a lawyer.

YEH Oh, very good. Very good, indeed. Is Mr. Fang here already?

SHEN He's out there. They're giving him a homecoming celebration.

YEH Hum—that's great—just great—fine, fine. [*Turning angrily to* OLD CHIN] How come you're just sitting there? Don't want to move? Don't want to get back?

CHIN You want me to take this to the back?

YEH Who told you to take it to the back? Just empty the load here and go back home with your pole and baskets!

CHIN It's early. The moon hasn't come up yet. You said we'd be eating supper here and then go back.

YEH Who said so? Who said so? Take the things out, fast. Then just take your pole and go.

SHEN Ya, Mr. Yeh, won't you be drinking your wine here?

YEH I have something to take care of. But, Mrs. Fang, there is something I wanted to get in touch with Mr. Fang about. He's come back at the right time. As you know, Mrs. Fang, this land was originally public property of the village. When Fat P'an wanted to come and take it over, it was I who put up the money to buy the building and grounds and then let you take care of it. But over the last year, the expenses have gotten to be too much, and I'm really going into debt because of it.

SHEN Ya, Mr. Yeh, last time you spoke about how you were going to expand and renovate—

YEH That was last time. This time I just don't have the money any more to maintain it.

SHEN So you're planning to—

YEH There are other uses for this property. Since Mr. Fang is back, it's best that—those rooms of yours in the rear you can return to me. I'll be renovating them.

SHEN Mr. Yeh—

YEH Old Chin, is everything taken out. Let's go.

SHEN Mr. Yeh, we can't possibly accept all these things—We— [*Voices clamor outside*]

[NANNY WANG *enters, steps aside to let* FANG CHING-SHAN *enter, and hurriedly closes the gate*]

WANG [*Shouting to outside*] Go on home, Mr. Fang needs to rest. [*The door is pushed and pounded from the outside, while* NANNY WANG *leans her weight against it*]

YEH [*Not looking at* FANG] Ai, let us out.

WANG Oh Mr. Yeh! [*To* FANG] Mr. Yeh San was most thoughtful looking after our young lady. This is our young gentleman! Mr. Yeh, did you come to welcome our young gentleman back?

YEH Mr. Fang, I've heard so much about you, indeed—

FANG Mr. Yeh.

YEH Just a little thing—

WANG Won't you sit with us a while? I'll go brew tea.

YEH I don't have the time. Old Chin! [*Exits arrogantly,* OLD CHIN *following*]

[SHEN HUI-LIEN *stands as though rooted to the spot, looking fearfully at* FANG *as though he were a stranger*]

FANG Hui-lien! Hui-lien! [*Advancing to greet her*] Don't let me fall and wake up to find you still not by my side.

SHEN [*Moving forward, quickly avoiding* FANG] Ching-shan, I couldn't get there on time to meet you.

FANG I didn't want you to meet me. I didn't want you to meet me. I wanted you waiting here for me, here in our nest.

WANG Aren't you starved? I'll go get some dinner ready.

SHEN I'll go.

FANG Hui-lien—

WANG [*With annoyed sarcasm*] I couldn't possibly do this little thing! I want you to go do it! [*Exits*]

FANG Hui-lien [*Embraces* SHEN, *who pulls away*] That's one more empty embrace. Ai, Hui-lien, Hui-lien. I don't know how many times, how many times, I'd see you and you'd slip away. Always I'd come that close to grasping you. [*Observing* SHEN] Don't you recognize me? Are you afraid of me? [*Smiling sadly*] This is a convict fresh out of prison, you know!

SHEN Ching-shan, you're tired. Rest a while, eat a little something—

FANG Haven't I rested enough! I've been resting for more than a year. What haven't I tasted? Is there anything else I still want to eat? [*Walking toward* SHEN, *who retreats into the hall*] Hui-lien, you've become a stranger.

SHEN Ching-shan, don't—don't— [*Dodging him*] There's something we have to talk about.

FANG Talk! When you were not at my side, I used to talk to you in my mind. Now you still want me to talk to myself? Hui-lien, come over here, give me the real, true you! I've been afraid, afraid I'd never hold you again all my life, that I'd forever hug a shadow. [*Drawing close to* SHEN]

SHEN [*Backing off*] Ching-shan, [*Forcing a smile*] don't put on that face.

FANG [*Suddenly noticing his mother's spirit tablet, he stops and looks searchingly at his mother's photograph*] Can this still be false? This is the mother who waited for me to come back! In my dreams I never saw such a cruel reality. [*Gazing on the photograph, he sobs—stopping, he addresses* SHEN] Hui-lien, Hui-lien. Before, you resented that I only thought of mother. Now, today, I can answer you: she used to be in my mind, but she's gone. Poor mother. To have a son who amounts to nothing, who would never be good, who dragged her out here. And that wasn't enough—I had to make her sick with worry—lonely and desolate—

SHEN Nanny and I were with her every minute.

FANG But I wasn't here—

SHEN Once she got ill she was disoriented, so she didn't understand that you weren't here. I was afraid she might become lucid and maybe have something to say, so I didn't dare take turns with Nanny. For several days and several nights, I was with her straight through, at her side—

FANG How sad that mother could forget where her son was. In her heart she was so unwilling to die, wanting still to wait for me to come back.

SHEN I took her to the clan association's headquarters in the city.

FANG So alone, so alone—ai, a son, a son! I just didn't know my place, for that, for nothing, I gave her a life of misery on my account. I sacrificed not only myself, but her as well. Hui-lien, I didn't have the right to sacrifice her!

SHEN You didn't have the right to sacrifice *anyone* else.

FANG But it's already done, can I take it back? People like you with mothers and fathers don't understand. Before, I was like a bamboo shoot in the mud, and now I've grown into a full shaft of bamboo. The skin that protected me I've cast off layer by layer. I'm no longer that tender shoot, but I must be that strong, resilient bamboo.

SHEN Poor hero in the wind and snow! Poor filial son!

FANG Filial son; now there's no way to be filial. Hero; I'm a piece of trash who's accomplished nothing. I've done nothing with my life, and the world won't miss me when I go. Hui-lien, if I didn't have you, I wouldn't have the strength to go on living. Come over here, Hui-lien, and let me gobble you up like a wild animal, let your blood run through my veins. Give me a bit of your heat and your energy.

SHEN Long ago you swallowed me, you digested me, all of me, all became you, you, you! [*Breaking away from him. With hatred:*] Poor you, poor, poor you! You don't have the right to sacrifice anyone but you want to swallow me, because you say you love me.

FANG Oh, Hui-lien, Hui-lien, you accuse me of sacrificing you? It was your own idea to come here and work. I only know I love you. You and I, I and you: is there any way to separate us? Your devotion is my devotion. Your strength is my strength. My success is your success. From today on, Hui-lien, I have only you.

SHEN Me. I ceased to be a long time ago. I became part of you. Except for the little bit that you couldn't digest.

FANG [*Looking at her in dismay*] What little bit? Look at the size of you. There's plenty there, all as hard as steel and cold as a block of ice.

SHEN [*With a forced smile*] I was afraid you'd eat me—Ai, go in and rest. Don't stand out here looking down on me. If I weren't as hard as steel, how would I have held up this past year? I've turned my back on my family for you, and they've never come to take me back. Am I still some tender bud?

FANG You were a tender bud that I snapped off. Now you are like the Monkey's magic staff for me.[1] [*Embraces* SHEN] Ah, Hui-lien, now this is my Hui-lien! [SHEN *stubbornly averts her face*] But who could have known that I was still embracing a shadow. You have never fully given yourself to me, and you will never be all mine—turn your head, look me in the eyes. What is in my heart, I can't put into words. Let you heart draw next to mine, let the words in my heart flow out to you.

SHEN [*Pushing away*] I know it all.

FANG You don't know how much I feel. Without you, without Shu-yuan, would today have happened? In the fall, when I caught a bad disease, I almost died of their abuses. When mother got sick, I could have died of worry. Without you both, I would have given up and died. There's nothing so rare about that. Who would know that the world lost someone who had wasted away? How ridiculous that I held on to such great hopes, shouldered such a heavy respnsibility.

SHEN Heaven didn't let you die.

FANG With you alive, how could I be willing to die! With you and friends like Shu-yuan in this world, life is still worth living. Hui-lien, I tell you, this last year I've thought it over carefully. How could we say this world is ugly? If we hadn't gone through this challenge, how would I have known how much courage you have, how firm you are, supporting me from beginning to end without flinching. And how would I have known how Shu-yuan could forget about his own safety, ignore everything, in order to save me. How can I say heaven is cruel, when for a bit of hardship it has shown me so much mercy.

SHEN I wish heaven would show mercy on me, too.

FANG And so I have returned! Hui-lien, I'm back! From today on, we don't ever again have to part!

SHEN From today on—

FANG Days without end! Every day, a step closer to our ideals. Hui-lien, someday this little village will have turned into a model town, to show everyone what a town should be like. On that day we'll let everyone who's laughed at us know we haven't wasted our time just for the purposes of feeding and clothing ourselves. If they call us fools, then we're matchless fools.

SHEN Only I'm not foolish. Don't say "we." I'm not foolish at all.

FANG [*Seeing clearly that* SHEN *is scorning and avoiding him, he releases her*] In that case you are truly pitiful, a stupid thing who thinks she's smart, who thinks she's seen through it all, that nothing is worth doing.

SHEN And still cannot but do it.

FANG Then you're finished! [*Angrily walking away*]

SHEN Perhaps— [NANNY WANG *enters*]What is it, Nanny?

WANG The chicken and the meat are done tender. We'll lose the juices if we let it cook any more.

FANG Nanny, I only want to eat some of the gruel we have every day, and the pickles you make yourself—

WANG Oh, today we've so many good things to eat— [*Suddenly seeing the presents at the base of the steps: fish, meat and so forth*] Aiya, miss, what are we going to do about all these things?

SHEN Take them to the back—

WANG There's food here for several days. [*Exits carrying food*]

FANG That man called Yeh something? I'm really grateful for his kindness. Tomorrow we'll get something together and invite him over to eat with us.

SHEN No need to invite him.

FANG And T'ang Shu-yuan, too.

SHEN He's busy getting ready for a long trip.

FANG He won't be gone by tomorrow!

SHEN He doesn't have the time to come.

FANG He'll find the time for me.

SHEN It's too late to invite him.

FANG I'll send him a note right away.

SHEN But, Ching-shan, why do we need to? I was hoping it would be just the two of us, with no one else.

FANG [*Impatiently*] Today we are alone together. Tomorrow we'll invite Shu-yuan over. I haven't had a really good talk with him. I want to keep him here for a few days and then let him go. And while we're at it, we might just as well invite that fellow Yeh, too. It's his food.

SHEN Ching-shan, I want you all to myself—

FANG You are a hopeless woman! You don't understand love, and still you like to flirt. Have me to yourself, second honeymoon! Unfortunately, I don't have any desire to talk love with you, in tears and laughter, playing hide and seek, poking here, testing there. My youth is gone. And you aren't a tender, pampered little girl any more.

SHEN So there's no time to talk about love. We can only talk about your projects? But I don't love your projects!

FANG Hui-lien, you are a woman, so you are jealous of your husband's work: to talk about projects amounts to not loving you. And you are jealous of your husband's friends: to have friends amounts to not having you. It's not that I'm not deeply grateful to you, but without Shu-yuan, how much help could you have been to me? Now that I've returned, you're pressing me to break off with my friend.

SHEN I haven't pressed, I only think—

FANG You're trying my patience to the limit.

SHEN Ah, Ching-shan, I really am not a good wife: how did I so utterly forget your personality; how can I defy you?

FANG Don't bother beating around the bush. I told you before: we're no longer young. One honeymoon in one lifetime is enough!

SHEN You're quite right—tomorrow invite T'ang Shu-yuan, invite Yeh San to come—

FANG Ai, Hui-lien, you're not angry with me? I still have such a temper—I was only being difficult when I said those things just now. You don't take me seriously, do you?

SHEN I almost forgot. I almost took you seriously.

[NANNY WANG *enters*]

WANG Where do you want dinner?

SHEN Ask him. [*Exits*]

FANG Hui-lien, Hui-lien! [*Exits*]

WANG [*Looking after them, nonplussed*] Quarreling again?

[*Curtain*]

ACT II

[*Same setting as Act I. As the curtain opens, urchins outside the wall are heaving stones and mud clods over the wall into the courtyard.* NANNY WANG, *arms akimbo, yells from inside the courtyard.*]

WANG Hey, hey! What are you up to? Who is it? [*Mud clods sail in from offstage*] All right, you better watch out! Who's throwing things into our place?

[*Offstage*] Your place? This isn't your place!

WANG [*Mounting a bench to look over the wall*] Well, if it isn't A Lung and Little Fish. What are you doing?

[*Offstage*] We're playing.

WANG Playing? Who taught you how to play that way? Slinging mud all around.

[*Offstage*] We're playing, and it's none of your business.

WANG You're making trouble, and I'm going to tell your fathers you didn't go home when you got out of school but came over here to throw rocks at people.

[*Offstage*] Who cares if you tell them. We want to throw them.

WANG If you want to throw them, go someplace else! When you come around here, watch out! I'll tell Mr. Fang!

[FANG *enters*]

[*Offstage*] Mr. Fang's no good!

WANG What?!

[*Offstage*] Mr. Fang's no good! This place isn't Mr. Fang's!

WANG A Lung, isn't that just fine. Just yesterday you were setting off fireworks and saying lucky things for us!

[*Offstage, two or three voices in unison*] Mr. Fang's no good. They're making him get out tomorrow.

WANG That does it! You watch out— [*Turns her head and sees* FANG, *cries out*] Master!

FANG Nanny, what are you doing?

WANG Listen to these savages! Yesterday they praised you to the skies, and today they're cursing you.

FANG Don't pay any attention to them.

WANG And I have no idea who put that into their heads.

FANG Ai, Nanny, are you the same age as they? Hui-lien has her hands full alone in the kitchen!

WANG Oh, she has her hands full! She's sitting by the stove staring at the tongues of flame and dreaming!

FANG Oh, so you're not going to help her?

WANG She kicked me out to sweep the ground.

FANG We have guests coming in a little while, so don't be late.

WANG She said there wouldn't be any guests today; no one is coming.

FANG [*Angrily*] What do you mean no one is coming? Why isn't anyone coming? [YEH SAN *enters*]

WANG Oh! They sure are coming! Master Yeh San is here now! [*Exits*]

FANG Mr. Yeh! Please come in, please come in!

YEH Please don't let me bother you—I'm looking for Mrs. Fang.

FANG She's in the back. Please have a seat.

YEH [*Hesitating*] Mrs. Fang must have told you, I suppose.

FANG Yes, I know. So today I especially wanted to invite you to come and chat. Things can always have new developments worth reconsidering.

YEH But I don't have the time. I came over to remind you.

FANG What I have in mind can be of great benefit to you, Mr. Yeh. I've already written up a brief proposal—Mr. Yeh, perhaps I ought to introduce myself—I have been studying agrarian economics for some time. Here I'm just running a small elementary school with a handicrafts class added on, but that is only my first step, it's a foothold, so to speak.

YEH Oh, I've learned of your reputation quite some time ago. Most commendable, really.

FANG You flatter me. With all my failings up to now, I haven't come to pay my respects to you. Let me thank you now, Mr. Yeh, for looking after my wife.

YEH It was nothing, really nothing. [SHEN *enters and stands in the background listening*]

FANG I don't know how to repay you. I can only take your consideration for me as encouragement. I want to devote my whole life to the prosperity of this place.

YEH Mr. Fang, you mustn't be so concerned. This area—

FANG This area is the most ideal. Not too small, not too large, and transportation is very convenient.

YEH [*Losing patience*] I've already told your wife—

FANG What's your hurry, Mr. Yeh? Why not have a seat, and we'll talk about it in detail.

YEH I'm sorry—

FANG If you really don't have the time, Mr. Yeh, please wait a moment. [*From his pocket he draws out a packet of papers*] Here, Mr. Yeh, there's no harm in taking these along and looking them over. My proposal—it's a rough draft, something I jotted down as it came to me last night.

YEH I don't understand this sort of thing.

FANG Mr. Yeh is too polite. This is a very simple outline. Perhaps, when you see it you'll feel it's not concrete enough. But the draft I have in my head has plenty of detail. I've been quietly thinking about it for over a year. It's based on a little theory of mine, and four or five years of experience. I think it's really worth an experiment. And now I've had the good luck to meet a person with as much enthusiasm as yourself, Mr. Yeh, here in this village. And you have the ability to match.

YEH In that case, Mr. Fang, you've got the wrong idea. In fact, I don't have the means to maintain this any more. [*Prepares to leave*]

FANG Mr. Yeh, there's no harm taking it with you and looking it over. Take your time giving it back to me. If, when you look at it, you feel it's—oh, well, we can talk about it again at our leisure. [*Forces the proposal on* YEH]

YEH [*With no choice but to take it, he stuffs it in his pocket*] It would be too bad if I lost it.

FANG It can't be lost. I have the original in my head—

YEH Goodbye.

FANG If you feel it's too sketchy, Mr. Yeh, I can talk to you about it in the most detailed and realistic terms— When you have time, come over, please— It's really a disappointment you couldn't stay today. Sorry, we'll be enjoying the fine things you brought over without you.

YEH Don't mention it! Don't mention it! [*Exits.* SHEN *emerges from her shadowy spot*]

SHEN Ching-shan, did you give your proposal to him?

FANG I'm just afraid he won't look at it.

SHEN What does he understand?

FANG How can he not understand? The phrases are simple enough. I've only added a little scientific management. What's so difficult about understanding what's good for him. Even he can understand *that*, at any rate. If I had land and fields, I'd do it right away.

SHEN Ching-shan, he's not your friend.

FANG Of course he's not my friend. You think I don't see that clearly? But what difference does that make? If you can't work with someone unless he's a good friend, then you'll never get anything done. If a person who wants to get things done takes other people's opinions to heart, would he ever be able to get anything done? Let them object, let them laugh and disapprove—don't pay attention. You have to be like a tank: it doesn't care what obstacles are in the way, it just rolls ahead over them. As long as you roll along, you'll flatten them out. Why do I need to have him as a friend? I just want him to face the same direction I am, and to harness his strength— [T'ANG SHU-YUAN *enters*] Oh, Shu-yuan, I knew you'd come! [*Shakes* TANG*'s hands with both of his*] I've been waiting for you. [SHEN *lowers her head and exits*] Hey, Hui-lien! You said he wouldn't come!— Ah, Hui-lien?— Heh, heh, she's lost so she's running away!

T'ANG It's because I told her I was leaving right away—

FANG But you had to come for my sake. I positively wanted you to come! The things I positively want done, I get done.

T'ANG Ching-shan, I envy you for your self-confidence.

FANG I don't have anything on this earth, except some self-confidence.

T'ANG Self-confidence is half the battle.

FANG Self-confidence is just a matter of forcing yourself—the thing just has to be done. And it means expending an uncommon amount of energy. Despair, dismay . . . are all so energy-saving—I say that amounts to laziness of the spirit.

T'ANG I have to respect you.

FANG [*Smiling*] I can't do without your respect. The life I have from now on is the one you have given me. I don't dare squander it!

T'ANG You're being too serious with that kind of talk.

FANG Shu-yuan, there aren't words enough to thank you for a favor as great as this. I wouldn't dare say how grateful I feel. I'm afraid of how puny it would sound if I relied on my tongue to express it. I'm a self-made man. When I'd had enough of the vanity of this world, out of my despair I forged a little self-respect, a little pride, and I thought that would be enough to support me for my life. It's too bad I wasted so much of my life before I realized that there can be such an unselfish sympathy on this earth, love that can set aside the self.

T'ANG [*Smiling*] Ching-shan. You want me to believe I am your Good Samaritan, is that it? Or do you want me to put on that I'm a saint, offering mercy and expecting nothing in return? I did nothing more than most selfishly protect my friend—

FANG But our relationship was nothing more than an ordinary one. You don't respect my ideals. I don't respect your success.

T'ANG My success! My burden, my responsibilities to my family—they're too heavy and too demanding. I can't have ideals.

FANG Now I understand that this, too, is your humaneness. You have sacrificed yourself for your mother and your sisters.

T'ANG [*With an embarrassed smile*] Oh, Ching-shan, don't embarrass me like this. Are we eating here? I'll have a seat. [*Sits*]

FANG [*Smiling and sitting*] I've turned into an out-and-out fool, as well! Making you stand around listening to me say all this extraneous stuff. [NANNY WANG *brings on dishes of food and pours wine*] Nanny, tell Hui-lien to hurry up.

WANG I already told her I'll take care of it, I'll take care of it, I don't need anyone else to help— [*Exasperated*] I'm just not to be trusted any more! I can't even cook a few dishes! Never laid eyes on any dinner party before— [*Exits*]

FANG Ha, ha. Just look at our Madame Nanny! [*Yelling toward the back*] Hui-lien! Hui-lien! [*Returns to his seat*] Shu-yuan, does Hui-lien still hold it against you that there's no woman you like? I always remember the first time she came to visit me in jail, quite in a huff, saying you didn't approve of her at all, as though all women were useless luxury items, and any trouble a husband got into was all the fault of a woman.

T'ANG [*Smiling*] That was because I'd never run into a woman like her before.

FANG Is that so? Never ran into one! There's not one in ten thousand like her for her—her— Ai, Shu-yuan, only since I met her did I realize how madly I could love someone. You said I have self-confidence. But in that instance, I didn't have any. I was simply— [*Shakes his head*] Now that I look back on it, it was really interesting how mad I went. You know [*Smiles*] I was ready to commit suicide. I had a pistol all ready to use.

T'ANG Oh, [*Pointing to the hole in the wall*] is that your pistol?

FANG That's it. Did you see it? I have a cousin who's a soldier. I got it from him. I was ready to kill myself! Heh, heh, heh.

T'ANG You've done all the romantic things.

FANG There was nothing romantic about it. That pistol has become nothing more than a souvenir. But, hey, Shu-yuan, at *that* time! I was half-delirious, half-intoxicated with that delicious, warm sensation. Shu-yuan, how is it you've never fallen in love? If you throw that away for your family's sake, you'll only taste the dregs your whole life.

T'ANG I'm afraid I'll have to sacrifice that.

FANG I urge you not to! I'm really not urging you on toward selfishness, I actually want to learn from your selflessness. But there are some things about yourself which you can't run away from, and there's no need to repress yourself. Only when you have a self can you be of use to others. It's just like a pig—he needs to amass all that fat before he's worth slaughtering. And turnips and sweet potatoes have to mature before they are fit to eat. If you've never gone mad with love for someone, you're just an empty shell, hollow and dry—

[SHEN *brings on dishes. Her gaze timidly moves toward* T'ANG's *face, but when it meets his eyes, she suddenly shifts her eyes away.* T'ANG *also averts his face*]

FANG Really, Shu-yuan, you must never sacrifice this one thing for anyone. You mustn't sacrifice the experience of love for anyone's sake. [*Draws* SHEN *over*] Hui-lien, what do you say, am I right or not?

SHEN Let go of me, I still have things to take care of.

FANG Nanny's angry; you've muscled in on her territory.

SHEN [*Dismissing him with a wave of her hand*] I'll be back shortly.

FANG [*Vacantly watching her walk away, he pauses for a while*] Shu-yuan, do you see any change in me?

T'ANG You're a lot thinner. Quite run down.

FANG Repulsively so?

T'ANG [*Smiling*] Why?

FANG [*Smiling sadly*] I feel that way. [*Pauses*] You said I have self-confidence. Sadly enough, I don't have any self-confidence at all. I only feel I'm repulsive. Oh, you don't know how this past year has worn me down to the point that I don't have any respect for myself. No one has any respect left for me. They've all given up on me.

T'ANG You haven't recovered yet.

FANG Recovery leaves a large scar, not smooth, clear skin. The only thing I take comfort in is—ah, now that you have finally come over, it's boring for me to sigh and mope in front of you. Shu-yuan, I tell you I've got a really large-scale plan—

T'ANG Back to making plans so soon?

FANG It's not my nature to be thrown off balance. It's as though you and Hui-lien were a lead base that keeps me from tipping over.

T'ANG Your wife is, yes. How do I fit in? What sort of large-scale plan? [NANNY WANG *enters, muttering to herself in exasperation, and sits down spitefully on the stone steps*]

FANG I have a copy of it written down— [*Searching himself*] I'll get it out for you to read. [*As he is about to go, he suddenly sees* NANNY WANG] Nanny, what is it? [NANNY WANG *pays no attention and goes on muttering to herself.* FANG *to* T'ANG] I'll be right back. [*Exits.* SHEN *enters and stands upstage*]

SHEN Nanny. Nanny.

WANG [*Spitefully*] I'm resting.

SHEN This is a fine fix. Nanny, come on, quickly!

WANG Still have to call on Nanny!

SHEN Quickly, Nanny. You can't take a break now!

WANG [*Smiling and getting up*] I told you! [*Exits, turning her head*] You just stay put.

SHEN [*Softly*] Nanny, the master?

WANG He's in the back. [*Exits*]

SHEN [*Somewhat indecisively, she draws closer to* T'ANG, *and asks in an accusatory tone*] Why did you come, Mr. T'ang?

T'ANG Ching-shan asked me to come. I didn't have any reason not to come. Tomorrow I'll be moving on.

SHEN Because Ching-shan asked you to come?

T'ANG Because of Ching-shan. [*They face each other in silence*]

SHEN [*Suddenly covering her face and sitting down with her elbows propped on the table*] But I can't stand it. I can't stand it!

T'ANG I can go right now.

SHEN No, no. I hoped you'd come. I hoped you'd turn back for one more look. I was afraid you didn't have the guts to.

T'ANG [*Forcing himself to remain composed*] It was for Ching-shan.

SHEN You're fooling yourself.

T'ANG [*Rising and taking a step*] Please forgive me. I shouldn't have come.

SHEN You should! I—I can't stand this place. I can't take it for another day. I must— [*Staring at* T'ANG, *swallowing the rest of her sentence*]

T'ANG You've got to calm down a little.

SHEN I've got to leave this place.

T'ANG And Ching-shan?

SHEN He has his projects.

T'ANG Without you he doesn't have a project.

SHEN His projects! His projects! I'm his cushion, so he'll have something comfortable to sit on. I'm his walking stick, so he'll have something to prop himself up when he walks down the road. He is a great pillar, and I am the mud supporting his base! He's a huge machine, and I'm the coal he burns! Am I not human? I'm not human! My whole life I'm to be a foil, a backdrop for him!

T'ANG [*Returning to his seat*] Ah, poor Ching-shan, he—

SHEN [*Slowly, with hatred, biting out each word*] Poor Ching-shan— Only I am supposed to pity him! But the day is coming when I won't have the strength to pity anyone—I want someone to have pity on me— [*Sobs and weeps*]

T'ANG [*Turning away*] Ching-shan—he loves you—

SHEN Ching-shan loves me! Better to say he loves himself. He only knows that he wants me to love him. If I turned into *him*, then he would love me as much as he loves himself—

T'ANG [*With certainty*] He loves you.

SHEN [*With hatred*] Oh, thank you, thank you very much for teaching that phrase. [*Rising*] No one in this world except me knows just how he loves me!

[FANG *enters.* SHEN *wipes her tears and turns away*]

FANG Shu-yuan, I simply got mixed up— [*Stops, looking after her*] Hui-lien! [SHEN *ignores him and exits*] What's she up to?

T'ANG Didn't she go to the kitchen?

FANG Oh! [*Suspecting something*] I thought she— I was saying,

Shu-yuan, that I forgot. In the first place, I gave the proposal to someone else, and in the second place, you wouldn't have the least bit of patience with it, anyway.

T'ANG Who said I would have no patience? I'm just a layman when it comes to this sort of thing—

FANG It's no use having patience. I just gave it to someone else.

T'ANG Who?

FANG Yeh San.

T'ANG What does he understand?

FANG That's what Hui-lien said. But if he doesn't understand then I'll have to make him understand. This land and this building are his. He just now came to repossess them and throw us out.

T'ANG So what are you doing giving him your proposal to read?

FANG So I should just go, eh? Heh, heh, just as easy as that! Meekness is a virtue for women. We men must be a little tougher.

T'ANG But there's no way for you to be tough.

FANG That depends on the situation. When the other guy is softening, then I get tough. When he gets too tough, then I soften.

T'ANG I'm scared of you just because of that. [*Smiling*]

FANG Scared of me? [*Smiles*] Heh, heh. Frankly, I'm making a strong effort to be obnoxious. If it were on my own account, there'd be no harm in making some concessions. For the sake of the project, I have to make a nuisance of myself. Have you seen anyone who has accomplished any venture who isn't obnoxious?

T'ANG A shrewd one who does not hesitate to make a nuisance of himself?—I just hope Yeh San is willing to let you use him.

FANG Don't worry. If he listens to what I say he'll make a fortune.

T'ANG All right. I hope that by the time I come back here Yeh San will have gotten rich, and your project will have succeeded.

FANG Oh? When do you think you'll be back? It won't be until after I've succeeded?

T'ANG I probably won't be back for some time.

FANG Then you have to stay on here for a few more days. Shu-yuan, for our sake, let your style be cramped here for a few days.

T'ANG But I must go today. [*Looks at his watch*] When we're done with dinner, I'll have to go.

FANG I won't let you go! [SHEN *and* NANNY WANG *bring on dinner together*] Hui-lien, we can't let Shu-yuan run off. [*Tugs at* SHEN] Sit down. Is there anything else to be cooked?

WANG Nothing. [*Stands to one side.* SHEN *sits*]

FANG [*Rises*] We have two toasts to drink before we eat. [*Pouring the wine*] This one is to thank Shu-yuan, to thank Hui-lien, and to thank Nanny. [*Everyone else defers*] This cup is to settle my temper [*Everyone laughs.* FANG *pours*] This cup is to send off Shu-yuan. [*Everyone drinks.* FANG *pours*] This cup is best wishes for our success, and best wishes to Shu-yuan—may heaven guard him, and give him a good wife just like mine— [FANG *drinks.* T'ANG *withholds his drink.*

SHEN *raises her cup, looking at* T'ANG, *and the two of them forget to drink.* FANG *notices them and suddenly, as though he has understood something, he sets down his cup*] Hui-lien, your eyes are all red from the smoke.

SHEN [*Rubbing her eyes*] Is that so? [*She helps* NANNY *serve the food*]

FANG [*Looking intently at* T'ANG, *and then again at* SHEN] Shu-yuan, did I say something wrong when I toasted you?

T'ANG [*Embarrassed*] Unfortunately, I don't have time for marriage.

FANG What has marriage got to do with it! When you have found your girl, love her! [SHEN *sits*] What do you say, Hui-lien? Right or wrong?

SHEN [*Looking coldly at* T'ANG] There you've misjudged Mr. T'ang. He's a great philanthropist with a sublime, fraternal love for all mortal creatures. He loves every living thing in creation—however, he does not have time to love anyone in particular.

T'ANG Fraternal love for all mortal creatures: that's Ching-shan. I don't have any such devotion. I despise everyone, including myself.

SHEN [*Smiling, to* FANG] So he'd happily follow the example of the saint Tripitaka T'ang[2] and carve all the flesh off his own body to feed the demons and goblins and let them live eternally, and ascend to the bliss of heaven.

T'ANG That's Ching-shan.

FANG I'm nothing more than a self-seeking, self-serving man. And my project also amounts to an expanded self.

SHEN So you only need to love yourself and you have loved others. When you do something for yourself, you are carrying out for heaven what it would want. And your mind is then the intent of heaven. Mr. T'ang—he carries out God's will. His mind is just what heaven wills. You two are a pair of close friends!

T'ANG Mrs. Fang, I'm no match for Ching-shan. He has ideals, he can make things move, and he can fight. I've made a mess of half my life, all by living for other people. I'm already finished. He has just begun.

FANG Shu-yuan, you've never paid me such respect before. You've never flattered me like that.

T'ANG Within me I've had that much respect for you, and that much disappointment in myself. [*He puts down his chopsticks, looks at his watch, and smiles slightly*] And now I have to go. We ought to say a few nice things when it's time to part company. With all our separate viewpoints, it really doesn't do to hold another debate at a time like this.

SHEN [*Rises, pouring him some wine and forcing a smile*] Mr. T'ang, first have a drink—to forgive me for speaking inappropriately. [*T'ANG drinks*]

FANG Shu-yuan, are you in such a rush?

T'ANG I have to go. I want to catch this next train.

FANG [*Without enthusiasm*] In that case, Shu-yuan, we won't hold you up.

T'ANG Goodbye.

SHEN [*Looking away*] Goodbye.

FANG [*Stealing a look at them both, deliberately*] But wait a minute. I'll have Nanny bring you some water to wash your face. [*Exits*]

T'ANG Mrs. Fang.

SHEN [*Putting her finger to her lips*] Hush.

T'ANG I don't know what's right. I hope that while Ching-shan was absent I never held any intention of being unfair to him.

SHEN You know the road to hell is paved with good intentions.

T'ANG And you, too, blame me?

SHEN I don't know who to blame. At any rate I can't blame myself.

T'ANG [*Hesitating, uneasy*] But— [FANG *enters*]

FANG Can you wait a moment? The water isn't hot yet.

T'ANG I don't need to wash my face. I have to go. [*Exits. FANG and* SHEN *see him off and return*]

FANG Hui-lien! There's nothing more joyful than meeting a new friend, and nothing sadder than parting company for a distant journey. To meet a new friend and send him off into the distance all at once really has an odd taste to it! Once you've separated, you don't know when you'll see each other again.

SHEN [*Pretending not to mind*] It's just a day or two away on the road; you can easily run over to see him.

FANG [*Smiling coldly*] Besides, though two persons are at a distance their hearts are close.

SHEN Indeed.

FANG Indeed! Even though the mouth is silent, there is nothing closer to the heart.

SHEN Is that so?

FANG Isn't it? [SHEN *gathers up the dishes, while* FANG *stands to one side smiling coldly.* SHEN *calmly ignores him, and is about to carry off the dishes*] Hui-lien.

SHEN Are you going to eat some more?

FANG Thank you, I am still hungry. [*They sit and eat*] Strange, nobody ate anything today—

SHEN Who says—

FANG I didn't see you eat one bite.

SHEN [*Forcing a smile*] It's not easy being a host. [*She sits and eats*]

FANG It's not easy being a lover.

SHEN Ching-shan. [FANG *smiles coldly*] What are you saying?

FANG Not something a lover says—but something a husband says.

SHEN Ah, my husband—

FANG Unfortunately, I am your husband.

SHEN I advise you to say no more.

FANG It doesn't matter if I do say more. I'm just a repulsive thing anyway.

SHEN [*Rising*] Ching-shan, I'm not going to quarrel with you. [SHEN *starts to exit.* FANG *pulls her back*]

FANG Was I quarreling with you? Actually, you've been avoiding me the whole day because everytime I open my mouth there's a quarrel! How sad, how sad. Why is it I can't seem to say anything right? I disgust people every time I open my mouth.

SHEN What's the point of this! You insist on making people angry—

FANG Do you need me to make you angry? Isn't just looking at me enough to make you angry! More dreadful than a snake; more venomous than a scorpion—keeping away from me, avoiding me, looking at me from a distance, despising me—

SHEN Whatever you say, Ching-shan. I've already made a resolution not to defy you in the least anymore.

FANG Heh, heh, heh, heh! Now there's a wise and virtuous woman! But let me ask you one question: why have you made this resolution? Is it repentance? Or do you want people to build a memorial arch to you commemorating your wifely virtue? Really, there are only memorial arches to chaste widows. Are there any for wise wives? It's a lot harder to be a virtuous wife than a chaste widow, especially to be the wise wife of such a repulsive husband. [SHEN *eats and ignores him*] Pardon me. This quarreling again. Ai, when I speak she ignores me. When I argue she doesn't answer back. Heh, heh, heh. This is a wise and virtuous wife. She doesn't defy me in the least. [SHEN *rises to exit.* FANG *blocks her*] Don't defy me! Where are you running off to?

SHEN What do you expect me to say?

FANG I wouldn't dare expect you to say anything. Any slight sound that escapes your lips, any slight expression that escapes your eyes, they all let out your secret. Go off and hide. Your conscience has grown mildewed. It can't stand the light.

SHEN [*Sitting down*] Ching-shan, an individual's patience is not made of tempered steel.

FANG Ah-ha, Hui-lien, you dislike me so, and still you are patient with me! I'm truly "ignorant of my blessings," pointlessly trying you in the fiery furnace!

SHEN Ching-shan! Oh, this is so ridiculous. I don't have the patience to argue with you.

FANG How could I dare hope you'd have patience with me!

SHEN I advise you to control yourself a little. Right now you're hurting me, and then in a little while you'll just say, "Hui-lien, don't take me seriously" and figure that it's all settled. But, Ching-shan, nobody's feelings can stand that kind of abuse.

FANG Is that a threat?

SHEN It's a plea. You know perfectly well that you're in the wrong. Don't let your temper go.

FANG Pardon me, I didn't know I'd said anything wrong.

SHEN Should I take what you said seriously?

FANG Heh, heh. The truth is nothing I say counts! Right, what am I to you? Does what I say amount to anything?

SHEN Ching-shan, Ching-shan, I forgot how you can be so—

FANG You should forget! Such a mean, selfish husband, why should you want him to come home. If you'd just let him die away from home it would have been a lot simpler! The flaw was that you forgot, Hui-lien! And now even if your eyes have grown hooks, it's hard to catch someone, isn't it? And it's too late to hide in the kitchen and cry. [SHEN *seethes.* FANG *smiles coldly*] You tell me, did I say anything wrong then? Ai, how sad! You couldn't fool me! Hui-lien, Hui-lien, it was my excessive optimism, thinking that in this world there really could be a sincere, devoted wife, and a sincere friend who would be willing to help me, who would selflessly help me out of loyalty.

SHEN Ching-shan, you're being so unfair.

FANG I should have died in prison, then I would have been fair to you two. You could use me as a subject you both have in common to bring you two together.

SHEN [*Enraged*] Ching-shan, if no one in the world has treated you sincerely, it's because you're not worth it.

FANG I'm not worth it! What do I have to offer you? To join me in suffering, to drag you into misery?

SHEN It's no use talking that way to me. You shouldn't talk that way to me— You are a mean, petty little person. I hate you. I hate you! I hate you!

FANG Ah, ah, Hui-lien, you hate me. I wanted to hear you say something sincere. I'd rather hear you say something genuine that cuts as deep as that—I can't stand your pretending and faking.

SHEN Sure! If you can take hearing the truth, you bet I have some truth for you to listen to. I despise you and I hate you. *I hate you!*

FANG [*Indifferently*] Since when?

SHEN Since the beginning.

FANG Ai, that's sad! "Blind love!" I remember you were what they call a rational girl, not one to love me blindly.

SHEN Go ahead and laugh—

FANG I have no desire to laugh—Hui-lien, I'll tell you why I got so angry with you—

SHEN [*Smiles coldly*] Say it's because you love me!

FANG And felt you don't love me. You couldn't fool me, even if you played the totally obedient and docile wife for me. It's nothing more than a screen made of silk. The surface is so soft, but I can feel what lies underneath; it's cold and hard as ice. I'd rather you get angry and vent your spleen—

SHEN So I can get angry and vent my spleen on you! The minute I pretend to be displeased the least little bit, you leap up in a rage! Is there any room in your heart for anyone else? Except you, you, you! What is there to get angry with you about, to argue about? Haven't you made up your mind to be as immovable as a mountain? So what is there to fight about?

FANG But you've fought with me more than once.

SHEN And each time is always proof I'm wrong. I don't need to waste my time fighting with you.

FANG May I ask what you're doing now?

SHEN Speaking the truth you so love to hear.

FANG But, Hui-lien—this isn't the truth.

SHEN The truth is— [*Smiles sarcastically*] I'm fighting with you because I love you!

FANG Hui-lien, before, you still thought you loved me, so you fought with me all the time. But since yesterday you've clearly despised me. You've ignored me. You haven't loved me at all. Hui-lien, tell me honestly, is what I say—

SHEN I don't know. There's no point in my saying anything, only what you say is correct.

FANG It's correct. Sometimes people can't admit the truth about something, not even to themselves.

SHEN Very good, Ching-shan. Heaven has gifted you with a pair of good eyes to see through me clearly. I'm still fooling myself! Why should I force it? [*Rises to exit*]

FANG Hui-lien, where are you going?

SHEN It's none of your business.

FANG [*Pulling her to a stop*] Where are you going?

SHEN To pack some things—I am leaving.

FANG Heh, heh, heh. What a display you can put on. How hard it was for you to get out those three words. You think I still don't know you're going. You only want to be able to say that I made you leave, that I forced you to leave. All right, you have your wish fulfilled. Get out! Someone's waiting for you!

SHEN Ching-shan, if you want to insult me, I'm too weary to argue with you. But please don't drag other people into it.

FANG Heh, heh. Still trying to cover up! I like dragging others into it. You two drag yourselves together. And you want me to play the fool. I'm grateful to you two, so I'm supposed to play dumb.

SHEN Ching-shan, Shu-yuan has never been unfair to you in the least. If he hasn't come to your rescue out of complete sincerity, if he's been the least bit selfish— Have you seen me paying attention to Yeh San? It's *because* Shu-yuan isn't like that that I respect him.

FANG You love him!

SHEN That's something else again.

FANG Say it! You love him! Because he doesn't love you.

SHEN Not because of anything.

FANG This time it's blind love!

SHEN *Not* blind. And not for a reason.

FANG Okay! Okay! Go on out of here. Go have a comfortable life! A car, a foreign-style house, good food, good clothes—

SHEN [*Laughs*] How pathetic can you get! Giving *me* this indignant rigamarole fit for gold-digging concubines and ballroom girls. You say that to *me*! I'm simply wasting myself on your account for nothing. [*Exits rear*]

FANG Get out! Get out! We'll see if you can leave! You won't leave, not even over my dead body. I won't let you leave.

[NANNY WANG *enters, bringing on the water for face-washing*]

WANG Ai-yo. It took forever for this water to heat up— Ai, Master, where is Mr. T'ang?

FANG He left. They're both going away. Just the two of us are left.

WANG Who's leaving?

FANG When you've made a mistake, you can correct it. When you've married the wrong person, you can switch. Your young lady is going away with Mr. T'ang. How about you, Nanny?

WANG Tut, tut, tut. Is this something you should take as a joke? You've got fifty or sixty years of life. A bolt of cloth is only twenty-five feet long. Once you cut out a long gown from it, you can't turn the long gown into a jacket and pants. Once you make a door curtain of it, you can't turn it into bedclothes. There won't be much material for you to ruin, and you won't have any chance to change your mind. What you have cut out is what you have to sew with. Really, what kind of a joke is this? Arguing is arguing! Are you two fighting again?

FANG [*With regret*] I'm no good.

WANG She's no better.

FANG I act like a wild dog.

WANG So now you are blaming yourself?

FANG But she won't ever pay any attention to me. She despises me. She hates me.

WANG I'm not defending her, but she went through so much misery thinking of nothing but how to get you out. She waited for you to come back to the point that she couldn't eat and couldn't sleep.

FANG For me?

WANG If it wasn't for you, then who was it for?

FANG She found another man. She—

WANG Lightning will strike you yet if you don't watch out. Look at her, as bristly as a porcupine. Who'd dare touch that creature, eh?

FANG But Nanny, I really am obnoxious. How can I blame her for despising me? Everyone rejects me, everyone steps on me. If she despises me, too, then what am I living for?

WANG It's all nonsense. You two fight at the drop of a hat about anything, for no reason at all. You even squabble in front of guests. Mr. T'ang was so polite— Where's Hui-lien?

FANG She's in the back. She's leaving. Oh, Nanny, Nanny, if she leaves, it's pointless for me to go on living. Quick, Nanny, go to the back gate and keep a lookout, don't let her leave.

WANG Where will she go?

FANG Go watch the back gate. Go, go! [*He pushes* NANNY WANG *off toward the back*] I'm like some wild dog. I am a wild dog. [SHEN *enters, carrying a small suitcase*] Hui-lien! [SHEN *ignores him*] Hui-lien, look at me once! [SHEN *ignores him.* FANG *blocks her path forward*] Hui-lien, look at me once! [SHEN *looks at him expressionlessly*] Forgive me. [SHEN *turns her face away, dismisses him with a wave of her hand, and starts to exit.* FANG *blocks her*] Hui-lien, I don't dare ask you to forgive me, but let me explain. Hui-lien, I'm jealous of him, so I didn't think what I was saying. And you didn't pay any attention to me. I'm a child who's done something wrong, tugging at his mother, wanting her to pay just a little attention. I'd rather make her angry and give me a slap, just so long as she'll pay attention to me.

SHEN But I'm not your mother. And you aren't a child.

FANG You've treated me as a child before. You've forgiven me—

SHEN I'm fed up, Ching-shan. *I'm* a spring that's snapped, a piece of rubber with no more elasticity. I'm sick of you, so let me go.

FANG Hui-lien. I've been unfair to you. Everytime I think of you, my conscience is upset that I've abused you. I constantly think how, how can I pay you back—

SHEN When you think of me in the future, please forgive me a little. [*Exits*]

FANG [*Pursuing her, pulling her back onstage*] You're not even looking back once as you go. Let's see if you can go!

SHEN [*Determined*] Ching-shan, let me go.

FANG Not unless I'm dead.

SHEN [*Smiling coldly*] You can't die! If you die, who else will come to reform the village and rebuild China? It's no use trying to hold me with death threats. I'm not a wide-eyed, dreamy little girl thinking that if you're willing to die for me I have to live for you! Let me go—

FANG [*Holding on*] I can't! Unless you want me to die.

SHEN You can't die. I'd rather die for you. I can't live for you any more! If you've got it in you, then kill me. Otherwise, let me go. [*She pushes FANG away, frees herself, and exits*]

FANG [*Blankly staring after SHEN*] She's gone. She's gone.

[*Curtain*]

ACT III

[*Setting same as in Act II. The time is early morning the following day. The dishes from the dinner party the night before have not been removed from the table, and a lamp still glows on the table. As the curtain opens FANG CHING-SHAN, who has not slept all night, dozes sitting on the stone steps. Offstage someone pounds on the gate. FANG jumps up, startled and overjoyed*]

FANG Nanny! Nanny! Are you back from the city? [*He exits to open the gate, while offstage the knocking on the gate continues*] Nanny, did you bring back Hui-lien? [*Offstage there is only the pounding on the gate with no answer. FANG holds his breath and stops, his voice trembles*] Hui-lien, is it you? [*Pounding on the gate continues. With trembling hands, FANG hastily unlatches and opens the gate. Outside are only some country girls, students in SHEN's handicrafts class. FANG is angry*] Well, what are you doing?

FIRST GIRL We've come for class, Mr. Fang.

[*Voices outside*] Mr. Fang.

FANG Go away, go away. Go, go on.

SECOND GIRL One more day of vacation? Teacher Shen only let us out for one day.

FANG Beat it! [*He pushes the girls back out the gate, then closes and bolts it. Again knocking on the gate is heard*]

[*Voice offstage*] Mr. Fang, Mr. Fang. Mr. Fang!

FANG [*Yelling angrily*] Go away!

[*Voice outside*] How many days more vacation? [*They knock on the gate, but* FANG *ignores them*]

FANG [*His voice low and angry*] The rest of your life! [*He returns to his seat on the steps, hanging his head in deep thought*]

[*Again there is knocking at the gate. After a while, there is silence. Those knocking on the gate walk around to the low wall and call out*]

[*Male Voice from outside the wall*] Is anybody home? [FANG *ignores him*] Open the gate! Open the gate!

FANG [*Shouting angrily*] No one's here.

[*Female Voice outside the wall*] Cousin?

FANG Who?

[*Female Voice*] It's cousin—cousin, open the gate.

[*Male Voice*] Ching-shan—

FANG Who?

[*Female Voice*] It's me, Chin-hsin, hurry up and open the gate, father's here!

[*Male Voice*] Ching-shan.

FANG [*Smiling coldly*] What an unexpected honor! [*Loudly*] Please, come in. [*Opens gate.* FANG'S UNCLE *and a* COUSIN *enter*]

COUSIN Cousin, I pounded till my hand was sore!

UNCLE Hey, Ching-shan— [*Looking around*]

COUSIN Father came especially to see you. Elder brother couldn't get time off from the bank to come.

FANG [*Coolly*] Thank you, uncle, for your concern for me!

COUSIN [*Setting out a bench for her father to sit on*] Father, sit down for a while. [*Seats herself*] I'm tired to death. There wasn't a single car we could rent—where's Hui-lien?

FANG She's not here.

COUSIN Don't kid us. Where have you stashed her? Don't forget I was the main matchmaker. I came especially to see her today.

FANG Is this the first time you've come?

COUSIN Yes. We looked round and round. I never thought there would be someone living inside this place.

FANG How well you did your job as matchmaker. First you ruined her life marrying her to such a nonentity of a husband, and then you didn't think of her until today!

COUSIN Aiya, aiya, how could I have managed to come out—I—

UNCLE Chin-hsin got married last year. She's just had a baby.

FANG Oh, oh, pardon me. I had no way of knowing.

UNCLE [*Coughs*] Now you two just slow down and relax. Ching-shan, when did you get out?

FANG Does my uncle also know what I just got out of?

UNCLE Everyone is aware of that.

FANG Everyone is aware of it! I thought you weren't.

UNCLE Ching-shan, there's no need to be resentful. I have something a bit unpleasant to say: You brought it on yourself.

FANG Sure, I didn't listen to the teaching of my elders. I deserved to be unjustly imprisoned on false charges.

UNCLE It's not all injustice either. It's that you show no restraint or judgment in your words or behavior. That pride, that arrogance of yours makes people hate you, turns them against you.

FANG [*Smiling coldly*] So I deserved it.

UNCLE It's not that you deserved it—it's that it was bound to happen.

FANG My uncle has the understanding of a god!

UNCLE Ching-shan, I rushed out here early this morning especially to see you, not to say "I told you so" and utter platitudes about what's past. There's no need to mention it anymore. What's important is the future. How are you preparing for it?

FANG Heh, heh. My uncle is still concerned about my future! It's fortunate that I didn't die, otherwise I really would have failed to live up to my uncle's kindness.

UNCLE That, too, is excessive and uncalled for. You talk about death so easily. Once you got into trouble, I sent Ching-yuan around to find out everything. We learned that it was nothing drastic, and that you'd be out in a few months. On top of that, we knew you had a very capable and dependable friend working on how to get you out. Ching-yuan is a simple-minded, useless fellow, and I was sick and confined to the house, with no way to be of any help. I could only watch and wait with concern and that's all. If you want to talk about dying—

[COUSIN *wanders about, looking at this and touching that*]

FANG If I died, that too would have been brought on by myself. I regret I didn't die last year. Then I could have left behind an example Uncle could have used to teach the next generation.

UNCLE Ching-shan, even now you don't understand what you're saying. You offend others, and yet you deny it. Obviously you are blaming your relatives for not doing all they could do for you. But do you think of anyone else? Each person has his own things to look after. Ching-yuan is tied down in his office every day until evening, and he has no choice but to go there. He has a wife and children to support. I had to put everything aside to help Chin-hsin. I knew you were in no serious trouble, and I couldn't divide my concern. To be sure, we didn't do everything we might have. But look at it another way: if Ching-yuan were in trouble, would you then be able to drop everything here, pay no attention to your own needs, and devote yourself entirely and unceasingly to help him?

FANG Absolutely correct. What you say is absolutely correct. I used to think I had a friend like that. Now I know that no such thing exists on earth. Everyone takes care of himself, period. Take care of yourself and don't burden others: that's morality and virtue!

UNCLE I thought that by going through these unpleasant, trying experiences some of your youthful arrogance would be subdued and you would learn some moderation. But you are as arrogant as ever.

FANG If I'm arrogant, then let me be arrogant! From today on, I'm relying only on myself. I have my own self, and no more.

COUSIN Cousin, look, what's eating you?[3] Elder brother couldn't get time off, so father came out here especially to see you. He's been sick now for a week and isn't over it yet.

FANG Why did you have to come out here to see me in the first place? Don't bother.

COUSIN What's the matter with you?

UNCLE Chin-hsin. Don't interrupt. Now it's this way: I've found something for you to do in the city—

FANG I won't go.

UNCLE And I have something more to say that you'll find unpleasant— you need food and clothing in order to live. As for the job I was talking about just now, the remuneration isn't bad, and there is a real opportunity for promotion—a lot of people are trying hard to get it through pulling all sorts of strings. However, they want a university graduate, and someone who's studied economics—

FANG I haven't studied economics.

UNCLE You've studied agrarian economics—of course, what you've studied is not applicable. But, a person also must adapt a little. Take Ching-yuan, for example. He studied literature, *literature*! How did he wind up working in a bank?

FANG I have only admiration for him!

UNCLE It's no use being condescending. Ching-yuan is an honest, loyal person, who knows how to behave himself and has his share of luck. I know my own son very well. He's not to be compared with you, but—here you have a gifted woman and she's miserable; and you have a gifted man, and he's miserable. A person must be able to find and know his place—

FANG His place—what is my place?

UNCLE I can't discuss this with you. Ching-shan, I've always said, when a young person first goes out into the world, to use your new style phrase—if he lacks that spirit of resistance, this person will be a failure. But if a person stubbornly resists everything his whole life, never satisfied with this, never satisfied with that, putting the blame on heaven and everyone else, then this person, too, will be a failure. When people are young, they all think that they're the greatest thing that's happened to mankind, they all think they're going to do something so unusual. Just look at Ching-yuan. Didn't he use to love writing that new-style vernacular poetry! Give them time for a few of life's experiences, and they will realize that one can't be so uncompromising.

FANG Some people can compromise and some people cannot—

UNCLE It's not necessarily so. You see me now, old and sick, working all all my life to earn some money and nothing more, with nothing to say about any great career— But when I was young, I had great ambitions! In the mind and eyes of a youth, everything is a bright rainbow. It's only with the eyes of middle age that it becomes the ordinary light of day. And these words are what my father, your grandfather, once said, too. When he was young he could talk big and act fast. He wasn't going to end up with mediocrity, no. What a pity he never got beyond "candidate" for a county magistrate's position; never held an actual post as such in his whole life! Ambition, ambition, ah—

FANG But it's not my ambition to be a bigtime official, or get rich, or be famous. I just want to accomplish a little something in this little place without a lot of fanfare. If you all are afraid I'll be a burden to you in the future, then let me make myself clear: if I get into trouble again, no matter whether I live or die, you needn't concern yourselves. There's no need for anyone to be concerned about me.

UNCLE [*Sighs, then rises*] To each his own.

COUSIN Are you living here, but how can you?

FANG I live quite well.

UNCLE It was sad, too, about your mother—

COUSIN How has Hui-lien gotten used to it? She even wrote a letter saying how great everything was. You two really are—

UNCLE Chin-hsin, we'll go now.

COUSIN Is Hui-lien coming back soon? I came all this way just to see her.

FANG You needn't wait for her—

COUSIN Where has she gone?

FANG I don't know

UNCLE Chin-hsin. [*Walks toward the gate*]

COUSIN Very well, we're going. Cousin, tell her for me that I couldn't wait—

UNCLE [*Turning his head*] Ching-shan, there's no harm in talking things over with your wife. I can wait for you for a day or two.

FANG You needn't wait.

UNCLE "You go ahead and do a thing even though you know it can't be done . . . I'm just trying to do what my heart dictates, that's all"⁴— If you have the time, drop by your home as often as you like.

FANG I have no home. [UNCLE *exits.* COUSIN *looks back startled at* FANG *once or twice, then also exits*] They've all cleared out. Go, get far, far away from me. No one needs to bother about me.

[OLD CHIN *enters from the back. He calls backstage*]

CHIN Good! Mr. Fang's here! [*He gestures to the men behind him to come on*]

FANG [*Turning his head*] Who are you?

CHIN [*To his rear*] Come on, come on! [*Two village men carry on baskets, suitcases, and bundles from* FANG's *apartment. Another two men move a table and chairs on*] Set 'em down here.

FANG Hey, hey, what are you doing?

FIRST VILLAGER The front gate was shut. We knocked, but no one opened it. The back gate wasn't latched, and there wasn't anyone around. Where did Nanny Wang go?

FANG Who told you to come?

CHIN Mr. Yeh San wants the apartment.

FANG If he wants the apartment there's no need to steal our things.

SECOND VILLAGER [*Angered*] Steal things! If we wanted to steal, wouldn't we take them out the back door?!

FANG If you want the apartment, let's talk about it. There's no need to move things helter-skelter first.

SECOND VILLAGER How do we know? We're not the ones who want the apartment.

FIRST VILLAGER We're farmhands working for Mr. Yeh San. He's the one who wants the apartment, not us.

FANG Even so, if you have something to say, it's easy enough to say it. You can't just barge in and move someone's things out.

CHIN The back apartment is going to be torn down and rebuilt. Tomorrow's a good day, they'll start work. You'll have to move into the temple to sleep for a few days.

FANG Sleep for a few days, I could sleep anywhere. But why is Mr. Yeh in such a rush?

THIRD VILLAGER For that, Mr. Fang, you'll have to go and talk to the boss. [THIRD VILLAGER *beckons to* FOURTH VILLAGER. *They exit together to move things*]

FANG Why didn't your boss come himself?

CHIN You think he has the time?

FANG Is he at home?

SECOND VILLAGER Yack, yack, yack! If you don't want your stuff moved, we'll go. Tomorrow when they come to rip up the apartment, you can move 'em yourself.

[NANNY WANG *enters through the front gate*]

WANG Aiya, aiya. Young Master, what is this?

FANG Nanny, you're alone?

WANG What is this, Old Chin? Ah, [*Toward* FIRST VILLAGER] Yu-ch'ing, what are you all doing? [*The two of them look at each other, too embarrassed to speak*]

FANG Nanny, are you alone? You didn't find—

WANG We'll talk about that later. Now what is this? That's my clothes bag!

FIRST VILLAGER Nanny Wang, relax, we haven't messed up your things. We came around through the back gate to find you. Where did you go?

WANG Why were you looking for me?

CHIN [*Impatiently*]Mr. Yeh San wants the apartment.

WANG Mr. Yeh San has a face like one of those broad, flat lacquer brushes. One side is all smooth, then you turn it over and it's all bristles. Why he just said he'd look after us, then the minute the young gentleman comes back he makes us move out. We're not snails carrying our houses around on our backs, and able to park ourselves anywhere.

FIRST VILLAGER Nanny Wang, don't blame us.

WANG Don't blame you! I was just going to ask you! You're a fine one. When your second baby had a fever for half a month wasn't it our lady's medicine that cured it? [THIRD *and* FOURTH VILLAGERS *enter carrying bedframe*] Ah, Hsiao Hei, you've come to throw us out! When your mother was going to throw you out, didn't I speak up for you—

FANG [*Dismayed and depressed that* SHEN *hasn't returned, abandoning all his courage*] Nanny, what is there to say? We'll go and that's that.

WANG So we have to go. At least in my head I'm not taking it sitting down. So Yeh San is pushing us around, okay. [*To the peasants*] Why are you helping him? Every lousy thing we've endured here, hasn't it been for you people?

SECOND VILLAGER What has been "for us"?

WANG Oh, pretend you don't know anything! Who set up the school? Who taught you how to read?

THIRD VILLAGER Don't bring up reading. Once people learn a few characters they're too lazy for the rough work in the fields. They just want to read and look at pictures. If it keeps up, tomorrow there won't be anyone to plant the fields.

SECOND VILLAGER Rich people learn to read. But learning to read won't make you end up rich.

FANG Well put. Really well put. [*Smiles bitterly*] There's no need for you all to move our things. Just have them come over tomorrow and rip out the apartment. [*He sees* OLD CHIN *and the others off.*]

FIRST VILLAGER That's more like it. And something more, Mr. Fang, I advise you to leave soon. [*He pulls* NANNY WANG *to him and whispers in her ear.*]

WANG They're going to come and arrest him again? On what grounds?

FIRST VILLAGER If Mr. Fang won't go, then—[*Speaks softly*]

WANG Did you hear that, Young Master? They're coming to take you away again. He has evidence! It's that proposal or something you wrote.

FANG Never mind him. Never mind him. Nanny—Hui-lien? She wouldn't come back?

WANG I didn't see her.

FANG You didn't go—

WANG She wasn't at her parent's home.

FANG Of course she wasn't there. I'm saying, you didn't go to T'ang's home and ask?

WANG She wasn't at T'ang's home, either.

FANG Oh? She didn't go to the city?

WANG There's no point in asking, Young Master! We can't stay on here.

In a little while everyone will know, and then we won't be able to face anyone.

FANG Nanny, what happened, Nanny?

WANG It was already late when I got into the city. I went over to her family's home as fast as I could. I haven't been there since you got into trouble and I delivered a message to them that time—I saw that she wasn't there—the Old Master and Mistress still didn't know anything had happened to you—

FANG How can that be?

WANG The Young Master and Mistress were afraid the shock might upset their parents, so they took very strict precautions to keep it from them. They didn't know until I told them. The Old Mistress was very anxious to fetch our Young Lady home to live, and she said to invite you also. Look—you hurt our Young Lady's feelings so badly, but all for nothing—

FANG Nanny, why do you go on talking about what doesn't matter—

WANG Listen—after I saw that she wasn't there, I could only say that the two of you sent me into town on some errand. The first thing this morning, I went over to the T'ang household to ask—they said Mr. T'ang wasn't at home. Last night he got a telephone call to go meet someone at the train station. After they met, they went together to a hotel. He didn't come home.

FANG Stayed in a hotel? Hui-lien, Hui-lien— [*He covers his face. Pause*] Nanny, you're making it up. Did you see them at the hotel?

WANG What really happened, we don't know—

FANG But I know—I know! It's true! She loves him. She loves him.

WANG I never thought of that—

FANG Why didn't I think of it sooner than I did? I should have died. I should have died.

WANG How is talking rubbish like that going to help? Seriously, Young Master, let's get our things together and get out of here fast.

FANG What am I doing still hanging around here? Nanny, why did I have to come here?

WANG If you don't get out of here, Yeh San's men will come—

FANG Oh, I'm really afraid of Yeh San! But to get locked up, with no one to come get me out again, with no one paying me any attention any more.

WANG Sure. What's Nanny good for? All I can do is pack your things for you and get you out of here in a hurry. [*Organizing things*]

FANG You say get out. Get out to where?

WANG Where can't we go! There are no starving sparrows in the sky, no ants freeze to death in the ground.

FANG So, no matter where or when, God looks after you, Nanny! God has seen a lot of birds freeze to death and a lot of ants stepped on. Does God look after them all? We small things are as miserable as worms. We can get crushed under someone's foot, and they'd never even feel it. Who's to care about our pain, our suffering?

WANG Who isn't in pain, who doesn't suffer?

FANG But Nanny, if I were a hero, a great man, there would be poets to sing of my misery, everyone would be broken-hearted over me, down through the ages men would weep for me. What's funny is that I'm just a very ordinary person, no different from a billion others. So what hardship do we deserve? Our misery isn't worth suffering. Nameless, silent, buried in the hearts of a billion people. To cry out these tiny, little miseries will only make people laugh; it's not enough to make them cry. Nanny, my suffering is wasted. My living is wasted. Alive, the world doesn't know I exist. Dead, they won't miss me.

WANG We have to live, no matter whether people know about us or miss us. That's what I say.

FANG Oh, Nanny, but I can't accept it. I cannot accept it! Make me content with my lot! What is my lot? To struggle through the day to make a living. Why should I go on living?

WANG Young Master— It's your temperament, that's what it is.

FANG Nothing more than my temperament! I've seen others incredibly contented and incredibly lucky. But I was born with this temperament. Since I've come into this world, what is mine amounts to my temperament. Oh, Nanny, this temperament of mine is like a fire, it's baked me dry and shrivelled, and I still have no way to put it out! [*In a low voice*] Hui-lien, Hui-lien—if only she were here, just one word from her, just one smile—

WANG Bringing her up again—

FANG She's discarded me, too. Everyone has discarded me. Can I hold it against them? They are the people who saved me. They met each other only because they were trying to save me. I should have died before, then I wouldn't have had to endure their contempt, their hatred. Perhaps they could still find it in their hearts to take pity on me. [*Sobs*] They're laughing at me! They're happy! You say they still take pity on me. I want their pity.

WANG We don't know what's with them. There's no point thinking about it any more. [*Closes the suitcase*] Your things are in here.

FANG Just leave it there.

WANG Our young lady doesn't have much. I'll take hers for her.

FANG It's up to you.

WANG What are we going to do with these tables and chairs?

FANG Throw them away.

WANG What we can move, we'll move.

FANG Move where? In any case, I can't bring them with me!

WANG Where are you going?

FANG Nanny, you go your way, and I'll go mine. This is where we part.

WANG Where would you have me go? I don't have a single relative in the countryside. And since I defied the Mistress at the Shen home to come here with the Young Lady, I don't have any face left to go back there.

FANG You can still stay with Hui-lien—

WANG I won't go to the T'ang household. Mr. T'ang is a good man, but I won't go there. I'll stick with you.

FANG But I can't take you where I'm going. Nanny, my paper? My pen? [WANG *gives* FANG *pen and paper.* FANG *writes a letter*] There is still mercy in heaven. I'm not wanted here, so there's someplace else nice and peaceful to rest quietly, and endless days to spend there.

WANG I'll go with you.

FANG No one can go with me, and I won't need anyone. Nanny, I advise you to stay with Hui-lien. Mr. T'ang and she—they'll make a fine couple—

WANG [*Angrily picking up her bundle*] Don't worry, I will have someplace to go.

FANG Nanny, don't be angry. You go on ahead. I still have some things to take care of. [*Gives her some money*] This is yours. And this is for you as a token to remember me by.

[NANNY *takes the money and the token and tucks them away*]

WANG Thank you, Young Master. Thank you. [*Wipes her tears*]

FANG Go ahead.

WANG I'm off, Young Master. [*Sighs*] Relying on other people: you might as well use a hollow reed for a walking stick.

FANG Nanny Wang, don't hold it against me—

WANG I'm going. I'll go out along the back path, say some goodbyes, and wait for you at the station.

FANG No need to wait for me. We won't be on the same train.

WANG Well, then, don't stay here long. [*Exits out the back way, wiping her tears*]

FANG [*To* NANNY WANG*'s back*] Go on. Go on. I should have quit this world long ago, and left it to others. I'm not fit to live. [*Rises, folds the letter, and places it on the frame of his mother's picture. He heaves a long sigh, standing silently*] Mama, Mama, will I see you once I'm dead? In a moment I'll leave my body behind, to come for you. Will I be able to find you? Will I exist? [*At the sound of footsteps outside,* FANG *leaps up startled, and says in a low voice*] Who's coming? Yeh San? [*Nods his head in the direction of the sounds*] All right, Yeh San, come! Come on, you win! [*Exits out the back*]

[T'ANG SHU-YUAN *enters, supporting* SHEN HUI-LIEN *and carrying her small suitcase.* T'ANG *puts down the suitcase and silently looks at* SHEN, *not knowing what to say.* SHEN *bites her lip with suppressed anger*]

T'ANG Hui-lien—

SHEN Fine, your mission is fulfilled. The unfaithful wife has been brought back home! You'll want a face-to-face scene to make sure the transaction is clear, too!

T'ANG If you want, I'll talk to Ching-shan—

SHEN If you're afraid of breaking your holy friendship, if you want to clarify your position, you might as well grab me by the hair and heave me back at Ching-shan.

T'ANG I'd rather have you hate me now, Hui-lien. I don't want you to feel regret in the future.

SHEN Oh, I'm feeling regret right now! A woman who abandoned her husband, who would dare have anything to do with her! [*Laughs*] I'll go find the master for you, to take back a lost sheep! [*Suddenly noticing the furniture in the hall*] Ai, Shu-yuan, what's all this doing here?

T'ANG It looks as though you're moving out.

SHEN I'll go to the back and see. [*Exits*]

T'ANG [*Depressed, sits down*] For whose sake have I become a punctilious Confucian prude?

SHEN [*Emerging from the rear*] There's no one here.

T'ANG He's gone looking for you for sure.

SHEN That's good. I can comfort myself that they're still looking for me and want me back! You can relax. It won't get to the point that I'm clinging to you like a sopping wet shirt you can't find a way to pull off! Please go ahead and leave!

T'ANG Hui-lien, listen to me. Have I ever lectured you before? The things I have no choice but to say you don't like to hear. You'll have to forgive my honesty, if you'll listen—

SHEN Whatever you say, I know it all. I could say it myself.

T'ANG You say you don't love Ching-shan—

SHEN I loathe him!

T'ANG You did love him. You abandoned your comfortable home for him—

SHEN I'm a fool. You don't mean to say you're going to teach me some lover's platitude about how love never changes—

T'ANG I'm not lecturing you, Hui-lien. You hate him and resent him so much because you still love him—

SHEN Well that's certainly a hopeful bit of news.

T'ANG It's true. Besides, the feeling you've had for me is because I've respected you and didn't let down a friend—

SHEN Yes? For that one thing I—

T'ANG Hui-lien, I don't have the right to say these things—but—but if I were to take this opportunity now to sell out Ching-shan, let alone that it would mean being unfair to him and that I couldn't stand myself, you, too, would despise me and leave me. And you will not be able to forget Ching-shan, you'll hate me and regret what you've done.

SHEN Shu-yuan, since you insisted on bringing me back here, you don't have to fantasize about who I love and who I don't love. You don't have the right to analyze what's going on in my mind. We can forget from now on that this ever happened. But if you think of me as a stubborn, wilfull child, then you're wrong. I can't force myself to love Ching-shan anymore. I loved him, I married him. But having married him, I don't love him. So what can I do? What can I do? I can take care of him, watch over him, fulfill my responsibilities. But, Shu-yuan, if a small plant growing in the shade of a wall one morning discovers the sun—do you say it should not fall in love with the warmth of sunlight?

T'ANG I didn't say "shouldn't"—

SHEN You said can't, right? You're probably right. Fortunately, it's not a long time between the dawn and the night. What can't be, we can forget. Shu-yuan, please forget what's happened. And I ask you sincerely to forgive me.

T'ANG But you won't forgive me. You refuse to understand me.

SHEN Why must I understand?

T'ANG I'm a mass of contradictions. I can't stand up if you poke down here and push a little there; this loose ball of sand will collapse. You think I'm a cold, priggish Confucian hypocrite.

SHEN You are a warm, genuine Confucian gentleman. You'll never go mad and forget yourself. You'll always be a true gentleman, an upright friend.

T'ANG Hui-lien, don't offer those cold-blooded eulogies. I'm nothing more than a luckless fellow. Since I was a child I had a hard life. All along I was well aware of my insignificance in this world. And I resented it, rebelled against it. What I resented was that I couldn't understand why I wasn't as good as others. But then the day came when I suddenly saw myself clearly, and I had to admit my insignificance. And then, too, I acknowledged that other people were as important as I was. From that day on, I felt calm and at peace. It was as though I was not simply living inside myself, but also living at the same time inside others. No aggravation, no misery was worth so much as a chuckle. Hui-lien, that's nothing more than the vision of an honest, thoughtful person. I don't have the ability to accomplish anything of consequence. You aren't laughing at me? [*She is silent, her head lowered*] I haven't said these things to anyone before. They don't move people as easily as words of resentment, the voice of hatred screaming out. It's a slight, gentle vision. It seems too timid. It can only stay tucked away inside. I'm afraid that somebody would laugh if I let it out.

SHEN Do you think I won't appreciate your vision enough? Do you think I'll laugh at you? When I'm thoroughly miserable and upset, I give up caring for myself. And then I arrive at the point of that calm and peace that you were talking about. I put my self aside, and do my best helping another person, and that's even more of a happiness I can't put into words. But I don't believe that anyone made of flesh and blood can truly escape from his own self.

T'ANG Would you say it's possible? Perhaps you can never be completely liberated from yourself, just temporarily lock yourself up in the cellar. Then by a careless slip, it frees the lock, leaps out and makes his way to your head—

SHEN Do you feel that way?

T'ANG [*Rising*] The more we talk the further away we get from where we started. Am I not made of flesh and blood? Yet you laugh at me, scold me, say I'm a priggish Confucian hypocrite, blame me for holding myself in check. Hui-lien, I'm going. In time you'll realize I wasn't mistaken.

[SHEN*'s head is lowered. She is motionless and unresponsive*]

T'ANG [*Suddenly seeing* FANG CHING-SHAN's *letter, he walks over to examine it*] Hui-lien, this is a letter for you from Ching-shan.

SHEN [*Looking at the outside, back and front*] Shu-yuan, what does this mean? [*She half opens it, then with trembling hands gives it to* T'ANG] I don't want to read it—

T'ANG [*Opening the letter*] Go on and read it.

SHEN You read it for me.

T'ANG [*Reading*] "Hui-lien, someday this letter will find its way into your hands. By that time, you'll be free." What's that supposed to mean?

SHEN [*Anxiously*] Go on.

T'ANG "There's no point in your hating me any more. Everything about me that you have hated and held in contempt is now finished . . ."

SHEN Shu-yuan—

T'ANG "You say I loved you as I loved myself. That is so. Once you went, my own self ceased to exist. You have despised me, so what is there of myself that I still cherish? Unfortunately my love for you came to nothing more than a blacksmith's furnace; it tempered you into steel. I want to hate you, but I cannot. I want to feel contempt for you, but I cannot do that either. Shu-yuan is a most honest and dependable husband. You are the warmest and dearest of wives. Heaven ought not to have played a joke, and stuck me in between you. Hui-lien, Hui-lien, living I loved you. I loved you so—this love is enough to redeem this pitiful soul of mine— If they destroy my body, I still have a soul; it must be redeemed. . . ."

SHEN [*Holding back her tears*] Go on.

T'ANG That's all. Below that is his name.

SHEN [*Snatching the letter, weeping as she reads*] I love him. Shu-yuan, I love him. You weren't mistaken a bit—if I believe that there is love in this world, how can I not love him? And if I don't believe there is any love, then what love am I still looking for?

T'ANG Hui-lien, don't cry. You must know where he is.

SHEN I've killed him. I've killed him.

T'ANG [*Goes to the place in the wall containing the pistol and draws out the brick*] Hui-lien, the pistol is still right there.

SHEN He wouldn't use the pistol. I know where he is. Past the edge of that field there's a place with ten or so willow trees. There's a deep pool there, deep and dark. [*Shivers*] Ching-shan often said that if he died he wanted to turn into a ghost there. [*Shaking*] That water is so cold! Shu-yuan, I couldn't have been more selfish than I have been. I've only wanted to take love. I haven't been willing to give it.

T'ANG But look, Hui-lien, the writing isn't dry yet. This letter was written just now.

SHEN Can we still get to him in time to save him?

T'ANG Are there usually people around there?

SHEN People fish there sometimes.

T'ANG It's still daylight. He won't have had an opportunity yet. Let's hurry to find him.

SHEN The paths in the countryside around here have so many twists and turns, so many dips. There are trees and pools everywhere—ai, Shu-yuan, how will we find him?

T'ANG Don't get upset. At this time of day he absolutely won't have had a chance, so don't worry. We're sure to find him and bring him back.

SHEN If he can come back. Shu-yuan, Shu-yuan, it's as though my heart has split in half. I say I love him. I also hate him. I'm afraid, but I'm hoping—I'm desperate. Shu-yuan, I can't leave him. And I can't let you go. I utterly despise myself. [*Raises her head, holding back her tears*] But, it's no great matter whether I love or not! Let me live inside another person—from now on I'll have done with myself—

T'ANG Let's hurry up and get going. [*They go together to the front gate*]

SHEN [*Turning around, losing her self-restraint*] But Shu-yuan, say you love me—let me store those words away within me. Then in a freezing, snow-swept land, I will also keep one strand of warmth—

T'ANG Hui-lien, let's get going, quickly.

SHEN [*Crying*] That's right, Shu-yuan, you don't have to answer me— come on. [*Exit together*]

[*Curtain*]

ACT IV

[*Same setting as in Act III. It is dusk. The stage is darkened. Dark clouds pass overhead in the faint moonlight. His hair disheveled,* FANG CHING-SHAN *enters*]

FANG Am I still alive? Am I still a living person? Ching-shan, Ching-shan, Fang Ching-shan— Is that a voice? How is it that the louder I yell, the more I feel the deathly stillness. I've really turned into a ghost, a solitary ghost returning to his home. If I had actually died, and still had a soul that did not die, that would truly be eternal solitude, endless loneliness. If I were to come back to look around, it would be just as it is now, only a cold, barren room. Everyone has gone. They're celebrating! They're happy! Do they still have me on their minds! I stepped aside, and did they do the same for me? Ha, look! I'm not that weak! In my life I've never given in to anyone! Now if she does not love me, and I just go quietly to my death, I'm giving in to them! While I'm alive, she's mine. If I die, she must die with me! [*Takes the pistol from the wall*] If I die without making a sound, and hold in this choking hatred, how can I hope for revenge? I am still flesh and blood; before I die, I first have to deliver my hatred. [*He clasps the pistol to him*] We're going to the city; to find a couple of cheap creatures, one that can cheat a friend, another that can turn its back on a husband. [FANG *hears the sound of voices outside and listens intently.* T'ANG SHU-YUAN *enters, supporting* SHEN *and carrying a lantern.* FANG *slips into a dark corner to hide*]

T'ANG Hui-lien, you're shaking. Are you cold?

SHEN [*Leaning on* T'ANG] I'm scared.

T'ANG Don't be afraid. I'm here.

SHEN This place is dreadful.

T'ANG Hui-lien, you're worn out. Sit down and rest. [*He sets down the lantern and sits on the steps*] Come, rest yourself against me. You didn't sleep at all last night, and you haven't eaten today.

SHEN [*Sits next to* T'ANG, *sobbing*] Even his death was cruel. His death is his revenge on me. To let me know I killed him.

T'ANG He really didn't blame you.

SHEN But I know that it was I who killed him. [*Weeps*]

T'ANG Perhaps there's still hope.

SHEN Did you hear what they said? Clearly people saw him there. Then he disappeared. The water in the pool was disturbed.

T'ANG He'll turn up tomorrow or the next day.

SHEN [*Shaking*] That water is so deep and so dark—

T'ANG Don't think, Hui-lien. Relax against me here. Don't think about anything.

SHEN [*Resting against* T'ANG, *she shivers*] Hold me tight— It's as if Ching-shan's eyes were glaring at me in the dark, fixed on me in hatred.

T'ANG Don't imagine things, Hui-lien.

SHEN He should hate me.

T'ANG What's past is over with, Hui-lien.

SHEN Who would have thought it would end like this. We were so concerned for him. This past year, all the worry, the anxiety—in the end, it was all in order to kill!

T'ANG Ai, we're cart-horses with blinders on, going down the road not knowing what's in front of our eyes. Who knows how heaven is arranging things.

SHEN If heaven meant to bring us together, why add a Ching-shan? If it couldn't let us be together, why has it caused us to meet? Why force me to forget you and love Ching-shan? I'd rather be dead. I've tried a hundred times, and I still can't. But with Ching-shan sacrificed, Shu-yuan, he'll weigh down my mind as long as I live. I'll never find any happiness. I'm worn out from this life. I don't have the strength for it. Let me shut my eyes and forget about everything—and never open my eyes again.

T'ANG Hui-lien, are you too tired to live for me—

SHEN Don't say you want me to go through all this again. Life is too short, you can't work up a draft and then revise it.

T'ANG Will you just shut your eyes, then, and leave me forever?

SHEN When I close my eyes, I still see you—

T'ANG Hui-lien, Hui-lien—oh, god. The day has finally come when I can enjoy hearing you say that. I thought I would go to my grave still not able to show my feelings for you. Hui-lien, you don't know how much weight it has taken to sink this secret to the bottom of my heart.

SHEN Don't talk about love any more. My feelings have died.

T'ANG You can't die. You mustn't die. While you have time to live, go on and live. Only the past is dead. This is a world of the living. Things past don't exist. And a person from the past no longer is. The past has no right to interfere with us in the present. Hui-lien, in our minds we can remember, we can pity. But we have to live. Hui-lien—you're shaking.

SHEN [*Shivering*] Because even as I feel in love with you—I can feel Ching-shan hating me.

T'ANG Say you love me! Say you love me! Until today I've had to force myself to keep from letting you know, and how I loathed the fact that you couldn't know. For others it is such a delicious experience, and for me it has been so miserable. Except when I didn't yet understand what I was feeling—for those few days even in my dreams I felt a happiness I couldn't put into words. It seemed I was ten or twenty years younger. I felt that the world was wonderful, that I loved everyone on earth. Then—suddenly I realized. From then on, I was only miserable.

SHEN You think I didn't know?

T'ANG I lied to myself. I told myself you wouldn't know. I acted so properly toward you.

SHEN You were extremely polite. And I was extremely distant.

T'ANG But just when I left you, suddenly I had a reason to come back. I came, and again I was too timid to say anything.

SHEN And when you were too timid to say anything, you didn't secretly find it a bit delicious?

T'ANG Hui-lièn, how did you know?

SHEN I knew before you did. I was waiting for you, waiting and waiting. I thought that my life would go by and you would never have anything to do with me, that you were contemptuous of me, that you never so much as gave me one look—

T'ANG But, Hui-lien, do you mean to tell me that you loved me since way back?

SHEN I don't know. I only remember that once your tongue slipped and you blushed so—and how I felt sorry for you. [*Laughs*] But what's there to be sorry about, really!

T'ANG When I hear you say that, Hui-lien [*Pulling* SHEN *to him*] I still don't know whether it is that I am too happy, for it seems like pain. Ai, Hui-lien, how did this day really come, when you could tell me, when I could tell you.

SHEN How much could you tell me! You are a fool! Before you told me, I had gone out in the middle of the night, throwing away everything, to come and find you. And all you could do was go on denying it! All you could do was keep me from speaking, and make me come back here—

T'ANG [*Smiling*] I'm just like those willow blossoms in the wind you talked about; how could I be in control? How could I pretend to be so calm and collected, and say I wasn't in love with you? I always thought that no one knew about my secret. So then, when I was dead and buried, my body would all decay, but my heart would not. It would still be like a seed, capable of sprouting blossoms.

SHEN [*Laughing*] Such a secret! You don't have any secrets!

T'ANG Is that so? Then I'll tell you one more. The day we were parting this corner of your mouth was quivering.

SHEN Oh?

T'ANG Then I almost did something, Hui-lien. And if I'd done it, perhaps you wouldn't have had any respect for me any more.

SHEN What was that?

T'ANG You know. [*He kisses* SHEN. FANG *emerges from the shadows, and walks up in front of them.* SHEN, *believing he is a ghost, clutches at* T'ANG, *her eyes growing wider and wider, staring at* FANG. *Finally, she gasps weakly*]

SHEN Shu-yuan, [*Points toward* FANG] do you also see him?

T'ANG Don't be frightened, Hui-lien.

FANG [*Laughing coldly*] Don't be frightened, Hui-lien! Don't be frightened, Hui-lien! I'm only Ching-shan—still alive. My blood still circulates; my bones aren't cold. This is your world; I have no right to interfere with you. The hell I want your remembrance of me! or want your pity!

T'ANG Ching-shan! Are you all right?

FANG [*Laughing*] Fascinating! Let all the dead come back to look at what they're missing! Fortunately I'm not dead. I still have a voice to speak with. I have hands and feet, so I can walk and move about. I'm all right, Shu-yuan, I'm all right! Too bad, I'm all right! I haven't given you that satisfaction. [*He draws the pistol*] Move away a little, Hui-lien. Don't hug him so close! I want to take you with me! So you two cannot be together, for ever and ever after. All right, Hui-lien. Shall we go and leave Shu-yuan behind? Or shall we send him off, and remain ourselves?

T'ANG Ching-shan, are you mad? If you dare harm Hui-lien— [*Moves to grapple with* FANG]

SHEN [*Comes forward and snatches the pistol*] Fight! Quarrel! Wretched things born in the morning and dead by nightfall! I'm so tired. [*Turns the pistol on herself. There is a burst of fire, and she falls speechless*]

T'ANG [*Quickly supporting* SHEN] Hui-lien, Hui-lien—

FANG [*Snapped out of his madness; transfixed, he looks at* SHEN *sprawling on the floor. Wails exhaustedly. He quivers, holding out his hand as though seeking help*] Shu-yuan—

[T'ANG, *ignoring him, does not move*]

[*Curtain*]

Notes

1. Monkey is a fabulous creature, the hero of a well-known traditional novel, *Journey to the West (Hsi yu chi)*, and many plays. His "magic staff" *(chin-ku-pang)* aids him in fending off and defeating numerous foes.

2. Tripitaka T'ang (T'ang Hsüan-tsang) was a famous explorer and promoter of Buddhism in the T'ang dynasty around whom many legends developed, including the one alluded to here of his actions as a Buddhist saint. The novel *Journey to the West (Hsi yu chi)* offers a highly fictionalized account of his travels to India to acquire the Buddhist texts known as the Tripitaka.

3. "What's eating you?" is a loose English rendering of a Chinese phrase which more literally reads, "You look as though you were chewing on uncooked rice."

4. "You go ahead and do a thing . . ." The uncle is quoting well-known lines from the *Analects* of Confucius.

Yang Lu-fang

Cuckoo Sings Again

Translated by Daniel Talmadge and Edward M. Gunn

Cast of Characters

KUO CHIA-LIN, Party member and disabled veteran—he has one arm

SHIH HSIU-O, Female Communist Youth League member and wife of Kuo

FANG PAO-SHAN, Agricultural Producers Cooperative Director and Party Branch Secretary

LEI TA-HAN, Cooperative member

K'UNG YÜ-CHENG, Party member, Youth League Branch Secretary, and Production Team Leader

SHEN HSIAO-CHIA, Youth League member and tractor-driver-to-be

AUNT LEI, mother of Lei Ta-han

AUNT MA, Aunt Lei's neighbor. An old matchmaker who has seen better days

T'UNG YA-HUA, wife of Lei Ta-han and older sister of "Cuckoo"

T'UNG YA-NAN, Female Youth League member, nicknamed "Cuckoo"

WANG PI-HAU, Youth League Branch Committee Member

OTHERS: CH'Ü HSIAO-TI and LI CHIN-FANG, female Youth League members; YEH YU-KEN and PAI T'IEN-SHUI, Youth League members; HUANG CHÜ-YING, a pregnant young woman; CHIA and I, Cooperative members

(The first three acts are presented in full; Act IV is summarized.)

ACT I

Scene 1

It is early 1956. Spring has not yet arrived; the winter lingers. In the fields of Chiang Nan, the tips of young wheat sprouts have pushed through a new layer of snow. On the side of a small hill is a highway, recently repaired. To one side of the road, willow trees have been planted which have not yet budded, and on the other side, the river flows by quietly. Across the river a small, temporary wooden bridge has been built. From the fields come the sounds of calling, shouting, and laughter, and of a Hsing Hua folksong, "The Blowing Wind." A female voice leads the singing:

> Production depends on our hard labor—hey!
> We must work hand and foot with this white soil clay.
> We must work hand and foot with this white soil clay.
> Important to us is this hard labor—hey!
> Butterflies dance on their colorful wings.
> Blooming roses and peonies bring the fragrance of spring.
> Important to us are such beautiful things.

Members of the co-op go back and forth, carrying mud from the river with which to enrich the clay soil of the fields.[1] One of these, the one-armed KUO CHIA-LIN, *enters, back from the fields with an empty basket. He encounters his wife,* SHIH HSIU-O, *coming the other way with a full load of mud.*

KUO CHIA-LIN Help me take off my shirt, Hsiu-o. [*He puts down his basket, and starts to take off his shirt*]

SHIH HSIU-O If you take it off, you'll catch cold. You're not going to take it off!

KUO Carry out orders and obey commands.

SHIH Then I'm ordering you!

KUO [*Imitates a soldier*] Yes, sir. As you say, sir. [*The two laugh.* SHIH *helps him button up.* FANG PAO-SHAN *enters on a bicycle*]

FANG PAO-SHAN Whew! The Women Generals have all ridden out.[2]

SHIH Ridden out? Where did they get the horses, Director Fang?

FANG You'll see. In two years you'll see, and it won't be any four-footed horses; it'll be four-wheeled—

SHIH Wagons—

FANG Cars—the kind that go "putt, putt." Hsiu-o, find your team leader K'ung, and bring him here on the double. [SHIH *exits;* FANG *turns to* KUO] Chia-lin. [*He props up his bicycle*]

KUO Secretary Fang? [LEI TA-HAN *enters, carrying river mud*]

FANG Wait a minute, Ta-han.

[FANG *goes over and grabs* LEI TA-HAN'S *baskets and carrying pole. He hefts the carrying pole on his shoulders and walks once around with it to get the feel of it. The other two men stare at him with curiosity, and look at each other; then they get the point and laugh.* FANG *laughs too and puts down the pole*]

FANG How many *chin*[3] does this weigh, Ta-han?

TA-HAN 150, give or take some.

FANG That's too few; when you were working for yourself you could carry 250.

TA-HAN [*Frankly*] You give so many work points, I put out so much work.

FANG Oh. Young Mr. Arithmetic has it all figured out. I'll put you down for three points.

Ta-han Then I'll make it 250 chin.

Kuo Look at what a stingy attitude you've got. [Ta-han *exits, carrying the mud*]

Fang So how's it going? Still going strong?

Kuo I come from peasant stock.

Fang Ai! Chia-lin, ever since I took this position they call "cadre disengaged from production" I've been deprived of my right to work. Watching everybody putting out all they've got just makes my hands and feet itch to join in. Like a young widow when she sees another girl get married. [*The two laugh*]

Fang [*To* Kuo] Eh!—one-armed general, do you dare to compete with the big muscle-man?

Kuo When it comes to farm work, then I'm happy to admit defeat. But if you're talking about hurdling obstacles, crawling through barbed wire, and throwing hand grenades, then he'll have to take commands from me.

Fang Why, you old salesclerk, you've got a high-quality sales pitch, but the less said about your goods the better. [*The two laugh again*]

Kuo Oh, may an old veteran make a suggestion?

Fang Go ahead.

Kuo Have you seen her? The pregnant one with the big belly carrying river mud; it's too much for her.

Fang You're right. [K'ung Yü-cheng *enters*]

K'ung Secretary Fang, you're back from the meeting?

Fang I'm back. [*To* Kuo] Chia-lin, we'll talk later. [Kuo *exits, carrying his baskets*]

Fang Yü-ch'eng, the young guys have put out a lot of effort, eh?

K'ung The young people are all full of energy.

Fang As soon as you get raised to an advanced co-op all the fires must be roaring.

K'ung They're all roaring!

Fang How many members of the Youth League team went out to work today?

K'ung Every living one went out today.

Fang Good. Yü-ch'eng, you know what they used to say: in the three months of spring, we were busy celebrating the new year, in the three months of summer we were busy with rice transplanting, in the three months of autumn we were busy harvesting, in the three months of winter we warmed outselves in the sun. But now, there's no one celebrating New Year, or sunning themselves. They're all busy laying in manure.

K'ung Right! This year our winter leisure has become winter work, Secretary Fang.

[*A pregnant woman,* Huang Chü-ying, *goes past gritting her teeth as she hauls the mud*]

Fang Chü-ying!

Huang Oh! Secretary Fang. [*She exits carrying the mud*]

FANG Isn't she pregnant, Yü-ch'eng?

K'UNG Mobilization can't be put aside. When you ask them they all say "I'm not. Now, the task of laying in manure is critical. Also, there is a labor shortage . . ."

FANG Yes. What can be done?

K'UNG And besides, men can't very well ask too many questions about that sort of thing.

FANG And what about the women's representative?

K'UNG I'm it.

FANG [*Unable to suppress his mirth*] You! That's news! And when did a scraggy-beard like you become the women's representative?

K'UNG Secretary Fang, it's like this: My Ta-mei had no experience in doing women's work, so I took her place.

FANG So what you're saying is you can have a baby for Ta-mei too. Aiya! Don't take on everything all by yourself. Look at you, you're the production team leader, the Youth League Branch Secretary, and the women's representative all at once. You're trying to do and be everything at the same time. What makes sense is for you to grapple with production instead. This and only this is the crux of the matter. And at this time the crux of the matter's crux is laying in manure. Eh!!

K'UNG [*Obediently*] Right!

FANG "All for production! All for laying in manure!" We must see that this slogan permeates the Youth League.

K'UNG Okay, "will do." I'll mobilize them to work from the crack of dawn 'til late at night.

FANG [*Satisfied*] Correct! Yü-ch'eng. The Youth League will take the leading role, eh! You, you women's representative, you!

K'UNG [*Embarrassed and uncertain*] Heh, heh, heh.

FANG Heh, heh, heh. [K'UNG Yü-CHENG *is about to exit*] Yü-ch'eng, at the meeting tonight, we'll look into which two youths we'll send to study tractor driving.

K'UNG I still have to hold a women's meeting—Okay, I'll come. [*Exits.* LEI TA-HAN *enters again*]

FANG Ta-han. 250!

TA-HAN Three points! [*They both exit*]

[*From afar the sounds of "Cuckoo" singing carries through the air, a Chiang Tu folksong, "When They Go Out and Play":*]

> Our love's a silk thread binding us heart-to-heart
> Through thick and thin, oh my sweetheart.
> The comb that you brought me
> I use on my hair.
> We'll go out together to have a good time.
> As soon as I see you I blush and it's clear
> That I'm crazy with love for you, dear.

[SHEN HSIAO-CHIA *returns from the fields carrying his baskets. He is enchanted by the song, and stands dreamily on the wooden bridge.*

AUNT LEI *and* AUNT MA *are nearby, collecting dung in baskets.* SHEN HSIAO-CHIA *spontaneously breaks into song:*]

> The comb that you brought me may not be pretty, no,
> But, my sweetheart, it's shiny and red, even so.
> When I pick up the comb
> Then I know I love you.
> We'll go out together to have a good time.
> As soon as I see you I blush and it's clear
> That I'm crazy with love for you, dear.

[AUNT MA *sees* SHEN's *expression. She tugs on* AUNT LEI's *sleeve and points to him*]

AUNT MA [*In a low voice*] Shhh—look, he's infatuated!

[AUNT LEI *brushes her finger against her cheek, in a sign of disapproval. The two turn away and start laughing.* SHEN *hears them and starts back in confusion, but, after a few steps, realizes he's going in the wrong direction. He turns around again and runs off toward the riverbank. Co-op members* CHIA *and* I *enter, carrying their empty baskets. The sound of "Cuckoo" singing gets louder as it gets nearer; it is a Mao Shan folksong, "The Cuckoo's Song":*]

> Loud sings the cuckoo, she'll chant
> To the peasants transplanting rice:
> Ko-li ko-san tuo, Ko-li ko san tuo.
> In row after row, oh my boy friend, we'll go,
> Ko-li ko san tuo.

[CH'Ü HSIAO-TI, LI CHIN-FANG, YEH YU-KEN, SHIH HSIU-O *and* KUO CHIA-LIN *enter one after another, carrying baskets of river mud as the song continues:*]

> The old and the young, every woman and man
> Is hard at work in the fields,
> For our co-op has set a production plan.
> Ko-li ko-san tuo, ah ko-li ko-san tuo.

[*"Cuckoo" is heard, laughing happily.* T'UNG YA-HUA *and "Cuckoo"* —T'UNG YA-NAN—*enter carrying baskets.* T'UNG YA-HUA *slips down the bank, and* YA-NAN *hurries to support her. She tumbles down too. All the others roar with laughter*]

YA-NAN [*Jumps right up*] What are you laughing at, "Heh, heh, heh. . . ."

[*All the others laugh, some goodnaturedly, some derisively*]

CHIA [*Sarcastically*] Women had better get back to bustling around the stove instead of coming out and falling all over themselves.

I Right! Only a rooster can be sacrificed to the Buddha. How can a hen be used instead?

YA-NAN What?

CHIA [*Tactlessly*] I said, women—

YA-NAN [*Rushing up to* CHIA *and* I] What? Are you sneering at the women?

YA-HUA [*Goes up to pull at* YA-NAN] Ya-nan. Don't . . .

YA-NAN [*Not paying her any heed*] How can you build socialism without women, huh? Try it and see. If you can carry 100 I won't be carrying only 99.

[CHIA *and* I *back down. Again everyone roars with laughter*]

CHIA Wow, tough girl!

I We've poked into a hornet's nest this time!

CH'Ü Humph! We women are all hornets. Do you want to mix it up with us?!

LI [*Trying to suppress a giggle*] Z-Z-Z—the big hornet!

YA-NAN You had better examine your point of view on women.

KUO All right! The women have counterattacked boldly.

ALL THE YOUTH Hurray for "Cuckoo".

[CHIA *and* I, *seeing that things are not going their way, decide to call off the battle*]

CHIA [*To* I] A good chicken does not pick a fight with a dog—a good man does not pick a fight with a woman. Let's go!

I [*With a parting shot*] Right. We won't waste words on a skirt.

[CHIA *and* I *hope to slip away.* T'UNG YA-NAN *grabs a fistful of mud and throws it at* I. I *ducks, but as luck would have it, a direct hit is scored on* WANG PI-HAU, *who is walking by carrying a basket.* YA-NAN *hurries over, embarrassed and uncertain what to do*]

CHIA The embroidered ball[4] has hit its mark.

[*Again everyone roars with laughter.* CHIA *and* I *exit quickly.* YA-NAN *laughs loudly*]

KUO They're deserting from battle. Grab them!!

ALL THE YOUTH Grab them!

KUO Such great courage—but "Cuckoo" makes them run like scared rabbits.

SHIH Scared out of their wits! Their souls have jumped out of their skins.

[*Laughing, the others go their separate ways.* AUNT MA *tugs at* AUNT LEI]

AUNT MA Old Sister, did you see that?

AUNT LEI I saw it.

[MA *and* LEI *exit, whispering conspiratorially.* WANG *sits to one side in a pout*]

YA-HUA Ya-nan, let's go . . .

YA-NAN You go ahead, sister, I'll be along later.

[YA-HUA *looks at her and at* WANG, *then exits.* YA-NAN *begins to question him gently and solicitously*]

YA-NAN Pi-hao. [WANG *won't speak*] Pi-hao, are you hurt? Where?

WANG It's nothing, let's get to work.

YA-NAN Pi-hao, I hit you by mistake just now. I didn't mean to—

WANG It's nothing! Let's get to work!

YA-NAN Pi-hao, are you mad at me?

WANG It's nothing. Let's get to work.

YA-NAN [*In a gentle voice*] Pi-hao, we'll go together tomorrow evening to dredge up river mud, okay?

WANG Okay. Let's get to work.

YA-NAN [*Shaking her head*] No, smile. After you smile, then I'll go. [*Watches* WANG, *waiting expectantly.* WANG *smiles*] Pi-hao, you aren't angry? Huh?

WANG Okay. Let's get to work. [YA-NAN *picks up her pole and baskets and is about to exit*] Ya-nan!

YA-NAN Eh, Pi-hao.

WANG . . . let's get to work.

[YA-NAN *exits, carrying mud.* AUNT LEI *and* AUNT MA *enter, carrying their baskets*]

AUNT MA Old sister, I saw it just now [MA *imitates* YA-NAN *heaving mud.* WANG *sees them and hurriedly hides*] Tsk, tsk, tsk. Boys and girls doing what they please, what kind of grownup girl is that! [*Then, whispering conspiratorially*] Didn't you hear about when her mother was young—[*Draws near to* LEI *and whispers in her ear. The two snicker*]

AUNT LEI Ai, you can make a good ladle out of a good calabash. But bad seeds mean a bad plant. As for that daughter-in-law of mine, Ya-hua, she and her mother are birds of a feather. . . .

[WANG *really can't stand this, and, feeling upset, runs off*]

AUNT LEI They all talk about women joining the labor force, earning work points. In their bones they just want to fool around with the men, the hanky-panky stuff. Tsk, tsk.

AUNT MA It's like this, sister, the old proverb says it best: "To keep a girl chaste, leave nothing to chance: Give her a whack with a yellow-thorn branch."[5] And you don't have Ta-han discipline her, either.

AUNT LEI If our Ta-han didn't discipline her nearly every day she'd probably walk on clouds by now.

AUNT MA Hai, kids nowadays really don't listen to reason. Sister, I won't lie to you, before all this I used to have to hustle all year round from one end of town to the other arranging marriage matches for every family I could. I couldn't do without those pig's heads, bolts of foreign cloth, and mandarin-duck slippers they'd give me for being a matchmaker. But the way it is these days, the young folks all hide behind the marriage law.[6] So even if I was one big mouth full of big tongues, who would listen to me?

AUNT LEI [*Melancholically*] It's not only the men who can't stand the young women of today, but we old women can't stand them either. Eh, what's the world coming to! If it was in the old days—it's really—look at these![*Rubs her legs*] Ai, the year I gave birth to Ta-han, once I was washing clothes by the river, Wang Lao-san on the other side said a few words to me. Unfortunately, my husband saw me. He grabbed me by the hair, and dragged me home. The minute the door was shut, he beat the daylights out of me, he nearly broke my legs . . . since then I've been deformed like this.

AUNT MA It's this way with me, sister, when I was young that devil of mine . . .

[*A whistle sounds—the signal to quit work*]

AUNT LEI A-yo, sister, while we were chattering away, they've finished work.

AUNT MA Right. We should be getting home. [*They pick up their baskets and start off*] After I've washed clothes for a long time, I feel faint, my vision is blurred, my legs are numb, my back aches, my feet hurt, and my hands tremble.

AUNT LEI Sister, you're much stronger than I am.

AUNT MA A-yo, sister, stop that talk right now. These old bones of mine are ready for the belly of a coffin.

AUNT LEI Get into a coffin, not me! Even if the King of Hell sent me a written invitation I wouldn't go. Imagine, with everyone enjoying socialism, and just me all by myself supposed to climb into an icy cold coffin. Whew! [*She spits a few times to drive away bad luck*]

AUNT MA Sister, fate is not determined by men; socialism is fine for young people, but it isn't our destiny to share in it.

[*They exit still talking.* K'UNG YÜ-CHENG *and* WANG PI-HAO *enter. Everyone else enters en masse*]

K'UNG Work is over until this evening.

ALL THE YOUTH Good.

[YA-NAN *enters carrying mud*]

KUO Cuckoo has arrived. How about singing another song with us?

ALL THE YOUTH Great! Let's sing, Cuckoo!

YA-NAN [*Puts down her basket and sings*] Up in the morning, so thick is the mist . . .

WANG [*Walks up to* YA-NAN] Ya-nan, everyone's tired; don't sing! [YA-NAN *stops*]

K'UNG Good. Don't sing. We'll all go home and eat, and this evening we'll dig mud again.

ALL THE YOUTH Cuckoo, let's sing.

KUO Right. Everyone is tired out from the day's work; if Cuckoo sings, our strength will return.

YEH [*Tugging on* SHEN HSIAO-CHIA, *pushes him into the group*] Her partner has arrived.

[SHEN *is bashful and tries to get away, but he is encircled and trapped by the others*]

ALL THE YOUTH Hsiao-chia, Cuckoo, sing!

YA-NAN Let's sing, Hsiao-chia.

ALL THE YOUTH Sing, sing.

YA-NAN *and* SHEN [*Sing lead, the others sing chorus to the tune "The water chestnut and lotus root entwined"*]

Up in the morning, so thick is the mist.
Sings the cuckoo, so loud and strong.
She'll sing her song, so her man comes to hear.
He'll sing his song, so she'll sing with him.

And the sun comes up in a blaze of light.
The tractor putt-putts through the fields.
The rich soil turns like the ocean waves,
Like a ship plowing on through the sea.

When the sun's high above, beaming down its warmth,
The tractor putt-putts through the fields.
It flings on its a way a million seed grain,
That fall all around like the rain.

When the setting sun is glowing so red,
The tractor putt-putts through the fields.
Grain-heavy rice in golden row on row,
In field after field bends low.

K'UNG [*Blows a whistle*] Okay. Everybody go home!

KUO Team leader K'ung, let them sing!

K'UNG [*Points to the alarm clock*] Do you see what time it is? Do you?
[*The others, deprived of an encore, begin to scatter.* YA-NAN *is about to leave;* WANG PI-HAO *goes over to her*]

WANG Ya-nan.

YA-NAN Ai, Pi-hao, what's up?

WANG Wait, I have something to say.

YA-NAN Are you still angry with me, Pi-hao? [*She gazes meekly up at him, then buttons one of his buttons;* WANG *pushes her hand away*]

WANG [*Seriously*] Ya-nan, you are a Youth League member, and I am also a Youth League member.

YA-NAN [*Puzzled*] What do you mean?

WANG Listen: I am a League branch committee member. I'm also your sponsor to enter the League. I must have concern for your progress.

YA-NAN [*Upset*] What did I do wrong? Tell me, what faults are there in my work?

WANG None. It isn't a question of work problems, it's your outlook and behavior style.

YA-NAN My outlook and behavior style?

WANG [*Lecturing her*] Yes. Young people should clamor for progress, reform their outlook, and rectify their behavior styles. . . .

YA-NAN Is it possible that I—

WANG Listen to what I say: recently your deportment has not been good; others have reported it.

YA-NAN [*More upset*] Reported *me*?

WANG I'm saying that not only can't the men stand you, but the women can't either.

YA-NAN Can't stand me?

WANG [*Seriously*] Yes, for the sake of your progress, for the sake of your . . . your . . . every aspect. I represent the Youth League authorities' position.

YA-NAN I don't understand a bit of what you're saying, Pi-hao.

WANG You don't understand?

YA-NAN I don't understand. How did this happen? Tell me right now!

WANG Listen: When you're carting mud, you grab some and splatter people with it, and you argue with others in front of everyone. Everyday you sing. some of that—some of that "the girl sings a song and the boy comes to listen"; some of that "I'm lovesick because of you" . . .

[YA-NAN *suddenly understands what this is all about and laughs out loud*]

WANG [*Wooden-faced*] Laugh, laugh, laugh, you're never serious. [*Lecturing*] A woman— [YA-NAN *laughs again*] Still laughing, still laughing. What are you laughing at; what's so funny?

YA-NAN [*Stops laughing; in a sing-song manner*] Sourpuss, sour-sour-sourpuss. You'll make me laugh until my stomach hurts, until my sides split, until my eyes cry big tears. Aiya, Pi-hao, you really make people die laughing.

WANG Too much laughing makes men silly, makes women queer!

YA-NAN Pi-hao, don't say it. You really are . . . comical.

WANG Listen to me: You are a Youth League member; you are also a girl. You must watch your actions in front of others and must set your behavior style straight. [*Suddenly at a loss for words in his speech-making*] Still there is something else that you must do . . . you must do . . . Right. Attitude. Your attitude should be serious.

YA-NAN I don't watch myself? I'm not upright? I'm not serious? [*Silence*]

WANG Ya-nan, I want to ask you something.

YA-NAN Eh, ask.

WANG You must answer me truthfully. The excellent qualities in a young person are sincerity and honesty. Falseness and cunning are—

YA-NAN Yech!

WANG What?

YA-NAN Just what are you trying to ask me?

WANG If I say it, don't be angry. I'm doing this solely for your own good, for the sake of my responsibility to other comrades, and for the sake of the influence the Youth League is to exert—

YA-NAN Yech!

WANG What?

YA-NAN You really can be annoying. [*Giving in*] Oh, all right. Let's get to what you have to say.

WANG Promise me now. Don't sing songs together with Shen Hsiao-chia, and don't giggle and laugh in front of everyone.

YA-NAN [*Not expecting this*] Oh! [*Silence*]

WANG Promise? [*Silence*] It's not your singing that I'm opposed to. Only just don't sing outside, and don't sing with Shen Hsiao-chia.

YA-NAN Oh!

WANG This is just a test to see if you really love me, understand? A test. [*Silence*]

YA-NAN [*Nods her head*] Okay. I promise you.

WANG [*Animatedly*] Good, Ya-nan, good. I knew you were willing to obey. [*Lecturing*] Young people shouldn't be afraid of having shortcomings. When they're in the wrong, as long as they have courage, and have resolve . . .

YA-NAN [*Picks up*] . . . then they can overcome their shortcomings and correct their mistakes.

WANG Right. Right. Now you've got it.

YA-NAN Yeah, I've got it all memorized.

WANG Good, I'll wait for you tomorrow night.

[YA-NAN *nods;* WANG *exits.* YA-NAN *is about to exit when from inside angry shouting is heard, then* YA-NAN *races on with* LEI TA-HAN *chasing her*]

TA-HAN Halt, devil woman!

YA-HUA Ya-nan! [*Runs to* YA-NAN*'s side*]

YA-NAN Sister!

TA-HAN Let's go. You're coming with me!

YA-NAN What are you doing, Brother Ta-han?

TA-HAN [*Fiercely*] You never mind. I ride my horse as I please; I'll handle my wife as I please. I'll do whatever I want.

YA-NAN Why don't you try talking sense instead of bullying someone for no reason at all?

YA-HUA Ya-nan, it's that bull's temper of his again.

TA-HAN [*Brandishes his fist*] What?

YA-NAN [*Stands in his way*] You . . . Brother Ta-han, if you've got troubles it's best to explain it. Out with it, what's going on?

TA-HAN We just finished dinner, and now she wants to go run out somewhere—the wild, lascivious badger.

YA-HUA Haven't I already told you, I'm going to the women's meeting.

TA-HAN I forbid you to go to the women's meeting, the old hag's meeting.

YA-NAN Ta-han!

YA-HUA Ta-han, I only want to go this once, just this once.

TA-HAN No! You're coming home with me.

YA-NAN Brother Ta-han. Our outlook can only progress if we attend meetings. Aren't you going to let my sister progress?

TA-HAN Progress. In your kind of progress men become cuckolds!

YA-NAN Yech! You!

TA-HAN [*To* YA-HUA] Are you coming with me or not? [YA-HUA *obediently starts to follow him*]

YA-NAN Sister [YA-HUA *halts again*] Sister, come! [YA-HUA *turns around again; she doesn't want to go back with him*]

TA-HAN The tramp is itching for a beating.

[*He takes off a shoe, and tries to grab* YA-HUA *by the hair.* YA-HUA *frantically dodges.* TA-HAN *pursues, striking out with the sole of his shoe, but not hitting her.* YA-NAN *cannot control herself any longer, and jumps into the fray. She snatches his shoe from him and flings it to the ground.* TA-HAN *glares menacingly at* YA-NAN. *Fearfully* YA-HUA *ducks behind her sister. There is a standoff*]

TA-HAN Okay. Defy the gods then! [*He whirls around and exits, then returns*]

TA-HAN [*To* YA-HUA] Since you've got resources, don't come back! [*He walks forward, glares at* YA-NAN *for a minute, humphs, and stalks off*]

YA-HUA [*Embraces* YA-NAN] Ya-nan!

YA-NAN Sister.

[*Momentary pause*]

YA-HUA Sister, what am I going to do?

YA-NAN Never mind about him. Let's go to the meeting.

YA-HUA No, I'm going home. [*She picks up* LEI TA-HAN'S *shoe and exits slowly*]

[*Curtain*]

ACT II

Scene 1

Inside the co-op's recreation club, on the following evening. It is almost dark. On either side of the entrance hang two scrolls; they read, "The CCP is like the sun" and "Organizing cooperatives is the way." The club is furnished with tables, chairs, and stools, and decorated with silk award pennants, slogans, and promotional posters. No lights are on, although it is almost dark; outside, the new crescent moon hangs in the evening sky. SHEN HSIAO-CHIA *is sitting on a stool playing a two-stringed fiddle; the tune is "Bird Calls on a Deserted Hill." The crisp notes of the fiddle waft through the air, lyrical and pleasant to the ear.*

Soon YA-NAN *comes in. When she sees* SHEN, *she considers withdrawing, but is drawn back by the graceful beauty of the music, and sits down quietly on a chair in the corner.* SHEN, *deeply absorbed in playing, isn't aware that anyone else is around. As he plays faster, a string breaks.*

YA-NAN [*Jumping up*] Oh, oh! [*Startled,* SHEN *too jumps to his feet*]

SHEN Who is there?

YA-NAN Me.

SHEN [*Pleasantly surprised*] Ahh, you gave me a fright, you know!

YA-NAN You really must be courageous if I could startle you! [*Walks over and picks up a kerosene lamp*] Hsiao-chia, have you got a match?

[SHEN *takes out a match to light the lamp, but his heart is pounding, and after a few tries, he still hasn't got it lighted*]

YA-NAN Hasn't anyone come yet?

SHEN No.

YA-NAN What's wrong? Can't you light it?

SHEN No, I can't—but I think it's catching now.

YA-NAN [*Not noticing* SHEN'S *flustered state*] Let me do it [*She lights it*]
Will we sing tonight or have a meeting?

SHEN I don't know. [*Silence*]

YA-NAN Things were so lively back when we formed the drama club.
Everyone who could sing was singing, the dancers were dancing, the
actors were acting . . . [*Silence*]

SHEN We were promoting the organization of cooperatives, the Forty
Articles,[7] the new conscription law, the—

YA-NAN And now nothing is really happening.

SHEN Yes, it's strange. [YA-NAN gets up and starts to leave] Ya-nan, don't
go! [*She stops*] Why don't we rehearse some songs until the others
come?

YA-NAN Rehearse? The two of us?

SHEN Hey! I really like this one. [SHEN *begins to sing. Without thinking,*
YA-NAN *joins in*]

YA-NAN and SHEN [*Sing*] Up in the morning, so thick is the mist. Sings
the cuckoo, loud and strong . . .

YA-NAN Don't sing. Don't sing.

SHEN What's wrong? [YA-NAN *lowers her head*] Are you mad at me?
[YA-NAN *shakes her head*] Ya-nan. What's the matter?

YA-NAN Nothing.

SHEN There is, don't try to fool me.

YA-NAN I want to ask a favor of you.

SHEN What is it? Just tell me, whatever it is I'll do it. [*Momentary pause*]

YA-NAN From now on, we won't sing together, okay?

SHEN Why?

YA-NAN Don't ask, I've already promised someone.

SHEN Whom did you promise?

YA-NAN Don't ask. Don't ask! [*Silence*]

SHEN Okay, I won't ask, and that's that . . . Anyway, I have to get going
also.

YA-NAN Leaving? Where are you going?

SHEN To enter the tractor-training course, to study tractor driving.

YA-NAN Really!?

SHEN Branch Secretary K'ung just told me.

YA-NAN Drive a tractor! Wow! That's terrific, terrific!

SHEN Why? Do you want to go too?

YA-NAN That's what I was thinking, Hsiao-chia. Do you think they'd
have me?

SHEN No. Well, I don't know!

YA-NAN Do you think I'm qualified enough? If I submitted a report, and
put in a request, would that do?

SHEN Okay. Let's try it and see.

[YA-NAN *takes out a pen.* SHEN *takes out his diary.* YA-NAN *reaches
for it.* SHEN *hurriedly hides it . . . then hastily rips out a blank page and
hands it to her*]

YA-NAN What should I say in the report?

SHEN I'll help you think of something.

  YA-NAN *and* SHEN *bend over the table and write the report.* KUO
CHIA-LIN *enters , humming a song*]

KUO Hey, you two zealots! Are you studying characters again? [*The two
  laugh.* KUO *walks over to the table*] What? What are you beating the
  drum about?

SHEN Ya-nan is filing a report to the Youth League authorities.

YA-NAN Don't tell him.

KUO [*Under the misconception that she wants to marry* WANG PI-HAO
  and is therefore filing a marriage request] Ah. Now I understand, you
  want to be a bride, right?

YA-NAN [*Embarrassed*] Ts'e!

SHEN [*Misconstrues what he has said and thinks that* KUO, *guessing
  what's in his heart of hearts, is playing a joke on them*] How did you—
  No, no, that's not it; we have no such intentions.

KUO [*Even more nonplussed*] Then . . . then what are you two up to?

SHEN We're going to study tractor driving together!

YA-NAN I want to make a request to the Youth League Committee for
  approval.

KUO [*Suddenly enlightened*] Ah. So this is it!

YA-NAN Do you approve?

KUO No, I don't agree.

YA-NAN Why not?

KUO You go and the songbird of the drama troupe flies off. Then who'll
  sing: "Up in the morning, so thick is the mist, sings the cuckoo, loud
  and strong"?

YA-NAN Don't! Don't sing!

KUO What's wrong? [*Silence*] Why doesn't the Cuckoo want to sing?
  [YA-NAN *turns away and is about to exit*] Ya-nan, where are you going?

YA-NAN To deliver my report to Branch Secretary K'ung.

KUO You have rehearsed the songs?

YA-NAN I'll come back in a bit. [*She runs off*]

KUO What's going on?

SHEN I don't know.

KUO Her mood has changed over the last few days, Hsiao-chia. Has she
  said anything to you?

SHEN Nothing. —Ah, she did say something. When I asked her, she
  simply said, "Don't ask, I already promised someone else."

KUO How can he do this?

SHEN Who's "he"?

KUO Wang Pi-hao.

SHEN Wang Pi-hao!

KUO If it's like this *now*, what's it going to be like later on?

SHEN Ah . . . [*Sits down sorrowfully*]

KUO What's the matter with you? [*Silence*] Don't keep it from me. I can
  see, there's no doubt, you have something on your mind . . . [*Silence*]
  Tell me, Hsiao-chia.

SHEN Brother Chia-lin, it's something I haven't been able to say . . .

KUO It's that you, too . . . [*Suddenly* SHEN *collapses against* KUO'S *chest and cries bitterly. There is a brief pause*] Hsiao-chia, don't be upset. All these things will eventually pass. [*Silence*] Hsiao-chia, there are lots of fine girls in our co-op. And later on you'll pick one who's just exactly right for you.

SHEN No. There is only one like her; only one; I'll never find another.

KUO No. You *will* find another. Look at me. Even someone like me with only one arm can find someone who loves him. You're still young, and if you just don't snivel, you'll find one for sure.

SHEN I don't want another. I don't want anyone else. I'm leaving tomorrow. Brother Chia-lin, don't ever let anyone know about this, and don't let her know either.

KUO Okay, I won't tell, I won't tell [SHEN *is about to go*] I want to talk to you, Hsiao-chia.

[KUO *and* SHEN *talk as they exit.* WANG *and* K'UNG *enter at the same time from different directions*]

WANG *and* K'UNG [*Simultaneously*] Ai!

WANG Did you see Ya-nan?

K'UNG Did you see Ya-nan?

WANG What, are you looking for her, too?

K'UNG Are you looking for her, too?

WANG Ai, Yü-ch'eng. You see, you see, yesterday she promised to go dig mud with me tonight. I waited for her by the river bank for a long time but she never came.

K'UNG Ah. I went to her home but didn't find her. Someone said she came to the recreation club.

WANG She's not at the club, and Hsiao-chia's not there either. They've gone off in the dark, for sure, to hug and sing "I'm longing for you" or whatever.

K'UNG Hai, you really are jealous. Don't jump to rash conclusions. I've got good news to tell her.

WANG What good news?

K'UNG The Youth League authorities have decided to send Hsiao-chia and Ya-nan to study tractor driving.

WANG What? What? Ya-nan and Shen Hsiao-chia?

K'UNG Oh.

WANG Shen Hsiao-chia with Ya-nan?

K'UNG Well, yes. I recommended both of them. Secretary Fang also agreed.

WANG Ai, I'm done for. It's all over for me.

K'UNG What's wrong?

WANG How could you double cross me like that? You!

K'UNG Double cross? I'm always on your side.

WANG On my side? You're out to get me!

K'UNG Out to get you?

WANG Yes, don't you know? Hsiao-chia and Ya-nan are together the whole day singing and jumping about, talking and laughing. That jerk has something rotten on his mind!

K'UNG Ah, is that really so?

WANG Isn't it? That jerk was born with a great voice. When he sings, it's like listening to a recording, and all the girls lose their minds. I'll never have a voice that good. This time they've really done it. There's the two of them in the tractor instruction class. The guy says yes, and the girl won't say no. Something *is* bound to happen even if nothing is going on now.

K'UNG Ai, actually I've heard enough about it. This time I wasn't thinking fast enough. I only looked at how energetic they are, at their education, and their "quick minds," and I just thought of using the most suitable material for the job. I never thought of this aspect.

WANG And there's more: I had talked with Ya-nan earlier, and we planned on getting married after the wheat harvest. Now with this, all my plans are ruined. Yü-ch'eng, are you deliberately against me or what?

K'UNG You're falsely accusing a good man, Pi-hao.

WANG So, what can I do?

K'UNG Okay. Okay. Fortunately I didn't get to see Ya-nan just now, she still doesn't know about this. So it will be easy to take care of.

WANG Tell me how you're going to do it.

K'UNG I'll go and discuss it with Secretary Fang, and then take Ya-nan's name off the list—that will keep her at home, so you and she can get a quick marriage. When the rice is cooked, it's cooked. And that will be that, okay?

WANG Good, good. We'll do it that way, we'll do it that way. But will Secretary Fang take her name off the list?

K'UNG Whew. Now that's . . . I'd better go have a talk with him and see. As for the marriage, there's no way for me to get involved in that; you take care of that yourself.

WANG Yü-ch'eng, I'll never forget this as long as I live, as long as I live!

K'UNG What's the point of saying this, we're like real brothers. What concerns you concerns me, and what concerns me concerns you.

WANG Right. Right. When it's all settled, I'll tell my bride to personally pour three cups of wine for you.

K'UNG Pi-hao, this plan of yours is too conservative. I wouldn't object to thirty cups!

WANG Great, thirty cups. It'll be thirty cups.

K'UNG Okay. Let's get to work. I'll go find Secretary Fang and you go find Ya-nan.

[K'UNG *and* WANG *exit. Laughter is heard outside the door.* LI CHIN-FANG *and* CH'Ü HSIAO-TI *enter.* SHIH HSIU-O *also enters, pulling* YA-HUA *along with her*]

CH'Ü Hey, there's no one here.

Lı It's always this way. When the gongs are ready the drums aren't.

SHIH Ya-hua. What are you doing moping around home? If you'd come out and listen to everyone singing, you'd feel much happier.

CH'Ü So happy you could die!

YA-HUA [Timidly] But later when Ta-han comes home, he will again . . .

CH'Ü You are really a softie; what are you afraid of? If he tries to gobble you up, you have us.

YA-HUA You don't know what a temper he has. In every other way he's good. It's just that he won't let me go out to meetings and study sessions.

SHIH No meetings? No study? How can you make any progress?

Lı Ai. Here we're all building socialism, and his head is still loaded with feudal remnants.

CH'Ü Humph! I'd really like to give him a rap on that head of his.

YA-HUA Hsiao-ti, don't talk like that, he'll change.

CH'Ü Change? Not unless the roosters start laying eggs and horses grow horns.

Lı Hsiao-ti, don't talk like this.

SHIH Girls, give her an idea.

CH'Ü I've got a good idea.

OTHERS Tell us. Tell us. Speak! Speak!

CH'Ü We'll all unite. No one will get married. Let them all stay bachelors; let them go a whole lifetime without wives and see if they still dare to insult women.

[Everybody bursts out laughing]

SHIH Stupid. This method of yours is unacceptable. I'm absolutely opposed to it. I've been married to Chia-lin for three years. He's good to me and I'm good to him, so why should I want him to remain a bachelor?

Lı I'm also opposed to it. I already have someone in mind. [She's greatly embarrassed, turns her face away and giggles]

SHIH and CH'Ü [Simultaneously] Which one?

Lı [Covers her face] I don't know. I don't know. But anyway whoever he is I want to marry him . . . [Bursts into giggles again]

CH'Ü [Angry] Okay, okay, fine, fine. You all go and get married! But I won't marry a man ever.

YA-HUA Stupid! Don't talk tough. We'll remember what you've said. The day will come when you'll meet—

SHIH Meet a young guy who's also sworn never to marry.

CH'Ü [Jumps up and starts after SHIH] You're going to die for that. I won't let you get away with it . . .

[Everyone doubles over with laughter]

CH'Ü You! You're all thick-skinned, no sense of shame!

[Everyone roars even more. PAI T'IEN-SHUI and YEH YU-KEN enter; the women immediately stop laughing]

PAI Why so happy? Why such excitement?

YEH When women get together, if they're not crying they're laughing, and if they're not laughing they're talking about us guys.

LI No one has mentioned you.

[*The girls all giggle again*]

CH'Ü We're not talking about you—we're cursing you.

SHIH Ai, the skin of your face is thicker than a city wall at its corners!

YEH So, I guessed right—cursing is also talking!

[*All the girls are embarrassed. They laugh in sputters*]

PAI Why do you want to curse us?

YEH Right. How have we offended you? Is it because we borrowed your rice and gave you back the chaff? Aahchoo! All that cursing of yours makes me sneeze. [*As if to confirm this remark, he sneezes again*] Aachoo!

[*Everyone laughs again*]

YA-HUA [*Suddenly*] Hsiu-o, I'm going home. I still haven't washed the clothes . . . [*Hurriedly exits*]

PAI What's wrong with Ya-hua?

SHIH She's afraid that Ta-han is looking for her.

LI Ta-han does nothing but bully her. That kind of man . . .

CH'Ü Men are really detestable. If it was me, I'd definitely get a divorce.

YEH You're not even married and you want a divorce?

PAI Don't joke about it; Ya-hua is too meek. Lei Ta-han needs to get straightened out.

LI That's more like a man's talk.

SHIH Cuckoo straightened him out that day. She threw away his shoe, and all he could do was pick it up and walk away.

PAI Right, Cuckoo did right.

YEH You clown. Now you're changing your tune. You all can bring him into your women's association—aachoo!

PAI Aachoo! [*Everyone laughs*] I haven't heard Cuckoo sing for days now.

YEH I really want to hear her sing:

"Our love's a silk thread binding us heart-to-heart
Through thick and thin, oh my sweetheart.
The comb that you bought me
I use on my hair.
We'll go out together to have a good time,
And as soon as you blush then it's clear
That I'm what's on your mind, oh my dear."

[SHEN HSIAO-CHIA *excitedly rushes on*]

SHEN Are you all here?

[*Everyone gets up to welcome him*]

ALL THE YOUTHS Come on and sing, Hsiao-chia!

SHEN There's been an accident!

ALL THE YOUTHS What is it? What happened?

SHEN Huang Chü-ying fainted!

SHIH How did it happen?

SHEN Everyday she's been hauling mud while she's pregnant, and today when she got home, she miscarried. Right now her condition is critical.

ALL THE YOUTHS Miscarried? What can be done?

SHEN Chia-lin is there. He says to change the date for the club to rehearse, and for us to carry her to the health station right away.

ALL THE YOUTH Let's go.

[*They exit en masse.* AUNT LEI *enters, leaning on a cane and carrying a lantern*]

AUNT LEI Ya-hua! Ya-hua! [*She sees no one, so she sits down to rest*] Ah, there's not a trace of anybody. Where did they all run off to? [*Rubs her legs*] I nearly fell off the mud levee. [*Resentfully*] Right now, I'd like to grab—

[LEI TA-HAN *hurries on*]

TA-HAN Ma, did you see her?

AUNT LEI Her? A ghost, maybe! Such a big man you are, and you can't even keep a woman under your thumb. And you have to get an old woman like me to grope in the dark looking for her. Calling her is like trying to call back a wandering soul.

TA-HAN Ma, it wasn't my idea for you to come outside. What if you should trip and fall, then what?

AUNT LEI Then what? Too bad that good wife of yours disappears the minute you turn your back. I just want to come out here to see what she's up to.

TA-HAN Ai. This time watch me and see if I don't give her a taste of what's coming to her.

AUNT LEI Right. This time you've got to lay into her good. No sense in being afraid. There's only three things a woman sets store by: weeping, fighting, and hanging herself. That's all, nothing much.

[YA-NAN *enters and hears them talking; she halts, unnoticed*]

TA-HAN Damn, I know. Anvils are made for hammering, and women are born to be whipped. If she can take it then she'll have to stay obedient to me. If she can't, then I'll throw her out like a pan of foot-washing water.

AUNT LEI Now that's like a man who's got a spine. There are many women in the co-op. You could get a string of them with your eyes closed.

YA-NAN [*Can't restrain herself any more and bursts out*] What are you talking about?

AUNT LEI Oh!

TA-HAN You!

YA-NAN Aunt, it's pitch black and you're still out!

AUNT LEI That's right, I came out, am I getting in somebody's way?

YA-NAN Brother Ta-han, what you just said is absolutely wrong. Women are people too, not anvils or foot-washing water.

TA-HAN I wasn't talking to you!

YA-NAN Brother Ta-han, in what way is my sister bad? Why must you be like this to her?

AUNT LEI You—it's none of your business, you.

YA-NAN When the road is uneven, others will level it. When it is unfair, others will interfere.

AUNT LEI Go mind your own man's business.

TA-HAN Go mind your own man's business. Let's go, Ma! [AUNT LEI *and* LEI TA-HAN *exit*]

YA-NAN [*Frustrated, irked, and vexed*] Why, why is there still this type of person today, and with this kind of outlook . . . ?

[WANG PI-HAO *enters*]

WANG Ya-nan.

YA-NAN Pi-hao.

WANG So you're here. I've been looking for you everywhere.

YA-NAN Why, Pi-hao? Have you seen Branch Secretary K'ung?

WANG Why are you looking for him?

YA-NAN You guess, Pi-hao.

WANG I can't, Ya-nan, let's talk about something serious.

YA-NAN No, guess! My business is also serious.

WANG Don't be silly. Listen to what I have to say.

YA-NAN [*Hands* WANG *the report*] Look!

WANG [*Looks at it*] Oh, so you want to drive a tractor?

YA-NAN Indeed I do.

WANG And you want to go with Shen?

YA-NAN Yes, together.

WANG You've really thought it all out.

YA-NAN Yes . . . being a tractor driver would be really good! [*Enthusiastically*] The tractor "putt, putt, putts" along over a stretch of flat land; it turns over big clod after big clod of rich earth; they look like the breaking waves; it sows row after row of seeds, as if it was sprinkling raindrops. Then row upon row the ripened golden rice and wheat will lie down . . . [*Realizes that his reaction is unsympathetic*] Pi-hao, do you agree to my going?

WANG No, I don't agree!

YA-NAN You don't, why?

WANG You are a woman.

YA-NAN A woman? Can't a woman drive a tractor? That's crazy. Haven't you seen the newspapers? A great many women know how to drive tractors, and there are train operators, and trolley operators, and—

WANG They're all putting on a show. Ya-nan, it's not proper for women to do these things.

YA-NAN Why isn't it proper?

WANG Listen to me: Women should get married, get pregnant, give birth, bring up children, look after the household, all year round. When they are involved in production, there will be so much interruption that would only hinder production.

YA-NAN Hinder production?

WANG Yes, I'm thinking of the good of production and I'm also concerned for your own good. Ya-nan, listen to me and you won't go wrong.

YA-NAN Give me back the report.

WANG What are you going to do if I give it to you?

YA-NAN I'm going to give it to the Youth League's Branch Secretary.

WANG I'm a Youth League committee member.

YA-NAN Okay. I'll ask for a higher level review.

WANG There's no use reviewing it. [*He rips it apart and throws it away*]

YA-NAN What are you doing—

WANG Ya-nan, listen to me: Don't go off on wild flights of fancy. Stay patiently at home. [YA-NAN *is not listening; she takes out a pen and starts writing another report*] Ya-nan, don't develop a subjective attitude. Look, spring is here, my family's house is all fixed up. So let's get married right away. After we're married you can stay at home, and we'll live happily ever after.

YA-NAN No, Pi-hao. I want to study; wait for me to come back, after my studying, okay?

WANG No. I won't wait; I won't even wait for one day!

YA-NAN Didn't I promise to marry you after the wheat harvest? Why are you getting so impatient?

WANG I've just got to ask you. Why are you making lame excuses?

YA-NAN I've got nothing else in mind, I only want to study.

WANG Why are you so set on going to study?

YA-NAN I want to study hard, so I can come back and build up our village.

WANG Don't give me this high-flown language! I am asking you for your real motive in wanting to study.

YA-NAN What motive? What do you mean?

WANG You tell me. Why must you study with Shen? Why won't you marry me now?

YA-NAN Hai! You . . . you . . .

WANG Say it. Am I right?

YA-NAN You've got it all cockeyed!

WANG You tell me why you didn't show up tonight after you promised me that we'd dredge up mud together!

YA-NAN Tonight was the night the theatrical troupe had settled on to practice singing.

WANG The place for practice is right here, in the club. So where did you and Shen go just now?

YA-NAN I went to Branch Secretary K'ung's home just now!

WANG Humph, you're lying. K'ung was just here!

YA-NAN I didn't know where he was. I went to his home and when I didn't find him I came back.

WANG You're lying! You really went off hand in hand with Shen. Say it. What were you two doing in the dark? What were you doing?

YA-NAN You're talking nonsense; aren't you ashamed of youself?

Hsiao-chia and I grew up together, and now we're in the same work team, the same Youth League group, sing songs in the same recreation organization, we're good comrades. It was that way before you became my boy friend and it's still that way now. You can think what you want.

WANG You're simply unwilling to acknowledge your mistakes, and you're simply unwilling to expose your thoughts.

YA-NAN What's wrong with you today, Pi-hao? Are you sick?

WANG I am sick, so sick I could die.

YA-NAN Pi-hao, don't be like this. Look at you, you're nothing like your usual self. Calm down. I'll talk things over with you.

WANG I don't want to listen, I don't want to listen, I've told you many times already that I'm fed up with this behavior of yours. When I see you singing together with others, dancing and play acting, it cuts at my heart like a file, it stabs at it like an awl, and cuts it like a knife. I can't sleep all night long. And when I dream it's nothing but nightmares. [*Starts crying*]

YA-NAN Pi-hao, stop this, stop this. This is something that's all in your head! In the past, I did what I pleased, and wasn't willing to listen to you. This is all my fault, all my fault . . .

WANG You let all the things that I've said go in one ear and out the other. You've never taken them seriously. If you really loved me then you wouldn't torment me this way.

YA-NAN Pi-hao, I know you like me, and I think highly of you. Your outlook is good and you are willing to help me progress. I promised you and I put my trust in you. But you don't trust me.

WANG I want to trust you. That is why I must alter your thoughts and behavior style.

YA-NAN I'll change in whatever way you want me to change.

WANG Do you sincerely want to change?

YA-NAN I sincerely do.

WANG Good, then promise me you'll stay at home and marry me immediately. [*Silence*] Ya-nan, what did you just say?

YA-NAN I'm thinking it over.

WANG Ya-nan, you said you sincerely wanted to change. How can you not listen to what I say?

YA-NAN Okay. I won't leave.

WANG Good, you're willing to listen, Ya-nan, very good, very good! [*Slight pause*] Then tomorrow we'll go and register. After that we'll get married, we'll invite Secretary Fang, and Yü-ch'eng, and others to come and celebrate. Oh, we'll invite the entire Youth team to the banquet. Everything will be splendid, a grand commotion. We'll make all the boys and girls envious when they see it.

YA-NAN Pi-hao, don't make such a big deal out of this. It's best to keep it simple.

WANG No. This is the biggest event in our lives, we simply can't let it be something haphazard.

YA-NAN Pi-hao.

WANG Ya-nan, don't be such a rightist-conservative. I will make all the decisions.

YA-NAN You will make all the decisions?

WANG Yes. We must construct a model family; let all the youth study us well. You see, I've even set up a five-point contract for our model family. [*Takes out a piece of paper and hands it to* YA-NAN]

YA-NAN What kind of contract?

WANG Look.

YA-NAN [*Reads aloud*] "1. Resign from the theatrical troupe; you are not permitted to sing, dance, or act with the boys and girls."

WANG You can sing at home.

YA-NAN [*Reads*] "2. You are not permitted to talk to boys when you are by yourself."

WANG If you do, you must report it to me the same day.

YA-NAN [*Reads*] "3. You are not permitted to giggle in front of the masses."

WANG Under special circumstances you can, but you must first obtain my consent.

YA-NAN [*Reads*] "4. If you see Shen, you must move off and keep your distance to avoid any untoward occurrence."

WANG If there is any public business to transact, I'll carry messages between the two sides.

YA-NAN [*Reads*] "5. Marry me now and swear not to study tractor driving."

WANG What do you say?

YA-NAN You're joking, aren't you?

WANG Who's joking? Ya-nan, if you want to progress, if you want to reform your thought and behavior style, if you're going to build a model family with me, then these guidelines must be implemented. Sign it! [*Silence*] Hurry up and sign it!

YA-NAN Are you for real?

WANG Of course.

YA-NAN Do you really want to do it this way?

WANG Yes, you definitely must do it this way.

YA-NAN So this is the sort of person you are after all.

WANG What's wrong? [*She rips up the paper*] You, you have the nerve to—[*She throws the paper away*] Okay. You've torn it up, torn it up!

YA-NAN Right, I've torn it up. What kind of person do you think I am? You think you can turn me into my sister, Ya-hua, but you can't!

WANG Ya-nan, listen to what I say.

YA-NAN No, I won't listen, I won't. You think you can tie me up hand and foot, but it can't be done! You think you can gag me, but it can't be done. You think you can lead me around by the nose, but you can't do it! You can't do it! You can't!

WANG Good, so that's—

YA-NAN Get away from me!

WANG That's it for good.

YA-NAN Okay.

WANG You'll regret it later.

YA-NAN I certainly won't.

WANG [*Stamps off, then comes back*] You're truly an ungrateful woman. If it wasn't for my concern for you, could you have joined the Youth League? If it hadn't been for my helping you, could you have become so literate? If it wasn't for me looking after you, wouldn't you have been nothing but an abandoned child no one wanted?

YA-NAN I appreciate your concern and appreciate your help, and I thank you for looking after me. But I still want to laugh and I still want to sing. I want to sing!

[WANG PI-HAO *exits angrily.* YA-NAN *suddenly breaks down. She bends over in the chair and cries bitterly.* KUO CHIA-LIN *enters*]

KUO Ya-nan, what's wrong? [*A pause*]

YA-NAN Pi-hao and I are finished. . . .

[*Curtain*]

Scene 2

Evening of the following day. The sun is about to set. In front of the door of the co-op management committee office there are brick tile steps. Alongside the steps a row of evergreens has been planted. On either side is a peach tree, not yet in blossom. Below the steps there is a newly laid out square. In the past there used to be a big road here, and travelers still pass through. At quitting time the co-op members, having worked all day, are dead tired. But as they pass by on the way home, they are still happily singing and chatting.

FANG PAO-SHAN *is squatting on his heels on the porch, engrossed in studying a scale-model rice paddy. He moves the pine needles representing the rice shoots back and forth in the sandbox as though he's onto an idea.* K'UNG YÜ-CHENG *enters.*

K'UNG Secretary Fang.

FANG Yü-ch'eng, come over here.

K'UNG Secretary Fang, are you studying the scale-model rice paddy again?

FANG Look, plant this way: plant with five spaces between rice sprouts and six spaces between rows. All in neat order. Everything evenly spaced. Helps with the weeding, too. Very scientific.

K'UNG [*Going right along with it*] Yes, before, the transplanting was like hen pecks—here a peck, there a peck—not much rhyme or reason anywhere.

FANG Right. This is scientific and technological reform. This year we will first demonstrate it with the Youth team. And then we'll expand the plan to include every plot. This way we're sure to hit the 3,000-kilos-per-acre[8] target.

K'UNG We're sure to do it!

FANG Yü-ch'eng, I've heard that the older farmers have some opinions about this.

K'UNG Yes, a few have some.

FANG Who? What are their opinions?

K'UNG Su Lao-han says: "I've been planting crops for forty years, I've never used these newfangled things and I've never starved. Ho! 3,000 kilos an acre, only if ears of wheat can grow all over the plant, starting from the roots."

FANG Yü-ch'eng, analyze it, analyze it. What kind of thought is that?

K'UNG [*Uncertainly*] This is . . . empiricism.

FANG Right, you've got it right. What are the other reactions?

K'UNG And also Grandpa Chiang says: "If we can pull it off, then we'll all be rich. If we can't pull it off, then we'll all be broke."

FANG Eh! What kind of outlook is this? Try and analyze it.

K'UNG This is a conservative outlook.

FANG Right! That's right!

[FANG *gives* K'UNG *a cigarette, and the two light up*]

FANG Yü-ch'eng, when you grasp a new thing you'll always run into some sort of "ism" or outlook. But to be a good cadre, you can't just chime in with whatever the masses clamor for. We must slowly establish a rapport with the way the masses are thinking. Some time later we will start a technical training class. Your Youth team must send more people over to study.

K'UNG Right. [*They walk off the porch*]

FANG Yü-ch'eng, are there any problems in the Youth team?

K'UNG Yes, Ya-nan has submitted a report. [*Hands over the report to* FANG]

FANG [*Takes a quick look at it, hardly noticing it*] Didn't you say her outlook and behavior style were poor and it's been decided to send Chou Huai-ch'ing instead?

K'UNG Yes. She still wants to make an urgent request. She still stubbornly requests it. Yesterday, she just went ahead with Wang Pi-hao and—

FANG Made eyes at him?

K'UNG No, they broke up!

FANG [*Paying it no mind*] Ah, so it's a different story now.

K'UNG Yes, and over a piddling matter, she argued with Wang.

FANG [*Laughs in spite of himself*] This is just like you: even if there is nothing, you'd find something. Now you're even involved in this trivial affair. The love between youths is like our April weather here in Chiang Nan. One minute it's clear, the next it's raining, so why bother with it? Yü-ch'eng, to be a cadre, all you have to do is to pay close attention to production. Don't grab for the sesame and lose the watermelon.

[*Co-op members* CHIA *and* I *enter, alarmed and anxious*]

CHIA *and* I Chief Fang, Chief Fang!

FANG What's the matter?

I Bad news. Something terrible's happened.

FANG What?

CHIA [*Panting*] I don't know why. She just lay down!

I [*Jumps in*] We chased her but couldn't make her get up.

CHIA She walked around in a circle then lay down again.

FANG Someone's sick? Who?

CHIA *and* I [*Simultaneously*] Yueh K'e-hsia.

FANG [*Upset*] Yueh K'e-hsia is sick? Ai, our co-op's only breeding pig!

CHIA An authentic pure breed!

I There's not a hair of her that's hybrid!

FANG [*Cutting them short*] What kind of sickness? How bad is it?

CHIA She ate a mouthful of feed in the morning, but at noon she didn't
    eat anything—

I Wrong, she ate two mouthfuls.

CHIA She ate two mouthfuls, then spit it up. In the evening—

I She'll throw up in the evening too.

FANG You're driving me nuts with all your chattering, speak one at a
    time.

CHIA Okay. I'll speak. While she was sleeping on the straw heap, she
    was breathing heavily. We didn't know if she was panting or snoring.

I Panting!

CHIA Snoring!

FANG Quick, go get the vet.

CHIA The vet can't come.

FANG Then carry her to the vet station right now! Yü-ch'eng, pick out
    a few hardy guys.

    [K'UNG *exits; so do co-op members* CHIA *and* I. FANG *is about to go
    when* LI CHIN-FANG *and* CH'Ü HSIAO-TI *hurry on*]

LI *and* CH'Ü Chief Fang!

FANG What?

LI Your wife just vomited!

FANG Oh!

CH'Ü I think she's expecting.

FANG It can't be!

LI Why don't you go back and see. [*Pause*]

FANG You two help me by keeping an eye on my wife. I've got to go to
    look at the pig first! [*He hurries off*]

    [LI *and* CH'Ü *exit. Pause.* WANG *comes out of the committee office.*
    YA-NAN *enters from stage right. The two meet accidentally. An
    extremely awkward moment; neither knows what to do.* YA-NAN *wants
    to greet him, but, spitefully, he turns his head away.* YA-NAN *sighs
    softly, and then runs into the committee office. As she exits, her
    headband falls off.* WANG *hears her go, turns around, looks at the door
    of the committee building for a moment, and then, with confused
    emotions, pauses. Suddenly he notices* YA-NAN*'s headband, and starts
    to pick it up, then changes his mind and agrily gives it a kick.* SHEN
    HSIAO-CHIA *enters, wearing a backpack. He too wishes to say hello to*
    WANG, *but* WANG *ignores him and exits. He then sees the headband,*

picks it up, and is about to hand it in to the committee office. YA-NAN *comes out of the committee office with lowered head and proceeds down the steps.* SHEN *'s first inclination is to dodge her, but he changes his mind and goes over to her*]

SHEN Ya-nan!

YA-NAN [*Startled*] Ah!

SHEN Did you drop something?

YA-NAN [*Ponders, and feels her clothes*] No.

SHEN What are you looking for?

YA-NAN I'm not looking for anything. I'm trying to find K'ung.

SHEN [*Takes out the headband*] Is this yours?

YA-NAN [*Elated*] Yes. It's my headband. Thanks a lot.

SHEN Ah, ah— [*Uneasily*] Well, see you. [*Turns and starts to go*]

YA-NAN Hsiao-chia, where are you going?

SHEN To report to the district office.

YA-NAN Just you alone?

SHEN Two of us are going.

YA-NAN [*Thinks that she herself has been approved to go*] Going together? Has it been approved?

SHEN Yes, I told you yesterday.

YA-NAN Yesterday?

SHEN Have you forgotten?

YA-NAN No. It can't be.

SHEN What "can't be"? I'm not kidding you.

YA-NAN It was only today that I gave my report to K'ung.

SHEN [*Doesn't understand*] What report?

YA-NAN Did you forget this too? The one that we wrote up together last night in the club.

SHEN [*It dawns on him*] Oh, studying tractor driving. Ya-nan, it's too late now. Chou Huai-ch'ing and I are leaving together right away.

YA-NAN Chou Huai-ch'ing?

SHEN Yes, he and I are going together.

YA-NAN [*Finally understands*] Oh . . . with him.

SHEN Look! The letter of introduction is all made up.

[*Gives the letter of introduction to* YA-NAN]

YA-NAN [*Looks at the letter with amazement*] What? They took off my name and put in Chou Huai-ch'ing's!

SHEN [*Takes the letter and looks at it*] That's true. I didn't see that!

YA-NAN What's going on here? First they approve me to go, then they take my name off.

SHEN I don't know.

YA-NAN [*Crushed, she sits down on the steps*] Ah . . .

SHEN Ya-nan, don't be crushed, don't be crushed. [*Silence*] It's all my fault. If I hadn't shown you the letter then it would have been all right.

YA-NAN I don't blame you. I know who did this.

SHEN Who? [YA-NAN *shakes her head but remains speechless*] Don't let your imagination run away with you, Ya-nan. It's windy out here. Go on home.

YA-NAN No, I've got to get to the bottom of this.

SHEN Don't be like this. I'll study hard, and when I come back, I'll teach you.

YA-NAN Teach me?

SHEN Sure! Wel'll set up a contract.

YA-NAN [*As if she's been scalded*] You want to set up a contract too?

SHEN Yes, we'll fix three targets, the first—to teach, the second—to study, the third—to know how. What do you think?

YA-NAN [*Sighs softly*] Ah . . . three fixed targets.

SHEN Okay?

YA-NAN Okay!

SHEN I'll see you when I get back. [*Starts to leave*]

YA-NAN Hsiao-chia, wait! [*SHEN halts. There is a slight pause*] Hsiao-chia, I've felt very bad the last couple of days.

SHEN Why?

YA-NAN In the club last night . . . [*She becomes choked with emotion and sobs. A voice calls out from inside:* "Shen, let's go!!"] It's nothing.

SHEN Then why are you crushed?

[*A shout from inside:* "Shen, let's go now!"]

YA-NAN We'll talk again later. Go, Hsiao-chia.

SHEN Okay. I'm off. [*Runs a few steps and turns around again*] I wish the both of you much happiness! [*He dashes off*]

YA-NAN "Both of us happiness"? [K'UNG *enters*] League Branch Secretary!

K'UNG Ya-nan, we've already gone over your report.

YA-NAN I know.

K'UNG Good. Do you have anything to say about it?

YA-NAN League Branch Secretary, why did you first decide that I could go and then retract it?

K'UNG This is a county-level matter. There's no use in your asking about it.

YA-NAN Why can't I ask?

K'UNG [*Getting angry and showing displeasure*] This is clearly a breach of discipline and insubordination.

YA-NAN This is a breach of discipline and insubordination?

K'UNG See. This cheekiness of yours and this attitude of yours—

YA-NAN League Branch Secretary, if my attitude is wrong, you can criticize me.

K'UNG You're really a tough one to handle.

YA-NAN I know only too well who played this trick.

K'UNG [*Furious*] Humph, T'ung Ya-nan. I'll tell it to you straight. The only reason we didn't approve you to go this time is because your outlook and behavior style are bad. A great many others despise you and you casually broke off with Comrade Wang Pi-hao; these are your mistakes. You'd better write out a detailed self-criticism for me. [*Turns around*] And it better not be a superficial one. [*Hurries off angrily*]

    [YA-NAN *sits down in a rage on the steps. Voices are heard from the back* "Wait for me, Chia-lin." "Woman, you don't have bound feet. Mother of my children." "Shame on you. Where are the children?" *A gale of happy laughter is heard.* KUO CHIA-LIN *and* SHIH HSIU-O *enter, carrying baskets. They're on their way home*]

SHIH [*Sees* YA-NAN *sitting on the steps*] Ya-nan!

KUO What are you doing here alone?

SHIH Ya-nan, what are you unhappy about?

KUO Is it because you didn't get selected?

[YA-NAN *nods*]

SHIH That's nothing to grieve over!

KUO Ya-nan, it doesn't matter who goes. Let's go home.

YA-NAN I won't go without a fight. Why did they select me and then strike my name off?

KUO *and* SHIH.[*Simultaneously*] Why?

YA-NAN K'ung says it's on account of my outlook and behavior style are poor.

KUO *and* SHIH [*Simultaneously*] Your outlook and behavior style are poor?

YA-NAN And breaking up with Wang Pi-hao is also my error. He wants me to write a self-criticism.

SHIH Have you written it?

KUO Don't be in a hurry to write it! Hsiu-o, you take Ya-nan home and cheer her up. I'm going to have a little chat with Secretary Fang.

SHIH Okay. Come on to our house, Ya-nan.

    [SHIH *and* YA-NAN *exit.* SECRETARY FANG *enters hurriedly*]

FANG [*Seeing* KUO] Chia-lin, oh good, it's a good thing we discovered it early, otherwise it would have been a big mess!

KUO What is so urgent?

FANG [*Can't help laughing*] Yueh K'e-hsia got sick today!

KUO Yueh K'e-hsia?

FANG Yes, she's the breeding pig that the prefectural Party committee gave us as an award.

KUO [*Bursts out laughing*] At first I thought you were talking about a person!

FANG I'm talking about a pig! [*Both laugh*]

KUO Secretary Fang, are you busy?

FANG Does it look like I'm busy or not? The old women have all lodged a serious challenge against me. They're determined to quit.

KUO The co-op?

FANG The family! [*They laugh*] You always like to "tie me up" in the middle of a busy time.

KUO But there is never any time when you're not busy.

FANG Good, let's talk, old pal. Although it's true that now I'm called a leader, in the past we grazed cattle together and cut grass on the landlord's estate. The blood-sucking devil wouldn't give us anything to eat or drink, and we were starving, so we'd sneak a ladle of pig slop for ourselves to eat. After we grew up we joined the militia together and fought as guerrillas. Once we went to the city to carry out our mission; we disguised ourselves as husband and wife. You were the one made up as a woman and had a black shawl wrapped around your head, and on your feet—

KUO Don't bring up the past. Let's talk about the present.

FANG Okay. Is it that your disabled veteran's allowance hasn't come through yet? Do you have some difficulties getting by?

KUO Ha, ha, I'm much obliged for your concern but you didn't guess correctly. I've got no problems in my life. Did you know that since Huang Chü-ying miscarried, she's become worse!

FANG Rest and relaxation will cure her.

KUO There's more, a good many co-op members have picked up schisto-somiasis;[9] their stomachs have all swollen up.

FANG [Unconcerned] Ah.

KUO [Imitating him] Just "ah," and nothing else?

FANG Let's research it.

KUO We'd best get these people to the hospital immediately.

FANG Look at you, all worked up. That's not a big thing. Right now we've got big problems all around—the need for farm work is at its peak, we're short on manpower—

KUO I think that thing is a little bigger than the business of Yueh K'e-hsia getting sick.

FANG [Staring] How can people be as important as pigs?

KUO [Doesn't believe his own ears] What? What!? Is there something wrong with my hearing?

FANG What happens to people is their own individual business. Pigs are the business of the whole co-op; so which is more important?

KUO That's really outlandish!

FANG There's nothing outlandish about it at all! [He starts to go into the committee office]

KUO Secretary Fang!

FANG [Impatiently halts] Now what's so important?

KUO There's the matter of Ya-nan.

FANG Has the flap about studying tractor driving got someone upset?

KUO I heard that the reason her name was removed was because her outlook and behavior style were poor.

FANG Yes. That was the report of the Youth League Branch organiza-tion. Her outlook and behavior style are poor. Many people have disapproved of her, so out of concern for the bad impression it might make, her name was taken off.

KUO Secretary Fang, what's *your* view on all this?

FANG I think it is a bit excessive.

KUO What's excessive? Is it the report that's excessive, or is it her outlook?

FANG She's a bit too lively.

Kuo How can you be too lively? Furthermore, what evil is there in liveliness? Young people *should* be lively. They should be happy. They should sing and dance, and talk and laugh. Why should we want to go and put restrictions on her kind? All this talk of "you're going overboard here" and "you're going overboard there," or "I do like it this way" and "I don't like it that way," or "this isn't according to the rules," and "that doesn't adhere to principle"—you don't mean to tell me that you want to change all these young kids into doddering, senile little old men and little old ladies? And only then would they be good youth all alike, cut from the same mold?

Fang Ha, ha. You're really being outlandish.

Kuo No I'm not. Socialist youth are just not like that.

Fang You drag such insignificant things into socialism. I tell you, these are trivial things.

Kuo [*Obstinately*] This isn't trivial!

Fang [*With an air of resignation*] Chia-lin, at this time we are engaged in grasping cooperativization and building socialism. Every day I must concern myself with many weighty affairs, with all this huge operation and all this production. You haven't shouldered the load I have to carry so you don't know how heavy it is. [*He walks toward the committee office*]

[*From inside comes* Lei Ta-han*'s voice:* "Take one step out the door and see if I don't break your legs." *The voice of* Ya-hua *crying is heard:* "Break them, go ahead." Ta-han *curses.* "Where are you going?"]

Ya-hua's voice "To find Chief Fang!" [Fang *hears the voices and halts.* Ya-hua *runs on stage, with* Ta-han *in pursuit. A gaggle of men and women follow them on*]

Ya-hua [*Crying*] Chief Fang!

Ta-han You'd better . . .

Fang What? Are you two brawling again?

Ya-hua Chief Fang, he's out of his mind. Last night . . .

Ta-han Last night she ran out. My mother and I looked for her everywhere; and she didn't come back home after work again today.

Ya-hua I got off work a little later today. When dinner wasn't ready he beat me again.

Ta-han You wild bitch! You're getting cheekier and cheekier. [*Goes over and jerks* Ya-hua *away*]

Kuo [*Steps in between*] Ta-han, we don't play rough here.

Fang You two. If you didn't fight for three days, even the kitchen god would get lonely.

Ya-hua Chief Fang, you speak for me.

Ta-han Chief Fang, don't listen to the womenfolk.

Fang An honest official does not meddle in family problems. Everyone can make a case for themselves. Don't anyone say any more. Go home and work well on production. [*He goes into the committee office*]

Ya-hua I'll die before I go home with him.

The Women Right, don't go.

Ta-han Not going home? Looking for a wild young stud?

YA-HUA I'll go to my mother's home.

TA-HAN Returning to your mother's? Good. Don't you ever cross my threshold again for the rest of your life.

[*YA-NAN and* SHIH HSIU-O *enter*]

CH'Ü It's all right, sister Ya-hua, you come home with me.

YA-NAN [*Going up to* YA-HUA] Sister, let's go to our home.

TA-HAN You've come again to fan the flames, I won't put up with it!

YA-NAN She's my big sister.

TA-HAN She is my wife.

[FANG, hauling his bicycle out, rings the bike-bell]

FANG Okay, okay. It's all in the same family, let's get going back.

[K'UNG *enters; sees* PAI T'IEN-SHUI *and* YEH YU-KEN *among the crowd of onlookers*]

K'UNG So you're here!

FANG What? Haven't you gone to the vet's yet?

K'UNG I was looking for the others. [*Pushes* PAI *and* YEH] Go, go!

PAI To do what?

K'UNG To do what? To carry the pig!

FANG Aiya! Get going now!

[K'UNG, PAI, *and* YEH *exit.* FANG *is about to leave*]

YA-NAN Secretary Fang.

[FANG *goes off riding his bike*]

KUO Ta-han, just let her go to her mother's house to live for a few days!

ALL THE YOUTH You go, Ya-hua!

YA-NAN [*Takes the bundle that's in* YA-HUA*'s hand*] Big sister, let's go!

CH'Ü Go quickly. We're here.

TA-HAN [*Angry*] Okay. Get lost. I don't give a damn.

YA-HUA Remember, I'll never take your abuse again. [YA-NAN *and* YA-HUA *go off together*]

TA-HAN Humph. Women have all gotten up on our shoulders now.

CH'Ü [*Comes running back*] Even if you come for her with a bridal sedan chair, she won't go back! [*She runs off*]

TA-HAN She's gone . . . [*Dejectedly, he sits down*]

[*Curtain*]

ACT III

Scene 1

It is late afternoon, a month later. In front of the entrance to YA-NAN*'s home,* YA-NAN *and* YA-HUA *are making straw rope.* YA-NAN *is standing, tying knots in the rope.* YA-HUA *is sitting, braiding it.*

YA-HUA Ya'nan, aren't you tired?

YA-NAN No. The co-op's waiting for this; let's hurry. [*Pause*]

YA-HUA [*Sighs*] Ai.

YA-NAN Big sister!

YA-HUA Ai.

YA-NAN Do you still miss him? [YA-HUA *is silent*] You're really too much. The way he bullies you, haven't you taken enough?

YA-HUA You don't understand. Being a woman is very hard.

YA-NAN I know, I know. I've been pushed around too!

YA-HUA But in your case it's a blessing in disguise. If it's not the way you want it, right away you act . . . Mine is not like that. Since I was little, I was promised to his family as a child bride; good or bad it's been almost fifteen years now.

YA-NAN Yes, you were only eight or nine at that time.

YA-HUA It's been a month since I left this time. Inside me, it feels like I've been stuck up on a hook. [*Embarrassed, she lowers her voice*] I really want to go back to take a look.

YA-NAN Big sister, you're too soft-hearted, just like a rush-stem, one flick and over it goes. Big sister, don't worry so much. Just stay on here for a while longer. If his outlook doesn't change, then just forget about him. We have a co-op here, the women themselves work, and they support themselves. Not like before, when you had to be married off to a guy to keep body and soul together. But nowadays, what's there to be afraid of?

YA-HUA Ya-nan, what you say makes sense. . . . But I wait for him, wait for him. . . .

YA-NAN What if he never changes?

YA-HUA Yes, he will. I know Ta-han. He's just got big ears, and listens to people's lies.

YA-NAN Ah. Big sister, you! You're really too nice. Brother Ta-han should drop dead. . . .

YA-HUA [*Hurriedly covers her mouth*] Don't!

YA-NAN Okay. Okay. I won't curse at him. If I do, you'll feel hurt again. But does he feel any hurt like you?

YA-HUA Sometimes . . . he hurts too.

[*The two can't help laughing.* YA-HUA *straightens out the rope and* YA-NAN *gathers it up*]

YA-HUA Let me ask you something—have you and Pi-hao really broken up?

YA-NAN Why do you ask?

YA-HUA Is there still a chance that you two. . . . ?

YA-NAN [*Shakes her head*] No chance.

YA-HUA Let me give you some advice: Don't be so inflexible. Everyone should show a little consideration and make the best of things . . .

YA-NAN Sis. You don't know. I've seen through him. I can't spend a lifetime with him. I look at you two like you are now, and then I think about myself. . . . I'm just afraid that . . . [*Picks up the rope*] That's good. Give it to me. I'll take it over to the supply custodian. [*She coils up the rope and exits*]

[YA-HUA *sighs, takes a pair of men's shoes out of her bosom and works on them.* AUNT MA *enters, looking around furtively, hiding and peeping*]

AUNT MA Oh! Sister Ta-han, you're here alone?

YA-NAN Aunt Ma, please—take a load off your feet.

AUNT MA Sister Ta-han, who are you making those for? [YA-HUA *starts to hide the shoes.* AUNT MA *snatches them in a flash*] Sister Ta-han, are you making them for Ta-han? [*Holds them up for inspection*] Sure enough, Sister Ta-han, you're really skillful. [*Sighs with admiration*] Tsk, tsk, tsk. You really can make the needle and thread fly; you're so good with your hands, embroidering phoenixes and things, a very capable daughter-in-law.

YA-HUA [*Embarrassed, takes back the shoes*] I'm actually awkward and clumsy. When have I ever done excellent needlework? It's just something to do with my hands when I'm not busy.

AUNT MA Sister Ta-han, you're really a good daughter-in-law. If you weren't married, old Auntie here would wear these old legs out to make sure you got just the groom you like.

YA-HUA [*Impatiently*] Auntie Ma, don't make fun of me. Sit for awhile; I've got to cook dinner. [*She's about to go inside*]

AUNT MA [*Frantically stops her*] Why so busy? Sister Ta-han, I'm asking you a straightforward question: why haven't you gone back home? A woman who's left home and gotten married, always staying at her parents' home, neither fish nor fowl—what sense does that make?

YA-HUA Auntie Ma, be quiet. In the past, Ta-han bullied me enough. Here at my own home I have my own work and my own life. I'm not bothered by anyone else's affairs, and I can do whatever I like.

AUNT MA Yo, yo! The old saying goes: The rabbit runs along the hill, but it still comes back to its old warren. You never can spend a whole lifetime in someone else's house. Sister Ta-han, husband and wife can't bear an overnight grudge. When the teeth bite the tongue, when the couple scream and fight, that's very natural—how can you take it seriously? Okay now, get your things together, and I'll take you back!

YA-HUA [*Starts to move, then stops*] Auntie Ma . . . no, I'm not going.

AUNT MA Don't put on an act. Do you take me for an old fool? Who are you making the shoes for? [YA-HUA *can't speak*] Do you think I can't read your mind? Where is there a woman who doesn't follow her husband no matter what? Marry a chicken, follow a chicken. Marry a dog—

YA-HUA [*Can't endure this*] Auntie Ma! [MA *stops talking and gapes at her*] They're not for him.

AUNT MA Then for who? [*With a flash of recognition*] Now I understand.

YA-HUA It doesn't matter whether you understand or not. Now, please excuse me. [*Goes inside*]

AUNT MA [*Spits angrily*] Tsk! So you're getting uppity too.

[AUNT LEI *enters stealthily on tiptoe*]

AUNT LEI Old Sister! How did it go?

AUNT MA No good, old sister.

AUNT LEI What's wrong?

AUNT MA It's hard for me to tell you. Come . . . [*Whispers in* LEI'*s ear*]

AUNT LEI [*Gives a start*] Really? It's really like this?

AUNT MA It can't be otherwise. I saw it with my own eyes and heard it with my own ears. Sister, do I look like an old tongue-wagger?

AUNT LEI [*Angrily*] Humph! I had kind of expected this. That slut is all puffed up now.

AUNT MA Yes, Sister, the ways of the world have really changed. These days I've worn out two pairs of shoes and when I mention your family, those bitches act like they were bitten by a ghost. They stop up their ears, pick up their feet and run. And their parents who should take responsibility for them just leave it up to those girls and won't take charge of the situation. The way things are today, this is hard to handle. I'd just as soon return that length of cotton you gave me.

AUNT LEI [*Downcast*] Ah, if it wasn't that things are difficult to manage now, I would have told Ta-han long ago to divorce her. Would I have asked you to go to so much trouble to beg her to come back? I'll tell you frankly, with Ya-hua gone we're short on manpower and our family has lost half its work points! And now that we have an advanced cooperative, you can't take a profit from your own share of the land. You just have to rely on sheer work effort. Look at what a fix that puts me in!

AUNT MA Yes, with this new marriage law and the collective system women have two magic weapons; so now they stand up straight, and act rude. They have plenty of nerve, and they've got no shame.

LEI and MA [*Simultaneously*] Ai!

[*The two exit dejectedly.* K'UNG YÜ-CH'ENG *and* WANG PI-HAO *enter*]

WANG I don't know if she's at home or not.

K'UNG Let's go in and look!

WANG I won't go.

K'UNG Why? Lost your nerve? Let's go. I'm here!

WANG Yü-ch'eng, if things go poorly, just jump in quickly.

K'UNG I know. Relax. I don't believe it! She's nothing more than a little girl and you can't keep her under control. Well, if she doesn't listen this time, then . . . heh, heh. [*Takes out a diary and slaps it in his palm*]

WANG And what if she goes looking for Secretary Fang?

K'UNG Do you think Secretary Fang is going to listen to me or to her? [*They laugh self-confidently*]

WANG Good, Yü-ch'eng. If she promises to go ahead with the marriage, then we'll leave it at that. But if she doesn't, then we'll get tough with her.

K'UNG It'll be a disaster if we don't get her under control. You didn't see it, but she was terrible the last time she presented her opinions to me. I told her to write up a self-criticism but as of now she still hasn't written it. It's imperative that we strengthen her sense of League organization. Let's go!

[*They are about to go in when* T'UNG YA-HUA *emerges in the doorway*]

YA-HUA Ah, League Branch Secretary, Pi-hao, come in and sit down!

WANG Is Ya-nan at home?

YA-HUA No. She just went out to deliver some rope.

WANG Ah-ha! [*They exit*]

[YA-HUA *looks after the two of them doubtfully then goes back inside.* LEI TA-HAN, *carrying a small sack, enters timidly. Seeing that nobody is around, he starts to go in, then hesitates outside the door.* SHIH HSIU-O, LI CHIN-FANG, CH'Ü HSIAO-TI, *and* HUANG CHÜ-YING *enter, each with a bundle of straw rope. Spotting* TA-HAN, *they wink knowingly at each other and pretend not to see him. When* TA-HAN *detects them he quickly hides*]

SHIH Hey! Did you see that?

LI See what?

SHIH The rough and tough hero who beats his wife. [*Everyone laughs*]

CH'Ü Ts'e! That guy. Whoever marries him has run out of luck.

HUANG Yeah, Ya-hua was always such a sweet person, and now she's a nice flower stuck in a dung-heap.

SHIH Of course she's not! Haven't you heard what they're saying: there are so many girls in the co-op that you can get a string of them with your eyes closed.

LI Oh, I get it, a string of tears. [*Giggles*]

[*All the women roar*]

SHIH And did you hear? "Go-Between Ma" is still working as a match-maker for him!

CH'Ü Damn it, grab Ta-han and we women will hold a struggle meeting against him.

LI Relax. No one's fool enough to get taken in by him.

SHIH Huh. I wouldn't be too sure about that.

THE GIRLS Why?

SHIH He's grown up into quite a strapping fellow.

HUANG . . . so he eats a lot.

CH'Ü . . . and loves to fight.

LI . . . and is willing to listen to matchmakers.

SHIH No wonder "Go-Between Ma" guaranteed to do the job for him.

THE GIRLS What job?

SHIH Find him a girl who's young and pretty and not a day over eighty!

[*Everyone roars.* LEI TA-HAN *can neither listen nor ignore this; he can neither go nor stay. The others thread their way by the front gate of Ya-nan's house as they exit. He comes out. Dumbstruck, he stands there, then, after a pause, walks to the doorway. Quietly and timidly he calls out: "Ya-hua, Ya-hua!"* YA-HUA *comes out; when she sees* TA-HAN, *she is disconcerted, but lingers uncertainly. There is a pause*]

TA-HAN Ya-hua!

YA-HUA Why have you come?

TA-HAN [*Speaks haltingly*] I came to see you . . . to see you.

YA-HUA [*Hiding her emotion*] I'm not sick and I haven't died, so there's no need for you to come visit me.

TA-HAN I was afraid you didn't have enough food. So I hauled over a little for you. [*Gives the small sack to* T'UNG YA-HUA]

YA-HUA [*She's touched and wants to accept it, but changes her mind,*

*afraid that the idea was his mother's, in order to trick her into going
back*] No. Take it back. I have food.

TA-HAN Ya-hua, take it. If I carry it back with me, my mother will
see it.

[*Now realizing it was his own idea, she accepts the sack. He turns and
starts to go*]

YA-HUA Ta-han!

TA-HAN Uh?

YA-HUA Wait! [*Hurries into the house, and brings out a pair of cotton
shoes*]

YA-HUA Ta-han, look at your shoes. They're separated from the soles.
How can you work in them? [*Holds out the new shoes*] Take them.
You! You've been hard on shoes since you were little. [*He is moved; for
a moment he can't speak*]

TA-HAN [*In a low voice*] You made . . . you made them for me?

YA-HUA You don't like them?

TA-HAN [*At ease and happy*] Uh! Yes. I do! [*Accepts the shoes*] Just
now Auntie Ma and my mother were saying that you and someone else
were . . .

YA-HUA I did that to provoke them.

TA-HAN Oh, provoking them. [*His courage suddenly increases*] Ya-hua,
let's you and I go home. [YA-HUA *doesn't answer*] Let's go home,
Ya-hua. A man without a wife is a family without a homemaker. Since
you left I felt so empty, like there's nothing left. And the house is like
some deserted mountain temple. I can't get through another day like
this. I just can't make it. . . .

YA-HUA [*Sobs brokenheartedly*] Who told you to be so mean?

TA-HAN I've been a brute, Ya-hua. Give me a whack. Whack me! [*Takes
off his shoes and gives them to* YA-HUA]

YA-HUA [*Picks up the worn-out shoes, but then casts them at his feet.
She's both loving and angry*] I hate you! Put them on now!

TA-HAN Go ahead, hate me. I hate myself too. When I gave you a bad time
I gave myself a bad time also.

YA-HUA Ta-han—

TA-HAN Ya-hua . . . from now on, if I so much as curse you once—my
tongue will rot. If I once lay a finger on you—break my finger. You
can do whatever makes you happy. If you don't believe me, I'll write
you out a pledge.

YA-HUA Who wants your pledge?

TA-HAN Ya-hua, rest assured, I'll never listen to their talk. I've wised up.
You act properly. It was only just this minute that I learned that my
mother got "Go-Between Ma" to act as matchmaker behind my back.

YA-HUA What? Making matches?

TA-HAN [*Frankly*] Nothing came of it. There was no girl who was
willing to marry me.

YA-HUA [*Relieved*] Ah!

TA-HAN Let's go, Ya-hua.

YA-HUA Okay. Wait a minute; I'll get my things. [*She goes inside.* YA-NAN *arrives*]

TA-HAN Ya-nan!

YA-NAN So you've come.

TA-HAN Ya-hua has agreed to go home with me.

YA-NAN Go home?

TA-HAN Yes, ah, I—

[YA-HUA, *carrying her bundle, comes out*]

YA-HUA Ya-nan, I'm going home.

YA-NAN Sister!

TA-HAN Ya-nan . . . I . . . I am not forcing her.

YA-HUA We've been reunited.

YA-NAN Good. Brother Ta-han, you must be good to my sister. Don't be blind to your conscience. You don't know how wonderful she is.

TA-HAN I know. I know. In the past, the windows to my brain were smeared with pork fat, my eyes were plugged with cheesy dregs of bean curd—

YA-HUA Yech. Come on, let's go.

TA-HAN Right. [*Sticks out his hand*] Give me the bundle. [*He grabs* YA-HUA's *bundle*]

YA-NAN [*See the small sack*] What is this?

TA-HAN The food that I brought. Keep it, Ya-nan.

YA-HUA Yes, keep it.

YA-NAN No. You take it home with you. [YA-NAN *gives the sack to* TA-HAN]

TA-HAN Ya-nan, when I get home I'll write up a pledge.

YA-HUA [*Urging him*] Let's go!

[TA-HAN *and* YA-HUA *go off blissfully.* YA-NAN *gazes after them and, feeling relieved herself, starts humming a tune.* K'UNG YÜ-CH'ENG *and* WANG PI-HAO *enter*]

K'UNG Ya-nan, you're back!

YA-NAN Secretary K'ung. What is it?

K'UNG Pi-hao wants to talk to you.

YA-NAN Talk?

K'UNG You two talk. I've got some other things to do. I'll be back in a while. [*He exits. Silence*]

YA-NAN What do you want to talk about, Comrade Wang Pi-hao?

WANG About us. I've got another idea.

YA-NAN Us? We've already settled the whole thing. What sort of idea have you got?

WANG Now listen to me: As for what's taken place, you were a little in the wrong and I was a little in the wrong. Neither was the fundamental problem.

YA-NAN I don't quite understand.

WANG In the past, your outlook and behavior style were poor; that was your shortcoming. And I criticized you too harshly: that was my shortcoming.

YA-NAN If you put it that way, it sounds as though you were in the right—

WANG No. It must certainly be considered a shortcoming. Your outlook and behavior style have changed now. From morning to night, you're serious and behave properly. Even K'ung has commended you.

YA-NAN You've made a mistake if that's what you think.

WANG No. We're quite correct.

YA-NAN No. You're quite incorrect. You criticized incorrectly, and now you've commended incorrectly. I don't accept it.

WANG Ai. You're some comrade. You won't accept criticism, and you won't accept praise. All right. We'll do away with both praise and criticism.

YA-NAN Comrade Wang Pi-hao, what are you driving at? What is it you want to talk to me about?

WANG Listen: You've made progress. The Youth League authorities are very happy, and I am too. Lately, I've been thinking it over a lot. It's not worth getting so riled up over such an insignificant matter. We two can still restore our relationship, can't we?

YA-NAN No. We aren't all riled up and this is no insignificant matter. When I think of your five conditions, I'm disgusted. You—

WANG So I have shortcomings.

YA-NAN You are too selfish!

WANG What? I, I, I—I truly love you.

YA-NAN No. It isn't me you love. *It's yourself!*

WANG [*Jolted*] Myself? [*Silence*] Okay. If you promise to restore our relationship I'll eliminate two conditions! No—three conditions!

YA-NAN It's not just eliminating three conditions—you're going to have to abolish that obnoxious outlook of yours, as well.

WANG Ya-nan, don't be too sharp with me. As for things like obnoxiousness and selfishness on my part, isn't your outlook selfish? Isn't your behavior style obnoxious?

YA-NAN If it bothers you so much, then ignore me.

WANG Humph. Don't lift your tail too high. There's no advantage to be gained by it.

YA-NAN There's no advantage in my going along with you either!

WANG I'll put it to you straight: You've got to go out with me. That's the view of the Youth League authorities.

YA-NAN The Youth League authorities?

WANG Yes. Branch Secretary K'ung's view.

YA-NAN The Youth League Branch Secretary can't force arranged marriages.

WANG All right. You dare—

[YA-NAN, *extremely angry, starts to go in.* K'UNG *enters hurriedly*]

K'UNG Ya-nan! [YA-NAN *stops*] All right, what's wrong, you two? [*There's a standoff*] Ya-nan, don't get mad! Come over here, I want to have a word with you.

YA-NAN Speak, Branch Secretary.

K'UNG Young people are apt to lose their tempers. Why don't you just have a good talk?

YA-NAN We've got nothing to talk about!

WANG I eliminated my criticism of her, and I even eliminated my praise for her and abolished my contract. But in spite of all that the more we talk the more smart-mouthed she gets.

K'UNG Ya-nan, if a Youth League member wants to progress, then she must get in step with the organization.

YA-NAN Hm. I am listening.

K'UNG Good. That's more like it. Pi-hao wants to restore the relationship with you. Have you thought it over?

YA-NAN There's nothing to think over!

K'UNG You'd better give it some real good thought. Pi-hao is a good comrade. His work is good. His outlook is good. And his behavior style is good. His every aspect is very good; why won't you go out with him?

YA-NAN He— I don't wish to.

K'UNG You got along very well with him in the past. Why can't you two be reconciled?

YA-NAN If I had wanted to keep our relationship, then I never would have broken it off. But since it's been broken off, there can't be a reconciliation.

K'UNG Ya-nan, don't be flippant about the Marriage Law and just break up whenever you feel like it. It's simply a bourgeois notion that one word can pull down a whole relationship.

YA-NAN What kind of bourgeois notion is this?

K'UNG Humph. You still want to be evasive . . . [*Takes out a diary*] Look. Do you know what this is?

YA-NAN No, I don't.

WANG This is a diary that was discovered in Shen Hsiao-chia's home.

K'UNG Listen to this: "It was only today that I learned that she and Wang were going together. In the evening, alone, I wept . . ."

YA-NAN Hsiao-chia. He—

WANG Yü-ch'eng, it isn't in this section.

K'UNG Ah. Ah. [*Turns to another page*] " . . . tomorrow I must go. As long as she's happy, I'll willingly stand aside. . . ."

WANG This is sheer jealousy.

K'UNG Yes. Jealousy. And there's more. "She sings very well, even better than the cuckoo . . ."

WANG Skip that!

K'UNG Isn't this proof? Huh?

[YA-NAN *wants to take the diary and look at it, but* K'UNG *draws his hand back*]

WANG What have you got to say to all this?

K'UNG So tell me. You're very fond of him, arent' you? [*Silence*]

WANG Speak! [*Silence*]

YA-NAN Yes. Very fond.

K'UNG *and* WANG [*Simultaneously*] What?

YA-NAN I can see it all clearly now. He's better than you, stronger than you, and I love him. You two get out.

[K'UNG *and* WANG *are dumbstruck*]

K'UNG Ya-nan, be sensible. If you and Wang go together, it will be good for your work; good for your future; good for the masses' impression of you.

YA-NAN My work, my future . . .

WANG . . . and so on, in every aspect. [*Pause*]

YA-NAN Youth League Branch Secretary, what's your intent in saying this? If I'm good to him then I'll have a future. If I'm not, then there's no future. What do you call this?

K'UNG It's for your own good!

YA-NAN No. I won't take my personal happiness and exchange it for your kind of "future." I won't; I won't.

WANG Ya-nan. Don't be stubborn.

K'UNG I'm not afraid of your being stubborn. If you're thinking of going out with Shen, it won't work. The Youth League authorities won't approve it.

YA-NAN I will. If I want to love, I'll love no matter what. It's no one's business.

WANG Ya-nan, don't speak angry words!

K'UNG Ya-nan, if you persist in your erroneous ways, I'll have to take away your Youth League membership!

[YA-NAN *jolted, stops*]

WANG Recant your errors, quickly.

YA-NAN No. I'm not in the wrong.

K'UNG Okay. I'm going to convene a Youth League branch assembly right now!

YA-NAN Go ahead. Go ahead. I'm not afraid!

[K'UNG *and* WANG *exit rapidly*]

YA-NAN Shen Hsiao-chia . . .

[*Curtain*]

Scene 2

KUO CHIA-LIN's *living room, that same night. Outside, the north wind is blowing. Snowflakes whirl in the wind; it's a big spring snowstorm. To the left is a bedroom; on the right is a kitchen. Hanging on the walls are pictures of Chairman Mao and Vice-Chairman Chu Teh, and in a picture frame is a certificate.* KUO CHIA-LIN *and* SHIH HSIU-O *are studying characters by the light of a kerosene lamp.*

SHIH Chia-lin, what is this word? I forgot again!

KUO Stick out your hand.

SHIH Why?

Kuo I'll tell you.

Shih [*Wondering whether she should or not*] All right, here!

[Kuo *gives her hand a slap*]

Shih [*With feigned anger*] Why did you hit me?

Kuo Do you know it now?

Shih Know what? Tell me quickly how to read this character.

Kuo Didn't I tell you already!

Shih [*Suddenly realizing*] Ahh, I know. "Hit," "hit," "hit." The word for "hit."

Kuo [*Shakes his head*] When I hit your hand, how did you feel?

Shih I felt that a person who hits his wife is too detestable. Yes, the word for "detestable."

Kuo [*Bursts out laughing*] You're really intelligent. I'll tell you: it's the word for "hurt." If I hit you, it hurts, doesn't it? If you don't believe me, then stick out your hand again.

Shih [*She wants to hit* Kuo] You're bad, so bad.

Kuo [*With mock pomposity*] Be a little more serious. A woman mustn't be "too excessively lively"! Ha! And she'll soon be the mother of my kids!

[*Both laugh in mutual understanding. The door opens and a blast of cold wind blows in.* YA-NAN, *snow-covered, dirty, and dishevelled, enters. Weak and exhausted, she leans against the door. The other two are astonished*]

Shih *and* Kuo Ya-nan!

[Shih *supports* YA-NAN *and leads her in.* Kuo *closes the door*]

Shih Ya-nan. What's wrong?

Kuo What's the trouble?

[*Suddenly* YA-NAN *embraces* Shih *and sobs*]

Shih Ya-nan, Ya-nan.

Kuo What's the matter?

YA-NAN [*Wiping her eyes*] My Youth League membership . . . has been revoked . . .

Shih *and Kuo* [*Simultaneously*] What?

YA-NAN Just now at the Youth League branch assembly.

Kuo An assembly? I didn't even know about it.

YA-NAN A lot of Youth League members didn't attend. K'ung just declared the meeting open. At the start of the meeting, a few got up to oppose it. They were all attacked by K'ung. And when I got up to appeal the grounds for their case, he told me I was persisting in error and wouldn't permit me to speak!

Kuo This is really outrageous!

YA-NAN Wang wants me to acknowledge my errors. I won't. I argued with them, then K'ung got furious. . . .

Kuo I don't understand a thing. Just exactly what is going on?

Shih Be quiet. Listen to her.

Kuo What was the reason? How was it pushed through?

YA-NAN K'ung said I made five big mistakes. He says I am seriously infected with bourgeois thought, have a serious lack of party discipline and spirit, have a seriously dissolute behavior style, a serious inclination to defiance, and seriously instigated discord between husband and wife.

KUO All this is nonsense! Nonsense!

SHIH Chia-lin, calm down!

YA-NAN Brother Chia-lin, you're a Party member; once and for all, do you think I have any errors? Why do they want to attack me like this? Why doesn't Secretary Fang even interfere? [*Pause*]

KUO These jerks, I'll . . . get them! [*Starts for the door*]

SHIH Chia-lin, where are you going?

KUO To find Secretary Fang!

YA-NAN I'm going with you.

KUO No. Rest a bit. I'll find him and bring him here. [*Exits*]

YA-NAN There's heavy wind and snow outside.

SHIH Let him do as he pleases. He's never given up acting like a soldier.

YA-NAN Hsiu-o!

SHIH Don't worry, Ya-nan, lie down for a bit. I'll cook up a bowl of ginger broth for you to get rid of your chill.

YA-NAN You mustn't, Hsiu-o. Let me ask you, doesn't a woman in our new society have the right to pick her own happiness?

SHIH You do. Of course you do. [*Pause*]

YA-NAN Hsiu-o, are you and Chia-lin happy?

SHIH We're happy. Ya-nan, why do you ask that?

YA-NAN I'm trying to understand a problem, Hsiu-o. Is happiness something that you choose yourself?

SHIH That's difficult. A long time ago, my Ma arranged a marriage for me. She gave me to a bad egg. He would only eat, drink, and gamble. Then I went with him to the court and broke off the marriage.

YA-NAN Then no one stood in your way? How did you happen to get together with Brother Chia-lin?

SHIH It wasn't all that easy! My mother despised Chia-lin for being a cripple. She said he was half-dead and refused to agree to the marriage. And then other people urged me, too, saying I was such a sweet girl, why pick a one-armed cripple? I still wouldn't listen.

YA-NAN Yes, so your happiness was of your own choice, Hsiu-o. I want to choose my happiness. But why do they want to interfere with me, to attack me?

SHIH Ya-nan, this will pass. You will be happy. You will. . . . Hsiao-chia is a fine young man. He really and truly loves you.

YA-NAN Hsiao-chia . . . Hsiu-o?

SHIH Now you know! Don't be bashful, go and get him. When I got Chia-lin, I wasn't thin-skinned at all. Would you believe he was not willing to take the vows with me? He said I was taking pity on his being crippled, and that it wasn't love. But I latched onto him and wouldn't let go. In the end I brought him around, and how! Now when I think of it, I get so embarrassed my ears turn red. [*The two laugh*]

YA-NAN Why hasn't Secretary Fang come yet? [*There's a knock on the door*]

SHIH Come in. [SHIH *opens the door.* T'UNG YA-HUA *and* LEI TA-HAN *enter*]

YA-HUA Ya-nan.

YA-NAN Sister.

YA-HUA So you're here, after all. We almost died looking for you.

TA-HAN My god. We knocked on every door in the village looking for you, like police on residence check.[10]

YA-NAN Why did you come?

YA-HUA We know you've had some trouble—

YA-NAN Sister—it's not important. Chia-lin has gone to find Secretary Fang.

YA-HUA Will he get involved in this type of thing?

YA-NAN He'll concern himself with it. If he doesn't there's always someone who will.

YA-HUA Ya-nan, we must have patience. Don't argue with cadres. It's all because you're always so headstrong that you've offended the cadres and provoked this whole fight.

YA-NAN No. It's not like that. Sister, since you've always given way to other people, why did Ta-han still bully you?

TA-HAN Oh, why pull at an old scab now? Let's go. Let's go!

YA-HUA Okay. Ya-nan, come with me. Look at you, you're soaking wet, you'll catch cold.

YA-NAN No. I want to wait for Secretary Fang.

YA-HUA So, I'll go back and fetch you a clean, dry change of clothes.

TA-HAN Let me go!

YA-HUA You big lug, you're so rough and heavy-handed; what can you do? I'll go and bring back something for you to eat.

TA-HAN All right. I'll go with you. [TA-HAN *and* YA-HUA *exit.* SHIH *closes the door and laughs*]

YA-NAN I'm afraid Secretary Fang won't come. [*There is a knock on the door*]

SHIH Come in! [FANG PAO-SHAN *and* KUO CHIA-LIN *enter.* FANG *has a waterproof cloth over his head*]

SHIH Secretary Fang.

KUO We're here. We're here.

FANG Chia-lin, where have you brought me?

YA-NAN Secretary Fang.

FANG Where's the ox?

SHIH What ox?

FANG Didn't you say there was a sick ox in the co-op who was about to die?

KUO Pao-shan, I really wanted to invite you to my home, but I was afraid you would not be willing to grace us with your presence, so I made up this fib.

SHIH Oh. [*She can't suppress a laugh and goes into the kitchen*]

FANG In the dead of a windy and snowy night, you pull me out from under my quilt. Are you going crazy or what?

KUO No, I haven't had a breakdown. I invited you to come because there is an urgent matter—

YA-NAN Secretary Fang, will you look into—

FANG Look into what? Once and for all, is it a pig problem, or an ox problem?

KUO It's a people problem.

FANG Whose?

KUO Ya-nan's.

FANG Her? Oh, we'll talk about it another day. [*He starts to leave*]

YA-NAN Secretary Fang. When someone has suffered this much, are you really going to ignore it?

FANG I don't care whether there's suffering or not. When girls and guys fall in love, there's always a little suffering. I've got too many things on my mind. I'm the director of this co-op, and the Party Branch Secretary at the same time. I go from dawn until dusk—my principal business is never finished. Where do I have the free time to concern myself with your babbling? [*He starts to leave again*]

KUO Secretary Fang, then a person is not as good as a pig, or an ox.

FANG What are you talking about?

YA-NAN Secretary Fang, you mean to tell me you'll only concern yourself with everyone's socialism, but not with my socialism?

FANG Your socialism? What socialism have you got?

YA-NAN My happiness!

FANG Happiness? Everyone is included in the co-op system. If anyone is still unhappy, don't worry, happy days are coming.

YA-NAN Secretary Fang, if a person has been falsely accused, is the Party concerned?

FANG What false accusation? What have you been falsely accused of?

YA-NAN My membership was revoked at the Youth League branch assembly.

FANG What? Who did this?

YA-NAN K'ung Yü-ch'eng.

FANG Really and truly?

KUO Falsely.

FANG That's going too far! I didn't know a thing about it!

KUO You only know about pigs and oxen.

FANG Ai. Okay. I am concerned about pigs and oxen. But it isn't because I personally like pigs' hooves or cows' tails. Don't I do it for the sake of everyone? Ya-nan, why did they expel you? Isn't it because you have shortcomings? For example, this outlook and behavior style of yours, isn't it too . . .

KUO A little too lively.

FANG Eh, for example, you casually broke off with Wang.

YA-NAN Do you know why we broke off?

FANG This . . . I still don't understand this too well.

YA-NAN First of all, in the beginning Wang harbored doubts about me, so he restricted me. I put up with it all. Later, he proposed his "Five-Condition Contract" thinking I wanted to live a life that's not even as good as my sister's, but I'm determined not to do that!

FANG Is that really what it's all about? But I heard that it was because of Shen Hsiao-chia.

YA-NAN That's all something that Wang thought up himself. But what I want to ask is, you originally chose me and Shen Hsiao-chia to go study tractor driving. Why did you later take my name off the list?

FANG Uh, that was what I agreed to. They told me . . .

YA-NAN They told you my outlook and behavior style were poor. Once and for all where is it poor?

FANG On this . . . I'm not at all sure.

YA-NAN Actually, it is Wang Pi-hao's pettiness. He's afraid I'll go off with Shen. That's not to his advantage so he thought of a way to deceive you. If you took my name off the list, then I'd have to stay at home and marry him.

FANG Marry him? I didn't know about this.

KUO You know very little about what happens to people.

FANG Now don't go on shooting sarcastic slugs behind my back, okay? I'm investigating and researching the matter, aren't I?

KUO Okay. Okay. I'll cease fire. Ya-nan, you tell him.

YA-NAN I was sweethearts with Wang in the beginning. I didn't know that Hsiao-chia liked me and Hsiao-chia didn't know that I was going with Wang Pi-hao.

FANG This is getting very complicated!

YA-NAN They read Hsiao-chia's diary to me today. Now I know how much character he has and how sincere his feelings are for me. But they insisted that I was going with Hsiao-chia earlier. Then they forced me to end my relationship with him, and only then did I clearly see what they were really up to.

FANG Where did Hsiao-chia's diary come from?

YA-NAN They took it from his home.

FANG They actually did that?

KUO This is cheap. [*Pause. In the next instant* SHIH HSIU-O *brings in hot soup*]

SHIH Drink some hot soup. Warm yourself up.

[FANG *is deep in thought and not conscious of the activity around him*]

SHIH Ya-nan is a good girl. Better drink it while it's hot. And she's a good Youth League member. Don't let it get cold . . .

FANG That's absurd.

SHIH [*Thinks that he's referring to her*] What? Absurd?

FANG Oh. I didn't mean you.

KUO Oh, you. Comrade-brother, trained personnel are the precious gems that build socialism. You just watch over the manure collecting, and when a pregnant woman miscarries from fatigue, you ignore it; when the co-op members get schistosomiasis, you don't care; when Ya-hua gets treated like dirt, you don't see. But when a pig gets sick, or when an ox suffers from the cold, then you get so worked up about it, you can't see straight.

FANG I really am a little "out of it," Ya-nan, so why did you want to break up the married life of Ta-han and Ya-hua?

YA-NAN I broke up their married life?

[LEI TA-HAN *and* T'UNG YA-HUA *enter, obviously on affectionate terms*]

YA-HUA Ya-nan, we've come to get you!

TA-HAN [*Simultaneously*] Let's go home!

FANG [*Surprised*] You two!

TA-HAN *and* YA-HUA [*Simultaneously*] Director Fang, we're back together!

TA-HAN Fortunately Ya-nan helped me to—

YA-HUA [*Embarrassed*] Ta-han, don't—

FANG [*Surprised*] Helped you—

TA-HAN Director Fang, from now on, if I curse her just once, cut my tongue out. If I lay a finger on her, cut if off. She can have whatever makes her happy. If you don't believe me, I'll write up a pledge for you!

KUO This is really too much!

FANG It is really too much. [*Looks out the window*] Has the snow stopped?

TA-HAN It looks like it has.

FANG [*Shakes* KUO CHIA-LIN*'s hand and is about to go*] I thank you, Chia-lin.

KUO Why? We haven't talked about our real business yet!

FANG What real business?

KUO The business about the ox.

FANG Old man, you're a tough one. [*To* YA-NAN] Take heart, Ya-nan. The Party will take care of your problem.

[*Curtain*]

ACT IV (SUMMARY)

The fourth and final act is set during the wheat harvest. Shen Hsiao-chia returns from his tractor course to find T'ung Ya-nan waiting for him, now vindicated and promoted to youth team leader. The thoughts of other young people, too, have turned to love. Although "Go-Between Ma" still holds her strict views, Aunt Lei has come to accept the freer life of the young. While Wang Pi-hao and K'ung Yü-ch'eng engage in mutual recriminations over the failure of their schemes, the cooperative as a whole turns with renewed strength to the tasks of production.

Notes

1. River mud (*ho-ni*) is the rich, fertile soil from the river bed which is being hauled and spread over the white clay soil mentioned in the song above by the peasants.

2. Traditional admiration for legendary women warriors made the phrase "women generals" a positive reference to the newly liberated, assertive woman envisioned by socialist policy. "Ridden out" in the Chinese phrase includes the notion "on horseback," a suitable reference to women warriors, but not to the actual circumstances of many peasant villages of the 1950s which had no horses.

3. A *chin* or catty is a weight measure fixed at 1-1/3 lb. avoirdupois.

4. "Throwing the embroidered ball" (*p'ao hsiu-ch'iu*) was a method by which a girl indicated her choice for a mate.

5. The yellow thorn tree (*huang-ching*), *Vitex negundo*, is known as the chaste tree.

6. The full title is "Marriage Law of the People's Republic of China." As passed in 1950, this law prohibits bigamy and concubinage, imposes voluntary marriage on both sides, equal status of spouses, divorce by mutual consent, and no payments for marriages.

7. "The Forty Articles on Agriculture" (*Nung-yeh ssu-shih t'iao*) comprised a twelve-year plan for agricultural development instigated by Mao Tse-tung in a speech in January 1956.

8. "The 1,000 Catty Mou" (*Ch'ien chin mou*) slogan for production put forth in 1957 called for an output of 500 kilos of grain from every *mou* (one-sixth acre) of land.

9. Schistosomiasis is a debilitating disease transmitted through the skin of man by parasites of water-dwelling snails. The peasants of China call the disease "big belly," as it results in distension of the abdomen, as well as emaciation, listlessness, and, if not treated, death.

10. Residence checks are made by security bureau personnel normally in searches for subversives.

T'ien Han

Kuan Han-ch'ing

Translated by the Foreign Languages Press, Peking

Cast of Characters*

MISTRESS LIU, proprietress of a tavern
ERH-NIU, her daughter
KUAN HAN-CH'ING, a physician and prominent playwright during the Yuan dynasty
HSIEH HSIAO-SHAN, an artist and authority on folk songs of the Kin dynasty
CH'IEN SHUA-CH'IAO, an actor
YOUNG LORD, Akham's 25th son
HENCHMAN
CHU LIEN-HSIU, a famous entertainer and actress
HSIANG KUEI, her maidservant
YEN SHAN-HSIU, Chu Lien-hsiu's pupil
MA ERH, Yen Shan-hsiu's husband
SAI LIEN-HSIU, another of Chu Lien-hsiu's pupils
ENTERTAINMENT HOUSE GUARDIAN
KUAN CHUNG, Kuan Han-ch'ing's old servant
YÜ MEI, the "Flute King"
WANG HO-CH'ING, Kuan Han-ch'ing's old friend
SUPERINTENDENT HO, superintendent of the Yu-hsien-lou Playhouse
BODYGUARD
PLAYHOUSE ATTENDANTS
WANG CHU, Military Commander of Yitu
HO CHEN, Akham's henchman
YEH HO-FU, a black sheep in theatrical circles
HORIKHOSON, a high minister, later Prime Minister
AKHAM, Deputy Prime Minister, Kublai Khan's favorite
WARDEN, GAOLER, WOMAN GAOLER, PRISON GUARDS
FIRST INMATE (LIU CH'ANG-SHENG)

---

*Scenes 3, 5, 9, and 11 have been omitted. Characters appearing only in these deleted scenes are not listed here.—EMG

YOUNG PEASANT
PEASANT CHOU
PEASANT LIU
YANG HSIEN-CHIH, nicknamed "Patchman Yang," a great dramatist
LIANG CHIN-CHIH, a composer and physician
WANG SHIH-FU, another great dramatist
LI WU and WANG NENG, deportation escorts

Setting

The capital city of Cambaluc (present-day Peking), during the reign of Kublai Kahn, in the year A.D. 1281.

SCENE 1

A small tavern on the corner of a street close to the city gate. The street is filled by a great multitude of people watching the procession of an execution squad. Amid a flourish of trumpets, a Mongolian execution supervisor gallops past. Next come attendants beating bamboo clappers and shouting: "Pedestrians, make way, make way!"

Then, to the booming of cracked gongs and drums, the executioner marches along, knife in hand, a long feather in his hat, escorting a mule cart in which a woman convict is seated, with her hair dishevelled, her head drooping, and on her back a tablet bearing her death sentence. An old woman follows closely behind the cart, crying frantically: "My child, my child! Heavens, spare my child! Don't let them do this!" The attendants, no less fiendish in their attitude than wolves and tigers, keep snarling at her, "Go away, you old hag! D'you want to have your head cut off too?"

MISTRESS LIU, proprietress of the small tavern, stands waiting, holding a bamboo basket containing some wine, meat, and sacrificial paper money. Apparently she intends to intercept the procession by elbowing her way through the crowd, but, finding this impossible, she retraces her steps, merely murmuring to herself, "Poor child, poor child!" A few household servants, clad in Mongolian attire, happen to pass by her. Discreetly she chokes back her tears, dries her eyes, and calls her daughter, ERH-NIU, who is looking on as though spell-bound. ERH-NIU, though plainly dressed and without any makeup, is a beauty.

MISTRESS LIU Come, Erh-niu, what can you gain by looking on? We must see to the house.
ERH-NIU I'm coming, mother. [*Nevertheless she stands watching*]
MISTRESS LIU I hear you say "coming," but I don't see you move. Spectacles of this kind can be seen on the street every month. What is there new to look at, I wonder?
ERH-NIU [*Turning back reluctantly and taking her mother's hand*] It's really a pity, mother! How could such a young woman be a murderess?
MISTRESS LIU Who says she is? She is just as sweet and innocent a child

as you are. Don't you remember that girl, Hsiao-lan, who came to see us the year before last in spring?

ERH-NIU Hsiao-lan? You mean Mistress Ch'en's daughter-in-law?

MISTRESS LIU That's right. [*Wiping her eyes*]

ERH-NIU But she is completely changed! Mother, we can still help her, can't we?

MISTRESS LIU How can we, foolish child? [*Pointing at the bamboo basket*] Here's some sacrificial wine and meat I have for her after she's executed, but even this I dare not try. Poor Hsiao-lan! To think she should have run into . . . [*Stopping short*]

[KUAN HAN-CH'ING, *a playwright of great renown, also a physician of the Royal Medical Service, who has been watching the procession from behind the throng, comes over to join mother and daughter the moment he hears their voices*]

KUAN HAN-CH'ING [*In a low voice*] I beg your pardon, Mistress Liu, do you know her?

MISTRESS LIU Good Heavens! You came here to see this too, Master Kuan?

KUAN HAN-CH'ING Not exactly. I was going out of town to see a friend. Coming this way, I found the street cleared of pedestrians. I was simply stranded here.

ERH-NIU Ah, Uncle Kuan, won't you come in and sit down for a while? [*She hastens to serve tea*] Please have a cup of tea.

KUAN HAN-CH'ING Thank you, Erh-niu. You are growing prettier every day. And you still remember me, eh?

MISTRESS LIU Of course, she does. Since we were old neighbors and you moved away only a little more than two years ago, how could she have forgotten you? Sit down, please.

KUAN HAN-CH'ING [*Taking a seat*] How's business?

MISTRESS LIU Not bad. Only we're short-handed and we can't afford any help. The old man spends most of his time in the country at Wanping, and comes home once or twice a month at best.

KUAN HAN-CH'ING I don't think you have too much of a problem. Erh-niu must be a great help.

MISTRESS LIU Yes, she is, but I wish she were a boy. To have a girl show herself in public is an invitation to trouble, I tell you.

KUAN HAN-CH'ING I know what you mean. . . . Tell me, Mistress Liu, do you know this woman convict?

MISTRESS LIU Yes, I do. As a matter of fact, I'm distantly related to her mother-in-law. [*Heaving a sigh*] To think I should see with my own eyes an innocent child sent to death and not to be able to do a thing about it. Really. . . . [*Drying her tears*]

KUAN HAN-CH'ING What's happened to her? She's such a young woman to have committed so great a crime!

MISTRESS LIU She did nothing of the kind. She is a good girl.

KUAN HAN-CH'ING Then, for what reason . . . ?

MISTRESS LIU [*In a hushed voice, seeing that the crowd on the street is beginning to disperse*] Master Kuan, this is what her own mother-in-law told me. I vouch for its truth. If you can't save the living, perhaps you will be able to avenge the dead.

KUAN HAN-CH'ING [*Eagerly*] Go on; I'm listening.

MISTRESS LIU This unfortunate girl is called Chu Hsiao-lan. She comes from a peasant family in Hsiangyang. Hsiangyang, as you know, had been under siege for a number of years. After its fall, Lord Alihaiya[1] grabbed a large tract of grazing land for his horses. He not only enclosed the whole piece that belonged to Hsiao-lan's family, a total of several *mou*, but also demanded the service of her father as a stablehand. Her father was highly indignant and ran away. Left behind, Hsiao-lan and her mother could find no means of livelihood and came to this city to look for an uncle. He happened to be away. They put up at the house of Mistress Ch'en, also from Hsiangyang. Then Hsiao-lan's mother fell ill and was laid up for more than six months. They had to borrow ten taels of silver from Mistress Ch'en to pay for a doctor's advice and medicine. Mistress Ch'en had a son, named Wen-hsiu, an honest young man, but since childhood his health had been poor. One day Mistress Ch'en wanted to collect the debt. Hsiao-lan's mother, of course, had no money to pay her back. Partly as a settlement of the account, she promised to wed her daughter to Mistress Ch'en's son. In the meantime her illness continued. Sometimes she felt better and sometimes worse until finally last autumn she died.

KUAN HAN-CH'ING [*With sympathetic concern*] What became of Hsiao-lan then?

MISTRESS LIU She married Wen-hsiu. The young couple lived happily together. Mistress Ch'en loved her like her own child. Financially, the family had no worries either. But then, somehow, misfortunes befell the house from within its walls!

ERH-NIU Mother, please, let's not talk about it. Let's do something to save Hsiao-lan, or I'll go mad. Can't we ask Uncle Kuan to think of some way? There's no time to waste. Let's hurry!

MISTRESS LIU My poor child, Uncle Kuan is a physician. His business is to save people when they are troubled by colds or coughs but not when their heads are to be cut off. Now, listen, I'm speaking to Uncle Kuan, don't disturb me.

[*Restless and frustrated,* ERH-NIU *runs outdoors again*]

KUAN HAN-CH'ING Tell me, Mistress Liu, how did misfortune come to the house from within?

MISTRESS LIU You see, Mistress Ch'en's maiden name is Li. She has a cousin on the paternal side, called Li Liu-shun, who is quite old. Mistress Ch'en had him stay with her and entrusted him with her household affairs, as she had no other help. The year before last, Liu-shun's son, who had been away for a long time, came back. His name is Li Yi, but people call him Donkey Li. He has been in the army for a number of years and he's a rogue. He's said to have enlisted in the southern expeditionary army under Commander Sa, but when he got to Linan,[2] he made a fine haul and then left the army. From the day he returned, he had his eye on Hsiao-lan and wanted to take her for his wife. Even after Hsiao-lan married Wen-hsiu, Donkey Li still wouldn't give up. One day, Wen-hsiu went out but he never came back. Two days later, it was discovered that he had been drowned. Some people said Donkey Li had pushed him into the river.

KUAN HAN-CH'ING [*Banging the table*] Scoundrel! He certainly had the good folk in the hollow of his hand. That was, of course, part of his scheme for marrying Hsiao-lan, if I am not mistaken?

MISTRESS LIU Precisely. After Wen-hsiu was buried, Hsiao-lan wept day and night. But the brazen-faced Donkey Li lost no time in paying his court to her. She rejected him, and swore that she would live with her mother-in-law for the rest of her life. As to Mistress Ch'en, she was so deeply grieved at the loss of her son that she cried herself sick. One day, she felt like eating a little mutton tripe soup. After Hsiao-lan had cooked it, Donkey Li, as an excuse to get rid of her, sent her on an errand. Then he put arsenic in the soup. His plan was to kill Mistress Ch'en so as to remove the last obstacle to his marriage with Hsiao-lan. But it so happened that the patient took a turn for the worse and didn't touch the broth when it was served. The old man, Li Liu-shun, who had a keen appetite for food, took it and ate it up. Almost immediately blood spurted from his mouth, nose, ears, and eyes and he died on the spot. Then Donkey Li threatened to drag Hsiao-lan to court, but said he would hush up the affair if she promised to be his wife. But Hsiao-lan replied with a clear conscience, "All right, go ahead and take me to the court." As ill luck would have it, however, out of all the judges, the poor girl ran into a corrupt one.

KUAN HAN-CH'ING H'mm, but there aren't many who're uncorrupted these days. Whom did she run into?

MISTRESS LIU [*In a low voice*] The case was brought before the Tahsing Prefecture. The prefect, Lord Khoshin,[3] as you well know, is a money-grabber. But then he is equally jealous of his reputation and often demands that the people present him with the 10,000-name homage umbrella.[4] He is a Semu.[5] Seeing that Hsiao-lan was the daughter of a "barbarian,"[6] who had run away from her home village, he was prejudiced against her in the first place. Then Donkey Li handed him a personal letter from Commander Sa and some silver to boot, so it was a foregone conclusion that he would decide the case against Hsiao-lan. At any rate, during the trial the prefect simply turned a deaf ear to her defense, but went on using cruel tortures to wring a confession from her that she had poisoned Donkey Li's father. Hsiao-lan, however, stoutly maintained her innocence, and refused to plead guilty.

KUAN HAN-CH'ING That's right! She shouldn't have pleaded guilty under any circumstances.

MISTRESS LIU Then Lord Khoshin said that since Chu Hsiao-lan would not confess, it must have been her mother-in-law who had mixed the poison in the broth and he ordered the old woman to be flogged with eighty lashes. When Hsiao-lan heard this, she realized immediately that her aged mother-in-law couldn't stand such torture. Courageously, she decided to plead guilty.

KUAN HAN-CH'ING But that's one thing she shouldn't have done. Didn't it occur to her that to plead guilty was to forfeit her life?

MISTRESS LIU I think it did. But her one thought at that moment was to save her mother-in-law, and she cared nothing about herself. She was always like that—straightforward and resolute.

KUAN HAN-CH'ING She certainly was a fine character. It's a pity that her case wasn't handled by a judge patient enough to give her a fair trial.

MISTRESS LIU But, Master Kuan, who could she expect to give her a fair trial? These days, the life of a Han is not worth as much as that of a donkey. Hsiao-lan was only granted one hearing the day before yesterday; today she was sentenced to be beheaded.

KUAN HAN-CH'ING You see them everywhere—these venal officials who trample on human life as if it were mere grass!

MISTRESS LIU [Lowering her tone] Master Kuan, watch what you are saying. [More people in the street rushing past the tavern. ERH-NIU runs back]

ERH-NIU [Holding her mother's sleeve] Mother, do something! Hurry! [Looking at KUAN] Think quickly, Uncle Kuan. You have many friends. Do something right away! [The report of a cannon is heard in the distance]

MISTRESS LIU It's too late now. She is gone already. Poor Hsiao-lan! [She sits down crying with her face buried in her hands. ERH-NIU begins to sob, too]

KUAN HAN-CH'ING [Sad and disturbed] What a world! [Rising from his seat] Mistress Liu, thank you. I must go. [Thinking aloud] Am I only fit to cure people's colds and coughs?

MISTRESS LIU Watch your step, Master Kuan. Come to see us again when you have time. Are you going home?

KUAN HAN-CH'ING No, I must go out of town to see a friend.

[He takes leave with a heavy heart, but before he can make his exit two friends, HSIEH HSIAO-SHAN and CH'IEN SHUA-CH'IAO, enter the tavern. The moment HSIEH HSIAO-SHAN sees KUAN, he takes him by the arm. The latter, absorbed in thought, gives a start]

HSIEH HSIAO-SHAN Lao Kuan,[7] I've been looking for you. I didn't know you were drinking here. I went to your house; you weren't in.

KUAN HAN-CH'ING I wasn't drinking. I was talking with Mistress Liu about the woman convict who was just executed.

HSIEH HSIAO-SHAN ·I heard something about it too. I understand it was unjust.

CH'IEN SHUA-CH'IAO I was told it was arranged by someone who demanded her hand and was rejected.

KUAN HAN-CH'ING Mistress Liu told me the whole story just now. My blood boiled!

HSIEH HSIAO-SHAN Why did you get angry? These days nine out of ten judgments are wrong. If you're going to take them too seriously, you might as well hang yourself. . . . Now, I've something to ask you. Won't you come over to our place for a drink?

KUAN HAN-CH'ING No, thanks, I have to go out of town. What's on your mind?

HSIEH HSIAO-SHAN A gentleman asked me to teach him one of the ballads you wrote.[8] The first line I remember runs, "Drink when thirsty; eat when hungry; and sing when you've had one too many." But Ch'ien Shua-ch'iao insists that it should be "Drink when thirsty; sing when you've had one too many" without the three words "eat when hungry." Now we've got to look up the original text; that is, to ask you. Tell us who's right.

KUAN HAN-CH'ING You're both right.

CH'IEN SHUA-CH'IAO We can't be. Tell me straight which one of us is right.

KUAN HAN-CH'ING You are, according to the original version. "Eat when hungry" was inserted later to make the lines easier for singing. But some people thought the alteration broke up the melody, and was not as ingenious as the original.

HSIEH HSIAO-SHAN That's right, too. I think I'll go by the original version in the singing lessons I give. That gentleman is particularly fond of these lines, "To till your own land, to retire into the mountain—in leisure and quiet one can brood over what came to pass. My rival may be wise; I may be a fool. But why should I fight?" He said he liked these ideas very much.

KUAN HAN-CH'ING [*From the bottom of his heart he really disapproves of this spiritless, idle, detached outlook on life*] No, it's no good at all. My rival is not necessarily wise, and I'm not necessarily a fool. We've got to fight it out to see who is wise and who is a fool, to decide what is right and what is wrong. Hsiao-shan, it seems to me that you'd better stop teaching that ballad.

HSIEH HSIAO-SHAN Why? You've changed! Then, what are you going to do with that piece called "Feng Liu Ti"?[9] Won't you study it any more?

KUAN HAN-CH'ING Yes, I will. I'll come over later. [*To* CH'IEN SHUA-CH'IAO] Is Fourth Sister Chu[10] in today?

CH'IEN SHUA-CH'IAO Probably.

KUAN HAN-CH'ING Probably? And Sai Lien-hsiu? Is she well again?

CH'IEN SHUA-CH'IAO [*Tossing his head*] I don't know.

KUAN HAN-CH'ING You don't know? I thought you two were getting along quite well.

HSIEH HSIAO-SHAN It's all over now. This fellow was drunk the other day, and forgot his lines on the stage. Sai Lien-hsiu gave him a good scolding. He couldn't take it and left her there and then.

KUAN HAN-CH'ING Tell me, Ch'ien Shua-ch'iao, can you allow a man in our profession to forget his lines on the stage, no matter how good an actor he is?

CH'IEN SHUA-CH'IAO Of course not.

KUAN HAN-CH'ING Then you knew the scolding was for your own good. Why did you take it so badly?

CH'IEN SHUA-CH'IAO Because . . . because. . . .

KUAN HAN-CH'ING Because you were scolded by a woman, right? Well, under the sun there's only one truth, which admits of no sex distinction. I want you to come along with me to Fourth Sister's place and apologize to Sai Lien-hsiu. [*To* MISTRESS LIU *and* ERH-NIU] Mistress Liu and Erh-niu. Good-bye. We're going now.

MISTRESS LIU Mind how you go.

[*They walk to the corner of the street*]

KUAN HAN-CH'ING [*Taking leave of* HSIEH HSIAO-SHAN *at the street corner*] Hsiao-shan, will you make an appointment for me with the drummer, Lao Jen-ssu, and the flutist, Yu Mei? I have a new play in mind, and I want to consult them about the P'ai Tzu[11] and Ch'ang Tzu.[12]

HSIEH HSIAO-SHAN Certainly I will. [*He moves in the direction of the town.* KUAN HAN-CH'ING *and* CH'IEN SHUA-CH'IAO *make for the city gate. At this juncture, the servants in Mongolian attire who have just passed turn back again, followed by a richly dressed* YOUNG LORD *and his* HENCHMAN. *They enter* MISTRESS LIU'*s tavern*]

MISTRESS LIU Young lord, sit down, please.

YOUNG LORD Never mind. [*To his* HENCHMAN] You tell her.

HENCHMAN Well, Mistress Liu, what do you say to the matter we talked about yesterday?

MISTRESS LIU The matter we talked about yesterday? Oh, yes, Fourth Master Tsui, but I thought I'd made it clear to you already. My daughter, Erh-niu, is engaged. Chang, you know, is the matchmaker. Her fiancé, Chou Fu-hsiang, comes of a peasant family at Wanp'ing. He works at the residence of His Lordship Horikhoson. The wedding will take place after harvest this fall. [*She makes a sign to* ERH-NIU *to go to the inner compartment.* ERH-NIU *does so*]

HENCHMAN You needn't repeat all that. I've heard it before and reported to the young lord already, but this is what he said, "That doesn't matter. Just a servant at the minister's residence! Why, even the minister's own son would have to yield. Give this man Chou some money and tell him to marry somebody else."

MISTRESS LIU But no rules of decency or propriety will ever permit such a thing. My daughter is in truth betrothed.

HENCHMAN Why should there be so many rules of decency and propriety? The 25th son of His Excellency Lord Akham has taken a fancy to your daughter, and that is the last word of decency and propriety. Few people ever have the chance of gaining access to our great house. The young lord has condescended to come over here a number of times. Don't tell me you still decline such an honor. Now, do you agree or not?

MISTRESS LIU Fourth Master Tsui, please put in a good word for me before the young lord. Being betrothed to somebody else, Erh-niu simply cannot accept this good fortune.

HENCHMAN [*To the* YOUNG LORD] What shall I say?

YOUNG LORD It's no use wasting words on her. Take the girl!

HENCHMAN [*To the servants*] Take her!

[*The servants start dragging* ERH-NIU *out of the inner room*]

ERH-NIU [*Resisting*] Mother! Help! Help!

MISTRESS LIU Young lord and Fourth Master Tsui, you can't do this! Her father has gone to Wanp'ing. I am in no position to decide. Can't you wait until her father comes back? Let me implore you on my knees. [*She sinks on her knees*]

HENCHMAN When her father comes back, send him over.

MISTRESS LIU But I won't allow you to take her.

HENCHMAN Yes, you will!

[*Without another word the servants drag* ERH-NIU *away, led by the* YOUNG LORD. HENCHMAN *follows behind.* MISTRESS LIU *clutches at his robe desperately*]

MISTRESS LIU How dare you kidnap someone's child in broad daylight! Don't you know there's a law?

HENCHMAN Don't be an ass. You should know, Mistress Liu, this is the way of His Excellency Lord Akham and his whole family, and it has been so for the last twenty years. If you want to talk about the law, go to the Tahsing Prefecture. You'll soon find out that the prefect of Tahsing, who is also the Governor of Tatu Province, is none other than Lord Khoshin, the first young lord of our House! [*He pushes* MISTRESS LIU *back and struts off*]

MISTRESS LIU Woe is me, woe is me! I shall die, I shall die! [*She throws herself down on the ground and cries loudly*]

[*Curtain*]

SCENE 2

Chu Lien-hsiu's sitting room, in the entertainment house, in the amusement quarter in the suburbs of the capital, where hang-yuan *(performers and courtesans) can be found. On the walls of the sitting room hang a guitar, a flute, a sword, and a whisk broom.*

CHU LIEN-HSIU *is the fourth child of her family, and is thus known to her friends as Fourth Sister. In the Yuan dynasty, female entertainers customarily took the word* hsiu *(elegance) as one component of their names.* CHU LIEN-HSIU *(pearl-screen elegance) had achieved renown early in her career. A versatile actress who has been gifted with a rare voice, she is a star of the first magnitude. She has a number of pupils, as well as a large circle of acquaintances. But her closest friend is* KUAN HAN-CH'ING, *who has presented her with a ballad[13] as a tribute to her performances in many of his plays, such as "Rescued by a Coquette," "The Cunning Maid," "The Riverside Pavilion," and "The Prayer to the Moon." * CHU LIEN-HSIU *comes from a fine family and is nobleminded and brave.*

As the scene opens, CHU LIEN-HSIU, *elegantly dressed in purple, conforming to the regulation requiring courtesans to wear this color, is listening to* KUAN HAN-CH'ING *as he finishes telling her the whole story about Chu Hsiao-lan. Her maid,* HSIANG KUEI, *is serving him tea from an exquisite tea set.*

KUAN HAN-CH'ING You see, they took a precious life so brutally and shamelessly, and yet call themselves "fathers of the people." [*He pounds the table*]

CHU LIEN-HSIU [*Hastening to save the teacup from tilting over*] Why vent your anger on the table and teacup, my dear Master Kuan?

KUAN HAN-CH'ING What kind of world is this? I can't help feeling angry, Fourth Sister, can you?

CHU LIEN-HSIU No, I don't blame you for feeling angry, of course. I'm so disgusted with everything that my heart has turned cold and numb. Some people are utterly resigned to the present state of affairs and regard it as a matter of course. Only you, though you're greying with the years, still have an unbridled youthful spirit and rage against injustice. [*She draws near him*] It is exactly because you have this courage that you have won people's love and respect. Don't you know that?

KUAN HAN-CH'ING That's enough! [*He rises and turns away from her*] Perhaps it's because I'm still immature that we feel differently about the matter.

CHU LIEN-HSIU It isn't that you are immature. Only you haven't quite outgrown that "child's heart in a man" about which you yourself have often spoken. But those who, unlike you, no longer lose their temper over the present state of things are not necessarily unworthy compared with you. It may be because they lead a more difficult life than yours. You men have a bright future if you are talented and learned. You may have some setbacks, but it's more likely you will see your dreams come true. But we miserable women are simply doomed. I came of a good family, too. I was sold to this house as an entertainer only when my father died in prison for defaulting on the payment of an interminable tax imposed upon him by Prince Puhua. I've been cooped up here for over a decade now. Haven't I suffered a wrong submissively all these years without having found a place to air my grievances? Even so, I consider myself lucky compared with others. There are 25,000 woman quartered outside the city gate of Cambaluc and not one lives like a decent human being. Some of them are hovering between life and death and they would be better dead—like the young woman executed today.

KUAN HAN-CH'ING The situation you are in is deplorable, of course. What kind of future do we educated men have? Remember, according to customary rating, artisans occupy the seventh place, courtesans eighth, Confucian scholars ninth, and beggars tenth.[14] So these days our position compares unfavorably with yours. On the other hand, I must confess that I've overrated myself. Tu Fu said, "Having pored over ten thousand volumes, one can write with godly power." I've always thought I was resourceful. But today when I saw with my own eyes a pack of bloodthirsty creatures dragging an innocent young woman to execution, I could do absolutely nothing. I wrote "The Butterfly Dream."[15] In that play, upon Wang Shih-ho's acquittal by Justice Pao, I made his mother sing: "Our sadness has turned to joy, our debt of sorrow is paid. We have left the castle of darkness." How I wished then we could have another Justice Pao to turn sadness into joy. But instead we are being confronted with these man-eating leopards and wolves, and in face of these beasts our hands are tied. "Black Whirlwind" Li K'uei,[16] who was an illiterate, had the courage to raid the execution ground at Chiangchou. And I? All I can do is to stand behind the crowd with folded arms and look on, restraining my indignation. This is me, the proud Kuan Han-ch'ing. How I despise myself!

CHU LIEN-HSIU [*Holding his hand in a warm clasp*] Li K'uei was very brave indeed. But could he have made the raid alone? It was, of course, a prearranged move planned by all the heroes of Liangshanpo. Now, what can you do, if you by chance see something outrageous?

KUAN HAN-CH'ING In ancient times, when one traveler saw another being attacked, he would unsheathe his sword and go to the rescue. In my case, I have no sword to unsheathe, only a worn-out brush.

CHU LIEN-HSIU Isn't your brush as good as a sword? Isn't your script your sword? In your plays you have exposed such wicked men as Lord Yang, Keh Piao, and Lu Chai-lang.[17] All the theatre-goers hate, as much as we do, those men who defy moral principles, persecute the innocent, and terrorize the people. Now, why don't you unmask Donkey Li, Khoshin, and their like, to right the wrongs done to many women?

KUAN HAN-CH'ING But these evil men aren't an isolated few. There's a whole group of them who work together in this man-eating business. Can you ever unmask them all? I have always thought that heaven and earth, deities and spirits have eyes and uphold justice and equity, though there is no justice on earth. Now I realize that heaven and earth, deities and spirits are blind too, and neither know nor care about justice and equity.

CHU LIEN-HSIU Well, then, if the evil ones are too many, just sort out the worst, the most hideous. If heaven, earth, deities, and spirits have no eyes, then give them a piece of your mind too.

KUAN HAN-CH'ING I will, as a matter of fact. On my way over just now, I was thinking about Chu Hsiao-lan's case and I've decided to make it into a play. I'll lay bare the hypocrisy of these vicious, corrupt officials to the blazing sun so that everybody can see. I'll give expression to the feelings and grievances of the wronged women. Let all know that in the hearts of the people there's still a sense of justice and that they know what's right and wrong.

CHU LIEN-HSIU Wonderful! I know something about this prefect Lord

Khoshin, too. Backed up by his all-powerful father, he is as lawless as he is reckless. Recently he was charged with mistrial in a sentence he handed down. Lord Hsü Heng[18] came to investigate the proceedings. Khoshin feigned illness and refused to receive Hsü. Hsü had to drop the matter because he could do nothing about it.

KUAN HAN-CH'ING Help me to collect more evidence of his crimes. He'll never get away. I have an outline of the script in my head, and I've the name of the female title role, too. There is one question, however. . . .

CHU LIEN-HSIU What is it?

KUAN HAN-CH'ING I'm worried in case no one dares act in the play after it is written.

CHU LIEN-HSIU [*After a moment's thought*] Han-ch'ing, go ahead and write. If you have no objections to our troupe, we'll have a try. How about it?

KUAN HAN-CH'ING Why should I object to your troupe?

CHU LIEN-HSIU Well, didn't you once say that only private performances by respectable people of good families can really be called stagecraft whereas we entertainers or professional actors are no different from slave-entertainers of the public and that our stage acting was "merely an unconventional, unrefined, crude entertainment."

KUAN HAN-CH'ING Really! I said nothing of the kind. Don't believe what Chao Meng-fu[19] said. Nowadays, it doesn't make any difference whether people are amateur artists from a respectable family or professional entertainers or actors. They are all part of the oppressed and downtrodden. They are all slaves.

CHU LIEN-HSIU In that case, if you'll dare to write, I'll dare to perform.

KUAN HAN-CH'ING For my part, then, if you dare to act, I'll surely write and finish the writing quickly.

CHU LIEN-HSIU Fine, it's agreed. I've acted Chao Pan-erh, T'an Chi-erh, Wang Jui-lan, and Yen-yen,[20] and people have spoken kindly of my performances in all these parts. Now, for Chu Hsiao-lan's sake, for the sake of all the wronged women in the world, I'll play the new role with heart and soul and make it a real success.

KUAN HAN-CH'ING Well said, Fourth Sister! [*Grasping her hands, visibly moved*]

CHU LIEN-HSIU What name will you give to the female role?

KUAN HAN-CH'ING I'll call her Tou Ngo.

CHU LIEN-HSIU Tou Ngo? How interesting! I remember you were once going to stage the story of a filial daughter called Tsao Ngo. I guess you'll simply change the filial daughter to a filial daughter-in-law and name her Tou Ngo instead. Am I right?

KUAN HAN-CH'ING Exactly. You're right.

[*Enter* YEN SHAN-HSIU, MA ERH, SAI LIEN-HSIU, *and* CH'IEN SHUA-CH'IAO, *talking and laughing*]

YEN SHAN-HSIU [*To* CHU LIEN-HSIU] Teacher, here's something very strange! Ch'ien Shua-ch'iao actually apologized to Sai Lien-hsiu!

MA ERH We should thank Master Kuan for that. For a while I thought the two had become mortal enemies.

KUAN HAN-CH'ING Ha, ha, ha! You'll be surprised to know how obstinate he was, though. On our way over here, I had to give him quite a lecture before I finally made him see his mistake.

CHU LIEN-HSIU That lecture from you was long overdue. He has been behaving as though he has taken a leaf out of your own book. He's always saying you call yourself "the prince of gentlemen" and the king of gallants." I can see he has made himself a little prince and a little king, to say the least.

KUAN HAN-CH'ING I don't see anything wrong with that. But the point to remember is this: Stagecraft should be tempered with reason. It is reason which makes man. If we depart from reason to the extent of totally disregarding it, then how can we consider ourselves gentlemanly and gallant?

CHU LIEN-HSIU [*To the others*] You all heard that? To be truly gentlemanly and gallant you must support reason and respect yourself. Oh, by the way, Sai Lien-hsiu, I have good news for you. Master Kuan is going to write a new play which has an excellent story. He said he would give it to our troupe.

SAI LIEN-HSIU Wonderful! I only hope we won't spoil it.

KUAN HAN-CH'ING You needn't be over-modest, Sai Lien-hsiu.

SAI LIEN-HSIU I hope you'll write it quickly. I'm perfectly well now. I'm dying for a new part.

MA ERH Master Kuan, Ch'ien Shua-ch'iao is dying for a new part, too. Why don't you write him something like "The Uncouth Li K'uei Tenders His Apology"?[21] [*Everybody laughs aloud*]

CH'IEN SHUA-CH'IAO Ha, ha, ha, ha! [*Changing the subject and turning to* KUAN HAN-CH'ING] By the way, I nearly forgot to tell you. There will be a party at Liulang Village in the western suburbs. We've been asked to perform your play "Lord Kuan Goes to the Feast."[22] Will you be able to come over?

KUAN HAN-CH'ING When will it be?

CH'IEN SHUA-CH'IAO The early part of next month. I'll let you know as soon as the date is fixed.

KUAN HAN-CH'ING Of course, I'll go, if I am free. I used to tread the boards myself at Liulang Village.

MA ERH We seldom see you on the stage now. How about joining us? I suggest we present your "The Jade Mirror-Stand."[23] Fourth Sister can play Liu Ch'ien-ying; you, Wen Ch'iao; Sai Lien-hsiu, Mistress Liu; Yen Shan-hsiu, the maidservant; Ch'ien Shua-ch'iao, the matchmaker; and I'll be Prefect Wang, of course.

KUAN HAN-CH'ING Ha, ha! Your casting sounds pretty good. But I'm afraid the Liulang villagers won't care for elegant things veneered like that. What about "The Wife-Snatcher"?[24] Fourth Sister can play Li's wife, you take Chang Kuei; Ch'ien Shua-ch'iao, the silversmith, Li Ssu; and I'll be Justice Pao.

MA ERH Good, I like that one better. [*He recites some lines*] "Lu is

so high-handed as to be fearless of Heaven. He is an official but knows
no law. Even the courts are under his thumb. He seizes people's wives
and daughters at will. Over the common citizen he rides roughshod.
Few officials have such power as he. . . ."

CH'IEN SHUA-CH'IAO Citizens today are just like wild geese shot with
arrows right through the mouth, no one can even cough. Such a play,
I am sure, will be more than welcome.

MA ERH [*To* KUAN HAN-CH'ING] Then we will look forward to seeing
you play Justice Pao.

[*Enter the* ENTERTAINMENT HOUSE GUARDIAN. *She greets* KUAN HAN-
CH'ING

GUARDIAN The Superintendent came over just now and said there would
be a reception at the Prime Minister's residence this evening in honor
of the guests from Persia. You'd better get ready immediately and
rehearse your program.

YEN SHAN-HSIU *and* OTHERS Excuse us, Master Kuan. [*They retire with
the guardian*]

SAI LIEN-HSIU Master Kuan, you will excuse me. I must go too. [*To*
CHU LIEN-HSIU] Teacher, will you make Master Kuan stay? [*She and*
CH'IEN SHUA-CH'IAO *exit*]

KUAN HAN-CH'ING [*Rising to his feet*] Well, Fourth Sister, I must leave
too.

CHU LIEN-HSIU Why, are you going home to write the play? [*Earnestly*]
Why don't you stay and do it here? I'll go to the rehearsal. Later on
we'll have dinner together. Sai's father sent over a few carp freshly
caught from the lake. You may as well have some to show your appreciation. [*To the maid*] Hsiang Kuei, please see to the tea. Use the
best brand I have. [HSIANG KUEI *nods compliance*] But don't disturb
Master Kuan. Close that door so that he won't hear the noise of the
drums and gongs.

HSIANG KUEI Yes, but Master Kuan won't be bothered by anything like
that. Didn't he write his script backstage the other day? He worked as
though he couldn't even hear the music and the singing up in the
front at all. He's a real genius.

CHU LIEN-HSIU Silly girl. I ought to know how capable Master Kuan is.
But the play he is going to write this time is quite different from his
previous ones. He needs a quiet atmosphere and shouldn't be
disturbed, that's all. Do you understand?

HSIANG KUEI Yes, of course.

KUAN HAN-CH'ING Fourth Sister, it's very thoughtful of you. Please
give my thanks to Sai Lien-hsiu, too. I haven't quite built up the plot
yet. I'm afraid it will take me a few days before I commit it to paper.
Right now I have to go to the Western Hills to see a patient.

CHU LIEN-HSIU See a patient?

KUAN HAN-CH'ING [*Smiling*] Don't forget I'm also a physician. The Royal
Medical Service sent for me. You have to go wherever they want you to.
Some patients don't want people to know anything about their station

in life. You may make several visits without even knowing their names.

CHU LIEN-HSIU Why do you want to carry on this profession? Why don't you resign and devote yourself to writing?

KUAN HAN-CH'ING Well, if I resign, I won't get any exemptions from this motley array of taxes. I'll be made to run some other errands. So it's better to be a professional, for at least I can take time out to do something of my own. Besides, physicians, you know, occupy the fifth rank in the social scale. As an author I am one step lower than you, but as a royal physician I am a few steps higher. Ha, ha, ha, ha!

CHU LIEN-HSIU So that's why! All right, then, I won't keep you any longer. Allow me to wish your patient health and yourself wealth, my dear Dr. Kuan.

KUAN HAN-CH'ING You!

[*Curtain*]

SCENE 3 (SUMMARY)

In Scene 3 Kuan Han-ch'ing uses his position as a physician on call to the Mongol aristocracy to secure the release of Erh-niu from the young lord's household.

SCENE 4

KUAN HAN-CH'ING *'s study. Hanging on the wall are a fiddle and a sword.* KUAN HAN-CH'ING *is seated beside a flickering candle which is fast burning out. Sometimes he hums and reads aloud, sometimes he stops to think or bends over the desk scribbling. Now and then he gets up to stretch his legs and does some swordplay for exercise. The drum tower reports third watch. The cock crows. KUAN is still busy writing. Enter KUAN CHUNG, an old servant, with his coat thrown across his shoulders.*

KUAN CHUNG You're still working, sir? It's high time to retire. It'll be dawn soon.

KUAN HAN-CH'ING Never mind. Wait till I've finished Act III, just so that I have an outline of the play set up.

KUAN CHUNG You're a doctor. You always caution people not to ruin their health by sitting up late. Why don't you practice what you preach?

KUAN HAN-CH'ING You don't understand. As a doctor I have to tell others not to sit up late, but as a writer I must sit up late myself. Those are two different stories altogether.

KUAN CHUNG I'm afraid I don't understand. All I know is, you are working much too late. You must be cold and hungry. There isn't much to eat in the house either. The best I can offer you is boiled eggs. In the old days when your wife was living, she took good care of you, and you used to listen to her too. She didn't allow you to work as late as you pleased. For a while I thought I'd be able to look after you, but these last few years my age is beginning to tell on me. Now even my eyes and ears fail me. I can't do as much as I'd like to.

KUAN HAN-CH'ING Why tell me all this? Who needs you here in the first place? Why don't you go to bed?

KUAN CHUNG Do you expect me to sleep peacefully with you working here like you're possessed? You ought to know better. I'm going to boil you an egg.

KUAN HAN-CH'ING Honestly I am not hungry. You can help me best by letting me alone and again I beg you to go to bed.

KUAN CHUNG All right, I'll leave you alone. But you must retire as soon as you've finished. Tomorrow, first thing in the morning, Mistress Liu and her husband will come over to thank you personally.

KUAN HAN-CH'ING What do they want to thank me for? Tomorrow I'll be busy. [*He stops writing*] What? Was Liu home when you took Erh-niu back?

KUAN CHUNG Not only Erh-niu's father but also her fiancé, Chou Fu-hsiang. There was a family reunion, and everybody was as happy as a lark. They feel so indebted to you they want to worship you as an ancestor. They said but for your help they could never even have found out Erh-niu's whereabouts. Chou Fu-hsiang told me he would come over tomorrow too. He works for Lord Horikhoson. Erh-niu will be married soon. This time, Sir, you have done a good deed equal to the goodness of Heaven. For this you deserve another good wife who may yet bear you five more boys and two more girls.

KUAN HAN-CH'ING Stuff and nonsense! Go and get yourself some sleep.

KUAN CHUNG [*Walking to the window*] Look, the eastern sky is grey already.

KUAN HAN-CH'ING Oh, by the way, get me a new candle, please.

KUAN CHUNG I pray you, Sir, change candles no more. I certainly hope you will call it a day when this one has burned out. [*He trims the wick and removes the melted wax*]

KUAN HAN-CH'ING All right, I will. [*He bends over the desk and resumes his work. The cock crows. Suddenly there is a knock at the door*]

KUAN CHUNG [*Answering the door*] Who is it?

A VOICE [*Outside the door*] Me.

KUAN CHUNG Who are you? At this time of night.

THE VOICE Why, don't you recognize my voice? I am Hsieh and I'm here to see Lao Kuan.

KUAN HAN-CH'ING Open the door quickly. It's Master Hsieh.

KUAN CHUNG [*Unbolting the door*] Oh, Master Hsieh. Isn't it rather late, though? [*The cock crows*]

HSIEH HSIAO-SHAN Why, I'm here before daybreak and still you complain that I'm late? [*A ringing laugh.* YÜ MEI *steps inside after* HSIEH. *He holds a long cloth cover containing a fife and a flute. He is known in stage circles as the "flute king"*]

KUAN HAN-CH'ING [*Rising to receive the visitors*]

Oh, so Yü Mei is here too. Sit down, sit down.

HSIEH HSIAO-SHAN You told me to bring over Jen Ssu and Yü Mei. Now Jen Ssu was called to Tung-chow. Yü Mei performed today, and I had to wait for him until just now. He wanted to go home to sleep but I kidnapped him.

KUAN HAN-CH'ING [*To* YÜ MEI] How is it you finished so late?

YÜ MEI We were singing at a reception at General Juri Timur's[25] residence. Our program started yesterday afternoon and lasted until now. We performed three long operas and five short ones. We only had a breathing spell when the audience was tired out. My lips were so parched they were literally bleeding. I really worked like a horse!

HSIEH HSIAO-SHAN Yü Mei hasn't had his dinner yet.

KUAN HAN-CH'ING Oh! . . . [*Looking at* KUAN CHUNG] Is there anything to eat?

KUAN CHUNG I'd better go and boil a few eggs. [*He serves tea*] I'm sorry the tea is a bit cold. [*Exit*]

KUAN HAN-CH'ING You are both here at the right time. [*To* HSIEH HSIAO-SHAN] You remember I told you I was going to write "Tou Ngo"? Well, when I came to Act III, I ran into a problem. I'm hoping that perhaps you gentlemen can give me some advice.

HSIEH HSIAO-SHAN Is the plot the same as we talked about last time? I thought it was pretty good. What's the problem?

KUAN HAN-CH'ING Please go over the ballads for the first three acts.

HSIEH HSIAO-SHAN [*Taking over the manuscript and reading with* YÜ MEI] I see the melodies you use: You begin with "Tien Chiang Chun" of Hsien Lu Kung in Act I; with "Yi Chih Hua" of Nan Lu Kung in Act II; and "Mu Yang Kuan," "Ma Yu Lang," "Kan Huang En," "Ts'ai Ch'a Ko," and so on of Nan Lu Kung again in Act III. So you use these tunes to let Tou Ngo sing when she addresses the court, when she is tortured, and when she is forced to plead guilty. "How could I let you be flogged, mother? And how could I save your life except by giving mine?" The finale here is quite good.

KUAN HAN-CH'ING But that's precisely where I'm at a loss. For immediately in the next episode Tou Ngo is to be executed. In the hour of death she is so overwhelmed with anger and so full of revenge that she vows her three wishes will be granted—that her blood will gush up and splash over the streamer on the flagpole, that snow will fall in the Sixth Moon and that there will be a drought for three long years. Obviously Nan Lu Kung won't fit in with such an outburst. So I've changed to Cheng Kung beginning from "Tuan Cheng Hao." The tune "Kun Hsiu Chiu" is fairly satisfactory to me. Then at the hour of execution, I've changed to "Shua Hai Erh," "Erh Sha," "Yi Sha." So, in a single act the Kung Tiao tune changes three times. I've done it all right, but I'm afraid it's against the rules. What do you think?

HSIEH HSIAO-SHAN I don't see anything wrong with that. The tune varies with your mood. If your mood changes, naturally it needs a different tune. [*To* YÜ MEI] Yü Mei, what do you say?

Yü MEI I quite agree with you. I feel it's high time to do something about these so-called theatrical rules. Ordinarily I've never given much thought to the matter. But last night when I went through the ordeal of playing the flute in three long operas, I began to feel the monotony these rules produce. Why, for instance, must a play always be limited to four acts, and each act have only one tune? Again, why must one whole act be performed by one singer only? It seems to me all these restrictions should be thrown overboard. Last year at Pien-ching,[26] I saw an adapted version of your "Madam Liu Gives a Feast."[27] It catered to the local taste, and it obeyed none of these rules.

KUAN HAN-CH'ING How interesting! So they made it into a southern drama.

Yü MEI Yes, that's what they did. I felt wonderful when I saw it. [To KUAN HAN-CH'ING in a serious tone] You're our leader in dramatic art. As such, you're expected to guide us in the right way. It'll be easier for all your followers and for yourself too. But don't take us into bumpy, meandering byways. They'll be difficult for us to negotiate and very likely you'll trip over too. Ain't I right, though, Master Kuan? [They all laugh]

HSIEH HSIAO-SHAN I must say byways aren't half as bad as the cul-de-sac which we're supposed to find ourselves in according to some literary lights, if you please! [Enter KUAN CHUNG with a bowl of boiled eggs]

KUAN CHUNG I'm very sorry. We only had three eggs left, and one was broken by the kitten. That leaves only two. What shall we do then?

KUAN HAN-CH'ING Well, there are two guests, so that's one for each.

HSIEH HSIAO-SHAN Please, I am not hungry. Give them both to Yü Mei.

Yü MEI No, that won't do.

HSIEH HSIAO-SHAN This is no time for ceremony. [Yü MEI starts eating the eggs]

KUAN HAN-CH'ING [To HSIEH HSIAO-SHAN] Hsiao-shan, while you're here why don't you read through the three acts line by line and see whether they're smooth enough or whether there is any place where it twists your tongue?

HSIEH HSIAO-SHAN With pleasure. [He starts reading the manuscript]

Yü MEI [Finishing eating] H'mm, I must declare the two eggs have saved my life.

HSIEH HSIAO-SHAN A friend in need is a friend to feed. [He discovers something wrong and points it out] Look, Yü Mei, you read this line. I feel it would be easier to sing without these two words.

Yü MEI Where? [He reads and then tries out with his flute] H'mm, you're quite right.

HSIEH HSIAO-SHAN I say, Lao Kuan, how about striking out these two words here? [No response from KUAN HAN-CH'ING]

Yü MEI He's fallen asleep!

HSIEH HSIAO-SHAN Lao Kuan, Lao Kuan!

Yü MEI Don't wake him up. He must be exhausted. You go ahead and strike out the words. I'm sure he won't mind.

Hsieh Hsiao-shan Just as you say. [*He does so*] Kuan Chung, help him to bed. We're leaving.

Kuan Chung [*Supporting* Kuan Han-ch'ing *by the arm*] Sir, sir. [*He helps his master to bed.* Kuan Han-ch'ing *snores*]

Hsieh Hsiao-shan Yü Mei, my home is quite near here. Why don't you come over and take a rest? Later on I'll treat you to a drink.

Yü Mei No, thanks. It's bright and early, and I have to go to Nan T'ien-hsiu's place right away to give her a singing lesson.

Hsieh Hsiao-shan What! Don't you want a life of your own any more!

Yü Mei I'm getting paid for it. What can I do?

Hsieh Hsiao-shan Well, Kuan Chung. We must be off. See you tomorrow. [Hsieh Hsiao-shan *and* Yü Mei *leave*]

Kuan Chung Goodbye and mind your step. [*He closes the door*] Good Heavens! At last I can get some sleep.

[*The cock crows. The dawn brightens the sky*]

[*Curtain*]

SCENE 5 (SUMMARY)

In Scene 5 Kuan Han-ch'ing explains and defends his use of historical allusions and situations as dramatic commentary on the injustice of his own time. He faces down the arguments advanced by the philistine Yen Ho-fu for making the play less controversial, and finally arranges for a performance of "Tou Ngo" with Chu Lien-hsiu and her associates.

SCENE 6

Backstage at the Yü-hsien-lou Playhouse.

Kuan Han-ch'ing *together with* Ma Erh, Yen Shan-hsiu, *and* Sai Lien-hsiu, *who have all removed their makeup and are peeping through the embroidered drapes, intently watching the performance on the stage and its effect upon the audience beyond the apron. They compare notes in whispers off and on. The attendants and the Mongolian guards keep moving about.*

The last scene of Act 4 of "Tou Ngo" is proceeding.

Female Spirit [*Singing*] *Pray, in the name of the Emperor, with the well-tempered, bestowed sword, put these evil, corrupt officials out of the way. You'll do His Majesty a great service by putting to death the enemies of the people.* [*The audience exclaims* "Bravo!" *Some voices shout out,* "Death to the people's enemies!"]

Female Spirit [*Speaking*] Father, my mother-in-law is old, and has no one to look after her.

Tou Tien-chang I'm glad you are aware of your filial duty, my child.

Female Spirit [*Singing*] *Father, I beg you to have my grandmother reburied and to take care of my mother-in-law out of pity for her infirmity, then reopen my case and reverse the unjust verdict.* [*The audience shouts approval:* "Good! Good!"]

Tou Tien-chang Dawn is breaking. Go and arrest all these officials of

Yangchow Prefecture who sat on the case of Tou Ngo.

CHANG CHIEN To hear is to obey. . . .

The final act is still going on. CHU LIEN-HSIU, *having finished her part as the spirit of Tou Ngo, withdraws backstage.*

KUAN HAN-CH'ING, *overwhelmingly impressed, helps her as she appears. All her pupils gather around her. Hsiang Kuei brings her tea.*

KUAN HAN-CH'ING Sit down and rest yourself, Fourth Sister. You played beautifully. Even I am surprised that the play has such a powerful effect.

CHU LIEN-HSIU [*Removing the tassels she wears in her role as the spirit*] Did I hear people shouting?

KUAN HAN-CH'ING Yes, some people cried, "Death to the people's enemies!"

[WANG HO-CH'ING *and* SUPERINTENDENT HO *enter excitedly*]

WANG HO-CH'ING Lien-hsiu, you were marvellous. Such a splendid performance with so few days' rehearsal! [*To* KUAN HAN-CH'ING] You are quite a tragedian, I must say. Of course, you mustn't forget it is only an occasion of this kind that allows this performance.

KUAN HAN-CH'ING I must thank you for that.

WANG HO-CH'ING You needn't. You'll do well by not ordering my deportation on my next visit. [*They all laugh*]

KUAN HAN-CH'ING Fourth Sister, you must be tired. You'd better change quickly.

SUPERINTENDENT HO Please don't. Put on the costume you wore in the first act. I'll present you to Her Ladyship. You have no idea what a marvellous evening she's had. She dried her tears with one yellow silk handkerchief after another, and said, "I've never seen such a good play in my life. I want to see that poor little daughter-in-law. Give her something. She deserves a reward." When Madame Po Yen saw Her Ladyship so exuberant, she also said, "The play is excellent." Well, it looks as though I'll keep my job as program director.

[*A bodyguard in Mongolian uniform rushes in*]

BODYGUARD Go quickly. Her Ladyship is anxious to see you.

SUPERINTENDENT HO Coming right away. [*To* CHU LIEN-HSIU] Now, stick another flower into your hair and put on a little more powder and rouge. Her Ladyship, you know, wouldn't like to see a young woman too simple and plain.

[CHU LIEN-HSIU's *pupils help her apply fresh makeup. Enter* ATTENDANT]

ATTENDANT [*To* SUPERINTENDENT HO] Sir, Commander Wang wants to see Chu Lien-hsiu and Master Kuan.

SUPERINTENDENT HO Is he Commander Wang Chu of Yitu?[28] Show him in. [*To* KUAN HAN-CH'ING *after the* ATTENDANT *has withdrawn*] You'll find in this commander a warm, open-hearted man. He was the one among the audience who cried out "Death to the people's enemies!" I suggest that you receive him.

KUAN HAN-CH'ING Certainly.

[WANG CHU, *a stoutly-built military officer, is ushered in by the attendant*]

WANG CHU [*To* SUPERINTENDENT HO] Who played the role of Tou Ngo?

SUPERINTENDENT HO [*Turning his eyes to* CHU LIEN-HSIU *who is dabbing her nose with a powder-puff*] There she is.

WANG CHU [*To* CHU LIEN-HSIU] Congratulations upon your excellent performance. You certainly took the words out of our mouths: "The officials have no heart for justice, and the people dare not speak out."

CHU LIEN-HSIU Thank you, but it is the playwright who should be credited with those words. [*She directs his attention to* KUAN HAN-CH'ING]

WANG CHU Just the same, it is the way you sing, your voice flushed with emotion and power, that holds the audience spellbound.

BODYGUARD [*To* CHU LIEN-HSIU] Let's go now. Her Ladyship is waiting.

CHU LIEN-HSIU [*To* WANG CHU] I hope to have another opportunity of hearing your critical opinions. I must go and see Her Ladyship immediately. Please excuse me. [*She spruces up before the mirror and then turns to her pupils*] You go home first. [CHU LIEN-HSIU *retires, flanked by* SUPERINTENDENT HO *and the* BODYGUARD. *Her pupils start packing; some are leaving*]

WANG CHU [*To* KUAN HAN-CH'ING] Master Kuan, I have seen many of your plays, but this one impressed me most. Among the audience this evening, many were deeply moved. If it is no indiscretion to ask you, may I know whether the plot was taken from the case of Chu Hsiao-lan?

KUAN HAN-CH'ING [*Embarrassed*] No, it wasn't. It's based upon a historical tale.

WANG CHU I see. Then you should write more of these tales.

[HO CHEN, *an assistant to the Prime Minister, struts up following the* ATTENDANT *and* YEH HO-FU]

HO CHEN Where is Chu Lien-hsiu?

ATTENDANT Your Excellency, Superintendent Ho took her to see Her Ladyship just now.

HO CHEN Then which one is Kuan Han-ch'ing? [*Silence*]

YEH HO-FU [*Pointing at* KUAN HAN-CH'ING] This gentleman here.

HO CHEN [*Sizing him up*] So you are playwright Kuan Han-ch'ing. Don't you know me? [*Silence*]

YEH HO-FU This is His Excellency Lord Ho Chen.

KUAN HAN-CH'ING Oh. . . .

HO CHEN I thought you were a royal physician. So you write plays too, eh?

KUAN HAN-CH'ING Not very good ones.

HO CHEN You needn't be so modest. You write quite well. Her Ladyship was one of many who were moved to tears. Ha, ha, ha! Even our Lord Akham saw part of the play. Tomorrow we'll have to trouble you with the same performance again. We've decided to put "Tou Ngo" on the program instead of "The Riverside Pavilion." Do you hear? [*Silence*] The program is definitely decided. But the script will have to be changed in a number of places by your esteemed self. [*To* YEH HO-FU] Did you note down the lines pointed out by His Lordship?

YEH HO-FU I did, Your Excellency.

HO CHEN Where is the list?

YEH HO-FU Here it is.

HO CHEN [*Taking the list from* YEH HO-FU *and handing it to* KUAN HAN-CH'ING] Will you change these lines?

KUAN HAN-CH'ING [*Taking the list and glancing it over*] I'm afraid I can't. If all this is to be changed, it won't be a play anymore. [WANG HO-CH'ING *takes over the list from* KUAN HAN-CH'ING *to read*]

HO CHEN It never was a play in the first place. Not only we officials, but heaven and earth, gods and spirits, are under fire. You call that a play? I'll tell you, but the for presence of Her Ladyship, Lord Akham would have flown into a rage. It was I who . . .

YEH HO-FU It was Lord Ho Chen who did all the explaining and apologizing for you until Lord Akham finally said, "All right, tell Kuan Han-ch'ing to make the changes and we'll see the play again tomorrow."

KUAN HAN-CH'ING But I can't do that.

HO CHEN You can't do it? Quite a smart answer, eh? But Lord Akham has ordered the play to be banned unless it's changed in places.

WANG HO-CH'ING Han-ch'ing, make a few changes, will you?

KUAN HAN-CH'ING No, I would rather withdraw it than change it.

HO CHEN You seem to be quite proud of your obstinacy. Didn't your great sage Confucius say, "Know your wrongs, and amend them with a good grace"?

KUAN HAN-CH'ING He meant wrongs. . . .

HO CHEN And you aren't in the wrong? . . .

[CHU LIEN-HSIU, *carrying an armful of gifts, returns with Superintendent Ho*]

SUPERINTENDENT HO Believe me, Her Ladyship was really happy today. Look at these lavish gifts she gave—something she has never done in her life.

HO CHEN [*To* SUPERINTENDENT HO] Listen, Ho.

SUPERINTENDENT HO [*Smelling a rat*] Yes, my Lord.

HO CHEN Tomorrow evening at the same time.

SUPERINTENDENT HO Yes, sir.

HO CHEN And this same theater.

SUPERINTENDENT HO Yes, sir.

HO CHEN And the same play. Lord Akham wants to see it once more. Understand?

SUPERINTENDENT HO Very well, sir.

HO CHEN But the play has to be changed and acted accordingly. Kuan Han-ch'ing has been given the slip of paper.

KUAN HAN-CH'ING [*With determination*] Lord Ho, may I ask you to advise

Lord Akham that I would rather withdraw the play. If it's changed the way he wants, it will be completely disfigured and no longer recognizable as the original "Tou Ngo."

Ho CHEN Ha, ha! You are very, very foolish indeed, Kuan Han-ch'ing. Do you suppose Lord Akham is really interested in seeing your original "Tou Ngo"? Well, I think I've made myself clear: We want the play changed and performed accordingly, else all of you will lose your heads. [Ho CHEN, *followed by his bodyguards, walks off in a fury.* YEH HO-FU *stays on*]

YEH HO-FU Han-ch'ing, didn't I tell you before that the play would make trouble for you? Look here, a wise man never fights at a disadvantage. Why don't you make some changes? Just now Lord Khoshin complained to his father Akham how you ridiculed him here and there in your play. Some of your words hurt the old man himself. Of course, he couldn't help getting furious. We of this trade know too well that we are only playing a game. So, why do you take it so seriously? Why can't you smooth it over a bit? A few words less, and the storm will be over. Well, Han-ch'ing, will you listen to the advice of an old friend?

KUAN HAN-CH'ING [*Forced to draw the line*] You . . . an old friend? Bah! A spy—that's what you are!

WANG HO-CH'ING [*Fearing* KUAN HAN-CH'ING *will give rein to his tongue*] Han-ch'ing!

YEH HO-FU Look here! I meant to help you, but you're as stubborn as ever.

WANG HO-CH'ING Lao Yeh, let's have no more of this, please. Can't you see Han-ch'ing is in a temper?

YEH HO-FU So is Lord Akham. Just see whose temper counts. Good night and goodbye! [*He walks away haughtily, revealing his true colors*]

WANG HO-CH'ING [*Trailing* YEH HO-FU *angrily with his eyes*] I never thought that he was such a scoundrel! [WANG CHU *brings himself face to face with* KUAN HAN-CH'ING *and grasps his hand in a warm clasp*]

WANG CHU Master Kuan, I consider it a great fortune this evening not only to have seen your excellent play but also to know you as a man. You love your work so much that you are prepared to answer for it with your life. In this way you are making even a deeper impression on us and our hearts are still closer to you. You are absolutely right—let them kill the play, but not a word shall be changed. On the other hand, such an excellent piece of work should be given the widest presentation. If it can't be staged in Cambaluc, then go somewhere else. If it can't be shown in the north, go south. After all, China is a big country. Any time you come over to Yitu, you can count upon my hospitality. This evening I found your play so exciting, I couldn't help shouting. I'm sure when you take it to the people, you will hear more of them calling out. Yes, indeed, we must wipe out the people's enemies, and not compromise with these evil, corrupt officials. Well, I bid you all farewell. Take good care of yourselves. [*He waves to everybody and strides off with a determined step*]

WANG HO-CH'ING Compare the two; here is a man, whereas Yeh Ho-fu is at best a mouse.

CHU LIEN-HSIU Han-ch'ing, what shall we do? When I heard the voices offstage, I knew there was trouble in the air. Besides, Sai Lien-hsiu somehow became excited and seemed to have added a few extra lines. I literally had my heart in my mouth.

SUPERINTENDENT HO Master Kuan, after all is said and done, I'm afraid it simply means more work for you. I hope you'll take the time this evening to make the changes written on that slip. Tomorrow morning Lien-hsiu and others will have to rehearse again so that everything turns out well, don't you think? I am inclined to agree with Lao Yeh. You needn't rewrite the whole thing. Just don't say certain things. Phrases like "the officials show no justice," for instance, might as well be deleted. As to your rebuking heaven and earth, well, keep it in if you can't sing without it. You won't kill people by singing these things. To tell you the truth, these officials are extremely touchy about any ridicule cast on officialdom. They don't mind your grievances against heaven and earth so much, for they feel it's none of their business.

WANG HO-CH'ING You are quite right.

SUPERINTENDENT HO Well, it's time for everybody to go home now. [*Looking at* CHU LIEN-HSIU] Lien-hsiu, you must have worked hard in the last few days to produce this magnificent show. You'd better turn in early, and reserve some energy for the play tomorrow. Apart from the storm-cloud, I should think you've every reason to be satisfied, since Her Ladyship gave you so many presents. She's so fond of you, she even talked about taking you as an adopted daughter. So, good night, everybody. See you all tomorrow. [*He turns away*]

EVERYBODY Good night.

SUPERINTENDENT HO [*Looking over his shoulder*] Master Kuan, don't forget: "A man of men is he who knows when to eat humble pie and when to hold his head high." You will make the changes, won't you? [*Exit* SUPERINTENDENT HO, *followed by the attendants. Left on the stage are* KUAN HAN-CH'ING, WANG HO-CH'ING, *and* CHU LIEN-HSIU, *who has removed her makeup*]

CHU LIEN-HSIU Well, Han-ch'ing and Ho-ch'ing, what shall we do? We must decide right now.

WANG HO-CH'ING [*After a momentary pause*] The performance this evening was a sensation. Even some of the officials were moved. Commander Wang was one of them. But it's obvious that the more impressive the presentation is, the more irksome it is to those with a guilty conscience. Akham has more power in the court than all the others. Many of his own colleagues have fallen at his hands. Of course, he won't let us get away with it. Luckily, being a celebrity, Han-ch'ing can't be so easily disposed of, and then Po Yen's mother was so taken with Lien-hsiu's performance that she sent for her. Otherwise, anything might have happened to us. The resolute stand taken by Han-ch'ing is admirable. But the play won't be allowed on the stage without the changes. On the other hand, it has to be shown, for they've already booked the theatre for the purpose. So, whether we shall live or die, whether fortune will smile or frown on us, entirely depends upon the course of action we choose.

KUAN HAN-CH'ING I've already chosen my course. Let them stop the play; I won't change a word.

WANG HO-CH'ING But didn't they say that the play must be presented?

CHU LIEN-HSIU [*Decidedly*] Then it will be shown as it is. There won't be any changes.

WANG HO-CH'ING But you can't fool these cunning old foxes. Didn't you hear what Ho Chen said? "We want the play changed and performed accordingly, else all of you will lose your heads."

CHU LIEN-HSIU [*After a moment's thought*] I've an idea, Ho-ch'ing. You help smuggle Han-ch'ing out of town tonight, please. [*To* KUAN HAN-CH'ING] Han-ch'ing, you go. Leave everything to me. They may have my head chopped off, but I'll see to it that your play doesn't receive so much as a scratch.

KUAN HAN-CH'ING No, that won't do. If you're ready to give up your head, I'll throw mine in too.

[*Curtain*]

SCENE 7

In the hall of the Yü-hsien-lou Playhouse.

Deputy Prime Minister AKHAM, *in the company of High Minister* HORIK-HOSON, *is watching the performance.*

Because in her performance CHU LIEN-HSIU *adheres to the original version of the play, of which not a single word has been changed,* HO CHEN *and other responsible officials have been trying time and again to seize an opportunity to explain the matter to* AKHAM *and to request further instructions, but have found it inexpedient to do so in the presence of* HORIKHOSON.

AKHAM *is very angry, his eyes wide open; nevertheless he feels obliged to humor his guest.*

HORIKHOSON It isn't bad at all, Lord Akham. No wonder Po Yen's mother likes the play. The playwright has something to say. I understand he is among the best pens of the day, isn't that so?

AKHAM That's right. Lord Horikhoson, have you seen any of his plays before?

HORIKHOSON Hardly any. As you well know, I am not much of a theatergoer. That's why I didn't attend the performance yesterday. But when you bade me come over this evening, I couldn't possibly decline the honor.

AKHAM I am the one who should feel honored with your presence, of course. You are quite right—the author of this play is something of a celebrity. I understand he has written fifty or sixty plays. You know, under our dynasty, these Hans with a semblance of education, no longer able to carve their way to renown through civil service examinations, have diverted their thoughts to this profession. But that's quite all right with us. After all, didn't His Majesty tell us to find them an outlet for their surplus energy? That's why I often take time out to see their shows. For one thing, it's recreational. Then too I can find out for myself what's on their minds.

HORIKHOSON Lord Akham, you are very wise indeed. Next time when there is another excellent performance of the kind, please let me know. I shall be only too pleased to bear you company.

AKHAM H'mm, but these monkeys, you know, aren't so easy to handle. One can never keep them in their place. They compare the present with the past or slander by insinuations. And they will do the very thing they are forbidden to. Haven't you heard just now how this one inveighed against us officials?

HORIKHOSON Yes, I have. Very forceful, I must say, the way he hits the corrupt bureaucrats. But what's that to do with us?

AKHAM Lord Horikhoson, you are much too fair-minded, I'm afraid. If he attacks them, certainly he attacks us.

HORIKHOSON Let them attack. It's a good thing. It'll help to strengthen morality and discipline.

AKHAM No, that's one thing we can't do—let them talk. Once the lid is loose, there'll be a deluge of rebellion and they'll take the law into their own hands. No, you can't let them go too far!

[HORIKHOSON, *for the moment unable to think of an appropriate comment within the bounds of politeness in response to* AKHAM*'s haughty remarks, remains mute. Their attention once again shifts to the stage*]

TOU NGO [Singing] *It is not that I, Tou Ngo, choose to make any such wish after my death. Rather it will be the voice of my deep grievances forced to cry out. If there were no such thing as the Spirit of Righteousness that governs through generations of mankind, then the sky wouldn't be bright and blue. I desire my blood splashed over the streamer on the eight-foot flagpole, and none to redden the soil. Once this becomes visible to all, far and high, my blood will become sanctified.*

EXECUTIONER Have you anything more to say? If you don't say it now in the presence of His Honor the Execution Supervisor, you'll never say anything again.

TOU NGO Your Honor, mind you, it's now the height of summer. But if justice is indeed denied me, after my death there will be a heavy fall of snow—three feet deep—to cover my dead body.

EXECUTION SUPERVISOR In such a hot summer, even if the spirit of your grievances travels sky-high, it couldn't find a single snowflake at its command. None of your nonsense!

TOU NGO [Singing] *Do you really suppose it never snows on a summer day?*

*Haven't you heard that Tsou Yen[29] once caused frost to fall in midsummer?
If only the spirit of my grievances spouts like flames, certainly it will
command snow to whirl like cotton-balls and protect my corpse from
exposure. I shan't need a horse-wagon in white to carry me to the open
country for entombment....[She kowtows again] Your Honor, I, Tou Ngo,
am truly dying an unjust death. When I am gone, this district shall suffer
from a drought for three consecutive years.*

EXECUTION SUPERVISOR Shut up! Such nonsense!

TOU NGO [*Singing*] *You say you can't depend on Heaven and it shows no
sympathy for human suffering, but you don't know Heaven sometimes
does grant man's wishes. Why then for three whole years did it not rain
in Tunghai? It was because of the wrong done to a filial daughter. Now
it is the turn of Shanyang County, all because the officials show no justice
and the people dare not speak out.*

AKHAM [*Roars*] Stop! Stop the play!

BODYGUARDS Stop the play!

AKHAM This is intolerable! [*To* HO CHEN] What have you done?

HO CHEN I told them to make the changes as you ordered. Even today
I have been assured by Chu Lien-hsiu herself that the orders had been
complied with only to discover after the performance started that not a
single word has been touched.

AKHAM [*Laughing in scorn*] I thought you had been doing your work
fairly well. How could you be such an ass all of a sudden? Bring that
woman Chu Lien-hsiu here at once!

HO CHEN [*To the bodyguards*] Bring Chu Lien-hsiu here!

[*The bodyguards rush away and return with* CHU LIEN-HSIU, *wearing
her stage costume of a condemned convict*]

CHU LIEN-HSIU [*To* AKHAM] Allow me to kowtow to you, Your Lordship.

AKHAM So you are Chu Lien-hsiu.

CHU LIEN-HSIU Yes, I am.

AKHAM You're very bold, I must say. [*To* HO CHEN] What did you
tell them yesterday?

HO CHEN Your humble servant told them that the play had to be
changed and performed accordingly or else their heads would be cut
off.

AKHAM And the playwright, Kuan Han-ch'ing? Is he here this evening?

CHU LIEN-HSIU No, he didn't come.

AKHAM Where's he?

CHU LIEN-HSIU I don't know. His mother is sick; perhaps he has returned
to the country.

AKHAM You people were told to make the changes but you deliberately
refused. Why was this?

CHU LIEN-HSIU Kuan Han-ch'ing did make the changes. But there was
only half a day left for rehearsal. As I couldn't learn the new lines in
such a short time, I had no choice but to fall back upon the original. I
deserve death a thousand times. I beseech you, Your Lordship, to have
mercy on me.

AKHAM You really couldn't learn the new lines by heart? Aren't you
good at cramming? Apparently you are no coward. To save the neck of
Kuan Han-ch'ing, just like Tou Ngo trying to save her mother-in-law,
you would take the whole load on your own shoulders. [*To* HORIK-
HOSON] A commendable virtue, don't you think? [*He turns to* CHU
LIEN-HSIU] Very well, your good heart shall have its reward. Guards!
BODYGUARDS Yes, Sir.
AKHAM Take her away and off with her head!

[*The bodyguards are tying* CHU LIEN-HSIU. KUAN HAN-CH'ING *rushes
on to the scene*]

KUAN HAN-CH'ING Stop! [*To* AKHAM] Lord Akham, it's I who have
forbidden any changes in the play. It has nothing to do with Chu
Lien-hsiu.
AKHAM [*To Ho Chen*] Who is this man?
HO CHEN He is Kuan Han-ch'ing himself.
AKHAM So he takes upon himself the consequences of relieving the
wench of her fate. I can see he is no coward either. Now, Kuan Han-
ch'ing, you've written quite a number of plays; don't you even know
that under the laws of our dynasty it's a crime to propagate
inflammatory literature against the authorities. This latest work of
yours is not only inflammatory but full of personal slanders and
satire. That alone ought to cost you your head. But, considering the
fact that you're a talented writer in a way and have something of a
name, I gave you a chance to amend the play and present it again. But
you openly disobeyed me and told that wench of yours to act according
to the original script. What you did was virtually a revolt. Well, I may
as well grant both of you your wish to be martyrs. Guards!
BODYGUARDS Yes, Sir.
AKHAM Take them out and behead both of them! [*The bodyguards
fiercely rush upon* KUAN HAN-CH'ING *and tie him up. Greatly
disturbed and unable to hold his peace,* HORIKHOSON *rises from his
seat next to* AKHAM's]
HORIKHOSON Lord Akham, if I put in a word for someone, would you
deign to accept it?
AKHAM Yes, of course, Lord Horikhoson. Please do not stand on
ceremony. May I know your wish?
HORIKHOSON I am not acquainted with the woman, but I had the
privilege of meeting Kuan Han-ch'ing before. He is a heart specialist.
He prescribed a draught for me and it worked wonders. There are
quite a few among our colleagues who have heart trouble. If there
should be inquiries about what has become of the doctor, it might be
annoying. I understand your mother also suffers from the disease, isn't
that so?
AKHAM Well, then, on the strength of Lord Horikhoson's recommendation, have Kuan Han-ch'ing locked up for the present.

[*The bodyguards take away* KUAN HAN-CH'ING]

HO CHEN What shall we do with Chu Lien-hsiu?

AKHAM Behead that wench alone!

BODYGUARDS Yes, Sir.

[*The bodyguards are just about to take her away when* SUPERINTEN-DENT Ho *comes up hurriedly*]

SUPERINTENDENT Ho Lord Akham, this woman can't be beheaded either.

AKHAM Why not?

SUPERINTENDENT Ho Yesterday Prime Minister Po Yen's mother received her in person and gave her many precious gifts. Her Ladyship also said something about adopting her. Now, if she should mention the matter again, what shall we say?

AKHAM What? All the eighth or ninth grade scum of society has managed to get itself patronized! All right, lock her up, too, until my next audience with His Majesty. [*The bodyguards lead away* CHU LIEN-HSIU]

AKHAM [*To* HO CHEN] The one who acted Mistress T'sai, what's her name?

HO CHEN Sai Lien-hsiu.

AKHAM These monkeys are a troublesome lot. One is just as bad as the other. What they need is a little discipline. Bring Sai Lien-hsiu here!

[*Presently* SAI LIEN-HSIU *appears, led in by the bodyguards. She is still wearing her stage costume*]

SAI LIEN-HSIU Allow me to kowtow to you, Your Lordship.

AKHAM Tell me, Sai Lien-hsiu, can you read?

SAI LIEN-HSIU Yes, Your Lordship, but not much. I can read the script.

AKHAM What you spoke on the stage just now, "The day shall arrive when Heaven will open its eyes and have these cruel officials skinned alive." Is that in the script, I wonder?

SAI LIEN-HSIU No, it isn't.

AKHAM If it isn't in the script, they why did you give mouth to such words?

SAI LIEN-HSIU They are adapted from another script. Couplets like "Flowers may blossom anew, but youth never returns" are often freely improvised in singing.

AKHAM There're so many good quotations. Why did you have to pick this one particularly? What is your background?

SAI LIEN-HSIU You mean the kind of family I come from? Well, I am the daughter of a peasant. I come from a village to the west of the capital city. We had a few *mou* of land, but they were seized by a servant of Your Lordship's. My father, unable to eke out a living, finally had to sell me to the entertainment house to learn singing.

AKHAM And you have no patron?

SAI LIEN-HSIU No, I have none.

AKHAM Very well. You do wish Heaven could open its eyes and avenge your wrongs, don't you?

SAI LIEN-HSIU How dare I dream of such a thing?

AKHAM Guards!

BODYGUARDS Yes, Sir.

AKHAM Gouge out her eyes! [*The bodyguards lay hands on* SAI LIEN-HSIU *and finish the job expertly*]

SAI LIEN-HSIU [*Shrieking*] Help! Help!

AKHAM Now, Sai Lien-hsiu, are you still thirsting for revenge?

SAI LIEN-HSIU How could a girl like me ever have her revenge? I . . . I only beg Your Lordship to have my eyeballs hung on the walls of Cambaluc.

AKHAM On the city walls? Why?

SAI LIEN-HSIU [*Bursting with indignation*] To see Your Lordship's downfall!

AKHAM [*Roaring*] Throw her into the condemned cell!

HORIKHOSON [*Springing to his feet thoroughly disgusted*] Pardon me, Lord Akham. I must leave.

[*Curtain*]

SCENE 8

In a prison at Cambaluc at the end of the Third Moon in 1282. Late at night. The WARDEN *presides over an interrogation. Fiendish-looking prison guards stand in a line on either side. Though it is late spring, the air is unusually raw and chilly. The* WARDEN *passes his eye over the dossier, and then casts a glance at the* GAOLER *and the* WOMAN GAOLER.

WARDEN Has Kuan Han-ch'ing been quiet these days?

GAOLER Fairly quiet.

WARDEN Any visitors?

GAOLER His servant, Kuan Chung.

WARDEN, Nobody else?

GAOLER Yang Hsien-chih, and Liang Chin-chih came, and Wang Shih-fu sent over some food and other articles. A certain Mistress Liu and her daughter wanted to present him with something, but weren't admitted.

WARDEN Did you let Kuan Han-ch'ing have everything given him?

GAOLER Yes, I did, in accordance with your orders, sir.

WARDEN From now on, no visitors will be admitted any more, and no one will be allowed to bring him anything. [*He looks at* WOMAN GAOLER] And that goes for Chu Lien-hsiu, too. Understand?

GAOLER *and* WOMAN GAOLER Yes, sir.

WARDEN Any visitors for Chu Lien-hsiu?

WOMAN GAOLER Her pupil, Yen Shan-hsiu, came and Superintendent Ho had something sent over.

WARDEN Who else?

WOMAN GAOLER That's all.

WARDEN From now on, watch her more closely.

WOMAN GAOLER Yes, Sir.

WARDEN How about that Sai Lien-hsiu? Does she keep swearing?

WOMAN GAOLER Yes, she does, but on the whole she has calmed down a little. Only her eyes are still bleeding. Shall we get her a doctor?

WARDEN They may summon her one of these days, you never can tell. I wouldn't want to see her die here. Give her the medicine prescribed by Kuan Han-ch'ing. Had she any visitors?

WOMAN GAOLER An actor by the name of Ch'ien Shua-ch'iao came to see her about every three days.

WARDEN From now on, don't let him in again. Now, bring Kuan Han-ch'ing here.

PRISON GUARD [*Repeating the order*] Bring Kuan Han-ch'ing here!

[*The* GAOLER *exits, and almost immediately one hears chains and fetters clanking. Enter* KUAN HAN-CH'ING]

GAOLER On your knees! [KUAN HAN-CH'ING *stoutly refuses to kneel down. The gaoler threatens to hit his legs with a cudgel*]

WARDEN [*Stopping the gaoler*] Don't be harsh with him! [*To* KUAN HAN-CH'ING] You may sit down. [*To the prison guard*] Bring him a stool.

[*The prison guard brings over a stool on which* KUAN HAN-CH'ING *sits*]

WARDEN Well, how do you find yourself these days?

KUAN HAN-CH'ING The sun and moon are warming my heart though my eyebrows and temples are frosted over. I haven't given up the ghost yet.

WARDEN I certainly don't want to see you die. Your literary works are beyond me, but I know for a fact that you are a good doctor. My mother has felt so much better ever since she took your prescription. She has suffered from rheumatism for years; we never expected her to recover so quickly. Now she's able to walk with a cane.

KUAN HAN-CH'ING A little walk is good for her. But she shouldn't try too much at her age.

WARDEN I understand perfectly. Thank you very much. Now, Kuan Han-ch'ing, your case is getting more and more serious. Frankly, I'm afraid no one can help you. I'm very sorry indeed! [*Some of the prison guards are whispering to one another*]

KUAN HAN-CH'ING [*Baffled*] Getting more and more serious?

WARDEN Can't be any worse. Do you know a certain Wang Chu?

KUAN HAN-CH'ING Wang Chu?

WARDEN Yes, Commander Wang Chu of Yitu, remember? Are you well acquainted with him?

KUAN HAN-CH'ING Oh, I remember him now. That evening when "Tou Ngo" was presented at Yü-hsien-lou Playhouse, he came backstage to see us.

WARDEN He was deeply stirred by your play, wasn't he?

KUAN HAN-CH'ING That was what he said. He was so excited that he even cried out in the theater, "Death to the people's enemies!" We met him just once, on that occasion, and I must say we hardly know him.

WARDEN Well, he is a man of deed, all right. And not a small deed either. Do you have an old friend by the name of Yeh Ho-fu?

KUAN HAN-CH'ING Well, there exists such a person, but I wouldn't call him an old friend.

WARDEN He wants to have a talk with you.

KUAN HAN-CH'ING I have nothing to say to him!

WARDEN See him anyway. You might find it profitable. [*He turns his head*] Master Yeh, please. [YEH HO-FU *enters from a back room*]

YEH HO-FU [*In a voice of exaggerated concern*] My dear old friend! To think we should meet here! You never listened to a word I said. I was worried from the very beginning lest there should be such a day. I told you—remember?—you had better not write "Tou Ngo," and that if you did, it would draw more frowns than smiles from fortune. Now, you see what has happened. Unfortunately my prediction has come true.

KUAN HAN-CH'ING [*With great disdain*] Tell me what you want, quickly.

YEH HO-FU You're as impetuous as ever. Don't you think it's high time you train yourself to be a little less temperamental?

KUAN HAN-CH'ING [*Annoyed*] If you have anything to say, speak up. [YEH HO-FU *whispers in the warden's ear*]

WARDEN [*To the prison guards,* GAOLER *and* WOMAN GAOLER*:* All of you leave this room. [*They exit*]

YEH HO-FU [*In a low voice*] Now, Han-ch'ing, I'm afraid I must first break a piece of horrible news to you. That friend of yours, Wang Chu, conspiring with the wizard-monk Kao, assassinated Lord Akham and Lord Ho Chen on the night of the 10th of the last month at Shangtu.[30]

KUAN HAN-CH'ING Oh, really?

YEH HO-FU It's absolutely true. The whole imperial court, high and low, is upset by this news. Such a misfortune to the nation!

KUAN HAN-CH'ING Is there anything else you want to tell me?

YEH HO-FU I want you to realize the calamity you've brought about, all because you wouldn't take my advice! That rebel Wang Chu, you know, began his designs on the life of Lord Akham only after he had seen your play.

KUAN HAN-CH'ING [*Angered*] What makes you think so?

YEH HO-FU Many people heard him shout "Death to the people's enemies" the other day in the midst of the performance of "Tou Ngo" at Yü-hsien-lou. Later, when he was brought to justice at Shangtu, he cried again, "It's the people's enemies that I, Wang Chu, have slain." And then in your play there is actually a line which says, "Put all the evil, corrupt officials out of the way."

KUAN HAN-CH'ING [*With restraint*] Don't you think the evil and corrupt officials should be done away with?

YEH HO-FU Well . . . yes, they should be.

KUAN HAN-CH'ING Should we or should we not get rid of the people's enemies?

YEH HO-FU We should, of course. But it was wrong of Wang Chu to believe that his assassination of Lord Akham would be a service to the people.

KUAN HAN-CH'ING Whether the assassination of Akham serves the interests of the people or not is for the people themselves to judge. But, granting, as you said, that Wang Chu attempted Akham's life under the sway of my play, why did the monk Kao, who didn't see my play, also want to kill Akham?

YEH HO-FU Well . . .

KUAN HAN-CH'ING In our characterization we playwrights either praise or censure. Take, for instance, the historical characters. We sing the praises of Yueh Fei but we condemn Ch'in Kuei,[31] and at times spectators are likely to be so aroused that they kill the same type of man as Ch'in Kuei out of righteous indignation. In such a case can you honestly charge the playwright with aiding and abetting?

YEH HO-FU Han-ch'ing, what you've said is reasonable, of course. But at the present moment when feeling is running high, how can you expect His Majesty and his ministers to listen to you? Besides, I am not here tonight to argue with you about the repercussions of your play "Tou Ngo." [*With bated breath again*] I am here upon personal instructions from Lord Khoshin to make an important bargain with you. You know, your case is quite serious, but if you promise to cooperate, it can be extenuated even to the point of having you released.

KUAN HAN-CH'ING I want no part of any bargain with Khoshin.

YEH HO-FU Come, my friend, calm down; you'll have nothing to lose anyway. Wang Chu is dead, and he can't be called to witness. All you'll have to do is to testify at your hearing that Wang Chu assassinated Lord Akham with the intention of getting rid of a minister loyal to the Yuan dynasty and of plotting against the court in collusion with the rowdy elements among the Kin and Han people throughout the country. If you only give this testimony, your offense will be extenuated and Lord Khoshin will give you a cash reward of one million *chung-t'ung-ch'ao*.[32] This, indeed, is a handsome fortune, old chap.

KUAN HAN-CH'ING [*Beside himself with anger*] Have you finished?

YEH HO-FU Yes, all I came here for tonight is to make you this momentous proposition.

KUAN HAN-CH'ING Come near and let me talk to you.

YEH HO-FU Do you agree? [*He steps over*]

KUAN HAN-CH'ING Do I? [*He gives* YEH *a box the ear, hitting him so hard he is thrown off balance*]

YEH HO-FU [*Staggering to his feet*] Han-ch'ing, I'm here to talk to you as a friend and in all sincerity. Certainly I didn't expect you to be so rude.

KUAN HAN-CH'ING You dog, you have two slits for eyes but you cannot see you have the wrong man. I, Kuan Han-ch'ing, am known to people as a bronzebean which can't be made soft by cooking nor flattened by beating. You try to bribe me and make me a tool of that stinking, corrupt bureaucrat, Khoshin. To think that a shameless beast of your kind was bred within our own ranks! I could tear you to pieces and devour your flesh!

YEH HO-FU [*Grimly*] You won't do it, eh? All right, then wait for your execution.

KUAN HAN-CH'ING Never again for the life of me will I speak another word to such a cur. Warden, please let me return to my cell.

WARDEN Well. [*To* YEH HO-FU] Master Yeh, you'd better go back. [YEH HO-FU *slips off. The prison guards return and resume their formation*]

WARDEN Kuan Han-ch'ing, you're right. If you ever consented to give testimony as he suggested, we Han people would have to bear the brunt. You are a good man, and moreover I'm personally indebted to you for having cured my mother. But with my petty office, my powers are limited. There isn't much I can do for you, but I can give you this tip: you only have a few days to live. Now, if you have certain personal affairs to be settled, or if you have a message to be delivered, so long as it doesn't openly embarrass my office, I shall place my service at your disposal. Is there anything you'd like to eat? I can buy it for you, you know.

KUAN HAN-CH'ING [*Trying to collect himself*] Thank you. I've no appetite for any particular food, nor is there any business that awaits my attention. But seeing that you are so devoted to your mother, I have here a letter for my own, and I wonder if I may trouble you to forward it to her after it's all over with me. Please take care not to frighten my old mother. This little request of mine is no different from that of Tou Ngo's when she asked not to be taken by the main street so as to avoid being seen by her mother-in-law.

WARDEN [*Taking the letter*] All right, I assure you I'll have it delivered accordingly. Don't worry.

KUAN HAN-CH'ING Would it be possible for Kuan Chung to make one more trip?

WARDEN I'm afraid not. I'm sorry.

KUAN HAN-CH'ING It's quite all right.

WARDEN Is there anything you want to tell any one?

KUAN HAN-CH'ING Plenty, only I don't know where to begin and who to tell. [*Suddenly it occurs to him*] Would you allow me to see Chu Lien-hsiu?

WARDEN Well . . . all right. I think I can make an exception and take the responsibility upon myself. But what good will it do to talk to her? She will share the same fate.

KUAN HAN-CH'ING It's just like "two fish swapping spit in a drying pond," as the saying goes. If you think you can manage it, I would appreciate it as a favor.

WARDEN [*To the* WOMAN GAOLER] Bring Chu Lien-hsiu here!

WOMAN GAOLER Yes, Sir.

[*She withdraws and in a short while brings in* CHU LIEN-HSIU, *still wearing the clothing of a convict as Tou Ngo, her chains and fetters clanking as she enters*]

CHU LIEN-HSIU [*Falling on her knees*] Allow me to kowtow to Your

Lordship.

WARDEN You may rise. Kuan Han-ch'ing wants to have a word with you. I'm giving you a few moments. [*To the* GAOLER *and* WOMAN GAOLER] When they are through, take them back to their cells. Mind your duty. [*To prison guards*] Let us retire.

[*Exeunt all except* KUAN HAN-CH'ING *and* CHU LIEN-HSIU]

CHU LIEN-HSIU Well, Han-ch'ing, here we meet once again.

KUAN HAN-CH'ING [*In a grave tone*] I'm afraid this is the last time.

CHU LIEN-HSIU [*In a tremulous voice*] Really?

KUAN HAN-CH'ING D'you remember that Commander Wang?

CHU LIEN-HSIU You mean Wang Chu whom we met backstage at the Yü-hsien-lou Playhouse?

KUAN HAN-CH'ING Yes, that's the one.

CHU LIEN-HSIU I spoke but a few words with him; somehow he impressed me as an honest and open-hearted man. But I must say I didn't quite expect him to embark upon this earth-shaking enterprise. For that we have every reason to be proud of him as a patron of our stirring play "Tou Ngo."

KUAN HAN-CH'ING I can see from the way you talk you feel quite triumphant. But do you know he killed Akham?

CHU LIEN-HSIU Of course, I do. Yesterday a new inmate came. She is Commander Wang's aunt and she lives at Cambaluc. She told me that Commander Wang shouted in protest even with the last breath, "It's the people's enemy I've slain. Now, I'm going to die, but in future someone will bear record to what I did." A remarkable man!

KUAN HAN-CH'ING Well, there are people who linked up what he did with this line in our script, "You'll do His Majesty a great service by putting to death an enemy of the people." And the charge is that we encouraged Wang Chu to assassinate the court ministers, which made our case more serious.

CHU LIEN-HSIU But he did kill an enemy of the people, didn't he? This heartless Akham was so cruel as to gouge out the eyes of my pupil.

KUAN HAN-CH'ING Wang Chu avenged her, and he avenged us too—as it so happens, I wish I could write a line about him, but unfortunately time is running out.

CHU LIEN-HSIU Time is running out?

KUAN HAN-CH'ING The warden informed me just now. In a day or two my number will be up. I'm afraid you'll be next. He advised us to tell him of the things we want cleared up and any message we may have for our friends or relatives in good time so that he can take care of them for us. I wonder if there is any note you'd like him to deliver. Incidentally, if there is anything you'd like to eat, he'll get it for you, too. [*Seeing her face*] Oh, Fourth Sister, I have frightened you, haven't I?

CHU LIEN-HSIU [*Turning pale but pulling herself together*] No, I'm not afraid.

KUAN HAN-CH'ING Fourth-Sister, I'm extremely sorry. It's all because of my play that you are made to suffer all this.

CHU LIEN-HSIU What nonsense! Didn't I give my word that if you dared to write, I would dare to act? When I said that, I was aware something like this would happen.

KUAN HAN-CH'ING But you didn't know it would come so soon.

CHU LIEN-HSIU What difference does it make—sooner or later? As a matter of fact, I've never found life so rich and meaningful as it is these days. I feel all the more keenly that I am one among a multitude. Don't you see? The people hate Akham; so do we. We dare to fight him and his like. Wang Chu killed an enemy of the people. He gave his life, and again we find ourselves on his side, battling with the wicked to our last moment. And isn't Tou Ngo this kind of woman who wouldn't yield to the evil forces even on pain of death? I admire such a woman and I want to answer with my life the way she did. Look at this costume I'm wearing, the same as Tou Ngo wore, and before long I'll fall as she did. But I won't fall so meekly. Like Tou Ngo, I'll protest aloud before I drop down. Perhaps I'll even shout out like Wang Chu, "Death to the people's enemies!" Shall I, Han-ch'ing? Right now I really don't know whether I'm off the stage or still on it, for I feel as though I'm standing face to face with thousands of spectators and I have perfect confidence in myself. Frankly, when you broke the news about our immediate fate, I felt a little upset. Now I'm over it. You can rest assured that I'll remain as firm and unflinching as Tou Ngo.

KUAN HAN-CH'ING I'll give you the same assurance, Fourth Sister. My family name is Kuan. Although I am now considered a resident of Cambaluc, my home town is Chiehliang, Puchow.[33] I'll lay down my life as fearlessly as that great heroic ancestor of our family. "The jade may be smashed, but its color will remain immaculately white; and the bamboo may be burned but its joints are indestructible and remain as evidence of its integrity and strength." These words express the feeling in my heart.

CHU LIEN-HSIU But there is one thing that makes it impossible for me ever to rest in peace. The other evening at the Yü-hsien-lou Playhouse, I asked Ho-ching to help you get away. Why didn't you? Instead you came to see the play the next evening. Are you that much of a theater fan?

KUAN HAN-CH'ING How could I leave? How could I let you accept such a heavy load alone?

CHU LIEN-HSIU But what am I? Nothing but an entertainer. How can I be compared with you? You are one of the great playwrights of this age, harbinger of contemporary drama. The theater will be dull without your plays. You should write more good plays for the people. You should speak more for the common people who dare not speak for themselves. You should carry on your fight for the wronged, oppressed women, for the sake of justice. But . . . but they'll kill you now in the same obscure way as they kill me! No, they can't do this to you! Let them kill me, but they must spare you . . . [She bursts into a convulsive sob]

KUAN HAN-CH'ING Fourth Sister, it's really good of you to think so highly of me. But isn't it precisely because we've spoken for the people that we must die? It's said that what is written with blood is more valuable than what is written with ink. Perhaps our death will only enrich and strengthen our voice. However, there is this difference between us: I'm approaching fifty, and you're young and talented; already you've made a name for yourself. I'm afraid people will blame me for your untimely death. Now, since Prime Minister Po Yen's old mother is so fond of you and even wanted to take you as an adopted daughter, why don't you write her a letter asking her to help you? I wager something will come of it. You may entrust your letter to Superintendent Ho; I'm sure it will reach her. Why don't you write now? Or, if you like, I'll write it for you.

CHU LIEN-HSIU How about yourself? You can ask her for help as well.

KUAN HAN-CH'ING How can I?

CHU LIEN-HSIU Then why should I write to her? After all, isn't she the mother of that Prime Minister Po Yen, who kills people in cold blood? She liked me simply because I've made her shed a few crocodile tears. I don't think she really appreciates or understands our art. That she laments over a tragedy is only a public gesture to make people believe she has a soft heart. But did she ever shed a single tear, when her son massacred the whole population of a city one day and another time killed all those who had surrendered to him? I hate that kind of woman. Beg of her? No, not for the life of me!

KUAN HAN-CH'ING If you don't, you'll . . .

CHU LIEN-HSIU Die? But what more can I hope for but to die together with you? Fate forbids me to enjoy your companionship in life, then may we rest in peace together, Han-ch'ing! [*She holds* KUAN HAN-CH'ING*'s hands in a warm clasp*]

KUAN HAN-CH'ING Fourth Sister, I feel our hearts are closer to each other at this moment than ever before. The very day we were imprisoned, I visualized this hour. The night before last, I wrote a song, called "A Pair of Butterflies."[34] I was going to show it to you, but nobody dared to take it to you. I didn't insist, of course. Now I want to hand it to you in person. I wish you could sing it.

CHU LIEN-HSIU Let me see it. [*She takes it out of his hand*]

KUAN HAN-CH'ING It's almost illegible. Can you make it out?

CHU LIEN-HSIU Certainly. [*She reads and sings by snatches*]

> *We shall lay down our lives like the martyrs of old,*
> *whose spirit keeps haunting the wicked.*
> *And our blood shall flow*
> *eternally like the Yellow River,*
> *like the Yangtse mingling with the souls of the*
> *heroes*
> *of times bygone.*

This is something nobler than writing about maidens
   embroidering in their chambers,
Or scholars in their silks
   visiting the royal court,
Or philanderers romancing by brightly painted windows.
These embellished lines may give the country
   something to read and think about,
   but to survive the rigors of a snowstorm
   takes the strength of a pine.
I studied thousands of volumes of the classics;
I wrote more than fifty plays.
And all these years the nation has been crushed,
   people have suffered untold misery everywhere.
We saw, and we fought,
   till "Tou Ngo" sped us to our deaths.
The moon wanes by itself,
   the single wick flickers out alone,
   but we shall die together.
Resting, we share
   the same glimpse of the clouds
   through our barred windows.
Walking, our chains clank in unison.
But like the rainbow
   our hearts are bright with faith and strength.
Who would waste tears?
If there is no place for martyrs
   in the nether world,
   are there not green vales reserved
   in which the pure and great may rest?
Years divide us, but our hearts are one.
Unwedded, we shall lie in the same grave.
Behold! When the fields again
   are red with azalea[35] blossoms,
   how two butterflies, you and I,
   will flutter in the breeze, loving each other,
   never to part!

CHU LIEN-HSIU Oh, Han-ch'ing! [*She hugs him*]
[*Enter the* GAOLER *and* WOMAN GAOLER]
GAOLER Time's up. Go back to your cells. [*He parts them*]
WOMAN GAOLER [*To* CHU LIEN-HSIU] I heard you talk, and indeed you're much to be pitied. Since you two will never see each other again, I'll give you a chance to say farewell.
CHU LIEN-HSIU That won't be necessary.
KUAN HAN-CH'ING There is no need for us to say farewell, for we shall never part.

WOMAN GAOLER Then back to your own ward. [*They are both led away, their chains and fetters rattling in unison*]

[*Curtain*]

SCENE 9 (SUMMARY)

In Scene 9 Akham is posthumously revealed as a tyrant by official investigation, and a petition to spare Kuan Han-ch'ing, bearing more than 10,000 signatures, is entrusted to Chou Fu-hsiang, now married to Erh-niu, for delivery to Horikhoson.

SCENE 10

The patter of chilly autumn rain. In a prison cell, an inmate sits huddled up in a corner, silent as the grave. Two prison guards are taking KUAN HAN-CH'ING *to this cell. They unlock the door and throw him on the ground with a loud rattling of his handcuffs and fetters. The guards fasten the door again and march away.* KUAN HAN-CH'ING *staggers to his feet, rubbing his legs and arms.*

KUAN HAN-CH'ING [*Thinking aloud with a deep sigh*] They are mine no more. But, [*Gnashing his teeth*] they will not make my heart waver and they will never claim it. [*Exhausted, he makes for the corner where the first inmate is seated*]

   [*The first inmate utters a sound*]

KUAN HAN-CH'ING [*Starting*] What? You're a human being?

FIRST INMATE [*Jeering at himself*] Well, for the present I still am.

KUAN HAN-CH'ING [*Sweeping the cell with a listless glance*] Only you?

FIRST INMATE There was another one last night.

KUAN HAN-CH'ING Where's he gone?

FIRST INMATE They pulled him out this morning and skinned him alive.

KUAN HAN-CH'ING [*With utter disgust*] H'mmm, they either gouge out your eyes or break your bones or skin you alive—and that has become their daily routine. But how did you find out?

FIRST INMATE They told me.

KUAN HAN-CH'ING Why were you sent here?

FIRST INMATE Because I'm a Han.

KUAN HAN-CH'ING For no other reason?

FIRST INMATE They demanded my wife of me. I refused. They beat me and I hit back.

KUAN HAN-CH'ING Is that all?

FIRST INMATE That's all.

KUAN HAN-CH'ING Being a man, you had to fight back.

FIRST INMATE And what brought you here?

KUAN HAN-CH'ING I was accused of "propagating inflammatory literature against the authorities." What is more . . .

FIRST INMATE So you're Kuan Han-ch'ing, I suppose?

KUAN HAN-CH'ING How do you know?

FIRST INMATE Well, among the playwrights nowadays there aren't many who dare to offend the authorities. Besides, when you came, the whole prison heard about it. Isn't there a certain Chu Lien-hsiu with you?

KUAN HAN-CH'ING Yes.

FIRST INMATE You're good people. You've the courage to speak for us. Unfortunately I haven't seen your new play. Isn't it called Tou something?

KUAN HAN-CH'ING "Tou Ngo" is the title. I hope you'll have a chance to see it some day.

FIRST INMATE [*With a sardonic laugh*] In my next life, you mean. [*His voice expressing sympathy and deep concern*] But how is it that you are transferred to this cell, too? That looks bad!

KUAN HAN-CH'ING Why?

FIRST INMATE Nobody in this cell has ever survived longer than three days.

KUAN HAN-CH'ING How many days have you been here?

FIRST INMATE I was moved here the day before yesterday.

KUAN HAN-CH'ING For Heaven's sake! What's your name?

FIRST INMATE Liu Ch'ang-sheng.[36] The name has become a mockery now.

KUAN HAN-CH'ING [*His voice earnest with conviction*] No, I don't think so. You are among the brave who dare fight back, and you will become an immortal.

FIRST INMATE Thanks. With such words I can die happily.

KUAN HAN-CH'ING Is there anything you want me to do? You may count upon my service.

FIRST INMATE But you yourself will have only a day or two to live.

KUAN HAN-CH'ING I shall do whatever I can even when I have only two days to live.

FIRST INMATE Well, then, will you please tell people if they all have the courage to fight back, happy times will come to them.

KUAN HAN-CH'ING You're right.

[*Enter the* WARDEN *on inspection duty, lantern in hand, and accompanied by prison guards*]

WARDEN [*Calls the roll*] Liu Ch'ang-sheng.

LIU CH'ANG-SHENG Here.

WARDEN Come out.

LIU CH'ANG-SHENG Good-bye, Kuan Han-ch'ing.

KUAN HAN-CH'ING I'll be coming.

[LIU CH'ANG-SHENG *goes out*]

WARDEN Tie him up.

[*The prison guards have hardly laid hands on* LIU CH'ANG-SHENG *when he hits one of them with his fist and sends him reeling. But more guards rush up and tie him hand and foot*]

WARDEN Take him away.

[*The guards withdraw with* LIU CH'ANG-SHENG]

WARDEN [*Searching for Kuan Han-ch'ing with his lantern*] Kuan Han-ch'ing!

KUAN HAN-CH'ING [*Perfectly calm*] Here

WARDEN [*Passing a slip of paper to Kuan Han-ch'ing, under his breath*] From Chu Lien-hsiu. [*He fastens the door and retires forthwith*]

KUAN HAN-CH'ING [*Spreads out the slip and reads it in the dim lantern light*]

> In fetters bound
> I sat and listened to the autumnal rain
> 　　till I fell asleep.
> I dreamed I was set free,
> 　　acting Tou Ngo again.
> I awoke with a start
> 　　at hearing the bell tower.
> We may go any minute,
> But our hearts shall shine
> 　　through all eternity.
>
> 　　　　　　　　—Dedicated to Han-ch'ing in prison.
> 　　　　　　　　Adapted to the tune "Chi-sheng-tsao."

KUAN HAN-CH'ING Don't worry about me, Fourth Sister, I have the courage to face it!.

[*Curtain*]

SCENE 11 (SUMMARY)

In Scene 11 the official Horikhoson is persuaded against his better judgment to release Kuan Han-ch'ing and allow him to go south into exile.

SCENE 12

Lukouch'iao is not far from Cambaluc. It is also called Marco Polo Bridge by some people, because Marco Polo, an Italian, who served under Kublai Khan, mentioned the structure in his writings. Actually the bridge was built some 88 years before the arrival of Marco Polo at Kublai Khan's court, being the monumental work of Chinese working people. It had nothing to do with Marco Polo. Its stone railings each have a carved lion on them. There are one hundred odd exquisite stone lions on its parapets in various attitudes. At the head of the bridge there is a pavilion and a row of willows. Underneath the bridge, the river is swollen with spring floods. This is where the south-bound highway begins and where the people of Cambaluc come to bid travelers farewell.

Two old peasants, one carrying a hoe on his shoulder, and the other a plough, come up across the bridge from one end and are greeted by a young peasant, who, plough in hand, is going the other way.

YOUNG PEASANT Uncle Chou and Uncle Liu, have you finished for the day?

PEASANT CHOU Almost finished.

YOUNG PEASANT Old people shouldn't work too hard, Uncle.

PEASANT CHOU What can I do? Thank Heaven I had my boy's help. I just managed to get my small plot returned to me. So I have to work it. And you, young fellow, are you going down to the fields?

YOUNG PEASANT No, I'm going to see about the flood. [*He crosses the bridge*]

PEASANT LIU [*Heaving a sigh*] Last year a great drought and this year too much water. Another flood and we'll be done for.

PEASANT CHOU You ought to be glad you are able to keep a small tavern in town, and that you have so capable a wife.

PEASANT LIU I've always suspected, however, that the capital city isn't such a peaceful place to stay. Look what's happened!

PEASANT CHOU Do you expect peace in the countryside either these days? Over there in Ts'ui Village the other day, wasn't old man Hu's daughter kidnapped by a *t'uluhun*?[37]

PEASANT LIU You're right. It makes no difference—town or country. Heaven only knows when we people shall ever have peace again.

PEASANT CHOU [*Putting his hoe on the ground*] I must be really getting old. What about stopping here for a smoke?

PEASANT LIU [*Laying down his plough*] All right, let's have a rest.

[*They strike a flint to light their pipes*]

YOUNG PEASANT [*Retracing his steps*] By the way, Uncle Chou, your daughter-in-law, the bride, is back and her mother came with her. Aunt Chou wanted me to tell you. I forgot it just now. [*Having delivered the message, he goes on his way*]

PEASANT CHOU Thank you very much. [*To* PEASANT LIU] Your daughter is here. Let's go.

PEASANT LIU What's the hurry? You have your daughter-in-law in your house now. Let's finish our pipe.

PEASANT CHOU All right. [*They sit down face to face, smoking*]

[*Enter* WANG HO-CH'ING *and his servants. They start to unpack a case they have with them, taking out cups, saucers, bowls, and chopsticks on the stone table in the pavilion. Around the table are seven or eight stone chairs. There are also stone stools between the stone pillars. The servants are cleaning up the place.* YANG HSIEN-CHIH *enters and greets* WANG HO-CH'ING]

YANG HSIEN-CHIH How do you do, Ho-ch'ing!

WANG HO-CH'ING Why, it's Hsien-chih. Have you just arrived?

YANG HSIEN-CHIH No, I came earlier. Then I went to Wanp'ing to see a friend. Are you here to see Han-ch'ing off too? Didn't you always argue with him? Ha, ha!

WANG HO-CH'ING I certainly did. But it looks like I'll have to carry on the argument alone, now that Kuan Han-ch'ing is going away.

Heaven knows what will happen next.

[*When he hears the name Kuan Han-ch'ing,* PEASANT LIU *steps up anxiously*]

PEASANT LIU Excuse me, Sir. What has become of Kuan Han-ch'ing?

WANG HO-CH'ING Well, old man! Do you know who Kuan Han-ch'ing is?

PEASANT LIU Who doesn't? Everybody in Cambaluc has seen his plays.

PEASANT CHOU In the play "Lord Kuan Goes to the Feast," Kuan Han-ch'ing depicts the hero in a way worthy of his illustrious ancestor. I've also seen him on the stage himself. In his younger days, he came to our village to perform quite often. I knew then that this young fellow would come to the top of the tree some day. Well, isn't he the best playwright today?

PEASANT LIU [*To* WANG HO-CH'ING] Sir, what has become of him? It's said he's been sentenced to death, is that true? There're few good men like him in Cambaluc. Why don't they let him live a few more years and write more plays like he's been putting out? I must say the ways of the world are queer indeed. The bad ones live on and on, whereas the good men get their heads chopped off, one after another.

WANG HO-CH'ING You needn't worry any more, my friend. Kuan Han-ch'ing's death sentence has been commuted to banishment. We are waiting here to bid him farewell.

PEASANT LIU What's that? Kuan Han-ch'ing is coming this way? Is he still alive? Is he leaving us?

WANG HO-CH'ING Yes.

PEASANT LIU [*Picking up his plough and turning to* PEASANT CHOU] I say, let's go and tell our folks. [*They set out immediately*]

WANG HO-CH'ING [*Moved*] Well, I concede!

YANG HSIEN-CHIH What do you concede?

WANG HO-CH'ING Well, in arguing and talking about nothing, I can always outdo Han-ch'ing. But now I've found out that in making friends with people or in the public estimation, I'm way behind, and I concede I am the loser.

[*Enter* LIANG CHIN-CHIH, *a great composer and physician and* WANG SHIH-FU, *a noted dramatist.* WANG HO-CH'ING *and* YANG HSIEN-CHIH *go up to meet them*]

LIANG CHIN-CHIH Hsien-chih and Ho-ch'ing, you two must have arrived here quite early.

YANG HSIEN-CHIH No, we've just come.

WANG HO-CH'ING [*To* WANG SHIH-FU] I've heard you have not been feeling well. Are you sure you can stand this wind from the river?

WANG SHIH-FU I always come out for a walk, but the moment I pick up my pen, it gives me a headache. Yesterday I received a letter from my son and learned that Han-ch'ing was to leave for the south. I set out in the dead of night to make sure I would get here in time to see him off. But the donkey I rode was in no hurry. I was worried lest I might be late. Fortunately everything has turned out all right.

WANG HO-CH'ING I can't help reciting those lines of yours which are really a stroke of genius: "Up in the blue sky the clouds travel high, and the earth is littered with yellowed flowers. The westerly wind sharpens, and the wild geese are hurrying south."[38] Although the season at present is one of greening willows and blue rippling water, yet spring is at the mercy of autumn, so that the northern wild geese have begun moving south.

WANG SHIH-FU The whole thing is indeed most unexpected. Cases of writers being persecuted are not wanting in history, of course. But among us I must say that Han-ch'ing has been victimized in the worst conceivable way. The second time I sent my boy over to the prison to take him something, they refused to accept it. I was very much worried lest I might never see him again. Then, all of a sudden, they softened again. Why? Could it be because they have reexamined the case of Wang Chu?

WANG HO-CH'ING I think so. From what I've heard, it was all because His Majesty said something about lessening the penalty on all cases in which Akham had a hand. The imperial censor, Lord Pai Tung, has been released. The penalties which were to have been imposed on Han-ch'ing and Chu Lien-hsiu, which might have been decapitation, were also reduced. Otherwise, we'd have to see them off at the execution ground.

WANG SHIH-FU Hsieh Hsiao-shan came to see me the other day soliciting my endorsement of a ten-thousand-signature petition. I signed my name. But I wonder if it has been presented.

YANG HSIEN-CHIH Yes, that's right. We all signed, and took part in drafting that petition. If it has been submitted, it will have had a certain effect, I'm sure.

LIANG CHIN-CHIH What I can't understand is this. If it's true that Akham deserved to be put to death, that Wang Chu did the right thing, and that the denunciations in "Tou Ngo" are all justified, then why isn't Han-ch'ing acquitted and a free man again? Why should he be banished?

YANG HSIEN-CHIH Don't forget the laws of this dynasty. Admittedly, Wang Chu had every reason to kill Akham, but it's a crime for a Han to kill a Mongolian or a Semu. By the same token, Han-ch'ing had every reason to denounce Akham and his son. But verbal attack against the authorities itself is an offense. I've heard that Han-ch'ing's sentence was commuted to banishment only because of his fame as a scholar.

WANG SHIH-FU So that's why.

[KUAN HAN-CH'ING *arrives in travel attire, under the escort of two guards,* WANG NENG *and* LI WU. KUAN CHUNG, *carrying the baggage across his shoulders, follows in the rear*]

WANG NENG Now, this is Lukouch'iao. Let's have a rest. Brother Li, you watch here. I'm going to the county center for a while.

LI WU All right. Go ahead. Nothing can happen here.

[*Exit* WANG NENG]

LI WU [*Glancing at the pavilion*] Kuan Han-ch'ing, sit down and relax. Your friends are here to see you off. [WANG HO-CH'ING *and the party come up hurriedly to extend their greetings*]

WANG HO-CH'ING Han-ch'ing, come over and sit with us. [*To the escort-guard*] You certainly need a rest too after such a tiresome journey.

LI WU I'm quite all right, thank you. [*He steps aside and looks on at a distance*]

LIANG CHIN-CHIH [*To* KUAN HAN-CH'ING] Big brother, in this package are new clothes and a sufficient supply of brushes and paper so that you can write us or compose some poems on your way.

YANG HSIEN-CHIH [*To* KUAN HAN-CH'ING] We have also procured two thoroughbreds for you.

KUAN HAN-CH'ING Thank you very much. [*He notices* WANG SHIH-FU] Look who's here! Shih-fu, you shouldn't have taken this trouble. I don't know how to thank you.

WANG SHIH-FU What a thing to say to an old friend! You must have suffered all this time. I hope it didn't ruin your health.

KUAN HAN-CH'ING Well, I'm still alive. But it was a close call and I was certain I would never see you people again.

WANG SHIH-FU It was a good fortune that the Wang Chu case was closed so soon.

WANG HO-CH'ING As I was saying just now, we certainly would much rather see you off here than at the execution ground.

KUAN HAN-CH'ING [*Smiling*] Well, I didn't believe I would come out alive myself. I even wrote my last letter to my mother. As it is, though, I hope Chin-chih will continue to withhold the news from her. After I've arrived in the south, I'll write to her myself.

LIANG CHIN-CHIH All right, I will. As far as your household is concerned, you may set your mind at ease. Hsien-chih and I will take care of everything.

YANG HSIEN-CHIH My home is near yours. We'll look after your mother, you can be sure.

KUAN HAN-CH'ING Please do. I appreciate it greatly. [*He takes a letter out of his pocket and hands it over to* WANG SHIH-FU] I wrote you this note in prison, and I thought it was to be my last.

WANG SHIH-FU [*Taking over the letter, his eyes running down the sheet avidly*] So, even in prison you thought of my "West Chamber." Your suggestions are all very good, I'll make the changes accordingly. As a matter of fact, I wanted to go over the play but had to put it off again and again because I've been ill. You are quite right in saying that one's writings are more valuable than one's life. A life span is limited, but writings last for generation upon generation. . . . So I'll work on the revision in good time, you can be sure. I understand the play is now being staged in the south too. Do let me know your opinion after you've seen it.

WANG HO-CH'ING [*Looking at a faraway point*] See! "The West Chamber" troupe is coming to Lukouch'iao.

WANG SHIH-FU [*He fails to catch the point*] Where?

WANG HO-CH'ING Look, isn't the caravan over there coming over to play Act Four of "The West Chamber"?[39] [*He recites*] "My eyes are fastened on the pavilion-post ten *li* out, and I'm growing thin with each passing day, but who would know this agony and this gnawing pang?" Now aren't these lines just right for the present scene?

[*Some distance away* CHU LIEN-HSIU *and* SAI LIEN-HSIU *are seen coming up.* SAI LIEN-HSIU, *wearing a white silk band to cover her empty eye sockets, is supported by* CH'IEN SHUA-CH'IAO *and the maidservant,* HSIANG KUEI. *The* ENTERTAINMENT HOUSE GUARDIAN *brings up the rear*]

LIANG CHIN-CHIH Now I see. Here comes Ying-ying! [*A peal of laughter*]

KUAN HAN-CH'ING [*In a deeply sympathetic voice*] Good Heavens! Sai Lien-hsiu has come too! Poor girl!

[CHU LIEN-HSIU, *wearing a new dress, looks more beautiful than ever. She greets everybody and walks straight up to* KUAN HAN-CH'ING]

CHU LIEN-HSIU [*With half a mind to protest*] Why didn't you tell me you were leaving?

KUAN HAN-CH'ING The warden pronounced the terms of my sentence and bade me leave without delay. I requested him to send you word only to find out that you had been released a day earlier. But I wrote you a note and had Kuan Chung deliver it to your house. Didn't you receive it?

CHU LIEN-HSIU No, I didn't. Maybe the superintendent kept it for fear that I might run away. [*After a moment's thought, in a determined tone as though coming to some kind of decision*] But never mind. [*She hands a gift parcel to* KUAN HAN-CH'ING] Here's a present for you from Sai Lien-hsiu.

KUAN HAN-CH'ING [*Taking the parcel in a solemn manner; to* SAI LIEN-HSIU] Thank you ever so much, Little Second Sister. I feel uneasy that you should come such a long way to see me off. Do your eyes still hurt?

SAI LIEN-HSIU Yes, but it's much better.

KUAN HAN-CH'ING What can I say to comfort you? You are a brave girl. As long as I live, you can count upon my help. My friends will all help you.

WANG SHIH-FU That's right, Sai Lien-hsiu, although you've lost your eyes, you've gained many new friends.

WANG HO-CH'ING Shih-fu is quite right. We are all your friends, and we'll all help you. Try to ease your mind.

SAI LIEN-HSIU Thank you all for your thoughtfulness. I feel quite satisfied. I asked them to hang my eyeballs on the city wall so that I could see Akham's downfall, and it came to pass so much sooner than I expected.

KUAN HAN-CH'ING Yes, and it called for universal joy and happiness. [*To* CH'IEN SHUA-CH'IAO] Ch'ien Shua-ch'iao, you should take very good care of Little Second Sister now. You mustn't drink so much.

CH'IEN SHUA-CH'IAO Master Kuan, don't worry. I've given up drinking ever since she was imprisoned. We'll have our wedding soon. I promise to make a good husband and take the best possible care of her.

KUAN HAN-CH'ING Wonderful! I know you are a conscientious man and that you deserve Little Second Sister's love.

CHU LIEN-HSIU Sai Lien-hsiu is very ambitious. She wants you to write more plays like "Tou Ngo" and she said she would act just the same even without eyes. She will make herself a name as the first blind actress in history, won't she?

WANG HO-CH'ING Of course. No disability can stop an ambitious artist. Besides, she *is* a good actress in the first place.

KUAN HAN-CH'ING Yes, Little Second Sister, I'll do it, although when I was released, the warden advised me to leave the evil men and scandals alone in my future plays.

CHU LIEN-HSIU What did you say then?

KUAN HAN-CH'ING I told him that one day when there are no more evil men and scandals, then I shall write no more about them. Then he said, "Isn't Akham dead already?" "Well," I replied, "Akham is dead, but are you sure that there won't be a second or third Akham?"

CHU LIEN-HSIU Good for you, Han-ch'ing.

WANG HO-CH'ING You are right, Han-ch'ing.

KUAN HAN-CH'ING Then the warden concluded his speech by warning me. "In view of your stubbornness," he said, "if you leave here today, it is not unlikely you will come back tomorrow. To tell you the truth, some of the royal laws and ordinances were made simply for men like you. Mark my word, one of these days your head will be removed to a new roof." I said, "Who knows? But I hope you won't mind my bothering you again, when that day comes." The warden was quite amused. [*Everybody bursts into laughter*]

WANG HO-CH'ING A prisoner once wrote on the prison wall: "No admission for timid souls; for the lion-hearted, reentry free." I propose to present Han-ch'ing with these words as our farewell message. [*Everybody laughs*]

[MISTRESS LIU, PEASANT LIU, *and* ERH-NIU, *in her best clothes, rush upon the scene*]

MISTRESS LIU Master Kuan, Master Kuan, at last I see you again.

KUAN HAN-CH'ING Who's this? Oh, I see, it's Mistress Liu! How are you? [*He turns his eyes to* ERH-NIU] And this young lady?

ERH-NIU Uncle Kuan, again you don't recognize me? Can't you see I'm the same Erh-niu whom you rescued?

MISTRESS LIU As soon as you brought her back the other day, I arranged for her wedding. We all owe you a debt of gratitude. [*To her daughter*] Erh-niu, aren't you going to kowtow to Uncle Kuan? [ERH-NIU *sinks on her knees and starts to kowtow immediately*]

KUAN HAN-CH'ING [*Hastening to make* ERH-NIU *rise to her feet*] Please, Erh-niu. I didn't recognize you because of your new clothes. You folks make me feel exceedingly guilty that you should make such a long trip just to see me.

MISTRESS LIU Ah, call that a long trip! Even if it were much longer, we'd come just the same. I told you before—you remember?—that my son-in-law's family lived right here at Wanp'ing, and that my husband worked his plot of land here, too. Well, Erh-niu came down from Cambaluc to see her father and her husband's parents, and I came along with her. While Erh-niu's mother-in-law and I were chatting about house-keeping, my husband came to tell me there was a party at the bridge waiting to see Master Kuan off and he wanted me to come over and have a look. Why, it's you, indeed! Erh-niu and I went to the prison a few times, but we weren't allowed to see you. We were worried to death. My husband reminded us time and again never in all our life to forget the great favor you did us.

PEASANT LIU [Raising his hands folded as a gesture of respect] Allow me, Master Kuan. Being an old peasant, I really don't know how to thank you in a proper manner . . . Erh-niu is my life. But for you, I would have lost this child.

MISTRESS LIU Then it was rumored that you and Fourth Sister Chu were to be sentenced to death. Every day I heard a prisoner's cart passing by, I would run into the street to have a close look and would feel relieved only when I found that none of the condemned looked like any of you. But then someone told me again that a number of prisoners were simply tortured to death in jail. I've asked Erh-niu's husband to inquire about you from time to time. I'm sure if he gets the news about your leaving today, he will come over in time to see you off.

ERH-NIU Master Hsieh came to us with a ten-thousand-signature petition the other day. My mother and I both put our finger prints on it. He told me later that it was finally presented by a Mongolian secretary.

KUAN HAN-CH'ING Many thanks to all of you. Without your help, we would never have been released.

MISTRESS LIU All's well that ends well. . . . It will do you good, Master Kuan, to go down to the south for a rest. The only regret is that Mistress Kuan is no longer living, and who is going to take care of you while you're so far away from home? I can't help worrying about you, really. [She turns to CHU LIEN-HSIU] Fourth Sister Chu, I admire you for what you have done. Your spirit is rare even among men. Pardon me for speaking my mind so bluntly, but I honestly believe that you and Master Kuan would make an ideal couple. Why don't you join him?

KUAN HAN-CH'ING Now, Mistress Liu. I'm afraid you don't know what you're saying.

WANG HO-CH'ING Ha, ha, ha! I should say Mistress Liu has the right idea. Why, it would be perfect, if it could be arranged.

LIANG CHIN-CHIH It so happens we have two horses here. [CHU LIEN-HSIU *is speechless*]

WANG HO-CH'ING I've never seen Fourth Sister ill at ease before company. Why so bashful all of a sudden? [*A peal of laughter*]

CHU LIEN-HSIU Of course, I'll go with Master Kuan. If I could make a thousand wishes, they'd all be one and the same. But will they let me go?

YANG HSIEN-CHIH That's just the question. Lien-hsiu's misgivings are not without cause. Under the laws of the present dynasty, actresses can only be wedded to musicians or actors, and they're not allowed to marry a scholar or a son of a noble man.

WANG HO-CH'ING [*Rubbing his hands as a gesture of resignation*] There's the difficulty.

WANG SHIH-FU Han-ch'ing is known in stage circles far and wide and he's well versed in music. Quite often he treads the boards himself; he sings and dances. He ought to be considered as an all-round actor; I think he has every qualification for marriage with Fourth Sister. But the trouble is, actresses are forbidden to ride a horse. Violators are punished by law, their horses are awarded to their captors. Now, in order to be able to ride with Han-ch'ing, it'll be necessary for Lien-hsiu to secure leave first to renounce her status as an actress. But there's no time for that.

LIANG CHIN-CHIH Heavens! So many restrictions!

KUAN HAN-CH'ING Fourth Sister, haven't you gained your freedom?

CHU LIEN-HSIU Nothing of the kind. I'm under strict supervision at the courtesans' house.

KUAN HAN-CH'ING Strict?

CHU LIEN-HSIU [*Nodding*] Yes, strict. But that's nothing new to me. Ever since I was taken to the house, I've been under strict supervision. A day will come when, like that butterfly you wrote about for me, I shall fly, fly, and fly to where you are. [*Her voice is choked with emotion*]

KUAN HAN-CH'ING Come to think of it, even in prison we had a chance to see each other and talk together. But after we're parted today, Heaven knows when we shall meet again.

CHU LIEN-HSIU Come, come, Han-ch'ing. [*To* YANG HSIEN-CHIH *and* WANG HO-CH'ING] Master Yang and Master Wang, can't you have a talk with them [*Pointing at the escort-guard*] and see if they will let Han-ch'ing stay for another half day?

YANG HSIEN-CHIH Why?

CHU LIEN-HSIU Well, while we were in prison with death hanging over us, Han-ch'ing told me to write to Po Yen's mother to plead for clemency, but I didn't. This time, however, when I heard Han-ch'ing was leaving, I did send her a letter through Superintendent Ho. I told Yen Shan-hsiu and her husband not to leave the house, as I expected a reply in the course of the day. [YANG HSIEN-CHIH *walks over to the escort-guard,* LI WU]

YANG HSIEN-CHIH What do you say? Would it be all right for us to keep Kuan Han-ch'ing for a day or two?

LI WU It's quite all right with me, sir. Only by imperial orders, we must proceed without delay and we are not allowed to make any stopover. We ought to be going right away, sir. [WANG HO-CH'ING *joins the parley, grabs* LI WU*'s hand and presses a silver piece into the hollow of his palm*]

WANG HO-CH'ING Look here, why can't you do us all a favor? You don't have to report back everything, you know.

LI WU Very well, sir. Let me go and have a talk with my partner. He went to the county center and hasn't come back yet. [*He sets out in the direction of the county*]

WANG HO-CH'ING We have brought along some wine and food. Let's make it a sendoff party for Han-ch'ing. [*Everybody is seated*]

YANG HSIEN-CHIH [*Raising his wine cup*] Brother Han-ch'ing, that we should have to part here on this bridge is indeed a sad thing. But considering what has happened, your departure is certainly the best thing we can expect. Your destination, Hangchow, is a scenic spot, famous for its lake and hills. People say it's like a paradise on earth. Moreover, it's the last stretch of the Sung dynasty taken over by the Yuan dynasty. I'm sure you'll find the place full of memories which will inspire you to write more poetry. Allow me, therefore, to toast to your health and your literary success!

KUAN HAN-CH'ING [*Picking up his cup*] Thank you, Hsien-chih.

WANG HO-CH'ING [*Filling a cup and passing it to* WANG SHIH-FU] Please, Shih-fu.

WANG SHIH-FU [*Raising his cup with a heavy heart*] What shall I say, Han-ch'ing? Old acquaintances, one after another, are seen no more. Do take care of yourself. [*His eyes are brimming with hot tears*]

KUAN HAN-CH'ING [*Drinking it down at one gulp*] Shih-fu, take good care of yourself, too.

LIANG CHIN-CHIH [*Raising his cup*] Big brother, good luck. Hsien-chih and I will take care of your home.

KUAN HAN-CH'ING [*Drinking another cup*] Here's my thanks. Please see my mother as often as you can and send word to my son.

YANG HSIEN-CHIH Rest assured, my friend. We'll do it.

KUAN HAN-CH'ING Well, in the future, I'll have to forgo your personal advice and the benefit of hearing your criticism of my work.

YANG HSIEN-CHIH You are flattering me. Besides, I'll come south to visit you sometime.

WANG HO-CH'ING [*Raising his cup*] My dear old friend, with you leaving me, I shall have one less with whom to argue. I'm at a loss to know how to fill this vacuum. I wish you would think from time to time of your home town and the Western Hills, of Lukouch'iao, as we see it now, and, last but not least, of pals like us. Write us often. If you can't, then curse us, so that at least we can feel our ears burning. [*Everybody laughs*]

KUAN HAN-CH'ING [*Drinking another cup*] I'll certainly write you all. I hope you'll write me too.

YANG HSIEN-CHIH Of course, you can rest assured that I'll keep you informed about your mother from time to time.

SAI LIEN-HSIU [*Pulling* CHIEN SHUA-CHIAO *by the sleeve*] Fill me a cup, please.

CH'IEN SHUA-CH'IAO [*Handing her a cupful immediately*] That's right. Let's drink a toast to Master Kuan too.

SAI LIEN-HSIU Master Kuan, I lost my eyes at the hands of the vicious, corrupt bureaucrats for performing your play. But I can still sing, and I will sing. If only there is one spark of fire in my singing, I will sleep in peace. Master Kuan, since people welcome plays like "Tou Ngo," please write more of them. Now, drink your cup, please.

KUAN HAN-CH'ING [*At one gulp, spiritedly*] Little Second Sister, I certainly will write more. No matter where I go, you will never leave my heart. You were maimed for denouncing the vicious, corrupt bureaucrats. The people will never forget you. Your friends will remember you and Ch'ien Shua-ch'iao will take good care of you. To your health, Little Second Sister.

SAI LIEN-HSIU Take good care of yourself, Master Kuan.

CH'IEN SHUA-CH'IAO Your health, Master Kuan.

WANG HO-CH'ING With all these speeches going on, our prima donna in "The West Chamber" is nearly snowed under. I say it's an outrage. Now. Lien-hsiu, come on.

CHU LIEN-HSIU I am sorry I don't drink, and I don't think we should make Han-ch'ing drink too much either. While we were in prison, Han-ch'ing wrote me a song, called "A Pair of Butterflies," which ends in these words: "loving each other, never to part." I will sing it again.

WANG SHIH-FU That'll be splendid. People spoke about the ordeal you two went through in prison and it was so touching. You certainly deserve to be rewarded with "loving each other, never to part." Now let's hear the song. [CH'IEN SHUA-CH'IAO *hands a guitar over to* CHU LIEN-HSIU]

KUAN HAN-CH'ING Go ahead and sing, Fourth Sister. I like to hear you sing it again.

[CHU LIEN-HSIU, *visibly moved, tunes the guitar, ready to start, when* WANG NENG, LI WU, *and a petty official rush over*]

PETTY OFFICIAL By imperial orders, Kuan Han-ch'ing shall leave the capital at once and be banished to Hangchow without delay. [*To everybody*] Those who've come to see him off please go home.

WANG HO-CH'ING Wait a minute. Chu Lien-hsiu has sent a letter to Prime Minister Po Yen's mother. I think we shall wait for Her Ladyship's reply.

PETTY OFFICIAL That doesn't change the situation. Kuan Han-ch'ing must leave the capital immediately. [*To the guardian*] Take Chu Lien-hsiu back.

GUARDIAN Yes, sir.

[WANG NENG *and* LI WU *try to part* KUAN HAN-CH'ING *and* CHU LIEN-HSIU. *The guardian joins forces by pulling her away*]

CHU LIEN-HSIU No, I won't leave him.

GUARDIAN What's the matter with you? Didn't you promise to behave? Come home with me!

CHU LIEN-HSIU I promised nothing. For the life of me, I won't go back!

[*The superintendent of the courtesans' house, accompanied by a subordinate, arrives and confers with the petty official in whispers.*]

PETTY OFFICIAL Well, Chu Lien-hsiu, your superintendent is here.

SUPERINTENDENT Listen, Chu Lien-hsiu, you go right back. There's a program this evening. They want you to play "The Cunning Maid." Now, go back and rehearse, do you hear?

CHU LIEN-HSIU I am not going.

SUPERINTENDENT Lien-hsiu, listen to me. I rushed over myself just to make sure that nothing should go wrong. Yen Shan-hsiu and her husband wanted to come. I didn't even let them for fear things might be all upset. Now, don't be foolish. You are a prisoner on parole and by imperial orders are to be placed under our strict supervision. Can we possibly allow you to run away with a man? I tell you, it's only because the high above have taken a fancy to your performances that we have treated you differently. Don't take things too much for granted.

CHU LIEN-HSIU You heard what I said. I won't go back for the life of me!

SUPERINTENDENT You won't, eh? Where do you think you're going? The great empire of Yuan is one and unified. Do you dare to violate the laws of the state? [*He puts on a grave face*] Now, go quickly!

CHU LIEN-HSIU No!

SUPERINTENDENT Since you are deaf to words, well, come men, put her on the wagon!

[*His subordinate draws up, threatening to lay hands on* CHU LIEN-HSIU. *She makes a dash for the bridge but her attempt to jump over is thwarted by* WANG HO-CH'ING *and others*]

KUAN HAN-CH'ING [*Shouting*] Fourth Sister!

SAI LIEN-HSIU Teacher!

WANG HO-CH'ING [*Looking daggers at the guardian*] What are you people trying to do? Force someone into suicide?

GUARDIAN She is a prisoner on parole. Can you be responsible for her?

WANG HO-CH'ING If something should happen to the adopted daughter of Prime Minister Po Yen's mother, and if Her Ladyship should send for her, would you be responsible?

GUARDIAN [*To the superintendent in a low voice*] Lien-hsiu wrote a letter to Prime Minister Po Yen's mother. . . .

SUPERINTENDENT [*With a change of expression*] Oh, I see. All right, then. [*To the petty official*] Let us wait. It's not unlikely that Her Ladyship will release Lien-hsiu from her present status. Why should we stand in her way?

[YEN SHAN-HSIU *speeds over on horseback*]

CH'IEN SHUA-CH'IAO Good, here comes Yen Shan-hsiu! [YEN SHAN-HSIU *dismounts and walks over*]

YEN SHAN-HSIU Well, I came on time.

CH'IEN SHUA-CH'IAO What's the news from Her Ladyship?

YEN SHAN-HSIU Superintendent Ho had Her Ladyship's letter delivered to me by a messenger. I borrowed a horse and left in such a hurry that I didn't ask him anything.

CHU LIEN-HSIU Where's the letter?

YEN SHAN-HSIU [*Taking the letter from his breast pocket and handing it to her*] Here it is. Read it.

[CHU LIEN-HSIU *hastens to open the envelope. Everybody is on tenterhooks*]

WANG HO-CH'ING [*Impatient to know*] What does the letter say?

CH'IEN SHUA-CH'IAO Fourth Sister, has Her Ladyship granted you your request?

CHU LIEN-HSIU [*Putting the letter away calmly, and taking up the guitar and playing a tune, her eyes on* KUAN HAN-CH'ING] Han-ch'ing, let me sing for you your song "The Intoxicating East Wind." [*She sings*]

> North and South,
>   So near, and yet so far,
> The moon wanes,
>   the flowers fade away
>   all in a fleeting moment.
> I raise my cup,
>   I hold my tears.
> But it's hard to say "Your health!"
>   without a tremor in my heart.
> Adieu, nevertheless,
>   a long future before you!

[*Hardly has she finished when she breaks down*]

KUAN HAN-CH'ING Fourth Sister, please. I knew all the time it would turn out like this. You sang beautifully. I never thought that what I wrote on the spur of the moment should today become a reality. North and south may part us in body but not in heart. May the heavens watch over you and keep you safe!

PETTY OFFICIAL [*Sensing which way the wind blows*] Well, Kuan Han-ch'ing, it's time you are on your way.

KUAN HAN-CH'ING [*Calmly*] Goodbye, Fourth Sister. Friends and neighbors, goodbye. It's hard to leave you all, but my thoughts will always be with you.

WANG HO-CH'ING, WANG SHIH-FU, YANG HSIEN-CHIH Han-ch'ing, take good care of yourself.

MISTRESS LIU, *her Husband and* ERH-NIU Master Kuan, farewell!

CH'IEN SHUA-CH'IAO, SAI LIEN-HSIU, YEN SHAN-HSIU Master Kuan, farewell!

[HSIEH HSIAO-SHAN *and* YÜ MEI *arrive in time*]

HSIEH HSIAO-SHAN *and* YÜ MEI LAO KUAN, we have come so late. All the members of our Book Society wanted us to say goodbye to you.

KUAN HAN-CH'ING Thank you all. Goodbye.

CHU LIEN-HSIU [*On a sudden impulse*] Oh, no, Han-ch'ing, I can't let you go. [*She runs over to* KUAN HAN-CH'ING *and clasps him in her arms*]

KUAN HAN-CH'ING [*Trying to compose his feelings and wiping away her tears*] Come, Fourth Sister; somehow, I have a feeling that we'll meet again. Let's say farewell with this verse: "Hold your pearly tears."

CHU LIEN-HSIU "Let the wild geese[40] come often."

KUAN HAN-CH'ING "The cockcrows announce each morn."

CHU LIEN-HSIU "Till the butterflies come out in pairs again."

KUAN HAN-CH'ING Right. The butterflies will come out in pairs. Fourth Sister, do take good care of yourself. [*He holds her hand in a warm clasp, and then again salutes* WANG HO-CH'ING *and the rest of the party with his hands folded, before he moves in the direction of the bridge, followed by* KUAN CHUNG *and the escort guards*]

CHU LIEN-HSIU [*With* WANG SHIH-FU, YANG HSIEN-CHIH, *and* WANG HO-CH'ING, *looking on quietly as the great playwright walks away, murmuring in spite of herself*] Han-ch'ing!

[*Curtain*]

Notes

(Editor's note: Notes to Kuan Han-ch'ing are those provided in the Foreign Languages Press edition, Peking, 1961.)

1. Lord Alihaiya was a Uighur warlord who served under Kublai Khan in his military conquests and was rewarded with important military positions. Chinese history records that while stationed in Hsiang-yang, Alihaiya plundered the people, seizing their land and committing other crimes.

2. Linan, present-day Hangchow, was the capital of the Southern Sung dynasty.

3. Lord Khoshin was Akham's eldest son. With his father's influence, he became governor of Tatu province (in modern Hopei) and prefect of Ta-hsing (near Peking). At the time of Akham's death, he was the chief executive official of the Kianghuai administrative area. Soon afterward he was convicted and executed by his father's political enemy, Chang Hsiung-fei.

4. Umbrellas bearing the names of 10,000 subscribers given to popular officials.

5. Semu (colored eyes) refers to the national minorities in China's northwest who had been conquered by the Mongols. They included the Hui, the Uighur, and the Tanguts. Khoshin was a Uighur. When the Mongol slave-owning aristocracy ruled China, the people in China were divided into four grades; at the top were the Mongols who held official positions in the central and local governments; next came the Semu; the Han people inhabiting the northern part

of China occupied earlier by the Mongols came third; the last were the Hans in South China—the "southerners" who came under the Mongol rule after the Sung dynasty fell.

6. A derogatory term used by the Mongol ruling class for the Hans and "southerners."

7. Lao, literally old, is a familiar form of address.

8. The ballad referred to here is called "Szu k'uai yü" of Nan Lu Kung. See note 11.

9. See note 11. Kuan Han-ch'ing wrote a long poem which could be sung in Shuang Tiao describing young people's true love.

10. Fourth Sister Chu refers to Chu Lien-hsiu. Kuan Han-ch'ing calls her "Fourth Sister" in a familiar way. But one can address a young woman as sister to show respect or politeness.

11. P'ai Tzu is a general name for melody. The plays of the Yuan dynasty are made up of dances and songs mainly performed by a *sheng* (male role) or a *tan* (female role). The melodies follow rigid rules. A play is usually divided into four acts, each of which has its melody belonging to one *kung* or *tiao*, which mainly denote the musical pitch. The different *kung* and *tiao* and the way they are sung express different ideas and emotions. Nan Lu Kung expresses lamentation and sorrow; Cheng Kung melancholy but prowess; Pan She Tiao mixed feelings or subdued sadness. The playwrights arrange suitable melodies and supply the words for the songs according to the play. For an operatic piece sung without costume, action, and scenery, one melody is often sufficient.

12. Ch'ang Tzu is a general name for stage direction, casting, and the division of a play into acts and scenes.

13. This ballad is called "I chih hua" of Nan Lu Kung. In it there is a verse describing the rolling up of the screen. Kuan Han-ch'ing dedicates this ballad to Chu Lien-hsiu whose name literally translates as Pearl-screen elegance.

14. Tradition had it that in the Yuan dynasty the Hans and the "southerners" were graded into ten classes: (1) high officials, (2) lower officials, (3) Buddhist priests, (4) Taoist priests, (5) physicians, (6) manual workers, (7) artisans, (8) courtesans, (9) Confucian scholars, and (10) beggars.

15. In this tragicomedy by Kuan Han-ch'ing, Mrs. Wang's husband is killed by a vicious nobleman, Keh Piao, and her three sons avenge their father by killing the murderer. When the case comes to court, Justice Pao Cheng (999-1062), known in Chinese history as a fair and honest judge, pronounces that the youngest and cleverest boy, Wang Shih-ho, should die. Secretly, however, he arranges to have a criminal who had been sentenced to death take the boy's place, and brings about a happy reunion of the mother and children. See *Selected Plays of Kuan Han-ching* (Foreign Languages Press, Peking, 1958), pp. 79-105.

16. Li K'uei is one of the 108 heroes of Liangshanpo (in Shantung) in the traditional novel *Shui-hu chuan* (Water Margin, or All Men Are Brothers), which describes the peasant uprising against the Sung dynasty rulers. Before the uprising, Sung Chiang, the leader, is arrested and sentenced to death in Kiangchow. Li K'uei and the other heroes cleverly enter the execution ground and rescue him. "Black Whirlwind" is the nickname given to Li K'uei to indicate his uncouth ways and brave character.

17. Villains in three of Kuan Han-ch'ing's plays: "The Riverside Pavilion," "The Butterfly Dream," and "The Wife-Snatcher" respectively.

18. Lord Hsü Heng, also known as Hsü Ping-chung (1209-1281), a Han, served the Yuan court as a jurist, philosopher, and literary writer. During Kublai

Khan's reign, he differed with Akham in political views.

19. Chao Meng-fu (1254-1322), a descendant of the Sung dynasty's imperial family, became an imperial academician after he surrendered to the Yuan rulers. A well-known scholar, painter, and calligrapher, he is said to have been responsible for the statement falsely ascribed to Kuan.

20. All female roles in four plays by Kuan Han-ch'ing: "Rescued by a Coquette," "The Riverside Pavilion," "The Prayer to the Moon," and "The Cunning Maid."

21. An incident from *Shui-hu chuan* (Water Margin), in which Li K'uei heard a malicious rumor to the effect that Sung Chiang, his leader, had forcibly abducted a woman. Furious, he denounced Sung. When he discovered his mistake and went to apologize to Sung, he carried a stick on his back to indicate that he was ready to be flogged. Here Ma Erh uses the story to draw a parallel to Ch'ien Shua-ch'iao's making up with Sai Lien-hsiu.

22. "Lord Kuan Goes to the Feast" is one of Kuan Han-ch'ing's plays in which Kuan Yü, loyal general and sworn brother of King Liu Pei of the period of the Three Kingdoms (220-280), shows his magnificent courage and heroic stature when he goes to a feast in the enemy's camp and returns unscathed, having overawed all his foes.

23. Another of Kuan Han-chi'ing's plays, a story of an old husband with a young wife, in which Wen Ch'iao (288-329), an academician of the Chin dynasty, invites his widowed aunt and her eighteen-year-old daughter to come to live with him in the capital. When he falls in love with his beautiful cousin, he cannot ask for her hand openly, as he is so much older than she. In the name of some other young man, he proposes marriage, and the mother gives her consent, and he presents a jade mirror-stand as a betrothal gift. On the wedding day the bride discovers who her husband is and protests. Eventually, after cajoling, deceiving, and mediating by Prefect Wang, she is reconciled to her fate.

24. Another of Kuan Han-ch'ing's plays, in which a lawless scoundrel named Lu Chai-lang, relying on the influence of the imperial house, takes the wives of the common people by force. He first snatches a silversmith's wife, then the wife of a petty official, thus breaking up two happy homes. Justice Peo Cheng has the villain killed and the families reunited.

25. A fictitious Mongol aristocrat and ruler.

26. Pienching is present-day Kaifeng, Honan province.

27. In this play, General Li Tzu-yuan of the Posterior T'ang dynasty (923-936) adopts a boy during a hunting trip. Eighteen years later the boy is reunited with his mother. The story is an intricate one, and in content similar to *The White Rabbit*, a popular opera of South China during the Yuan dynasty.

28. In the Yuan dynasty military commanders were ranked according to the number of men under their command—100, 1,000, or 10,000. Commander Wang Chu had 1,000 men under him stationed in Yitu (in present-day Shantung province).

29. Tsou Yen, a loyal subject of the Prince of Yen during the Warring States period (475-221 B.C.), was imprisoned after a sham trial. Thereupon frost appeared in summer.

30. Shangtu is near present-day Tolun County, Silingol League, Inner Mongolian Autonomous Region.

31. Yüeh Fei (1103-1142) was a famous patriotic general of the Southern Sung dynasty (1127-1279) who resisted the Kin invaders. Ch'in Kuei, then Prime Minister, collaborated with the enemy and advocated truce and compromise. He

plotted Yüeh Fei's death. People came to love Yüeh Fei as a national hero and despise Ch'in Kuei as a traitor.

32. *Chung-t'ung-ch'ao* is a term for paper currency of the Yuan dynasty.

33. Chiehliang, Puchow (P'u-chou), is now Chiehhsien County of Shansi province. The chronicles of the Yuan dynasty state that Kuan Han-ch'ing was a native of Chiehliang. By "that great heroic ancestor," Kuan Han-ch'ing means Kuan Yü, born in Chiehliang, the famous general in the period of the Three Kingdoms who gave his life for his country and became a hero admired and respected by the people. Kuan Han-ch'ing's play "Lord Kuan Goes to the Feast" was written to extol him. The quotation here is attributed to Kuan Yü before his execution according to the traditional novel *Romance of the Three Kingdoms* (*Sankuo yen-i*).

34. This song was written in classical style by the author of this play, T'ien Han, in Kuan Han-ch'ing's name.

35. Traditional symbol of love.

36. Meaning long life or immortality.

37. T'u-lu-hun, a term from Mongolian, denotes a steward who serves a commander of one to ten thousand men.

38. This quotation is taken from "The Western Chamber" by Wang Shih-fu. (See note 39).

39. "The Western Chamber" is a drama attributed to Wang Shih-fu, Kuan Han-ch'ing's contemporary. It portrays a love affair between Chang Chun-jui, an impoverished young scholar, and Ts'ui Ying-ying, daughter of a prime minister. Ying-ying's mother separated the lovers by sending Chang to take the imperial examinations. Act IV is the climax of the work, from which the quotation above is taken, in scene 3, "The Farewell."

40. Geese are an emblem of letter-carriers.

Wu Han

Hai Jui Dismissed from Office

Translated by C. C. Huang and Edward M. Gunn

(Acts III, VI, and IX are presented in full. The other acts are summarized).

ACTS I AND II (SUMMARY)

The play opens in Hua-t'ing county in the Soochow-Nanking region of central China in the sixteenth century. Hsü Ying, the forty-year-old son of a retired prime minister, seizes the land of a local peasant, Chao Yü-shan, and abducts his sixteen-year-old granddaughter, Chao Hsiao-lan, severely beating the old peasant when he attempts to intervene. The peasant family brings suit in court, but the local magistrate accepts a bribe from Hsü Ying, allowing his servant Hsü Fu to present an alibi, and has Chao Yü-shan flogged to death.

This case brings to a head the tension between the peasants and the local gentry, the scholar-official group collectively known as the *hsiang-kuan*, who have been engaged in unrestrained seizure of peasant land. It is at this point that Hai Jui arrives in Soochow to take up his new post as governor-general of the region that included Hua-t'ing county.

ACT III: TAKING OFFICE

Cast of Characters

CHENG YÜ, prefect of Soochow, 55 years old. He is fairminded and conscientious

HSIAO YEN, magistrate of Wuhsien, 45, a corrupt official

LI P'ING-TU, prefect of Sung-chiang, about 50. He fawns upon the *hsiang-kuan*. Greedy and lawless, he is well known as "The Grafter"

Acts III and VI, from Wu Han, *Hai Jui Dismissed From Office*, trans. C. C. Huang. Copyright © 1972 by the Asian Studies Program, University of Hawaii. Reprinted by permission.

WANG MING-YU, magistrate of Hua-t'ing county
HAI JUI, 54, grey-bearded, in civilian clothes
LADY HSIEH, his mother, 71, strict and upright by nature
LADY WANG, Hai Jui's second wife, 30. Gentle and timid, but loyal
HEI P'ENG his old servant, honest and reliable
An ARMY OFFICER and a number of SOLDIERS
HUANG AH-LAN and VILLAGERS.

Setting

The Pavilion of Official Reception outside the Gate of Heaven, Soochow, early in June 1569.

[*Officials, the army officer, and the soldiers enter, bearing flags and canopies*]

CHENG YÜ Good day, my lords. Governor Hai Jui left Nanking quite some time ago, but he still has not arrived. I'm afraid we will be waiting for him in vain.

HSIAO YEN When it was heard that Governor Hai Jui was coming, the number of sedan-chair carriers of grandpa Huang Ching, eunuch and Commissioner of the silk industry, was reduced from eight to four.

LI P'ING-TU Yes. Some of the *hsiang-kuan* in our area hurriedly painted their red doors[1] black during the night to be on the safe side.

WANG MING-YU My lords, everybody says Governor Hai Jui is an honest and upright official. Just what kind of man is he?

CHENG YÜ When I was in the capital several years back, I knew Governor Hai Jui pretty well. Allow me to describe him for you.

> He was most honest and upright,
> So he named himself *Kang-feng* accordingly.
> Toward the end of Chia Ching's reign,
> He made criticisms that angered the Throne.
> He tried to convince the Emperor
> That seeking longevity was a futile effort:
> "From the ancient times to the present day,
> There has never been a mortal man who didn't die.
> Wealth is being wasted in practicing superstition,
> Yet blocked are channels of civil administration.
> Miserable poverty is now widespread,
> And serious disturbances occur everywhere.
> Even the Emperor's name's become a distasteful word.
> Should this condition go on unchanged,
> It will lead the state into disaster,
> And bring disgrace to our ancestors."

[*Speaks*] He scolded the Emperor rather harshly. The Emperor became so enraged that he wanted to chop off Hai Jui's head. He sent people to keep an eye on Hai Jui to prevent him from escaping. Later, when the Emperor learned that Hai Jui was already prepared to die, he was astounded, and did not know what to do. Hai Jui was then jailed in a prison for officials where he was tortured in every way. He was pardoned and released after the Emperor passed away. Now that he is coming here, you must be very careful, my lords.

[HSIAO YEN, LI P'ING-TU, *and* WANG MING-YU *are shocked. Their faces turn pale*]

CHENG YÜ The weather is scorching. Why don't we all go and take a rest inside the Pavilion of Official Reception? We'll come out when the advance guards arrive. We won't be late. Come, attendants. Clear the way to the Pavilion of Official Reception. [*All exit*]

HAI JUI [*Off stage*] Let us hurry!

[HAI JUI, LADY HSIEH, LADY WANG, *and* HAI P'ENG *enter*]

HAI JUI [*Sings*]

> By Imperial order to inspect ten prefectures,
> I have come directly to Ching-ch'ang County.
> To fulfill my grand plans and ambitions,
> I'm going to help the weak and suppress tyranny.
> The South here is affluent and rich,
> They pay heavy taxes in grain and cash.
> People often say, "There's a paradise in heaven,
> But we have Soochow and Hangchow here on earth."
> The *hsiang-kuan* and officials are greedy and vicious,
> Unable to endure the hardship and suffering,
> From their native land they are fleeing.
> The people are wretched, their wealth drained,
> Our national life is following a dangerous trend.
> Being grateful and loyal to the Emperor,
> I am resolved to do my duty, whatever the cost.

LADY WANG [*Sings*]

> My sweat flows like drops of rain,
> I'm drenched to the very skin.
> There's beautiful scenery by the roadside,
> Which I'm simply too weary to admire.

LADY HSIEH Son, how much further is it to Soochow?

HAI JUI The city of Soochow is just ahead. The weather is scorching. Mother, how about resting awhile before we proceed?

LADY HSIEH As you say, son.

HAI JUI I see a forest beyond. Please take a rest there, Mother. Hai P'eng, lead the way.

[LADY HSIEH, LADY WANG, *and* HAI P'ENG *exit.* HUNG AH-LAN *and* VILLAGERS *enter*]

VILLAGER C The weather is burning hot. Let's take a rest before we continue. [*Seeing* HUNG AH-LAN *weep*] Lady, why are you crying? What's the trouble?

HUNG AH-LAN I'm going to the Governor's yamen in Soochow to lodge a suit.

VILLAGER C Against whom?

HUNG AH-LAN Against Third Young Master Hsü and the magistrate of Hua-t'ing County, for their seizure of my land and my daughter, and the beating to death of my father-in-law.

VILLAGER C Tell us the details, please.

HUNG AH-LAN O, Heavens!

[*Sings*]

> Having power and an iron hand,
> The wicked Hsü Ying seized our land.
> I could do nothing but cry to the heavens
> When my daughter was kidnapped and grandfather killed,
> We were further wronged by the magistrate of Hua-t'ing,
> Because he wanted to protect the defendant.
> Rushing toward Soochow for my redress,
> My heart pounds till it burns under this stress.

[HAI JUI *listens and nods*]

VILLAGER C Such injustices! Can it really be true?

VILLAGER A Of course it's true. We all saw it happen.

[*Sings*]

> The two graves, old and new, are there,
> Burying both generations, son and father.
> The former died of anguish, the latter of beating,
> Then they kidnapped the girl in addition.

HAI JUI Why don't they go to the court?

VILLAGER B Pardon me, sir. You don't know it, but they did go to the court. The wronged plaintiff was beaten to death there.

HAI JUI Can this be true? Which article of the law allows them to do that?

VILLAGER A The magistrate said they made false charges against the *hsiang-kuan*.

HAI JUI How could they be false charges? Did anyone testify to that?

VILLAGER A Yes, the defendant's house servant, Hsü Fu, did.

HAI JUI Ha! How can a house servant testify for his own master? Anyway, what did he try to prove?

VILLAGER B He said on the day of *Ch'ing-ming* Third Young Master Hsü was studying all day at the house of a county school student of the same city, so he never left town.

HAI JUI Which Third Young Master Hsü was that?

VILLAGER A It was none other than the third young son of Prime Minister Hsü.

HAI JUI So. Since Third Young Master Hsü did not leave town, how could he have done things like kidnapping and beating in the countryside?

VILLAGER A Rubbish! That's like seeing ghosts in broad daylight. We all saw him do it, kidnapping and beating, both.

HAI JUI It's your fault, in that case. Since you saw it happen, why didn't you go and testify?

VILLAGER B Listen, my dear sir.

[*Sings*]

> At the court we all truthfully testified,
> But it meant nothing to the magistrate bribed;
> He accepted the *hsiang-kuan's* words,
> Yet he would not trust our eyes.

HAI JUI So the words of the *hsiang-kuan* were true, while the testimony of the poor was false.

VILLAGER Precisely.

HAI JUI The *hsiang-kuan* was alone and you were many. Even then the magistrate would not believe you?

VILLAGER A How would you, sir, know the grievances of the poor? We are all tenant farmers of the Hsü family. We dare not say too much.

HAI JUI I see. So you are all tenant farmers of the Hsü family.

VILLAGERS All our lands have been seized by the Hsü family. In addition, we still have to pay taxes and do labor service. You don't know how we suffer.

HAI JUI Again, this is your own fault. Why didn't you sue?

VILLAGERS A *and* B Sir, since you are not a local man, we can't blame you for not knowing. The prefect is the notorious "Grafter," and the magistrate is infamously corrupt. How would we dare sue? [*Sings*]

> The doors of the official yamen are open wide,
> But cash alone can determine who is right.
> Big or small, they are officials just the same;
> The poor people have only their misfortune to blame.

HAI JUI Well, since neither the magistrate nor the prefect will help you, where will you go now?

VILLAGER C We'll go to lodge suits with the governor of Soochow.

HAI JUI The governor of Soochow is not interested in money and will act in your behalf?

VILLAGER That's right. The new governor Hai Jui can definitely act in our behalf. Listen here.

> When I was a rice merchant,
> Many years ago, in Ch'un An,
> Everybody spoke highly of Hai Jui,
> As an honest and upright man.
> He reduced the number of post-stations and simplified
>   taxation;
> He abolished labor service and other old practices.

Agriculture and the people's welfare were his sole concerns,
Consequently, all the refugees did return.
His daily life was simple and frugal,
No one ever saw such a good official.
Jailing the young rascals and removing the despots,
His judgment on each case was clear and fair;
When he was transferred to another town,
The people's hearts were filled with despair.

HAI JUI You really believe he will act in your behalf?

VILLAGER C Of course. Even before he arrived to take office, there were already announcements encouraging the people to air their grievances. If he didn't act in our behalf, he couldn't have been called "the clear and blue sky above."

HAI JUI Oh, I see.

[Sound of music comes from offstage]

VILLAGER B The officials have arrived to welcome the new governor, "Hai, the azure sky." Let's see what he's like.

[HUNG AH-LAN and the VILLAGERS crowd forward and bump into the oncoming officials and soldiers. VILLAGER C is knocked over by a soldier. No sooner than HAI JUI helps him up, he again collides with LI P'ING-TU]

LI P'ING-TU You blind old fool, how dare you bump into me. Guards, give the old fool a thrashing.

[The soldiers swing their whips, but are stopped by CHENG YÜ. Officials and soldiers exit. Frightened, HUNG AH-LAN and VILLAGERS also exit]

HAI JUI He is merely a minor official, yet he is so pompous and overbearing. It's easy to imagine how he preys on the common people every day.

[Sings]

The common people come here in crowds,
With lawsuits against those tyrants.
Helping the old and leading on the young,
They have traveled to this distant town,
Because the local officials, greedy and cruel,
Are just packs of foxes and wolves.
Exacting illegal taxes and coveting bribes,
They bring untold suffering to the masses.
That bureaucrat pushes the people around,
In order to show that his power abounds.
His behavior tells the simple story
That he is despotic and haughty.
Now that I am governor of this region,
The commoners will be treated as my own children.
I will suppress evil and help the good people,
And get rid of all those vicious officials.

[*Chants*]

> To uphold the law and tighten discipline,
> To destroy tyranny and protect the innocent,
> I am determined to do all within my power,
> Because I must fulfill my long-cherished ambition.

[*Exit*]

ACTS IV AND V (SUMMARY)

In Act IV Hai Jui visits Hsü Chieh, father of Hsü Ying. It is clear that while the two men are old allies in the Imperial court, Hsü Chieh is intent on protecting his son, while Hai Jui sees the need to bring him to justice.

In Act V Hai Jui's mother counsels him that while he may feel gratitude for Hsü Chieh's past support in disputes at the Imperial court, his first duty now is to uphold the law and seek justice regardless of personal consequences. Hai Jui determines to re-open the case against Hsü Ying.

ACT VI: JUDGMENT

Cast of Characters

HAI JUI
OFFICIALS of Soochow and Sung-chiang
HUANG AH-LAN and other VILLAGERS
HSÜ YING
HSÜ FU, dressed as a student
INSTRUCTOR of the Hua-t'ing County School
ADJUTANT, ARMY OFFICER, SOLDIERS, COURT RUNNERS

Setting

Central hall of the Soochow Governor's yamen, ten days later.

[*Officials of Soochow and Sung-chiang enter*]
CHENG YÜ [*Chants*]
> Daily at the yamen gate await summons.

LI P'ING-TU [*Chants*]
> Our hearts pounding with worries.

HSIAO YEN [*Chants*]
> Why have orders still not come?

WANG MING-YU [*Chants*]
> I feel like I'm on pins and needles.

HSIAO YEN My lords, we went to welcome the Governor, but we missed him because he was wearing civilian clothes. He has since shut himself up inside the yamen, not wishing to receive any officials, civil or military. Every day he goes to the river to supervise the work, and he only talks with poor peasants, workers, and small traders, I don't know why.

CHENG YÜ We missed him because he came to town in civilian clothes. I suppose he would not feel offended by that. However, he has not opened the official seal and held court since his arrival. There are a hundred matters waiting for his decision to start. It worries me that he does not come out and take charge.

LI P'ING-TU It's strange, indeed. He asked me to come and see him; yet I have been here several days and he has not summoned me. I have no idea what has happened.

WANG MING-YU Every day I come and wait outside the yamen, but nothing happens. I'm really worried. [ADJUTANT *enters*]

ADJUTANT The governor has given orders to open the yamen doors and hold court. [*Exit all officials*]

[*Music plays. Army officer, soldiers, yamen runners enter. HAI JUI also enters, wearing his official silk hat and scarlet robe*]

HAI JUI [*Chants*]

> I must strengthen law and order,
> And redress grievances for the masses.
> The people have suffered more than they can bear,
> Because the *hsiang-kuan* are cruel and lawless.
> To kill the dragons and tigers is a man's duty;
> And I need no monument to serve my country.

[*Speaks*] I am Hai Jui, Governor of Ying-t'ien. Since I took office I have learned that the *hsiang-kuan* and the rich people here are despotic and lawless. The officials are corrupt and oppressive. Positive criminal evidence has been found concerning all those involved. The law clearly prescribes that all evil men must be gotten rid of. In today's court trial I definitely must uphold this ideal, to wipe out the blot of evil, to protect the people. Men, summon the officials.

ADJUTANT Officials of Soochow and Sung-chiang, enter the court, please.

[*All officials enter, with heads bowed*]

OFFICIALS Allow us to pay our respects to Your Excellency. When Your Excellency arrived, we went to welcome you, but didn't see you. We earnestly hope that you will forgive us.

HAI JUI I'm grateful that you went to meet me. You missed me because I traveled without horses, and in civilian clothes. You are not to blame. Besides, since we have all already met, there's no need for this ceremonious greeting.

LI P'ING-TU May I ask Your Excellency where we met?

HAI JUI In front of the Pavilion of Official Reception. Please look up, so we can recognize each other.

[*The officials look up in alarm. LI is frightened and at a loss*]

HAI JUI Please be seated. I have something to discuss with you.

OFFICIALS Thank you.

CHENG YÜ May I venture to ask Your Excellency if a date has been chosen to open the seal and make official announcements?

HAI JUI It won't be necessary to choose a date because we shall do it today. Adjutant, pass the order to open the seal in order to make official announcements.

ADJUTANT Yes, Your Excellency.

[ADJUTANT *holds the official seal and stamps the announcement on the bulletin board. Soldiers hold the bulletin board and leave the stage*]

HAI JUI My lords.

OFFICIALS Your Excellency.

HAI JUI How have you performed your official duties?

OFFICIALS We have always been honest and careful, serving the Imperial Court on the one hand and sharing the worries of the common people on the other.

HAI JUI Is it really so? You have really been serving the Imperial Court on the one hand and sharing the worries of the common people on the other?

OFFICIALS Yes.

HAI JUI Ha, ha! Since you are all honest officials, then, I will request your participation in the trial of this case. Who's the magistrate of Hua-t'ing County?

WANG MING-YU I'm here, Your Excellency.

HAI JUI Let me ask you, how did you handle the case concerning Hung Ah-lan?

WANG MING-YU That? That case has been tried and concluded according to the dictates of justice.

HAI JUI How, precisely, did you settle it according to the dictates of justice?

WANG MING-YU Hung Ah-lan accused Hsü Ying of having abducted her daughter and of having injured her father-in-law. I summoned the defendant. It turned out that Hsü Ying was studying at county school student Chang's house and never left town that day. It was clear that the wicked woman was making false accusations. I thought it reasonable to expel her from the court and refuse to consider her case further.

HAI JUI Who testified that Hsü Ying did not leave town on the day of *Ch'ing-ming*?

WANG MING-YU The Hsü head servant Hsü Fu was with Hsü Ying that day. He testified at the court.

HAI JUI Aha! So there was a witness, and he was a servant of the Hsü family. Now let me ask you another question. How did Chao Yü-shan die?

WANG MING-YU Well, well, I merely hit him lightly a few times. Who'd have thought that he would suddenly die on account of his age?

HAI JUI Ha, ha! "Died suddenly; settled according to the dictates of justice." Adjutant, summon all parties involved in Hung Ah-lan's case to court.

[ADJUTANT *passes the order.* HUNG AH-LAN, VILLAGERS, HSÜ YING, *and* Hsü Fu *all enter*]

HUNG AH-LAN [*Howling bitterly*] My lord, Your Honor, you must redress the injustices done to me!

HAI JUI There's no need to cry. Tell me the whole story truthfully.

HUNG AH-LAN Your Excellency!

[*Sings*]

> Ever since they wronged me,
> I've born the injustices to this day.
> The tyrant seized our land,
> So my husband died grievously.
> Then they abducted my young daughter,
> And beat my father-in-law to death.
> Magistrate, how could you have done it,
> Relying solely on false testimony?

HAI JUI Seizure of her land, her husband's grievous death, her young daughter's abduction, her father-in-law's being beaten to death—how pitiful! What injustice! This is truly outrageous! Hsü Ying!

HSÜ YING *Ying-kuan* Hsü Ying is here, Your Excellency.

HAI JUI You've heard Hung Ah-lan's accusations. Are they true?

HSÜ YING I'm the son of a Prime Minister. Book learning and the teaching of propriety have been our traditions. How could I do such unlawful things? Besides, I positively did not leave town on the day of *Ch'ing-ming*; county school student Chang can testify to it. The case has been tried and concluded according to law by Magistrate Wang of Hua-t'ing County. I do hope that Your Excellency will not believe the onesided accusations made by the wicked woman, and that Your Excellency will also take into consideration my father's humble name so as to settle this case justly.

HAI JUI Since you have a witness, it should be easy to settle the case, should it not?

HSÜ YING It's a universal court practice to rely on witnesses and evidence. If there is falsehood, I am willing to take the punishment.

HAI JUI Well said—"willing to take the punishment." Student Chang!

HSÜ FU Here I am, Your Excellency.

HAI JUI You must tell the truth. Was Hsü Ying in fact studying at your house on the day of *Ch'ing-ming*?

HSÜ FU Positively. There's not the slightest doubt. Third Young Master Hsü not only studied that day, he also wrote an essay!

HAI JUI What essay did he write?

HSÜ FU [*Stammering*] He wrote the . . . "Thousand-Character Text." No . . . he wrote the "Hundred-Surname Text."[2]

[*Hsü Ying pales. He stamps his foot*]

HAI JUI [*Banging the desk*] Nonsense! You brazen dog! How dare you try to pass yourself off as a county school student? You will be severely punished for this!

HSÜ FU Forgive me, Your Honor. But my hat is genuine.

HAI JUI Genuine? Well, let me ask you. When did you enter school?

HSÜ FU Well . . . well . . .

HSÜ YING May I report to Your Honor, he really is a county school student. I can vouch for that.

HAI JUI Shut up! Is the instructor of the Hua-t'ing county school here?

INSTRUCTOR I am here, Your Excellency.

HAI JUI Is this a student of yours?

INSTRUCTOR I've never seen him before. He's not a student at our school.

[HSÜ YING trembles, and HSÜ FU kneels down]

HAI JUI You brazen scoundrel! How dare you pretend to be a student, acting as a false witness in order to harm the good people. Guards, take him away. He will be flogged to death at once.

HSÜ FU [Kowtowing] My great lord, Your Honor, please, spare my life. I will make a truthful confession.

HAI JUI If you confess truthfully, your life will be spared. Who are you?

HSÜ FU My name is Hsü Fu. I am Third Young Master Hsü's servant.

HAI JUI If you are a servant, why did you then pretend to be a county school student?

HSÜ FU Forgive me, Your Excellency. I was ordered to do so; it was not of my own will.

HAI JUI You wretch. Let me ask you again, exactly, where was Hsü Ying on the day of Ch'ing-ming?

HSÜ FU He was visiting ancestral graves and Heng-yü Mountain and was having a good time.

HAI JUI Was Chao Hsiao-lan abducted by Hsü Ying, and, if so, where is she now?

HSÜ FU I myself grabbed her under orders from the young master. She was tortured in every way, but she refused to submit. She is even now shut up in the Hsü residence.

HAI JUI And why did you beat Chao Yü-shan?

HSÜ FU When we were seizing Chao Hsiao-lan, Chao Yü-shan tried to stop us. So the young master ordered us to beat him.

HAI JUI Was he seriously injured?

HSÜ FU Yes, very seriously. Wounds all over his body.

HAI JUI Why, then, did the Hua-t'ing magistrate say that Chao Yü-shan was not injured when they examined him?

HSÜ FU By orders from the young master I bribed the prefect, the magistrate, and the coroner. The coroner received money so he had to say that Chao was not injured.

[LI P'ING-TU and WANG MING-YU stand up, trembling]

HAI JUI How much was the bribe? Who witnessed it? Speak the truth!

HSÜ FU Three hundred ounces of gold for the prefect and two hundred for the magistrate.

[WANG MING-YU, LI P'ING-TU, *and* HSÜ YING *kneel down, trembling*]

HAI JUI Did you deliver the gold personally?

HSÜ FU Yes, I did.

HAI JUI How did Chao Yü-shan die?

HSÜ FU He was beaten to death by the Hua-t'ing magistrate; that was how the case was settled.

HAI JUI You witnessed it?

HSÜ FU Yes, I saw it with my own eyes.

[WANG MING-YU, LI P'ING-TU, *and* HSÜ YING *kowtow to admit their guilt, and beg for mercy*]

HAI JUI [*Sings*]

> You heartless creatures, so corrupt and filthy,
> You've soiled your official robes with infamy.
> Heavy as the mountain, the law cannot be lenient;
> To punish you for crimes, I will not relent.

[*Speaks*] I will now pass sentences upon you. Hsü Ying abducted a young girl by the name of Chao Hsiao-lan, and brutally beat her grandfather Chao Yü-shan. Furthermore, he bribed the Hua-t'ing magistrate who, relying on false testimony, beat Chao Yü-shan to death. Hsü Ying will be hanged in accordance with the law. Of his property, the portion which he seized from other people shall be returned to its lawful owners. The rest shall be confiscated. Chao Hsiao-lan shall be released and reunited with her mother. Wang Ming-yu broke the law by accepting a bribe and flogging the plaintiff to death. His head shall be chopped off. Li P'ing-tu, nicknamed "Grafter," accepted bribes and broke the law. He shall be dismissed from office and imprisoned while waiting for final decisions from the Imperial Court. Hsü Fu pretended to be a county school student, delivered bribes, and gave false testimony. But considering the fact that he was forced to do these things, and since he has confessed everything, he deserves leniency. Therefore he shall receive one hundred floggings and three years' imprisonment. The coroner accepted a bribe and made false testimony. He shall be dismissed from duty, and shall receive one hundred floggings and two years' imprisonment. My lords, are the sentences fair?

CHENG YÜ Your Excellency is doing all this to eliminate public evils, which deserves all my respect and admiration.

HSÜ YING [*Kowtows*] Governor, my great lord, please consider my father's humble name and spare my life.

HAI JUI Say no more. If a prince breaks the law he will be punished just like a common man. Take them away!

[*Soldiers bind* WANG MING-YU, LI P'ING-TU, HSÜ YING, *and* HSÜ FU. *Exit*]

HAI JUI Hung Ah-lan, is there anything else you'd like to say?

HUNG AH-LAN My great lord, Your Honor. You've avenged the people. May you have dukes and marquises in your family for ten thousand years. [*She kowtows*]

HAI JUI Elders, many thanks for the enlightenment I received from you when we chatted together the other day. Now that the case is concluded, is there anything else you wish to say?

VILLAGER A My great lord, your sentences are most fair. But our lands were seized by the Hsü family and other *hsiang-kuan*. And yet, we still have had to pay taxes. The peoples' lives are extremely hard. We hope Your Honor will do something.

VILLAGERS B *and* C My great lord, you must please do something.

HAI JUI Adjutant, make a written announcement ordering all *hsiang-kuan* to return to the people, within ten days, all the land they have seized. There must be no delay. Those who refuse to obey the order shall be punished in accordance with the law.

ADJUTANT Yes, Your Excellency.

VILLAGERS [*Kowtowing*]

Your Excellency has acted in our behalf. The common people of Kiangnan will have a better life from now on. We are deeply grateful. When we return home we shall paint your portrait and worship it morning and night.

[*Sing together*]

> Today we've seen the cloudless blue sky;
> To rebuild our homes, we shall work diligently.
> Having land, we shall lack neither clothes nor food,
> In the near future, we shall find a better livelihood.

[*Speak*] We thank your great lordship!

HAI JUI There's no need. You may go home now.

[HUNG AH-LAN *and* VILLAGERS kowtow and leave]

CHENG YÜ *and* HSIAO YEN Your Excellency, may we take leave of you?

HAI JUI Wait. Magistrate of Wu County.

HSIAO YEN Yes, Your Excellency.

HAI JUI Your reputation is bad because you are grasping and wasteful. Are you aware of your crimes?

HSIAO YEN Yes, Your Excellency.

HAI JUI You are dismissed from office, to be sent home. Adjutant, remove his official silk hat.

[ADJUTANT *removes* HSIAO*'s silk hat.* HSIAO *leaves the stage*]

HAI JUI Prefect of Soochow.

CHENG YÜ Yes, Your Excellency?

HAI JUI Announce to all officials that they should remain at their posts with peace of mind; they need not worry.

CHENG YÜ Yes, Your Excellency. I'll take leave of you now. [*Exit*]

HAI JUI Well! It has taken more than ten days to settle this case. Flood control work in the Wusung River is going well. But the Pai-mao River needs dredging also. The simplified and unified tax system must be introduced into new regions. After all this is done, the people can breathe a sigh of relief.

[*Chants*]

> Exerting great effort to wipe out corruption.
> I'm trying to wash clean the administration.
> To aid the oppressed against the strong,
> It's an official's duty to right a wrong.

[*Exit*]

[ADJUTANT *and soldiers enter, holding a written announcement. A soldier beats the gong and the* ADJUTANT *reads the announcement aloud*]

ADJUTANT Listen carefully, everyone; especially the *hsiang-kuan*: Hai Jui, Third-Class Censor of the Censor General's Office and Governor of the ten prefectures of Ying-t'ien, makes the following announcement to all regarding the question of giving back the land to its lawful owners: the *hsiang-kuan* and other ferocious despots have, in the past, seized many people's land. Consequently, the peasants have become unemployed and lived miserable lives. The law demands that all the land thus seized must be returned to its lawful owners. Anyone who dares to disobey this order will be duly punished.

[*The common people listen quietly, then leave the stage happily.* ADJUTANT *and soldiers also depart*]

ACTS VII AND VIII (SUMMARY)

In Act VII Hsü Chieh begs Hai Jui to spare his son's life, recalling their past friendship. Hai Jui adamantly refuses, invoking his higher loyalty to the Emperor and revealing his demand that the local *hsiang-kuan* return huge amounts of land which they have forcibly seized from the peasants. Hsü Chieh threatens to use his connections at the Imperial court to have Hai Jui dismissed. And, in Act VIII, Hsü Chieh arranges to impeach Hai Jui and have him replaced by a new governor-general.

ACT IX: DISMISSAL FROM OFFICE

Cast of Characters

HAI JUI

ADJUTANT, ARMY OFFICER, SOLDIERS, YAMEN RUNNERS

TAI FENG-HSIANG, 50 years old, newly appointed Governor of Ying-t'ien

TAI'S ADJUTANT, ARMY OFFICER, SOLDIERS, YAMEN RUNNERS

HSÜ CHIEH, former prime minister, father of Hsü Ying

HSÜ YING, WANG MING-YU

Setting

The main hall in the Governor's yamen, Soochow, five months after Hsü Chieh has begun impeachment proceedings.

[TAI FENG-HSIANG *enters in his official silk hat and scarlet robe, under*

a parasol canopy and banners, attended by his ADJUTANT, ARMY OFFICER,
SOLDIERS, *and* YAMEN RUNNERS]
TAI FENG-HSIANG [*Chants*]

> What brings me to Kiangnan with all this commotion—
> nothing less than official promotion.
> What fits with ease in my well-padded sash—
> a hundred thousand in strings of cash.
> Don't give offense to the powers that be,
> act as dumb as you please,
> And in the search for the life of ease,
> it's a must to bend with the breeze.

[*Speaks*] I am the newly appointed Governor of Ying-t'ien, Tai Feng-
hsiang. Recently a letter from Prime Minister Hsü urged me to come
without delay, and so, spurring my horse, I ride on. [*Exit with his
retinue*]
[*Enter* HSÜ CHIEH]
HSÜ CHIEH [*Chants*]

> I'm riding out fast to greet our next governor,
> Sparing no effort to rescue my son.

[*Speaks*] The Execution Office of the Governor's yamen has sent a
messenger to report that Imperial orders to hold the autumn assize
will arrive any time now. Our new governor, Tai Feng-hsiang, is also
on his way. To save my son's life I'm riding out to greet the new
governor, for there's no time to lose. [HSÜ *exits, lashing his horse with
his riding crop*]
[ADJUTANT *for* HAI JUI *enters*]
ADJUTANT By order of the governor, court is now in session.
[HAI JUI *enters in his official silk hat and scarlet robe, attended by*
OFFICIALS, ARMY OFFICER, SOLDIERS, *and* YAMEN RUNNERS]
HAI JUI [*Chants*]

> We are commanded by the Throne to enforce the law,
> By removing the heinous and upholding the right.

[*Speaks*] Guards, bring out the condemned, Hsü Ying and Wang
Ming-yu, and carry out the sentence at the time appointed.
[HSÜ YING *and* WANG MING-YU *enter, escorted by* GUARDS]
HAI JUI [*Speaks*]

Hsü Ying and Wang Ming-yu, the Imperial orders to hold Autumn
assize have arrived, condemning you to be executed on the spot.
Criminals!
[*Chants*]

> You have snared yourselves in the legal nets of the state:
> Let those who will, reform, or see in you their fate.

HSÜ YING *and* WANG MING-YU Spare us, Your Honor. [*Both kowtow*]
HAI JUI Remove them for immediate execution.

[Hsü Ying *and* Wang Ming-yu *exit, escorted by* Guards. Tai Feng-hsiang's Adjutant *enters*]

Adjutant All hear the Imperial decree!

[*Drums beat and* Tai Feng-hsiang *enters with* Hsü Chieh *and their retinue*]

Tai Feng-hsiang In accordance with the will of Heaven as entrusted to His Majesty, the Emperor decrees: "Hai Jui, Governor of Ying-t'ien, is dismissed from office to return to the fields of his home. Tai Feng-hsiang is herewith appointed Governor of Ying-t'ien. Obey this."

Hai Jui Long live the Emperor! May it please His Majesty's Emissary, for what offense is Hai Jui dismissed and ordered home?

Tai Feng-hsiang Officials at court have impeached you for misusing the people and abusing the *hsiang-kuan*.

Hai Jui As Heaven is my witness!

[*Sings*]

> The people are the victim of the *hsiang-kuan*'s violence,
> Driven from their fields as if by tigers and wolves.
> Any charge I've mistreated the *hsiang-kuan* is nonsense;
> To dismiss me on these counts is absurd.

[*Speaks*] May it please His Majesty's Emissary, when is the new governor to arrive and assume office?

Tai Feng-hsiang I am the new governor. Your Excellency, it is an honor to meet you.

Hai Jui An honor to meet you, Your Excellency. Since Your Excellency has arrived, allow me to offer some views to you.

Tai Feng-hsiang Please proceed.

Hai Jui [*Sings*]

> The people are the victim of the *hsiang-kuan*'s violence,
> Driven from their fields as if by tigers and wolves.
> Any charge I've mistreated the *hsiang-kuan* is nonsense;
> To dismiss me on these counts is absurd.

[*Speaks*] May it please His Majesty's Emissary, when is the new governor to arrive and assume office?

Tai Feng-hsiang I am the new governor. Your Excellency, it is an honor to meet you.

Hai Jui An honor to meet you, Your Excellency. Since Your Excellency has arrived, allow me to offer some views to you.

Tai Feng-hsiang Please proceed.

Hai Jui [*Sings*]

> The greatest evil in Kiangnan are the *hsiang-kuan*.
> With their lands seized, the farmer's lot's near to hopeless.
> An injustice so grave, it demands strong redress:
> Till their lands are returned the people will live in distress.

Tai Feng-hsiang Silence! The Emperor has dismissed you precisely

because you have used the people as so many tigers and wolves to ruthlessly force the *hsiang-kuan* off their own lands.
[*Sings*]

> It is fate that ordains each man's status and wealth;
> Leave the ignorant in hardship, it's where they belong.
> Thinkers live well and laborers suffer:
> You've read so in classics now for so long,
> How could you use people like tigers and wolves
> To savage the *hsiang-kuan*, you know that is wrong.

HAI JUI Who is in the wrong?
TAI FENG-HSIANG You are.
HAI JUI Silence!
[*Sings*]

> You speak of the people as tigers and wolves;
> Do you know what the *hsiang-kuan* have left them to eat?
> "Lo, the poor *hsiang-kuan*" rings the cry at the Court;
> Does it know about people left grain husks to eat?
> With lip-service to peasants as the empire's foundation,
> Officials plunder them behind a façade of virtue and right,
> Shielding exploiters and deceiving the Throne,
> Their own shadows shame them by day, their beds by night.

TAI FENG-HSIANG You can't talk to me that way! I am outraged!
HSÜ CHIEH Your Excellencies, let's not carry this too far. Kang-feng, I meant well when I warned you before that you can't get away with offending so many people and abusing the *hsiang-kuan*. But you were adamant; you wouldn't listen, and now that you've been dismissed to go home I have this to say:
[*Sings*]

> In your prime you've had spirit but not learned submission,
> So you've courted failure now for some years.
> Excessive in pursuing the law as your mission,
> You have gone to extremes by injuring others.
> We talked once before, but you would not listen.
> You slipped this time to face the world as it it.
> I'd advise you, in future, seek self-cultivation,
> Be a "civil" official and keep your blade sheathed.

HAI JUI Sir!
[*Sings*]

> You've spoken without weighing the ideas in your words.
> I may be dismissed, but my name will remain.
> What's inside a man should match his appearance,
> And plotting to ruin a friend is profane.

HSÜ CHIEH Who's been plotting to ruin you?
HAI JUI You!

[*Sings*]

> At court you worked for the harmony that upholds the state,
> Through Confucius, Mencius, and tales of former kings.
> In the country you let your son plunder its wealth,
> Through briberies, extortions, and unconscionable rapings.
> You may deceive the Emperor with false judgments;
> You may smear the people as tigers and wolves;
> You may claim for the *hsiang-kuan* unspeakable torments;
> But where will you hide from the common man's hate?
> I have lost the silk hat of office, but not my conscience.
> The day will come when I hold office again,
>> and uphold the laws of the state.

Hsü Chieh If you're that stubborn there's no point saying anything more.

Adjutant It is the appointed time. I request orders to execute the condemned.

Tai Feng-hsiang *and* Hsü Chieh [*Alarmed*] Execute whom?

Hai Jui By order of the Imperial court we are executing Hsü Ying and Wang Ming-yu immediately.

Hsü Chieh No! [*He pales and trembles*]

Tai Feng-hsiang Pass the order to halt the execution.

Hai Jui Execute them.

Tai Feng-hsiang As the newly appointed governor, I order the execution cancelled.

Hai Jui As the present governor I order the execution to proceed.

Tai Feng-hsiang Your Excellency, they must not be killed.

Hai Jui Why not?

Tai Feng-hsiang I have a directive from State Secretary Li and the Venerable Feng, Minister of Rites, to stay the execution of Hsü Ying in view of Prime Minister Hsü's advanced years and distinguished service to the state, and to await further instructions.

Hai Jui And where is this directive?

Tai Feng-hsiang It will be here shortly.

Hai Jui And in the meantime?

Tai Feng-hsiang In the meantime I am ordering a stay of execution as directed by Secretary Li and Minister Feng.

Hai Jui But you have no authority to issue orders.

Tai Feng-hsiang What do you mean "no authority"?

Hai Jui How can you issue orders while I still hold in my hands the *ling-chien*[3] and the seal of office? I have not yet given away this authority.

Tai Feng-hsiang Very well, give them to me.

Hai Jui I absolutely refuse. I am under Imperial orders to conduct the autumn assize. And when the execution has been carried out, then I will surrender my authority to you.

Tai Feng-hsiang Sir!

[*Sings*]

To ignore the Court's edict is no small offense.
You're looking at death for you and your clan.
Show Minister Hsü consideration due a venerable man,
And keep impulse from leading to a regrettable stand.

HAI JUI Ha, ha!
[*Sings*]

It is by edict that I've judged and passed sentence,
And a matter of course it be carried out promptly.
How can I base judgments on personal sentiments.
So be it, then, if that's judged an offense.

TAI FENG-HSIANG Then you don't fear death?

HAI JUI A true man stands his ground and accepts the burden heaven places upon him. To let his fear of death decide in favor of the guilty is to grovel shamelessly. [*He holds up the* ling-chien] Adjutant, give the order for execution.

ADJUTANT [*Taking the* ling-chien] Yes, Sir.

[*The* ADJUTANT *exits. Three cannon shots sound.* HSÜ CHIEH *falls to the ground in a faint.* TAI FENG-HSIANG *is so startled he's at a loss what to do.* HAI JUI *holds up the seal of office*]

HAI JUI Your Excellency, here is the seal of office. I pass it to you now, and take my leave.

[TAI FENG-HSIANG *is numb with astonishment.* HAI JUI *is still holding out the seal of office to him as the curtain falls*]

CHORUS [*Behind curtain, sings*]

Swept by the moaning wind, heaven and earth turn cold.
A thousand times ten thousand, the ties that fail to hold
The Patriarch Hai, powerless to protest his southern
    journey, homeward bound.
Yet in the lighted incense of ten thousand homes
    as a living Buddha, the memory of him is found.
[*The End*]

Notes

1. Red doors indicated great merit and wealth.

2. The "Thousand-Character Text" and the "Hundred-Surname Text" were well-known primers used by schoolchildren in those days, but hardly suitable exercises for an advanced scholar like Hsü Ying.

3. The *ling-chien* is a flag attached to an arrow, signifying the authority to issue orders.

Revised collectively by
the China Peking Opera Troupe

The Red Lantern

Translated by the Foreign Languages Press, Peking

Cast of Characters

SERGEANT, in the Japanese gendarmerie
HOU, auxiliary gendarme of the Japanese gendarmerie
HATOYAMA, chief of the Japanese gendarmerie
GRANNY LI
LI YÜ-HO, railroad switchman, member of the CCP, and son of Granny Li
T'IEH-MEI, Li's daughter
HUI-LIEN, Li's neighbor
AUNT T'IEN, Hui-lien's mother-in-law
"KNIFE-GRINDER," platoon leader of the guerrillas of the Eighth Route Army in the Cypress Mountains
WANG LIEN-CHU, puppet police inspector, former underground Communist who has turned traitor
GUERRILLA LEADER
OTHERS: Japanese gendarmes, spies, Chinese guerrillas of the Eighth Route Army in the Cypress Mountains

Setting

North China, during the War of Resistance to Japan (1937–45)

(Scenes 1 through 7 are summarized. Scenes 8, 9, 10, and 11 are reprinted in full.)

SCENES 1–7 (SUMMARY)

Li Yü-ho, a railroad switchman, lives with his adoptive mother, Granny Li, and adopted daughter, T'ieh-mei. Each of the three is the sole survivor of worker families wiped out by warlords, and each has become a firm supporter of the Communist Party in its underground guerrilla warfare against the Japanese during the War of Resistance to Japan, 1937–45.

Li Yü-ho has been assigned the task of delivering a secret code to a guerrilla unit in the Cypress Mountains; he is to identify himself by carrying a red lantern. However, Wang Lien-chu, a former member of the underground, informs Hatoyama, Chief of the Japanese gendarmerie, of Li's mission. Arrested and tortured, Li will not reveal the location of the code. Hatoyama now arrests Granny Li and T'ieh-mei, hoping to use them to extract information from Li, who earlier did inform them of the code's location. Just before their arrest, Granny Li has told T'ieh-mei for the first time that no blood relationship exists among the members of their little family.

SCENE 8: STRUGGLE ON THE EXECUTION GROUND

[*Night. A corner of the prison in the headquarters of the Japanese gendarmerie. As the curtain rises,* SERGEANT *and* HOU *stand waiting. Enter* HATOYAMA]

HATOYAMA It seems direct questioning won't get us the secret code. The hidden microphone?

HOU Already installed.

HATOYAMA Good. We'll hear what they say when the old woman meets her son. Perhaps we'll find out something this way. Bring the old woman in.

HOU Yes, sir. [*To offstage*] Come along!

[*Enter Granny*]

HATOYAMA Do you know this place, madam?

GRANNY It's the gendarme headquarters.

HATOYAMA This is where your son will ascend to heaven! When a man has committed a crime and his mother refuses to save his life when she has it in her power, don't you think she is cruel?

GRANNY [*Sternly, putting the vile enemy on trial*] What kind of talk is that! You've arrested my son for no reason. Now you want to kill him. You are the criminals; it's you who are cruel. You kill the Chinese, and you want to shift the blame onto the Chinese people, onto me, an old woman?

HATOYAMA All right! Go and see your son!

[GRANNY *walks off resolutely.* HATOYAMA *signs to* HOU *to follow her*]

HATOYAMA Take Li Yü-ho there.

SERGEANT Bring Li . . . Yü-ho! . . .

[*Dark change*]

[*A corner of the execution ground: A high wall, a steep slope, a sturdy pine reaching to the sky. In the distance a high mountain pierces into the clouds*]

LI [*Offstage, sings "erh huang tao pan"*]

At the gaoler's bloodthirsty cry . . .
[*Enters and strikes a dramatic pose*]
I stride forth from my cell.

[*Two Japanese gendarmes push him. With a strong sense of righteousness,* LI *stands chest out, undaunted. Then he performs a series of characteristic Peking Opera dance movements: moving briskly sideways on both legs, backing a few steps on one leg, a pause; turning round on one leg and then swinging the other and striking a dramatic pose. He advances boldly, forcing the gendarmes to retreat*]

[LI *rubs his wounded chest, then places one foot on a rock and nurses his knee. He casts a contemptuous glance at his chains and fully displays his noble spirit*]

LI [*Sings "hui lung"*]

Though heavy chains shackle me hand and foot,
They cannot fetter my spirit that storms the heavens.

[*Feeling a sharp pain in his wounded legs, he backs a few steps on one leg, nurses his knee, and finally stands on one leg in a dramatic pose*]

LI [*Sings "yuan pan"*]

That villain Hatoyama used every torture to get the code,
My bones are broken, my flesh is torn,
But my will is firmer than ever.
Walking boldly to the execution ground, I look afar:
The red flag of revolution is raised on high,
The flames of resistance spread far and wide.
Japanese bandits, let's see how much longer you can age!
Once the storm is past [*changes to "man san yen"*] flowers will bloom,
New China will shine like the morning sun,
Red flags will fly all over the country.
This thought heightens my confidence
And my resolve is strengthened. [*Changes to "yuan pan"*]
I have done very little for the Party,
I'm worried that the code hasn't got to the mountains.
Wang's only contact was with me,
The wretch can betray no one else;
My mother and daughter are as firm as steel.
Hatoyama, try and get the secret code!
You may ransack heaven and earth,
But you will never find it.
Revolutionaries fear nothing on earth,
They will forever march forward. [*Enter* GRANNY]

GRANNY Yü-ho!
LI [*Looks back*] Mother!
GRANNY [*Runs over to support* LI, *sings "erh huang san pan"*]

Again I live through that day seventeen years ago,
And burn with hate for the foe of my class and country.
These . . . Japanese devils, cruel and treacherous,
Have beaten you black and blue,
My son, my son!

LI Don't grieve for me, mother!
GRANNY [*Continues to sing*]

With such a fine son . . . I shouldn't grieve.

LI My good mother!

[*Sings "erh huang erh liu"*]
Brought up by the Party to be a man of steel,
I fight the foe and never give ground.
I'm not afraid
To have every bone in my body broken,
I'm not afraid
To be locked up until I wear through the floor of my cell.
It makes my heart bleed to see our country ravaged,
I burn with anger for my people's suffering.
However hard the road of revolution,
We must press on in the steps of the glorious dead.
My only regret if I die today
Is the "account" I have not settled.
[*Gestures to indicate the secret code*]
I long to soar like an eagle to the sky,
Borne on the wind above the mountain passes
To rescue our millions of suffering countrymen—
Then how gladly would I die for the revolution!

[*Enter* HOU *followed by two Japanese gendarmes*]
HOU Old woman, Captain Hatoyama wants to have a talk with you.
GRANNY [*To* LI] Son, I know what he is going to say.
HOU Come on.
[GRANNY *goes out fearlessly, followed by the gendarmes*]
HOU Bring Li T'ieh-mei here! [T'IEH-MEI *runs in*]
T'IEH-MEI Dad!
[*Exit* HOU]
T'IEH-MEI [*Sings "erh huang san pan"*]

Day and night I've been longing to see you again,
And now you . . . so battered and covered with blood . . .
Dear father!

LI You mustn't cry, child! [*Strokes* T'IEH-MEI'*s hair lovingly, with determination*] Be brave, daughter! [*Helps* T'IEH-MEI *to her feet, with feeling*] My child! [*Continues singing*]

One thing I have wanted to tell you many times,
It's been hidden in my heart for seventeen years.
I . . .

T'IEH-MEI [*Quickly stopping him*] Don't say it, dad, you are my own
father. [*Kneels*]
[*Sings "erh huang k'uai pan"*]

Don't say it, father,
I know the bitter tale of these seventeen years. [Li *helps* T'IEH-MEI *to her feet, his feelings like turbulent waves*]

Li [*Sings "erh huang yuan pan"*]

People say that family love outweighs all else,
But class love is greater yet, I know.
A proletarian fights all his life for the people's liberation.
Making a home wherever I am,
I have lived in poverty all these years.
The red lantern is my only possession,
I entrust it to your safekeeping.

T'IEH-MEI [*Sings "erh huang kuai san yen"*]

Dad has given me a priceless treasure
To light my path forward forever.
You have given me your integrity
To help me stand firm as a rock;
You have given me your wisdom
To help me see through the enemy's wiles;
You have given me your courage
To help me fight those brutes.
This red lantern is our heirloom.
Oh dad, the treasure you leave me is so vast,
That a thousand carts and ten thousand boats
Cannot hold it all.
I give you my word I will keep the lantern always safe.

Li [*Sings "erh huang san pan"*]

As wave follows wave in the great Yangtze River,
Our red lantern will be passed on from hand to hand.
[*To* T'IEH-MEI]
If some day to home you return,
Find our relatives, make a living, clear that "account."
[*Gestures to indicate the code*]
I'll have no worries.

[*Japanese gendarmes enter, pushing* GRANNY. *Enter* SERGEANT]
SERGEANT Captain Hatoyama gives you five more minutes to think it over. If you still refuse to give up the secret code, you will all be shot. [*Drags* T'IEH-MEI *away*] Only five minutes left, girl. Give up the code and save the whole family. Understand? Speak up!
[*Firmly,* T'IEH-MEI *walks back to her dear ones*]
SERGEANT Where is the code?
T'IEH-MEI I—don't—know!
SERGEANT Shoot them all.
GENDARMES Yes.

LI No use baring your fangs! T'ieh-mei, Granny, let's link arms and go
together.

[*"The Internationale" is played. Bravely and firmly, the three walk
arm in arm up a slope with their heads high. Enter* HATOYAMA]

HATOYAMA Wait! I give you one more minute to think it over.

LI [*With a spirit that shakes the universe*] Hatoyama, you can never kill
all the Chinese people, all the Chinese Communists. You must think
of the end in store for you scoundrels!

HATOYAMA Terrible! [*To* SERGEANT] Act according to plan! [*Exit*]

SERGEANT Shoot them!

[*To the militant strains of "The Internationale," the three revolutionaries of three generations, heads high, walk up the slope, defying
death. They go out. Japanese gendarmes follow. Silence. Offstage,* LI
shouts: "Down with Japanese imperialism! Long live the Chinese
Communist Party!" *The three of them shout with their arms raised:*
"Long live Chairman Mao!" *A volley of shots. Two Japanese gendarmes
drag* T'IEH-MEI *in and throw her down*]

T'IEH-MEI [*Standing up, turns to call*] Dad! Granny! [*Enter* HATOYAMA]

HATOYAMA Give me the code, Li T'ieh-mei.

HOU *and* SERGEANT Speak up! [T'IEH-MEI *glares at* HATOYAMA]

HATOYAMA Let her go!

SERGEANT Yes, sir. Get out! [SERGEANT *pushes* T'IEH-MEI *away. They go
out, followed by the gendarmes*]

HOU Why did you let her go, sir?

HATOYAMA It's called using a long line to catch a big fish.

HOU Right! [*Lights fade*]

[*Curtain*]

SCENE 9: ADVANCING WAVE UPON WAVE

[*Immediately after the last scene. Dawn. Li's house, interior and exterior view.
As the curtain rises,* T'IEH-MEI *enters the room, leans back against the door.
Looking around, full of sorrow and hatred, she thinks of her martyred father and
grandmother*]

T'IEH-MEI Dad! Granny! [*Rests her head on the table and sobs. A pause.
Slowly rising, she sees the red lantern, hurries over and takes it*]
Granny, dad, I know what you died for. I shall carry on the task you
left unfinished and be the successor to the red lantern. I'm determined
to deliver the code to the Cypress Mountains and avenge your bloody
murder. Hatoyama, you may arrest me or release me at will, but you'll
never get the secret code!

[*Sings "hsi p'i tao pan"*]
I burst with anger when I think of the foe!
[*Changes to "k'uai san yen"*]
Repressing my rage I grind my teeth.

Using every trick to get the code,
Hatoyama has killed my granny and dad!
[*Changes to "erh liu"*]
Biting my hate, chewing my rage,
I force them down my throat,
Let them sprout in my heart.
I'll never yield, I'll never retreat,
[*Changes to "k'uai pan"*]
No tears shall wet my cheeks,
Let them flow into my heart
To nourish the bursting seeds of hatred.
Flames of rage, ten leagues high,
Will burn away this reign of the forces of darkness.
I'm prepared: arrest me, release me,
Use your whips and lash, your locks and chains.
Break my bones, you will never get the code.
Just wait, you villain Hatoyama,
This is T'ieh-mei's answer!
I'll go now! [*Picks up the red lantern, ready to leave*]

[HUI-LIEN *comes out of the inner room*]
HUI-LIEN T'ieh-mei!
T'IEH-MEI Sister Hui-lien! [*Puts down the lantern and bolts the door*]
HUI-LIEN My mother has come to see you.
   [AUNT T'IEN *emerges from the inner room*]
AUNT T'IEN T'ieh-mei!
T'IEH-MEI Aunty. . . . [*Runs into her arms*]
AUNT T'IEN Child, we have heard what happened to your dad and
   grandma. We'll see how much longer those beasts can ravage our
   land! There are spies outside, T'ieh-mei, you mustn't leave by this
   door. Slip out through our house. Hurry, change jackets with Hui-
   lien.
T'IEH-MEI No, aunty, I mustn't get you into trouble.
AUNT T'IEN My child! [*While helping* T'IEH-MEI *to change jackets with*
   HUI-LIEN *she sings "hsi p'i san pan"*]

None but the poor help the poor,
We are two bitter gourds on the same vine;
We must save you from the tiger's jaws,
So that you can go forward on your course.

T'IEH-MEI But what if something happens to you?
AUNT T'IEN We are both working-class families. We have shared
   bitterness and hatred for many years. No matter how risky it is, I must
   see you safely away.
T'IEH-MEI [*With gratitude*] Aunty . . .
AUNT T'IEN Hurry up, child!
HUI-LIEN Be quick, T'ieh-mei!

T'IEH-MEI I shall never forget you, sister and aunty.

AUNT T'IEN Go quickly.

[*Picking up the red lantern, T'IEH-MEI goes into the inner room. Exit*]

AUNT T'IEN Be very careful, Hui-lien.

[AUNT T'IEN *goes into the inner room. Exit.*]

[HUI-LIEN *wraps T'IEH-MEI's scarf round her head, covering the lower part of her face. She steps out of the house with the basket and closes the door behind her. Exit.*]

[SPIES B *and* C *emerge from behind an electric pole and trail her. Lights fade*]

[*Curtain*]

SCENE 10: AMBUSHING AND ANNIHILATING THE ENEMY

[*Immediately after the last scene. On the road leading to the Cypress Mountains. As the curtain rises, enter* KNIFE-GRINDER *with two guerrillas dressed as peasants. Enter* T'IEH-MEI. *They meet*]

T'IEH-MEI Uncle Knife-Grinder! [*Takes the red lantern from the basket and holds it aloft*]

KNIFE-GRINDER T'ieh-mei! [*Turns to the guerrillas*] Keep guard!

T'IEH-MEI I've found you at last, Uncle! My dad and granny . . .

KNIFE-GRINDER We know everything. Don't grieve, T'ieh-mei. Turn your sorrow into strength. We'll be avenged! Have you got the code with you?

T'IEH-MEI Yes.

KNIFE-GRINDER That's fine.

T'IEH-MEI Uncle, my neighbor Hui-lien helped me. She disguised herself as me and led the spies off after her. That's how I was able to get the code and bring it here.

KNIFE-GRINDER The enemy must be suspecting Hui-lien's family. [*To* GUERRILLA A] Old Feng, help the T'iens move as quickly as possible.

GUERRILLA A Right! [*Exit*]

[*A police car siren is heard*]

GUERRILLA B The enemy's coming, Old Chao.

KNIFE-GRINDER You take T'ieh-mei up the mountain. We'll deal with them. [GUERRILLA B *leads* T'IEH-MEI *off*]

[WANG *shouts offstage:* "Halt!" *Japanese gendarmes enter, with* HATOYAMA *and* WANG *in the lead.* KNIFE-GRINDER *blocks their way.* HATOYAMA *shouts:* "Take him!" KNIFE-GRINDER *snatches* WANG's *pistol and kills a Japanese gendarme. Then he strikes* WANG *with his bench.*

[*The guerrillas jump out of a grove. Dramatic pose.*

[*On the crag a guerrilla kills a Japanese gendarme.* HATOYAMA *and* WANG *run off;* KNIFE-GRINDER *and the guerrillas pursue them. The guerrillas dash down from the crag and chase the enemy.*

[*A guerrilla with a red-tasselled spear fights two Japanese gendarmes. They flee, followed by the guerrilla.*

[KNIFE-GRINDER *chases* WANG. *They lock in struggle.*

[*Enter* HATOYAMA *with Japanese gendarmes. Fighting at close quarters. The guerrillas wipe out all the enemies, shooting down the traitor* WANG, *and running* HATOYAMA *through with a sword.*

[*The ambush has been a great success. The guerrillas form a tableau of heroes, in a valiant, dramatic pose. Lights fade*]

[*Curtain*]

SCENE 11: FORWARD IN VICTORY

[*Immediately after the last scene. The Cypress Mountains. As the curtain rises, red flags flutter against a clear blue sky. The* GUERRILLA LEADER *walks down the hill slope.* KNIFE-GRINDER *enters with* T'IEH-MEI. *All the guerrillas enter. Solemnly,* T'IEH-MEI *hands the code to the* GUERRILLA LEADER. *Brandishing their rifles and swords, all rejoice in their victory.* T'IEH-MEI *holds aloft the red lantern while crimson light radiates. The curtain slowly falls*]

[*The End*]

Tsung Fu-hsien

In a Land of Silence

Translated by Shu-ying Tsau

Cast of Characters

LIU HSIU-YING, a retired grade school teacher, 52 years old

HO SHIH-FEI, her husband, director of the revolutionary committee of an important export company, 60

HO WEI, their son, surgeon in a hospital, 34

HO YUN, their daughter, cadre of the Municipal Public Security Bureau, 30

OU-YANG P'ING, a waiter in a small diner in a Peking suburb, former friend of Ho Yun, 31

MEI LIN, his mother, an old cadre who has been ordered back to her home town, 58

ACT I

It is a muggy morning on a stifling day in the early summer of 1976, in the living room of Ho Shih-fei's house, a detached two-story building with a garden. The living-room decor is somewhat luxurious but not vulgar. Furnishings include a couch, a large bookcase, a piano, and an electric fan. There is a stairway at stage left leading upstairs. In front of the stairs is a corridor leading to Ho Yun's room. There is a door at stage right leading to Ho Wei's bedroom. There is another door toward the front leading to the kitchen. At stage center there is a big sliding glass door leading to the garden outside.

It is the rainy season in southern China. Although it is not raining at the moment, the thick overlapping clouds keep even a sliver of blue sky from showing. Inside the room it is unbearably muggy.

As the curtain goes up, the clock strikes ten. LIU HSIU-YING opens the glass door; the persistent droning of the cicadas is heard from outside. LIU HSIU-YING had never, in her entire life, told a lie. She used to be a grade school teacher who delighted in teaching her pupils to be as morally upright, as trustworthy, as honest as she was herself. She was also gentle and submissive; she loved and admired her husband, and took his word as law. But in recent years a change has come over her. She cries easily and often sits motionless, or mumbles wild, meaningless phrases. When asked what is wrong, she refuses to utter a word. At other times she seems perfectly normal. She has had to take early retirement because of her condition, and now keeps herself busy within this small world of a few dozen square meters taking care of the household for her husband and her children. Now, after listening to the heavy chimes of the clock, she becomes motionless again.

Footsteps are heard on the stairs. Ho Shih-fei *is coming down. Although eight years his wife's elder, he appears much younger because of his glossy black hair, tanned complexion, and energetic movements. He is of medium height and slightly overweight. He speaks softly but with authority. Clearly, this is a man of some importance, who is in prime physical condition. One might find it difficult to believe that before Liberation he was only a minor clerk in a foreign company, kicked out without compensation when he came down with tuberculosis. With the help of a neighbor, a person in charge of an underground unit, he was cured. From then on he became close to the Chinese Communist Party and joined it in early 1949. Since Liberation he has been working in the field of foreign trade.*

At this moment he comes down with a bottle of Kweichou Mao-t'ai liquor and a bottle of Gold Medal Brandy in his hands.

Ho Shih-fei Hsiu-ying! . . . You're in a trance again. Ah, we'd have such a happy life if only you . . . [Liu Hsiu-ying *remains silent*] Hsiu-ying, what is it that's been making you unhappy these last two years? Tell me, all right? In our life we've been through a lot of hard times together. Now what on earth could be troubling you that you cannot let me know? [*She looks frightened. He sighs*] Where are the kids? [*She shakes her head. He turns toward the corridor*] Hsiao Yun! Hsiao Yun! [*No answer*] She's gone out again? This is her affair and she doesn't give a damn. Ta Wei! Ta Wei!

[Ho Wei *comes out of his room. He is a surgeon, and once was considered to have a promising future. Now he has turned slovenly and lazy, and is rarely serious about anything. He shuffles out in slippers; part of his shirttail is hanging out; he has a book in one hand and a big straw fan in the other*]

Ho Wei Dad.

Ho Shih-fei [*Sarcastically*] Young master, it's time for you to shake a leg, don't just stand there and leave your mom with all the work.

Liu Hsiu-ying He's sick, let him rest, I'll do it.

Ho Shih-fei You don't have to shield him all the time. I thought you used to be quite strict with the kids! He's sick? What sickness? Sick in the head! Sluggish attitude toward the revolutionary cause! You won't take part in the class struggle that's heated up out there but just hang around doing nothing serious!

Ho Wei [*Brandishing the book*] I am studying the world classic recommended by our Great Cultural Standard-Bearer:[1] *Gone with the*

Wind. This is the most serious, the most, most serious, the most, most, most serious business indeed!

HO SHIH-FEI [*Furious*] You—

[HO WEI *yawns idly*]

HO SHIH-FEI [*To* LIU HSIU-YING]You'd better go to prepare the meal, it's already past ten. You don't want to wait until the guest comes. Well, Hsiu-ying, where did you put the white tablecloth?

LIU HSIU-YING In the wardrobe, bottom left.

HO SHIH-FEI [*On his way upstairs, turns around to* HO WEI] Take a good look at yourself: do you look at all like a young revolutionary? [*He goes up. Lying down on the couch,* HO WEI *starts reading his book*]

LIU HSIU-YING [*Approaching* HO WEI] Ta Wei, don't be lying there, your father will get mad again.

HO WEI Well, tough, who told him to give birth to a son without ambition like me?

LIU HSIU-YING Ta Wei, this friend of your sister who's coming today, is he a good person?

HO WEI Mom, you've asked me that at least twenty times! I've told you that according to the official recommendation he is the world's top-ranking good guy. Not a single flaw can be found anywhere on his body, not even on his bellybutton.

LIU HSIU-YING I wonder if he is an honest person?

HO WEI Honest? Extremely honest! No matter what it is, persuasive debate or armed fighting, he is this: [*Sticks up his thumb*] His profession is to catch people and kill them!

LIU HSIU-YING What?!

HO WEI But, Mom, you should never be afraid of him. I've heard that the ones who are afraid of him are all bad guys; the good guys are not afraid of him. He's pretty fine in Dad's eyes. Ah, well, you'd better go and ask Dad about him. This son-in-law was his choice. [*He turns back to his book*]

[HO YUN *walks in from the corridor. She is a pretty, good-natured girl, who has led a rather simple life. After graduating from high school she was sent to a farm; later she was transferred back to town, to a position at the Municipal Public Security Bureau. Her way of thinking is somewhat naive, but she is not content to let things drift, or to ignore the struggle in the world around her. Recent events have deeply troubled her; she has been wracking her brain in a futile effort to make sense of what has been happening. Today she is more depressed then ever, for she is facing yet another turning point in her life*]

HO WEI You were inside? Dad was calling you, are you deaf?

[HO YUN *does not reply*]

HO WEI [*Noticing her red eyes*] Why must you shed tears on such a great and joyful day? So you don't have the guts to resist the marriage; all you can do is cry your eyes out!

Ho Yun [*Angered*] Brother!

Ho Wei [*Also suddenly angered*] If I were you, I would definitely wait for Ou-yang; go look for him, search for him all over the place. I wouldn't even give that T'ang Yu-ts'ai a glance.

Liu Hsiu-ying Hsiao Yun, you are not going out with T'ang. You are not, you are not! [*Grasping* Ho Yun *tight and shaking her*]

Ho Yun Mom, what's the matter with you? [*Worried, she puts her arms around* Liu Hsiu-ying *and leads her to a seat on the couch*] Brother! What nonsense did you tell Mom?

Ho Wei Me? I just praised her son-in-law for you. Oh, why should I care about some petty business of yours! Look: *Gone with the Wind*—poof . . . I'm just drifting with the wind. [*Exits*]

Ho Yun Mom, don't listen to my brother's nonsense.

Liu Hsiu-ying That man is not honest.

Ho Yun I don't know him either. But Dad said he was good; probably he's all right.

Liu Hsiu-ying No, your Dad—he—he doesn't know how to judge people!

Ho Yun Mom, here you go getting confused again. Do you mean that Dad is so limited he can't even judge a person?

Liu Hsiu-ying Child, you really don't understand this!

[Ho Shih-fei *comes downstairs carrying a tablecloth and a small, framed picture.* Liu Hsiu-ying *swallows the rest of her words, stands up slowly, and exits into the kitchen sobbing*]

Ho Shih-fei Hsiao-yun, where were you a while ago? [*Putting the small picture on the bookcase and fixing the angle, he admires it for a moment. Then he turns around to discover* Ho Yun*'s red eyes and after a moment realizes the reason for them*] Hsiao-yun, come over here.

[Ho Yun *sits down obediently on the couch with* Ho Shih-fei]

Ho Shih-fei T'ang Yu-ts'ai is coming today. What do you think about that?

Ho Yun Nothing.

Ho Shih-fei For the past few years this family of ours hasn't really been looking after your interests. Your brother is so selfish he only cares about himself. As for your mother, God knows why she had to lose her mind. Well, the fault is mainly mine . . . to have kept you waiting until now. You're already thirty.

Ho Yun Stop it, Dad.

Ho Shih-fei [*Standing up to put the tablecloth on, he suddenly turns to* Ho Yun] It's Ou-yang P'ing, isn't it? You still can't get him out of your mind?

Ho Yun Dad! [*He gives her a searching look. She avoides his eyes*]

Ho Shih-fei Well, I know that you and Ou-yang P'ing grew up together, you enjoyed being together and playing together. There was an innocent affection between you two in childhood. I used to think that he wasn't such a bad kid. But then he became mean.

Ho Yun [*Stands up, her chest heaving rapidly*] Dad, stop it!

Ho Shih-fei It's time to put an end to all this! Nine years ago wasn't
  it he who dropped you for no reason at all? For nine years you've been
  looking for him everywhere. You've waited for him and searched for
  him. But what has he done? Who would have believed that he could be
  that cruel, without even writing you a word, like a stone dropped into
  the ocean without a ripple . . .

  [*Ho Yun sits down at the piano*]

Ho Shih-fei Hsiao-yun, your Dad doesn't mean to rub salt into your
  wounds. I simply think it's time you stopped letting this thing haunt
  you. Please give it careful thought. As for T'ang Yu-ts'ai, his
  background is good: his origins are beyond suspicion; he is alert and
  firm in struggles over political line. I heard that the Central
  Committee leaders have a rather high opinion of him!

Ho Yun But some people say that . . .

Ho Shih-fei In a society with so many people there's bound to be all
  kinds of gossip. He's the man in charge of the Shanghai Militia,
  responsible for carrying out the class struggle. It is unavoidable that in
  this society there should be some people who hate him bitterly. In fact,
  was there ever a Legalist in history who was not cursed?[2] [Ho Yun
  remains silent] Hsiao-yun, your own father wouldn't do anything to
  harm you. Won't you trust me?

Ho Yun I will, Dad!

Ho Shih-fei That's fine then. Of course, I don't mean to force you
  into anything. You should be introduced to him today, and then when
  you have more contact, you will get to know each other better, right?
  And if you really decide it won't work out, then we'll talk about it
  again, all right?

Ho Yun [*Pauses for a moment, reluctantly*] All right.

  [Liu Hsiu-ying *enters carrying a basket*]

Ho Yun [*Rising*] Mom, let me do the shopping.

Ho Shih-fei Better let your Mom do it—Oh, well, let me do it then, I'd
  better do some work too. You two stay at home and get things going
  quicker! [*Exits*]

Ho Yun Mom! [*Suddenly embraces* Liu Hsiu-ying] Mom, where do
  you think Ou-yang and Aunt Mei are now?

Liu Hsiu-ying I keep dreaming that they're both dead, both dead!

Ho Yun [*Frightened*] Mom!

  [Liu Hsiu-ying *enters the kitchen, weeping. After a short while* Ho
  Yun *walks back to the piano and, hardly aware of it, plays a simple song.*
  Ou-yang P'ing*'s soft, tender voice echoes from nine years before:* "Come,
  Hsiao-Yun, let's sing our favorite, the *Red Plum Ode.* I'll sing, you play
  for me, how about it?" *Suddenly she sits down and starts playing the
  'Red Plum Ode,' totally absorbed in the music.*

  [Ou-yang P'ing *enters with two traveling bags. Though his weather-
  beaten face is dark and thin, his eyes are sparkling. He has lived through
  rough weather and completely lost his student ways. He looks calm, but*

in his heart the flame of the Revolution burns unceasingly. Like a rock, he is firm, unyielding, and solid. Hearing the familiar, enchanting, somewhat melancholic music, he stands motionless, staring at HO YUN*'s back, and listens eagerly. At the end of the song* HO YUN *slumps onto the keyboard; the piano makes a mournful noise.*

[OU-YANG P'ING *opens his mouth to speak, but quickly shuts it and quietly retreats toward the doorway.* HO YUN *stands up and covers the piano with a bang*]

HO YUN It's all over, it's over for good! [*Turning around, all of a sudden she sees* OU-YANG P'ING] Ah!? [*Time, air, eveything freezes*] You? Ou-yang?

OU-YANG P'ING It's me.

[HO YUN *runs to him, carried away by her feelings;* OU-YANG P'ING *quickly stretches out a hand; the two grasp each other's hands and gaze in silence*]

OU-YANG P'ING [*Moving his eyes away from her*] My mother is still outside.

HO YUN Aunt Mei?

[OU-YANG P'ING *turns away and walks out through the central door*]

HO YUN [*Standing there perplexed for a while, she tries to calm herself*] Brother! [*She follows* P'ING *through the central door.* HO WEI *comes out of his room, with the book and the big straw fan still in his hands*]

HO WEI [*Glances at the piano*] Plays that tune day after day, how annoying! [*Sits down on the couch, lost in thought*]

[HO YUN *and* OU-YANG P'ING *enter through the central door, supporting* MEI LIN. MEI LIN *is only in her early fifties but already looks as spent as a candle nearly burnt down in the wind. Her hair has turned completely gray, her face is wrinkled, and her body is thin and stiff. Yet she smiles frequently, is active and talkative, takes a great interest in life, and is calm and composed in a crisis. It is amazing that such a frail body can house such a strong character.*

[HO WEI, *at the sound of footsteps, quickly lies down on the couch and lifts his book to read*]

HO YUN Brother, we have guests.

[HO WEI *simply turns his face toward them*]

OU-YANG P'ING Ta Wei!

HO WEI [*Gets up slowly*] Ou-yang?

MEI LIN Right, it's Ou-yang and me.

HO WEI [*Hesitantly*] Aunt Mei?

MEI LIN Little Imp, can't even recognize me any more?

HO WEI Aunt Mei! [*They support* MEI LIN *to the couch, but she does not sit*]

HO YUN [*Goes to the kitchen door*] Mom, come see who's here. [*Enters the kitchen*]

MEI LIN P'ing, go see your Aunt Liu. [OU-YANG P'ING *also goes into the kitchen*]

Ho WEI [*Trying to find something to say*] Aunt Mei, have you been well?

MEI LIN What sort of a doctor are you? Can't even tell from the way I sag and look worn?

[*Uncomfortably* Ho WEI *looks away from her. From the kitchen comes a loud crashing sound*]

Ho WEI Aunt Mei, please sit down.

[*Looking concerned,* Ho WEI *exits to the kitchen.* MEI LIN *observes the room carefully. After a moment she appears to be exhausted, and puts her hand against her side near her liver, leaning back at an angle against the couch.* Ho SHIH-FEI *walks in through the central door and sees her*]

Ho SHIH-FEI Who do you want to see?

[MEI LIN *looks at him without answering*]

Ho SHIH-FEI [*Speaking loudly into her ear*] Old woman, who do you want to see?

MEI LIN I am not deaf.

[Ho SHIH-FEI *is astonished, but gradually recognizes her. He takes two steps backwards*]

MEI LIN Right, a dirty old woman sitting like a beggar in this clean room of yours. . . .

Ho SHIH-FEI Mei . . . Sister Mei!?

MEI LIN Yes, it's me, Mei Lin.

Ho SHIH-FEI I almost failed to recognize you! Sister Mei!

[LIU HSIU-YING *stumbles out of the kitchen.* OU-YANG P'ING, Ho YUN, *and* Ho WEI *follow her out.* LIU HSIU-YING *walks over to* MEI LIN *in silence and embraces her*]

MEI LIN Hsiu-ying.

Ho YUN Mom, Aunt Mei isn't feeling well now. [LIU HSIU-YING *cries*]

MEI LIN We haven't seen each other for over ten years. We should be happy, shouldn't we?

HSIU-YING I didn't expect to see you in this life!

Ho WEI More of your depressing talk.

Ho YUN [*To* MEI LIN] It's just that Mom's so excited. When she heard you were here she dropped a pot. [LIU HSIU-YING *smiles through her tears*]

MEI LIN We haven't seen each other since 1965 when I was transferred. Hsiu-ying, are you well?

LIU HSIU-YING I'm fine. Sister Mei, you've suffered a lot, haven't you?

MEI LIN What do you mean? Don't I look terrific?

Ho YUN Aunt Mei, for the past few years you— [*Glancing at* OU-YANG P'ING]

Ho WEI Right, all of a sudden there was no word from you.

MEI LIN Just got caught in a bit of a rainstorm! Old Ho, you caught a few drops too, didn't you?

Ho SHIH-FEI Well, well, Sister Mei, now you . . .

MEI LIN I was sent back to my home town to sweep floors for the Township.

HO WEI Yet another tale of "Revolutionary Rebirth":[3] a grade eleven cadre sent back home to sweep the floor.

HO YUN But for what reason?

MEI LIN They said that I was a traitor.

HO YUN Traitor?

HO WEI And the evidence?

MEI LIN I heard that "circumstantial evidence was substantial and an ironclad case was established"!

OU-YANG P'ING But when they passed their verdict on this case, they did not allow my mother to read it.

MEI LIN But how come none of you knew any of this?

HO SHIH-FEI It's absurd! Didn't any of those people have any notion of due process?

LIU HSIU-YING Sister Mei was wronged! You were wronged! [*Weeping bitterly*]

HO WEI Ugh, I'd really like to write a letter to the leaders in the Party Central Committee, the ones in charge of the struggle between the Confucians and the Legalists, and ask them to reverse the case against the old traitor Ch'in Kuei.[4]

MEI LIN To reverse whose case?

HO WEI Ch'in Kuei, the medieval traitor who suppressed Yueh Fei. That conspirator should be recognized as the greatest, most revolutionary Legalist in history.

MEI LIN That's interesting. Why?

HO WEI Because he was the one who invented the method of Passing Judgment without Evidence; now it works like magic for a certain group taking more and more control of the country!

MEI LIN [*Laughing*] But now they are much smarter than the old traitors. The false accusations are loaded with tricks!

HO SHIH-FEI Sister Mei, we must trust the masses and the Party; we must be tested . . . ah, it really confuses me. You are an old revolutionary; surely you understand this far better than I do.

LIU HSIU-YING He . . . I mean they made you suffer! [*Holding* MEI LIN *and weeping bitterly*]

HO SHIH-FEI Hsiao Yun, will you take your mother up for a rest? [HO YUN *helps* LIU HSIU-YING *upstairs*]

MEI LIN What's the matter with Hsiu-ying?

HO SHIH-FEI It's a long story; Hsiu-ying is insane.

OU-YANG P'ING Insane?

HO WEI Two years ago Mother suddenly fell ill, and when she recovered she was like this. At times she's quite lucid, but sometimes she rambles and keeps saying that she dreamt that you both were gone for good.

MEI LIN Perhaps she's had some emotional trauma?

HO SHIH-FEI We've puzzled over it for two long years now but haven't figured out what kind of emotional shock she could have suffered. She's had a very easy life. And when we ask her, she won't say a word Ai!

MEI LIN P'ing, my son, hand me a couple of biscuits. [*He does so*] Old Ho, are you still in the same work as before?

HO SHIH-FEI Yes.

HO WEI Father was promoted, Aunt Mei. Now he's the director of the revolutionary committee of the import-export company!

MEI LIN Old Ch'en and Old Hsün are both fine, I suppose?

HO WEI Aunt Hsün died in '69, it's not clear why. Uncle Ch'en is still in the cadre school labor camp doing manual labor. [MEI LIN *and* OU-YANG P'ING *look at each other in silence*]

HO SHIH-FEI Are you looking for them, Sister Ho?

MEI LIN Not especially, I just wanted to know. They were old wartime comrades, and we hadn't seen them for years. [HO YUN *comes downstairs*] Hsiao Yun, is your mother any better?

HO YUN I made her take a tranquilizer.

MEI LIN You, where do you work?

HO YUN At the Municipal Public Security Bureau.

HO SHIH-FEI She's been very busy since the T'ien-an-men Square Incident.[5] Well, Hsiao Yun, tell them about the nationwide alert for that counterrevolutionary.

OU-YANG P'ING A nationwide alert? And what are his crimes? [*He and* HO YUN *exchange looks*]

HO YUN [*Reluctantly*] He has distributed poems commemorating Premier Chou.

MEI LIN I can't understand that at all. Why is commemorating Premier Chou a counterrevolutionary act?

HO SHIH-FEI Ah, Hsiao Yun, it's not that simple is it? We were told that commemorating Premier Chou was only a front. Their real target was the Central Committee of the Party!

OU-YANG P'ING How could anyone find a link between these two things, commemorating Premier Chou and opposing the Central Committee of the Party? I wish someone could explain it to me. [*He and* HO YUN *exchange glances*]

HO WEI Ou-yang, you take everything too seriously; this is something which can be understood only through the imagination, words can't convey it! Do you understand?

MEI LIN Very interesting. How about you, Ho Wei, are you still a surgeon?

HO WEI Mm, but I'm far from busy. I'm just dawdling away my time, that's all.

MEI LIN I can tell that from this outfit of yours. It's like Lord Slob's.[6] [*Embarrassed*, HO WEI *quickly straightens his clothes*]

HO SHIH-FEI For the past few years he's been impossible! He groans nothing's wrong. He takes plenty of time off when he's slightly ill. He loafs around, cares about nothing. He'd be all set if he had a bird cage in one hand and a dog on a leash! He is simply unworthy of living in this great era of Mao Tse-tung!

MEI LIN Is it that serious?

HO WEI Mm, just about.

MEI LIN Interesting! I thought you'd worked very hard on surgery! You and your teacher were planning to go into liver transplants, weren't you?

HO WEI Well, that was because we were infected with the poison of seventeen years of wrong policies carried out by the Medical Department, when people were encouraged to develop the most advanced science. But now the top level really hopes we'll do some research on a kind of popular operation.

MEI LIN What kind of operation is it?

HO WEI "Mouth Closure." [*He gestures*] That is to drill a hole in everyone's lower and upper lips, run a steel wire through the two holes, and then twist the wire. . . .

[MEI LIN *and* OU-YANG P'ING *laugh.* HO YUN *also bursts into laughter*]

HO SHIH-FEI You're well over thirty, why do you have to behave so inanely?

MEI LIN No, it's rather interesting. I was going to ask you to treat me, but I couldn't bear this "Mouth Closure" operation. I love talking too much.

HO YUN Do you need medical treatment, Aunt Mei?

MEI LIN Recently my liver has given me a lot of pain, makes me feel nauseated, and I can't eat.

HO SHIH-FEI Let Ta Wei take good care of you. Ta Wei, you're now in charge of Aunt Mei's health.

MEI LIN Never mind. We're only passing through Shanghai, just stopping for a quick visit with you, and then we'll leave shortly.

OU-YANG P'ING I want to take mother to Peking for treatment. But, Mother . . .

HO WEI How about coming over to our hospital first for a checkup?

MEI LIN Never mind. I heard that in Shanghai they've carried out class struggle very thoroughly, and neither of us has brought along a letter of recommendation.

HO YUN It doesn't matter, Aunt Mei.

HO WEI Stay with us.

OU-YANG P'ING We don't want to trouble you.

HO WEI I don't think you're quite normal either. So don't talk nonsense. Stay. [*Looking at his watch*] First eat and then we'll talk things over.

HO YUN The meal should be almost ready. Give me a hand, brother. [*Exits into the kitchen*]

HO WEI Right. Dad knew you were coming, so he got out two bottles of good liquor—Kweichow Mao-t'ai and Gold Medal Brandy, and Mom cooked a tableful of delicious dishes. [*He follows his sister*]

OU-YANG P'ING [*Looks around*] Uncle Ho, do you have company coming today?

HO SHIH-FEI Ah, Hsiao Yun's boyfriend is coming for dinner.

[*The water spills from* OU-YANG P'ING*'s cup.* MEI LIN*'s liver suddenly hurts.* HO WEI *carries out two dishes and puts them on the table*]

HO WEI Come to eat! Aunt Mei . . .

OU-YANG P'ING Mother! Mother!

[*Hearing him,* HO YUN *comes out of the kitchen*]

MEI LIN [*Clearly in pain*] It's all right, P'ing, my son . . . you always make a fuss about me.

HO SHIH-FEI Take her to the hospital, quick!

HO WEI Go to my room and rest first.

[OU-YANG P'ING, *supporting* MEI LIN, *takes her into* HO WEI*'s room.* HO WEI *and* HO YUN *follow them off.* HO SHIH-FEI *looks at his watch, takes the telephone off the hook, hesitates for a moment, then hangs it up and exits through the central door. After a while,* OU-YANG P'ING *and* HO YUN *enter from the room*]

HO YUN Aunt Mei always used to be so healthy. What happened to her to make her so ill?

OU-YANG P'ING [*Shakes his head mournfully*] Mother was imprisoned for six whole years during the Cultural Revolution. It was all spent in a dark room, three meters square, where she ate, drank, went to the toilet, and slept. There was no window. Once she didn't see sunshine for fourteen months in a row; that was the longest time. They beat her, hung her by the hair, and kicked her with their boots. They weighted her down with bricks. . . . They used what they called "Exhaustion Tactics," not allowing her to sleep for thirteen days in a row. The moment she'd close her eyes they'd whip her . . .

HO YUN [*Upset*] Stop it! Stop it!

OU-YANG P'ING That's when mother got her liver trouble. But they wouldn't give her any treatment; they went on torturing her even worse! [*Silence*]

HO YUN Ou-yang, stay here, will you? For the sake of Aunt Mei's health, stay here.

OU-YANG P'ING [*Smiles bitterly*] You'd be accepting two people with ambiguous status, you know that, don't you?

HO YUN Don't I? Don't I know your background? Our two families lived together for close to twenty years. I used to play with you every day. Do you mean that I—I don't understand Aunt Mei, that I don't understand you?

OU-YANG P'ING This Ou-yang P'ing is completely different from the one you used to know. [*He gazes at* HO YUN. *She remains silent.* HO WEI *enters*]

OU-YANG P'ING How is she now?

Ho WEI Her ascites is quite severe. She has cirrhosis, if nothing worse.
. . . Ou-yang, you haven't handled this very well. Why didn't you take
her to a doctor much earlier?

OU-YANG P'ING I . . . I haven't been around for the past few years, you
know! She was in the countryside, and there was no one in the local
clinic there who would dare to treat her. The first page of her hospital
case history was stamped in large print: "Stinking Reactionary."

Ho WEI You should have taken her away from there sooner and come
to me!

OU-YANG P'ING Mother didn't have a cent of her own. And I was forced
to leave the Army because of Mother's problems. Now I'm working as
a waiter in a small diner in the suburbs of Peking, making thirty-two
dollars a month. [*Silence*]

Ho WEI Go call a taxi. Let's take Aunt Mei to the hospital immediately.
[Ho WEI *exits into the sickroom.* Ho YUN *starts to go outside*]

OU-YANG P'ING Hsiao Yun, let me go. Don't you have guests coming
today?

Ho YUN Who told you that?

OU-YANG P'ING Don't try to hide it from me. . . . [*Exits through
central door.* Ho SHIH-FEI *enters*]

Ho SHIH-FEI Hsiao Yun, I've just telephoned T'ang Yu-ts'ai and he has
already left. He may be here any minute.

Ho YUN [*With her head lowered*] I want to take Aunt Mei to the
hospital.

Ho SHIH-FEI What if T'ang Yu-ts'ai arrives?

Ho YUN I don't know.

Ho SHIH-FEI Hsiao Yun, you've started dreaming again.

Ho YUN Father, leave me alone, will you? At least I'm not seeing
T'ang Yu-ts'ai today! [*Telephone rings*]

Ho SHIH-FEI [*Answering the phone*] Hello . . . [*Hands the phone
to* Ho YUN] It's for you. Uh-oh, what's burning on the stove? [*Exits
to kitchen*]

[OU-YANG P'ING *enters through the central door.* Ho YUN *is about to
call him, but he goes straight into the bedroom*]

Ho YUN Hello . . . speaking. . . . Come to the Bureau now? I have
something important to do at home. . . . I have to go? . . . All right.
[*Ho YUN hangs up and walks to the corridor.* OU-YANG P'ING *and*
Ho WEI *enter, supporting* MEI LIN]

MEI LIN P'ing, son, my bag!

OU-YANG P'ING Yes. [*Returning to the room*]
[Ho WEI *helps* MEI LIN *through the central door.* Ho YUN *enters
wearing her police uniform.* OU-YANG P'ING *enters with a leather
bag*]

Ho YUN Ou-yang, I can't go to the hospital now.

OU-YANG P'ING [*Smiling*] I've told you to stay at home. [*Starts to go*]

Ho YUN [*Upset, blocks his path*] No, I have to get over to the Bureau.

OU-YANG P'ING You may go anywhere you want to!

HO YUN I'm not kidding. I have to attend an emergency investigative session. That activist counterrevolutionary fled to Shanghai today.

OU-YANG P'ING Ah?

HO YUN After the checkup at the hospital, please don't leave. Let's have a good talk, all right?

[HO WEI *calls from offstage: "Hurry up, Ou-yang!"* OU-YANG P'ING *dashes out through the central door*]

HO YUN [*Following him*] Ou-yang, wait for me at home! [*Exits*]

[HO SHIH-FEI *enters with a pot in his hand*]

HO SHIH-FEI This rice is burnt to charcoal. How can we eat!? Hsiao Yun! Hsiao Yun! Ta Wei! [LIU HSIU-YING *walks slowly downstairs*]

HO SHIH-FEI [*Furious*] They've all gone!

[*Outside a car suddenly brakes to a stop. After a few quick honks on the horn, someone quacks: "Old Ho! Damn it! Old Ho!"*]

HO SHIH-FEI [*Scared*] T'ang Yu-ts'ai!? [*He walks respectfully to the doorway to receive the guest*]

[*Curtain*]

ACT II

Four in the afternoon of the same day, in the same room. With no breeze at all, it is even more stifling. Leaves on the trees now and then quiver nervously, as if they were ready to dance on the branches. But then they droop dejectedly. It seems that there will be more rain. As the curtain goes up, the clock strikes four.

LIU HSIU-YING *stands motionless at the door for a moment, looking out, then walks to the table and stands there briefly. Suddenly she picks up a message on the table and reads it. Looking around in panic, she clenches her teeth and tears the message in half.* HO SHIH-FEI *enters from the central door.*

HO SHIH-FEI Hsiu-ying! Were you home alone? [*She does not answer*] It's past four already. Aren't they back from the hospital yet?

HSIU-YING Yes, they are. They're all in Ho Wei's room.

HO SHIH-FEI Ah. Was anyone from the local militia here?

LIU HSIU-YING Local militia? No. [*She quickly walks over to the table, grabs the torn pieces of the message, and hides them behind her back*]

HO SHIH-FEI [*Noticing her guilty pose*] What's in your hands?

LIU HSIU-YING Nothing.

HO SHIH-FEI Nothing? Let me take a look. [*Goes over to her and seizes the message, smoothing it out furiously*] You're really crazy! How can you tear up this sort of thing? Eh? I asked you, did anyone come from the local militia, and you lied! [*She looks at him in panic. He softens his voice*] Hsiu-ying, when you were a teacher, didn't you always teach the children to be honest, never to tell lies? But here you . . .

[*As if her heart had been pierced by a knife*, LIU HSIU-YING *runs upstairs weeping*. OU-YANG P'ING *and* HO WEI *enter from the sickroom*]

OU-YANG P'ING Uncle Ho, you're back.

HO WEI [*Staring after* LIU HSIU-YING] She was all right a while ago. Now here she goes again. How come?

OU-YANG P'ING Ta-wei, can't you try harder to find a way to cure Aunt Liu?

HO WEI Illnesses with unknown causes are incurable.

HO SHIH-FEI Ah! Ou-yang. Sister Mei's condition . . .

HO WEI Cirrhosis and ascites were both confirmed. As for . . . well, we haven't received the results of the other tests yet. I'll go to fetch them in a while.

HO SHIH-FEI Then why didn't you let Aunt Mei stay in the hospital, Ta Wei?

HO WEI There are no beds available in the hospital; she has to wait a couple of days.

HO SHIH-FEI Oh. Don't worry, Ou-yang. Your mother's condition is hopeful, I'm sure it's hopeful. You should feel free to stay with us.

OU-YANG P'ING Thank you, Uncle Ho.

HO SHIH-FEI Oh. Hsiu-ying said that Comrade Chang from the local militia was just here and left a message. He wanted you two to apply for a temporary permit to stay here; you'll need identification and recommendation letters from your units. Look, here it is, it was torn up carelessly by Hsiu-ying.

OU-YANG P'ING I have my own identification, but my mother . . .

HO WEI Did you get it? You need recommendation letters from your units, too. Do you have them?

OU-YANG P'ING No, we don't.

HO SHIH-FEI Ou-yang, you'd better take a little time over this matter. Luckily it's not all that troublesome. I'll go to see your Aunt Liu. [*Goes upstairs*]

OU-YANG P'ING [*Pauses for a while*] It's not so bad for me; anyhow, I don't care what happens to me. But my mother . . . her generation followed Chairman Mao for several decades, risking their lives to master the country, all nine million square kilometers of it, yet now there's not so much as an inch where they can stand.

HO WEI This is the "All-Inclusive Dictatorship" of T'ang Yu-ts'ai and his kind.

OU-YANG P'ING Forget it, we'll leave today!

HO WEI That won't do. In Aunt Mei's condition she can't take the strain of a trip like this. [OU-YANG P'ING *does not reply*] Just stay here! Who gives a damn about that jerk Yu-ts'ai?!

OU-YANG P'ING After all, what sort of person is this T'ang Yu-ts'ai?

HO WEI He is a rare, unique, remarkable—big thug. As for talent, he doesn't have any; as for integrity, he is without it; as for looks, he's a hippopotamus!

OU-YANG P'ING [*Laughs*] Watch your mouth; that's pretty bold!

HO WEI It's true. Let me tell you, one day this guy received some foreign guests. He swore "t'a niang" over a hundred times: "mother-fuckin' this" and "fuck your mother" that. As his conversation went on for an hour and a half, he must have said it a hundred times, two curses per minute. After a while even the foreigners could recognize the sound and they asked the interpreter: "What is 't'a-niang'?" The interpreter froze for a minute before he could answer: "That's Mr. T'ang's native dialect. It's probably a greeting word!"

OU-YANG P'ING But how could it be possible for Uncle Ho to introduce him to Hsiao Yun?

HO WEI T'ang Yu-ts'ai is powerful, influential, with plenty of backers, don't you know? He once saved the life of the "Rebel Commander-in-Chief" of Shanghai.[7] They became sworn brothers. That's why though his official title is only a lousy head of militia, he can put his finger in every pie, he can interfere with industry, transportation, finance, commerce, public security, literature and arts, our hospital, all the way to sanitary management units. Who's got the nerve to touch him!?

OU-YANG P'ING Those "East Overlords" and "West Overlords" Chairman Mao once talked about have returned! But do you mean that Uncle Ho has changed as much as this?

HO WEI Ugh, that "Uncle Ho" of yours . . . anyway there's been a change—if it isn't him then it must be me.

OU-YANG P'ING You have changed, drastically. I remember you used to be serious about everything.

HO WEI I'm afflicted, incurable!

OU-YANG P'ING What affliction could be so fearful?

HO WEI I'm afflicted with seeing through.

OU-YANG P'ING Seeing through?

HO WEI The "political line struggles" for all these years have made my head spin. Speaking the truth—that's a crime; telling lies—that's meritorious; parroting official jargon—that's safe; bullshitting—earns a promotion! To hell with all that. I've vowed, I've sworn, I don't care about anything any more, except to fill up on three meals a day and get enough sleep. [*Lying down on the couch again*]

OU-YANG P'ING That isn't so. A while ago when we were in the hospital, the moment you put on your surgeon's coat you seemed to become another person. You were very serious and very meticulous!

HO WEI [*Sitting up*] I'm a doctor. When I see a patient can I be careless? But it was just because I was so serious that I kept getting criticized! They said that I devoted myself to research in my profession out of concern for fame and prestige, that I was taking a nonpolitical road of expertise . . . to hell with it! Now I am taking an idiotic road to become a colossal fool, a satisfied one, right?

OU-YANG P'ING [*Laughing loudly*] This affliction of yours is curable. And I have the medicine for you.

HO WEI What medicine? D.D.T.?

OU-YANG P'ING How about ten bottles?

HO WEI Do you really want to send me to heaven?

OU-YANG P'ING I think living like this is a drag. You're imitating Lord Slob, pretending to be a fool but torturing yourself inside. What for? The three meals a day?

HO WEI [*Interrupting*] To me it seems yu're still the same as in the old days when you were an Air Force pilot: "Let my ideal give me wings and carry me all over the sky!"

OU-YANG P'ING I returned to solid ground long, long ago.

HO WEI Then what do you think I can do? I admit, my life is simply—

OU-YANG P'ING [*Softly*] Pathetic!

HO WEI [*As if he's been whipped*] True, it's pathetic. But I . . .

OU-YANG P'ING Ta Wei, you were never such a person and you shouldn't become such a person!

HO WEI Do you understand? If I had continued to be serious, I would have been smothered alive.

OU-YANG P'ING Then shout! Shout out the bitterness, the love, the hatred in your heart. Shout aloud!

HO WEI Shout? Me, an average guy . . .

OU-YANG P'ING There are eight hundred million average people in China!

HO WEI But the Chinese people have an enormous capacity for endurance.

OU-YANG P'ING Nonsense! Don't forget what Lu Hsün once wrote: "When you pass judgment on the Chinese . . . you must look at the ground."

HO WEI What is there on the ground? Rocks, mud.

OU-YANG P'ING Right, sturdy rocks, plain mud, and—erupting lava! [HO WEI *keeps silent*] Ta Wei, during the days when we mourned for Premier Chou you didn't go to T'ien-an-men Square to take a look. The wreaths were like mountains, the flow of people was like an ocean. The evergreen pines and cedars were decorated with tear-soaked white paper flowers. In front of the most solemn, the most sacred cloth scrolls, people whispered: Where are you, Premier Chou? The proud Monument of the People's Heroes was covered with oaths written in blood: Wipe away tears of mourning for the Premier, shed blood to quell the powerful conspirators! Thousands, millions of people formed a constant stream day and night. . . . Ta Wei, you only had to go to that furious billowing ocean and stay a moment; you would have understood right away: having been educated by Chairman Mao and the Party, having undergone the tempest of the Cultural Revolution, the Chinese people have matured! There is hope for the Chinese nation!

HO WEI [*Pauses*] But now? Pitch dark once again, silence everywhere!

OU-YANG P'ING Silence, the present frightening, uncommon silence foretells an even more frightening storm to come! [*Taking out a booklet*] I've collected the poems that appeared in T'ien-an-men Square into a booklet. Read it.

Ho Wei *The Proud Sword Is Drawn!*

Ou-yang P'ing Now, the summer of 1976, this is exactly what the average Chinese is like! [Ho Wei *thumbs through the pages eagerly.* Ou-yang P'ing *exits*]

Ho Wei [*Spontaneously reads aloud*]

>The last generation, whose blood was shed,
>What hopes for the living had they, the dead?
>Rather die than let a witch's head[8]
>Crown revolution they once led.

[Ho Shih-fei *enters, coming downstairs*]

Ho Shih-fei Ta Wei, hasn't your sister come back?

Ho Wei No. [*Turns his head away and exits*]

[Ho Shih-fei *paces anxiously.* Ho Yun *enters through the central door*]

Ho Yun Dad.

Ho Shih-fei Here you are, Hsiao Yun. Did T'ang Yu-ts'ai go to the Bureau to look for you?

Ho Yun Dad, that person is frightening!

Ho Shih-fei Frightening?

Ho Yun And he treated me in such a flippant way. I was disgusted with him.

Ho Shih-fei You shouldn't base a judgment of him on nothing but a subjective impression! Do you know why the Bureau assigned such a serious case to you today? T'ang Yu-ts'ai has been using a little influence on your behalf.

Ho Yun Why do I need his influence?

Ho Shih-fei You're still blind! You've given your director a rather bad impression recently. He said that in the past year your political stand was unstable, you've been wavering, hesitant, and quite often uncommitted.

Ho Yun But I've told you all the reasons. I had a suspicion some people were attacking Premier Chou.

Ho Shih-fei That's nothing but your fantasy.

Ho Yun [*Slowly shaking her head*] Didn't you hear just now that Aunt Mei and Ou-yang have the same view?

Ho Shih-fei Them? . . . Ah, didn't T'ang Yu-ts'ai tell you anything about them?

Ho Yun Yes, he did. He wanted me to draw a clear line between the traitors and myself, and he also wanted me to—drive them out.

Ho Shih-fei Did he? T'ang is coming for dinner later. I can see this is not an easy matter to handle!

Ho Yun Dad, could Aunt Mei really be a traitor? She used to be your director in the Party underground before Liberation. You should understand her!

Ho SHIH-FEI Of course, but I don't know if she was or wasn't a traitor. You know that before Liberation I was kicked out of my company by my boss because I had tuberculosis. It was Sister Mei who had me cured. I can never forget that she saved my life. When I witness her present misfortune, can I feel at ease? But we are all Communists; we can't place our personal feelings above the interests of the Party. We still must trust the organization, trust the Party. . . . Hsiao Yun, as your father, I want to give you a piece of advice. Quit torturing yourself! [Ho YUN *stands up*] You are a Public Security cadre; he is the son of a traitor. Between you, no relationship is possible.

[*Standing motionless for a while,* Ho YUN *suddenly turns away from him and runs out.* OU-YANG P'ING *and* Ho WEI *enter, supporting* MEI LIN*]*

Ho WEI Aunt Mei!

MEI LIN All right, I won't go out on the street, but let me walk around inside, will you?

Ho SHIH-FEI Sister Mei! You're feeling better, aren't you?

MEI LIN Me? According to Ta Wei, this simply can't be considered an illness, yet the strange thing is he won't let me move around. Who knows what kind of trick he is playing on me. [*With support,* MEI LIN *sits on the couch*] P'ing, son, hand me two biscuits.

Ho WEI Aunt Mei, you've just thrown up. . . .

MEI LIN You see, here we go again. I should eat after throwing up, shouldn't I? If I don't eat, how can I get better? [*She takes the biscuits and chews with great difficulty.* Ho SHIH-FEI *hurriedly hands her a cup of water.* Ho WEI *signals to* OU-YANG P'ING *not to let Mei Lin go out. He starts to exit*]

MEI LIN Old Ho, it must have been difficult to handle foreign trade these past few years.

Ho SHIH-FEI We've been trying our best, that's all.

Ho WEI [*Unable to restrain himself*] Dad, why should you be so humble? Aunt Mei, my father has worked extraordinarily hard the past few years. Let me show you something. [*Taking down the picture from the bookcase to show* MEI LIN] This is the picture taken when Chang Ch'un-ch'iao received my father. You might say it's an historical memento![9] [MEI LIN *puts on her glasses to look at the picture*] The one sitting in the middle is Chang Ch'un-ch'iao; behind him, the third on the left, the one waving the *Quotations of Mao* is my father.

MEI LIN I was locked inside a dark room at that time!

Ho WEI But from that time on father seemed to bask in the light of a lucky star, soaring higher and higher like the clouds! [*Sweeps out*] [*Pause. The telephone rings.* Ho SHIH-FEI *answers*]

Ho SHIH-FEI Hello? . . . speaking . . . register for staying here overnight? Fine, fine. [*Hangs up*] Sister Mei, Militia Headquarters is urging you to register for staying here overnight.

MEI LIN Tell them I'm planning to sleep in the streets tonight. If they have anything to say to me, they can look for me in the streets!

HO SHIH-FEI Sister Mei, don't get upset. Let's talk about it later.

MEI LIN The Cultural Revolution is really a priceless opportunity.

HO SHIH-FEI Right, right, unprecedented! It has washed away all filthy mud and sewage!

MEI LIN You're quite right! The Cultural Revolution has not only cleansed the souls of the revolutionaries, but it will also wash the makeup from the face of every political clown!

HO SHIH-FEI Profound, profound! It shows you haven't been a Communist these forty years for nothing.

MEI LIN No, I was expelled. A traitor, I think you should know. [*Pause*]

HO SHIH-FEI Let me take a look at Hsiu-ying, Sister Mei. You take a little rest. [*Exits upstairs*]

MEI LIN Turn on the fan.

OU-YANG P'ING Mom, drafts are no good for you.

MEI LIN Turn it on; the air is so oppressive!

[OU-YANG P'ING *turns the fan on, then moves it further away from* MEI LIN]

MEI LIN [*Mumbles*] Shouldn't have turned out like this . . . He used to have the smell of a businessman, but he improved after Liberation.

OU-YANG P'ING Mom, that's just what's so frightening. What is it that has brought to the surface the dregs of society, the scum sunken in some people's minds, floating up now so majestically? It seems that it's taken until the present day for these masters of travesty to find their golden opportunity.

MEI LIN Certain people need such clowns for their political purposes, so these clowns have appeared like a new fashion. They've done a lot of harm to others, and to the Party and the nation!

OU-YANG P'ING Mom, maybe we shouldn't have come here today.

MEI LIN I came to locate your Uncle Ch'en and Aunt Hsün. I have something important to tell them. Besides that, I also came to find out about the prospects for you and Hsiao Yun . . .

OU-YANG P'ING Mom!

MEI LIN You handled it foolishly nine years ago!

OU-YANG P'ING Mom, please never mention it again.

MEI LIN Why?

OU-YANG P'ING Because . . . it's becoming an impossibility for me!

MEI LIN What's the reason? [*Stares at him. He avoids her gaze*] P'ing, my son, I feel you're hiding something from me.

OU-YANG P'ING No, Mom.

MEI LIN [*Sadly*] Yes. Something important! [*Her liver hurts again*]

OU-YANG P'ING Mom! [LIU HSIU-YING *comes downstairs and approaches* MEI LIN]

LIU HSIU-YING Sister Mei, you'd better leave. Take Ou-yang and leave here!

MEI LIN Hsiu-ying, what's the matter with you? Hsiu-ying?

LIU HSIU-YING Hurry up and leave, I beg you, leave my house!

OU-YANG P'ING Aunt Liu!

LIU HSIU-YING Go, go! [HO SHIH-FEI *comes downstairs*]

HO SHIH-FEI Is she at it again? Alas! I really don't know what I've done to deserve such punishment! [*He pulls* LIU HSIU-YING *away from* MEI LIN *and drags her upstairs, as she weeps miserably and unceasingly*]

MEI LIN Strange. What on earth has happened to Hsiu-ying?

OU-YANG P'ING You'd better take a rest.

MEI LIN Got to go see your Aunt Liu and get to the bottom of it, see what's the matter with her. [*Exits*]

[HO YUN *enters. She and* OU-YANG P'ING *face each other in silence*]

OU-YANG P'ING Has Aunt Liu gotten any better? [*Turning away from her, about to go upstairs*]

HO YUN [*Losing control*] Ou-yang! [*He stops abruptly.* HO YUN *pauses a moment*] How is Aunt Mei's condition?

OU-YANG P'ING The medical report will be out soon. [*Starts to walk away*]

HO YUN Ou-yang! [*Sadly*] Don't tell me you don't even feel like talking to me any more?

OU-YANG P'ING Why should it be that serious?

HO YUN Then come over here, sit for a while. [*He does so*] You've lost too much weight.

OU-YANG P'ING I'm perfectly healthy.

HO YUN You're full of energy.

OU-YANG P'ING Can a waiter in a small diner be listless? Every day from dawn to dark I have to shout out: "Hey, beef noodle soup, one bowl, fried meat pie, two ounces!"

HO YUN [*Smiles*] You're still a mischief-maker. [*Pauses*] Tell me, what was the matter nine years ago?

OU-YANG P'ING Ancient history. What's the need for going into it now?

HO YUN Tell me. Otherwise I'll never feel at peace.

OU-YANG P'ING It all happened in one day. All of a sudden I was the son of a counterrevolutionary. "Son of a bitch," they called me. I didn't want to involve you.

HO YUN You thought that I was too confused to understand?

OU-YANG P'ING [*Shakes his head*] I was the one who was confused in those days. I had always imagined that making a socialist revolution was as comfortable and smooth as traveling by train in a soft sleeping car; I didn't really understand what the word revolution meant until I went through this decade of turmoil during the Cultural Revolution.

HO YUN [*Silent for a moment*] Maybe I haven't thought it through so deeply. But you should have trusted me; we are both Communists. .

OU-YANG P'ING [*Interrupts*] No, I'm no longer a Communist.

HO YUN How is that possible?

Ou-yang P'ing They suspended my probationary status. Later I made several dozen applications for permission to join the Party, and they didn't give a damn. The reason is that I have such a "seditious" mother, a good mother!

Ho Yun Ou-yang, don't be so upset. Maybe eventually they will take you into the Party.

Ou-yang P'ing "They"? Long ago Mom said that the Party is not theirs, it is ours. The Party will eventually defeat "them"! Wasn't the Lin Piao Anti-Party Clique smashed by the Party?[10] So will "they" be, soon!

Ho Yun [*Silent for a moment*] Why did they label Aunt Mei a traitor?

Ou-yang P'ing [*Smiles bitterly*] Do you know that they said Mother was under arrest from March to May in 1947?

Ho Yun [*Jumps up*] From March to May in '47!? That's impossible! That's exactly the time Aunt Mei was treating my Dad's illness, and she took us all in—Mom, Brother, and me, just a baby then. She stretched everything she had, pickled vegetables and turnips, to feed everyone. We lived together like that for exactly eight long months! No, our whole family can prove it, Aunt Mei was simply never arrested! Ou-yang, this is very simple. All we need is for Dad to write a letter to prove it. . . .

Ou-yang P'ing It's not that simple. Those people know very well that the charges of sedition are a frame-up. My mother's real crime is that she offended two big figures.

Ho Yun Who?

Ou-yang P'ing Mother worked under Premier Chou during the war against Japan. They were beating around the bush in an attempt to dig up some material to make an accusation against Premier Chou. But Mother exposed them to the Central Committee.

Ho Yun So these kinds of guys did exist then? They were against the Premier? [Ou-yang P'ing *fixes his eyes on* Ho Yun] You know, I've had suspicions all along. Recently, among the active counterrevolutionaries we've arrested there have been quite a few whose only crime was that they mourned the death of Premier Chou. The top level has gone all-out. They've ordered us to trace the links and arrest whoever has been behind those people, catch the "capitalist-roaders in the act." The latest national conference for Public Security heads passed a resolution on this question. I heard that it was withheld by Premier Hua, who didn't give permission to distribute it. But in our area in Shanghai someone insisted on issuing it. I don't know what their intentions are.

Ou-yang P'ing Just think back a bit: why, two years ago, did some people raise that damn slogan "Condemn Lin Piao, Condemn Confucius, and Condemn Lord Chou"? Why were some people in such a great hurry to attack China's modernization drive right after the Premier's death, when his body was still warm? Why was

mourning Premier Chou considered a crime and cause for persecution and suppression? . . . It was all because they wanted to
uproot the huge tree that towers into the sky. How could we not
draw the proud sword?

Ho Yun Draw the proud sword? You know the person I talked about
this morning, he is an active counterrevolutionary precisely because
he distributed a collection of poems titled *The Proud Sword Is Drawn!*
He had the guts to mail a copy directly to Chang Ch'un-ch'iao, and it
really struck home. Chang Ch'un-ch'iao had a fit and gave the order
for immediate arrest and trial. He was seen in the Northern Train
Station this morning. Apparently he is in Shanghai now. My
director's put me in charge of cracking the case. [Ou-yang P'ing *is
dumbfounded*] Ou-yang, what's the matter with you?

Ou-yang P'ing Nothing.

Ho Yun Are you sick?

Ou-yang P'ing I'm a little tired.

Ho Yun [*Gently*] Ou-yang, when we were small you always told me
whatever was troubling you. Why not now, tell me what it is?

[*The tune of the "Red Plum Ode" is heard*]

Ou-yang P'ing All right, let me tell you the whole story! When we
were little we both complained that we were born too late, that it
would have been better to take part in the struggles of the forties, like
Chiang Niang-niang in the novel *Red Cliff*.[11] If necessary we could
have given our blood to the cause without any fear. But now I begin to
understand that during the period of Socialist Revolution we can also
suffer "deep winters" and "chilly frost," so we still need the dignity
and the defiance of the Red Plum to resist the frost and snow. Hsiao
Yun, I am willing to give every drop of my blood for our country, a
country that the old generation fought for, to defend Chairman Mao
and Premier Chou. I am ready now!

Ho Yun [*Sinking deeper into thought*] You, you're still the Ou-yang I
knew! Trust me, Ou-yang, if there are really people who are fighting
against Chairman Mao and Premier Chou then I'll give my blood
together with yours!

Ou-yang P'ing Hsiao Yun! [*On an irresistible impulse, he grips*
Ho Yun*'s hand*]

Ho Yun [*Suddenly leans on his shoulder*] Ou-yang, you've hurt me so
much these past nine years!

[Ou-yang P'ing *suddenly stands up;* Ho Yun *almost falls forward; she
looks at him in astonishment*]

Ou-yang P'ing [*With a forced smile*] I, let me tell you something while
I am here, I . . . have a girl friend.

Ho Yun What!?

Ou-yang P'ing I'm deeply, entirely, devoted to . . . to her!

Ho Yun Don't say anything more!

Ou-yang P'ing [*Pauses a while*] I—I'd only let you down! [*Unable to
control his feelings, he dashes off*]

[Ho Yun, *heartbroken, sits down on the couch with her face in her hands. Ho Wei enters*]

Ho Wei I'm going to the hospital to fetch the test report for Aunt Mei. What, unhappy again? I thought you were going to buy me some wedding candies!

Ho Yun [*Weeping, griefstricken*] Brother!

Ho Wei All right, all right, let me show you something. It's extremely interesting, a book of poetry edited by Ou-yang, *The Proud Sword is Drawn.*

Ho Yun [*Lifts her tearful eyes, extremely frightened*] Ah!? [*Faints*]

[*Curtain*]

ACT III

Five o'clock the same afternoon, in the same room. It is darker now, about to rain. As the curtain rises, Ou-yang P'ing is sitting on the couch with Ho Wei pacing in front of him impatiently.

Ho Wei Speak. Tell me what happened between you two. [Ou-yang P'ing*'s head is buried in his large hands; he is silent*] Since Hsiao Yun came to she has been like an idiot; and you, you won't even say a word! [Ou-yang P'ing *is still silent*] Now speak, for god's sake!

Ou-yang P'ing [*Lifts his head*] I can only tell you one thing: I'm not good enough for Hsiao Yun. I've made her wait . . . for nothing.

Ho Wei [*Pauses a moment*] That's what it is, eh! "Waiting for nothing"!? How casual you are when you say it! Do you know how she got through the past nine years of waiting for you? She was like a crazy person, trying to find out where you were, and how you were. She looked for you, hoping so much that one day, all of a sudden, you would come back to be by her side. Everyday she'd play the *Red Plum Ode* on the piano until it even tore my heart! So now, get out. Get out, right now.

Ou-yang P'ing Ta Wei!

Ho Wei With my father the way he is, and my mother ill, my sister's all I have, do you understand? I can't just look on while she's driven crazy like my mother!

Ou-yang P'ing Ta Wei!

Ho Wei And me, your criticism of me was correct: I was ruining myself; D.D.T. is what I deserve. But my sister, she should have a good future. She should lead a life that's happy, and full, and secure!

Ou-yang P'ing I can say that no one in the world hopes that she leads such a life more than I do!

Ho Wei That's a lie. If you wanted to you could offer her all this. You're the only one in the world who can offer all this to her!

Ou-yang P'ing I want to. But I'm not the one who can bring her any of this. [*Bites his lip bitterly*]

Ho Wei Why?

OU-YANG P'ING Don't ask me, please, Ta Wei. Don't ask me any more!

HO WEI Then you'd better leave.

OU-YANG P'ING I'm going to. What's more, I'm afraid that I won't be able to come back again. Tai Wei, I want to ask you a favor.

HO WEI Shoot.

OU-YANG P'ING I want to ask you to take care of my mother.

HO WEI Where are you going?

OU-YANG P'ING I mean, you are a doctor. I hope you'll do your best to treat her.

HO WEI You don't have to go through all this with me. I have always treated her like my mother. [*Looking at his watch*] I must go over to the hospital to get the test report. [*As he goes to the door he stops and turns around slowly*] Or else, you can leave after I get back and have a chance to look at the test report. [*They walk toward each other. Ho WEI grasps OU-YANG P'ING's hand without a word. After a moment Ho WEI exits. Ho SHIH-FEI enters from the corridor*]

HO SHIH-FEI [*Anger showing on his face*] Ou-yang, what a fine thing you've done!

OU-YANG P'ING [*Surprised*] Uncle Ho?

HO SHIH-FEI [*Shouting*] Do you mean to destroy Hsiao Yun?

OU-YANG P'ING Uncle Ho!

HO SHIH-FEI You! You go take a look at her. How far do you want to drive her? I'm going to have a talk with your mother! [*Starts to exit*]

OU-YANG P'ING No, Uncle Ho, if you want to blame someone, blame me. Mother has just fallen asleep; her health is very poor. . . .

HO SHIH-FEI I have nothing to discuss with you. [*Insists on opening the door*]

OU-YANG P'ING [*Angrily*] Don't go in!

HO SHIH-FEI This is my house!

[*The door opens and* MEI LIN *appears, staring at* HO SHIH-FEI]

OU-YANG P'ING [*Quickly supporting her*] Mom!

MEI LIN Well, it looks like you are going to throw me out.

OU-YANG P'ING Mom, you'd better get some more sleep.

MEI LIN How can I sleep with your Uncle Ho shouting at the door? [OU-YANG P'ING *can only help* MEI LIN *to sit on the couch*] It's all right, son. I still have enough energy to listen to what he has to say. [*She presses her hand against her liver*]

HO SHIH-FEI Your liver is hurting again?

MEI LIN Yes, but I have to listen to you. What do you want to say? Say it quickly.

HO SHIH-FEI Well, Sister Mei, this is something that I don't feel I should say.

MEI LIN If you don't feel that you should say it, then don't say it!

HO SHIH-FEI But I . . .

MEI LIN You want to say what you feel you shouldn't, am I right?

HO SHIH-FEI How should I put it?

MEI LIN Put it plainly.

HO SHIH-FEI When you came here today I welcomed you from the bottom of my heart.

MEI LIN That's fine. Ou-yang, let's pitch our tents, set up camp, and stay for three or four years.

HO SHIH-FEI . . . but, who knows why, Hsiu-ying has been making a big scene; Hsiao Yun is crying; the whole family is turned upside down.

MEI LIN This is an announcement to the guests that they are unwelcome?

HO SHIH-FEI There's nothing I can do!

MEI LIN I understand. We've invaded your privacy. We have an odor quite incompatible with the fragrance of your house.

HO SHIH-FEI No, no, that's not what I meant!

MEI LIN That's what I meant! Originally I was going to have a good talk with you, but I didn't expect you would be driving us out so soon. [*She presses hard against the region of her liver*]

HO SHIH-FEI No, no, I'm not. Don't misunderstand me. But . . .

MEI LIN But what? [*He is speechless*] You have even lost the courage to utter the words on the tip of your tongue, haven't you? [HO YUN *enters slowly*]

HO SHIH-FEI No, no, it's Hsiao Yun who wants to get you out!

MEI LIN Hsiao Yun?

HO YUN Yes, it was I who said it. Dad, let me talk with Aunt Mei alone for a while. I'll tell her myself what I wanted to say.

HO SHIH-FEI Fine. Tell her what you have to graciously. Aunt Mei's health is poor, don't upset her. Sister Mei, please forgive me. [*Goes upstairs*]

MEI LIN Hsiao Yun, why are you so pale?

[HO YUN *looks after* OU-YANG P'ING *bitterly as he exits the room*]

HO YUN Aunt Mei! [*Putting her arms around* MEI LIN, *her tears streaming. Pause*]

MEI LIN [*Growing too weak to support herself*] What's happened, Hsiao Yun?

HO YUN Aunt Mei! . . . Let Ou-yang leave, let him leave, quickly!

MEI LIN Did he do anything?

HO YUN No, no, nothing. But I want him to leave, and right away!

MEI LIN [*Pondering for a moment*] We are going to leave soon. But before we leave, I want to ask you something bluntly. Did you, did you love him?

HO YUN Yes, I did.

MEI LIN And now?

HO YUN Now? I don't know. . . . maybe. I've never loved him so much as now!

MEI LIN He loves you too, do you know? Ou-yang is a tough boy; for the past few years he's been fighting against those people without yielding an inch. He's suffered no less than I have. There are only two things he couldn't bear: that he wasn't accepted into the Party, and

. . . that he can't forget you. He never says anything about it, but he
can't hide it from his mother, can he?

Ho Yun But he told me that he has a steady girlfriend.

Mei Lin Talking through his hat with a straight face!

Ho Yun He told me himself that with all his heart, with his whole
being, he was . . . [*Stops suddenly, realizing* Ou-yang P'ing's
intention; she is moved to tears] Aunt Mei, he is really very kind. You
both are very kind!

Mei Lin You two should stop behaving like little kids. The struggle
now is ruthless; when you know that the one you love stands firmly at
your side you will be stronger, braver, lose your fear! You should be
together always and never apart.

Ho Yun Good! . . . Then again, no, Aunt Mei, you'd better let him leave
right away. Get out of Shanghai!

Mei Lin Leave . . . Shanghai? [*The pain in her liver is excruciating*]
Hsiao Yun, what . . . happened?

Ho Yun Aunt Mei, what's wrong?

Mei Lin Tell me, hurry up, tell me the truth!

Ho Yun Aunt Mei! Aunt Mei! [Ou-yang P'ing *enters*]

Ou-yang P'ing Mom!

Mei Lin P'ing, son . . . tell me . . . (Faints)

Ou-yang P'ing Mom! Mom! [*To* Ho Yun] What were you talking
about with her?

Ho Yun [*Bitterly*] I . . .

[Ou-yang P'ing *carries* Mei Lin *into the bedroom.* Ho Yun *tries
to follow them in, but he blocks her way, so she walks sadly to the
couch and sits down.* Liu Hsiu-ying *comes downstairs*]

Liu Hsiu-ying [*Mumbling*] Something's up today! Something's up
today!

[Ho Shih-fei *appears at the stairs like a spectre*]

Ho Yun [*Griefstricken*] Mom! They are going to arrest Ou-yang,
arrest Ou-yang, do you know, Mom! [Ho Shih-fei *comes downstairs*]

Ho Shih-fei Who is going to arrest Ou-yang?

Liu Hsiu-ying [*Turns pale*] Hsiao Yun!

Ho Shih-fei Don't interrupt. Hsiao Yun, who is going to arrest him?

Liu Hsiu-ying Hsiao Yun! [*Pounding her with her fists*] Don't talk
nonsense! Don't talk nonsense!

Ho Yun Mom, what's the matter with you?

Ho Shih-fei Ah, she's getting worse and worse! Leave her alone. Tell
me quickly, who is going to arrest Ou-yang?

Liu Hsiu-ying [*Imploringly*] Hsiao Yun! [*Wailing*]

Ho Yun Mom, what is it you want to tell me?

[Liu Hsiu-ying *starts to say something, then bursts into tears*]

Ho Yun Mom! [*Hugging her*]

Ho Shih-fei Hsiu-ying, you can talk with me about it later, all right?
Hsiao Yun, you first, what is it? Maybe we can still find a way out.

HO YUN Ou-yang is . . . [LIU HSIU-YING *is on the verge of shouting.*
  HO SHIH-FEI *grabs her hand ferociously*] The "counterrevolutionary"
  who's wanted nationwide is Ou-yang! [*She runs off, her hands
  covering her face. Her parents are dumbfounded*]

HO SHIH-FEI Is that so! [*Paces impatiently and turns to the door*]

LIU HSIU-YING [*Suddenly sane, she stands up*] What are you going
  to do?

HO SHIH-FEI Hsiu-ying, what's the matter with you today? [*Pushes her
  away*]

LIU HSIU-YING [*Stubbornly hinders him*] Where are you going?

HO SHIH-FEI Don't get involved. I have something important to do!

LIU HSIU-YING [*Very clearly and soberly*] What important thing?

HO SHIH-FEI You— [*Tries to push her away*]

LIU HSIU-YING [*Not giving an inch*] You shouldn't do that kind of
  thing any more!

HO SHIH-FEI I shouldn't do what?

LIU HSIU-YING You shouldn't . . . you shouldn't do . . . any more of the
  harmful things to others the way you did . . . the way you did nine
  years ago!

HO SHIH-FEI [*Shocked*] What? What did you say? What did I do nine
  years ago? [*Suddenly panicked*] How—how did you know?

LIU HSIU-YING I know, I know it all . . .

HO SHIH-FEI Hsiu-ying?

LIU HSIU-YING I beg you, this mother and her son have suffered enough
  because of you! If it had not been for Aunt Mei, who knows where your
  bones would be rotting. I beg you, don't harm them any more!

HO SHIH-FEI So these two years you . . . [*Sits on the couch*]

LIU HSIU-YING I have been lucid all along. I haven't been insane, but
  what an agony it's been! And nowhere to turn. . . . [*Cries*]

HO SHIH-FEI Hsiu-ying, I was forced into it, you know! It was not
  all that easy for me to gain the confidence of the Rebels, and finally I
  made the connection with T'ang Yu-ts'ai. When they forced me to say
  that Sister Mei was a traitor, did I have the guts to refuse? Moreover,
  that was the intention from the top, Proletarian Headquarters! I only
  had to hesitate for a second and I would have been smashed on the
  spot!

LIU HSIU-YING But what a tragedy you have made of Mei Lin's life!

HO SHIH-FEI No, she can't blame me; she can only blame the harsh
  political struggles! For the last few years staying with T'ang Yu'ts'ai's
  clique has been as nervewracking, dangerous, and frightening as
  trying to make a living in the old days in the foreign company or on
  the stock market. I knew what they were up to and took the plunge
  with them, come hell or high water. I've staked everything on it,
  hoping I'll come out ahead. Otherwise . . .

LIU HSIU-YING What? What have you been saying?

HO SHIH-FEI [*Realizes he has been indiscreet*] Oh! Nothing serious.

Hsiu-ying, you shouldn't get mixed up in all this. I can guarantee you a comfortable, peaceful life in your old age. You should be at ease; I can get you anything you like.

LIU HSIU-YING I have never in my life asked you for anything. I've listened to everything you said and done whatever you wanted. Today let me ask you this favor: Save Ou-yang! Save Ou-yang, will you?

HO SHIH-FEI Save Ou-yang and then, what am I going to do? T'ang Yu-ts'ai will be here soon; if he finds out such an important active counterrevolutionary as that is hiding in my house, then all I've achieved in years and years of wracking my brain will be destroyed!

LIU HSIU-YING Then you don't care if Ou-yang dies?

HO SHIH-FEI He's looking for it! Don't tell me that he can't judge things. The course of events has been clear! What sort of heroic tough-guy figure does he think he cuts as a waiter? Ou-yang can't get away anyhow. But it makes all the difference in the world to me if he comes in and out of our house. [*Starts to go out*]

LIU HSIU-YING [*Catches and pulls him back*] No, it won't do, you can't . . . [Ho SHIH-FEI *gives her a kick. She falls to the floor, and he runs out*]

LIU HSIU-YING [*On the floor, hand pressing her chest, lifting her head up*] Hsiao Yun! Hsiao Yun! [Ho YUN *enters*]

HO YUN Mom! What happened?

LIU HSIU-YING Hurry up and call Ou-yang for me!

HO YUN Mom! [*Tries to help her up*]

LIU HSIU-YING [*Pounding* Ho YUN*'s leg furiously*] Call him! Call him!

HO YUN Ou-yang! Ou-yang! [OU-YANG P'ING *enters*]

OU-YANG P'ING Aunt Liu? What happened to you? [*Helping* Ho YUN *support* LIU HSIU-YING *to the couch*]

HSIU-YING Hurry, Ou-yang. Carry your mother on your back and leave right away. There is a . . . ghost . . . a ghost in the house . . . [*Faints*]

HO YUN Mom! Mom!

[Ho YUN *puts her arms around her mother and gets her upstairs.* OU-YANG *returns to the bedroom, and soon comes out with a traveling bag in his hand. For a moment he stands bitterly at the doorway, then turns to leave.* Ho YUN *comes downstairs*]

OU-YANG P'ING I was going to wait for the test report from Ta Wei, but now I can't. Tell Ta Wei I'll go to the hospital to see him tomorrow, and my mother still hasn't come to.

HO YUN What!?

OU-YANG P'ING I really can't bear leaving her here alone.

HO YUN I'll take responsibility for looking after her. Don't worry. Now leave quickly.

OU-YANG P'ING There is a small bag next to the bed. She has kept it with her constantly for the past few years. Keep it in a safe place for her, will you?

HO YUN Yes, I will. Goodbye!

OU-YANG P'ING Thank you!

HO YUN "Thank you," a phrase we haven't needed between us since we were little.

OU-YANG P'ING Off I go. [*He starts to shake hands with* HO YUN *and sees the collection of poetry in her hand*]

HO YUN It was edited by you, wasn't it? I've read it, and I enjoyed it very much! This one sounds like you:

> An offense on All Soul's Day? Tears are wept
> At the tombs all blood-rained and wind-swept.
> People, Party—these hearts shall know no shame.
> In a land of silence, thunder will erupt.[12]

OU-YANG P'ING I only hope that when people see the dagger flash, their faith will be strengthened: People will not keep silent forever!

HO YUN People will not keep silent forever! But why didn't you let me know? You misjudged me as badly now as you did nine years ago! When the time comes, I too can be a dagger!

OU-YANG P'ING Hsiao-Yun! [*Affectionately puts his arms around* HO YUN*'s shoulders*]

HO YUN [*Pauses*] You should go. [OU-YANG P'ING *turns toward the central door.* HO YUN *is too sad to say anything.* HO SHIH-FEI *appears outside the door*]

HO SHIH-FEI [*Blocking his way*] Ou-yang! How come you're leaving? [*He pulls him back in again*]

OU-YANG P'ING Mother is still unconscious; she really can't leave. I'll go first.

HO SHIH-FEI What? Aunt Mei is unconscious? Could it be that . . . ah, it was my fault. How stupid I was to get so angry with her on an impulse. In case Aunt Mei . . . I was so foolish! . . . Well, come in, come in [*Seizes* OU-YANG P'ING*'s travel bag*] Ou-yang, none of you must leave; this is your house. It must be old age that made me so mixed up a while ago . . . .

OU-YANG P'ING [*Grabs back his travel bag*] I've thought it over carefully. It's not right for me to stay here.

HO YUN Dad, just let him go, will you! [OU-YANG P'ING *starts to go out through the central door*]

HO SHIH-FEI [*Swiftly blocks the door*] It's going to rain soon, and your mother is still unconscious. If I make you go I won't feel right about it. Hsiao Yun, I think it's hardly convenient—to go out. He should stay here, and we'll find a way to solve the problem. [*Grips the travel bag*] [OU-YANG P'ING *has no choice but to come back in. The telephone rings, and* HO SHIH-FEI *answers it*]

HO SHIH-FEI Hello? Old Chang? . . . What? To register for staying here overnight? Ha, ha, don't you even trust my old friends? . . . No, no, it's a misunderstanding, a misunderstanding. . . . All right! I'll talk it over with Old T'ang! Fine, fine, sorry to trouble you!—There, everything is solved. Come on, let's take a rest. Ou-yang, don't be angry with your Uncle Ho! [LIU HSIU-YING *appears on the stairs*]

Liu Hsiu-ying Ou-yang, why haven't you left?

Ho Shih-fei Oh no, what are we going to do with your madness! [*Frantically pushes* Liu Hsiu-ying *back upstairs*]

Liu Hsiu-ying I am not mad! Your Aunt Liu is not insane! [*Struggles, fails, and finally is pushed up the stairs*]

Ho Shih-fei Ou-yang, don't, don't go away. [*Goes upstairs*]

[Ou-yang P'ing *is determined to leave. He picks up his travel bag and is about to step outside when* Mei Lin*'s voice is heard from behind the curtain: "P'ing, son! Come here quickly."* Ou-yang P'ing *goes to her.* Ho Yun *is motionless.* Ho Shih-fei *comes downstairs*]

Ho Shih-fei Ou-yang didn't leave, did he?

Ho Yun No. What are we to do, dad?

Ho Shih-fei What do you think?

Ho Yun Send him away by night to Grandma's house!

Ho Shih-fei Would that be proper?

Ho Yun It's out in the country, safer than here.

Ho Shih-fei [*Smiles indifferently*] You didn't get the question. I said, is it proper to do so? You and I are both Communists, I remind you.

Ho Yun Aunt Mei and Ou-yang are both better Communists than we are!

Ho Shih-fei Now you're talking nonsense, too. Mei Lin was expelled from the Party nine years ago; Ou-yang never joined!

Ho Yun But both are the most loyal fighters for the Party there are.

Ho Shih-fei Your "loyal fighters for the Party" are wanted by the law. How do you explain that?

Ho Yun The Party doesn't want to arrest Ou-yang; "they" do! The Party doesn't belong to "them"; the Party will defeat "them"! Ou-yang knows how to say it! [*Holds the collection of poems to her chest*]

[Ho Shih-fei *takes the book and thumbs voraciously through the pages. After a while he turns to the door and starts out*]

Ho Yun [*Suddenly alert*] Dad! What do you think you're doing?

Ho Shih-fei We should not flinch. We'll have to accuse and expose the active counterrevolutionary Ou-yang P'ing!

Ho Yun What! [*Seizes the book*]

Ho Shih-fei Hsiao Yun, I know you're very attached to Ou-yang, but the interests of the Revolution come before everything. We must uphold justice, even if it means sacrificing our own blood relations. Hand him over!

Ho Yun [*Waves the book*] But all he's doing is mourning Premier Chou . . .

Ho Shih-fei Mourning Premier Chou won't do either!

Ho Yun What?

Ho Shih-fei Didn't T'ang Yu-ts'ai show his hand to you? Chou En-lai has become a banner in the minds of certain people. Under that banner they resist the leaders of the Central Committee. That is why we must—[*Maliciously makes a chopping gesture*]

Ho Yun Ah! Now I understand, only too late!

Ho Shih-fei Better late than never. Pull yourself together, Hsiao Yun. Since Ou-yang P'ing has become a champion under a black banner, we should hate him, hate him deeply!

Ho Yun [*Sneers*] Hate *him* deeply! No, hate *you*!

Ho Shih-fei [*Horrified*] Hsiao Yun, are you out of your mind?

Ho Yun My Mom is, my brother is, and I—am also mad!

Ho Shih-fei Hsiao Yun!

Ho Yun Ever since I was little, I've treated you as an old revolutionary, an old cadre, happy and proud to have a father like you. For so many years, especially after Ou-yang went away, you were the person I trusted most. I've loved you, respected you. When I had any happy news I would tell you first. When I had problems, when I felt bad, even then I came to you first to beg for advice. . . . Though sometimes I wondered about some of your actions, you explained to me that secretly you loved Premier Chou, too; you felt very disturbed, very bitter, too. I believed every word you said. . . . Was this all just an act? Just a put-on? [Ho Wei *enters through the central door*]

Ho Wei My god, such a heavy rain! Eh, strange, what are all those shadows doing out there around our house? [*Enters the corridor*]

Ho Yun [*Goes out to look around and then steps in*] Did you do that?

Ho Shih-fei [*Mercilessly*] Yes, I did. I telephoned. T'ang Yu-ts'ai was going to come and arrest him in person, but out of consideration for your reputation he decided to grant you an opportunity to earn an easy merit. [*Looking at his watch*] It's six now; he ordered you to arrest Ou-yang P'ing by your own hand before seven! Otherwise . . .

Ho Yun Filthy!

[*Clock solemnly strikes six*]

[Curtain]

ACT IV

Immediately after the third act; the setting is the same. Outside it is raining hard; the wind roars. Curtain. Ho Yun paces back and forth nervously.

Ho Yun What should I do? What should I do? It's all my fault, all my fault! [Ou-yang P'ing *enters from the bedroom*]

Ou-yang P'ing Hsiao Yun! [Ho Yun *shivers*] What's going on with you? [Ho Yun *looks at him; tears spill from her eyes*] I've noticed a great change in you since I came here this time. You've learned how to shed tears. You were someone who always loved to smile. [*She continues to weep*] I really dislike crying. Ever since I can remember, I've only cried twice: once was when Premier Chou died, and the other time when Mother was released after six years in "isolation" and I went to fetch her.

[Ho Wei *enters, wiping the rain from his head. Seeing* Ou-yang P'ing *and* Ho Yun *sitting together, he starts to leave but, fascinated by* Ou-yang P'ing *'s words, stops and listens*]

Ou-yang P'ing Mother was so skinny she simply didn't look like a living person any more. But when she saw me, the first question she asked was: "Have you joined the Party?" I couldn't tell her it was impossible because of her problem. I could only lie to her. I told her: "The scum are in power in our unit; I don't want to join it now!" Would you believe that Mother got furious at that answer?

Ho Yun I've never seen Aunt Mei lose her temper!

Ou-yang P'ing But that time, you should have seen her terrible face! She said the thing that disturbed her most was this: during the Cultural Revolution, when some young people saw that not every-thing inside our Party was clean as they had expected, and they saw the twists and turns and the complications of the struggle within the Party, then suddenly they panicked, they lost their self-confidence, they imagined that they'd seen through the vanity of life! But if everywhere was so clean, so smooth, then what would people need to join the Party for?

 [*The music of "The Internationale" echoes in the air*]

Ou-yang P'ing Mother said that in 1936, when she joined the Revolu-tion, she set her jaw and prepared to lose her life. Today, when we join the Revolution, do we have the same determination? Can we set our jaws and be ready to lose our lives in defense of the Party, the ideas of Chairman Mao and Premier Chou?

Ho Yun Ou-yang!

Ou-yang P'ing That's enough, stop crying now. I'll come back to see you tomorrow, all right? [Ho Wei *starts to walk away*]

Ho Yun [*Losing control*] Ou-yang, they've already surrounded this house to arrest you! [*Pause*]

Ho Wei What? What for?

Ho Yun For *The Proud Sword Is Drawn*, the book he's been dis-tributing! [Ho Wei *is shocked*]

Ou-yang P'ing [*Opens the glass sliding door, looks out, bursts out laughing*] Me, just a waiter serving wonton soup and meat pie in a small diner; I wrote several poems, said a few truthful words, and guess what? I shocked Chang Ch'un-ch'iao, Great Lord Chang. He's declared me the nation's most wanted criminal, going all over the place trying to arrest me. He's mobilized troops and stirred up the people, didn't even leave the chickens and dogs in peace. Just imagine if ten people stood up to speak the truth? If one hundred, one thousand, if all the people of China boldly stood up to say what they have in their minds, what would great Lord Chang do then?

Ho Wei Ou-yang, that day is not far off! You . . . [*Grips his hands tightly*]

Ou-yang P'ing Wei! What's my mother's condition?

Ho Wei Aunt Mei—she . . .

Ho Yun How is she, Brother?

OU-YANG P'ING Tell me quickly. There is not much time left for me.

HO WEI Nothing, relax, just a little cirrhosis, not all that serious.

OU-YANG P'ING Wei, you still haven't learned how to lie and cheat these past few years.

HO YUN Brother, just what is her condition?

HO WEI [*Suddenly furious*] How is she, just how is she? [*Turns to* OU-YANG P'ING, *sadly*] Aunt Mei . . . her condition is terminal cancer of the liver.

HO YUN Ah! [OU-YANG P'ING *is numb. He walks slowly to the couch and sits down. Pause*]

OU-YANG P'ING For decades she survived one battle after another in the face of enemy bullets and artillery shells, but now she falls from a shot in the back! [*Pause*] Wei, Yun, please don't let my mother know.

HO YUN Trust us.

HO WEI I'll tell her everything is normal.

OU-YANG P'ING No, I meant don't tell her anything about my being arrested. You can say that I—well, you can say that I've gone somewhere. Please take care of her, comfort her for me, and also bury her . . . for me. [HO YUN *breaks down and cries.* HO WEI *turns away*] I've given you a hard job, haven't I? Well, the time I have left to trouble you—is not all that long anyway.

HO WEI Trust me, let me take care of Aunt Mei. [*The bedroom door opens to reveal* MEI LIN]

HO YUN Let me take care of her.

MEI LIN Oh, my, I must be some treasure! Do you mean an old woman like me deserves fighting over?

OU-YANG P'ING Mom, what are you doing out of bed? [*Quickly moves to support her*]

MEI LIN Life lies in movement. If I had listened to you and simply stayed in bed all day long, I'm afraid that I'd have gone to see Karl Marx long, long ago. [*They support* MEI LIN *and seat her on the couch, but no one dares to look her in the eye*]

MEI LIN What's the matter with you people?

OU-YANG P'ING Nothing, Mom! [HO YUN *if griefstricken, on the verge of tears.* OU-YANG P'ING *shakes his head to stop her;* MEI LIN *notices*]

MEI LIN Playing God behind my back! I can guess without being told. Ta Wei, my condition—is terminal, isn't it?

HO WEI No! I've just come from the hospital. Everything is normal.

MEI LIN You've been to the hospital again? [HO WEI *clears his throat.* MEI LIN *looks carefully at the three, one by one*] P'ing, son, bring me that bag of mine.

[OU-YANG P'ING *goes into the bedroom*]

MEI LIN [*Recites*]

> Against a sky of fire in its tenth year,
> On China's portals, my severed head will appear.
> You who live to hear we have won, tell me
> By offerings burnt for spirits in the air.

Do you know whose poem this is?

Ho YUN Ch'en I, the old general, wrote that.[13] [OU-YANG P'ING *brings in the small bag*]

MEI LIN [*Takes the bag*] One of these days, I'm afraid, I may pass out and never wake up again. Ou-yang, I have to explain two things to you clearly. [*Taking things out of the bag layer by layer*] Here are my Party membership dues for the past nine years, two dollars per month.

OU-YANG P'ING Mom! Where did you get all this? I mailed you so little every month.

MEI LIN Eating frugally, you'd save enough, wouldn't you? Before Liberation I paid my Party dues the same way, didn't I?

OU-YANG P'ING No wonder your health is so . . .

MEI LIN A Communist should pay his dues with his life.

Ho YUN [*Sinks down beside* MEI LIN] Aunt Mei!

MEI LIN Why are you all so gloomy? I dislike seeing this the most. Hsiao Yun, don't be like that. In the past few days I have relived my whole life: I took part in the Revolution at the age of sixteen, joined the Party at eighteen, by now I've been a member for over forty years. I regret nothing and only wish I could— Children, remember this, you must follow Chairman Mao, follow the Party, walk forward firmly, don't let your legs go soft, don't sway!

Ho WEI We'll remember!

MEI LIN P'ing, son, in this bag there is also an important document that I . . . in case I . . . you must find a way to deliver it to Peking. [OU-YANG P'ING *is about to take it, but retracts his hand and takes a few steps back*]

Ho YUN Aunt Mei, give it to me, won't you? I assure you I will fulfill this task!

MEI LIN [*Doubtfully*] Eh? [*See the travel bag*] P'ing, son, you're leaving aren't you?

[*The clock strikes once.* Ho SHIH-FEI *comes downstairs*]

Ho SHIH-FEI It's six-thirty already.

MEI LIN Hm! You don't have to rush us now!

Ho SHIH-FEI You're right, I don't have to rush you any more. Someone is here. He'd like Ou-yang to go with him.

MEI LIN Who?

Ho SHIH-FEI Hsiao Yun, you know what T'ang Yu-ts'ai is like. [Ho YUN *furiously pushes away* Ho SHIH-FEI's *hand*]

MEI LIN What's up?

OU-YANG P'ING Nothing, Mom.

Ho SHIH-FEI Nothing? How relaxed you are! Sister Mei, your son is the active counterrevolutionary who has been committing disgusting crimes, and the men who have been ordered to arrest him are waiting outside. [MEI LIN *feels dizzy*]

OU-YANG P'ING [*Holding* MEI LIN, *worried*] Mom!

MEI LIN Tell me, what have you done?

OU-YANG P'ING I edited a collection of elegies on Premier Chou, titled *The Proud Sword Is Drawn*

MEI LIN [*Relaxes*] Why didn't you tell me?

OU-YANG P'ING I was afraid you would worry about me.

MEI LIN How little you understand. Is your Mom, this old Communist, made of clay? Haven't I flung away the scabbard of my own sword? When the day comes to settle accounts with that scum, the Party will need it!

OU-YANG P'ING Good Mother!

MEI LIN Good son! [*Hand on* OU-YANG P'ING*'s head*] Don't worry about me, go! [*Pushes* OU-YANG P'ING *with all her energy*] Go to the prison and the court; make a final—struggle! [*Exhausted, she falls back on the couch panting*]

HO YUN *and* HO WEI Aunt Mei!

OU-YANG P'ING Mom, I'm going. When the day comes that we win, I'll come back to see you again.

HO SHIH-FEI No! Mei Lin has to leave here together with you.

HO YUN What? With it pouring outside and Aunt Mei as sick as she is?

HO SHIH-FEI Humanitarianism! I can't keep the mother of a counter-revolutionary, a traitor, in my house! If I did, what kind of proletarian would I be?

HO WEI [*Roars*] Humanitarianism!? Do you still have the slightest human feeling? Do you know that there may be only a few days for Aunt Mei . . .

HO YUN Brother!

OU-YANG P'ING [*Swiftly rushing to support* MEI LIN] Mom! [*Pause*]

HO YUN Aunt Mei!

MEI LIN [*Calmly*] P'ing, son, give me a few biscuits!

OU-YANG P'ING Mom!

MEI LIN I'm waiting! Ta Wei, I'm going to try to challenge the doctor's verdict of execution! Who knows, maybe one day I will be ready to lead troops again to fight on the battlefield!

HO YUN *and* HO WEI Aunt Mei!

[LIU HSIU-YING *enters through the central door, her face and hands covered with blood*]

OU-YANG P'ING Aunt Liu! [*Goes to support her*]

HO YUN Mom, what happened to you?

LIU HSIU-YING Your father locked me in the room. . . .

HO YUN What?

LIU HSIU-YING [*Gripping* MEI LIN*'s hand, expressionlessly*] Sister Mei, he's the one who wants to harm Ou-yang; he's also the one who nine years ago said that you were a traitor!

ALL [*Shocked*] Ah?

MEI LIN So, that's it!

[*Pause.* HO SHIH-FEI *shivers*]

LIU HSIU-YING One night two years ago I was straightening up his things when suddenly I found something he had written. Then I understood it was he, nine years ago. . . . I wanted to speak out, but I was afraid it would destroy Ta Wei and Hsiao Yun's futures, so I hid it inside of me, hid it . . . I used to be a teacher. I had always taught the children to be honest, to have integrity, but as for myself . . . I could never have imagined [*Softly*] the kind of person he is. [*She becomes very still*]

MEI LIN [*Embracing her*] Hsiu-ying!

HO WEI [*To* HO SHIH-FEI] And so it turns out that it was you who made Aunt Mei and Ou-yang, and Mom and Hsiao Yun, suffer so much for nine years!?

[*In a rage, he grabs a large vase and slowly approaches* HO SHIH-FEI, *who keeps retreating in terror.* HO WEI *lifts the vase, then puts it down softly*]

HO WEI Just consider yourself lucky. Yesterday I would have exchanged my worthless life for yours without hesitation. But today I feel there is still a little meaning to my life.

HO SHIH-FEI [*Panicky*] The situation was quite complicated then. . . . Originally I was . . . but . . .

OU-YANG P'ING Traitor! In the age of Socialist Revolution, you're a traitor who sold out the Revolution, its soul, our comrades!

HO SHIH-FEI [*Escaping upstairs*] You can damn me, damn me! There's only five minutes left anyway! [*Exits*]

OU-YANG P'ING Mom, it's time for me to go.

MEI LIN [*Quietly embraces* OU-YANG P'ING, *then pushes him away*] You . . . you can go now!

OU-YANG P'ING Hsiao Yun, did they say they wanted you to take me there?

HO YUN Ou-yang, I'm going to prison together with you!

OU-YANG P'ING Don't forget the task my mother has given you!

HO YUN [*Throwing caution to the winds, she hugs* OU-YANG P'ING *and cries*] Ou-yang!

OU-YANG P'ING Don't. In the Revolution we shed our blood, never tears! On T'ien-an-men Square, Hsiao Yun, I once saw with my own eyes how those people used clubs to strike . . . I'm going now, maybe . . . here is a picture of us when we were little, a memento for you.

HO YUN Ou-yang! I will wait for you, wait as long as I live.

MEI LIN Hsiao Yun, don't talk such nonsense. You know what he has committed is a capital offense!

HO YUN [*Walks to* MEI LIN, *pauses, suddenly kneels down and throws herself into* MEI LIN's *arms*] Mom! After I see him off, I'll come take care of you. I'll never leave your side. Mom, my good Mom!

MEI LIN Hsiao Yun!

LIU HSIU-YING [*Sobs*] Sister Mei, please accept her, please! [HO WEI *quickly goes into the bedroom wiping his eyes*]

MEI LIN Child, my good child! [HO WEI *enters with a leather suitcase in his hand*]

OU-YANG P'ING Ta Wei, where are you going?

HO WEI You think I can still stay in this house? I'll take Aunt Mei to my teacher's, try and see if we can challenge the god of death, and "them" as well.

OU-YANG P'ING [*Gratefully*] Ta Wei!

LIU HSIU-YING I'm leaving, too!

HO YUN Good! Mom, we'll all go together.

[HO SHIH-FEI *appears at the stairs, but doesn't dare come down*]

HO WEI You should get together whatever you want to take.

LIU HSIU-YING No need. Thirty-five years ago I came empty-handed like this; today I'll leave empty-handed as well.

HO YUN Ou-yang, do you have any more copies of your poems?

OU-YANG P'ING Yes, I do.

HO WEI Give them to us. We'll distribute them for you. [OU-YANG P'ING *takes out several volumes to divide between the two*]

OU-YANG P'ING I'll keep one for the Public Security Bureau.

[HO SHIH-FEI *is unable to stay upstairs any longer. He comes down, quivering*]

HO WEI [*Looking at him*] You don't have to walk like a thief! Eh, look at this carefully. I have four volumes in my hands; there are three in Hsiao Yun's hands; tomorrow you can betray us for a good price! [HO YUN *goes into the bedroom*]

MEI LIN Might as well tell you the whole secret of getting rich and promoted: If you betray everyone in this room that's a mere five people. What you should do is to go out on the streets to look for more business.

OU-YANG P'ING Right, there are eight hundred million Chinese out there!

[HO YUN *enters wearing her police uniform*]

HO YUN The only problem, Dad, is that people will not keep silent forever!

[*The clock strikes seven.* HO YUN *hugs* OU-YANG P'ING, *pauses;* OU-YANG P'ING *walks over to* MEI LIN]

OU-YANG P'ING [*Grief-stricken*] Mom! Goodbye, Mom! [HO YUN, HO WEI, LIU HSIU-YING *all weep*]

MEI LIN There was a rule among our revolutionary troops. When we said goodbye to our husbands and sons as they set out for the battlefields we always beat the drum and gong happily. Today let's also say goodbye with a smile!

[*They now restrain their feelings*]

MEI LIN [*Stands up with great effort*] All right, let's get going!

[MEI LIN *walks one step forward to hand the bag over to* HO YUN, *who accepts it solemnly. The five walk together to the door*]

HO SHIH-FEI [*Rushing down, speaks in a husky voice*] Wait a minute!

[*The five turn around quietly and with great contempt look at this pathetic worm who seems suddenly to have grown old*]

Ho Shih-fei You—are you all leaving? [*No one answers*] Ta Wei, Hsiu-ying, I did it all for this family, all for you! [Liu Hsiu-ying *slowly pushes* Ho Shih-fei*'s hand away from her*] Sister . . . Sister Mei, you can stay here too. I'll go talk it over with T'ang Yu-ts'ai. . . .

Mei Lin [*Walks closer and closer to him, then turns away*] Let's go!

[Ho Wei *opens the sliding glass door. The wind and rain are howling outside.* Ho Wei *and* Liu Hsiu-ying *support* Mei Lin. *Suddenly* Ho Shih-fei *grabs* Ho Yun]

Ho Shih-fei Hsiao Yun! I'm old. You can't leave me alone all by myself . . . [Ho Yun *pushes him away*]

Ho Shih-fei Your father's loved you ever since you were a child. Everything I did was for you, for you! Don't you understand?

[*She turns away from him, proudly facing into the wind and rain together with* Ou-yang P'ing. *Exit all but* Ho Shih-fei]

Ho Shih-fei Everyone has gone. I'm the only one left behind. How quiet it is.

[*Suddenly there is a frightening flash of lightning.* Ho Shih-fei *jumps in terror, waiting fearfully. After what seems like an eternity there is a tremendous clap of thunder*]

[*Curtain*]

Notes

1. The phrase "our Great Cultural Standard-Bearer" refers to Chiang Ch'ing, who, as the wife of Mao Tse-tung and as a member of the powerful Politburo, dominated cultural activities in China from 1966 to 1976 and in particular imposed programs on the performing arts and literature at the expense of much of the cultural establishment. The play, set in the summer of 1976, takes place a few months before her arrest by her rivals following Mao's death.

2. During the Cultural Revolution period under Mao Tse-tung and Chiang Ch'ing the Chinese tradition of Legalist thought was championed in opposition to the dominant Confucian tradition, hence the later sarcastic remarks by Ho Wei. See also n. 4.

3. "Revolutionary Rebirth" (more literally, "new-born thing") is a sarcastic reference to slogans praising the programs of the Cultural Revolution.

4. Ch'in Kuei (A.D. 1090-1155) was chief councilor of the Southern Sung dynasty who arranged for a peace treaty with the Chin dynasty to the north, acknowledging the Sung emperor's subordination to the Chin emperor. Ch'in Kuei also had the patriotic Sung general Yueh Fei(1103-41) recalled and imprisoned on false charges in order to crush any opposition to the treaty.

5. The T'ien-an-men Square Incident took place on 5 April 1976. In January of that year Premier Chou En-lai had died. Widely regarded as an opponent of Chiang Ch'ing's policies, Chou was not accorded the official show of mourning normally due someone of his stature. In April, at a time traditionally devoted to

honoring the dead, crowds placed wreaths at the Monument to the People's Heroes in T'ien-an-men Square to commemorate Chou. When these were removed by official order the crowd reassembled, voicing veiled criticism of Chiang Ch'ing and her associates, and was dispersed with violence.

6. Lord Slob is an allusion to Chi Tien (Chi kung), an ill-kempt, irreverent zen monk of the Southern Sung dynasty, known as a folk hero concerned with the welfare of the common people and portrayed in several Ch'ing dynasty novels and plays.

7. The Rebel Commander-in-Chief refers to Wang Hung-wen, one of the associates of Chiang Ch'ing, collectively known as the "Gang of Four."

8. The "witch's head" refers to Chiang Ch'ing, and by extension, her associates, arrested and charged with attempting to usurp power several months after the T'ien-an-men Square Incident.

9. Chang Ch'un-ch'iao was a journalist and propagandist who, as an associate of Chiang Ch'ing, was appointed chairman of the Shanghai Municipal Revolutionary Committee (1967) and member of the Communist Party's powerful Politburo. As a member of the Gang of Four he was arrested in late 1976.

10. Lin Piao (1908-1971) was minister of defense and commander of the People's Liberation Army, appointed to succeed Mao following his implementation of Mao's policies during the Cultural Revolution in 1966-68. However, he apparently attempted prematurely to seize power from Mao and was killed. There followed a mass political campaign condemning ideological heresies attributed to him.

11. *Red Cliff (Hung yen)* is a novel by Lo Kuang-pin and Yang I-yen, published in 1962. An English-language translation under the title *Red Crag* is available (Foreign Languages Press, Peking, 1978). The novel deals with the Communist underground during the Civil War in the 1940s against the Nationalist Party and the United States government backing it.

12. All Soul's Day is known in Chinese as Ch'ing-ming and here refers to the time of the T'ien-an-men Incident of 5 April 1976 (see note 5 above). The last line of the verse is taken from a poem by Lu Hsün (1881-1936), "Untitled," on the theme of revolution. A translation appears under the title "A Poem" in Gladys Yang, *Silent China* (1973), p. 133.

13. Ch'en I (1900-1972) was a high-ranking military leader, closely associated with Chou En-lai, and served as foreign minister until he was attacked by Red Guards during the Cultural Revolution and stripped of authority.

Chou Wei-po, Tung Yang-sheng,
Yeh Hsiao-nan

The Artillery Commander's Son

Translated by Stanley Dubinsky and Edward M. Gunn

Cast of Characters

Master Fang,[1] a worker who provides hot water for tea and such, heated on a so-called "tiger stove"
Section Chief Sun, section chief in a government bureau
Hsiao Chi,[2] daughter of Section Chief Sun, a worker, 24 years old
Hsiao Fang, son of Master Fang, Hsiao Chi's boy friend, a worker, 27 years old
Hsiao Ch'en, son of the chief of the bureau, former grade school classmate of Hsiao Fang, now a university student, 27 years old

Setting

The home of Section Chief Sun in the city, on a spring day in 1977, not long after the downfall of the Gang of Four.

[Master Fang *enters in front of the curtain, carrying a thermos bottle*]
Master Fang [*Bowing to the audience*] Good evening! If any of you happen to be thirsty please don't hesitate to let me know. Oh, don't thank me, please, it's nothing special, nothing out of the ordinary. Then again, if you look into the ordinary things of life and give them some thought you're apt to come up with quite a few mysteries, and quite a few insights, too. Look over there, for instance! [*Pointing to the audience*] There's a man sporting a pretty besotted proboscis. From here I'd say his nose is bigger than his entire face, bigger than his entire body, oh, and really, really red. Of course, you're going to ask why I can see so clearly? Well, I'll tell you: I use this thing here to see with. [*Taking out a large magnifying glass from his pocket and holding it in front of his eye*] There now, clear as day! I'd like you all to make use of this gadget to take a close look at the people I'm about to introduce to you.
[*The sound of a loud yawn comes from behind the curtain*]
Master Fang Well, speak of the devil and he's sure to show up.

[SECTION CHIEF SUN *enters, carrying a tea mug*]

SUN [*Looking at his watch*] Master Fang, you're late today! I *must* have my tea every day at this time.

MASTER FANG Oh, Section Chief Sun, your thermos bottle is broken, so I was just fixing it.

SUN Broken? [*Squinting, fishes around in his pocket for something*]

MASTER FANG [*Taking the magnifying glass out of his pocket*] Is this what you're looking for, Section Chief Sun? You left it on my hot water stove yesterday.

SUN Oh, right, right! [*Taking the magnifying glass, examines the thermos bottle*] Where is it broken?

MASTER FANG Not this one, the other one. The bottom's all ruined. I'll have to take it with me and fix it for you.

SUN Master Fang, you put yourself out too much. Not only do you bring me hot water every day, but now you're fixing my thermos bottle! I'm sorry to put you to so much trouble.

MASTER FANG It's no trouble at all. Besides, you're ill.

SUN The moral character of a worker is truly remarkable. Thank you very much.

MASTER FANG Not at all! [*Gives him a thermos bottle and starts to leave, then turns back*] Section Chief Sun, just what is your illness, anyway?

SUN Oh, my nerves are weak, and on top of that, I have a constant headache.[3]

MASTER FANG Well, you just rest up. When I've fixed this thermos I'll send it over. [*To audience*] That's a strange illness for sure. [MASTER FANG *exits*]

[SECTION CHIEF SUN *yawns repeatedly, puts down the thermos, and begins stretching his legs, reaching around to massage his back, and groaning.* HSIAO CHI *enters, carrying an open book*]

CHI Daddy, what's the matter? Are you all right?

SUN Oh, Hsiao Chi, your father's an old man. My back is sore, my shoulders hurt, my legs are numb. It's sheer misery! [*He gestures toward the thermos, and* HSIAO CHI *picks it up off the floor*]

CHI The windows are all closed; no wonder it's so dismal in here! It's spring already! With your health so poor you ought to be outside, taking in the sun and the fresh air. Come on, let's open the curtains!

SUN [*With an air of resignation*] All right. Open them.

[HSIAO CHI *and her father each pull open one side of the curtain. As it opens we see a huge magnifying glass set up stage front; behind it is a spacious, comfortable living room. A sofa faces stage front, flanked by two arm chairs. To stage left of the sofa is a three-cornered table, with a telephone and several illustrated magazines on top.* HSIAO CHI *enters the living room through the frame of the magnifying glass with* CHIEF SUN *following her.* HSIAO CHI *pulls the window curtains open, and bright sunlight streams in through the French windows, to the sounds of spring—willow branches rustling in the breeze, the humming of bees, the singing of birds*]

CHI Spring is here! It's such a beautiful time!

SUN [*Shielding his eyes from the sunlight*] It's so bright you can't open your eyes.

CHI Daddy, the spring sun can restore the sick to health, and turn old folks into children! [*The phone rings*]

SUN Just listen to you! [*Sits down on the sofa and picks up the receiver*]

CHI Dad, I'm going out! [*About to leave*]

SUN Eh, don't go yet! There's something I want to talk to you about. [HSIAO CHI, *obliged to sit down at his side, begins to read her book.* SUN *points to a soft cusion on the sofa, which* HSIAO CHI *passes to him*]

SUN [*Speaking loudly into the telephone, reprimanding*] What is it? I told you, I'm sick! [*Realizing that his tone of voice is all wrong, he quickly stands up, and with great deference bows at the waist and continues in an unctuous tone*] Ah, so it's Bureau Chief Ch'en, indeed it's the Bureau Chief himself. I knew it was you calling. . . . How did I know? . . .

[SUN *signals to* HSIAO CHI *to bring him his usual tonic, heavily laced with alcohol. She pours a glassful and gives it to him*]

SUN . . . ya, Bureau Chief Ch'en, there's no need to explain that, is there? The phone rings a different way when you call, not the way it does when other people do. It sounds more dignified, more . . . [*Sips a mouthful of tonic*] What flavor! It reminds me of your qualities: mildness within strength, and strength within mildness. The moment I taste . . . no, no, the moment I hear it, I can tell . . . My health? Ai, it's still the same, but I'm bracing up and holding on. . . . I was just reading your report, it's brilliant! [*Holds the report up to the receiver*] Bureau Chief Ch'en, you see . . . I'm right in the midst of reading it now! Oh, yes, right. It's a telephone, so of course you can't see through it. When I hear you ringing, I get so excited that I forget everything else. . . . What happened? Deputy Bureau Chief Li has been transferred out? Aiya, it must be even harder for you now. . . . Oh, Bureau Chief Ch'en, why hasn't your son come over yet? He's on his way? I'm waiting for him right now! O.K., goodbye, goodbye! [*Hangs up receiver; something suddenly occurs to him and he says to himself*] Ai, Deputy Chief Li has been transferred out, and then he asked me how my health was; it could be that there was something he didn't say. Could it be that he wants me . . . of course! It must be! [*Hurriedly picks up the receiver again*] Bureau Chief Ch'en! I'm quite recovered already, as strong as a bull. In fact, compared to a bull . . . [*places the receiver on his stomach*] Listen! I'm completely able to carry this important revolutionary burden, completely able! Bureau Chief Ch'en! Hello! Hello! Hung up already. [*Hangs up telephone*] Some unscrupulous devil disconnected me. If I find out who it was, I'll have him dismissed. [*About to pick up the telephone again*] Ai, Hsiao Ch'en is coming over. If Hsiao Chi and he can hit it off well together . . . then the position of Deputy Bureau Chief . . . right, I've got to have a talk with Hsiao Chi. Hsiao Chi! Hsiao Chi!

[*As* SECTION CHIEF SUN *circles the garden calling for* HSIAO CHI, *she dutifully follows him, hidden inadvertently behind his back for a moment*]

CHI Daddy, here I am!

SUN Oh, there you are. What is so fascinating about that book?

CHI [*Holding up the book*] It's a play by Schiller called "Intrigue and Love"—*Kabale und Liebe*.

SUN [*Inspecting it with his magnifying glass*] Love, young people only like to talk about love! Now, what is love? It's not so wonderful as you imagine it to be, so full of poetic sentiments and pretty thoughts. It's much too complicated for you to understand at your age. What's the book called again?

CHI [*Annoyed*] "Intrigue and Love."

SUN "Intrigue and Love"? . . . Why, that's a good book!

CHI Have you read it?

SUN I can tell from the title! Where there's love there's intrigue, and where there's intrigue there's love. Intrigue is shameful, so it follows that love also is shameful . . .

CHI Father, you're talking nonsense again!

SUN Be a good girl then and explain it to your father.

CHI Once upon a time there was a prime minister who was so concerned with wealth and status that he forced his only son to part with the woman he loved. And as a result he brought down a tragic ending on them all.

SUN So what I said does make sense: where there's love there's intrigue. If it's not handled properly it can turn into a tragedy. [*Earnestly*] Hsiao Chi, does your daddy love you or doesn't he?

CHI He does, and then again he doesn't.

SUN Is he concerned about you or not?

CHI He is, and then again he isn't!

SUN What kind of talk is that?

CHI From a material point of view, you're concerned enough about me . . .

SUN [*Happily*] That's my good little girl!

CHI But from an emotional point of view, you're not concerned about me one bit. You're just a . . . a very average father!

SUN [*Studies* HSIAO CHI] An average father! Hsiao Chi, you're being unfair to your daddy! Today, daddy is going to help you resolve your emotional dilemma!

CHI You! This I can't believe!

SUN [*Takes a sheet of paper from his pocket*] Right here is a wonderful prescription to cure the disease of an unsettled spirit!

CHI I don't want to see it!

SUN [*Reading in a loud voice*] Chao, Ch'ien, Sun, Li . . . Young Chao, son of the Public Health Bureau Chief; Young Ch'ien, son of the Light Industry Department Bureau Chief; Young Sun, the university president's son . . .

CHI [*Covering her ears with her hands*] I don't want to hear it! I don't want to hear!

SUN Aiya! Do you have any idea how much trouble your father has gone to, how much rebuke he's had to face, in order to arrange this for you? This list of names was not easy to come by!

CHI You're about to get yet another rebuke!

SUN Impossible. Who asked me, a Department Chief, to have such a bright and beautiful daughter? [*Sees that* HSIAO CHI *has her back to him*] What, are you shy?

CHI Let me have that paper of yours! [*Grabs the paper and throws it to the ground*]

SUN [*Carefully picking it up*] You're embarrassed? Well then, your father will pick one for you! Young Ch'en, Bureau Chief Ch'en's son; he's a top student at a major university, the best catch for a hundred miles around!

CHI I'm leaving!

SUN You can't go now, Hsiao Ch'en is coming soon!

CHI So let him come! It's not as though I don't know him!

SUN [*Mimicking* HSIAO CHI] "So let him come!" You say it so casually! He's not coming today for an ordinary visit!

CHI Not ordinary?

SUN There's a lot more to this visit!

CHI A lot more to it?

SUN He's coming especially for you!

CHI I didn't invite him! I'm leaving!

SUN You first answer your father one question, then you can go.

CHI What question?

SUN Do you . . . do you like Hsiao Ch'en?

CHI What are you asking me that for?

SUN You must answer!

CHI If I must answer, then I'll give you the truth! He's a passionately sincere person; he is incredibly talented, and has the innate qualities of a poet and the wisdom of a philosopher as well; whenever anyone has a problem, and he can be of help, he always stands up to volunteer . . . of all those who know him, there isn't anyone who doesn't like him!

SUN I'm asking *you*! [*Emphatically*] You!

CHI From the time I was little, he's been coming to our home. I've always regarded him as an older brother. Of course I like him, too.

SUN Aiya! My precious girl, why didn't you say so before?

CHI No, Daddy!

SUN Then, that settles the matter! I've already spoken with the Bureau Chief and Hsiao Ch'en myself. The Bureau Chief smiled and said

Hsiao Ch'en could decide for himself . . .

CHI [*Impatiently*] And Hsiao Ch'en?

SUN Although he didn't say anything at the time, my old, experienced eyes could see "willing" clearly written all over his excited face!

CHI Daddy, you . . . [*To herself*] Everything has happened so suddenly, so disastrously! Like a small deer suddenly finding itself looking down the barrel of a hunter's rifle. . . . No! I can't hesitate any longer, I mustn't be so shy, I've got to let father know just exactly what's on my mind.

SUN [*Deliriously happy*] Heh, heh . . . The son of a Bureau Chief will be my son-in-law! Within this shadowy mist of love, it's as if I can already see the position of Deputy Bureau Chief beckoning to me!

CHI [*Looks in agony at her father*] Now how can this be the father I've always looked up to? Selfish ambition has exposed the mean and vulgar man hiding deep inside him. And when all is said and done, what happens to his daughter means nothing next to being made Deputy Bureau Chief. . . . No, I have to be firm! Hsiao Fang is on his way over, too; when I think of him, I'm filled with determination.

SUN Hsiao Chi, you don't know how happy you've made your father today! It's all settled between you and Hsiao Ch'en!

CHI Right! Settled! [*Pauses for a moment*] I'm never going to marry him!

SUN [*Shocked*] What? Child, are you joking?

CHI I've already given my heart to someone else!

SUN [*Suddenly angered*] Oh no! I won't permit it! You're *my* daughter. I've got rights, as well as an obligation to . . . protect you!

CHI Dad, please don't get so carried away that you forget you're my father. I'm trying to express some of my most intimate feelings and looking for some sympathy and support. But I'm definitely not about to come begging for your approval! My heart is a free bird, and to me life is no more than the sky through which it can soar!

SUN What? Free bird? Sky? . . . Her father's heart shatters like glass to hear her say that. So much like her late mother she is: such a gentle exterior, and beneath it an incomparably obstinate heart!

CHI [*Remembering*] Mama! Mama, come back quickly to help your daughter! How she needs your compassionate embrace!

SUN She's calling for her mother! Ai, I've been so eager to work this out quickly that I've failed to be patient, to do some reflection. I should be winning her over through fatherly compassion! [*To* CHI] Hsiao Chi, your father was a bit impatient and made you angry. You must forgive daddy, he truly loves you, too! You haven't forgotten, have you, that you're my only daughter; that ever since your mother passed away I've struggled to bring you up, since you were a baby . . .

CHI Dad, please don't talk about Mama; it makes me feel so sad. [*Weeps*]

SUN If you don't let your father know what's on your mind, how can you blame him?

CHI Daddy, for some time now I've wanted to let you know just what my feelings are, but then, several times, I've stopped myself just when I was on the point of speaking up. Shyness for a young girl is like a stern bodyguard, standing at the pretty gate of her lips . . .

SUN So then, speak up now!

CHI Ai! Why is it that every time I start talking about Hsiao Fang, my voice begins to tremble like a lute string? Daddy, it's hard to express exactly what it is about him that's so fine, but the moment I set eyes on him I knew he was a good person. It's as if there was a marvelous power urging me forward . . .

SUN Ai, you've truly become possessed by that sinister romantic spirit! How is it that you've come to know him?

CHI We see each other every day. He's in charge of our lathe shop.

SUN He's been taking advantage of his position as foreman to . . .

CHI No, no! Daddy, you mustn't accuse him unjustly! He's bright, but he's practical; he's modest, but also full of self-confidence; he's passionate, but wise as well; he can see into people's hearts, but he also treats everyone sincerely . . .

SUN Since he's so fine, then it's certain that his father's a Party Committee Secretary at the very least, correct?

CHI No, he's not!

SUN A District Secretary?

CHI Not that either!

SUN Then, Hsiao Fang himself must be . . . [*Shakes head*]

CHI No, father, he's no brilliant diamond or pearl, nor is he made of costly gold or agate. He's simply another clod of mud on the face of the limitless earth. He even smells like the earth. He is a common worker, and his father too is nothing more than an ordinary, common worker.

SUN So that's the way it is!

CHI Daddy, have you changed your mind?

SUN You're the one who's going to have to change her mind!

CHI Daddy, do you mean to say that a man's worth is determined by his father's position?

SUN That's exactly the way it is! In this society, the parent's position determines that of their children. Moreover, marriage can strengthen that position and make it endure.

CHI [*Angrily*] Dad, you can keep your social position! What our nation needs are people who would contribute to the establishment of the "Four Modernizations,"[4] not those who would seek after their own social position. I believe that one day the people will rid themselves of this sort of hypocritical superficiality, and become a people dedicated to the "Four Modernizations," a *just* people.

SUN Hsiao Chi, do you really think that I'm doing all this just for myself, an old man? My experience in this world tells me that to change all these things will be extremely difficult! Connections come first! Connections come first!

CHI How did he get like this? [*Looks at her watch*] Dad, he's coming soon. If you think that love has beclouded my vision, then examine him for yourself; I'm positive you'll like him . . .

SUN [*Turning away*] I'm not interested in seeing him, and I don't want him setting foot in my house either!

[YOUNG FANG *rushes in, carrying a book*]

FANG Hsiao Chi, I've brought that book you wanted to borrow!

[*She looks at him strangely*]

FANG [*Puzzled*] Hsiao Chi, what's the matter?

CHI [*Dissembling*] Nothing, nothing at all. Hsiao Fang . . . [*Points to* SUN] this is my father! [*To* SUN] Father, Hsiao Fang is here.

FANG [*Respectfully*] Hsiao Chi's father, how do you do!

[SUN *ignores him*]

FANG [*Looking at* HSIAO CHI] What . . .

[HSIAO CHI *signals to him to come over and whispers a suggestion that he address her father as Section Chief Sun*]

FANG Section Chief Sun, how do you do!

[SUN *yawns loudly*]

CHI Father!

FANG What is all this about?

CHI [*Blurting it out*] Hsiao Fang, this is all because you're the son of a worker!

FANG What? What did you say? [*Ponders*] Are you saying that a section chief is not a cadre of the worker class? That there's some sort of impassible wall between the son of a worker and the daughter of a section chief?

CHI Oh, what have I said? This is so painful for him! Oh, Hsiao Fang, I didn't mean it like that . . .

SUN [*His back to* HSIAO FANG] Honorable comrade Fang, your visit today is a bit inopportune. We are expecting a very important guest any moment now. He's—

CHI Father, you—

SUN He's the son of the Bureau Chief, Hsiao Chi's boy friend. Therefore, your presence at this time is a bit inconvenient!

FANG [*Angrily*] So that's the way it is! Well, I'm leaving! [*To* HSIAO CHI] *You* should have made things clear before this! [*Turns to leave*]

CHI Hsiao Fang, you can't go; I've got to tell you—

FANG There's nothing more to say! I'd be an imbecile to stay a moment longer in a place as obnoxious as this!

[HSIAO FANG *angrily turns and stalks out.* HSIAO CHI *starts to run after him*]

SUN [*Blocking her path*] No! You're my daughter: I won't permit you to go.

CHI Let go of me! Let go!

SUN To chase after him? Is he worth chasing after?

CHI Get out of my way! [*Struggles free and runs*]

SUN Stop! . . . All right, go ahead and run after him, but don't set foot inside this house again if you do!

CHI That's fine. I'm going. [*Starts forward*]

SUN No! [*Entreating*] Please come back!

[HSIAO CHI *angrily sits down.* HSIAO CH'EN *enters behind* SUN *who, assuming it is* HSIAO FANG, *addresses him without turning to look*]

SUN Will you please go? I've already asked you to leave!

CH'EN Uncle Sun, you don't want me here?

SUN [*Turns*] Oh, Hsiao Ch'en! It's *you*! Come in, come right on in!

CH'EN Didn't you just ask me to leave?

SUN No, no, I was telling Hsiao Chi . . . no, I mean I was just telling myself . . .

CH'EN You seem to get pretty angry talking to yourself.

SUN That . . . that . . . come, come, sit down and have some tea.

[HSIAO CH'EN *sits down.* SUN *pours a cup of tea for him and in his confusion hands him the thermos bottle. Embarrassed, he then offers him the teacup. Meanwhile* CHI *ignores him completely*]

CH'EN What's the matter with you, Hsiao Chi? [*She turns away*]

SUN Oh, nothing's wrong with her, she just doesn't feel too well.

[SUN *signals to* HSIAO CHI *to converse with* HSIAO CH'EN. *She ignores him also*]

SUN Hsiao Ch'en, you chat with her. I'll be right back.

[SUN *exits. After a short silence* HSIAO CH'EN *stands and paces silently, deep in thought.* HSIAO CHI *sits absolutely still*]

CH'EN Hsiao Chi, what's this all about anyway?

CHI [*Icily*] Nothing. Nothing at all.

CH'EN So you're angry with me, is that it?

CHI If you already know, why do you ask?

CH'EN You're being unfair with me. The truth is, it wasn't my idea to come here today; it was my father's. He said he understands your father and wants me to handle this properly. As far as I'm concerned I have plenty of homework to do and being a student at the university I have better things to do with my time than take this very seriously.

CHI [*Feeling better*] Then you'll have to forgive me. Father has made me so angry I can't see straight.

CH'EN Hsiao Chi, let me ask you something. Just as I got here a young fellow stalked out in quite a temper. Who was he?

CHI He . . . he's . . .

CH'EN Let me guess. He would be none other than the Honorable Comrade Fang, correct?

CHI What! Either you were eavesdropping or you really are what people call you, "the rival of Chu-ko Liang"![5]

CH'EN Tell me everything. I'd love to help. Think of me as a sort of "Captain Lu" defending everyone against injustice.[6]

CHI I guess there's no use not telling you the truth. Yes, the fellow who just left is my boy friend, Hsiao Fang.

CH'EN Were you having a fight?

CHI No, my father drove him away.

CH'EN Why?

CHI Because he's the son of an ordinary worker.

CH'EN [*Thinking*] The son of an ordinary worker . . . No, that's definitely not the essence of the problem. If the social status of a worker were higher than that of a bureau chief, then your father would probably do almost anything to get him to come back. The real object of his adoration isn't so much social position itself as it is the prerogatives that go with it! As far as he's concerned, his daughter's marriage is nothing more than a means to strengthen and extend those benefits!

CHI [*Standing up, excitedly*] Brother Ch'en, you're absolutely right!

CH'EN While the Gang of Four carried out their subversion our lives went through a period of turmoil that truly could be called "Soaring through the heavens and plummeting into hell"![7] Nevertheless, even now, after our fathers have restored order to the government, these kinds of people go on, having learned nothing from the recent chaos. Even though the Gang of Four has been toppled, the blight they spread is still corrupting the people. Yet, we can come to realize through our own personal experience that in a socialist society the cadres are all servants of the people. They have only the obligation to serve the people earnestly, not special political or personal privileges! A worker's son and a cadre's daughter ought to stand as absolute equals. There are neither servants nor aristocrats.

CHI My father never gives a thought to how he can serve the people, just to how he can establish better connections with the higher-ranking cadre. He figures that he'll be able to maintain or elevate his own social standing that way. The power of this kind of sloth is such a great obstacle to the implementation of our nation's "Four Modernizations"!

CH'EN Making connections, seeking special privileges, these are examples of decadent, feudalistic thinking! If our Party was able to cut down the poisonous Gang of Four then it surely should be able to uproot these corrupt practices!

CHI [*Sadly*] Brother Ch'en, tell me, what can I do now? I'm afraid that my father will never consent to Hsiao Fang.

CH'EN Don't worry! . . . What's his full name?

CHI Fang Hua.

CH'EN No wonder he looked so familiar!

FANG Do you know him?

CH'EN Of course! He was my classmate in grade school! I haven't seen him for over ten years. He has gotten quite handsome, hasn't he?

CHI [*Embarrassed*] Listen to you.

CH'EN If I were a young woman, *I* might fall in love with him; then your plans would be in trouble!

CHI Cut it out!

CH'EN Don't worry, I'm definitely going to help you and Hsiao Fang get together, and teach your father that his antiquated ways won't work any more!

CHI That would be impossible.

CH'EN "Where the mountains stretch endlessly, and streams wind about, I doubted there was a road. The willows were dim, but the flowers were bright—suddenly there was another village ahead!"[8]

CHI What do you have in mind?

CH'EN Come here, I'll tell you!

[*They sit on the sofa together, conspiring.* SUN *enters, and watches stealthily from the doorway*]

SUN Where just a moment ago dark clouds filled the sky, now the sun is shining! It seems the Bureau Chief's son has managed all right after all! [*Exits*]

CHI Don't overdo it!

CH'EN Don't worry. I know just how to handle this! Well then, I'm on my way. [*About to leave, he turns back*] Hsiao Chi, wait a little while, and then tell your father that I already have a girl friend. May Cupid watch over you!

CHI May Chu-ko Liang watch over you! [HSIAO CH'EN *leaves.* SUN *enters bringing sweets*]

SUN [*Looking around*] Is he gone?

CHI Yes.

SUN [*Searchingly*] Did the two of you get along?

CHI Uh huh.

SUN [*Happily*] Did you say yes?

CHI He's got a girl friend!

SUN [*Worried*] What? What did you just say?

CHI Hsiao Ch'en said that he already has a girl friend!

SUN [*Unconvinced*] Impossible. Couldn't be.

CHI If you don't believe me then go ask him yourself.

SUN Well, in that case he's even been keeping it from his own father. I still think that you two are a match made in heaven! Ai, the cooked duck has flown away!

CHI It's no great loss.

SUN [*Agreeing*] Right, it's no great loss! [*Again producing his list*] I've got many more right here! [*Sits down, reading carefully with his magnifying glass*] There's Chao, and Ch'ien, and Sun, and Li . . .

CHI I wouldn't have any one of them!

SUN Hsiao Chi, when I was younger I was just like you are now; I looked at life as though it were a piece of crystal, pure and transparent. But these last ten years or so I've been knocked around enough to see that everything depends on your connections.

CHI Not necessarily. That's your own brand of logic.

SUN If you'd consider carefully what your father is saying you'd change your mind.

CHI I'm afraid you're the one who'll have to change his mind.

SUN No! My mind isn't going to be changed!

[*A car is heard pulling up outside; a horn honks*]

SUN [*Looking out*] Who's here now? Isn't that a Shanghai Motors make? Ooh, this must be someone with status!

[HSIAO CH'EN *enters, accompanied by a young man in military uniform*]

SUN Aha, Hsiao Ch'en, you've come back after all! [*To* HSIAO CHI] Now here's a young man with style!

CH'EN Uncle Sun!

SUN [*Reproachfully*] If you had a girl friend already why didn't you just say so?

CH'EN [*Affecting a conspiratorial air*] Uncle Sun, I've hooked a really big one for you! [*Soberly*] His name is Fang Hua, he's a classmate of mine, *and* he's the son of the Artillery Commander!

SUN What? An artillery commander's son!—Why, how rude of me! Please, sit down. Be comfortable.

FANG Uncle Sun!

SUN [*Overwhelmed*] Please, don't stand on ceremony! Just call me "Old Sun," okay? Hsiao Chi, let's have some tea right away!

[SUN *takes out his magnifying glass and carefully scrutinizes* HSIAO FANG]

SUN Ah, a very handsome fellow!

CH'EN Handsome indeed!

SUN Smooth and poised like—just like . . .

CH'EN Like a powerful cannon!

SUN Exactly, like a mighty cannon! A real general's son!

CH'EN [*Whispers*] Uncle Sun, do you like him?

SUN Of course! At a glance you can see there's nothing ordinary about him; by the second glance you could really begin to respect him; and just one more look [*Looks at* HSIAO CHI] and a person might find herself falling in love with him in spite of herself.

CH'EN That's wonderful! [*He winks at* HSIAO CHI *who covers her mouth to hide her laugh*]

SUN Why, I've completely forgotten to introduce you two; you're—

FANG —Fang Hua. Just call me Hsiao Fang.

SUN What? Another one called Hsiao Fang?

CH'EN What's the matter? Doesn't Uncle Sun approve of the name Fang?

SUN Oh, yes. I like it! Fang sounds very right—like Mr. Right: upright, forthright, just exactly right!

CH'EN And, of course, there's the "right" of "right side up and upside down," as well!

SUN Right! Right side up! . . . Hsiao Fang, my daughter, Hsiao Chi.

[HSIAO CHI *and* HSIAO FANG *give each other a look*]

CHI So, you're the son of an artillery commander?

SUN [*To himself*] Things are looking good!

FANG [*Embarrassed*] Yes, an artillery commander's . . . oh, I'm not—

CH'EN [*Quickly interjecting*] He's not the one who thought of coming here. It was my idea to bring him over!

SUN Just so long as he's here, that's fine. Please, have a seat.

[HSIAO CHI *and* HSIAO FANG *sit down together on the sofa.* HSIAO CH'EN *and* SUN *each sit in one of the armchairs*]

SUN Hsiao Fang, help yourself to some sweets! Please don't stand on ceremony in my house, just make yourself at home. Hsiao Ch'en, pass these around for me, please.

[*They all eat sweets*]

SUN Old Fang, no—Young Fang, Hsiao Fang, as a commanding officer your father must be quite busy, I would think.

FANG Yes, he is very busy. He goes from morning til night, nonstop.

SUN When you see your father, Commanding Officer Fang, you'll be sure to give him my regards!

FANG I'll be sure to tell him. Thank you, Uncle Sun.

SUN Please, don't thank me! I'm simply showing the proper respect due a superior!

CHI Father, how does an artillery commander come to be your superior? Are you an artilleryman?

SUN Ai, [*Pats his stomach*] an artilleryman? The heart is willing, but the body unable.

CH'EN Hsiao Chi, what your father means is that, if a person is of higher social standing than he, then he must show due respect; and if he's lower . . .

SUN Absolutely correct!

FANG Uncle Sun is truly a forthright person; he speaks whatever is on his mind.

SUN Ingenious!

CHI Ingenious?

SUN [*Suddenly*] Oh, ingenuous!

FANG Uncle Sun corrects himself when he knows he's made a mistake, truly an example for us young people to follow!

CH'EN Uncle Sun is completely modest; when he talks about reform, he reforms. When he talks about change, he changes.

SUN Aiya, I don't deserve all this praise. I'm always happy to have my errors pointed out! Hsiao Fang, how old are you?

FANG Twenty-seven.

SUN [*Nudging* HSIAO CHI] Just the right age! Are you very busy with your studies?

FANG Uncle Sun, at the factory, I—

SUN Factory?

CH'EN [*Quickly interrupting*] He used to be at the factory.

FANG Right, I was originally at the factory; afterwards—

CH'EN Afterwards he became my classmate.

SUN Where is your father stationed?

FANG The— he's— In Shanghai . . .

SUN Shanghai? What? I've never heard of an artillery commander—

CH'EN Uncle Sun, Commanding Officer Fang recently went to Shanghai for a meeting; his unit is stationed along the defense perimeter, so . . .

SUN [*Suddenly understanding*] Oh, confidential military affairs! [*He gives* HSIAO CH'EN *a knowing look and smiles*] Hsiao Fang, how many brothers and sisters do you have?

FANG None. I'm an only child.

SUN Ah, an only child! [*Points to young* FANG] An artillery commander's only son! [*Points to young* CHI] And a section chief's only daughter! Fascinating!

CHI You can't compare the daughter of a section chief with the son of an artillery commander!

SUN Hsiao Chi, your father will criticize you for talking too much. Every revolutionary cadre should—

FANG [*Looking at his watch*] Hsiao Ch'en, we've got to go.

CH'EN Uncle Sun, you see?

SUN [*Quickly pulling* HSIAO FANG *back*] No, no, at least have something to eat before you go!

FANG Next time, okay?

SUN Then it must be that you have no patience for your Uncle's chatter.

CHI Since my father's asking you to stay, you really shouldn't leave.

CH'EN Hsiao Chi is also asking you to stay, Hsiao Fang. Show us a little courage and sit down to eat. You'll certainly want to come again, anyway.

FANG All right, I won't stand on ceremony.

SUN I've never been able to have you over before this. Now, this first time we're strangers, but next time you'll be like one of the family.

CHI Hsiao Fang's welcome any time.

SUN Certainly. You three chat while I bring out something to eat.

[SUN *exits. After a pause the three burst out laughing*]

CHI We're lucky you could come up with a plan as devious as this one!

CH'EN Chiang T'ai-kung went fishing—and just let whoever wanted to, hook himself.[9]

FANG I was really afraid we couldn't pull it off!

CH'EN Right about now the fish is ready to take the bait, so let's just have a little patience . . .

[*Putting their heads together, the three have a quiet discussion. Suddenly* CHI *leaps up, somewhat upset*]

CHI Now that's going a bit too far!

FANG This way, maybe your father will wise up a little!

CH'EN I'm directing this little charade, and I'd like to see people learn something insightful from it.

[HSIAO CHI *calms down. From offstage,* SUN*'s voice is heard:* "Hsiao Chi, come here!" *She glances at* HSIAO CH'EN, *who gives her a sign to go*]

CHI Coming! [*Leaves*]

FANG I'm really afraid that it's going to be tough to carry off this little play as we've planned!

CH'EN Don't worry, to pull off a charade like this, you just have to give it a good opening, and it will certainly work itself out!

FANG Well, I'll just follow your directions then!

[SUN *and* HSIAO CHI *enter, bringing with them an assortment of snacks*]

CH'EN Uncle Sun, you've brought out so many things to eat and drink, it's as if you were throwing a banquet!

SUN Really, it's nothing!

FANG I honestly feel terrible for making you go to all this trouble. I'm eating you out of house and home!

SUN Not at all, not at all. Hsiao Chi, come with me to carry out the rest.

FANG Uncle Sun, you sit down and rest a bit. Let me go help Hsiao Chi.

[FANG *and* CHI *exit*]

SUN No, no, you can't do that! [*About to chase after them, but held back by* HSIAO CH'EN] Eh?! What do you think you're doing, holding me back? How can I allow the son of an artillery commander to go fetch . . . [*Struggles*]

CH'EN Uncle Sun, what's got you so mixed up today?

SUN Me? Mixed up?

CH'EN Yes, you really seem to be in a total fog!

SUN In a fog?

CH'EN The two of them have gone inside together; what do you want to go in there for?

SUN [*Understanding*] Of course, of course! Hsiao Ch'en, you have no idea what a terrible temper Hsiao Chi has! I'm just afraid that she may show it in there!

CH'EN Hsiao Chi told me everything that happened today, and I reprimanded her for it! I told her that her father only has her best interests in mind, and that the children of cadres are generally much more powerful than those of workers. These two are well matched for marriage.

SUN [*Impatiently*] Well, what did she say?

CH'EN Hsiao Chi thought it over carefully for a while and then realized that she was wrong!

SUN [*Elated*] What, what? Hsiao Chi admitted that she was in the wrong? That's wonderful, just wonderful! Thank you, thank you so much! [*Shakes hands with him*]

CH'EN Don't thank me yet. What do you think of Hsiao Fang?

SUN He's good! I like him!

CH'EN How would you say he stands up to the "Honorable Comrade Fang"?

SUN There's nothing to compare! One is the son of an artillery commander and the other is the son of a common worker; their social standing is completely different . . .

CH'EN Uncle Sun, did you notice that Hsiao Fang has taken a liking to Hsiao Chi?

SUN [*Pleasantly surprised*] What? What did you say?

CH'EN Hsiao Fang really likes Hsiao Chi!

SUN If that's true, it's wonderful! [*Calming down a little*] You wouldn't be fooling me, now, would you?

CH'EN It's just love at first sight. Didn't you notice the affectionate way they were looking at each other?

SUN Ha, ha . . . really?

CH'EN Truly!

SUN [*Talks to himself, ecstatically*] An artillery commander's son for my son-in-law! Ah, forget about being Deputy Bureau Chief; my prospects are now absolutely radiant . . . glorious!

[SUN *is on the point of keeling over, and sways back and forth, rubbing his forehead.* HSIAO CH'EN, *with considerable difficulty, helps him back onto the sofa*]

SUN Hsiao Ch'en, I'm really too fortunate! It seems as if this flood of good fortune's going to sweep me away! [*He stands up again and looks* HSIAO CH'EN *in the eye*] Is it actually true?

CH'EN Hsiao Fang said so! And he's asked me to help him out!

SUN Did you agree?

CH'EN Of course not!

SUN [*Worried*] What's the matter with you?

CH'EN Love has to come from both sides!

SUN Hsiao Chi will agree, just leave that to me!

CH'EN That's great. You should go and talk it over with Hsiao Chi yourself!

SUN [*Takes a few steps, then turns back with embarrassment*] You go!

CH'EN I'm not going!

SUN To tell you the truth, on account of what I tried to arrange between the two of you, Hsiao Chi almost had an all-out battle with me!

CH'EN I'm not going to do it!

SUN When a real gentleman helps people fulfill their wishes, he helps all the way! [*Gives* HSIAO CH'EN *a push*]

CH'EN But it's nearly impossible to talk about something like this.

SUN [*Bows to* HSIAO CH'EN] Uncle Sun is asking you, please!

CH'EN [*With a helpless expression*] Since Uncle Sun thinks so much of me, I guess I really have no choice but to do the best I can.

SUN When this matter is settled successfully, I'll certainly thank you many times over.

CH'EN I'll be very glad if you just don't curse me when the time comes! Look, Hsiao Fang is coming. Here I go. [*Exits*]

[HSIAO FANG *enters carrying edibles;* SUN *quickly takes what he's carrying from him and sets it on the table*]

SUN Hsiao Fang, please sit down; you're probably all tired out!

[SUN *pulls* HSIAO FANG *over to the sofa to sit down, and takes out a handkerchief for him to mop the sweat from his forehead with*]

SUN Hsiao Fang, Hsiao Ch'en just told me everything!

FANG Damn! He told you everything?!

SUN If he hadn't told me, I'd still be in the dark! Young people must show a little courage when it comes to matters of the heart. It's just like a huge cannon: when the barrel is loaded and you've got something to say, you just have to blast away, "boom," and let it all out!

FANG Well, that is the way I am, straight out and direct, like the barrel of a gun.

SUN I like that kind of spirit! It marks a real man!

FANG Uncle Sun, did you agree?

SUN I've been favorably disposed for some time now!

FANG Then, you've really consented?

SUN I wholeheartedly approve!

FANG Uncle Sun, you . . . [*Pauses*] . . . don't know whether or not Hsiao Chi . . .

SUN Don't you worry, Hsiao Ch'en is in there right now talking to Hsiao Chi! Look, here they come!

[HSIAO CHI *is carrying a tray of edibles;* CH'EN *nudges her out, and she bumps into* FANG; *they look at each other and quickly separate*]

CH'EN Uncle Sun, Hsiao Chi has also agreed!

SUN My precious daughter, I never imagined you had your sights set higher even than your father's.

CH'EN Does that mean you don't want me, a Bureau Chief's son, for your son-in-law any more?

SUN Of course I want you, I want both of you . . . oh, that won't do, will it?

CHI Father, you . . .

SUN Your father is genuinely happy today. Come, sit next to me. And you, too, Hsiao Fang. [*Pulls* CHI *and* FANG *down on either side, then realizes he shouldn't be sitting between them, and quickly gets up*] Marvelous, just marvelous!

CH'EN You should give Hsiao Fang a token to remember an occasion as happy as this!

SUN How fortunate I am that you reminded me! But what shall I give him? Oh, of course . . . [*Produces a diary*]

CH'EN Uncle Sun, you ought to inscribe a few words.

SUN What should I write?

CH'EN Whatever you think is appropriate.

[SUN *quickly sits down, takes out a ballpoint pen and writes, while* FANG *and* CHI *sit on the sofa talking happily.* SUN *finishes writing and stands up*]

SUN [*Holding up the diary and reading aloud*] "Presented to my most honorable artillery commander's son, classmate of the Bureau Chief's son, Hsiao Ch'en, my beloved son-in-law—Comrade Hsiao Fang!"

CH'EN Why Uncle, is Hsiao Fang already your son-in-law? [*Laughs*]

SUN Well, it amounts to that!

CH'EN You're really impatient, aren't you?!

SUN They say, "Strike while the iron is hot"! [*Hands the diary to* HSIAO FANG]

FANG Uncle Sun, have you thought the matter over completely?

SUN What? *You* still don't trust my sincerity . . . [*Hastily*] I can swear to it!

FANG Uncle Sun, might not the difference in social standing between our two families be too great?

SUN Difference in social standing? What difference does that make? Even though your father is an artillery commander and I am merely an insignificant section chief, if we are talking about the essentials, your father and I are both diligent servants of the people! To be a true revolutionary, one must always bear in mind this essential point! Otherwise, how is the revolution to be carried out? Your father is an old revolutionary, and I'm sure he has a high level of consciousness. And since you're his son, I'm sure you possess an even higher level of revolutionary consciousness! Remember: "the student surpasses his teacher"!

FANG But, Uncle Sun, our social standing may be . . .

SUN Do you think that the reason I'm letting you marry Hsiao Chi is on account of your being the son of an artillery commander? Do you think I'm after your social position? You don't seem to think very highly of your Uncle Sun! Social standing! What good is social standing? A man's value is to be found only in his own character and abilities! There are some people who simply want to rely on the social status of their parents in making their way up; I have very little regard for those types!

CHI Father!

SUN Just speaking about social standing brings my blood to a boil! Everybody is putting out their utmost for the sake of the "Four Modernizations," yet still there are some people whose only concern is their own social standing! It's a real shame!

FANG Uncle Sun, you're right! So I'm going to level with you completely; I'm actually the son of an ordinary worker!

CH'EN [*Surprised*] Hsiao Fang, what kind of joke are you playing?

CHI [*Anxiously*] Hsiao Fang!

SUN Hsiao Ch'en, don't rebuke Hsiao Fang; and Hsiao Chi, you shouldn't think of him merely as a common worker's son! This is merely Hsiao Fang's admirable modesty! Hsiao Fang, do you think that I don't realize that you're testing me? Did you think that I wouldn't pass your little test? There are no people I despise more than that petty bunch of philistines who only pay attention to status, and none at all to people! In all seriousness, I announce to you: regardless of whose son you are, I want to wish the best for my daughter and yourself, the very best! Hsiao Fang, now it'll be for the two of you to stand the test of love!

FANG Uncle Sun, I really am the son of an ordinary worker!

CH'EN Hsiao Fang! [*Gives* HSIAO FANG *a kick; he falls back onto the sofa*]

SUN [*Disbelieving*] You're really an ordinary worker's son? That's just wonderful! If there weren't workers, where would we all live? What would we wear? So, I want a worker's son like yourself to be my son-in-law!

CHI Father, you mean you know everything? And you're really going along with it?

SUN How can a father not know what's in his daughter's heart? I'm in complete agreement!

CHI Oh, dad! My wonderful dad!

CH'EN You've truly made some people happy today! Let us drink a toast to love!

EVERYONE A toast to love!

[MASTER FANG *enters, carrying a thermos bottle*]

MASTER FANG Section Chief Sun, I fixed your thermos.

SUN [*Cheerfully welcomes him in*] Ah, older brother, you've come to my home on a most joyous occasion!

MASTER FANG What's happened to make you so happy?

SUN My daughter's engaged to be married! To an artillery commander's son!

MASTER FANG An artillery commander's son?

SUN Come, I'll introduce you to him. [*Brings* MASTER FANG *face to face with his son, young* FANG] This is the artillery commander's son!

FANG Dad!

MASTER FANG Aiya, isn't this *my* son?

SUN [*Steps back, startled*] What? He's your son? Then who are you?

MASTER FANG [*Thinks a moment, then it dawns on him*] The artillery commander's son? . . . Well, older brother, the chimney of the "tiger stove" at our house rises straight up into the sky, so that folks have nicknamed it "the antiaircraft gun," and they call me "The artillery commander." So, I suppose he would be "the artillery commander's son." [*Hands thermos to* SUN]

SUN [*Stands before the magnifying glass*] Aiya! So this is the son of the "artillery commander"!

[*The thermos drops from his hands, shattering. Music comes up, as* SUN *stands staring blankly before the magnifying glass*]

[*Curtain*]

Notes

1. "Master Fang" is a courtesy title, indicating that Fang qualifies as a master worker, as distinct from an apprentice.

2. The "Hsiao" that precedes the names of Chi, Fang, and Ch'en is a familiar form of address, meaning "young" (literally, "small").

3. Sun's illness appears to be neurasthenia, a form of depression not uncommon among cadres and intellectuals.

4. The Four Modernizations denote programs for agriculture, industry, science and technology, and defense adopted as official government policy after the death of Mao Tse-tung and the arrest of the Gang of Four.

5. Chu-ko Liang, the prime minister of the state of Shu during the Three Kingdoms period, is an exemplar of resourcefulness and perspicacity.

6. Captain Lu (or Lu Chih-shen) is a fighting hero in the popular traditional novel *Water Margin (Shui-hu chuan)*.

7. "Above he went to the vast blue void; below to the yellow springs of Hades" is a quotation from the poem "Song of Unending Sorrow" (*Ch'ang-hen ko*) by the T'ang dynasty poet Po Chü-i.

8. The quotation is from a regulated verse poem, "A Trip to Mount West Village," by the Sung dynasty poet Lu Yu.

9. The allusion is to the *Records of the Historian (Shih-chi)*, chapter 32: King Wen, founder of the Chou dynasty, one day received an oracle predicting that what he would catch on that day's hunting would aid him as a ruler. That day he met an old sage, Chiang T'ai-kung, who was out fishing, and made him first an advisor and later prime minister.

Sha Yeh-hsin, Li Shou-ch'eng,
Yao Ming-te

If I Were Real

Translated by Edward M. Gunn

(Scene 5 is presented in its entirety. The remaining scenes are summarized.)

SCENES 1–4 (SUMMARY)

If I Were Real is in large part a satirical play set in the late 1970s following the overthrow of Chiang Ch'ing and her associates, collectively known as the Gang of Four, and at the start of widespread economic and social changes. The central character, Li Hsiao-chang, has for years been assigned as an educated youth to work on a state farm. When his girl friend, employed as a worker in a nearby city, becomes pregnant she pressures Li to arrange for a transfer to the city where they will be married, in preference to life in the countryside. Posing as Chang Hsiao-li, son of a high-level influential cadre, Li Hsiao-chang visits the city and ingratiates himself with Party cadre there, who arrange for his transfer to the city in the belief that a favor to him will redound to their benefit. Scene 5 portrays the visit to the state farm of Sun, chief of the municipal cultural bureau, to arrange for Li's transfer in the belief that he is a friend of Chang Hsiao-li and his father. His authority for this action is Wu, secretary of the Party municipal committee. Li Hsiao-chang himself has quietly returned to the farm to resume his actual identity and receive the transfer orders.

SCENE 5

The office of the Director of the Hai-tung State Farm is in a state of complete disarray. Every utensil used at work or in the office seems to be set out of place in some improbable location. A aging silk banner hangs on the battered wall near the floor. A broken broom has been tied onto a light switch cord. It seems certain that any order emanating from such an office as this cannot have much effect, and probably no sooner does it get past the door than it dies an early death. Several tufts of grass sprouting arrogantly at the corners of the room have a symbolic significance. Through them the audience can thoroughly conjure up the sort of spectacle the farm fields present.

As the curtain rises Director Cheng *enters carrying a canister of pesticide spray on his back. He then sits despondently on top of a desk and drinks wine.*

[Youth A *enters, running*]

Youth A Director Cheng!

Cheng What is it?

Youth A [*Taking out a telegram, with a sad face*] My grandmother is critically ill! A telegram came from home, asking me to return immediately!

Cheng What's her illness?

Youth A Cancer!

Cheng Don't try to scare people, okay? If you want time off then ask for time off. What's the point of crying that your grandmother has cancer!

Youth A But she really does have cancer!

Cheng So, you're not a doctor. If you go back will that cure her cancer? If it will cure her cancer, then when I get cancer I won't go to the hospital. I'll come and see you every day instead, and all the cancer cells will vanish.

Youth A [*Pleadingly*] Director Cheng!

Cheng All right, all right. Have you spoken with your company commander?

Youth A The company commander's father is ill. He went home a few days ago.

Cheng And the assistant company commander?

Youth A The assistant company commander's mother is ill. He just left yesterday afternoon.

Cheng How come everybody is ill? Oh, yes, they've probably all caught a contagious disease. All right, how many days do you want?

Youth A That depends on when my grandmother is cured.

Cheng When you have a relative like this who's ill, they never get cured quickly. It will take at least half a month, at most half a year. So how many days do you want?

Youth A A month, to start with.

Cheng Okay. Leave the telegram here.

Youth A Director Cheng, you're all right!

[Youth A *exits gaily on the run.* Youth B *enters, running*]

Youth B Director Cheng!

Cheng Is your father ill?

Youth B No, no.

Cheng Then is your mother ill?

Youth B No. My older sister is getting married. Here— [*Taking out a letter*] —a letter just arrived.

CHENG Do you want to ask for time off to go back?

YOUTH B Uh-huh.

CHENG If you don't go back then your sister will refuse to marry her fiancee, is that it?

YOUTH B No, no, no. I want to attend the wedding!

CHENG Have you talked with your company commander?

YOUTH B The company commander's brother is getting married and he's gone to attend the wedding.

CHENG And the assistant company commander?

YOUTH B His sister got married and he hasn't come back yet.

CHENG Good. The contagious disease is over with and everyone's back to collective weddings. How many days do you want?

YOUTH B Not many. Just a week.

CHENG All right. Leave the letter here.

YOUTH B Oh, Director Cheng! I'll bring you some of the wedding sweets when I come back!

[*Without looking up,* DIRECTOR CHENG *dismisses* YOUTH B *with a wave of his hand, and* YOUTH B *exits, running. With mournful nostalgia* DIRECTOR CHENG *hums a tune from the era of "Resist America Aid Korea." The sound of an automobile horn is heard from a distance, and* DIRECTOR CHENG *leans out the window to take a look. The sound of brakes is heard, and after a moment,* BUREAU CHIEF SUN *enters*]

CHENG I've been expecting you for days now. I just knew you'd be back.

SUN Good grief, are you drinking?

CHENG What about it—would you like a shot or two?

SUN You're drinking on the job. Maybe you're not worried about creating a bad impression, but I am.

CHENG There you go again putting on the straight-arrow act! What do you mean "on the job"? At this point there isn't any job to do! Take a look out the window at those fields. Who is there on the job? Who's working? Come on, come on. Have a drink!

SUN [*Taking a swig while he talks*] Then you shouldn't be drinking. You should be going around to each company, working on their ideology, immersing yourself among the masses!

CHENG The masses? They're all gone with the wind, back to the city: to replace their parents at factories, or by transfer orders, or through back-door connections. They've all been let go.

SUN What are you complaining about? You can thank your own mismanagement for this!

CHENG Mismanagement? You try managing this place. Yes, I'll abdicate, and if you'll take over I'll kowtow at your feet.

SUN All right, you've made your point. [*He produces the order written by Secretary Wu and hands it to* CHENG] Here!

CHENG [*Takes it, then reacts with a start*] So Secretary Wu has actually put an order in writing?

SUN Before I came here I also went over to the labor bureau and used this to get a transfer order from them. So let's hurry up and get Li

Hsiao-chang and his files transferred out of here. Secretary Wu says the sooner the better.

CHENG But it can't be done. You've just missed the boat.

SUN What do you mean?

CHENG The Party committee here has decided that for the present we're at a stage of reviewing the whole problem of transfers for educated youth. We have to make every effort to narrow down the battlefront on back-door connections. So the decision is that for the last half of this year the roster of people getting out through the back door is limited to no more than twenty.

SUN Secretary Wu's taking over this case does not count as back-door connections!

CHENG Aiya, my dear old Sun, don't be embarrassed. [*Giving Secretary Wu's note a shake*] This is a back-door connection through and through, one hundred percent!

SUN You've got nerve saying the Party municipal secretary uses back-door connections.

CHENG Why, there are heads of ministries and members of the Central Committee who use the back door, let alone a municipal committee secretary!

SUN You're drunk! This is not using the back door!

CHENG It *is* using the back door!

SUN It *isn't!*

CHENG It *is!*

SUN It *isn't!*

CHENG It *is!*

SUN It absolutely is not. We didn't go to Chang for favors, he came to us! [*Realizes his slip*] Ah, no, that's not it. That's not what I mean. I'm drunk too. All right, all right. What do you think, is there any way to work this out?

CHENG Not unless you cut someone else from the list.

SUN What do you mean cut someone else from the list? You mean seriously reconsider their status. Let me see the list.

CHENG [*Handing a roster to SUN*] The names of the twenty people are all at the top. Whom do you want to drop?

SUN [*Pointing on the roster*] What about this one?

CHENG Can't cut him. He's a nephew of Feng, the chief of staff for the regional garrison!

SUN Whew! [*Pointing on the roster*] This one?

CHENG The daughter of a nephew of the sister of the vice-minister of health.

SUN Look at this slug! [*Pointing at the roster*] What about that one?

CHENG Son of the son-in-law of a cousin of the vice-premier.

CHENG This just gets heavier and heavier! [*Pointing on the roster*] Is this one also related to a high-level cadre?

CHENG No, not a high ranking one.

SUN Oh, terrific!

CHENG But that's no good, either. She's the girl friend of the son of the farm's party committee secretary.

SUN Oh, well, aren't there any related to ordinary cadre . . .

CHENG [*Pointing on the roster*] This one. His father is the eighth assistant bureau chief of the housing bureau.

SUN An assistant bureau chief, and the eighth, at that? That's the one, all right. Ask him to be patient till next year, and put Li Hsiao-chang in his place. How about it?

CHENG [*With a wry smile*] Sure. An eighth assistant bureau chief naturally ought to give way to a party municipal committee secretary. The higher the rank, the greater the privileges. Privilege. If you have power, then you have privileges to go with it. This is what some people hold to be true, and it's been proven through practice and experience!

SUN So it's settled.

CHENG [*Opening drawers and taking out files*] Li Hsiao-chang's dossier, his ration documents, his change of residence certificate: they're all here. Take them.

SUN Oh! So you already arranged all the departure procedures for him?

CHENG With all this high rank and strong backing can I afford not to bend with the breeze?

SUN So you were putting me on after all?

CHENG No. I've been waiting for an order from the Party municipal committee secretary.

SUN [*Picking up the dossier and other materials*] You're going to get in touch with Li Hsiao-chang now and let him go as soon as possible, aren't you?

CHENG Fine. I'll call him right now. [*Picks up the telephone receiver*] I want the 57th Company. [*Pause*] 57th Company?—Is this Company Commander Ch'en? This is Cheng. Is Li Hsiao-chang there in your unit?—He just came back at noon today? No, don't criticize him, he's leaving right away!—Transferred, back to the city, right! What? You don't approve? Well good, so we still have a little of the old spirit of rebellion!—What—you're asking if it's all according to proper procedure? Using the back door? Hold on a minute. [*He hands the receiver to* SUN] Here, would you answer him, please!

SUN [*Taking the receiver, slightly tipsy*] Hello. You're asking who I am? I'll tell you; I'm the Party municipal committee secretary—

CHENG [*Surprised*] You're the municipal committee secretary?

SUN Secretary's deputy!

CHENG Oh . . . that's really enough to scare the daylights out of them!

SUN That's right! You're asking if it's according to proper procedure? I can tell you for a certainty that it isn't—

CHENG Huh?

SUN —in any way a violation of proper procedure.

CHENG Huh!

SUN Everyone knows that for cadres to have special privileges and use the back door is legal—

CHENG What?

SUN —is all a Gang of Four line.

CHENG Okay. Enough. Enough. I'll take it. [*Taking the phone receiver out of* SUN*'s hand*] Ch'en, old man, the municipal committee secretary has written an order, specifying that he wants Li Hsiao-chang transferred immediately—Right, right. You want to turn it down? That's all very well, only I'm afraid we can't!—Go tell Li Hsiao-chang to get up to headquarters. Right, and immediately! [*He hangs up*] Do you want to wait for him and take him back with you?

SUN No, if he has packing to do and so on how long would I have to wait for him? I'll go now. Actually I seem to be a bit drunk. No, no, I'm not, no I'm not! See you.

CHENG See you. You know the way out. [SUN *exits. After a moment the car is heard starting up.* CHENG *looks out the window at the departing* SUN. *He shakes his head and goes back to drinking. Suddenly he reaches for a piece of paper on the desk and hastily jots something down on it*]

[CHANG HSIAO-LI *enters, having reassumed his original identity as* LI HSIAO-CHANG. *First he cautiously looks the building over inside and out and then enters. Now from the way he talks and acts it is clear he is once again his old self*]

LI [*With more than a hint of wit*] Li Hsiao-chang, 57th fighter of the 57th Company firmly struggling for the glory of the Hai-tung Farm, reporting as ordered!

CHENG So you're Li Hsiao-chang?

LI The real thing in person, I can guarantee you. Height, one meter seventy-six. Weight, 66 kilograms. Age, 26 *sui*. And in just 66 days . . .

CHENG What?

LI It will be the eighth anniversary of my struggle at Hai-tung Farm. Let me join you in a toast now.

CHENG Cut the act. No need to pretend you're such a jovial guy. You've been miserable all along.

LI Good for you, Director Cheng, you're discerning.

CHENG Has your company commander told you? You've got a transfer.

LI I heard something like that.

CHENG We've carried out all the procedures for you. I've given Bureau Chief Sun your file and verification documents to take with him. You're free to leave our farm.

LI Thank god.

CHENG Should I offer my congratulations to you, or should I express my envy?

LI [*Puzzled*] Your envy?

CHENG [*In bitterness laced with alcohol*] Why not? The farm has been a failure. It's been a waste of land, and . . . and yes, it's been a waste of your youth, for all of you. So . . . so everyone just wants to get out and forget it. And each time one more person goes I . . . I just can't take it. It's as if I owed you a debt. But then what else . . . what else is there for me to do? Even the secretaries of municipal committees . . . even municipal committee secretaries are pulling rank and using their influence. They don't care about the farm . . . they don't care. How are we supposed to devote ourselves to the revolution any more? It's hopeless no matter what we do. Now it's not . . . it's not just you young people on the farm who want to get out through the back door . . . even the cadres . . . the cadres who run these farms, don't they want to pull strings and get out, too?

LI [*Not without sympathy*] And you?

CHENG Mi—miserable. [*Points to the wine*] This here is what I rely on to forget, to find release. I want to make something of this farm, but the way things are it's absolutely impossible. If things go on like this, then I . . . I don't want to rot here any more either. The way I'm going, the more I feel I'm . . . I'm just about fed up.

LI [*Surprised*] So you want to get out too?

CHENG [*Aggrieved*] Put in a memo . . . for a transfer order. There is a son of a high-level cadre; Chang Hsiao-li is his name. You know him, don't you? Ask him . . . to help me . . . to put in a word for me with the municipal committee secretary, and have me transferred.

LI [*Nonplussed*] But . . . but how can I do that?

[YOUTH A *enters*]

CHENG Why not . . . why can't you do it? [*Producing the note written by Secretary Wu*] Ask him, if he can write an order to transfer you, why can't he write an order to transfer me? [*Picking up the transfer request statement which he has just written*] Here's my . . . request for transfer, based on two reasons: The first, my grandmother has cancer; the second, my sister is getting married!

[CHENG *hands the transfer request to* LI, *who stands motionless in stupefaction. Abruptly,* CHENG *withdraws it, shakes his head in sadness, then waves* LI *out the door.* LI *exits. Slowly and vehemently* CHENG *tears the transfer request to shreds.* YOUTH A, *standing behind* CHENG, *slowly tears up his leave request form*]

[*Curtain*]

SCENE 6 AND EPILOGUE (SUMMARY)

Li Hsiao-chang is finally exposed as an imposter and brought to trial for fraud. Although admitting his guilt at the trial, he challenges the witnesses against him with the reminder that if he were really the son of a high-ranking cadre, then all the special favors and arrangements for him and all his actions to gain them would have been legal, normal behavior for members of society's elite.

Yang Mu

Wu Feng

Translated by Cissie Kwok and Yang Mu

Cast of Characters

ANG-LIN, a Taiwanese tribesman, aged 26
TU-LU-WAN-TO, a tribesman, aged 27
TA-NAO-AN, a tribesman, aged 22
OLD TRIBESMAN A, aged 65, blind
OLD TRIBESMAN B, aged 60
PO-TI-LUN, a tribesman, aged 21
WU FENG, a Chinese liaison interpreter appointed by the Ch'ing government, aged 71[1]
HSIU-KU, a girl of the tribe, aged 18
YI-FENG, an apprentice to the shaman, aged 14
SHAMAN, a tribesman, aged 65
A dozen young tribesmen

Time

The eighth to the tenth day of the eighth month, in the thirty-fourth year of of the reign of Ch'ien-lung is the Ch'ing dynasty (1769). It has been over a century since Chinese of the previous dynasty invaded and colonized Taiwan.

Place

The mountain known as A-li-shan in Taiwan.

ACT I

Scene 1

The eighth day of the eighth month, afternoon till sunset; in front of Wu Feng's house. Enter ANG-LIN and TU-LU-WAN-TO.

ANG-LIN Plague. I say it's the plague—
　　The god's rebuke on A-li-shan. Moaning,
　　Everywhere moaning, and the smell of death,

The grieving and the shrieking. Oh! Tu-lu-wan-to,
I cannot stand any more of it.

TU-LU-WAN-TO Cannot stand any more! Look,
Here is Wu Feng's home. Ang-lin,
We must make the old man accept
What we're asking for; it's not so much
To ask for, a simple request . . .

[TA-NAO-AN *and about ten other young tribesmen enter in single file from left and right*]

TU-LU-WAN-TO Look, Ta-nao-an and the others have come—
It's a small and simple thing to ask for, we
Must make Wu Feng understand: for the
Thousand lives of A-li-shan
Why can't we sacrifice the life
Of a man, just one man—
With no name.
It's not so much to ask for: a head,
The head of an outlander with no name.
Besides, the god is angry.
You've been through many villages and forests
And you've seen plague everywhere, haven't you?
The god is really angered.

THE YOUNG TRIBESMEN He is angered!

TA-NAO-AN Ang-lin, Tu-lu-wan-to,
I've climbed plenty of mountains, crossed
Plenty of streams to gather these men,
The true hunters, respected fighters.
But you can hardly imagine
How shaken, bewildered they were. Some of them
Had just come back from the wilderness smeared with muck.
Their wet eyes looked like a leopard's,
Sparkling and suspicious, even foretelling,
Grimly foretelling their own destruction
—So frightened and dazed; they may be
True hunters and respected fighters but—
Some wandered empty-handed through the woods,
Lost in thought. They grabbed my arms
And said to me, "Oh, Ta-nao-an, we're better
Dead! Better to die like this than
Go hunting every morning and tread the dew
Only to see the game
Lying dead on the ground, or else
Hiding in caves, or already
Fleeing far away into the Misty
Mountain beyond, the farthest place!"

THE YOUNG TRIBESMEN Even in the water the fish,
Even the fish, died by the school in the water,

Turning up their disgusting white bellies.

YOUNG TRIBESMAN B Even the small millet crop has
    Withered in the smothering
    Bloodstained wind, and crumpled. Our crops . . .

ANG-LIN Plague. I say it's the plague,
    The god's rebuke on A-li-shan!
    Ta-nao-an, we're grateful to you for your trek through
    Mountains and streams to gather our
    Fighters. This is a difficult task.
    It has just begun . . .

    [*Enter two* OLD TRIBESMEN. *A is blind, led by* B *with a stick. They stand silently, listening*]

ANG-LIN We've said we'll meet here
    To begin a difficult task . . .

    [*Enter* PO-TI-LUN, *drawing close to the group*]

ANG-LIN Here comes Po-ti-lun, at the right time.
    Po-ti-lun is the most outstanding hunter,
    A fighter who commands respect. Let's hope
    He isn't an aged coward.

OLD TRIBESMAN A [*To* B] He said,
    He said we are cowards, didn't he?

PO-TI-LUN Ang-lin, Tu-lu-wan-to,
    You are my friends. And Ta-nao-an,
    You as well. I am your friend.
    A hunter's character is not to be
    Ridiculed. Ang-lin, we'd
    Like to hear you continue.

ANG-LIN Eh, we're about to begin
    A difficult task,
    An earth-shaking reform—
    All for the lives on A-li-shan, for
    Hopes, our tribe's present and future.
    For the sake of A-li-shan: life, hopes, future,
    We must change the present. Only by changing
    This unreasonable present can the plague be stopped.
    You must know, Ta-nao-an, what you see
    Is plague. In their eyes you see
    The hesitation and fear of the leopard; that is
    The shadow of death. And you,
    You see the color of the bellies of fish:
    That is the color of death. And you,
    You smell the bloodstained wind in the millet fields:
    That is the smell of death.

ALL YOUNG TRIBESMEN [*Softly*] Ah, death . . .

ANG-LIN A plague is here, now.

ALL YOUNG TRIBESMEN [*Softly*] Ah, plague . . .

ANG-LIN I know. All this

I know: death goes stealing in the night,
Killing our loved ones, killing
Beasts, fish, and crops. During the day
He is hiding, in the floating
Fish belly and the flaming bloodstained wind, hiding
In your eyes. Next it may be
Your turn to die, you, you, you . . .
He comes out in the night, silently
Floating into our valley. He has no
Fixed shape. He sweeps through
Over our roofs, spying—
While you are asleep, while
You think your lids have closed and
Shut him out, but actually not, never
—He has chosen you tonight.
It may be your turn tomorrow night, you,
You, till one day we all fall dead
Beneath the roof, among the woods, in the wilderness,
Until no one can bury your body
Because we will all be dead—even he . . . [*Pointing at* Wu
   Feng's *house*]
Cannot bury you; sooner or later he
Will be snatched away by the huge hands of death.
OLD TRIBESMAN A We all die, sooner or later.
   Ang-lin, I'm a blind old man, this
   I know. The moment we're born
   We're destined to die.
OLD TRIBESMAN B We're destined to die.
   I, too, was once a brave and agile hunter . . .
ANG-LIN It's wrong to die tomorrow; it's wrong to
   Die silently in bed!
   [*Sighing*] Hunters, hunters should die
   In combat—fighting boars or bears,
   Fighting wind, rain, and thunder,
   Fighting against the unreasonable present. And
   Death can be resisted. We're not supposed
   To sit on the ground sighing and waiting for death.
   The plague can be stopped.
PO-TI-LUN Ang-lin, you are a wise man,
   How do you think we should stop the plague?
TU-LU-WAN-TO Human sacrifice.
ANG-LIN Wait, Tu-lu-wan-to.
   Yes, we must resume the *ambush*.
   We must offer the god of A-li-shan
   The head of someone down the road.
OLD TRIBESMEN A *and* B [*Simultaneously*] The *ambush*?
ANG-LIN The god of A-li-shan is furious, but

He's been patient for forty-eight years.
Now he is furious.
To resist death, we must first repent, and pray to him
To protect us. Wu Feng cannot, he cannot
Protect us—to resist
Death, we must first challenge the present
Wu Feng insists upon. We have to hunt a man and,
With blood, drive away the dark plague.

THE YOUNG TRIBESMEN Yes, we have to kill a man.
Wu Feng will approve of our plan—
He loves us. Wu Feng is a good man,
Ang-lin is a good man too.

PO-TI-LUN Ang-lin, I've some doubt in you.
I don't share your views. Yes, death
May be coming and going at A-li-shan,
As you say, destroying our
Tribesmen. We're all mourning
And, as you say, perhaps
We don't have time even to mourn for ourselves.
But, I wonder very much, why
The god of A-li-shan should permit death to prevail,
To harm his people? Is it that
The god has died? I'm really afraid.
Is it that he's gone far away from us—
Gone far, since the first day
When we accepted Wu Feng; or perhaps
He never existed at all? Are we
Already forsaken by the god? Let's suppose
This is true, but how can we
Turn away from Wu Feng? He brings us up,
He heals us, and loves us. If
We've already lost the god of A-li-shan
And if we now reject Wu Feng, and so
Lose Wu Feng, we won't know
How lonely and helpless we'll be. I'm really afraid . . .

TA-NAO-AN That's what I'm thinking too. Is it that
The god of A-li-shan has died,
Or else how can he bear to see us suffer?
Can a deceased god be revived to protect me
With a head I chopped off someone down the road?

THE YOUNG TRIBESMEN Quite impossible!
We'd better believe in Wu Feng.
Wu Feng is a good man, he
Heals us. Wu Feng loves us.

ANG-LIN Oh! You blind cowards . . .

OLD TRIBESMAN A [*To B, in a low voice*] He—
He's really swearing at me this time.

ANG-LIN You think that I don't know Wu Feng,
That I don't know Wu Feng is a good man? More than you
I love him. I was born, delivered by him, to
A-li-shan. But I know
He's now lost the glow of wisdom
In the raging gusts of Death,
Wu Feng has turned into
A shivering weed, brittle like us,
And he is unable to save
Either us or himself.
I have a feeling that he
May die before we do
Because his will has collapsed.
We can no longer rely on him. We
Must change his ways, or else
Follow him to destruction. We
Must bring back the god of A-li-shan,
Repent before him, and make up
For the sins of these past forty-eight years.
He is our true patron saint.
We must offer him blood and show him
Our resolve to return to him.
THE YOUNG TRIBESMEN Ang-lin is asking us to choose a god.
But one may have died a long time ago,
And the other perhaps is soon to die.
ANG-LIN But there is one who has never died.
In his fury he has forsaken A-li-shan.
We must offer blood sacrifice to win him back.
But as for the other one? The other one is Wu Feng.
He is mortal. Wu Feng is no god . . .
[*A shower of rain. The stage gradually fades into darkness. The group exits, dispersed*]

Scene 2

The same setting, light shining from the windows. The stage brightens gradually. The rain lets up and finally stops. WU FENG enters, holding an umbrella, his clothes soaked.

WU FENG Now the rain has stopped, and yet
I am soaked, like a sacrifice. Home?
Why is this thatched earthen hut,
Why is it alone home?
A lifetime in the hills, woods, and streams,
The wind of A-li-shan, the rain, sunshine: all are my home.
But then why should I falter and hurry on my way?
Why am I compelled to struggle in the mud? Is it that
I do have fears? Can it be that I am

Honestly frightened by this raging downpour, afraid that it's
A warning by some spirit? Why should I
Come looking for a familiar shelter
In the security of books and tea fragrance?
[*The light in the house goes off*]
Ah, maybe it's not fear. I, Wu Feng,
I've always been true to myself, for so many years,
So then why do I waver and shudder in the face of a storm?
Time causes the *ka-dang* tree to grow, until
It stands upright in the sun, spreading over an expanse,
And unfurling its huge canopy of benevolence, yes,
In Weissnichtwo[2] . . .
But why should this be a Weissnichtwo?
Even though it's remote, once my long roots
Grasp the warmth of the earth, once they
Stretch out boldly, cutting through crags and springs
To reach into the source of life, then Weissnichtwo
Will come to know, I will come to know,
My homeland is the Weissnichtwo. Oh, earth!
I am always a son of A-li-shan,
Oh, yes, an aging son of A-li-shan—
Even older it seems than a knotty ka-dang tree.
Even so, I cannot out-silence the ka-dang,
Shedding leaves in the summer showers;
Trembling and shivering in the winter chills.
Never have I compromised. Footprints . . .
[*Examining the scattered footprints*]
Something has happened, happened
Here. Many things
Happen at A-li-shan— Is the old tree
Soon to be crushed by the wind and rain?
It is late summer now; yet it's as if
The frosty autumn of my life, or even
A severe winter, were at hand, like . . .
A tree, in due season, shedding its leaves, but still
Persevering with its eternal branches,
Waiting for the spring to sprout brightly
Fresh new leaves, even to shoot up
Toward the broad sky. This is not surrender,
This is respectful obedience—under the power of time—
Cognizance of the grandeur and vastness of time.
A great tree will, in no event, succumb to a sudden rain.
The rain in A-li-shan's summer would come and go
Swiftly—that's not my fear. What I fear is whether
Time, the irresistible time, perhaps,
Will sweep away my courage of persevering.
But I know, I will die in a sudden rain

If I can live in eternal time.
I am resisting.
[*Enter* Hsiu-ku *from the house*]

Wu Feng Hsiu-ku, look at this mud all over the ground, and
The scattered footprints. Did the kids come again?

Hsiu-ku Yes, they did. Oh, master,
My exhausted master, look at yourself,
Your clothes are wet through—
The wind and rain scare me.
Is some cruel force going to rule
Over our A-li-shan, our lives?
Why are you so pale and tired,
As if back defeated in a fierce combat?
Your opponent, who is he . . .

Wu Feng My opponent? For many years
It has never really occurred to me
That I too have a ruthless opponent.
Yes, there's a ruthless
Opponent—your frightened look says,
It says, there's a rain god at A-li-shan,
Who is my opponent—doesn't it?
You think that this storm
Is his snipe, don't you?

Hsiu-ku No, no. I don't think it is a snipe.
I don't believe in the rain god. I believe in you.

Wu Feng Neither do I believe in a rain god like this,
Even if one day I cannot believe myself.
Yet I should believe myself—
If rain is commanded by a god, it should
Always be a timely shower, floating lightly
As it falls, or even when it is a downpour,
It should be tender and peaceful.
Because a god is what he is for nothing but
Being tender and peaceful. The ancients say:
"God, pleased with the sacrifices, cares for and cherishes us"—
A raging and brutal force cannot be god—
Such wind and rain, the ruthless storm is not god.

Hsiu-ku But master, why are you,
Why are you so pale and weary? You're
Struggling to resist, I can see that.

Wu Feng I'm struggling to resist, good child,
I'm fighting. My enemy is
Time. Time presses me,
Threatens me, makes me feel I'm unable
To accomplish the self-appointed task of my life.

Hsiu-ku Oh, it's persecution by time, I understand,
The wind and rain originally are not fearful;

But can we resist time, brush aside
Time's huge net and jump into life's cycle
And in the struggle transcend time,
Defeat time?
WU FENG Do you mean sacrifice and eternity?
Sacrifice and eternity. Better than I
You read my mind: but
I only know that for love we sacrifice, and
Eternity lies beyond the realm of our concern. Perhaps
You've never thought of this. You're not
Disturbed by unnecessary worries. Fine, fine,
That is a youthful and optimistic spirit you have,
And I must learn from this spirit; never again
Should I worry about the future. I must finish
The task before me in this way. Hsiu-ku,
They came again, those young men, didn't they?
HSIU-KU Those agitated boys, yes:
Ang-lin, Tu-lu-wan-to, Ta-nao-an,
And others. They're all kind-hearted,
My kind-hearted tribesmen . . .
WU FENG And mine, too.
HSIU-KU They argued outside the house
About plague and death, about blood
And blood sacrifice, and then
Scattered in the rainstorm. I heard Po-ti-lun say
They've begun downhill to harass
The passing travelers. Sometimes they've threatened to kill,
And grudgingly backed off once they heard
The name Wu Feng. But I'm afraid
This is just the beginning, I'm afraid
Bloodshed won't be stopped so easily.
WU FENG Ah, Wu Feng, your name,
Like a leaf about to fall in the rain . . .
Hsiu-ku, you may go.
I'll be in right away to change.
[HSIU-KU exits]
WU FENG Ah, Wu Feng, a leaf about to fall in the rain.
That is your name,
A shuddering, shivering leaf.
You drifted over the ocean into the mountains, a tiny
Thing appended, weak and ignorant.
And a name being known and accepted
Is in fact a man's countenance—
No, not countenance—but his character,
Known and accepted by strangers. So
When they said, "I want Wu Feng,"
They chose me,
The persistence and the honesty I stand for.
Yes, the persistence and honesty that is basic to the conduct

Of us educated in tradition, and which
In this wilderness has become
Supreme integrity—so what they've chosen
Is an integrity common to all educated men in general,
The interweaving of the values tradition has taught,
Something abstract, which because of me seems to have
     become something one can hold on to.
But I am myself just a minute entity,
Appearing by chance in the stream of history,
Destined to grow and age at A-li-shan . . .
They've chosen a man who rises and falls in a moment,
And yet not me, not my name. Ah, Wu Feng,
Love is their pretext for choosing you—
But your name is your phantom
—Just as you are the towering shadow identified with
The educated of three thousand years.
How can you fail them and their
Love? Still less can you disgrace that lofty image—
Their belief, which is your belief.

[*He stands motionless. The stage gradually fades to blackout*]

Scene 3

The same setting, now evening, at the door of Wu Feng's house. Light is streaming through the windows.

[*Enter* ANG-LIN, TU-LU-WAN-TO, TA-NAO-AN, *and the young tribesmen, proceeding to the door of Wu Feng's house; enter* PO-TI-LUN; *enter* OLD TRIBESMEN A *and* B, *guiding each other with a stick.* ANG-LIN *walks to the door, looks back and gestures to the others; the others gesture their agreement. All are silent*]

ANG-LIN [*Tapping on the door*] Master, teacher!

[*No response.* ANG-LIN *turns his head to the others. The group seems to stir a little*]

ANG-LIN [*Knocking at the door, slightly louder this time*]
     Teacher, teacher,
     [*Louder still*] Teacher, Wu Feng, Wu Feng . . .

OLD TRIBESMAN A [*To* B] What a beast! How can he call Teacher by his name?

ANG-LIN [*In a loud voice*] Wu Feng, open the door . . .

[PO-TI-LUN *steps forward, trying to stop him. The door opens. Enter* HSIU-KU]

HSIU-KU Ang-lin, you're too rowdy!
     Since when have you lost your manners?
     Though you're a brave hunter, a warrior of A-li-shan,
     Your voice's like that of a sulky boar,
     Trapped in its own fantasy. You—
     You should feel ashamed. Po-ti-lun,
     Are you one of them?

Po-ti-lun I, I'm not.

I've come to stop him from disturbing Teacher.

Hsiu-ku Teacher is taking care of a patient.

[*To* Ang-lin] You come with me.

[Hsiu-ku *turns back, and exits through the house.* Ang-lin *follows timidly. The door remains open. The others stand still outside, like statues. The stage is in dead silence. The light in the house gradually brightens, shining through the window and spilling out from the door. At times it flickers. About three minutes later,* Wu Feng*'s voice is heard behind the door*]

Wu Feng You know killing is sin.

[*On the stage, the people move again, turning to the door together. Enter* Wu Feng, *followed by* Ang-lin *and* Hsiu-ku]

Wu Feng Floods may kill people, earthquakes

And mountain fires may kill people, these are

Heaven and earth's cruelties; beasts may kill people,

Thugs may kill people, and selfish and greedy

Officials may kill people—these we can still

Bravely resist. . . . How can we join in

Heaven and earth's slaughter and rascals' ravage?

All these years, I've always been

Advising you that the bright world of

Life relies on our willing courage

To construct and embrace. Love alone is everything.

Ang-lin The god of A-li-shan is furious.

Teacher, the god doesn't love us.

Wu Feng He who loves us not is no god.

The selfish and greedy are not god. You must know:

When a ruler cheats and oppresses us,

He'll be overthrown and driven to dust. That's what's meant

When the ancients say, "Heaven's mandate is not to be slighted."

If there is a god of A-li-shan,

He must love you, protect you.

He has no reason to be angry.

Tu-lu-wan-to We aren't offering sacrifice.

Surely he has reason to be angry.

Wu Feng Tu-lu-wan-to, my good child,

Who says we aren't offering sacrifice? Haven't we

For all seasons offered livestock and the five grains,

Following the precept created by our ancestors,

Praying for peace on A-li-shan?

Besides, each year we offer

A skull to worship him; and, already,

Already it's been forty-eight years . . .

Old Tribesman A [*Raising his voice*] Forty-eight years,

Yes, it's been forty-eight years. I still remember

The last man-hunt. Oh, those bloody days!

Luckily our Teacher came to A-li-shan.

It's Wu Feng who delivered A-li-shan . . .

ANG-LIN Old skulls do not count.
We've been cheating the god, cheating him
For forty-eight years; therefore, he's grown angry
And sent down the dark mist of death; therefore,
Plague prevails at A-li-shan.

WU FENG Plague we can resist.
Tomorrow at dawn, we will mobilize all the villages
To dispose of the decaying corpses and garbage at A-li-shan.
I'll heal the ill, in my years,
I'll heal A-li-shan.
I tell you, Ang-lin, the plague and sacrifice
Have nothing whatever to do with any god.

ANG-LIN Plague is the god's punishment upon us.
Teacher, I can no longer believe you—
How can you, by yourself alone, heal
All the patients at A-li-shan? I am
A hunter of A-li-shan, they too.
The thing you can't do, we
Must do with our own effort, and do it
In our ancestors' way. We have to resume
The true sacrifice, we have to ambush and get a man.

OLD TRIBESMAN A *and* B [*Simultaneously*] Oh,
Oh, those bloody days!

TU-LU-WAN-TO We have to kill a man.
We must use a human head for sacrifice.

TA-NAO-AN Use a human head, oh, human head.
We must kill a man, to save A-li-shan.

THE YOUNG TRIBESMEN Right, right,
We should save A-li-shan, or else
Tomorrow we'll die . . .

YOUNG TRIBESMAN A Among the branches in the woods.

YOUNG TRIBESMAN B On the dews in the plains.

YOUNG TRIBESMAN C Over the cold streams.

YOUNG TRIBESMAN D In the withered millet fields.

ANG-LIN We cannot rely on you any more,
Teacher, old teacher, we've decided
To do it our way.
[*Turning to the group*]
He cannot help us any more,
Only we can help ourselves.
Now everything is settled,
Isn't it? Let's go!
When the moon rises tonight,
Let's meet in the *ka-dang* field.

[*The group applauds and disperses. The old tribesmen hesitantly
sigh, and exit, one leading the other slowly.* WU FENG *stands still,*

looking into the distance. PO-TI-LUN, *leaving, takes a look at* WU FENG *and* HSIU-KU, *then sits on a rock, feeling lost. He stands up again, walking toward* WU FENG]

PO-TI-LUN Master.

WU FENG Don't worry, they aren't going to kill.
  I trust them. A-li-shan's
  Children, my good children,
  They will come back to me.
  I'll find them a road,
  A broad way of love and light. You know,
  Po-ti-lun, you, Hsiu-ku, all of
  You, all are children I delivered at birth—
  Ang-lin, Tu-lu-wan-to, Ta-nao-an.
  I saw you come into this world, one by one,
  So tender and lovely, like lambs,
  And so full of curiosity, and your cries were loud and clear,
  Your eyes darker and prettier than those of the people downhill.
  This shows that you, my children,
  Were born to be shrewd hunters,
  Smarter and faster than leopard cats;
  And, your lips are thicker than theirs.
  This means that you are simple and honest;
  Your mouths open wider than those of the people in town—
  You are children skilled in singing.
  I watched you play on slopes and streams, calling me
  "Teacher." I taught you to read and calculate,
  For all of you I've prescribed medicine.
  And you've all grown up through hardship.
  Yet I cannot let you
  Grow up and go down the hill to kill.

HSIU-KU I have to stop them.
  I won't let the hunt happen.
  Po-ti-lun, tonight at moonrise, are they
  To meet and start out from the ka-dang field?
  You and I must stop them.
  This is our duty.

PO-TI-LUN I don't know. I'm afraid.
  I don't have enough power to stop them.
  When a person has smelt blood,
  Especially when he's lost his reason,
  He is like a wounded beast—oh, when one loses his reason
  Isn't he like a beast which, mad from its wound,
  Rampages in panic? And their reason?
  I fear that they're rejecting the guidance of reason,
  And are, instead, searching and seeking, following
  The odor of blood, fumbling, yet self-confident that all is for
  The lives of our A-li-shan, for love—

Ang-lin believes that for the lives of many, many others
He can sacrifice the life of *one* other . . .
HSIU-KU Teacher, did you hear what Po-ti-lun said?
WU FENG I heard it all. For
The lives of many many others,
Sacrifice the life of *one* other.
Why not for the lives of many many others,
Sacrifice one's own life? Po-ti-lun,
You're a thoughtful and understanding boy.
You'll run into many obstacles in your life.
I know you'll be courageous in judging, and
Courageous in declaring your judgment. Don't
Be afraid. Tonight at moonrise, they meet in
The field of ka-dang; that's only
A ritual prayer before the ambush. They, oh!
Their soul will for a while be entrusted
To the bewildering shaman. Oh my children,
My poor children! But I reckon, I believe
They won't go downhill until noon tomorrow,
And I believe, before going down the hill
They'll come back and ask me for permission—
They hope I'll agree with them, so that
All the responsibilities will rest on Wu Feng:
It's Wu Feng who kills, not my children.
HSIU-KU We know you won't permit it,
You will never agree with them.
WU FENG Now we can't discuss these problems.
Po-ti-lun, you and Hsiu-ku go tonight to
The ka-dang field, and stop them with good brotherly words.
You're a thoughtful person, don't be afraid
To declare your judgment before them. Also
I want to give you an important task:
At noon tomorrow, before they go downhill,
In case they don't come to seek my permission,
Your duty is to excite them, make them
Come to me first—a minute delayed
Is a minute gained. You understand?
PO-TI-LUN I understand, teacher.
WU FENG Good. Hsiu-ku, come with me.
We must heal the patients.
[*Exit* WU FENG. HSIU-KU *follows him to the door, then turns round
and looks at* PO-TI-LUN *affectionately. She steps forth to him, holds
his hand, and soon lets it go. She walks to the door, exit.* PO-TI-LUN
*paces up and down. The light suddenly goes off. The curtain quickly
falls*]

ACT II

Scene 1

The night of the eighth day of the eighth month. In the open fields, with a ka-dang tree to one side. The curtain goes up. The stage is very dark. In a moment the clouds disperse and a crescent moon appears. The stage brightens gradually. YI-FENG, *an apprentice shaman, enters.*

YI-FENG [*Sings*]

Old ka-dang, old ka-dang,
You be the sky and I be the wind.
Up in the morning chopping wood,
Back in the evening pounding rice.
Out to fish while sister cooks.
Into the river clear and swift,
Deep the swirl and fathomless.
In the river so clear, in the river so swift,
The current is deep and fathomless.
Down so deep, how will I catch the little fish?
So I ask the sun as it goes to set
To put in its leg to test its depth.
He says it's seven foot seven and more,
Then slips and slides to the bottom of the swirl.

Old ka-dang, old ka-dang,
You are the grandpa of A-li-shan.
You're our screen from sun in spring,
You're our shelter from rain in fall.
While sister weaves I draw a bow.
The bow is too heavy, the arrow's too light.
The knife has no point, the spear is not right.
When it comes to these weapons I've got no skills.
"You're stupid," say people, "How can you fight
With those big bears that roam in the hills?"
So the drunken old guru takes me in,
To dance and sing and catch ghosts wandering.
Old ka-dang,
You're not the sky and I'm not the wind.

[YI-FENG *dances alone, changing the rhythm of "Old ka-dang" to a dance. The autumn wind whistles, the shadows of trees and* YI-FENG'S *dancing blend. The dance stops.* YI-FENG *is tired and rests on the ground. Suddenly drums are heard, distant and mysterious.* YI-FENG *is startled and stands up*]

YI-FENG Drums, where are they?

Oh, yes, the hunters' drums.
[*A trumpet sounds*]
    The hunters' trumpet, someplace
    Far away. I, someplace far away,
    Waiting—waiting for what?
    I wish I were a traceless wind,
    Homeless and nameless,
    Sweeping over the water, drifting toward
    The dark, strange woods. Without childhood,
    Without memory, like wind,
    Sweeping the cultivated land, drifting,
    Drifting down the hill, drifting to the seas,
    Drifting to a place where they don't know me.
[*Drums and trumpets sound intermittently*]
    They all know me, Ang-lin and the rest,
    Tu-lu-wan-to, Ta-nao-an, and guru
    And Po-ti-lun, and Hsiu-ku
    And also Wu Feng, and
[*Sings*]
    Old ka-dang, old ka-dang,
    You be the sky and I be the wind.
[*He rises, dances and sings. The drums and trumpets sound intermittently*]
    Up in the morning chopping wood,
    Back in the evening pounding rice.
    Out to fish while sister cooks.
    Into the river clear and swift . . .
    [*A young tribesman enters. He squats and watches the dance. Ten or so tribesmen enter one by one before* YI-FENG *finishes his dance. They sit or squat here and there; some lying down or standing, and forming a part of* YI-FENG's *dance*]
    Deep the swirl and fathomless.
    In the river so clear, in the river so swift,
    The current is deep and fathomless.
    Down so deep, how will I catch the little fish?
[*All the young tribesmen have appeared on the stage. They softly sing the dance song*]
    So I ask the sun as it goes to set
    To put in its leg to test its depth.
    He says it's seven foot seven and more,
    Then slips and slides to the bottom of the swirl.

    Old ka-dang, old ka-dang,
    You are the grandpa of A-li-shan.
    You're our screen from sun in spring,
    You're our shelter from rain in fall.
    While sister weaves I draw a bow.

The bow is too heavy, the arrow's too light.
The knife has no point, the spear is not right.
When it comes to these weapons I've got no skills.
"You're stupid," say people, "How can you fight
With those big bears that roam in the hills?"
So the drunken old guru takes me in,
To dance and sing and catch ghosts wandering.
Old Ka-dang,
You're not the sky and I'm not the wind.

[*The dance and the music stop.* YI-FENG *sits under the tree and rests.*
The autumn breeze is heard. ANG-LIN, TU-LU-WAN-TO, *and* TA-NAO-AN
enter]

ANG-LIN Under this moonlight, anything
    Can happen. All of us are here.
    Po-ti-lun alone hasn't come—
    Recently I've had my doubts about him.
TU-LU-WAN-TO Po-ti-lun is our
    Good brother; he's been brave and a
    Delightful companion. No need to doubt him.
    Of course I've also noticed these days
    His eyes have an unusual look, always
    A tender light sparkling in anxiety,
    Like a robin's feathers in spring,
    When they're flaunting themselves,
    Flying openly in the sun.
    Yet there's some shyness, a fear that someone
    Discerns his deep feelings. I think
    Po-ti-lun is in love, in love with
    Hsiu-ku, the pretty, clever girl.
TA-NAO-AN A person in love is never
    An ordinary person, his actions
    Are always a bit different, but all these
    We can understand and excuse.
[YI-FENG *silently walks to the group*]
YI-FENG A person in love is never
    An ordinary person. Do you want
    To hear me sing a not-so-ordinary song?
    [*Sings*] On the cascade cliff is a lily . . .
    [*Speaks*] The lily is a simile.
THE YOUNG TRIBESMEN We like similes.
YI-FENG [*Singing and dancing slowly*]
    On the cascade cliff is a placid, white lily.
    Through the thundering water I silently row.
    From the flood-ravaged hamlet I have come up the river.
    Toward the mountainous inlet my boat sets its will.
    Searching the cause for god's fury,

Going upstream, I've questions to ask him . . .

TA-NAO-AN That's an unusual song,
Yi-feng, I don't know what you're singing about.

YI-FENG You wouldn't since you're not in love.
Ang-lin will surely know.

[*He sings and dances slowly*]
On the cascade cliff is a placid, white lily . . .

ANG-LIN I don't know either, Yi-feng,
Don't sing any more. The moon has risen
Very high. We're busy tonight.
We can't listen to you sing.
Where's your guru?

YI-FENG Guru is sleeping at home.
He's drunk sleeping at home.

ANG-LIN Go and invite him here, invite him
To the field under the ka-dang tree.

YI-FENG Guru is drunk sleeping.
If Yi-feng wakes him up,
He'll beat Yi-feng with a large club.

ANG-LIN Don't be afraid, go and wake him up,
Tell him Ang-lin has an important task for him.
After it's done there'll be a pot of wine for him.

YI-FENG All right, I'll go.
I'll go and wake him. When his eyes open,
I'll say at once, "Ang-lin has wine,
A pot of wine for you to drink in the field
Under the ka-dang tree." Then
Guru won't beat Yi-feng.

[*Singing*] On the cascade cliff is a lily . . .

[ANG-LIN *waves his hands;* YI-FENG *dances off stage. Enter* OLD TRIBES-
MAN *B, leading A. Both are hesitant and uneasy. They sit down smoking
in silence*]

ANG-LIN [*To himself*] In this desolate night,
With some doubts, but endless
Courage—we wish to change the present,
Resuming an ancient sacrificial rite,
The gem of our ancestors' great wisdom,
To prove that wisdom, as we show it
By acting in accordance with the set rite,
Will lead us away from the black disaster,
Will open our hearts, and secure peace
Not only for us, but also for our descendants.
Therefore, this is not only a resumption, but a creation.
We admit that our ancestors' souls exist forever,
Guiding us to choose a safe path.
Yes, there's some doubt.
A cool autumn wind blows in my heart, which
Can't help shivering a little,

Like the old ka-dang leaves shaking,
Indifferent, as if without any passion or love.
All these seem to point at dejection,
A flaw. I can't help worrying,
Fearing that this autumn moon will never be full.
[*Enter* YI-FENG, *dancing*]

ANG-LIN You're back, Yi-feng. Where's the guru?

YI-FENG Guru's come too. He got drunk,
Lying on a wooden bed snoring.
I woke him up, saying:
[*Singing*] On the cascade cliff is a lily.
Now there's a ghost Ang-lin asks you to catch . . .

He turned and got up, grabbing a club to beat me.
I said immediately, "Guru, don't beat me.
Ang-lin's inviting you to drink under the ka-dang tree."
He then came with me.
[*The* SHAMAN *staggers in*]

YI-FENG Look, here he is, here he is,
Here is the drunken guru.
Ang-lin, give him wine.
I have to rest. [*Retires to the tree*]
I really have to rest. [*Resting against the tree, singing*]
Old ka-dang, old ka-dang,
You're not the sky 'n' I'm—not—the—wind.

ANG-LIN Guru, do you see the moon?
The moon is our witness.
Tomorrow we'll go man-hunting.
Do the dance of warriors for us!

SHAMAN [*Raising his voice*] Bring me wine—
[*Tu-lu-wan-to and Ta-nao-an come forth with wine and pour
it into a large gourd. The* SHAMAN *drinks. The wine is passed
around among the young tribesmen*]

OLD TRIBESMAN A Following the ancient rite they now drink.
Tomorrow they're really going man-hunting. Though
I can't see the moon, yet I know
The moon is of a bleak color.

OLD TRIBESMAN B Wu Feng won't allow it.
[*The wine is passed back to the* SHAMAN. *The drums rise, as does
the wind. The* SHAMAN *drinks without pause. Suddenly he dances to
the drums, at first slowly, then fast, and finally slows down. When he
dances slowly,* YI-FENG *is heard singing softly*]

YI-FENG [*Singing*]
The mountains are blue,
The green water long flowing.
The lost souls are wandering,
Passing the weeds, passing the clouds,

Lonely and gloomy like the bats.
The lost souls are very lonely,
Wandering in the dark.

OLD TRIBESMAN A [*Continuing the singing*]
The blue mountains wither,
The blue mountains decay,
The tears of A-li-shan flow with the water,
Flowing through my heart with drops of blood,
Regretting the courage for disaster.
The lost souls regret much,
Wandering in the dark.

[*The* SHAMAN *stops dancing. The drums gradually die down and then cease. All is silent. The clouds cover the autumn moon. The stage gradually darkens, and finally blacks out*]

Scene 2

The same setting. The stage brightens slightly. Those present in the last scene, except YI-FENG *and the* SHAMAN, *are all on the stage, standing motionless, like so many trees and rocks, in shadow. Enter* HSIU-KU *and* PO-TI-LUN.

PO-TI-LUN The hazy autumn moon
Can't testify to my love:
It's too weak, and cold, and unstable.
It may be an omen of sorrow.
Even so, whenever I'm by myself
I'll pour out my feelings to it.
Oh, Hsiu-ku, where do I find the nerve
To tell you this secret?

HSIU-KU [*Sighs*] Oh—

PO-TI-LUN This world naturally should be
A prettier and better world than it is.
Trees, streams, meadows, all these,
Singing, dancing, needlework, all these,
All belong to you. The untainted heart,
The unworried face like a morning flower,
The happiness I meet every day going into the mountains . . .

HSIU-KU Po-ti-lun, oh, Po-ti-lun,
You know how time after time I can't help
Bringing destruction on my own young heart. I,
I live in worries and fears—
Like a half-opened flower in the early sun,
Feeling in its roots a strange pain,
Forcing myself to close up in shyness. I,
I'm not willing to let my happiness show
Because I have felt the earth's shudder.
Distress unfolds its black veil before our eyes,

You know, in the convulsive sobs of our people.
When disaster stalks us everywhere
At A-li-shan, a flower in full bloom
Is more fate's mockery than anything else.
I don't have reason to be happy.

PO-TI-LUN You are the glory of our tribe.
Your heart is kind.
I know you're not one to chatter or boast;
You're always quietly hard at work for us all.
Your love is like the shyness of moonlight,
Shining everywhere on A-li-shan,
And shining on me too, Hsiu-ku.
Yet I can't help being so selfish,
That I'm like a greedy well, hoping
To possess every bit of your light
And have the serenity and the intimacy all to myself.

HSIU-KU Don't blame yourself, that's not selfishness.
It's the force of the heart's blood condensed,
Drawing to it what little warmth there is in life.
That is love. Don't I understand love?
Young and heedless, our blood surges
And rolls like a storm in our hearts.
I know love; I only wish
I were the moon hidden at the bottom of the well
But not exposed in heaven to invite the chatter of gossip.
But I can't escape, I can't hide,
I love our tribe, I love Wu Feng. Before the clash
Between life and death leads to greater darkness,
I must suppress my desire, and give a little light,
A little warmth to the whole A-li-shan.

PO-TI-LUN Hsiu-ku, you're the honor of
A-li-shan. I understand and respect you.

[PO-TI-LUN *draws near to* HSIU-KU. *They hold each other's hands,
standing close together. The lights suddenly go on, and the young
tribesmen are seen moving across the stage, pointing at the two, showing
their anger.* ANG-LIN *walks to the front*]

ANG-LIN Oh—oh—oh, Po-ti-lun,
Your courage is very doubtful,
Very doubtful.

TU-LU-WAN-TO Calm and secure like a well
Waiting for the moon to case its light. Is this
What a hunter should be? Plague is
Ravaging A-li-shan, our people are moaning,
Po-ti-lun is in love, in love with
Wu Feng's—

PO-TI-LUN Wu Feng's what?

[*The young tribesmen are taken aback, unable to answer*]

HSIU-KU Wu Feng's disciple. My mind and heart are in
    Great sorrow, because I'm Wu Feng's disciple.
PO-TI-LUN I'm lost and wavering, because
    I'm Wu Feng's disciple. I believe in
    Wu Feng more than in the senseless rain god.
ANG-LIN So you're defending Wu Feng
    You know how to choose, Po-ti-lun,
    So you've already chosen . . .
    The most clever warrior of A-li-shan,
    The hero in my mind—but you
    At this most crucial moment
    Have chosen another road.
TU-LU-WAN-TO You've chosen Wu Feng's road,
    Not to fight for the brightness of A-li-shan.
    I'm afraid you've already deserted the god.
    You've already deserted your tribe.
PO-TI-LUN Tribe, oh my tribe!
    Sometimes I am a lost cloud in the sky,
    Only that eternal thought, a summon,
    Encourages me, so that I am not disembodied,
    Dissolving into mist and dust. Sometimes
    I lose my direction among beasts and the storm.
    In the misty hollows, in the shady forest,
    I trace our ancestors' footprints,
    Searching for a return to my tribe—
    With only a scimitar I chop away all poisonous vines.
    On my way, carving out a heroic world. I bleed,
    Proudly spilling the blood of our tribesmen.
    All these I do to share our ancestors' heroic will,
    So that the hunters in the future, our sons and grandsons,
    Can, at times when they are lost,
    With more calm find a way home.
    I rely on my ancestors' spirit to defeat darkness.
    I offer every drop of my life to the hunters to come,
    My sons and grandsons. I want to enlighten their
    World. Perhaps you think I die in the present,
    But I live in the past, the present, and the future.
HSIU-KU You are my true hero,
    You've already enlightened my world,
    Po-ti-lun. And you will use your courage
    To enlighten the world of all our tribesmen—oh!
    Isn't that also our world?
    The world in which we live and in which we strive?
ANG-LIN We have only one world:
    Dark, ruined, moaning.
    This world is being punished by the god,
    Because we've been stupid, stumbling down a vain and empty
        path.

Wu Feng has usurped A-li-shan. Come,
Po-ti-lun, Hsiu-ku, the brightness of A-li-shan
Needs us to plan and create together.
But Wu Feng? Wu Feng's only a declining, failing
Old physician. Perhaps he can heal
A man, but he cannot heal the whole world.

PO-TI-LUN Ang-lin, my brother,
Your hotblooded nerve has clouded
Your superior judgment and your discerning heart.

[*Exit* PO-TI-LUN *and* HSIU-KU *slowly. The stage gradually darkens. The half moon is in the sky. The rest of the people are standing or squatting.* YI-FENG *enters as the light shines on him*]

YI-FENG [*Looking around at the shadows of the people*] Ang-lin,
Tu-lu-wan-to, Ta-nao-an, all of you,
You are all unhappy, unhappy men.
[*To the audience*]
They are all unhappy,
Unhappy men. Let me sing.
Let Yi-feng sing for the unhappy ones:
[*Singing*] Old ka-dang, old ka-dang,
You be the sky 'n' I be the wind.
Love breeds hate, the heart's perplexed.
Your brave will is to be cherished.
Light is too uncertain, now in the east,
Now in the west, glittering and marvelous.
Now in the east, now in the west,
Glittering and marvelous. How can I
Rely on you to set my mind at rest?
The long years are in your memory.
Suddenly you come to yourself. Old ka-dang,
Old ka-dang, what a pity I'm the lost wind.

[*The curtain slowly descends*]

ACT III

Scene 1

The ninth day of the eighth month. Early dawn, in front of Wu Feng's house. As the curtain rises dawn gradually brightens. WU FENG *has been sitting alone for some time. All is quiet except for the birds' chirping to the dawn. Enter* HSIU-KU *from inside the house. As she walks to the well to draw water she turns around and sees* WU FENG.

HSIU-KU [*Surprised*] Oh, master, you—
Why are you sitting out in the dew so early in the morning?
It's still not dawn, and the heaven seems to be holding
    back deliberately
Grudging us its true light.

WU FENG Hsiu-ku, my good child, don't be startled.
Soon, very soon,
The day will break.

HSIU-KU Have you been sitting here alone,
Sitting all alone through the dark night, the long
Dark night? How can you shoulder
This immense pressure by yourself? Besides,
I sense that phantoms are all around,
And countless spying eyes tormenting you.

WU FENG I've been sitting here a long time,
Alone, thinking, struggling with the night.
Some of the cold dew wet me.
But there are also stars suggesting
The mysteries of life, the moon inspiring love, and
The sun promising light within my heart.

HSIU-KU You're meditating.
I know you're searching for a way out
For A-li-shan. Oh, master, you are straining
Nerves that have grown old yet strong,
I know. The whole of A-li-shan
Is in your mind—but how abstract that is—
I know the indomitable ranges seem like
Your lofty forehead; though white hair
Caps it like snow in the winter,
Though wrinkles line it like drifting
Evening clouds, those ranges endure in all their dignity.
Still, in that austere gaze is love.

WU FENG Why is your faith so firm?
Sometimes I have doubts too, even
Wondering whether all I've done in my life
Is real or illusion.
I'm even afraid that perhaps
All along I've simply been walking
A devious, predestined road, dazzling
And perplexing, leading not only myself but others to death.

HSIU-KU All roads lead to death.
But I see beyond the sign of death,
Gloriously ringing, the new life and immortality,
With songs and praises that shake heaven and earth,
A never-ending beauty and richness.
These I've learned from your love and patience,
And your kindly sense of devotion.
Can there be something wrong in what I've said?

WU FENG No, nothing. We are born once
In ignorance into this world.
Through days of folly we learn to understand,
We learn to stand up and walk, we come to know plants,

We come to know insects, fish, birds, and beasts, and
In happiness and sorrow we come to know people.
We memorize some names well, yet forget again
Those names; but names are only illusions.
At last we understand life and death. True life
Must lead to true death, yet
Only with true death is there true life:
The realization complete, in the courage
Of affirmation we are born again.
[*The sky brightens*]

HSIU-KU I have never doubted
The life that you have stood for. That is
Hard work and more work. Yes,
It's a struggle through hardships of blood and tears.
I've never feared death.

[HSIU-KU *exits, carrying the water bucket.* WU FENG *is left alone on stage for a moment. The sun rises. The unceasing chirping of birds is heard.* HSIU-KU *enters, walking from the well*]

WU FENG When you're done drawing the water,
Sew me a red cap,
And a red cloak . . .

[*Taken aback,* HSIU-KU *stops and looks at* WU FENG]

WU FENG Finish it today before midnight.
The threads should be pulled close and tight.
Have it done before midnight.

HSIU-KU [*Perplexed*] Well, master,
I'll make the threads close and tight,
And have it done before midnight.

[HSIU-KU *draws some water, then exits. The sun shines down*]

WU FENG Deities of heaven and earth,
I, Wu Feng, have never wished to oppose you,
Because I have not dared to. I'm a weak,
Lonely old man, that is all.
In fact what I desire more than anything is peace,
To be allowed to rest in quietude. Often
In my dreams I return to the distant homeland
Of my childhood. The cities of China,
The trim attire of the scholars and officials,
Their self-important look, I know
I once admired with fascination.
But that was merely the shadow of knowledge,
The frame of learning rather than the true scope
That knowledge and learning open up.
Though I used to yearn for repose in the classics
And the comfort which they brought . . .
Only when I had drifted across the ocean and trekked
    into the hills

Did I, Wu Feng, discover—
Oh! How lucky I was to be able to discover—
The fortitude and grandeur of life
Towering like the verdant mountain chains,
And dazzling like the vast seas, the glistening seas.
In people's tears and laughter
Was my life steeped and exercised its strength;
Since then comfort has gone far away from me; and yet
Deities of heaven and earth,
I have always been mild and meek,
Haven't I? I read the books of the sages;
Of course, I know the words of the sages
Are intangible and evanescent.
When the mounted barbarians fought through the gate, the
    proud and incompetent
Monarch could do nothing but slay his own wife and daughter.
In the name of integrity (nothing but a concept,
Merely a trivial concept) he hanged himself
At Mei-shan, with the result
That the *huai*-tree was made a sinner;
That Ku Yen-wu closed his doors in shame, knives and ropes
Ready close by; that Wang Ch'uan-shan formulated his ideals;
That Chang Huang-yen died a martyr; Chu Shun-shui took
    to a raft and drifted on the ocean;
And Cheng Ch'eng-kung burned his scholar's attire
And mapped his strategy in Southern Taiwan—too late![3]
The classics make us hesitant and indecisive.
Brilliant concepts remained fixed, yet disasters in life
Are real. I came to understand the concern
The scholars claimed for the world is empty.
Words are their pathetic escape, while
I chose commitment to life to prove that the sages are
Not to blame; it's the critics who are stupid and blind . . .
Watch how I, Wu Feng, crossed the ocean to this small island,
Tracing the path of Cheng Ch'eng-kung—
By coming to the mountains to teach the barbarians
I did no less than Chu Shun-shui;
For bringing institutions to a primitive land,
Even Ch'uan-shan, were he to live again, would take me
    as his colleague.
If my ways should not work, I, Wu Feng,
I will offer my own aging life, and through death
Explain what charity and benevolence mean.
If they remember me, so that
A-li-shan forever refrains from bloodshed and killing,
If my death can prove as significant as the willing
    martyrdom of Chang Huang-yen,

Then Wu Feng's life is not worth treasuring,
Though I am still afraid; ah!
Deities of heaven and earth!
Life's not worth treasuring, though still I'm
So afraid. And besides, once I am dead,
They may forget Wu Feng.
[*Sunlight fills the stage. After a brief silence the sound of cicadas
rises gradually.* Hsiu-ku *enters*]
Hsiu-ku [*Softly*] Master.
[Wu Feng *does not respond.* Hsiu-ku *raises her voice*]
The sun has risen.
Wu Feng [*His back to* Hsiu-ku] It has risen,
The sun has risen,
A fine day. [*Turning around*] How old are you now, Hsiu-ku?
Hsiu-ku Eighteen.
Wu Feng What about Po-ti-lun, how old is he?
Hsiu-ku He's twenty-one, master.
Wu Feng You've all grown up
And you're able to look after yourselves.
Ang-lin and the rest are also brave kids,
No need for me to worry about you.
Hsiu-ku We worry about you,
We worry about A-li-shan.
Wu Feng Worrying about A-li-shan. That's right.
But A-li-shan is forever A-li-shan.
A-li-shan will not perish.
Hsiu-ku Man perishes;
A-li-shan forever exists.
Wu Feng A man may vanish from the world,
But he may also live forever in the memory
Of others, in the hearts of his descendants.
Isn't this true, Hsiu-ku?
Hsiu-ku Oh yes, when we sing and dance for him
At the sacrificial ceremonies,
He's clearly with us.
Wu Feng At the sacrificial ceremonies he comes out
From our hearts and memory.
But at other times,
His image and personality have already
Merged with our image and personality, and
They have shaped our lives,
So that we are not stupid and childish,
So that we are cautious—we,
Because we have him in our hearts, we're cautious.
Because we love him, and imitate him,
So as not to let him down, we are cautious.
Hsiu-ku I see, master.

We're cautious of life and death, because
We always have him in our hearts.
WU FENG [*Smiling*] Hsiu-ku, my good child,
Go prepare me paper and the writing brush.
[*Exit* HSIU-KU]
WU FENG I understand now,
Deities of heaven and earth.
We're cautious of life and death, because
We always have him in our hearts.
[WU FENG *paces up and down. A moment later, enter* HSIU-KU]
HSIU-KU The paper and writing brush are ready,
Master, in your study. [*Exit* WU FENG]
Oh I, I can't stop
My slight shivering, not sure
Whether I'm frightened, excited, or . . .
Not knowing whether I, too, am sick—
Fear and excitement are sickness.
My hands tremble, my feet are heavy.
There's a violent tempest in my mind,
Where waves surge high, gulls cry in alarm,
And the atmosphere suffocates amidst black clouds and
Heavy rain. But in the boundless revolving universe,
There appears to be an unmoved star,
Burning in every minute, in dead silence
Or din, becoming brighter and brighter.
I know you, oh eternal star!
Yet I seem not to know you, strange
Star—we're searching,
Seeking a path to be close to you.
Bleeding, weeping, adjusting
Will and belief, with the nascent fondness of
A babe and the old regrets of a senile man,
We crawl and prostrate ourselves to be near you.
[*Exit. The sound of cicadas becomes clearer and louder. The sun
rises higher and higher*]

Scene 2

[*The same. Near noon. Amidst the sound of cicadas, enter* WU FENG, ANG-
LIN, TU-LU-WAN-TO, TA-NAO-AN, PO-TI-LUN, *and about ten young tribes-
men. Enter* OLD TRIBESMEN A *and* B, *supporting each other with a stick.*
HSIU-KU *follows.* ANG-LIN *and the other young tribesmen, except* PO-TI-
LUN, *are all dressed for hunting*]

ANG-LIN Master, we don't want to disobey you.
I need your permission, because
I know you, respect you, love you,

And I don't want to offend you. We
Won't make you disappointed and sad.
[WU FENG *is silent*]
TU-LU-WAN-TO We've made up our mind
To resume the sacrificial rite our ancestors handed down.
We're now going, going downhill to ambush a man.
TA-NAO-AN But, oh master!
We don't want to offend you.
ANG-LIN We need your approval,
Permitting us to do it, to do it
In the fashion of our ancestors. We
Need your blessing, or we'll be
Ill at ease. We're your children.
[WU FENG *paces up and down, silent*]
OLD TRIBESMAN A [*To B*] Our ancestors
Were all wrong; though I'm blind, I know
They were wrong.
OLD TRIBESMAN B A-li-shan cannot go wrong a second time.
WU FENG [*To himself*] A-li-shan,
Magnificent and melancholic A-li-shan.
ANG-LIN We have everything ready.
We aren't reckless. I've seriously
Thought about it. I was sleepless the whole night,
Picturing the courageous examples of our ancestors,
Imagining them, for the fortunes of A-li-shan,
Striving and struggling through fire and water,
Risking themselves, endangering themselves, to glorify
The joyless god of the mountains, seeking in life
A meaning and something to rely on to support and raise us.
TA-NAO-AN We've discussed it.
The disaster at A-li-shan cannot continue like this.
We're not willing to die senseless deaths,
To subject our ancestors to this unprecedented disgrace.
TU-LU-WAN-TO Kill, only by killing a man,
By a sacrifice to the great god of rain, and by repentance
to him
Can we purge ourselves of the dust.
PO-TI-LUN Tu-lu-wan-to, what makes you
So self-confident? Do you know the god?
Do you know our ancestors? Do you
Know yourself? Ah, Ang-lin,
Ta-nao-an, aren't you afraid?
Do you know him? Do you know
Wu Feng, our master?
Oh what a shame, you warriors of A-li-shan!
When the black plague is murdering everywhere,
Snatching your loved ones and friends,

At a time when death runs rampant,
You won't listen to reason,
But feed violence with fiery courage instead,
And ignorantly uphold the way to folly.
In the name of the rain god and your ancestors
You're senselessly groping along the road that smells of blood.

ANG-LIN I don't know you, Po-ti-lun.
Don't use wisdom as an excuse to cover up
Your cowardice. I know you're
A-li-shan's brightest, Po-ti-lun,
Yet I know you not.

TU-LU-WAN-TO Po-ti-lun, don't use words
To put out the fire in our hearts for sacrifice.

THE YOUNG TRIBESMEN We don't know you,
Po-ti-lun; we can no longer
Trust Wu Feng. Let's go!
Follow Ang-lin!

OLD TRIBESMAN A [*Turning his face to the sky*] Oh heaven—

WU FENG Don't get excited, don't bewail.
Anger and despair do not avail.
Keep calm, for A-li-shan, calm!
In honor of the dead, the ghosts,
The spirits of your ancestors will protect you.
You must remember, remember that today
All the rights and wrongs will flow into your children's
Blood, changing the color of their spirit.
My boys, listen to me, oh I think
I've said all I can say.
But, be calm, be calm, hear Wu Feng,
Hear my compromise, hear my promise:
Wu Feng will find you another human head.

PO-TI-LUN Master . . .

WU FENG Tomorrow morning at the first light of dawn,
Go to the fields, go under the ka-dang tree,
Wait there under the ka-dang tree. Remember this:
A man in a red cloak and red cap, on horseback,
Will pass by from an eastern path.
You can shoot him, kill him, and take his head.
Offer that to the rain god of A-li-shan.
[*All the tribesmen fall silent for a moment, then scream*]

THE YOUNG TRIBESMEN Tomorrow morning!
A passerby in a red cloak and red cap!
[*The young tribesmen exit, screaming.* WU FENG *stands alone.*
PO-TI-LUN *and* OLD TRIBESMEN A *and* B *stand to one side, bewildered.*
HSIU-KU *is horrified*]

HSIU-KU Master, master, you shouldn't,
You can't die, you shouldn't!

[WU FENG *stands alone, silent*]

HSIU-KU [*To* PO-TI-LUN] He . . .
 Po-ti-lun, he—the one in the red cloak and red cap
 Is he. I sewed them myself.

PO-TI-LUN [*Suddenly answers*] Oh!
 Master, no, master,
 You can't do that, you need not
 Offer yourself! Hsiu-ku . . .

HSIU-KU Master!

WU FENG Everyone in his heart worships
 What he thinks is an illustrious god.
 He is lofty and bright; he is gloomy,
 Covered with the dust of falsehood. And yet,
 Once he occupies the temple in your heart,
 He sits there fast. He is benevolence and kindness
 Incarnate, so abstract that it is for you,
 Through fearless decision, to prove him with action,
 To get to him and to manifest him with your life—
 Your sacrifice can prove to future generations
 The concept you worship in your heart is truth,
 Is eternal good and surpassing beauty,
 Not a hidden fiend, not a
 Usurping phantom, the illusion of illusion.

PO-TI-LUN Oh master, in my heart
 I worship you; aren't you
 The great god in my heart?
 So, to be near you, I must
 Understand you, glorify you. My sacrifice
 Can also prove to A-li-shan
 That you're the force that resists darkness.
 If heaven wills someone
 To receive the arrows of folly, I shall go.

WU FENG Po-ti-lun, don't be reckless,
 Don't take a mortal as god in your heart.
 I'm mortal, an aging mortal.

PO-TI-LUN I too am mortal, and you
 And I are worshipping one high, illustrious
 God. Please let me take your place
 To be near him, to understand him, to glorify him.
 I can bear the pains of our tribe,
 And cleanse A-li-shan's sins.

HSIU-KU Po-ti-lun . . .

WU FENG I'm an aging mortal. My life
 Drifts like the puffs of reed catkins,
 About to fall and perish in the heavy rain.
 A spark could still set me aflame, and
 In burning I should give light to the next generation.

The light I emit may be short-lived,
But so am I short-lived. Po-ti-lun,
You must live on for A-li-shan, and
For the action Wu Feng has chosen, prove to your tribe
That in you is my real life.

Po-ti-lun Is Wu Feng god?

Wu Feng Wu Feng is not god. [Wu Feng *exits quickly*]

Hsiu-ku When we were small and ignorant
We waited to grow up; worries have helped us
Grow, and happiness now disappears where knowledge goes.

Po-ti-lun Happiness is something that floats on the
wings of the pheasants,
On the hooves of deer, in the water.
The years rush on to trample the laughter on the reed-pipes.

Hsiu-ku The years unravel the clothes I've woven.
My mind left in tatters flutters
In the wind; disasters surge into A-li-shan.

Po-ti-lun Disasters, ah disasters pass,
More passing even than my transient life.
A sacrifice could prevent regret in life.

Hsiu-ku Your sacrifice and mine would only prevent
your regret and mine. A-li-shan will think that
We're lambs led along to death by Wu Feng.

Po-ti-lun Oh Wu Feng, you say that you aren't
God, but mortal. Yet being mortal,
How can you foretell if sacrifice is avoidable or not?

[*The sun is high up in the middle of the sky. The curtain descends amidst the crying of cicadas*]

ACT IV

The tenth day of the eighth month. From dawn till noon. In the field, there is a big ka-dang tree to one side (as in Act II). When the curtain goes up, heaven and earth are dim. Enter Yi-feng, *dancing a little.*

Yi-feng [*Singing*]
Old ka-dang, old ka-dang,
You be the sky 'n' I be the wind.
Clouds are like lead, mists are dim,
The bats' wings, all at rest.
Dews fill the earth, wet my hair,
Drench my clothes, drip in my dreams.
Wet my hair, drench my clothes,
Drip in my dreams. How should I
Fumble and search for you?
The eternal heaven and earth are in your secret,
Regrets hidden at the bottom of my heart. Old ka-dang,
Old ka-dang, what a pity I'm the lost wind.

Old ka-dang, old ka-dang,
You be the sky 'n' I be the wind.
Love breeds hate, the heart's perplexed.
Your brave will is to be cherished.
Brightness too uncertain, now in the east,
Now in the west, glittering and marvelous.
Now in the east, now in the west,
Glittering and marvelous. How can I
Rely on you to set my mind at rest?
The long years are in your memory.
Suddenly you come to yourself. Old ka-dang,
Old ka-dang, what a pity I'm the lost wind.

[YI-FENG *stops singing. He dances slightly and languidly. Enter*
OLD TRIBESMEN A *and* B, *guiding each other with a stick*]
OLD TRIBESMAN A I heard Yi-feng.
  Yi-feng was singing.
OLD TRIBESMAN B Yi-feng is dancing.
OLD TRIBESMAN A Oh! Yi-feng is dancing.
  That I can't see. What a pity!
  Yet I should be glad, because
  I don't see anything.
OLD TRIBESMAN B I'd rather be like you,
  Seeing nothing.
OLD TRIBESMAN A I see darkness . . .
  Is Yi-feng still dancing?
  [YI-FENG *stops dancing*]
OLD TRIBESMAN B Yi-feng has stopped.
OLD TRIBESMAN A Let Yi-feng dance, though
  I can't see anything. Songs
  Are wings of the soul and dancing is the soul,
  The soul itself, that flies and flourishes
  Without the help of wings.
  [YI-FENG *dances sporadically. Enter four young tribesmen, two from
each side, bows and arrows in hands, swords on waists, quick, nimble,
and soundless.* YI-FENG *leans on the ka-dang tree. Each young tribesman
occupies a spot, squatting or standing*]
OLD TRIBESMAN A I heard four men's
  Footsteps . . .
OLD TRIBESMAN B Here they come.
  [*Enter* ANG-LIN, TU-LU-WAN-TO, *and* TA-NAO-AN; *and, then,* PO-TI-LUN]
PO-TI-LUN Listen to me, Ang-lin,
  You can't afford not to believe me.
ANG-LIN I cannot believe you any more.
  You are a coward, because you fancy.
  You're confused by your own fancy.
  [*Enter more young tribesmen one after another, followed by* HSIU-KU]
HSIU-KU [*Proceeding directly to* ANG-LIN] Ang-lin,

You must believe me . . . [*Turning to others*]

You, you

Cannot kill Wu Feng. You . . .

THE YOUNG TRIBESMEN Hsiu-ku is out of her head.

ANG-LIN You'd better go home.

Don't stand in the way of the hunters.

HSIU-KU Your way leads to bloody death.

Ang-lin, Tu-lu-wan-to, you

Listen to me, you can't kill Wu Feng.

TU-LU-WAN-TO We are not killing Wu Feng.

It's a death convict Wu Feng's arranged for us,

Coming up the hill, in red garb and red cap, to meet his
death.

We're just executioners,

Offering a convict to the rain god,

Praying for the plague to depart, and for prosperity to
return to

This disaster-stricken A-li-shan.

[*The sky gradually gets brighter*]

PO-TI-LUN It's not a death convict, it's Wu Feng

Himself. The man dressed in red is Wu Feng,

The old loving and caring Wu Feng.

ANG-LIN Ha, Po-ti-lun,

Your imagination is really terrific—

Wu Feng is human, like you and me.

You and I will not surrender ourselves to death.

How would Wu Feng surrender himself to death?

PO-TI-LUN [*Frightened*] You listen to me,

Wu Feng is not like us, he—

He isn't human, he may be god . . .

[*Enter* WU FENG *from afar, dressed in red garb and red cap, among
the mist*]

HSIU-KU Oh oh, Po-ti-lun.

[*The young tribesmen are quickly on the alert, getting their bows
ready*]

PO-TI-LUN You, you people are mad!

[*The young tribesmen place arrows on their bows, drawn full*]

PO-TI-LUN Master, oh Wu Feng!

[PO-TI-LUN *rushes forth, trying to stop the young men.* YI-FENG *stands
up, perplexed.* ANG-LIN *shoots. The rest follow suit. The man in red
garb falls, disappearing in the bushes*]

HSIU-KU Oh heaven!

[ANG-LIN *and five young tribesmen swiftly run to where* WU FENG *fell.*
HSIU-KU *and* PO-TI-LUN *too, rush out.* YI-FENG *turns to the audience*]

YI-FENG [*Facing the audience, singing*]

The eternal heaven and earth are in your secret,

Regrets hidden at the bottom of my heart . . .

[*Beyond the woods, the people scream in great horror*]

ALL Wu Feng, Wu Feng, it's Wu Feng.

    Oh master, our old Wu Feng.

OLD TRIBESMAN A [*To B*] Oh, oh!

    They've really killed Wu Feng. Oh—

[*Suddenly, thunder tears the sky; lightning, fierce winds, torrents.*
OLD TRIBESMAN A, B, *and the young men, in panic, run in a circle on the
stage.* YI-FENG *whirls and dances among the crowd, then drifts off. Enter*
ANG-LIN, *followed by the others*]

ANG-LIN [*Wails*] Oh wind, oh rain!

    Today A-li-shan sinks into the dark sea.

    Oh heaven, Wu Feng has abandoned us!

    Oh wind, rain! Lash me, tear me

    With your violent whip, beat me—

    I know you hid away for a long time

    In the shady valley, in the woods,

    In the ferocity of the hunters' arrows,

    In the ominous hooting of the night owl.

    Oh wind, rain! Maliciously you've waited

    And waited for this moment,

    Storing up the brutal might of a thousand years

    To lash and beat me. I, I, I've

    Killed Wu Feng.

[TU-LU-WAN-TO *howls and tosses his bow and arrows on the ground,
trampling on them*]

TU-LU-WAN-TO Get away, get away,

    Swords and weapons. Now I wail

    Like a child lost in the wind and rain.

    I leave you to weep in the mud.

[TA-NAO-AN *draws his sword and strikes a rock. Some of the other
tribesmen toss their bows and arrows on the ground, others draw out
their swords and strike the ground*]

TA-NAO-AN Blind hunters,

    Absurd swords! If I cannot

    Behead the stubborn devil in my heart I'll

    Surrender to my cowardice. The bloody days . . .

    [*Violent wind and stormy rain*]

HSIU-KU I can see that this is wind,

    This is rain. This is thunder and lightning

    Racing and flying at A-li-shan.

    The wrath, sorrow, and lament of heaven and earth

    Are hovering, heaving, and whirling in my heart,

    Pounding my bones and veins,

    Like a thousand catties of stones beating upon

    My forehead and chest, which can hardly endure.

    I can't blame you, because you're ignorant.

    Because you lacked the solemn faith,

You sinned in ignorance. And I can't hastily forgive you
For your repentence. I can't forgive,
I can't forgive myself, because
All the way I kept my knowledge intact,
I foresaw the storm of my spirit would eventually
Involve you, and yet I couldn't save you,
I couldn't save Wu Feng, I couldn't save you.
ANG-LIN I understand. By now this shattered
Faith should have found another level of meaning.
Even the rain god of our A-li-shan
Is so grieved that he is crying loud. He
Is mourning for Wu Feng, having the storm as witness:
The rain god is crying in agony. So then, from the olden days
Was he already on the list of gods?
Oh Wu Feng, are you the god who once descended
Unto this mountain, cleansed my tribe with blood,
And wiped off the stain of the bloodthirst in our hearts,
Delivering us to a bright world?
Now then, my rain god,
You've poured off all cosmic might
To receive Wu Feng back to the lofty sky.
You should stop your terrifying mourning,
As we do, awakening in regret,
Swearing to our ancestors and descendants
Never again to ambush and kill a man,
Never again to use human heads for sacrifice.
[*The wind and rain gradually die down. All people are silent, looking
up at the sky. The wind and rain completely stop*]
PO-TI-LUN Let's make an oath to Wu Feng . . . [PO-TI-LUN *walks to a rock,
and tries to move it*]
ANG-LIN We should bury this rock,
The rock of the strongest will and faith.
[ANG-LIN, TU-LU-WAN-TO, *and two young tribesmen go forth to help*
PO-TI-LUN. TA-NAO-AN *and three other young men dig a pit under the
ka-dang tree. The new sun shines on the stage*]
OLD TRIBESMAN A [*Looking into the sky*] A-li-shan's
Children are working hard. The cleansed
Hearts will be pure forever. Wu Feng has died,
Wu Feng will live in their hearts forever.
[*They bury the rock in the pit. Some sitting, some squatting, and
some standing, facing the ka-dang tree, they chant a poem. The accom-
panying music is led by the pipe, majestic, grave, and desolate, changing
from weak to strong. The old tribesmen are smoking, while the young
move about from time to time. Now and then there are drums from far
away. The sun, moon, and stars repeat their rise and fall three times.
The crying of cicadas rises and falls in accordance with the shifting of
day and night*]

ANG-LIN Deep under the ka-dang tree we bury a rock.
   This rock is our eternal oath.
   In the ruined millet fields we observe silence,
   Sitting long hours on broken branches and tattered
      leaves left by the storm.
   Daisies of the early autumn must patiently grow,
   Steam waters must flow; mountains must cast their shadows,
   The sun on A-li-shan must stop at
   The Tropic of Cancer that circles a life,
   To insure that the temperate zone you have given us
   Is that temperate zone you have given us.
TU-LU-WAN-TO Bows are sobbing and arrows silent.
   Swords stare at the blood in repentence.
   A reed-pipe blows in the tribal hamlets, and
   People scatter to the windless knoll.
   Today it is not right for us to talk face to face.
   The old are watching the white clouds as they smoke,
   The young are squatting and ruminating.
   Today we smoke and ruminate.
TA-NAO-AN Never before was there a surging stream so
      bloody,
   Yet so cleansing when it flowed.
   The great earth has awakened, but today
   It is not proper for us to look at each other in the eye,
   Though we are like newborn babies,
   Presently learning to know. Today,
   Under the ka-dang tree we bury deep
   A rock of oath.
ANG-LIN To the snapped-off shadows we make gestures,
   We open our arms like a half moon to show our love—
   Love must illuminate a road,
   A well. Oh! Wu Feng,
   To the tired bows and arrows and scimitars,
   We make gestures, we bid them to go away;
   To the vocal cords, we make gestures, we bid them shut.
   To all things permissible and impermissible we make gestures.
   Today it is not proper . . .
PO-TI-LUN Not proper for us to make conclusions, but we can
   Reminisce. You can no longer help us drive away
   The totemic thunders, but with silence we will
   Smother them in the valleys. The days
   Will come again, you will come again;
   You will not scold us: you have
   Cleansed our bows and arrows and scimitars
   So our boys can walk by the swaying lilies,
   And go into the distance to learn hunting.
HSIU-KU Not proper for us to make conclusions, but we can

Guess. You can no longer help us dissipate
The fogs of taboos but with longings we will
Weave them into a cloth. The days
Will come again, you will come again;
You will not scold us: you have
Mended our spinning wheels and winches
So our girls can walk by the sheds laden with gourds
To the riverside to learn laundry.

PO-TI-LUN The mourning drums are echoing in the hills.
We don't know how we should bury you.
It seems that today, among the stars,
You're the morning star, closest to the drums,
Taller than the totem poles,
Tenderer than the hero's dance,
Truer than the joy of harvest . . .
We're gathered in the field,
Sleepless for one night, sleepless for two nights,
Sleepless for three nights, keeping vigil over you.

HSIU-KU Quietly in this way we keep vigil over you.
We wish to talk to you, tell you
The plague has ceased; it's your blood
That has cleansed the earth, sparkling with
Daylily flowers, areca fruit, and little costume bells, and
     with
Every sound from the pestles heralding new rice. You will be
     happy,
Oh! Wu Feng, you will be happy to know
Under the ka-dang tree we bury a rock deep,
We open our arms like a half moon,
To show that we yearn for a union in love.

ALL We open our arms,
We yearn,
We love.

[*The sun is in the middle of the sky. The music and the sound of
cicadas fill the stage. The curtain slowly descends*]

Notes

1. Wu Feng (Wu Yuan-hui, 1699-1769) was born in Fukien province and
moved as a child with his father to Taiwan, eventually settling in the hill
country around the mountain known as A-li-shan to conduct trade with the
aborigines of the area. He was subsequently appointed liaison-interpreter to the
non-Han Taiwanese peoples by the Chinese government. The customs of the
Taiwanese tribesmen and the martyrdom of Wu Feng are based on historical
record. Wu Feng was posthumously revered as the spirit, or god, of A-li-shan.

2. *Weissnichtwo* is an imaginary city in Thomas Carlyle's satirical *Sartor Resartus*. Weissnichtwo ("I know not where") is adopted by the author as an approximation of the Chinese phrase appearing in the original text, *wu-ho-yu chih hsiang*.

3. The historical figures alluded to in this passage all shared the experience of the collapse of the Ming dynasty in the face of massive bandit attacks and invasion by the Manchu Ch'ing dynasty. Chu Yu-chien, the Ch'ung-chen Emperor, was the last Ming monarch to govern in Peking. He ended his life by hanging himself and his chief consort on Coal Hill (Mei shan) when the city was invested by bandit forces under Li Tzu-ch'eng in 1644. Ku Yen-wu was a noted scholar who fought to save the Ming and thereafter steadfastly declined to accept official position under the Ch'ing regime, though hounded and imprisoned by enemies and enticed by friends. Chang Huang-yen (1620-1664) for years fought to restore the Ming, conducting raids up the Yangtze River with Cheng Ch'eng-kung. After Chang's retirement one of his former aides betrayed him to the Ch'ing government and he was executed together with his family. Chu Shun-shui (Chu Chih-yü, 1600-1682) was a Ming loyalist who eventually settled in Japan as tutor and advisor to the Prince of Mito, winning a distinguished reputation among Japanese scholars and later becoming a figure of great interest to Chinese studying in Japan at the end of the Ch'ing dynasty. Wang Ch'uan-shan (Wang Fu-chih, 1619-1692) abandoned active support of the cause of Ming restoration in 1650, but refused thereafter to take office in the Ch'ing government and built a reputation as a private scholar of moral and political philosophy challenging the legitimacy of the Ch'ing regime. Cheng Ch'eng-kung, the famous Koxinga (1624-1662), was the most powerful of the Ming loyalists who led raiding parties against the Ch'ing government and seized the island of Taiwan as a base of operations, displacing a Dutch colonial force. The Ch'ing government took control of the island some years after his death.

Notes on Authors and Texts

Ch'en Pai-chen (1908–) attended several universities. His activities in Communist youth organizations led to his imprisonment from 1932 to 1935. Subsequently his stories of prison life, such as "Hsiao Wei ti chiang-shan" (The realm of Hsiao Wei), attracted notice, and he also began writing drama. He spent the period of the War of Resistance to Japan in Chengtu and Chungking, participating in theater and film groups and writing a series of satirical plays, among them *Luan-shih nan-nü* (Men and Women in Wild Times), *Chieh-hun chin-hsing ch'ü* (The wedding march), and *Sheng-kuan t'u* (Plan for promotion). After joining the Party in 1950 he wrote a series of satirical sketches critical of United States policies. Weathering the purges of the Cultural Revolution period, Ch'en completed the historical play *Ta feng ko* (Song of the great wind) in 1977. As of 1979 he was teaching at Nanjing University and serving as vice-chairman of the Playwrights' Association.

The translation given here is based on the script published in book form as *Luan-shih nan-nü* (Chunking: Shanghai tsa-chih kung-szu, 1939; repr. 1945).

Chou Wei-po, Tung Yang-sheng, and Yeh Hsiao-nan were students at Fudan University, Shanghai, in 1979 when their satirical comedy, *P'ao-ping szu-ling ti erh-tzu*, was produced. It has also been televised.

The translation, The Artillery Commander's Son, is based on the text published in the newspaper *Wen-hui pao* (Shanghai), 10 June 1979.

The China Peking Opera Troupe (Chung-kuo ching-chü t'uan) included such well-known performers as Ch'ien Hao-liang (in the role of Li Yü-ho), Liu Ch'ang-yü (as T'ieh-mei), and Yuan Shui-hai (as Hatoyama), who developed the model revolutionary version of *Hung teng chi* (The Red Lantern) between 1963 and 1970, based on regional operas and under the direction of Chiang Ch'ing.

The translation of *Hung teng chi* included here may also be found in the monthly *Chinese Literature* (Peking), August 1970 (no. 8), and in Lois Wheeler Snow, *China on Stage* (Vintage Books, 1973). For a full text of the revised version of May 1970 with illustrations, stage directions, and musical scores, see the edition of Jen-min ch'u-pan she, 1972.

Hsia Yen (Shen Tuan-hsien, 1900–) studied electrical engineering in Japan but was drawn to literature and Communist ideology. Joining the Party in 1927, he soon became an influential figure in the Shanghai underground, noted for his dramas, especially the controversial historical play *Sai Chin-hua* (1936), and *Shanghai wu-yen hsia* (Under Shanghai Eaves, 1937). His patriotic plays during the War of Resistance to Japan are among the best known of the period, and he was honored with several important positions in the 1950s, including the vice-presidency of the Federation of Literary and Art Circles (FLAC). During the 1930s Hsia Yen and three associates had bitter arguments with the famous writer

Lu Hsün, who dubbed them "the four villains" (szu-t'iao han-tzu). In 1966 this term was resurrected when Hsia Yen and his associates were charged with subverting Maoist policies, and he was imprisoned and tortured. In 1978 he was restored and the following year named to head the Committee to Safeguard Writers' Rights and Interests of the Chinese Writers' Association.

The translation of *Shanghai wu-yen hsia* is based on the text in *Chung-kuo hsin wen-hsüeh ta-hsi hsü-p'ien* (Continuation to the comprehensive anthology of modern Chinese literature) (Hong Kong, n.d.).

Hu Shih (1891–1962) is a figure more prominently associated with the intellectual history of twentieth-century China than with drama. However, as a student of philosophy in the United States, Hu Shih made pioneering proposals for literary reform in China which he illustrated in poetry, prose, and the one-act comedy *Chung-shen ta-shih* (The Greatest Event in Life). He later achieved eminence as a leading scholar and academician in China, serving as ambassador to the United States, president of Peking University, and finally president of Academia Sinica in Taiwan.

Chung-shen ta-shih was originally published in *Hsin ch'ing-nien* (New youth), vol. 6, no. 3 (March 1919). The translation is based on the text in Chao Chia-pi, ed., *Chung-kuo hsin wen-hsüeh ta-hsi* (A comprehensive anthology of modern Chinese literature: 1917–27), 1935–36, vol. 9, *Hsi-chü chi*.

Hung Shen (1894–1955) was a student of ceramics in the United States when he became interested in the theater. He was strongly influenced by the early Eugene O'Neill, as shown in Hung's *Chao yen-wang* (Yama Chao), written upon his return to China. As a professor of literature and drama at several universities in Shanghai during the 1920s and 1930s, his allegiance to left-wing movements increased steadily, and he turned away from such successful ventures as his production of Wilde's *Lady Windemere's Fan* to write and stage some notable early Communist plays, among them *Wu-k'uei ch'iao* (Wu-k'uei bridge, 1930). Although remaining active in film and drama through the 1940s, his work was gradually overshadowed by later writers.

Chao yen-wang first appeared in *Tung-fang tsa-chih* (Eastern miscellany), vol. 20, nos. 1–2 (10 and 25 January 1923). The translation is based on the text in Chao Chia-pi, ed., *Chung-kuo hsin wen-hsüeh ta-hsi*, vol. 9.

Li Chien-wu (1906–) studied at Tsinghua University and in Paris (1933–35), returning to teach in Shanghai. During the 1930s he was well known for his comedies, such as *I-shen tso-tse* (To take as a model) and *Che pu-kuo shih ch'un-t'ien* (This is but the spring), while in the 1940s he wrote historical plays and adapted works by Scribe and Sardou, besides writing his notable comedy *Ch'ing-ch'un* (Springtime). Li was also quite active as an actor and prominent as a critic under the penname Liu Hsi-wei. Since 1949 he has continued to write, chiefly as a critic of drama, this work being interrupted by the Cultural Revolution period but reappearing thereafter.

The translation of *Ch'ing-ch'un* is based on the text first published in *Wen-i fu-hsing* (Literary renaissance) (Shanghai), vol. 1, nos. 1–2 (February–March 1946). The play was subsequently published in book form.

Ou-yang Yü-ch'ien (1889–1962), as a student in Japan, participated in the Spring Willow Society, a drama club formed by Chinese students that pioneered the production of Chinese spoken drama in 1907 with performances of *Uncle Tom's Cabin* and *Camille*. Following his return to China, Ou-yang was active in a series of dramatic and film organizations, and became a skilled female impersonator in Peking Opera. His special interest was in combining traditional forms of opera with techniques learned from the West. Ou-yang rendered increasing support to the Communist Party, and following the establishment of the People's Republic he served as administrator of several national theatrical organizations.

Pan Chin-lien was first published in *Hsin-yüeh yüeh-k'an* (Crescent moon monthly), vol. 1, no. 4 (June 1928), and published the same year in book form. **Sha Yeh-hsin, Li Shou-ch'eng, and Yao Ming-te** were members of the Shanghai People's Art Theater in the summer of 1979 when they wrote and staged *Chia-ju wo shih chen-ti* (If I Were Real) for a restricted audience. Performances were given in several cities until the Party decided the play's excesses and ideological flaws were grounds for curtailment. Sha Yeh-hsin, while protesting Party criticism of this play, was accorded a positive response from the Party for his next work, *Ch'en I shih-chang* (Mayor Ch'en I, 1980).

The translation is based on the text published in the Hong Kong monthly *Ch'i-shih nien-tai* (The seventies), January 1980.

T'ien Han (T'ien Shou-ch'ang, 1898–1968) studied medicine in Japan but there joined with other Chinese students interested in literature to form the Creation Society. His particular interest in theater led him to organize the Southern Society (Nan-kuo she) and to embark on a prolific career as a dramatist, culminating in his late works, *Kuan Han-ch'ing* and *Hsieh Yao-huan* (1961). The latter work was declared a "poisonous weed" offensive to Maoist thought. T'ien Han and three associates (Hsia Yen, Yang Han-sheng, and Chou Yang) were branded as "the four villains" and removed from their influential cultural positions in 1966. A member of the Communist Party since 1932, T'ien had long served its propaganda programs, and in 1979 his name and work were posthumously rehabilitated by the Party.

Kuan Han-ch'ing underwent several revisions. The first version, composed of nine scenes, was published in the monthly *Chü-pen* (Playscripts), May 1958 (no. 5). It included a final scene in which Kuan Han-ch'ing and Chu Lien-hsiu, his companion, are reunited. The play was subsequently expanded to twelve scenes and the ending revised. However, when it was performed later that same year by the Peking People's Art Theater, the tenth scene was cut. The remaining eleven scenes were published in book form by Jen-min wen-hsüeh ch'u-pan she, 1961. The translation into English by Foreign Languages Press (Peking, 1961) conforms to this script, but restores the deleted scene 10; this version thus consists of twelve scenes.

Ting Hsi-lin (1893–1974) studied in England and taught physics at universities in Peking, Nanking, and Tsingtao, also joining the Academia Sinica. His one-act comedies of the 1920s and 1930s, including *Ya-p'o* (Oppression), are generally considered among the most carefully crafted of their time. During the War of Resistance to Japan he also wrote two full-length plays. After the founding of the People's Republic he held numerous positions in cultural and political organizations but wrote no more plays.

Ya-p'o was originally published in *Hsien-tai p'ing-lun* (Contemporary review) (Anniversary commemorative issue, 1926). The translation is based on the text appearing in Chao Chia-pi, ed., *Chung-kuo hsin wen-hsüeh ta-hsi*, vol. 9.

Tsung Fu-hsien (?1947–) began writing during his spare time as a worker at the Shanghai Heat Treatment Plant. *Yü wu-sheng ch'u* (In a Land of Silence) is his first play to attract national attention.

The translation is based on the text published in *Jen-min hsi-chü* (People's drama), December 1978. Another translation of this play may be found in the monthly *Chinese Literature* (Peking), April 1979 (no. 4).

Wu Han (Wu Ch'un-han, 1909-1966) was beset with financial difficulties as a youth, and had to work part-time as a librarian and school teacher in order to complete his studies at Tsinghua University. During the War of Resistance to Japan he taught history at Southwest United University in Kunming and in the late 1940s committed himself to underground work for the Communist Party. During the 1950s he was both chairman of the history department at Tsinghua and a deputy mayor of Peking. His published research focused on the Ming dynasty, which furnished him with the background for his essays and for the drama about Hai Jui, intended as veiled criticism of Mao Tse-tung's policies and his treatment of those expressing loyal dissent. This led to his condemnation by Maoists in 1966.

The translation of *Hai Jui pa-kuan* is based on the text published by the Peking Publishing House, 1961.

Yang Chiang (Yang Chi-k'ang, 1911-) studied foreign languages in Soochow, Shanghai, and in Peking at Tsinghua University, where she met and married the scholar-writer Ch'ien Chung-shu. After study in Europe the couple returned to China in 1937 and eventually settled in Shanghai where Yang taught at Aurora Women's College, wrote short fiction, essays, and four known plays between 1942 and 1947. Since the founding of the People's Republic Yang Chiang has been a member first of the Institute of Literature and then the Institute of Foreign Literature of the Academy of Social Sciences. Following the Cultural Revolution she published translations of *Don Quixote, Gil Blas,* and *La Vida de Lazarillo de Tormes*; a collection of critical articles titled *Ch'un ni chi* (Spring soil, 1979); and an account of life during the Cultural Revolution, *Kan-hsiao liu-chi* (Six chapters from a cadre school, 1981).

The translation of *Feng hsü* (Windswept Blossoms) is based on the text published in *Wen-i fu-hsing* (Literary renaissance) vol. 1, nos. 3-4 (March-May 1946).

Yang Lü-fang (dates unknown) remains an obscure figure who wrote drama in the early 1950s based on his experiences in the navy before settling in the countryside of Kiangsu province to gather material for his popular play *Pu-ku-niao yu chiao-le* (Cuckoo Sings Again). In the wake of the controversy surrounding his play he was not heard of again.

Pu-ku-niao yu chiao-le was first published in *Chü-pen* (Playscripts), January 1957 (no. 1). The translation is based on a subsequent edition published in book form (Peking: Chung-kuo hsi-chü she, 1957).

Yang Mu (Wang Ching-hsien, 1940-), a native of Taiwan, studied at Tunghai University and received a doctorate in comparative literature from the University of California at Berkeley. Establishing himself as a poet in Taiwan during the 1960s under the penname Yeh Shan, he has continued to experiment with varying forms and styles, turning to verse drama with the writing of *Wu Feng*. Since 1974 he has been an associate professor of Chinese and Comparative Literature at the University of Washington.

Wu Feng first appeared in the newspaper *Lien-ho pao* (Taipei), 7-12 February 1979, and was subsequently published in book form (Taipei: Hung-fan shu-tien, 1979).

Notes on Translators

Carolyn T. Brown teaches at Howard University, District of Columbia, and has translated fiction by Lu Hsün and Eileen Chang.

Stanley Dubinsky is a doctoral candidate at Cornell University in Modern Languages and Linguistics.

Edward M. Gunn is an assistant professor of Chinese literature at Cornell University and has published studies on twentieth-century literature, including *Unwelcome Muse: Chinese Literature in Shanghai and Peking, 1937–1945*.

George Hayden is an associate professor of Chinese at the University of Southern California, Los Angeles, and has written on aspects of Chinese theater, traditional as well as modern, including *Crime and Punishment in Medieval Chinese Drama: Three Judge Pao Plays*.

Cissie Kwok is a graduate student at the University of Washington, Seattle, in comparative literature.

Joseph S. M. Lau (Liu Shao-ming) is a professor of Chinese and comparative literature at the University of Wisconsin, Madison, and has published extensively in Taiwan and the United States, including a critical study of the playwright Ts'ao Yü, titled *Ts'ao Yü: The Reluctant Disciple of Chekhov and O'Neill*.

David Pollard is professor of Chinese at the School of Oriental and African Studies, University of London, and has published a variety of studies on modern Chinese literature, including *A Chinese Look at Literature: The Literary Values of Chou Tso-jen in Relation to the Tradition*.

Catherine Swatek teaches Chinese literature at Hunter College, City University of New York, and is preparing a doctoral dissertation on the dramatic works of the seventeenth-century writer Feng Meng-lung, at Columbia University.

Daniel Talmadge is a doctoral candidate in Chinese literature at Cornell University, Ithaca.

Shu-ying Tsau received her B.A. from Peking University and is now assistant professor of Chinese at York University, Toronto. She has contributed to several anthologies of modern Chinese literature, including *Revolutionary Literature in China* (ed. John Berninghausen and Ted Huters) and *Literature of the People's Republic of China* (ed. Hsü Kai-yu).